SOCIOLOGY

McGraw-Hill Book Company • New York • St. Louis • San Francisco
Auckland • Düsseldorf • Johannesburg • Kuala Lumpur • London
Mexico • Montreal • New Delhi • Panama • Paris • São Paulo
Singapore • Sydney • Tokyo • Toronto

SOCIOLOGY

Paul B. Horton & Chester L. Hunt

Professors of Sociology • Western Michigan University

Fourth Edition

SOCIOLOGY

Copyright © 1964, 1968, 1972, 1976 by
McGraw-Hill, Inc. All rights reserved. Printed in
the United States of America. No part of this
publication may be reproduced, stored in a retrieval
system, or transmitted, in any form or by any
means, electronic, mechanical, photocopying,
recording, or otherwise, without the prior written
permission of the publisher.

3 4 5 6 7 8 9 0 D O D O 7 9 8 7

This book was set in Primer by Black Dot, Inc. The
editors were Lyle Linder, Helen Greenberg, and
James R. Belser; the designer was Hermann
Strohbach; the production supervisor was Sam
Ratkewitch. The part title illustrations were done
by Susanne Strohbach; cartoon drawings were
done by Frederick J. Ashby; other drawings were
done by Vantage Art, Inc.
R. R. Donnelley & Sons Company was printer and
binder.

Library of Congress Cataloging in Publication Data

Horton, Paul B
    Sociology.

    Bibliography: p.
    Includes indexes.
    1. Sociology. I. Hunt, Chester L., joint
author
HM51.H64   1976   301   75-20189
ISBN 0-07-030426-2

Contents

Three/Social organization

10 • The family 190

11 • Formal organizations 215

12 • Social class 233

13 • Social mobility 263

Four/Social interaction

14 • Social processes 289

15 • Social power 311

16 • Race and ethnic relations 333

17 • Collective behavior in mass society 364

Five/Human ecology

18 • Population 391

19 • The community in mass society 416

Six/Social change and social policy

Preface

What should an introductory sociology textbook try to do? First and most important, we believe it should capture the interest of the student and demonstrate both the process and challenge of scientific observation and analysis of social behavior in a readable and interesting way.

Second, an introductory sociology textbook should seek to cultivate in the student the habit of scientific analysis of social data. Unless students gain a sophisticated awareness of their own ethnocentrism and some ability to objectify their observations, the sociology course has failed in one of its major objectives.

Third, an introductory sociology textbook should present the basic concepts and descriptive materials of sociology clearly and intelligibly. These should be illustrated so vividly that they "come alive" and become part of the student's thinking vocabulary. Concepts should not be learned simply as definitions to be memorized, but as accurate, descriptive names for the ways people act and the things people build. Concepts are far more than a professional vocabulary to be used in advanced studies: They are even more important as tools for identifying and understanding a process or idea. Many sociology students will find that the introductory course is a terminal course as well, and the basic concepts should be tools for continuing social observation and analysis.

In this textbook we have tried to do these things. Whether we have succeeded is for the reader to judge. We have generally avoided esoteric sources in favor of others more easily available to most students. We have often used literary and popular sources for purposes of illustration. We have done this to emphasize the fact that sociology is the disciplined observation and analysis of everyday life and that the concepts and insights of sociology are applicable to all that goes on around the student.

We note that some recent textbooks contain very few footnotes or citations. It is true that footnotes and citations *do* clutter up a book. But we believe that students should constantly be reminded of the evidential basis for the conclusions of sociology. Therefore we have documented heavily in order to present sociology as a scientific and scholarly discipline, not as an exercise in popular journalism.

We have sought to incorporate recent research in this new edition, but have not slavishly deleted significant earlier research and theory simply to gain a more current dateline. We seek to describe new and controversial developments in sociology analytically and objectively, in the belief that advocacy and espousal are not proper in an introductory textbook.

We have tried to minimize the overlap with other sociology courses. This textbook is not an encapsulated encyclopedia of the entire sociology curriculum. We have intentionally not emphasized "social problems" material in the belief that the introductory course should concentrate upon principles and concepts and should leave specialized topics and problem-oriented materials for later courses.

This fourth edition is the most extensive revision of our textbook. The chapters on Social Institutions, Social Class, Social Mobility, Race and Ethnic Relations, and Population have been very heavily rewritten, and nearly all chapters have been substantially revised. We have sought to eliminate sexist vocabulary and sexist analysis.

Many instructors may find the *Instructor's Manual*, prepared by the authors, a useful aid. It provides a wide range of teaching suggestions and an expanded supply of objective and essay examination questions for each chapter.

The accompanying *Study Guide and Source Book* has been revised by Bruce J. Cohen for this fourth edition of *Sociology*. Many students find it helpful during study and review, a source of related materials, and a yardstick by which to measure their mastery of the text materials.

We owe a debt of appreciation to many people, and especially to the McGraw-Hill staff for their dedicated competence, to a number of our colleagues for their candid criticisms and helpful suggestions, to Bruce J. Cohen for his careful preparation of supplementary materials, and to Frederick J. Ashby for his imaginative line drawings.

Paul B. Horton
Chester L. Hunt

One/Sociology and society

For centuries people have pondered the societies they have developed. Some of our oldest documents, going back five thousand years or more, record their efforts to analyze and understand their social order. In this search people have sought truth from many sources by using many methods, some highly successful, some less so. Some of the sources of truth are described in Chapter 1, "Science and the Search for Truth." This chapter shows that although each source of truth has its uses, only through scientific investigation can reliable knowledge about human society be discovered. Chapter 2, "Fields and Methods of Sociology," tells how scientific methods are used in sociological investigation. All phenomena can be studied scientifically, but the techniques of study must be fitted to the materials studied. Just how sociologists try to make this adaptation is described in Chapter 2.

Chapter 1 • Science and the search for truth

In our time and for some centuries to come, for better or worse, the sciences, physical and social, will be to an increasing degree the accepted point of reference with respect to which the validity (Truth) of all knowledge is gauged. *(Copyright 1961 by G. A. Lundberg,* Can Science Save Us?, *2/e, Longmans, Green & Co., Ltd., London, p. 36. Reprinted with permission of the David McKay Co., Inc.)*

Sociology: The systematic study of the development, structure, interaction, and collective behavior of organized groups of human beings. (By permission. From *Webster's New Collegiate Dictionary* © 1975 by G. & C. Merriam Co., publishers of the Merriam Webster Dictionaries.)

Sociology: The intellectual discipline concerned with developing systematic, reliable knowledge about human social relations in general and about the products of such relationships. . . . *(Thomas Ford Hoult, Dictionary of Modern Sociology,* Littlefield, Adams & Co., *Totowa, N.Y., 1969, p. 307.)*

Sociology is the taking of what everyone knows and putting it into words that nobody can understand. *(Anonymous)*

A pathologist after elaborate preparation places a slide under the microscope and adjusts the lens carefully. A Purari war party watch carefully as they place their canoe in the water, for unless it rocks, the raid will not be successful. A man steps from a new station wagon, cuts a forked twig, and carries it around holding it above the ground, while a well-drilling crew stands by, waiting to drill where the twig tells them water will be found. A woman in Peoria, anxious over her teen-age daughter, prays to God for guidance. A physician leafs through the pages of a parasitology textbook as he tries to identify the puzzling skin rash of his patient. A senator scans the latest public opinion poll while wondering how to vote on the farm bill.

Each of these persons is seeking guidance. Their problems vary, and their sources of truth are different. Where shall human beings find truth? How can they know when they had found it? In the million years, more or less, of our life on this earth, we have sought truth in many places. What are some of them?

Some sources of truth

Intuition

Galen, a famous Greek physician of the second century, prepared an elaborate chart of the human body, showing exactly where it might be pierced without fatal injury. How did he know the vulnerable spots? He just *knew* them. True, he had learned a good deal of human anatomy through his observations and those of his associates; but beyond this, he relied upon his intuition to tell him which zones were fatal. *Intuition is any flash of insight (true or mistaken) whose source the receiver cannot fully identify or explain.* Hitler relied heavily upon his intuition, much to the distress of his generals. His intuition told him that France would not fight for the Rhineland, that England would not fight for Czechoslovakia, that England and France would not fight for Poland, and that England and France would quit when he attacked Russia. He was right on the first two insights and wrong on the last two.

Intuition is responsible for many brilliant hypotheses, which can later be tested through other methods. Perhaps intuition's greatest value is in the forming of hypotheses. As a source of knowledge, of conclusions, intuition is less satisfactory. True, sometimes intuition takes the form of a shrewd leap to a sound conclusion, based upon a mass of half-remembered experience and information. But how can such intuitive knowledge be tested and verified? Often it can't be. Anaximander propounded a theory of evolution in the sixth century B.C., but not until the nineteenth century A.D. were the facts available to indicate that his theory was essentially correct. Intuitive knowledge often can't be tested at the time it is offered. Sometimes it cannot be tested at all, or at least not until it is too late to make any difference, as Hitler eventually discovered.

Authority

Two thousand years ago, Galen knew more about human anatomy than any other mortal; as recently as 1800, physicians were still quoting him as an authority. Aristotle was credited with the suggestion that a barrel of water might be added to a barrel of ashes without overflowing, and for two thousand years thereafter, a student who might suggest trying it out would be scolded for his impertinence. For many centuries, creative thought was stifled by Aristotelian authority, for since an authority is *right*, any conflicting ideas must be wrong. Authority does not discover new truths, but it can prevent new truth from being discovered or accepted.

Dangerous though authority may be, we cannot get along without it. Our accumulation of knowledge is too great for anyone to absorb, so we must rely upon specialists who have collected the reliable knowledge in a particular field. An authority is a necessary and useful source of knowledge—*in the field in which that person is an authority.* Science recognizes no authorities on "things in general."

The layman's problem is finding a qualified authority

Authority is of several sorts. *Sacred* authority rests upon the faith that a certain tradition or document—the Bible, the Koran, the Vedas—is of supernatural origin. Or it is a faith that a certain group or institution—the medicine men, the priests, the church—is constantly receiving supernatural guidance. *Secular* authority arises not from divine revelation but from human perception. It is of two kinds: *secular scientific* authority, which rests upon empirical investigation, and *secular humanistic* authority, which rests upon the belief that certain "great men" have had remarkable insight into human behavior and the nature of the universe. The search for truth by consulting the "great books" is an example of the appeal to secular humanistic authority.

Some fields—counseling and psychological services, health and diet, for example—are cluttered with many self-styled "authorities" without professional training in these fields. The most reputable of authorities is likely to become a foolish incompetent when he[1] strays beyond his specialty. The general who pontificates on crime prevention, the business executive who endorses a food fad, the physician who gives prescriptions for labor-management problems—each of these may be making a fool of himself. He may also be making fools of his listeners.

The layman (and everyone is a layman in all fields except that of his or her specialty) has no choice; (s)he *must* rely upon authority since (s)he cannot become an expert on everything. It is presumptuous for the layman to disagree with the qualified authorities on a question of fact upon which the authorities have reached an agreement. The layman's problem is how to find and recognize a qualified authority in the area of concern.

No scientific authority, however, has the final word on human knowledge. The scientist respects the qualified authority, but still questions his basic assumptions and verifies his conclusions. A person who is considered an expert in a given field deserves to have his views considered seriously, but the weight of authority does not close the door upon further investigation. Today's scientific authority becomes the springboard to tomorrow's research. Thus knowledge grows, relentlessly converting today's "final" pronouncements into tomorrow's midpoints and side streets along the road to expanding knowledge.

Tradition

Of all sources of truth, tradition is one of the most reassuring. Here is the accumulated wisdom of the ages, and the person who disregards it may expect denunciation as a scoundrel or a fool. If a pattern has "worked" in the past, why not keep on using it?

Tradition, however, preserves both the accumulated wisdom and the accumulated bunkum of the ages. Tradition is society's attic, crammed with all sorts of useful customs and useless relics. A great deal of "practical experience" consists in repeating the mistakes of our ancestors. One task of social science is to sort out our folklore into the true and the merely ancient.

Common sense

For thousands of years people's common sense told them that the earth was flat, that big objects fell faster than small ones, that stone and iron were perfectly solid materials, and that true character was betrayed by facial features; yet today we know that none of these statements is true.

When we do not know where our ideas come from or what they are based on, we sometimes call them "common sense." If we call them common sense, we do not have to prove them, for then others will join us in the collective

---

[1] *A note on the problem of textbook sexism:* Every author and publisher is keenly aware of the widespread resentment of textbook sexism. The terms, "man," "he," "him," and "his" are commonly used to refer to both the entire human race and the male sex. The English language lacks a set of neuter equivalents for these terms. Sometimes such terms as "one," "person," or "they" can be used, but often this makes for clumsiness and lack of clarity. The repeated use of "he or she" or of "she/he" is also clumsy and interferes with the free flow of ideas. But a usage which many perceive as insulting also interferes with the free flow of ideas. The authors of this textbook are well aware of this problem and have removed nearly all the generic uses of the male gender terms.

Should anecdotes and illustrations show women in the roles which most women actually fill (housewife, mother, waitress, secretary, nurse, etc.)? To depict women *only* in such stereotyped roles would be objectionable. Such language usage helps to perpetuate these stereotypes and thus to limit women's choices. Yet to depict women *only* in unconventional roles (astronaut, engineer, truck driver) would be a distortion of reality, for this would be a failure to "tell it like it is." This textbook seeks to avoid the unconscious stereotyping which helps to imprison women, while also avoiding the "stereotyping in reverse" which would distort the truth in a manner unacceptable in a textbook.

TRADITION AND COMMON SENSE SAY:	SCIENTIFIC INVESTIGATION FINDS THAT:
Men are intellectually superior to women.	Neither sex is superior in inherited intellectual capacities.
Colds are caused by chills and wet feet.	Colds are caused by viruses, although exposure may lower resistance.
One's character shows in one's face.	There is no dependable association between facial features and personality characteristics.
A person who cheats at cards will cheat in business.	Honesty in one situation tells little about one's behavior in a different situation.
Spare the rod and spoil the child.	Serious delinquents usually have been punished more severely than most nondelinquents.
The genius or near-genius is generally delicate, impractical, unstable, and unsuccessful.	The genius and near-genius group is above average in health, emotional adjustment, and income.
Pornographic literature encourages sex crimes and perversions.	There is no evidence to link pornographic literature with disapproved sexual behavior.
The black race is especially talented in music but inferior in intellect.	Scientists find no convincing evidence of differences in innate racial capacities.

self-deception of assuming that they have already been proved. If one presses for proof, one is told that the idea has been proved by experience. The term "common sense" puts a respectable front on all sorts of notions for which there is no systematic body of evidence that can be cited.

Common sense and tradition are closely interwoven, with many common-sense propositions becoming part of a people's traditional lore. If a distinction is to be drawn, it may be that traditional truths are those which have long been believed, while common-sense truths are uncritically accepted conclusions (recent or ancient) which are currently believed by one's fellows.

What often passes for common sense consists of a group's accumulation of collective guesses, hunches, and haphazard trial-and-error learnings. Many common-sense propositions are sound, earthy, useful bits of knowledge. "A soft answer turneth away wrath," and "Birds of a feather flock together," are practical observations on social life. But many common-sense conclusions are based on ignorance, prejudice, and mistaken interpretation.

When medieval Europeans noticed that feverish patients were free of lice while most healthy people were lousy, they made the common-sense conclusion that lice would cure fever and therefore sprinkled lice over feverish patients. Not until the fever subsided would the lice be removed. Common sense, like tradition, preserves both folk wisdom and folk nonsense, and to sort out one from the other is a task for science.

Science

Only within the last two or three hundred years has the scientific method become a common way of seeking answers about the natural world. Science has become a source of knowledge about our *social* world even more recently; yet in the brief period since we began to rely upon the scientific method, we have learned more about our world than had been learned in the preceding ten thousand years. The spectacular explosion of knowledge in the modern world parallels our use of the scientific method. What makes the scientific method so productive? How does it differ from other methods of seeking truth?

Characteristics of scientific knowledge

Verifiable evidence

Scientific knowledge is based on verifiable evidence. By <u>evidence</u> we mean <u>concrete factual observations</u> which other observers can see, weigh, measure, count, or check for accuracy. We may think the definition too obvious to mention; most of us have some awareness of the scientific method. Yet only a few centuries ago medieval scholars held long debates on how many teeth a horse had, without bothering to look into a horse's mouth to count them.

At this point we raise the troublesome methodological question, "What is a fact?" While the word looks deceptively simple, it is not easy to distinguish a fact from a widely shared illusion. Suppose we define a fact as a *descriptive statement upon which all qualified observers are in agreement.* By this definition, medieval ghosts were a fact, since all medieval observers agreed that ghosts were real. There is, therefore, no way to be *certain* that a fact is an accurate description and not a mistaken impression. Research would be easier if facts were dependable, unshakable certainties. Since they are not, the best we can do is to recognize that a fact is *a descriptive statement of reality which scientists, after careful examination and cross-checking, agree in believing to be accurate.*

Since science is based on factual verifiable evidence, science can deal only with questions about which such evidence can be found. Questions like, "Is there a God?" "What is the purpose and destiny of the human race?" or "What makes a thing beautiful?" are not scientific questions because they cannot be treated factually. Such questions may be terribly important, but the scientific method has no tools for handling them. Scientists can study human

beliefs about God, or human destiny, or beauty, or anything else, and they may study the *personal and social consequences* of such beliefs; but these are studies of human behavior, with no attempt to settle the truth or error of the beliefs themselves.

Evidence consists of verifiable facts

Science then does not have answers for everything, and many important questions are not scientific questions. The scientific method is our most reliable source of factual knowledge about human behavior and the natural universe, but science with its dependence upon verifiable factual evidence cannot answer questions about value, or aesthetics, or purpose and ultimate meaning, or supernatural phenomena. Answers to such questions must be sought in philosophy, metaphysics, or religion.

Each scientific conclusion represents the most reasonable interpretation of all the available evidence—but new evidence may appear tomorrow. Therefore <u>science has no absolute truths</u>. An absolute truth is one which will hold true for all times, places, or circumstances. All scientific truth is tentative, subject to revision in the light of new evidence. Some scientific conclusions (e.g., that the earth is a spheroid; or that innate drives are culturally conditioned) are based upon such a large and consistent body of evidence that scientists doubt that they will ever be overturned by new evidence. Yet the scientific method requires that *all* conclusions be open to reexamination whenever new evidence is found to challenge them.

This receptivity to new evidence is easy to state but not always easy to maintain. Scientists are also human beings, and despite their commitment to scientific detachment, they sometimes refuse to examine new evidence if it conflicts with established scientific traditions. Galileo's colleagues refused to look through his telescope and see the moons of Jupiter; Lavoisier insisted that stones (meteorites) could not fall from the air because there were none up there; all the scientists of the Paris Academy pronounced Edison's phonograph a humbug because they knew that the human voice could not be reproduced from a disk. Harvey's circulation of the blood, Pasteur's microbes, and Simmelweis's discovery that physicians spread childbed fever were all rejected for many years after their discovery. A more recent survey [Warner, 1938][2] found that many of the psychologists who rejected Rhine's findings on extrasensory perception had read none of his published research. To maintain an open-minded willingness to examine new evidence is so difficult a task that even scientists do not always succeed.

Ethical neutrality

Science is knowledge, and knowledge can be put to differing uses. Atomic fission can be used to power a city or to incinerate a nation. Every use of scientific knowledge involves a choice between values. Our values define what is most important to us. Science tells us that overeating and cigarette smoking will shorten our life expectancy. But can science tell us which we should choose—a longer life or a more indulgent one? Science can answer ques-

tions of fact, but has no way to prove that one value is better than another.

Science, then, is ethically neutral. Science seeks knowledge, while society's values determine how this knowledge is to be used. Knowledge about bacteria can be used to preserve health or to wage germ warfare. Knowledge about group organization can be used to preserve a democracy or to establish a dictatorship.

Since science is ethically neutral, no field of inquiry is too sacred to explore. Scientific discoveries sometimes destroy revered myths, undermine established institutions, and challenge cherished values. When Vesalius was laying the foundations of anatomy by dissecting the human body, he was forced to rob graves to get corpses to dissect, since people considered the human body too "sacred" to cut up. Kinsey's studies of human sexual behavior a few years ago and Masters and Johnson's more recent studies [1966; 1970] aroused a chorus of protest from those who feel that human sexual behavior is "too intimate" for scientific inquiry. But science recognizes no "improper" questions. *Any* questions on which verifiable evidence can be secured is a proper question for science. Science acts on the belief that, if scientific knowledge undermines established beliefs, institutions, and practices, then these beliefs, institutions, and practices need to be revised.

Science may be ethically neutral, but *scientists* are not. Each scientist has his own value system which he cannot totally divorce from his work. Perhaps he should not. There is sharp debate among scientists as to whether their scientific disciplines should be committed to a neutral search for knowledge, or to the attainment of certain social goals. For example, should the physicist accept an assignment to develop a more deadly bomb, or should the sociologist show an oppressive, undemocratic government how to keep its people enslaved? These questions are discussed in the next chapter in a section on the roles of the sociologist.

[2]Bracketed references in the text are to sources described in full in the Bibliography at the end of the book.

Observation—the basic technique of scientific method

The word "evidence" keeps popping up in discussions of scientific method. What is evidence and where is it found? Evidence consists of verifiable facts of all kinds and is found through scientific observation. But scientific observation is not the same as looking at things. All of us have been looking at things all our lives, but this activity does not make us scientific observers, any more than a lifetime of swatting flies makes us entomologists. Wherein does scientific observation differ from just looking at things?

Accuracy

Scientific observation is *accurate*. The scientific observer is extremely careful to make certain that things are exactly as described. The statement, "My backyard is full of dead trees," is of uncertain accuracy unless the trees have been examined by an expert to be sure they are dead and not merely dormant. Or the statement, "Families are larger than they used to be," is of low accuracy. *What* size families, and *where,* are more numerous than they were *when?* If we say, "The proportion of American families with four or more children has grown substantially in the past decade," the statement is more accurate. Painstaking checking, rechecking, and cross-checking to produce carefully stated propositions are the price of scientific accuracy.

Precision

Scientific observation is *precise.* The statement, "My backyard is full of dead trees," is not precise, even though it may be accurate. What is meant by "full of" dead trees? If the sentence reads, "All the trees in my yard are dead," or "There are twenty dead trees in my yard," the statement gains in precision. While accuracy refers to the truth or correctness of a statement, *precision refers to degree or measurement.* If the above statement about family size is revised to read, "The proportion of American families with four or more children currently living with them increased from 6.6 percent of all families in 1948 to 11.1 percent in 1965, then declined to 8.6 by 1972," the statement is more precise.

In a laboratory experiment the scientist weighs, measures, counts, or times each development with great care. A report which read, "I took some hot salt water, added a pinch of copper sulfate and a little nitric acid, let it cool for a while . . ." would be almost useless. How much water? How hot? How much salt, copper sulfate, and acid? Cooled for how long, and to what temperature? Unless quite precise, an observation is of limited value to science.

Since scientific writing seeks precision, science avoids colorful or extravagant language. While literature may aim to arouse the feelings of the reader, science aims to convey accurate information. Tennyson's lines, "Every moment dies a man; every moment one is born," is good literature. To be good science, it should be written, "In the entire world, according to 1972 figures, every 0.5956 seconds, on the average, dies a man, woman, or child; every 0.2448 seconds, on the average, an infant is born." Literary writing may be intentionally vague, imprecise, and fanciful, stimulating the reader to wonder what is meant (e.g., whether Hamlet was really insane). The dramatic sweep of the novelist and the provocative imagery of the poet have no place in scientific writing. Yet good scientific writing need not be dull, and should never plod through an insufferable mass of ill-arranged detail. Good scientific writing is clear, is easily understood by a qualified reader, and gets its suspense from a readable procession of significant facts and interpretations.

How much precision is needed? This depends upon what we are studying. In measuring atoms, a millionth of an inch may be too large an error, whereas at an agricultural experiment station, a variation of several feet may be unimportant. A social scientist might observe the behavior of a mob of "several hundred" persons without counting them, just as an entomologist can describe a "large" swarm of bees without counting them. Science, however, always seeks *as much precision as the particular problem requires.* If the conditions of observation make this degree of precision impossible, the scientist must suspend judgment until more precise observations can be collected.

System

Scientific observation is *systematic.* A scientific investigation defines a problem, then draws up an organized plan for collecting facts about it. Suppose the question is, "How does the dropout rate of college students who marry while in college compare with the dropout rate of unmarried students?" One might try to answer the question by simply recalling the students one has known; but this sample would be small; it might not be typical; and one's memory is imperfect. Conclusions based on casual recollections are not very reliable. If our research plan calls for a systematic check on the college records of several thousand students, then our dropout rates for single and married students are based on dependable factual data. Unless these data have been collected as part of an organized systematic program of scientific observation, they are likely to be spotty and incomplete. Anecdotes, personal recollections, offhand opinions, and travelogue impressions may suggest an hypothesis which is worth testing; but no scientist would base a conclusion upon such data.

Records

Scientific observation is *recorded.* Human memory is notoriously fallible. Data which are

not recorded are not dependable. No laboratory scientist would attempt to memorize a detailed experiment. He or she writes it out completely, recording each operation and reaction, so that the procedures and findings described can be accurately known and verified by other scientists.

In the field of human behavior, the need for recorded observation is less fully realized. Suppose a professor were to say, "A number of women students have majored in this field, and while some do excellent work, on the average they don't quite measure up to the men students in this field." What, exactly, is this professor saying? Unless he has actually recorded and computed average scores for both groups, he is in effect saying, "I have mentally recalled the grades of hundreds of my students, and have mentally added the scores and mentally computed averages for male and female students; and I have found the female average to be lower." Such a feat of memory would be impossible. All conclusions based on recalling a mass of unrecorded data are untrustworthy.

In fact, such conclusions based on informal recollection may be worse than useless, for they generally express the prejudices of the observer, masquerading as a scientific conclusion. Since memory is imperfect, we often "remember" things the way we prefer them to have been rather than as they actually were. Prejudice, wishful thinking, and habitual attitude all operate to twist our observations to fit our preferences. It is important, therefore, that evidence be recorded as quickly as possible; the longer we wait the more greatly our prejudices, preferences, and afterthoughts may have distorted it. The following accounts of a disaster as reported by one of the survivors show the progressive changes made by time:

Man's memories of themselves aren't accurate. One month after the sinking of the Litch I questioned the survivors for a second time. The stories had altered—in some cases radically. When the ship blew up it was honorable and acceptable to save one's own skin. Later, as we got closer to civilization and normal society, many men remembered something new, how they had struggled to save others at the risk of their own lives.

My notes on a signalman, made ten minutes after he was rescued, read, "After I jumped over, I swam as fast as I could, I swam upwind like you always told us. I had no life jacket and got scared. I saw someone floating with his head under water. It was Mr. —. His back was broken; I could tell by the funny way it angled just below the neck. I said to myself if he's dead there's no use in his wasting the life jacket. I took the jacket from him and held on to it. I don't know what happened to Mr. —'s body."

When I interviewed the same man a month later he told me this: "I swam from the ship as fast as I could. I swam upwind just like you always told us. I saw someone floating with his head under water. It was Mr. —. Although his back was broken and his head had been submerged, I figured maybe the doctor could do something for him. I pulled his head out of the water and tied the jacket tie under his chin so that his head'd stay in the air. I trod water for about an hour, just holding onto Mr. —'s life jacket for a rest occasionally. I saw a raft about five hundred yards away. I thought maybe the doctor or a hospital corpsman might be on it. I swam over to it. The doctor wasn't there. We paddled over where Mr. — had been, but there was no sign of him."

I met the signalman on the street in Washington a couple of months ago—five years after the Litch sank. His story had changed more. Now it was he, the signalman, who had the life jacket. When he saw that Mr. — had a broken back, the signalman removed his life jacket and gave it to the injured officer. "I knew he was dead, but figured maybe there was a chance in a thousand he might be saved. It was my duty to try to help him, so I gave him my jacket." (From William J. Lederer, *All the Ships at Sea,* William Morrow & Company, Inc., New York, 1950, pp. 203–204. Reprinted by permission of Harold Ober Associates Incorporated. © 1950 by William J. Lederer.)

Objectivity

Scientific observation is *objective*. This means that, insofar as is humanly possible, the observation is unaffected by the observer's own belief, preferences, wishes, or values. In other words, *objectivity* means the *ability to see and accept facts as they are, not as one might wish them to be.* It is fairly easy to be objective when observing something about which we have no preferences or values. It is fairly easy to study objectively the mating practices of the fruit fly, but less easy to view the mating practices of the human being with objective detachment. On any matter where our emotions, beliefs, habits, and values are involved, we are likely to see whatever agrees with our emotional needs and values. Few Americans, for example, could record a detailed description of the workings of the polygamous family system without including many words and phrases which would betray their disapproval. If a set of scientific observations is reported objectively, the reader will be unable to know whether the observer likes or dislikes what he or she has reported. Yet many experiments have shown that even our simplest observations are affected by our feelings and expectations. For example, in one investigation [Harvey, 1953] most observers judged a white disk imprinted with the name "Eisenhower" to be larger than disks of the same size with random names from the phone book; poor children generally estimated the size of coins to be larger than did children from prosperous homes; and a leaf-shaped piece of green cloth was judged to be greener than a donkey-shaped piece of the same cloth.

Many questions which should be clear-cut scientific questions arouse violent controversy because we find it hard to be objective or even to be sure *when we are* being objective. The question, "Does cigarette smoking promote lung cancer?" is not an impossibly difficult scientific question; yet each new study provokes bitter emotional reaction. The data are now quite conclusive, but this conclusion is displeasing to many people. The tobacco industry, which can draw a mountain of conclusion from a molehill of scientific evidence when preparing advertising claims, insists that we need more evidence before drawing conclusions on *this* question. Cigarette smokers with an appetite to defend are also practicing their newly discovered habit of withholding judgment until more data are available. Some ardent battlers against the cigarette "knew" the answer long before any studies were conducted. On this question few are disinterested and few can be fully objective.

Objectivity means the ability to see and accept facts as they are, not as one might wish them to be

To be objective is perhaps the most taxing of all scientific obligations. It is not enough to be willing to see facts as they are. We must know what our biases are if we are to guard against them. A _bias_ is simply *a tendency, usually unconscious, to see facts in a certain way because of one's habits, wishes, interests, and values.* Thus, in a racial incident one observer sees a white person insulting or abusing a black while another observer sees a black acting presumptuously and provocatively. One observer sees black people courageously asserting their democratic rights, while another sees them making outrageous demands.

Seldom are "the facts" so undebatable that bias does not distort them. *Selective perception is a tendency to see or hear only those facts which support our beliefs and overlook the others.* Many experiments have shown that most people who observe a social situation will see and hear only what they expect to see

and hear. If what we expect to see isn't there, we see it anyway! This is dramatically shown in a famous experiment [Allport and Postman, 1947] in which observers were shown a picture of a roughly dressed white man holding an open razor and arguing violently with a well-dressed black man who was shown in an apologetic, conciliatory posture; then the observers were asked to describe the scene. Some of them "saw" the razor in the black man's hand, where they expected it to be. Others perceived it correctly, but in passing on a description of the scene (A described it to B, who described it to C, and so on), they soon had the razor in the black man's hand, where it "belonged." Even though they were not emotionally involved in the situation, had ample time to study it, and were making a conscious effort to be accurate in what they saw and reported or heard, the observers' unconscious biases still led many of them to "see" or "hear" a fact that wasn't there.

The student who is inclined to doubt that people often see and hear what they expect to see and hear should try a simple experiment. At a party, greet each arriving guest with a broad smile, a hearty handshake, and a murmured, "Pity to see you here this evening," and speed each departing guest with, "Glad you must leave so early!" Many will hear what they expect to hear, not what was actually spoken. This is why, if one is convinced that black people are lazy, Jews are pushy, businessmen are crooked, or cops are brutal, one will seldom "see" anything that conflicts with these expectations. Bias is like a sieve which allows to pass through it only what is supposed to pass through. Bias screens out our perceptions, generally admitting to our consciousness only those perceptions which agree with the biases.

Some common threats to objectivity, then, are vested interest, habit, and bias. Objectivity does not come easily to an observer, but it can be learned. One can become more objective as one becomes aware of personal biases and makes allowance for them. Through rigorous training in scientific methodology, through studying many experiments and noting many examples of objective and nonobjective uses of data, an observer may eventually develop some ability to cut through many layers of self-deception and to perceive facts with a greater degree of scientific objectivity. The scientist also has another powerful ally—the criticism of colleagues. The scientist publishes work so that it may be checked by other scientists who may not share his or her biases and who come to the problem with a different point of view. This process of publication and criticism means that shoddy work is soon exposed, and the scientist who lets bias dictate the uses of data is open to severe criticism.

In writing observations, the scientist uses objective language. For example, consider these statements:

The increasing American military commitment in Vietnam was accompanied by more frequent peace demonstrations and by increasing public debate over the wisdom of this policy.

Increasing American aggression in Vietnam aroused a mounting chorus of public indignation at our arrogant and brutal denial of self-government to the Vietnamese people.

Our rising determination to prevent the Communist enslavement of Vietnam was harassed by the mounting frenzy of our own Communist sympathizers and peace-at-any-price appeasers.

The first of these statements is written in the neutral, descriptive language of the social scientist, while the other two are fiercely partisan. Polemical writing may be appropriate in debate, but not in science.

In recent years, polemical papers have been appearing at the annual meetings of academic societies such as the American Sociological Association, and in the new journals devoted to "radical" sociology. In these papers, objectivity, neutrality, and rigorous passion for accuracy are secondary to sweeping generalizations, strident accusations, and passionate commitment to social action. This does not mean that the scientific method is changing. Instead, it reflects a debate, currently raging in all the sciences, over whether their authors' primary commitment is to scientific knowledge or to social action [Horton and Bouma, 1971].

Trained observation

Scientific observations are made by *trained observers*. A billion people watch the sun and the moon sweep across the sky, but more sophisticated observers possess certain knowledge which tells them that is not exactly what happens. Untrained observers do not know what to look for or how to interpret it. They do not know the pitfalls which lead to inaccurate observation, nor are they fully aware of the tricks their own limitations and biases may play on them. Startling reports of weird phenomena generally come from uneducated, unsophisticated persons, and are discounted by the experts. When some remarkable observations are reported, the scientist will want to know: (1) What is the observer's general level of education and sophistication? Is this person a member of a superstition-ridden folk group, or of a well-informed and somewhat skeptical population? (2) What is his or her special knowledge or training in this particular field? Does this observer have the knowledge to discern whether this event has a perfectly natural explanation? Thus the biologist among the ship's passengers is less likely to see a sea monster than are the members of the crew, and the meteorologist sees fewer flying saucers than people with no special knowledge of atmospheric phenomena.

At the present moment, public interest in psychic and occult phenomena is exploding. A book claiming that plants have consciousness and are responsive to human feelings has become a best seller [Tompkins and Bird, 1973], although scientists are generally unimpressed [First, 1973], and there are no authenticated reports that anyone has yet "hated" the crabgrass out of the lawn. A one-time stage magician, Uri Geller, is currently attracting great attention as a psychic, and has even impressed a team of physicists at Stanford Research Institute [*Science News,* July 20, 1974, p. 46]. But physicists and other scientists, whatever their credentials as scientists, are *not* trained observers of sleight-of-hand deception. Stage magicians consider scientists as easy to fool as anyone else, and generally dismiss Geller and other psychics as showmen with no psychic powers. [Weil, 1974; *Business Week,* Jan. 26, 1974, pp. 76–78]. Obviously, a "trained observer" must be trained in the particular kind of observation he or she is conducting.

Many events happen without any scientific observer on the sidelines. If each sea monster broke water before a panel of ichthyologists, each ghost materialized before the searching gaze of psychologists, and each revolution were staged before a team of visiting sociologists, our knowledge would be far more complete. But for many phenomena, the only reports we have are the casual impressions of untrained observers who happened to be there; these reports may be interesting and possibly useful, but must be interpreted most cautiously by scientists.

Controlled conditions

Scientific observation is conducted under *controlled conditions.* Laboratories are popular with scientists because they are handy places to control heat, light, pressure, time intervals, or whatever is important. We have a scientific experiment when we *control all important variables except one*, then see what happens when that one is varied. Unless all variables except one have been controlled, we cannot be sure which variable has produced the results. For example, if we wish to study the effects of phosphates on plant growth, all other factors—seed, soil, water, sunlight, temperature, humidity—must be the same for all the sample plots; then the varying amounts of phosphates on different test plots can be held responsible for different growth rates. This is the basic technique in all scientific experimentation—allow one variable to vary while holding all other variables constant.

There are procedures for *multivariate analysis* which enable the researcher to work with two or more variables at a time. But this is only a refinement of the basic procedure of holding all other variables constant in order to measure the impact of the one (or more) under study.

Failure to control all variables is a most common error in scientific method and accounts for most false conclusions. For example, the promotion of antihistamines as a cold cure a few years ago was based on several experiments in which half the patients reporting with cold symptoms were given an antihistamine pill, while the other half were given a blank pill which contained no medicine. This latter half were the "control group," used as a base for measuring the effectiveness of the new pill upon the test group. The findings were encouraging, with many more of the test group reporting that their colds had gone away. These findings were enthusiastically and uncritically reported in popular magazines, and dozens of "cold-stopper" manufacturers climbed on the gold-filled band wagon.

These experiments were honestly conducted, but further research disclosed a serious error in method. Although the men reporting for treatment believed they were all getting the same pill, the physician knew which pill each man received. Thus when the man made his before-and-after reports to the physician, the unconscious bias of the physician apparently led him to shade the reports in the direction which would support the findings he hoped to get. When a national test of the Salk polio vaccine was arranged, the standard safeguards were used to guard against the unconscious bias of the persons conducting the experiment. Using the "double-blind" technique, identical appearing doses of vaccine and of blanks were numbered and recorded in a secret code book, so that neither the patients nor the physicians giving the injections and reporting each case had any way of knowing which way to shade their reports. This meant that we could *know* that the findings were due to the vaccine and not due to unconscious bias. Deliberate dishonesty is exceedingly rare among serious scientists, but unconscious bias is a constant hazard, requiring research controls which make it more difficult for bias to operate.

Since laboratories are such convenient places to control the conditions of observation, scientists use them whenever possible. But much that is important cannot be dragged into a laboratory. Volcanoes and earthquakes cannot be staged in a test tube, nor can we study the courtship process very realistically by herding some couples into a laboratory. Both physical and social scientists frequently must observe phenomena in their natural setting. Techniques may range from lowering a bathysphere to the ocean floor to giving a questionnaire to a group of army recruits. If we remember that the basic scientific procedure is the conducting of accurate observations, while laboratories, instruments, and IBM cards are merely *tools* of observation, this difference in technique will not confuse us.

When phenomena—riots, panics, disasters, flying-saucer sightings—must be observed in their natural setting where the conditions of observation are not under the scientist's control, the scientist can only evaluate the observation in the light of the surrounding conditions and circumstances. Was the observer an interested bystander or an emotionally involved participant? Was the observer calm, relaxed, and comfortable, or excited, terrified, exhausted, hunger-crazed, or otherwise incapable of accurate observation? What were the lighting conditions and other visual circumstances? It is not surprising that sailors, traditionally a highly superstitious group who often suffered prolonged isolation, danger, hunger, thirst, and exhaustion, should have peered through ocean spray or evening haze and seen enticing mermaids and terrifying monsters which other observers have been unable to verify.

The scientific critic will trust a reported observation only insofar as the conditions of observation have been controlled. On this basis, science is skeptical of the claims of spiritualism and mind reading. Spiritualists can conduct a very convincing seance in their own stage setting but are loath to attempt a seance where the room, furnishings, and lighting are controlled by the scientist. The professional mind reader is very convincing in a theater setting but is unwilling to attempt a reading under scientifically controlled conditions. Until spiritualists and mind readers will make demonstrations under conditions which preclude the possibility of deception, scientists will dismiss them as either entertainers or frauds.

Spiritualists can conduct a very convincing seance in their own stage setting

Is it not strange that most of those who claim to foresee the future are performing in shabby carnivals and nightclubs instead of raking in the millions in Wall Street? Why has no professed mind reader ever won a world chess or bridge championship? If telekinesis (moving physical objects by mental power) is real, why aren't psychics spiriting wads of banknotes from locked vaults instead of fussing around with teacups and collar buttons? Although there are occasional newspaper reports of some psychic having "solved" a crime, is it not significant that police departments and intelligence agencies do not employ psychics? Yet although many exposés of the tricks of psychics, mentalists, fortune tellers, astrologers, and spiritualists have been published [Barber and Meeker, 1974], their popular following today seems greater than at any time in recent history.

In these several respects, then, scientific observation differs from looking at things. We spend our lives looking at things, and this activity brings us much information, many impressions, and numerous conclusions. But these conclusions are clouded by accident of coincidence, by selective memory, and by personal bias. Therefore, before accepting any generalization as true, the critical observer wants to know what it is based upon. Is this conclusion based upon a systematically collected body of scientific evidence, or is it an offhand reaction to haphazard observation?

The scientific method of investigation

The scientific method (some would prefer to say scientific methods) includes a great deal. The scientist must accumulate considerable background information on the problem. Then he or she formulates an *hypothesis.* This is a carefully considered theoretical statement which seeks to relate all the *known* facts to one another in a logical manner. The hypothesis is then tested by scientific research. For example, the hypothesis that cancer is a virus disease is based upon a great deal of observation; it relates known facts in a logical manner; and it is now being tested through many research projects. Eventually an hypothesis is confirmed, rejected, or revised, and in this manner a science grows.

There are several steps in scientific research. They are easy to list but not always easy to follow.

1. *Formulate the problem,* that is, find a problem of some apparent scientific importance and define it so that it can be studied scientifically. Suppose the question arises as to whether fraternity membership is a hindrance to academic success. Our hypothesis might be, "Fraternity members receive lower grades than comparable nonmembers."

2. *Plan the research design,* outlining just what is to be studied, what data will be sought, and where and how they will be collected, processed, and analyzed. In the above example, we should need to decide how to select and match the samples of fraternity members and nonmembers, where to secure data on the grades, and what mechanical and statistical procedures to use in analyzing these data and in arriving at conclusions.
3. *Collect the data* in accordance with the research design. Often it will be necessary to change the design to meet some unforeseen difficulty.
4. *Analyze the data.* Classify, tabulate, and compare the data, making whatever tests and computations are necessary to help find the results.
5. *Draw conclusions.* Was the original hypothesis confirmed or rejected? Or were the results inconclusive? What has this research added to our knowledge? What implications has it for sociological theory? What new questions and suggestions for further research have arisen from this investigation?

Normative methods of investigation

The term *normative* means "to make conform to or support some norm or pattern." The scientific method of investigation consists of stating a question, collecting evidence, and drawing conclusions from the evidence, however surprising or unwelcome they may be. The normative method, by contrast, states the question in such a way that the conclusion is implied, and then looks for evidence in support of this conclusion. This is the method of "investigation" most people use most of the time, and which even scientists sometimes fall into. For example, the question, "How does the traditional family thwart emotional growth?" (or, conversely, "How does the traditional family promote emotional growth?") really states a conclusion and asks for evidence to support it. Most popular thinking and a good deal of scientific research is normative, for it is a search for evidence to support a conclusion which has already been assumed. Most Marxian scholarship is normative, for it begins with the conclusion that class oppression is the cause of most social ills. Much conservative-biased research is equally normative, for it begins with the conclusion that most social ills stem from the personal defects and failings of the individuals involved, while the actual "research" consists of an effort to identify these failings. The findings of normative research are not necessarily "wrong," but they are always incomplete, because the researcher looks for only the kinds of evidence which support the preconceived conclusion.

Sociology as a science

Science may be defined in at least two ways: (1) A science is a body of organized, verified knowledge which has been secured through scientific investigation; (2) a science is a method of study whereby a body of organized, verified knowledge is discovered. These are, of course, two ways of saying much the same thing.

If the first definition is accepted, then sociology is a science *to the extent that it develops a body of organized, verified knowledge* which is based on scientific investigation. To the extent that sociology forsakes myth, folklore, and wishful thinking and bases its conclusions on scientific evidence, it is a science. If science is defined as a method of study, then sociology is a science *to the extent that it uses scientific methods of study.* All natural phenomena can be studied scientifically, if one is willing to use scientific methods. Any kind of behavior—whether of atoms, animals, or adolescents—is a proper field for scientific study.

During human history, few of our actions have been based on verified knowledge, for people through the ages have been guided mainly by folklore, habit, and guesswork. Until a few centuries ago, very few people accepted the idea that we should find out about the natural world by systematic observation of the natural world itself, rather than by consulting oracles, ancestors, or intuition. This new idea

created the modern world. A few decades ago, we began acting on the assumption that this same approach might also give useful knowledge about human social life. Just how far we have replaced folklore with knowledge in this area will be explored in the chapters which follow.

The development of sociology

Sociology is the youngest of the social sciences. Auguste Comte in France coined the word "sociology" in his *Positive Philosophy,* published in 1838. He believed that a science of sociology should be based on systematic observation and classification, not on authority and speculation. This was a relatively new idea at that time. Herbert Spencer in England published his *Principles of Sociology* in 1876. He applied the theory of organic evolution to human society and developed a grand theory of "social evolution" which was widely accepted for several decades, then discarded for several decades, and is today regaining a partial acceptance in modified form. Lester F. Ward, an American, published his *Dynamic Sociology* in 1883, calling for social progress through intelligent social action which sociologists should guide. All these founders of sociology were basically social philosophers. They proclaimed that sociologists should collect, organize, and classify factual data, and derive sound social theories from these facts: but very often their own method was to think out a grand system of theory and then seek facts to support it. So while they called for scientific investigation, they did relatively little of it themselves. Yet they took the necessary first steps, for the *idea* of a science of sociology had to precede the building of one.

A Frenchman, Emile Durkheim, gave the most notable early demonstration of scientific methodology in sociology. In his *Rules of Sociological Method,* published in 1895, he outlined the methodology which he pursued in his study *Suicide,* published in 1897. Instead of *speculating* upon the causes of suicide, he first planned his research design and then collected a large mass of data on the characteristics of people who commit suicide, and then derived a theory of suicide from these data.

Courses in sociology appeared in many universities in the 1890s. The *American Journal of Sociology* began publication in 1895, and the American Sociological Society (now the American Sociological Association) was organized in 1905. Whereas most of the early European sociologists came from the fields of history, political economy, or philosophy, many of the early American sociologists had been social workers, ministers, or ministers' sons; and nearly all were from rural backgrounds. Urbanization and industrialization were creating grave social problems, and these early sociologists were groping for "scientific" solutions. They saw sociology as a scientific guide to social progress. The early volumes of the *American Journal of Sociology* contained relatively few articles devoted to scientific description or research, but carried many sermons filled with exhortation and advice. For example, a fairly typical article in 1903, "The Social Effects of the Eight Hour Day," contains no factual or experimental data, but is entirely devoted to a recital of all the social benefits which the writer assures us will follow from the shorter working day [McVay, 1903]. But by the 1930s, the several sociological journals were well filled with research articles and scientific descriptions. Sociology was becoming a body of scientific knowledge, with its theories based upon scientific observation rather than upon armchair speculation or impressionistic observation.

Summary

In our search for truth, we have relied upon: (1) *intuition,* ranging from brilliant imagination to naïve guesswork; (2) *authority,* which tells us what is true; (3) *tradition,* which finds truth in whatever has been long accepted as true; (4) *common sense,* a convenient catchall which includes casual observation plus any or all of the above sources; and (5) *science,* the newest method of seeking truth. Science differs from other sources of truth in that (1) since scientific truth is based on verifiable evidence, science studies only those questions on which verifiable evidence can be secured, making no attempt to answer many important questions of value, purpose, or ultimate meaning; furthermore science realizes that all scientific truth is tentative, subject to revision in the light of new evidence; and (2) science is ethically neutral, seeking to discover knowledge no matter what values or institutions it may undermine or reinforce.

The basic technique of scientific investigation is *observation.* Scientific observation differs from just looking at things in that scientific observation is: (1) *accurate,* seeking to describe what really exists; (2) as *precise* and exact as is necessary; (3) *systematic,* in an effort to find all the relevant data; (4) *recorded* in complete detail as quickly as possible; (5) *objective,* in being as free from distortion by vested interest, bias, or wishful thinking as is humanly possible, (6) *conducted by trained observers,* who know what to look for and how to recognize it; (7) *conducted under controlled conditions* which reduce the danger of fraud, self-deception, or mistaken interpretation. The several steps in a scientific research project are: (1) Formulate the problem; (2) plan the research design; (3) collect the data; (4) analyze the data; and (5) draw the conclusions. While the scientific method proceeds from evidence to conclusion, the popularly used *normative* method starts with a conclusion and hunts for evidence to support it.

Whether the study of our social relationships is a science is often debated. Sociology is a very new discipline, recently emerged from the speculations of nineteenth-century social philosophers and social reformers. To the extent that human social life is studied through scientific methods so that a body of verified knowledge is developed—to that extent these studies become social sciences.

Questions and projects

1. Does the rigorously trained scientist make use of any sources of truth other than scientific observation in daily life? Which ones? How often?
2. Distinguish between the critical and uncritical uses of authority.
3. Will a scientist ever make use of sacred authority?
4. Discuss the proposition: "We should discard all ideas which are not scientifically verified." Should we? Can we?
5. Can scientists prove that ghosts and spirits do not exist, or that fortune telling and mind reading do not work? Why are scientists so skeptical?
6. Suppose a foreman says, "I've supervised all kinds of workers, and the black workers just don't measure up to white standards." What would be necessary for this statement to be a scientifically justified conclusion?
7. Suppose you were a reporter for the campus paper, writing a news account of a violent confrontation between students and police. Should you try to write it with strict objectivity, or should you "slant" it, using polemical language and omitting certain facts while emphasizing others in order to support the side which you felt to be morally right?
8. Suppose you wished to get an accurate description of a riot which happened five years ago in a city of 100,000 people. Make an outline showing where you would look for data, and suggest the limitations or inadequacies of each type or source of data.
9. Read Sinclair Lewis's novel *Arrowsmith*. What are some of the difficulties Martin had to meet in becoming rigorously scientific?
10. Suppose you, a college student, were to take a summer job working as a laborer in a factory. Make a list of the biases which might distort your impressions of factory workers as you size them up. Subject these lists to class comparison and criticism.
11. Prepare three statements of some issue or event, one written as a neutral scientist, the second as a supporter, and the third as an opponent.

Suggested readings

BLUME, STUART S.: *Toward a Political Sociology of Science,* The Free Press, New York, 1974. A discussion of how science is influenced by politics and of how science may be used in making political decisions.

*CHASE, STUART, with EDMUND DE S. BRUNNER: *The Proper Study of Mankind: An Inquiry Into the Science of Human Relations,* 2d ed., Harper & Row, Publishers, Inc., New York, 1962. A highly readable little book on the contribution of social science to the solution of human problems.

*DUNHAM, BARROWS: *Man Against Myth,* Hill and Wang, Inc., New York, 1962. A critical examination of some of the major myths of the Western world.

*EVANS, BERGEN:*The Natural History of Nonsense,* Alfred A. Knopf, Inc., New York, 1946. An entertaining examination of many popular myths and superstitions, which are demolished with wit and learning.

*GARDNER, MARTIN: *Fads and Fallacies in the Name of Science,* Dover Publications, Inc., New York, 1957. An interesting account of many unscientific and pseudoscientific theories and the cults which promote them.

HOMANS, GEORGE E.: *The Nature of Social Science,* Harcourt, Brace and World, Inc., New York, 1967. A brief philosophical discussion of what social science is all about.

HUTECHEON, PAT DUFFY: "Sociology and the Objectivity Problem," *Sociology and Social Research,* 54:153–171, January, 1970. A state-

An asterisk before the citation indicates that the title is available in a paperback edition.

ment of the argument that detached objectivity is obsolete.

*INKELES, ALEX: *What Is Sociology: An Introduction to the Discipline and the Profession,* Prentice-Hall, Inc., Englewood Cliffs, N.J., 1964. A brief description of what sociology is and what sociologists do.

*KUHN, THOMAS S.: *The Structure of Scientific Revolutions,* University of Chicago Press, Chicago, 1970. A sophisticated discussion of how major shifts in scientific approach and method are developed.

*MACDOUGALL, CURTIS D.: *Hoaxes,* Dover Publications, Inc., New York, 1958. An entertaining survey of frauds in art, history, science, literature, politics, and journalism.

Chapter 2 • Fields and methods of sociology

This study represents an experimental test of deterrence hypotheses. The relative effects of moral appeal and a sanction threat on college classroom cheating were assessed. The moral appeal was found to have no effect, but a clear and substantial impact was observed for the sanction threat. The sanction threat was found to be most effective in deterring cheating among females and least effective among those who had the greatest incentive to cheat. The applicability of the findings to deterrence theory is discussed. *(Charles R. Tittle and Alan R. Rowe, "Moral Appeal, Sanction Threat, and Deviance: An Experimental Text,"* Social Problems, *20:488, Spring, 1973. Used with permission.)*

The above paragraph is an example of a research abstract, *a very condensed summary of a research study. Just what sociology and sociological research are all about is the subject of this chapter.*

What will you say when you go home next weekend and your younger sister asks, "Sociology? Well, what *is* sociology?" If you reply, "Sociology is the scientific study of human society with special emphasis upon groups and institutions," she may say, "Oh," and you will guess that she is as confused as you are. If you tell her, "Sociology is the scientific study of social problems such as race conflicts, crime, divorce, etc.," your definition will give her *some idea* of what sociology is about, and may be a pretty good description to give to someone who would be puzzled by a more technical definition. But your answer will not be entirely correct, for sociology is much more than the study of social problems. As a student of sociology, you need a better definition.

The field of sociology

First of all, *forget whatever you have read about sociology in popular magazines and newspapers,* for most of it is absurd. A magazine writer who wishes to make some offhand guesswork sound more impressive may preface it with the phrase, "Sociologists fear that . . . ," "Sociologists are alarmed by . . . ," or "Sociologists are wringing their hands over. . . ." This journalistic device helps a writer to speak authoritatively without knowing very much about the subject. Often a writer sets up a "straw man" by attributing to sociologists the viewpoints which (s)he is about to demolish. For example, a reviewer for the *New York Times Book Review* (Oct. 20, 1974, p. 34) writes of ". . . the myth—treasured by sociology professors everywhere—that we are a middle-class society." It would be difficult to find even one reputable sociologist teaching this. A week later (Oct. 27, 1974, p. 34), the *Times* reviewer refers to Angela Davis, the black revolutionist, as "a good sociologist." Miss Davis is a philosopher and social critic, not a sociologist. If the olympian *New York Times* doesn't know what a sociologist is or does, no wonder other people are confused.

Sociology is interested in the way groups interact with one another.

Careless use of the term "sociologist" is very common. Magazine and newspaper writers, social workers, labor leaders, government officials, or anyone else who is interested in social relations may be described as sociologists. This is incorrect. A sociologist is one who has earned advanced degrees or pursued other advanced studies in sociology (not in psychology, theology, social work, or some other field) and is engaged in teaching, research, or other professional work in the field of sociology.

No formal definition of sociology is very satisfactory. Short definitions do not really define; long, explicit definitions are usually cumbersome. Yet a definition of some sort is needed, and sociology is often defined as *the scientific study of human social life.* Human beings behave differently from other animals. They

have unique forms of group life, pursue customs, develop institutions, create values. Sociology applies scientific methods to the study of these phenomena in the search for scientific knowledge. It may be helpful at this point to discuss some definitions in reverse—to state through comparison what sociology is not.

Sociology is science, not social philosophy. A science is a body of knowledge; a philosophy is a system of ideas and values. A social philosophy is a set of ideas about how people *ought* to behave and treat one another; a social science studies how they actually *do* behave, and the consequences of this behavior.

Sociology is social science, not socialism. Socialism is a social philosophy with a political program, whereas sociology is a body of scientific knowledge. Socialists sometimes find in sociological research some material they can use in their propaganda; so do Republicans and Democrats. Some sociologists are socialists; many more are Republicans or Democrats.

Sociology concentrates its study upon the group life of human beings and the product of their group living. The sociologist is especially interested in the customs, traditions, and values which emerge from group living, and in the way group living is, in turn, affected by these customs, traditions, and values. Sociology is interested in the way groups interact with one another and in the processes and institutions which they develop. Sociology is subdivided into many specialized fields, of which a partial list includes:

Applied Sociology
Collective Behavior and Mass Communication
Community
Comparative Sociology
Crime and Delinquency
Cultural Sociology
Demography
Deviant Behavior
Formal and Complex Organizations
Human Ecology
Industrial Sociology
Law and Society
Leisure, Sports, Recreation, and the Arts

Marriage and the Family
Mathematical Sociology
Medical Sociology
Methodology and Statistics
Military Sociology
Political Sociology
Race and Ethnic Relations
Rural Sociology
Social Change
Social Control
Social Organization
Social Psychology
Sociological Theory
Sociology of Education
Sociology of Occupations and Professions
Sociology of Religion
Sociology of Small Groups
Sociology of Knowledge and Science
Stratification and Mobility
Urban Sociology

These topics are not the exclusive property of sociology, for other fields share our interest in them. For example, our interest in communication and public opinion is shared by psychology and political science; criminology is shared with psychology, political science, law and police science, and so on. No science can fence itself off from other sciences, least of all sociology. Our field is especially close to those of psychology and anthropology, and overlaps theirs so constantly that any firm boundaries would be arbitrary and unrealistic. The more we learn about human behavior, the more we realize that no one field of knowledge can fully explain it.

The methods of sociological research

The methods of sociological research are basically those outlined in the preceding chapter and used by all scientists. As Karl Pearson has remarked, "The unity of all science consists alone in its method, not in its material. The man who classifies facts of any kind whatever, who sees their mutual relation and describes their sequences, is applying the scientific method and is a man of science" [1900, p. 12].

While scientific methods are basically alike for all sciences, scientific *techniques* differ, for techniques are the particular ways in which scientific methods are applied to a particular problem. Each science must, therefore, develop a series of techniques which fits the body of material it studies. What are some of the techniques of sociological research?

Cross-sectional and longitudinal studies

Every study has some sort of time setting. A study which limits its observations to a single point in time is called a *cross-sectional* study. For example, Freedman, Whelpton, and Campbell [1959] interviewed a national sample of 2,713 young married women to discover their childbearing frequency and expectations. If the study extends over time, describing a trend or making a series of before-and-after observations, it is called a *longitudinal* study. The national public opinion polls (Gallup, Harris, and others) are cross-sectional studies, but if the same set of questions is repeated at intervals over a period of years, longitudinal comparisons can be drawn.

Longitudinal studies may be either *prospective* or *retrospective*. A retrospective study (often called an *ex post facto* study) works backward in time, using data that are recorded somewhere. For example, Wynder and Graham [1950] used hospital records of 605 lung cancer victims and found that all but eight were cigarette smokers. When a retrospective study shows strong evidence of a relationship, the next step often is to see whether a prospective study will confirm the relationship. A prospective study begins with the present and carries observations forward over a period of time. Thus Dorn [1959] and Kahn [1966] followed the health history of 200,000 veterans for eleven years, finding that the pack-a-day-or-more smokers were sixteen times as likely to die from lung cancer as were nonsmokers. Prospective studies take a long time to complete and are often very costly, making them one of the least common types of research study.

All sciences use experiments. An experiment may be either a laboratory experiment or a field experiment. In the laboratory experiment, the materials or people are brought into the laboratory for study. In laboratory experiments with people, the people are recruited, assembled, and perhaps paid for engaging in the experiment. Dollard's famous frustration-aggression studies [1939] were conducted by assembling a number of students as experimental subjects, supposedly to study the effects of fatigue upon task performance; then these students were subjected to intense frustration through prolonged boredom, nonarrival of promised food and games, and other intentional annoyances, while their aggressive responses were cataloged.

The field experiment takes the research out among the people instead of bringing the people to the research laboratory. A massive field experiment involving the vaccination of several million children established the value of the Salk polio vaccine. A continuing series of field experiments are seeking to find effective ways of promoting the practice of birth control in underdeveloped countries and among disadvantaged groups in the United States [Berelson, 1966].

The concept of any experiment is quite simple: Hold all variables constant except one; cause it to vary and see what happens.

A *variable* is anything which differs from person to person, group to group, time to time, or place to place—age, education, income, and many others. As an example, suppose we want to know whether abolishing grades would increase learning or increase loafing. To test this by experiment, we would need a *control group* of classes which follow the usual teaching and grading procedures, and an *experimental group* of classes using whatever experimental procedure is being tested. To "hold all other variables constant," the control and experimental groups would need to be alike in caliber of student, subject studied, quality of teaching,

students' work load, students' finances, and anything else likely to affect their performance. We would also need a reliable instrument to measure learning outcomes (after reaching agreement upon *what* learning outcomes were important). Then the results of the trial could be objectively determined. If the experimental group shows greater or lesser learning gains than the control group, and this difference is confirmed by repetitions of the experiment conducted by other scholars (replication studies), then significant conclusions can be drawn.

There are two common ways of setting up experimental and control groups. One is the *matched-pair* technique. For each person in the experimental group, another person like him or her in all important variables (such as age, religion, education, occupation, or anything important to this research) is found and placed in the control group. Another technique is the *random-assignment* technique, in which statistically random assignments of persons to experimental and control groups are made—such as assigning the first person to the experimental group, the next to the control group, and so on. Suppose we wish to measure the effectiveness of an experimental treatment program for delinquents in a reformatory. Using one technique, we should match each delinquent who received the experimental treatment (experimental group) with another delinquent, matched for other variables thought important, who received only the usual treatment (control group). Using the random-assignment technique, every second (or third, or tenth) delinquent would be assigned to the experimental group upon arrival at the reformatory, with the others becoming the control group. Wherever the researcher is permitted to make assignments in this way, the random-assignment technique is far easier and at least as accurate; but often, when the research situation precludes this technique, the matched-pair technique may be used.

Experiments in sociology face certain difficulties. An experiment involving thousands of people may be prohibitively expensive. It may take years to complete a prospective study. Our values forbid us to use people in any experiments which may injure them. The scientific world reacts strongly in those infrequent instances where human subjects have been used in a hazardous or harmful manner [Katz, 1972]. When people are unwilling to cooperate in an experiment, we cannot force them to do so (although we may occasionally trick them into unconscious cooperation). Furthermore, when people realize that they are experimental subjects, they begin to act differently, and the experiment may be spoiled. Almost any kind of experimental or observational study upon people *who know they are being studied* will give some interesting findings which may vanish soon after the study is ended. This is known as the Hawthorne effect, named after some experiments with temperature, humidity, rest periods, and other working conditions at the Hawthorne plant of Western Electric Company [Roethlisberger, 1949]. It was found that *any* change in the working conditions—more humidity, less humidity, longer rest periods, shorter rest periods—was followed by a temporary gain in work output. In medicine, this is known as the "placebo effect." In medical research, many subjects in the control group who are given placebos (pills containing no medicines of any kind) report that they feel much better [Evans, 1974]. These show how the findings of many experiments may be due to the attention the subjects are getting, not to the factor which is being tested.

Planned experiments upon human subjects are most reliable when these subjects do not know the true object of the experiment. They may be given a rationale, a reasonable explanation of what the experimenter is doing, but this rationale may be a harmless but necessary deception which conceals the true purpose of the experiment. For example, McClelland [1971] wished to study the effects of alcohol upon normal people in a party atmosphere but told the subjects that he was studying the effects of a party atmosphere upon fantasy,

and had them write imaginative stories about pictures he showed them at intervals. But as Kelman points out [1966], the use of deception in social research poses the ethical question of distinguishing between harmless deception and intellectual dishonesty, and may even produce errors in the outcome (subjects may detect the deception and begin second-guessing the researcher!).

Because of all these limitations, social sciences (excepting psychology) make limited use of planned experiments. We use them wherever practical, but depend more heavily on other techniques.

Observational studies

Observational studies are like experiments in all respects except one: In the experiments the scientist arranges for something to happen in order to observe what follows, whereas in the observational study the scientist observes something which happens, or has already happened, by itself. Both rely upon systematic observation under controlled conditions in a search for verifiable sequences and relationships. Both are used in all the sciences, but the procedures for using them vary according to the material being studied. The types of studies which follow are not mutually exclusive, for a study may fit into more than one of these several categories.

Impressionistic studies. These are informal descriptive and analytic accounts, based on observations which are less fully controlled than in more formal studies. They definitely are *not* a rambling, incoherent recital of whatever one happens to recall having seen, but are an organized presentation of thoughtful, purposeful observations. Suppose a sociologist with a special interest in the family makes a tour of Russia. (S)he is alert for information on the Russian family, asks questions about Russian family life of most of the people (s)he meets, scans the papers and magazines for their pictures of family life. (S)he returns home with some very definite impressions of Russian family life, but they are not based on a systematic, scientifically controlled investigation—on an orderly search of the published literature, on a scientifically constructed sample of informants, and so on. If (s)he is a responsible scholar, (s)he will call his or her judgments impressions, and will not state them as scientifically established conclusions.

No matter how elaborate, carefully planned, and systematically conducted a study may be, if the recorded data consist of the impressions of the observer, it is classed as an impressionistic study. Thus the Lynds [1929, 1937] spent many months in "Middletown" (Muncie, Indiana); they systematically searched the newspaper files, interviewed virtually everyone who held a position of authority or was locally said to be important, and participated in community life. They ended up with a large mass of impressions which were highly perceptive and probably accurate, but largely unverifiable except through long and costly research.

Impressionistic studies are highly useful in social science. They provide many hypotheses and research leads, and suggest many insights which might be overlooked by other methods. The best of the impressionistic studies hold an honored place in sociological literature.

Statistical comparative studies. If information obtained from an experiment has already been written down somewhere it is sensible to look up the record. Much sociological research consists of looking up recorded statistical facts and comparing and interpreting them. For a simple example, consider the question, "Now that women have greater freedom to lead an interesting and independent life without marriage, are more women remaining single?" The answer is easily derived from census data, which show the proportion of single women dropping from 24.3 percent in 1890 to 12.3 percent in 1971. (These figures give the percentage of all American women fourteen years old or older, who had never been married, with

correction for changes in the age distribution of the population.) Many such questions can be answered quickly by checking data in the annual *Statistical Abstract of the United States,* which summarizes statistics collected by many government and other agencies and should be found in any library. Other questions may require study of more specialized statistical sources, such as the many *Special Reports* issued by the Bureau of the Census.

Many research questions involve a comparison of several kinds of statistical data from several sources. For example, Lander [1954] wondered about the relation between juvenile delinquency and overcrowded, substandard housing. From court records he compiled delinquency rates for 155 census districts in Baltimore, and from census data he found the average number of persons per room and the percentage of officially substandard housing units for each census district. He found that delinquency rates closely followed rates of overcrowding and substandard housing, but that this association disappeared when he controlled the other variables, such as race, income, education, and occupation. However, he found one variable—home ownership—which remained highly associated even when all others were controlled. He concluded that home ownership was an index of family stability, and that this connection helped to explain the lower delinquency rates in areas where home ownership prevailed.

Sometimes the research scholar must go out and collect the raw statistical data. For example, what factors have produced the fairly large nonstudent "fringe" which hangs around the edges of the major universities? In seeking an answer, Whittaker and Watts [1969] administered a standard psychological test to a sample of nonstudents and to a sample of students at Berkeley. They found the students and nonstudents to be from similar backgrounds, but found the nonstudents to be more interested in the arts than practical concerns, more impulsive, less self-disciplined, less integrated in personality, less distinctly masculine or feminine (more nearly "unisex") in personality, and more socioemotionally maladjusted.

Many people "have no use for statistics." Often they do not like statistics because they do not understand them. Statistics, like shotguns, are dangerous when handled by the ignorant, as is shown in Huff's entertaining little book, *How to Lie with Statistics* [1954]. Those who know the uses and abuses of statistics realize that statistics are nothing more or less than *organized, measured facts.* They are as trustworthy or untrustworthy as is the scientific method of the person who compiles them. To reject statistics is but a way of rejecting facts.

Sociologists make a great many comparative statistical studies. As almost any kind of research is likely to involve statistical organization and comparison of facts at some point or other, the sociologist must be something of a statistician, and the citizen who hopes to be intelligently aware of the world he or she lives in must have some understanding of statistical interpretation.

Questionnaire and interview studies. Sometimes the facts we need are not recorded anywhere, and we can find them only by asking people. For example, what is the "ideal-size family" in the eyes of American young people? This question has some importance for population prediction, business planning, educational planning, and many other purposes. We can find the answer only by asking people what they think is the ideal size for a family. Questionnaire and interview studies are systematic ways of asking questions under scientific controls. A questionnaire is filled out by the informant personally; an interview schedule is filled out by a trained interviewer who asks the questions of the informant. Both methods have their pitfalls, which the trained sociologist should be able to avoid. While it is fairly easy to get purely factual information quite accurately (e.g., "Do you own or rent your home?" "Are you married?"), surveys of attitudes and opinions have greater margins of error. The informants may not understand the question; they

may pick an answer even though they do not have any firm opinion on the matter; they may give an "acceptable" answer rather than the real one; or they may be swayed by the way the question is worded. A survey may also give false conclusions because the sample of persons surveyed is not a representative cross section of the population. Questionnaire and interview studies, like other research methods, must be used by trained scholars who are aware of their pitfalls.

Even though questionnaire and interview studies have a margin of error, they may still be useful, for they are more reliable than guesswork. For example, after victory over Germany in 1945, the Army had more men in uniform than were needed. *Which* men should be demobilized? This was an explosive question, with grave consequences for morale. The Army made a questionnaire study [Stouffer, 1949, chap. 11] in which several thousand servicemen were asked:

After the war when the Army starts releasing soldiers back to civilian life, which of these two groups of men do you think should be released first? (Check only one.)
——Men with dependents
or
——Men over 30 years of age

This question was repeated several times, each time presenting an answer choice between a different pairing of such criteria as overseas service, combat experience, length of time in service, age, and number of dependents. Responses showed that the largest number of servicemen would give first priority to men who have seen combat, next priority to married men with children, and so on. Using these responses, the Army developed a point system for determining eligibility for discharge. That this approach was highly practical was shown by the fact that the Army discharge policy proceeded with very little criticism or resentment, either from servicemen or from civilians.

Participant-observer studies. No man will fully know what it feels like to be a mother, nor will any civilian completely understand army life. Some things can be fully understood only by experiencing them. The *participant observer* seeks insight by taking part in whatever (s)he is studying. If (s)he wishes to study labor unions, (s)he will join one, work in the shop, attend the union meetings, possibly become a minor union official or a union organizer. If (s)he wishes to study a religious sect, (s)he will join it and try to share in its worship. Through personal participation, together with the opportunity for very intimate observation, (s)he may gain insights which no amount of *external* observation would provide.

The participant observer seeks insight by taking part personally.

At the height of the flying-saucer craze, an interesting cult arose in a Midwestern American city. A small group of believers received certain "revelations" that the earth would soon be destroyed, and that only a faithful few would be rescued by flying saucers and carried to a friendly planet. Several participant observers joined the group, concealing their scientific identities and taking part in the group's activities until it dissolved some months later [Festinger, 1956]. In another instance, a white novelist [Griffin, 1961] was commissioned by *Ebony* magazine to make a participant-observer study of black life. With his hair

trimmed short and his skin darkened by a drug, he traveled about the South, where everyone identified him as a black. Although he was a native Southerner, he found that his view of black life from the inside brought many surprising revelations.

There are pitfalls in this technique. The participant observer may become so emotionally involved as to lose objectivity and become a dedicated partisan instead of a neutral observer. Or (s)he may overgeneralize—that is, assume that what (s)he finds in the group (s)he studies is also true of all other groups. Since the data are largely impressionistic, the conclusions are not easily verified. Yet the participant observer is not just "looking at things," but is applying a sophisticated scientific methodology [Bruyn, 1966] which has given us many insights and suggested many hypotheses for further study.

Is it ethical to pretend to be a loyal member of a group in order to study it? Is such a deception justifiable? It is not easy to say when a deception ceases to be harmless. Perhaps the best answer is that a reputable scientist will be careful not to injure the people (s)he is studying.

The *eyewitness account* is an amateur, small-scale participant-observer study. How do people act after a disaster, such as a tornado or an explosion? What happens at a religious revival, a riot, a picket-line disturbance? Rarely is there a visiting sociologist, pencil in hand, ready to record the event. Social scientists often seek eyewitness accounts from persons who were there. A detailed eyewitness account, collected as soon as possible after the event, is a useful source of information. Such accounts must be used with care, for the eyewitness is usually an untrained observer, and his or her own excitement or involvement may have impaired his accuracy and objectivity. Yet the eyewitness account is a priceless source of data for the social scientist.

Case studies. The case study is a complete, detailed account of some phenomenon. It may be a life history of a person, a complete account of an event, or a detailed study of an organization. The case history of a group—a family, a clique, a union, a religious movement—may suggest some insights into group behavior. An accurate, detailed account of a riot, a panic, an orgy, a disaster, or any social event may have scientific value. An unhappy family, a happy family, a community, an organization—almost any phenomenon can be studied by the case-study technique.

Perhaps the greatest value of the case study is in the suggestion of hypotheses, which can then be tested by other methods. Most of our reliable knowledge about juvenile delinquency, for instance, has developed through the testing of hypotheses which were suggested by early case studies of delinquents [Thomas, 1923; Shaw, 1931]. Much of our present knowledge of personality disorganization stems from hypotheses suggested by a classic collection of case studies in Thomas and Znaniecki's *The Polish Peasant in Europe and America* [1923]. These hypotheses are not often *tested* by the case-study method, but by other methods.

A generalization cannot be based upon a single case, for a case can be found to "prove" almost anything. Generalizations must be based upon a large mass of carefully processed data, and the collection of a great many case studies is expensive. Also it is difficult to "add up" a number of case studies or compute averages or other statistical computations. Therefore we seldom use case studies when seeking to test a hypothesis. But after the hypothesis has been tested and we have arrived at some sound generalizations, a good case study may give a beautiful illustration of these generalizations. For example, there is conclusive evidence that juvenile delinquency is closely associated with unsatisfactory family life [Glueck and Glueck, 1959]. A case study showing how unsatisfactory family life has apparently encouraged delinquency in a particular family makes a vivid illustration of this generalization.

Some difficulties in sociological research

Complexity of phenomena

Social phenomena are so complex, subtle, and elusive that the sociologist sometimes wonders where to begin. Yet a science is defined, not by the simplicity of its raw materials, but by the rigor of its methods. To some extent, the subtlety and elusiveness of phenomena are in proportion to our ignorance about them. The causes of a patient's fever, which may elude the layman, may be easily perceptible to the pathologist. As any science gains in maturity and knowledge, its confusing complex phenomena become somewhat more orderly and systematic, and its data somewhat less puzzling and elusive.

It is unlikely, however, that any amount of knowledge will ever make our phenomena appear as orderly as those of the natural sciences. Boyle's law deals with only three variables—volume, temperature, and pressure of enclosed gases, all of which are easily controlled; criminal behavior deals with two or three dozen variables, none of which is very easily controlled. The truly great complexity of social phenomena poses a lasting challenge to the methodology of sociological research.

Constant change

Social phenomena are constantly changing. How can scientific truth be based upon data which are so slippery that today's truth is untrue tomorrow? This real difficulty is not peculiar to the social sciences, for many sciences must make allowance for changing phenomena. The geographer's landscape is constantly changing, although very slowly. The meteorologist must allow for shifting wind systems. The immunologist and the entomologist must concern themselves with changes in the tolerance or resistance of bacteria, viruses, and insects. The social sciences, however, study phenomena which change far more greatly and rapidly than the phenomena of the physical sciences. Sometimes the data change so rapidly that a research study is out of date before it can be published. A typical research schedule might allow a year to prepare a research design and get funding, a year to collect and process data, a year to analyze, interpret, and write up the findings, and one or two years more for acceptance and final appearance in print. Thus Farley and Tauber [1974] studied racial segregation in the public schools for the 1967–1968 school year, but by the time of publication in 1974, it had become history, not current research.

But, as already stated, it is not the materials but the methods of study which identify a science. Since many of the phenomena of sociology are constantly changing, each sociological generalization must have a time-and-place qualification. Therefore, when we speak of "the family," we must show whether we are speaking of the family in all its forms and variations or whether we are speaking of, say, the contemporary, urban, American, middle-class family.

All sciences must qualify their generalizations by stating the conditions under which they hold true. The physicist must say, "Water boils at 100 degrees centigrade—providing it is chemically pure and at an atmospheric pressure of 14.7 pounds per square inch." And the sociologist may say, "Contact and association between members of prejudiced groups will reduce prejudices, *provided* these contacts are cooperative and equalitarian in nature."

The very great changeability and variability of the phenomena of sociology compel the sociologist to qualify his generalizations with especial care. The student will find many carefully qualified statements such as, "In the contemporary American middle-class family, education and the drive to 'get ahead' are major goals," or "among the small, nontypical samples studied to date, young American married couples living with in-laws are as often happily married as those living by themselves." This incessant hedging may become tiresome to the student, who may be tempted to agree with the definition of sociology as "the science that is never sure of anything." Yet careful qualification is the price of accuracy, and the scientist never intentionally generalizes beyond the limitations of available data.

Unpredictability of behavior

Some critics maintain that, since all people are different, human behavior is unpredictable. People may even deliberately change their behavior in order to upset our predictions. A science can predict and sometimes control. Can sociology?

It is true that all persons are different in some respects. It is also true that all persons are alike in some respects. Sociology seeks to learn more about the ways in which people are different and the ways in which they are alike and act alike, so that their behavior can be understood and predicted.

The sociologist can rarely predict what any one person will do.

In considering scientific prediction, the student must grasp two principles. First, *predictions hold true only under certain stated conditions.* The physicist can predict with great exactness the behavior of a specially manufactured ball rolling down a perfectly smooth plane in a vacuum chamber. If asked to predict the behavior of a driverless truck rolling downhill, the prediction must be less exact, since the conditions are not fully controlled.

Accurate and exact prediction, in any science, is possible only when all variables can be controlled or mathematically calculated. The agronomist may predict, "About 20 percent of these seeds will fail to germinate, if placed in good Indiana soil about May 15 and if temperature and rainfall conditions are similar to those of last year." Likewise, the sociologist may predict, "About 20 percent of the male teenagers in this particular slum area will be officially recorded as delinquent this year, if social influences and law-enforcement practices in the area remain like those of last year." But if several of the variables cannot be controlled, then accurate prediction is impossible. For example, will we have a "white Christmas" next winter? The meteorologist cannot make a prediction without knowing what the wind systems and pressure areas are going to be next December. Or, what will the population of the United States be by the end of the century? The demographer cannot predict this without knowing what the birth rates, death rates, and rates of migration are going to be during the rest of the century; and these, in turn, hinge upon such variables as age at marriage, the popularity of large families, the level of prosperity, the progress of medical science, and several other variables. The problem of prediction, then, is similar in all sciences. Our success in prediction is in proportion to our ability to predict or control all of the variables involved.

A second principle of scientific prediction derives from the fact that *most scientific prediction deals with collectivities, not individuals.* The agronomist predicts what proportion of seeds will grow, without telling which little seed will die. The chemist predicts the behavior of several billion hydrogen and oxygen atoms, without predicting the behavior of any single atom of hydrogen or oxygen. The sociologist can rarely predict what any one person will do, although he or she may be able to predict what most of the members of a group will do in a particular situation. In other words, the sociologist may predict the *probability* of an action, just as the life insurance actuary predicts the probability that an insured will die. Predictions may be useful even when we cannot predict the behavior of any particular individual. It is not necessary to know *which* persons will die of typhoid fever to know that polluted water is deadly. Nor need we stop predicting population movements just because we cannot name the persons who are going to move. Sociological prediction can be a useful basis for social policy if it can foretell what certain *groups or proportions* of people are going to do; it is quite unnecessary to predict the behavior of each individual.

In the making of *socially significant* predictions, neither the natural nor the social scientist can claim any great success. The natural scientist can predict to the minute the next eclipse of the sun, but cannot predict the next flood or drought as accurately as the social scientist can predict the next recession. Natural science prediction is most accurate in artificial laboratory situations, and least accurate when directed to those matters upon which important social decisions hinge. On questions like, "How soon can we expect a major breakthrough in cancer research?" or "Which raw materials will be indispensable and which will have become inessential by the twenty-first century?" natural science is not very helpful.

The debate over positivist empiricism

For some decades most sociologists have viewed sociology as a positivist empirical discipline—that is, one based purely upon objectively verified evidence, after the model of physics or chemistry. But there have always been some sociologists who have felt that the dispassionate recording and processing of data sometimes "misses" a great deal that is significant.

Verstehen is a German word which translates approximately as "insight" or "understanding." Spokesmen for verstehen in sociology claim that positivist empiricism must be supplemented by less formal methods of inquiry if complete understanding is to be achieved. The difficulty is that there is no recipe or formula for verstehen. Some scholars believe they have achieved it but cannot tell others exactly how to do so.

Can only the rich study the rich?

Phenomenology and *ethnomethodology* are two terms which describe somewhat similar attempts to bring a more "true" or perceptive set of insights into sociological research. Again, no recipe or set of research "steps" can be outlined. Phenomenology and ethnomethodology are not sets of research procedures; they are comprehensive philosophical systems which embrace a series of assumptions about the nature of social reality and scientific observation which differ substantially from those of positivist empiricism. For example, the positivist is likely to assume that any competent scholar, if properly trained in scientific methods, should be able to study any topic within his or her field of study. An ethnomethodologist, however, would be likely to hold that only a black scholar is equipped to study the black family, or that only one who has been poor is equipped to study poverty. Traditional methods

of observation may describe the observable facts about two men fighting, but (according to ethnomethodologists and phenomenologists) a different method is needed to discover the motives and feelings of each man and his reactions to the other. According to Denzin [1970, p. 28], "The terms *phenomenology* [and] *ethnomethodology* . . . represent different attempts to confront empirical reality from the perspective of those who are being studied."

To attempt any satisfactory explanation of these alternative methodologies in a few paragraphs of an introductory textbook would be futile. We mention them in order to indicate that there *are* alternative methodologies in sociological research, and that no single perspective may be entirely adequate.

Pure and applied sociology

A distinction between pure and applied science is drawn in every scientific field. *Pure science* is a search for knowledge, without primary concern for its practical use. *Applied science* is the search for ways of using scientific knowledge to solve practical problems. A biochemist who seeks to learn how a cell absorbs food or how a cell ages and grows old is working as a pure scientist. If (s)he then tries to find some substance or procedure which will control the aging process, (s)he is working as an applied scientist. A sociologist making a study of "the social structure of a slum neighborhood" is working as a pure scientist; if (s)he then follows with a study of "how to prevent delinquency in a slum neighborhood," (s)he is working as an applied scientist. Many people view sociology entirely as an applied science—trying to solve social problems. Properly viewed, it is both a pure and an applied science. For unless a science is constantly searching for more basic knowledge, its "practical applications of knowledge" are not likely to be very practical.

Practical applications of sociological knowledge are not widely appreciated. Some sociologists are employed by corporations, government bureaus, and social agencies, usually as research scholars, and sociologists are sometimes consulted by legislative committees who are planning new legislation. But the private citizen rarely bases his or her social decisions upon sociological knowledge. If we want to know how to fertilize artichokes, we generally collect some scientific data before deciding. But how are social-policy decisions made? For many years, citizens' groups have been crusading against pornography, although until 1970 there was virtually *no scientific evidence* upon whether pornography was a dangerous stimulant or a harmless outlet for salacious impulses. But when, at long last, the first substantial body of research evidence was finally presented by the President's Commission on Obscenity and Pornography, the report was condemned and its recommendations rejected by President Nixon and by the Senate *before the entire series of reports was published.*

On many social questions, such as the causes and treatment of crime and delinquency, drug and alcohol addiction, sex offenses, the causes and consequences of racial discrimination, or the adjustment of the family to a changing society, there *is* considerable scientific knowledge, but this knowledge is rejected by many persons who prefer their prejudices. As a nation, we have only begun to apply scientific methods to our thinking about social issues.

Popular sociology

A great deal of sociological material gets into print through the agency of people who are not sociologists. The popular magazines are studded with articles on crime, family life, sex, education, suburbia, social class—practically every sociological topic imaginable. This is popular sociology—treatment of sociological topics, nearly always by writers without much formal sociological training, and aimed at a popular audience. Popular sociology at its worst is seen in articles like the "sex-and-sin"

exposés upon which certain men's magazines dwell so fondly. Such articles are generally descriptively inaccurate, with a total lack of the interpretative analysis which would fit the facts into a relevant social context. At the opposite pole are many magazine writers who do a fairly creditable job of popularizing sociological findings. Perhaps the best-known popular "sociologist" is Vance Packard, whose books on social class [*The Status Seekers,* 1959; *The Pyramid Climbers,* 1962] and other topics [*The Sexual Wilderness,* 1968; *A Nation of Strangers,* 1972] have been read by millions—and severely criticized by sociologists [Petersen, 1960; Goldner, 1963; Simon, 1969]. The writings of the sociological popularizers often contain inaccuracies and instances of misplaced emphasis, doubtful interpretation, oversimplification, and too-sweeping generalization. Yet it is likely that popular understanding of sociological topics has been greatly increased by such writers.

Why isn't popular sociology written by professional sociologists? For the same reason that popular science is usually written by journalists, rather than by scientists. Popular writing is a special skill which few scientists or professors have mastered. Furthermore, the scientist's passion for accuracy and for a careful qualification of his statements is a positive handicap in popular writing. Unwillingness to oversimplify, to overdramatize, or to indulge in grandly sweeping generalization all make the professional's writing more accurate but less exciting. Sociologists write for the scholarly audience, while journalists popularize sociology, more or less accurately, for the public.

The roles of the sociologist

What is the proper task of the sociologist? Is it merely to observe human action with the calm, detached curiosity of the ecologist who counts the lemmings as they dive into the sea? Or should the sociologist plunge into social action to avert the dangers (s)he foresees? Should the professor of sociology encourage students to develop a detached understanding of social phenomena or inspire them to man the barricades for social reform? What is the proper role for the sociologist in a changing society?

The sociologist as research scientist

Like all scientists, sociologists are concerned with both collecting and using knowledge. They share in these tasks in various ways.

Conducting scientific research. As a scientist, the sociologist's foremost task is to discover and organize knowledge about social life. A number of full-time research sociologists are employed by universities, government agencies, foundations, or corporations, and many sociologists divide their time between teaching and research. Many university sociologists are engaged in "funded" research, with all or part of their salaries and their research expenses paid from research grants made by government agencies, foundations, or corporations. These grants are made to sociologists who submit an acceptable proposal for research on a particular topic. Since little research can be conducted without research funds, this gives the funding agencies great power to influence the direction of sociological research.

Radical critics of sociology (including some sociologists) claim that, behind a facade of ethical neutrality and objectivity, sociologists have prostituted their research talents to the support of the interests of the funding agencies, and have thus supported militarism, racism, and other forms of oppression [Gouldner, 1962, 1970; Frederichs, 1970, pp. 82–85; any issue of *The Insurgent Sociologist* or *Social Policy*].

Whether sociological research has been widely corrupted in this manner may be debated [Horton and Bouma, 1971]. What is indisputable is that problems of bias and partisanship are present in all research, and that research findings are often helpful to the interests of some people and damaging to the interests of some other people [Becker, 1967]. Even the definition of a research problem may carry an implicit bias. For example, if we state a research problem as, "What characteristics of poor people contribute to their poverty?", we imply that the "blame" rests mainly on the poor people themselves; but if we define the problem as, "What social arrangements produce poverty?", then the blame is placed upon "society."

Throughout most of the history of sociology, sociologists were often accused of being radical subversives whose research and teaching were a threat to established institutions and vested interests. Many older sociologists today, still bearing the scars of the anti-Communist witch-hunts of the 1950s, are puzzled and hurt when students and younger sociologists accuse them of having been lackeys of capitalistic oppression all their lives! But the question of the responsibility of the scientist to his society is as old as science itself, and will not soon be settled.

Another task is to clear away the intellectual rubbish.

Correcting popular nonsense. Another task of the sociologist as a scientist is to clear away the intellectual rubbish of misinformation and superstition which clutters so much of our social thinking. Sociologists have helped to bury a great deal of nonsense about heredity, race, class, sex differences, deviation, and nearly every other aspect of behavior. It is due partly to the findings of sociology that today we rarely hear an educated person argue that the white race is innately superior, that women are intellectually inferior to men, that behavior traits are inherited, that punishment reforms criminals, or that rural people are less "immoral" than urbanites—ideas which nearly every educated person accepted a half century ago. By helping replace superstition and misinformation with accurate knowledge about human behavior, sociologists are perhaps performing their most important function.

Making sociological predictions. Although the track record of sociologists in making social predictions is not impressive, *someone must* make social predictions. Every policy decision is based upon certain assumptions about the present and future state of the society. A legislator who says, "We need more severe penalties to curb drug pushing" is predicting that more severe penalties actually will curb the narcotics business without creating even greater problems. Another legislator who says, "Legalize marijuana" is making a set of predictions about the consequences of this action. Thus every policy recommendation inevitably implies a set of assumptions and predictions. What sort of predictions do sociologists offer? Here are a few samples, offered without explanation or documentation at this point, as examples of the kind of predictions sociologists can make:

Urban sprawl will spread rapidly along the super-highways and will result in the eventual creation of regional planning and administrative authorities.

The trend toward the employment of mothers will continue until most women are working for a substantial portion of their married lives.

Birth rates will, sooner or later, fall to approach death rates, or death rates will rise to approach birth rates.

Despite some experimentation with alternatives,

the monogamous nuclear family will remain the basic family type in the United States for at least the next few decades.

Sociologist–Conducts research into origin and development of groups of human beings and patterns of culture and social organization which have arisen out of group life in society; collects and analyzes scientific data concerning social phenomena, such as the community, associations, social institutions, ethnic minorities, social classes, and social change. May teach sociology, direct research, prepare technical publications, or act as consultant to lawmakers, administrators, and other officials dealing with problems of social policy. (Definition in *Dictionary of Occupational Titles,* U.S. Department of Labor.)

Most social science prediction consists not of predicting specific developments, as the astronomer predicts an eclipse, but of forecasting the general pattern of trends and changes which seem most probable [E.g., Bell, *The Coming of Post-Industrial Society: A Venture in Social Forecasting,* 1973]. All such predictions or forecasts should be offered with a certain humility, for no certainty attends them. Instead, social scientists offer them as the best, most informed guesses available upon which to base our policy decisions and expectations for the future.

The sociologist as policy consultant

Sociological prediction can also help to estimate the probable effects of a social policy. Every social policy decision *is* a prediction. A policy (e.g., federal grants for Head Start) is begun in the hope that it will produce a desired effect (e.g., narrow the educational gap between poor and more prosperous children). Policies have often failed because they embodied unsound assumptions and predictions. Sociologists can help to predict the effects of a policy, and thus contribute to the selection of policies which achieve the intended purposes. For example:

What effect would the removal or the addition of the death penalty have upon the murder rate? (Probably none.)

What effects do brotherhood propaganda and "education for brotherhood" efforts have on race prejudices? (Practically none.)

What effect does dropping out of high school have upon a youth's future earnings? (Little or none, when other facts are equal.)

What would be the effect of intensified law enforcement upon campus marijuana use? (Little or no reduction, with aggravation of other student-police problems.)

Would lower birthrates and a small-family norm increase marital happiness? (Yes; there is research evidence that smaller families are better in every way.)

Would publishing the names of juvenile delinquents help to reduce delinquency? (No; it would more likely increase it.)

Would the suppression of obscene literature help to reduce sex crimes and sex immorality? (Our limited evidence suggests that it would not.)

These are a few of the many social-policy questions which sociologists could help to settle. So far our society has not generally accorded the sociologist a status as technical expert on social-policy matters. The image of the sociologist as a professional bleeding heart, so often reflected in the popular press, does not help the public to visualize the sociologist as a technical expert. Congressional committees, however, often consult·sociologists and other social scientists when holding hearings on proposed legislation. In some areas, especially in criminology and race relations, the conclusions of sociologists (and other social scientists) have had considerable influence. It was, in considerable part, the findings of sociologists and psychologists which led the United States Supreme Court to rule that "segregated schools are inherently unequal" [*Brown v. Board of Education of Topeka,* 1954].

One of the greatest services any scholarly group can offer is to show the society what policies are most likely to work in achieving its objectives. This is a service which sociologists are qualified to perform.

The sociologist as technician

Today sociologists are increasingly finding employment with government departments, corporations, hospitals, large welfare agencies, and other large organizations. Aside from research, they are engaged in planning and conducting community action programs; advising on public relations, employee relations, problems of morale or of "intergroup relations" within the organization; working on human relations problems of many sorts. The "staff sociologist" is found in all kinds of large organizations [*Business Week,* 1959]. Often this person has specialized in social psychology, industrial sociology, urban or rural sociology, or the sociology of complex organizations.

In such positions the sociologist is working as an applied scientist. He or she has been engaged to use scientific knowledge in pursuing certain values—a harmonious and efficient working force, an attractice public image of the industry, or an effective community action program. This role raises a question of ethics. When a sociologist accepts employment as a technician, pursuing values chosen by an employer, has scientific integrity been compromised? To take an extreme example, there is evidence [Monroe, 1962] that gambling operators engaged social scientists to find out why people do or do not gamble, so that the operators could learn how to attract more customers. (We do not know whether any sociologists were included.) Would this be a form of scientific prostitution?

The radical critics of "establishment sociology" charge that sociologists have "sold out" whenever they serve as technicians or research scholars in any kind of effort to maintain or improve the efficiency of the government, military, capitalistic, or welfare establishments. Thus, not only are sociologists (if any) working in war-related activities condemned, but even sociologists working in programs to improve the health of poor children in Mississippi, to increase agricultural output in Peru, or to teach birth control in Indian villages are accused of supporting "oppression." This is the classic view of the revolutionist—any attempt to make the present system work better, or to help people to find better lives within the system, is "oppressive" because it helps to perpetuate the system.

There is no simple answer to the question of what technician appointments it is proper for the sociologist to accept. Each sociologist's answer will be found partly in the prevailing views of the academic world at that moment and partly in his or her own conscience.

The sociologist as teacher

Teaching is the major career of most sociologists. In addition to the concerns and problems of teaching in any field, the problem of value neutrality versus value commitment is a particularly acute question. For example, in a course on "poverty," should the sociologist supervise an objective study of facts, theories, and policies—possibly sympathetic but as objective as possible? Or should he or she design the course to produce dedicated advocates of a particular action program? Should the sociologist seek to convert students to conservatism, liberal reformism, or revolutionary activism? For some decades, the ethics of university teaching have demanded that the teacher refrain from all conscious "indoctrination," but this question is now under spirited debate [Horton and Bouma, 1971].

The sociologist and social action

Scientists seek to discover knowledge. Should scientists also tell the society how this knowledge *should* be used? For example, the geneticists already know something about human heredity, and before very long it may be possible to control the genetic makeup of babies, and "order" babies according to a specifications list. Who should decide what sort of baby should go to whom? The scientists? The parents? The government?

The basic question is whether science—specifically sociology—should be value-free. For example, sociologists know some things about population growth, race relations, urban development, and many other matters involving questions of public policy. Should sociologists become public advocates of birth-control programs, legalized abortion, women's liberation, legalized marijuana, racial integration, and many other programs which they may consider socially desirable?

Early sociologists gave an emphatic "yes" to this question. Without an adequate foundation of scientific knowledge, they rushed to support all sorts of public policies they believed wise. Between 1920 and 1940, many sociologists shifted to the view that sociology should be a more nearly "pure" science, discovering knowledge but not attempting to decree how it should be used. They sought to build sociology on the model of physics or chemistry, as a value-free science. As such, it should be committed to no values except those of free scientific inquiry. Sociologists generally avoided involvement in controversial issues and sought the status of "pure" social scientists.

More recently, this view has been challenged in both physical and social science. *The Bulletin of the Atomic Scientists* carries many articles by scientists urging their fellows to claim a larger role in making the decisions relative to the uses of nuclear science discoveries. Many sociologists today believe that sociologists should claim a major role in making decisions about public policy and should involve themselves in the major issues of our society [Lindesmith, 1960; Horowitz, 1964; Stein and Vidich, 1964; A. Lee, 1966, 1973; Becker, 1967]. They charge that sociologists have buried themselves in "safe" research topics, leaving the really important questions to nonsociologists—questions such as, "How can poverty be reduced?" "How can schools be integrated?" "How can communities be organized for more civilized social living?" "Should the goals and values of American society be altered to promote human welfare?" They feel that sociologists not only should say what society *might* do about problems of race conflict, population growth, birth control, drug addiction, divorce, sex deviation, medical care, etc.; they feel that sociologists have a duty to say what our society *should* do about such problems. Books like Shostak's *Putting Sociology to Work* [1974] provide concrete examples of how sociologists are involving themselves in social issues and constructive social action and show what they have learned from these experiences.

Sociology today, in common with all the other social sciences, has some members who insist that, both individually and as an academic discipline, sociologists should openly and publicly support the "radical reconstruction of society" [Szymanski, 1970; Colfax and Roach, 1971; D. Horowitz, 1971]. This question is receiving much attention in sociological literature [Douglas, 1970; Lee, 1973]. Whether sociology should be value-free is an unsettled question, but sociologists are agreed upon the following propositions:

(1) Sociologists should show the relationships between values. In short, sociologists may say, "If *this* is what you want, *here* is what you must do to get it." If stable, enduring marriages are more important than happiness in marriage, then divorce should be made more difficult; if *happy* marriages represent the more important value, then fairly easy divorce should permit the unhappily married to separate and try again. If we wish to arrest urban blight and suburban sprawl, some private property rights will have to be sacrificed. If we wish to clean up polluted rivers, we must be prepared to spend a lot of tax moneys in doing

so. Sociologists may clarify what value sacrifices must be made if we wish to attain certain other values.

(2) A sociologist *as an individual* may properly make value judgments, support causes, and join reform movements, like any other citizen. As a scientist, (s)he may not know whether television violence is harmful to children, and therefore make no public recommendations; but as a parent will make a decision according to his or her personal beliefs and values. As a scientist, the sociologist may not be able to say whether gambling or marijuana should be forbidden, but as a citizen (s)he is free to express opinions and support personal value judgments.

As a citizen, the sociologist is perfectly justified in supporting causes.

Beyond this, there is no complete agreement among sociologists concerning what role they should assume. Most sociologists have some firm opinions on what policies society should follow and are in considerable agreement with one another upon many of these policies. Possibly the time will come when the social policies which seem best to most sociologists will also seem best to the rest of the society. As persons who cannot and would not divorce themselves from the society in which they live, most sociologists hope so.

The study of sociology

Some students will learn little in a sociology course because they feel that they already know everything worth knowing about social life. Confident that more wisdom is found by opening a lid than a book, and having made the same encounters in a score of different bars and exchanged the same insights in a dozen different pads, they already know all about LIFE. Those who feel this way will learn very little, here or elsewhere. A lifetime of eating food does not make one a dietition. Each student, true enough, has been having social experiences all his life, and from these he has learned many things, some true and some false. To separate truth from falsehood is one of the objectives of sociology. Only those students who are willing to learn—who are willing and able to subject their beliefs, assumptions, and practices to objective scientific scrutiny— will gain much from the study of any of the social sciences.

The use of concepts in sociology

Every field of study makes the student memorize many words to which that field attaches special meanings. This is not an idle ritual; it is done because precise concepts are necessary. First, *we need carefully expressed concepts to carry on a scientific discussion*. How would you explain machinery to a person who had no concept of "wheel"? How useful to a specialist would a patient's medical history be if her physician had recorded it in the language of the layman? The several dozen sociological concepts which will harass the student in this book are necessary for a clear discussion of social phenomena. Secondly, *the formulation of concepts leads to increased knowledge*. Some accurate descriptive knowledge must be organized before a concept can be framed. Then the analysis and criticism of this new concept point up the gaps and errors in present knowledge. The *use* of the concept often calls attention to the facts and relationships which may have been overlooked. Years ago, while studying migration, Park [1928] framed the concept of the *marginal man* who is on the fringes of two groups or two ways of life while fully belonging to neither. The use of this concept quickly led to the recognition that there were many kinds of marginal persons— the person of mixed racial ancestry, who belongs clearly to neither race; the foreman, who is not clearly either "management" or "labor"; the ambitious climber, no longer in the working class yet not securely a middle-class person; and many others. Sound concepts like that of the marginal man lead to increased knowledge.

Most of the concepts of sociology are expressed in words which also have a popular meaning, just as the term *order* has one meaning in zoology, another at the restaurant table, and still another at a law-and-order political rally. Every science appropriates some common words and makes them into scientific concepts by giving them a specific definition. Sociology is no exception.

Careers in sociology

If a subject interests a student, (s)he may wonder what possibilities it holds for a career. A combination of courses which constitutes an undergraduate major or minor in sociology is not, in itself, preparation for a professional career as a sociologist. Undergraduate majors and minors are useful mainly as background preparation for other careers: (1) In *social work,* the better jobs demand a graduate degree in social work, and usually recommend a strong undergraduate major in sociology. (2) In *the professions*—medicine, law, engineering—it has been found that undergraduate social science courses are useful. (3) *Secondary schools* present a growing demand for sociology teachers, with about one-fourth of the schools offering sociology as a separate course and another one-fourth including sociology in a composite course [S. Anderson et al., 1964; Wright, 1965]. (4) *Civil service positions* often include undergraduate sociology among the acceptable educational qualifications for a wide variety of positions in lower and middle brackets. (5) *Newly emerging careers* are to be found in many sorts of action programs—local human relations councils, fair employment practices commissions, economic opportunity programs, foreign aid programs, and many others. Such careers are too new and too rapidly expanding to have developed any rigidly standardized courses of professional preparation, but sociology majors are often sought for these positions.

An M.A. degree is usually sufficient to obtain a teaching position at a junior college or community college, but promotions and university appointments usually require a Ph.D., which is even more necessary for a distinguished career in sociology than it is in the other sciences. Among those scientists with enough "professional standing in the scientific community" to be listed in the 1970 National Register of Scientific and Technical Personnel, a doctor's degree was held by 76 percent of the sociologists, as compared with 66 percent of the psychologists, 42 percent of the economists, 41 percent of the physicists, 36 percent of the chemists; the sociologists were exceeded only by the anthropologists, 90 percent of whom held a doctorate. Of all sociologists, about 84 percent are employed by educational institutions, with the remainder scattered among many employers, mainly government agencies and private foundations. Teaching is the major activity of 58 percent of sociologists, with 22 percent engaged primarily in research, and 16 percent in management and administration, most often management and administration of research.

Until recently, the demand exceeded the supply of persons with doctorates in practically all fields. About 1970, cutbacks in government funding and in weapons and aerospace research cost many Ph.D.'s their jobs, especially in the physical sciences and engineering. Meanwhile, the rate of growth of college enrollments began to slow down, while graduate school output of Ph.D.'s was still rising. Consequently, the employment outlook for graduating Ph.D.'s for the decade of the 1970s is not encouraging [McGinnis and Solomon, 1973].

For most students, sociology will not be a career but merely a part of their general liberal arts education. Whatever career they enter, they will be members of a society, residents in a community, participants in many groups, and carriers of the culture to the next generation. The study of sociology may aid them to fill with greater insight these varied roles which are their destiny.

Summary

Sociology attempts to study society scientifically. Each social science has its own focus, and sociology's is upon the group life of the human race and the social products of this group life.

The methods of sociological research include *experimental* and *observational* studies. Observational studies are of several kinds: *impressionistic studies, participant observer studies, case studies, cross-sectional studies, longitudinal studies* (which may be either *prospective* or *retrospective*), *questionnaire* and *interview studies,* and *comparative statistical studies.* A single study may fit into more than one of these categories (e.g., a longitudinal participant observer study). Some difficulties in sociological research pose a challenge to our methodology—the complexity of social phenomena and the limitations of possible prediction when one is working with many variables.

Sociology, like all sciences, may be either *pure* or *applied. Pure sociology* searches for new knowledge, while *applied sociology* tries to apply sociological knowledge to practical problems. A good deal of more or less accurate sociology is popularized by professional journalists, who are sometimes incorrectly called sociologists.

The sociologist in the professional role of social scientist tends to be a pure scientist devoted to discovering and teaching truth and occasionally making sociological predictions. The sociologist may function as an applied scientist when employed as a technician or consultant, or in the role of private citizen. Whether sociologists as scientists and teachers should select, recommend, and actively promote those policies which they believe society *should* follow is an unsettled question.

The study of sociology will be successful only if the student is willing to learn about matters which already appear to be familiar. The student must learn some concepts which are needed for a precise scientific discussion. Granted a willingness to engage in serious preparation, (s)he may even find a prospective career in sociology.

Questions and projects

1. How would you define sociology to an uneducated person with no understanding of academic fields of knowledge? How would you define it to a well-educated person whose education had included no sociology courses?
2. What is a sociologist? How is the term often misused?
3. What is the difference between social science and social philosophy? Which do you think is more important?
4. Are sociologists interested in social reform?
5. Why are sociologists sometimes confused with socialists? What is the difference? Can one be both?
6. How do you "control" a variable? In studying the possible effects of student marriage on college achievement, what other variables would need to be controlled? How could they be controlled?
7. Why are experimental studies rather rare in sociology?
8. What precautions are needed in using eyewitness accounts as sources of scientific data?
9. How does the participant-observer technique differ from merely looking at things? Isn't everyone a participant observer?
10. What are the pros and cons of defining the sociology teacher's role as including the active promotion among students of the values, goals, and social policies (s)he believes right?
11. When you are in an informal student "bull session," listen to each statement with these questions in mind: "How scientifically sound is this statement? Is it based upon scientific fact or upon guesswork, folklore, and wishful thinking? Could it be documented with adequate scientific support?" At the conclusion, try to estimate what proportion of the statements could be scientifically substantiated.
12. Write a brief, impressionistic account of some group or some community you have observed. Then list several of your generalizations about the group, and outline a research project for collecting the empirical data which would enable you to test the accuracy of these statements.
13. A community makes a cross-sectional study of school achievement in 1974 and finds that black children equal whites in achievement in the lower grades, but fall progressively farther behind as grade level advances. How can this be interpreted: (*a*) as evidence of school failure? (*b*) as evidence of school improvement?

Suggested readings

ADAMS, SAMUEL HOPKINS: "The Juke Myth," *Saturday Review,* Apr. 2, 1955, pp. 13ff.; reprinted in EDGAR A. SCHULER ET AL. (eds.): *Readings in Sociology,* 4th ed., Thomas Y. Crowell Company, New York, 1971, pp. 47–51. An amusing account of the method whereby the author of a famous study arrived at some highly dubious conclusions about heredity and crime.

ALLPORT, GORDON W., J. S. BRUNNER, AND E. M. JANDORF: "Personality under Social Catastrophe: Ninety Life-histories of the Nazi Revolution," *Character and Personality,* 10:1–22, 1941; reprinted in CLYDE KLUCKHOHN AND HENRY A. MURRAY (EDS.): *Personality in Nature, Society, and Culture,* Alfred A. Knopf, Inc., New York, 1953, pp. 347–366. Shows how a collection of life histories can be used in arriving at scientific generalizations.

*BATES, ALAN P.: *The Sociological Enterprise,* Houghton Mifflin Company, Boston, 1967. A brief paperback telling what sociologists do and how they become sociologists. Chap. 5, "Training for Careers in Sociology," and Chap. 6, "Careers in Sociology" are especially recommended.

DENZIN, NORMAN K.: *The Research Act in Sociology: A Theoretical Introduction to Sociological Methods,* Aldine Pub. Co., Chicago, 1970. A rather sophisticated discussion of alternative methodologies and their theoretical presuppositions. Chapter 9 has a good presentation of the participant observer technique.

*DOUGLAS, JACK R..(ed.): *The Relevance of Sociology,* Appleton Century Crofts, 1970. Significant essays on the question of objectivity, value neutrality, and value commitment in sociology.

DYNES, RUSSELL R.: *Organized Behavior in Disaster,* D. C. Heath & Co., Lexington, Mass., 1970. A summary of research on behavior in disaster situations, showing how different research procedures are used.

*FREEMAN, HOWARD E., AND CLARENCE C. SHERWOOD: *Social Research and Social Policy,* Prentice-Hall, Inc., Englewood Cliffs, N.J., 1970. A brief statement of how social research can be designed to contribute to humane social policy.

*LABOVITZ, SANFORD, AND ROBERT HAGEDORN: *Introduction to Social Research,* McGraw-Hill Book Company, New York, 1971. A brief, readable explanation of research methodology, giving enough information to enable a student to interpret fairly sophisticated research.

LANTZ, HERMAN R.: *People of Coal Town,* Southern Illinois University Press, Carbondale, Ill., 1971. A largely impressionistic case study of a community. Gives few statistics and no sweeping generalizations, but presents some hypotheses and interesting sociological description.

LAZARSFELD, PAUL F., WILLIAM H. SEWELL, AND HAROLD L. WILENSKY: *The Uses of Sociology,* Basic Books Inc., Publishers, New York, 1967. A comprehensive review of the practical applications of sociology to a wide range of problems.

*PETERSEN, WILLIAM (ED.): *American Social Patterns,* Doubleday & Company, Inc., Garden City, N.Y., 1956. An Anchor paperback containing a good collection of sociological research examples.

PHILLIPS, BERNARD S.: *Social Research,* The Macmillan Company, New York, 1971. A standard text in social research methods.

SHOSTAK, ARTHUR B. (ed.), *Putting Sociology to Work: Case Studies in the Application of Sociology to Modern Social Problems.* David McKay Co., New York, 1974. Shows how sociologists may share in sound action programs.

Statistical Abstract of the United States, published annually by the Bureau of the Census, and *The World Almanac and Book of Facts,* published annually by the Newspaper Enterprise Association. Two useful sources of statistical and factual information on practically any subject, available in any library. Every student should be familiar with them.

Two/Culture and personality

Part Two shows how human beings create an intricate type of adjustment to life called *culture* and how culture in turn shapes their behavior. Chapter 3, "The Structure of Culture," tells what culture is and how it becomes a part of human life. Chapter 4, "The Evolution of Culture," deals with the processes through which culture grows and develops. Chapter 5, "Personality and Socialization," shows how individual personality is developed through the interaction of heredity, environment, culture, and both group and unique experience. In Chapter 6, "Role and Status," we see how most behavior is organized into a series of roles which men and women can fill easily only if they are properly prepared. Chapter 7, "Social Control and Social Deviation," shows how most people are led to act as they are expected to act, and attempts to explain the deviations of the minority.

Chapter 3 • Structure of culture

Let us consider the morning of an American college student. He awakens on a large, rather soft pad held above the floor on a wooden framework and covered with several layers of soft woven material between which he sleeps. He is roused at a carefully predetermined moment by a tinkling sound from a tiny box on a platform near his sleeping pad. He reaches out and silences it and after various scratchings and gruntings arises and enters a small adjoining room and gazes intently at a large shiny surface that reflects his image. He strokes his face and meditatively fingers a small object with a sharp cutting edge, then lays it down and shakes his head. He turns some knobs, and water gushes from small stems and fills a bowl into which he dips and splashes. He squeezes some white stuff onto a small tufted stick and stirs it about in his mouth while he foams and sputters. He dries himself on a large soft cloth, returns, and makes several selections from a large number of variously colored fabrics that are shaped to fit different parts of his body. He then leaves his room and walks to a much larger room where he and many

other students form a single line. Each is served some food, which he loudly criticizes and greedily consumes. After eating, he leaves the building and approaches a wide pathway filled with passenger wagons that move very fast and pass very close to one another without striking, since each stays on a certain side of this pathway. He stares at a colored light above the pathway until it changes color, whereupon the wagons stop and he crosses the pathway. Ahead of him he observes a young female and considers asking her for an appointment to face each other and jump up and down whenever loud noises are made by a team of professional noise makers. Deciding against this, he hurries into a large building, seeks out a particular room, slumps into a chair and whispers to another student, "What's that 'culture' stuff this prof's always talking about?"

A Purari youth in New Guinea awakens at sunrise from his sleep on a woven reed mat on the floor of the men's house. With other unmarried young men, he sleeps here because it would be shockingly indecent for him to sleep in the same house with his female relatives.

He yawns, stretches, and rises to perform his first assigned task of the day—he checks the row of human skulls on the display racks to see that they are in neat and orderly array. He gazes at them and remembers the mighty enemies they represent. He wishes he were old enough to share in the next cannibal feast. Then the enemy's powers would surge through his own muscles, and his enemy's craft would lodge in his own brain! Truly, it will be wonderful to be a Purari warrior!

But meanwhile there is work to do. He takes a quick plunge into a muddy stream, then goes to his father's house for a breakfast of sago sticks. He finds his mother and sisters in the house, so he returns to the men's house to eat his breakfast, as any well-mannered young man should do. Since today's work is to be a pig hunt, he collects bow and arrows and joins several other young men, mostly relatives on his father's side of the family. While they are waiting, a Purari maiden strolls casually by with her grass skirt swinging gaily, and he chats with her for a moment. He suspects that she may like him, but their fingers do not even touch, for both are above any vulgar public display. As the party leaves for the jungle, her younger brother appears and unobtrusively falls into step with him. Quietly and wordlessly this boy slips a small gift—which happens to be a roll of tobacco leaves—into his hand and then drifts away. Now his step becomes more elastic and the set of his shoulders more assured. Now he knows that she likes him and that the costly love-magic he placed under his sleeping mat last night has worked well. Truly it would be good to be a Purari warrior, but meanwhile, it is good to be a Purari young man!

For descriptions of the Purari, see F. E. Williams, The Natives of the Purari Delta, Anthropological Report no. 5, *Port Moresby, Territory of Papua, 1924; J. H. Holmes,* In Primitive New Guinea, *G. P. Putnam's Sons, New York, 1924. Robert F. Maher,* The New Men of Papua *(Madison: The University of Wisconsin Press, © 1961 by the Regents of the University of Wisconsin).*

As these two sketches indicate, a particular social situation gets its meaning from the culture in which it appears. A situation has very different meanings in two different societies. The members of each society are so completely immersed in their own body of beliefs and customs that they generally fail to sense that they are obeying *belief* and *custom,* and fail to wonder why they believe and act as they do. Only by imaginatively stepping outside one's own body of belief and custom can one become aware of their actual nature. From their life experiences, people develop a set of rules and procedures for meeting their needs. The set of rules and procedures, together with a supporting set of ideas and values, is called a *culture.* This chapter and the one which follows are devoted to the explanation of this very important concept.

We commonly say that a person is cultured if (s)he can identify operatic arias, read a French menu, and select the right fork. But people who are bored by the classics, eat peas with their knives, and speak in four-letter words also have culture. Like most sociological concepts, *culture* is a word with both a popular and a sociological meaning.

The classic definition of culture, framed by Sir Edward Tylor [1871, vol. 1, p. 1], reads, "Culture . . . is that complex whole which includes knowledge, belief, art, morals, law, custom and any other capabilities and habits acquired by man as a member of society." Stated more simply, *culture is everything which is socially learned and shared by the members of a society.* The individual receives culture as part of a social heritage, and, in turn, may reshape the culture and introduce changes which then become a part of the heritage of succeeding generations.

This social heritage may be divided into *material* and *nonmaterial culture.* Nonmaterial culture consists of the words people use, the ideas, customs, and beliefs they hold, and the habits they follow. Material culture consists of manufactured objects such as tools, furniture, automobiles, buildings, irrigation ditches, cultivated farms, roads, bridges, and in fact, any physical substance which has been changed and used by people. Such manufactured objects are called *artifacts.* In the game of baseball, for instance, the gloves, bats, uniforms, and grandstands are a few elements of material culture. The nonmaterial culture would include the rules of the game, the skills of the players, the concepts of strategy, and the traditional behavior of players and spectators. The material culture is always the outgrowth of the nonmaterial culture and is meaningless without it. If the *game* of baseball is forgotten, a bat becomes just a stick of wood.

Material culture consists of any physical substance which has been changed by human intervention.

The destruction of World War II, while the most extensive in history, has left little lasting physical impression because people retained the knowledge and skills (nonmaterial culture) needed to rebuild their ruined cities. The Pyramids of Egypt, on the other hand, would not be rebuilt, for they are entirely divorced from the nonmaterial culture that led to their construction—a culture that would include both the methods of construction and the values that inspired the Pharaohs to want to build such monuments. Today the value system that motivated their behavior has disappeared, and the Pyramids are merely monuments to a dead culture, of interest only as a tourist attraction. People are likely to place a great value on impressive parts of the material culture, even though these may easily be replaced if the relevant nonmaterial culture is active, or may be completely useless if the nonmaterial culture which produced them has disappeared. Since *the heritage of ideas is the most important part of human culture,* the major emphasis of this book will be on this nonmaterial culture.

Whereas a culture is a system of norms and values, a *society* is *a relatively independent, self-perpetuating human group who occupy a territory, share a culture, and have most of their associations within this group.* They may have some contacts with other societies, but if these become too numerous, the societal boundaries become blurred. For example, the American Indian tribes were undoubtedly societies before the coming of the Europeans, but today so many of their activities are with other groups that it is doubtful whether each tribe is still a society. As Lenski defines it, "A society exists to the degree that a territorially bounded population maintains ties of association and interdependence and enjoys autonomy" [Lenski, 1970, p. 9]. Thus societal boundaries may be more or less clearly defined according to how much social interaction is with people outside that society.

The ties of association and interdependence which bind people together into a society are obviously a part of culture. Without societies, culture could not develop. Yet the boundaries of culture and society are not always identical. For example, Roman law is the foundation of the legal systems of both France and Germany, yet these are usually considered separate societies. Conversely, some aspects of a culture may fail to spread throughout the entire society. A single society may include two or more languages and several religious faiths. Cultures exist within societies; however, some aspects of the culture may not be shared by all members of the society, and some aspects of the culture may extend beyond the society's boundaries.

Culture as a system of norms

Since culture tells us the way in which things should be done, we say that culture is *normative,* which is another way of saying that it provides standards of proper conduct. For shaking hands, we extend the right hand; our culture defines this as proper. For scratching our heads we may use either hand; our culture has no norm for head scratching. The term "norm" has two possible meanings. A *statistical norm* is a measure of what actually exists; a *cultural norm* is a concept of what is expected to exist. The famous Kinsey studies sought to find some statistical norms of sexual behavior in the United States. The effort infuriated many people who confused statistical with cultural norms. A statistical norm is a measure of actual *conduct* and does not indicate either approval or disapproval of the action measured. A cultural norm is a set of behavior *expectations,* a cultural image of how people are supposed to act. A culture is an elaborate system of such norms—of standardized, expected ways of feeling and acting—which the members of a society follow more or less perfectly. Except where otherwise indicated, it is the cultural norms to which the sociologist refers. These norms are of several kinds and several degrees of compulsion, as seen in the following classification.

Folkways

Social life everywhere is full of problems—how to wrest a living from nature, how to divide up the fruits of toil or good fortune, how to relate ourselves agreeably to one another, and many others. Human beings seem to have tried every possible way of dealing with such problems. Different societies have found a wide variety of workable patterns. A group may eat once, twice, or several times each day; they may eat while standing, seated in chairs, or squatting on the ground; they may eat together, or each may eat in privacy; they may eat with their fingers or use some kind of utensils; they may start with wine and end with fish, start with fish and end with wine, or they may reject both fish and wine as inedible. And so it goes for thousands of items of behavior. Each trait is a selection from a number of possibilities, all of which are more or less workable. Through trial and error, sheer accident, or some unknown

influence, a group arrives at one of these possibilities, repeats it, and accepts it as the normal way of meeting a particular need. It is passed on to succeeding generations and becomes one of the ways of the folk—hence, a folkway. *Folkways are simply the customary, normal, habitual ways a group does things.* Shaking hands, eating with knives and forks, wearing neckties on some occasions and sport shirts on others, driving on the right-hand side of the street, and eating toast for breakfast are a few of our many American folkways.

Folkways are simply the customary ways a group does things.

New generations absorb the folkways, partly by deliberate teaching, but mainly by observing and taking part in the life about them. Children are surrounded by folkways. Since they constantly see these ways of doing things, they become the only real ways. If the child chances to hear of the customs of other groups, they appear as quaint oddities and not as practical, realistic ways of getting things done. Even the most primitive society will have a few thousand folkways; in modern, industrialized societies they become even more numerous and involved. Sorting out the proper folkway becomes so difficult that Emily Post was able to earn a sizeable fortune as an interpreter of our folkways, even though her fat volume does not catalog those followed by all Americans, but lists only some of the nonoccupational folkways of the urban upper class.

Mores

Some of the folkways are more important than others. If one uses the wrong fork for one's salad, there is momentary embarrassment but no great injury. But if, in our society, a woman chooses anyone but her husband to sire her child, many aspects of financial obligation, property inheritance rights, family relationships, and sentimental linkage become disrupted. We therefore recognize two classes of folkways: (1) those which should be followed as a matter of good manners and polite behavior and (2) those which *must* be followed because they are believed essential to group welfare. These ideas of right and wrong which attach to certain of the folkways are then called *mores.* By the mores we mean *those strong ideas of right and wrong which require certain acts and forbid others.* ("Mores" is the plural of the Latin word *mos,* but the singular form rarely appears in sociological literature.)

The members of a society normally share a sublime faith that violation of their mores will bring disaster upon them. Outsiders, however, often see that at least some of the group's mores are irrational. They may include food taboos which make cattle, hogs, or horses unfit to eat; modesty taboos which forbid exposure of the face, the ankle, the wrist, the breast, or whatever is considered "immodest"; language taboos which forbid misuse of certain sacred or obscene words; and many others. Such taboos seem very important to their believers but may be entirely unknown in other cultures and seem to have no necessary connection with group welfare. It is not necessary that the act forbidden by the mores should actually be injurious. If a society believes that the act is injurious, it is condemned by the mores. Mores are *beliefs* in the rightness or wrongness of acts.

Mores are not deliberately invented or thought up or worked out because someone decides they would be a good idea. They emerge gradually out of the customary practices of the people, largely without conscious choice or intention. Mores arise from a group decision that a particular act seems to be harmful and must be forbidden (or, conversely, that a particular act is so necessary that it must be required). Originally, then, mores are a practical group judgment about group welfare. For example, suppose that through some coincidence several members of a tribe have nasty accidents after swimming in a certain pool. The tribe draws the logical conclusion that there is something dangerous about the pool. As soon as they firmly agree that people should stay away from the pool, the mores have defined this act as wrong. Persons who swim in the pool thereafter are likely to expect misfortune, and others who know of their act will wait to see how they are punished. Thus any misfortune will be interpreted as a punishment and will reinforce these mores. Before long, their origin is forgotten and people think of a dip in this pool as being wrong *in and of itself,* not just because it seems to have been followed by misfortune. In this way, mores, which originate as practical group judgements of the effects of actions, become transformed into absolutes—into things which are right because they are right, and wrong because they are wrong. In other words, *mores become self-validating and self-perpetuating.* They become sacred. To question them is indecent, and to violate them is intolerable. Every society punishes those who violate its mores.

Mores are taught to the young, not as a set of practical expedients but as a set of sacred absolutes. Wherever the mores are firmly established, obedience is automatic. When fully internalized, the mores control behavior by making it psychologically very difficult to commit the forbidden act. For example, we do not refrain from eating our children or our enemies because of an intellectual decision that cannibalism is impractical or wasteful, but because the idea of cannibalism is so repellent to us that the thought of eating human flesh never seriously occurs to us. Most of us would be unable to eat human flesh even if we tried to do so. Mores function by making their violation emotionally impossible. In a society with a clearly defined, firmly implanted set of mores, there is very little personal misconduct.

Some people claim that mores are just group opinions and are not the same as "real" right and wrong. They argue for absolute standards of morality, claiming that the nature of the universe makes certain actions definitely wrong and others definitely right, regardless of time, place, or circumstances. This is an important ethical issue but one which usually has had meaning only for philosophers and theologians. As far as the behavior of most people is concerned, "mores" is simply another word for "real" right and wrong. For, as Sumner [1906] has observed, the mores can make anything right and prevent condemnation of anything. Examples of contrasting definitions of wrong and right by the mores are numerous. Some of these moral views seem bizarre indeed to a Western observer: the Kurtachi defecate in public and eat in private; the Balinese expose the breast and hide the legs; Buganda men must be fully clothed, the women may go naked [Stephens, 1970].

Similarly, the mores of Western societies have often endorsed standards which seem peculiar to a contemporary observer.

Medieval mores made it right for the church to tolerate prostitution and even share in its income. Most of the Reformation churchmen, both Catholic and Protestant, who ordered the torture and burning of heretics were not cruel or evil, but were decent and often kindly men who did what the mores of the time and place required them to do. Mores of our recent past have approved child labor, slavery, and persecution of minorities, and have condemned pacifism, woman suffrage, and sex education. At all times and places, good people feel pure and righteous when following the mores, whatever they may be.

Institutions

Some clusters of folkways and mores are more important than others; for example, those con- cerned with forming families and raising children are more important than those concerned with playing football. Organized clusters of folkways and mores dealing with functions which the society considers to be highly important are embodied in the *social institutions* of the society. Institutions include behavior norms, values and ideals, and systems of social relationships. For a formal definition we suggest: *An institution is an organized system of social relationships which embodies certain common values and procedures and meets certain basic needs of the society.* In most complex societies there are five "basic" institutions which consist of family life, religion, government, education, and the organization of economic activities. Beyond these the concept tapers off into less significant clusters of behavior patterns like those surrounding baseball, hunting, or beekeeping, which are sometimes loosely called institutions, but probably should not be included because they are so much less important.

Institutions are among the most formal and compelling of the norms of a society. As already outlined, folkways emerge from the trial-and-error experience of the group; some of the folkways come to be viewed as essential to group welfare, and are therefore supported by the mores; when the folkways and mores surrounding an important activity become organized into a quite formal, binding system of belief and behavior, an institution has developed. For example, banking, corporate enterprise, investment markets, checking accounts, and collective bargaining are economic institutions which began with simple barter thousands of years ago and passed through many stages of development. An institution thus includes a set of behavior patterns which have become highly standardized, a set of supporting mores, attitudes, and values, and generally a body of traditions, rituals and ceremonies, symbols and vestments, and other paraphernalia. Social institutions will be treated in detail in later chapters, but are introduced here because the concept must be used throughout our discussion.

Laws

While some of the mores function simply as mores, there is a strong tendency for them to become incorporated into the laws of a society. Many people will obey the mores automatically or because they want to do the "right" thing. A few people, however, are tempted to violate the mores. These people may be forced to conform by the threat of legal punishment. Thus the law serves to reinforce the mores. Those who still will not conform are punished, imprisoned, or even executed. Sometimes laws are passed which do not really harmonize with the mores, and their enforcement then becomes difficult—a topic which we discuss more fully in Chapter 15.

Sometimes laws do not harmonize with the mores

Mores do change, and the actions that they command in one era they may forbid in another. The change, however, is seldom conscious and deliberate but is rather a gradual adaptation to changing circumstances. Sumner referred to this kind of change as *crescive,* a type of natural development little affected by specific human decisions [Sumner, 1940, 53–55]. No legislature, for instance, decreed the end of chaperonage; it was simply phased out as the rise of automotive transportation effectively limited the control of the older over the younger generation. Similarly, it was not formal changes in the laws, but the advance of scientific knowledge which finally ended the burn-

ing of unfortunate women as alleged witches.

By its nature, crescive change is usually slow, while the rapid changes in modern life often seem to require rapid modification of our practices. Such changes are designated as *enacted,* indicating that they were the result of deliberate choice rather than of unplanned drift. In contrast to a gradual crescive shift, enacted change may seem harsh and abrupt and may even be resisted by many people. However, the pace of modern life requires rapid decision making in many areas, and much modern legislation is an example of enacted change.

A vast array of laws and regulations—building codes, zoning ordinances, business law, traffic codes, and many others—has developed to regulate matters which are too detailed, specialized, technical, or changeable to be controlled successfully by mores. Some sociologists [Odum, 1947, pp. 227–229] have used the term *stateways* to include all this regulatory machinery of the state, and this is a useful label since the term *law* is used in many other contexts. Scientific laws, for instance, are statements of an "orderly and dependable sequence presumably of a causative character" [Fairchild, 1957, p. 171].

The structure of culture

A culture is not simply an accumulation of folkways and mores; it is an *organized system* of behavior. Let us see some of the ways in which it is organized.

Cultural traits and complexes

The smallest unit of culture is called a *trait.* This is a somewhat arbitrary definition, since what is a single unit to one individual may appear as a combination of units to another. Hoebel's definition [1949, p. 499] is apt at this point: "A reputedly irreducible unit of learned behavior pattern or material product thereof."

Traits of the material culture would include such things as the nail, the screwdriver, the pencil, and the handkerchief. Nonmaterial culture traits would include such actions as shaking hands, tipping hats, the practice of driving on the right-hand side of the road, the kiss as a gesture of affection between the sexes, or the salute to the flag. Each culture includes thousands of traits, and some widespread traits are a part of many cultures.

Is the dance a trait? No; it is a collection of traits, including the dance steps, some formula for selecting the performers, and a musical or rhythmic accompaniment. Most important of all, the dance has a meaning—as a religious ceremonial, a magical rite, a courtship activity, a festive orgy, or something else. All these elements combine to form a *culture complex,* a cluster of related traits. Another cluster of objects, skills, and attitudes forms the football complex.[1] The saying of grace, the reading of the Bible, and evening prayers may form a family religious complex. Similarly, there is a dating complex which includes many activities and attitudes with which students may have some familiarity.

The complex is intermediate between the trait and the institution. An institution is a series of complexes centering upon an important activity. Thus the family includes the dating complex, the engagement-and-wedding complex, the honeymoon complex, the child-care complex, and several others. Some complexes are parts of institutions; others, revolving around less important activities— such as stamp collecting—are simply independent complexes.

Subcultures and countercultures

Every modern society includes some groups of people who share some complexes which are not shared by the rest of that society. Immigrant groups, for example, develop a blend of

the culture of their host nation and of the mother country. Economic groups, whether of high, low, or middle status, usually develop ways of behavior that mark the group off from the rest of society. The adolescent has special styles of behavior, thought, and dress, and a private vocabulary which adults can scarcely translate, so that one may speak of "teen-age culture." Institutions tend to produce behavior patterns not required outside of the institutional setting, and the expressions "culture of the school" or "culture of the factory" suggest special sets of behavior patterns. Such terms as "army life," "preacher's kid," and "ivory tower" evoke pictures of a specialized cultural setting.

Clusters of patterns such as these, which are both *related to the general culture of the society and yet distinguishable from it, are called subcultures.* The subcultures in our society include occupational, religious, national, regional, social-class, age, and sex subcultures, and many others. Literature abounds in descriptions of subcultures, ranging from serious studies like Howell's study of lower class family life, *Hard Living On Clay Street* [1973] or Liebow's study of black men in *Talley's Corner* [(1967] to Clausen's lighthearted description of carnival life in *I Love You Honey, but the Season's Over* [1961].

Subcultures are important because each complex society has, not a single, uniform culture, but a common core of traits and complexes plus an assortment of subcultures. The individual lives and functions mainly within certain of these subcultures. The immigrant may live within the immigrant subculture, and the army wife on a military post may have very little contact with civilian people or civilian values. The child passes through several age subcultures and behaves according to their values, often distressing the mother, who applies the values of a different age subculture.

Among intellectuals, C. P. Snow believes that there is a major communication block between the scientific and the literary subcultures. Scientists, he finds, seldom read the books or magazines in which literary figures

[1]This term should not be confused with the term in psychology (e.g., inferiority complex) where the meaning is quite different.

argue the issues of the day, while the literary world is generally unaware of even the most basic of scientific developments. Hence, two important segments of our society are so confined within mutually exclusive attitudes, standards, and patterns of behavior that any exchange of ideas is difficult in the extreme [Snow, 1963].

The individual lives and functions mainly within certain subcultures.

There is a major communication block between the scientific and the literary subculture.

Several sociologists feel that the term *counterculture* should be applied to designate those groups which not only differ from the prevailing patterns but sharply challenge them. The delinquent gang, for instance, is not a group with no standards or moral values; it has very definite standards and a very compelling set of moral values, but these are quite the opposite of conventional middle-class precepts. Youth trained in this culture are influenced *against* the dominant cultural norms; hence "countercultural." Similarly, the "hippie" conforms to a culture depicting work as undesirable, chastity as "square," flag-waving patriotism as passé, and the accumulation of material possessions as irrelevant. [Yablonsky, 1968; Roszak, 1969].

Most subcultures serve to reinforce the dominant cultural patterns by offering a variety of ways in which the individual may respond to the basic values of the larger society while still retaining allegiance to his or her particular subculture. The counterculture, on the other hand, serves to reinforce the individual's rejection of the patterned ways of the society. Delinquents may be accused of being disloyal to the conventional mores, but they comfort themselves by resolute adherence to the mores of the gang. The gang mores sustain them in deviant behavior by proclaiming that everyone steals, that "squealing" is the worst possible sin, and that only dopes go to school, save money, or try to hold steady jobs.

Countercultures arise out of the needs of individuals to find group support for their failure to follow the dominant patterns [Yinger, 1965, p. 233]. The growth of such countercultures may be expected to reflect the quality of frustration within a society.

Cultural integration

The culture of the Plains Indians centered upon the buffalo. From its carcass they drew most of their material culture, as they used its flesh, hides, tendons, bones, sacs, membranes, and many other parts for one purpose or another. Their religion was mainly directed at ensuring the success of the buffalo hunt. Their status system measured success largely according to the man's hunting skill. Their nomadic way of life was attuned to the buffalo migrations. In other words, the different parts of the culture all fitted together in an interrelated system of practices and values. When the white man killed off the buffalo, the Indian tribes were demoralized because a focal point of their culture had been destroyed.

Just as a pile of bricks is not a home, a list of traits is not a culture. A culture is an *integrated system* in which each trait fits into the rest of the culture. It is no accident that hunting peoples worship hunting gods, fishing peoples worship sea gods, and agricultural peoples worship sun and rain gods. The different parts of a culture must fit together if the culture is to function efficiently. Over a period of time, a people tends to reject or discard inharmonious elements, gaining from their elimination a reasonably integrated culture.

Failure to appreciate the integration of culture leads to many failures in dealing with other cultures. When the American Indians were herded onto reservations and supplied with cattle by the government, the Indians hunted the cattle instead of tending and milking them as expected. The idea of tending and milking cows did not tie in with anything in their culture; to introduce a completely foreign complex was a far more complicated task than had been first imagined. Today, the industrialization of the underdeveloped areas of the world is delayed because "backward" patterns are tightly interwoven into the native culture. For example, the Bantu of South Africa are overgrazing their lands with oversized herds of scrawny, infected cattle. Reduction of herds and selective breeding are clearly indicated; but in the Bantu culture a man's wealth and status and his ability to purchase wives are measured by the number, not the quality, of his cattle. To introduce scientific livestock practices will require changes in customs and values which weave through the entire culture. Since a culture is integrated, we cannot change one part of it without producing some change in the whole.

Ethnocentrism

There is a tribe of Greenland Eskimo who call themselves the *Inuit,* which translates as "the real people" [Herbert, 1973, p. 2]. Sumner called this outlook *ethnocentrism,* formally defined as "that view of things in which one's own group is the center of everything and all others are scaled and rated with reference to it" [Sumner, 1906, p. 13]. Stated less formally, ethnocentrism is the habit of every group of taking for granted the superiority of its culture. We assume, without thought or argument, that monogamy is better than polygamy, that young people should choose their own mates, and that it is best for the young married couple to live by themselves. Our society is "progressive," while the non-Western world is "backward"; our art is noble and beautiful, whereas that of other societies is grotesque and degraded; our religion is true; others are pagan superstitions. Ethnocentrism makes our culture into a yardstick with which to measure all other cultures, which are good or bad, high or low, right or queer in proportion as they resemble ours. It is expressed positively in such phrases as "chosen people," "progressive," "superior race," "true believers," and negatively by epithets like "foreign devils," "infidels," "heathen," "backward peoples," "barbarians," and "savages." Like the Bostonian who "didn't need to travel because he was already here," we are usually quick to recognize ethnocentrism in others and slow to see it in ourselves. Thus it was often remarked that Americans could not possibly believe Hitler's claim that the Germans were a nation of supermen, because they knew this could be true only of Americans!

All known societies are ethnocentric. The "backward" native peoples, to whom we feel so superior, have a similar feeling of superiority to us. Even while they are adopting our technology, they generally consider most of the rest of our culture quaint and absurd. Worsley describes the New Guinean's evaluation of white men:

The Europeans were not regarded as all-powerful, but as rather pathetic, ignorant people who could be easily cheated or stolen from. Their ignorance of sorcery was lamentable. "These are not men; they are merely gods," said the natives, judging the whites to be beings whose lives were inferior to those of living men. Again, they spoke the indigenous tongues very badly; why should one bother trying to make out their uncouth speech? (Reprinted by permission of Schocken Books, Inc., New York, and Mac Gibbon & Kee, Ltd., London, from *The Trumpet Shall Sound,* by Peter Worsley, pp. 208–209. Copyright © 1968 by Peter Worsley.)

WHICH OF THESE STATEMENTS ARE ETHNOCENTRIC?*

1. Labor productivity is lower in Guatemala than in the United States.
2. Never trust anyone over thirty.
3. Turn off that junk so I can study.
4. I don't like rock music.
5. I don't like classical music.
6. Hard hat workers are selfish and narrow-minded.
7. My religion is the only religion which embodies truth.
8. I believe in my religion.
9. Politicians are crooks.
10. Sociologists have the answer to social problems.
11. Orientals are inscrutable.
12. Americans know how to handle business.
13. The United States has the greatest industrial production of any nation.

---

*Items 1 and 13 are simple statements of fact. Items 4, 5, and 8 state beliefs or preferences without any ethnocentric reflections upon the beliefs or preferences of others. The rest of the items are ethnocentric.

Most, if not all, groups within a society are also ethnocentric. Caplow [1958, p. 105] studied 55 sets of six organizations each, including fraternities, churches, insurance companies, colleges, and many others. He found that members overestimated the prestige of their own organizations eight times as often as they underestimated it. Levine and Campbell [1972] list twenty-three facets of a "universal syndrome of ethnocentrism," that is, ethnocentric responses which they find in all societies. Ethnocentrism is a universal human reaction, found in all known societies, in all groups, and in practically all individuals.

In an apparent exception to ethnocentrism a few persons reject their group or some part of its culture. There are anti-Semitic Jews, blacks who reject and deny their black identity, aristocrats who lead revolutions, priests who abandon their faith, and so on. This rejection of one's group or its culture is a form of deviant behavior that will be discussed in Chapter 7.

No one can help being ethnocentric.

Although ethnocentrism is partly a matter of habit, it is also a product of both deliberate and unconscious cultivation. We are trained to be ethnocentric to such a degree that it is doubtful whether anyone can avoid being ethnocentric. Our culture complex of nationalistic patriotism is perhaps the greatest source of deliberately cultivated ethnocentrism. From early childhood we learn about national heroes and the national mythology. Self-appointed patriotic organizations comb our textbooks and pounce upon any statements lacking in ethnocentric coloration. Anybody who is of doubtful commitment to nationalistic loyalties may be denounced as an undesirable citizen. Thus, the United States and the Philippines have had "un-American" and "un-Philippine" activities committees which investigated people who were suspected of deviating from true ethnocentric devotion to national principles.

College students should find ethnocentrism easy to understand, since they experience so much of it. They are subjected to a barrage of ethnocentric cultivation from before they arrive until the moment of graduation—when the alumni office takes over. College newspapers and annuals, pep rallies, trophy cases, and countless "bull sessions" all combine to convince the neophyte that Siwash U. has unique virtues denied to all lesser institutions. Rush week reaches a high point in ethnocentric indoctrination. An elaborate drama is staged to allow the pledge to perceive how only this particular fraternity or sorority has the social values, the illustrious membership, the burnished traditions, and the shimmering prestige which make joining it a privilege. All others are counterfeits, to whose members one condescends; the unaffiliated student one simply ignores. Without the successful cultivation of ethnocentrism, few fraternities or sororities could meet the payments on the mortgage, and every college "homecoming" would be a flop!

There are many other sources of ethnocentrism. Almost every race, social class, regional or sectional group, occupational group, recreational group, or group of any other kind encourages the ethnocentrism of its members.

Personality and ethnocentrism

All groups stimulate the growth of ethnocentrism, but not all members of the group are equally ethnocentric. There is some evidence that many people in American society develop a personality which is basically more ethnocentric than that of other people. How can we explain this? One answer is that some of us are

strongly ethnocentric as a defense against our own inadequacies.

At one time, it was believed that social science had established a definite link between personality patterns and ethnocentrism. In *The Authoritarian Personality,* Adorno [1950] found that ethnocentric people tended to be less educated, more socially withdrawn, and religiously more orthodox. In this approach, ethnocentrism was defined primarily as intense and uncritical loyalty to an ethnic or national group coupled with prejudice against other ethnic or national groups. The trouble with this definition is that it tends to exclude consideration of some other types of ethnocentrism. If an intense and uncritical loyalty to the views of one's own group is to be the criterion of ethnocentrism, then members of supposedly liberal circles may be just as ethnocentric as those in conservative circles. The conservative may be uncritical of religious orthodoxy and national patriotism and quite sure of the superiority of his or her own ethnic group and of the inferiority of others. The self-styled liberal may be equally rigid in the opposite direction: sure that the national foreign policy is always wrong, that orthodox religion is mere superstition and that businessmen, blue collar workers and politicians are invariably either stupid or corrupt [Greeley, 1970; Hoffer, 1969; Lerner, 1969; Lipset and Ladd, 1972].

In either case, the apparent explanation of the appeal of ethnocentrism is that it simultaneously reaffirms the individual's "belongingness" to the group while it offers comfortingly simple explanations of complex social phenomena. It may be that there are personality characteristics associated with an overly rigid adherence to the standards of judgment of the groups of which we are members but, so far, this has not been proved. The old, the socially secluded, the less educated and the politically conservative may be ethnocentric but, frequently, so are the young, the well educated, the widely traveled, the politically "left" and the well-to-do [Ray, 1971]. It is obvious that different types of people vary in the ideas about which they are ethnocentric, but it is far less clear that there is any significant variation, by social background or personality type, in the degree to which people are subject to ethnocentrism.

Effects of ethnocentrism

Is ethnocentrism good or bad for people? First, we should have to decide how to define "good" and "bad," and even then we might find the question very unsettled. Ethnocentrism gets us into many of our muddles; yet it is doubtful whether groups can survive without it.

Promotion of group unity, loyalty, and morale. Ethnocentric groups seem to survive better than tolerant groups. Ethnocentrism justifies sacrifice and sanctifies martyrdom. The attitude, "I prefer my customs, although I recognize that, basically, they may be no better than yours," is not the sort of faith for which dedicated believers will march singing to their death.

Ethnocentrism reinforces nationalism and patriotism. Without ethnocentrism, a vigorous national consciousness is probably impossible. Nationalism is but another level of group loyalty. Periods of national tension and conflict are always accompanied by intensified ethnocentric propaganda. Perhaps such a campaign is a necessary emotional preparation for the expected sacrifices.

Protection against change. If our culture is already the world's most perfect, then why tinker with alien innovations? From the Biblical Hebrews to nineteenth-century Japan, ethnocentrism has been used to discourage the acceptance of alien elements into the culture. Such efforts to prevent culture change are never entirely successful; change came to both the Hebrews and the Japanese. Yet if people share a serene, unquestioning faith in the goodness of their culture—a conviction so completely

accepted that no proof is necessary—then change is delayed.

Ethnocentrism also acts to discourage change.

While ethnocentrism provides rationalization for the privileged, it also brings compensation to those of low status. An example is seen in the attitude of Southern "poor whites" toward blacks. Myrdal [1944, pp. 597–599] found that the poor whites, low in income and social status, were the strongest exponents of the doctrine of white supremacy. As Sinclair Lewis writes, "Every man is king so long as he has someone to look down upon." Black Power advocates today who promote racial pride ("black is beautiful") are essentially pleading for a greater degree of ethnocentrism among blacks as a means of building self-esteem and group loyalty while providing emotional protection against white disrespect.

Japan's economic progress has exposed some possibly ethnocentric thinking in American business circles. American firms feel that they have to lay off employees when business is down and they expect management employees to move fairly frequently from company to company. Similarly, they often try to deemphasize seniority and to pay according to contribution rather than length of service. Japanese firms give a major emphasis to seniority in promotion and pay, encourage lifelong employment and keep employees on the payroll even when business is declining. According to American thinking, the Japanese patterns would slow economic progress by making labor costly, and reward "time serving" rather than initiative. However, the fact that Japan's economic growth rate has been two or three times the American rate most of the time in recent years has raised some question about the superiority of American practices.

An American business consultant now suggests that the traditional Japanese patterns may have real advantages [Diebold 1973]. He suggests that lifetime tenure (*sushin koyo*) frees Japanese executives from the fear of losing out if their particular project is abandoned or if the bright idea of someone else is accepted. Therefore, they can accept developments which require a longtime payoff since they expect to be with the firm for a lifetime. Finally, lifetime tenure increases corporate loyalty and a feeling that what's good for the company is also good for the individual.

Economic development is a complicated process, and Japanese practices do raise some problems. Further, much of the Japanese success has been due to a willingness to learn from other countries. Nevertheless, the preceding examples do raise the possibility that even supposedly hard-headed American businessmen are not immune to ethnocentrism. The fact that a practice has apparently been successful in the past and still appears logical today is no guarantee that some other approach may not be better. We accept new ideas fairly easily when they come from people like ourselves, whose innovations are simply a modification of existing patterns. Ethnocentrism is likely to become a major hazard when we are appraising practices which have originated in societies we consider exotic, strange, or less prestigious than our own.

In discouraging culture change, ethnocentrism is undiscriminating. It discourages both the changes which would disrupt the culture and the changes which would help it attain its goals. Ethnocentrism led the Biblical Hebrews to reject both the pagan gods who would have disrupted their culture and the superior farming techniques of their neighbors which would have advanced their culture. Since no culture is completely static, every culture must make some changes if it is to survive. Ethnocentrism in India today helps to keep it from turning Communist, but India may not remain non-Communist unless it rapidly modernizes its technology and controls its population growth, and these changes are delayed by ethnocentrism. In an age of atom bombs and push-button warfare, when the nations must probably either get together or die together, ethnocentrism helps to keep them tied to concepts of national sovereignty. Under some circumstances, then, ethnocentrism promotes cultural stability and group survival; under other circumstances, ethnocentrism dooms the culture to collapse and the group to extinction.

Cultural relativism

We cannot possibly understand the actions of other groups if we analyze them in terms of *our* motives and values; we must interpret their behavior in the light of *their* motives, habits, and values if we are to understand them. Consider, for example, the administration of justice in the far North. The Canadian Mounties are occasionally called to go into the arctic region to apprehend Eskimos who have committed a murder. This action in terms of our culture is a crime, and the individual has violated the mores. In the culture of many Eskimo tribes, however, the killing may have been justified, since their mores demand that a man avenge an injury committed upon a kinsman. This type of revenge is not considered unruly or deviant but is the only kind of action which an honorable man could take. We would condemn the man who takes the law into his own hands and seeks revenge, while they would condemn the man who has so little courage and group loyalty as to allow his kinsman to go unavenged.

Few culture traits are so disturbing to most Americans as the primitive practices of head hunting—an apparently useless and bloodthirsty pastime. However, this trait nearly everywhere has a fairly complex meaning. The Marindese of New Guinea, a quite gentle and affectionate people, hunted heads in order to provide names for their children [Van der Kroef, 1952]. Since they firmly believed that the only way a child could get a name and a separate identity was to take it from a living person, they hunted heads from neighboring tribes. A Marindese husband had a moral obligation to have one or two head names on hand, in case he was presented with a child. Thus head hunting, like any other important trait, was deeply integrated into a total cultural system within which it was moral and necessary.

The goodness or badness of a cultural trait depends upon its setting.

These illustrations show what we mean by cultural relativism—that *the function and meaning of a trait are relative to its cultural setting*. A trait is neither good nor bad in itself. It is good or bad only with reference to the culture in which it is to function. Fur clothing is good in the arctic, but not in the tropics. Premarital pregnancy is bad in our society, where the mores condemn it and where there are no comfortable arrangements for the care of illegitimate children; premarital pregnancy is good in a society such as that of the Bontocs of the Philippines, who consider a woman more marriageable when her fertility has been

established, and who have a set of customs and values which make a secure place for the children. Adolescent girls in the United States are advised that they will improve their marital bargaining power by avoiding pregnancy until marriage. Adolescent girls in New Guinea are given the opposite advice, and in each setting the advice is probably correct. The rugged individualism and peasant thrift of early America would produce great unemployment if they were widely practiced in our present mass-production economy. From such examples we see that *any cultural trait is socially "good" if it operates harmoniously within its cultural setting to attain the goals which the people are seeking*. This is a workable, non-ethnocentric test of the goodness or badness of a culture trait.

The concept of cultural relativism does not mean that all customs are equally valuable nor does it imply that no customs are harmful. Some patterns of behavior may be injurious in any milieu, but even such patterns serve some purpose in the culture, and the society will suffer unless a substitute is provided.

Sociologists are sometimes accused of undermining morality with their concept of cultural relativism, and their claim that almost "everything's right somewhere." If right and wrong are merely social conventions, say our critics, one might as well do whatever one wishes. This is a total misunderstanding. It is approximately true that "everything's right somewhere"—but not everywhere. The central point in cultural relativism is that in a particular cultural setting, certain traits are right because they work well in that setting, while other traits are wrong because they would clash painfully with parts of that culture. This is but another way of saying that a culture is integrated, and that its various elements must harmonize passably if the culture is to function efficiently in serving human purposes. Persons who invoke cultural relativism to excuse their own unconventional behavior are showing they do not understand the concept, and perhaps that they have no concern for the welfare of their society.

Real and ideal culture

In most societies some behavior patterns are generally condemned yet widely practiced. In some places these illicit behavior patterns have existed for centuries side by side with the norms which are supposed to outlaw them. Malinowski cites as an example of this type of behavior, the Trobriand islanders, a group whose incest taboos extend to third and fourth cousins.

> If you were to inquire into the matter among the Trobrianders you would find that . . . the natives show horror at the idea of violating the rules of exogamy and that they believe that sores, disease and even death might follow clan incest . . . .
> [But] from the point of view of the native libertine, *suvasova* (the breach of exogamy) is indeed a specially interesting and spicy form of erotic experience. Most of my informants would not only admit but actually did boast of having committed this offense or that of adultery (kaylasi); and I have many concrete, well-attested cases on record. (Bronislaw Malinowski, *Crime and Custom in Savage Society,* Routledge & Kegan Paul, Ltd., London, 1926, pp. 79, 84. Used with permission of Routledge & Kegan Paul, Ltd., and Humanities Press, Inc.)

Like all societies, the Trobrianders have some standardized ways of evading punishment. Malinowski [p. 81] observes, "Magic to undo the consequences of clan incest is perhaps the most definite instance of methodical evasion of law."

This case illustrates the difference between the real and ideal culture. The ideal culture includes the formally approved folkways and mores which people are supposed to follow (the cultural norms); the real culture consists of those which they actually practice (the statistical norms). For example, Warriner [1958] found that many residents of a town in Kansas,

a legally "dry" state at the time of his research, drank in private while supporting the "temperance" morality in public. He concluded that the official morality served to prevent a disruptive public controversy, without interfering with their drinking behavior. There are many such divergences between the real and the ideal culture in our society. As a sample, Williams lists ten examples of "patterned evasion" of our formally approved norms:

1. Prohibition vs. the bootlegging and speakeasy industry, prior to repeal of the Eighteenth Amendment; organized gambling.
2. Impersonal, disinterested governmental services vs. political graft, "fixing," "status justice."
3. Family mores vs. prostitution.
4. Classroom honesty vs. accepted patterns of "cribbing."
5. Promotion by technical competence vs. nepotism, racial discrimination (as seen, for example, in the systematic evasion of civil service laws).
6. Universalistic legal justice vs. white-collar crime, the public defender system, bias in jury selection, racial discrimination.
7. Prescribed patterns of sexual behavior vs. the patterns revealed by studies of actual behavior.
8. Legal rules regarding divorce vs. actual court practice ("void" divorces, the "alimony racket").
9. Professional codes vs. such practices as fee splitting among doctors, violations of state and federal statutes and administrative regulations by retail pharmacists, ambulance chasing among lawyers.
10. Ethical concepts of truth vs. some advertising, financial transactions, etc. ("business is business"). (Robin M. Williams, Jr., *American Society, copyright* © by Alfred A. Knopf, Inc., New York, 1970, pp. 421–422.)

A clash between the real and ideal culture patterns is generally avoided by some kind of rationalization which allows people to "eat their cake and have it." For example, Lowie [1940, p. 379] describes some Burmese villages which are Buddhist, and whose inhabitants are therefore forbidden to kill any living thing, yet are dependent upon the murderous occupation of fishermen. They evade this contradiction by not literally killing the fish, which ". . . are merely put out on the bank to dry after their long soaking in the river, and if they are foolish and ill-judged enough to die while undergoing the process, it is their own fault."

No society is free of such inconsistencies, and complex societies like ours have many patterns which are formally condemned, enthusiastically practiced, and skillfully rationalized. We cherish monogamous marriage but tolerate quasi-legalized prostitution. The practices seem to be incompatible, but there is little conflict between them since our culture trains us both to applaud the virtuous woman and to tolerate the prostitute. Tax evasion is legally and morally wrong, but apparently it is practiced by most people who have a good opportunity. Business life demands rigid honesty, but alongside this uprightness may be found a pattern of bribery and special favors which is said to facilitate the making of business agreements. Such contradictions could be extended into an impressive list for any modern society.

In the long-run viewpoint, the clash between real and ideal culture patterns may simply illustrate the fact that we have gone only part way in developing social control, and that eventually there may be a greater consistency between the actual behavior and the moral precepts of the culture. The extension of the voting privilege regardless of race or sex narrows the gap between precept and practice in our democratic mores. The abolition of child labor and the social security provisions for the aged and the handicapped are fulfilling the implications of the humanitarian mores in areas which have often been neglected. These and many other developments exemplify what Sumner [1906, p. 66] called a "strain toward consistency in the mores." In spite of frequent discrepancies, there is still a strong tendency for a society, sooner or later, to bring its various ideas and practices into harmony with one another.

On the other hand, in some circumstances it may be possible that the illicit patterns of behavior allow society to engage in conduct which seems essential to the welfare of the group but for which it has not been able to find a moral sanction. Thurman Arnold expressed this viewpoint in a book called *The Folklore of Capitalism* [1937]. He argued that the large-scale consolidation of industry was an essential part of modern technological development. This trend, however, is inconsistent with the American mores which sanction the value of small-scale competitive business. To meet the situation, he claimed that the United States evolved unenforceable antitrust laws which expressed our moral condemnation of bigness in business, and at the same time permitted business to gain the advantages of continued consolidation. This procedure reminds us of the practice in some primitive societies in which courtship and marriage regulations are so complicated that most marriages occur through a type of elopement which is vigorously condemned by the mores. If the couple are unusually awkward, they may be caught and severely beaten, but ordinarily they are able to make good their escape. After a period of penance, they are welcomed back into the social group. Thus society is able to maintain the expression of sentiments sacred to the mores, along with the existence of a useful practice in violation of the mores, thereby promoting a type of adjustment which seems necessary to the smooth functioning of the society.

Real and ideal patterns are both definitely a part of the culture. The real patterns are not mentioned in formal statements or deliberately taught as part of the program of church and school, but they are transmitted by an informal communication network of gossip and advice which may be even more effective than the formal channels. For this reason it is sometimes suggested [Yinger, 1965, p. 75] that the terms *overt* and *covert* might indicate their nature. Ideal patterns are overt, that is, openly announced, while the real patterns are often covert, transmitted in an unofficial and perhaps clandestine fashion.

Culture and human adjustment

Is culture a help or a burden to human beings? Some of each. It helps them to solve some problems, gets in their way as they grapple with others, and itself creates still others.

Culture and biological adjustment

Culture contains many gadgets which help people in their unremitting battle with nature. Since people freeze and sunburn easily, they wear clothes and build houses. Nature offers wild fruit, seeds, and berries; people domesticate them and increase their yield. Hands are poor shovels, but bulldozers remake the surface of the earth. Human beings cannot run fast, swim well, or fly at all; yet no living thing travels so fast as they. Men and women were created fragile, delicate beings, quickly prey to death through heat or cold, thirst or hunger. Through culture, they can moisten the desert and dry the swampland, can survive arctic cold and tropic heat, and can even survive a trip through outer space.

While culture helps people to adjust to their environment, it also interferes with their biological adjustment in many ways. Every culture offers many examples of patterns harmful to physical well-being. The Hindu belief that people should not kill anything has filled India with stray dogs, scrawny cattle, and all manner of parasites, wasting food and spreading diseases. Through culture, we have improved our weapons until we can destroy the entire human race. We follow methods of agriculture and land use which destroy the soil and flood the land. We pollute the air, foul the streams, and poison our foods. If we are rich enough, we generally eat, smoke, and drink more than is good for us. We eat polished rice or white bread which is stripped of vital food elements, while passing up beef, pork, horse meat, snake meat, snails, milk or whatever valuable source of nourishment is under taboo in our particular society. If we were descended from cats instead of anthropoids, we would be better equipped for the night hours we like to keep.

In nearly every culture men and women have twisted, stretched, squeezed, gouged, painted, trimmed, and scarred the human body in an effort to be beautiful. The clumsy platters inserted in the slit lips of the Ubangi, the foot binding as practiced upon upperclass female children in classical China, and the precarious high heels of women are all efforts to improve upon nature by deforming and distorting the natural body contours—along with those interesting Western devices intended to squeeze, shift, uplift and supplement various parts of the female anatomy. Our culture causes men to wrap themselves in useless garments in the summer while in winter women expose their legs to the icy blasts. Our culture encourages men to dangerous overexertion in sports, yet encourages them to miss healthful exercise by taking a car for a trip to the corner, and by hauling their children to school even when they would be better off walking. Automobile buyers have been more interested in a stylish appearance than in passenger safety, and only a minority of drivers fasten their seat belts. Our culture includes traits that lead communities to build new hospitals and other traits that cause them to oppose fluoridation programs to reduce tooth decay. American culture includes both the scientific milieu that developed an effective polio vaccine and the folkways and vested interests that make it difficult to pursue an effective mass-immunization program for making efficient use of this vaccine. When the values of the culture are not in harmony with the needs of biological adjustment, the culture may cause people to work against their own physical welfare.

Is culture, then, good or bad for us? It may be either. Culturally sanctioned behavior may prolong life, or it may prevent us from using nature for our own physical welfare.

Culture and social adjustment

Just as culture may either promote or impair the individual's physical health, so it may either encourage or impede the harmonious operation of the society and the development of well-adjusted personalities. World birth rates have barely begun to fall in response to worldwide recognition that the large-family pattern has plunged the world deeply into a population crisis. In the Ottoman Empire the military and agricultural activities were highly valued, while commerce was disdained to such an extent that the Turks could not maintain their leadership in a world increasingly dominated by industrialism. In the Philippines the culture encourages an extremely high status for the legal profession with the result that other occupations are neglected while the country has thousands of lawyers without a practice.

The cultural guides to family formation may also have mixed effects. A family-determined choice of marriage partners may lead to a rule of the elders which retards social change, while the belief in romantic choice of mates by individuals may lead them on a fruitless round of divorce and remarriage in search of ecstatic happiness probably unattainable by the human family.

The culture includes patterns of behavior, organized into a series of ascribed and achieved roles, and thus provides for getting the routine work of society accomplished. The culture may ascribe roles to people without providing adequate preparation for them, or may require a succession of roles which impose painful transitions upon individuals. It may build conflicting pressures into a role so that few individuals can possibly avoid mental conflict, or it may require difficult role choices of individuals or encourage role ambitions which doom most persons to failure. It may overelaborate these roles to a point of impracticality. It is said that Marie Antoinette was unable to get a glass of cold water; court etiquette required it to pass through so many hands that it was always tepid by the time it reached her. Rivers [1912] tells how on Torres Island in Melanesia, canoe building was surrounded with such an elaborate set of magical rites and taboos that only a small group of hereditary canoe builders dared to try to build one. Others were familiar with the manual skills for canoe building, but since they lacked the secret magic, it was unthinkable that they should build the craft. Therefore when the hereditary canoe-builder families died out, the Torres Islanders went without canoes despite their desperate need for them. If this deliberate frustration seems stupid to the reader, let him or her try to explain why in our society, building codes, union rules, and other monopolistic practices in the construction industry make building unnecessarily complicated and costly. In every society the culture organizes the work of the society in ways that are sometimes cumbersome and impractical; yet, without a culturally organized system for getting things done, most of them would not get done at all.

Summary

Culture consists of the socially learned behavior norms and values shared by a human group. *Material culture* is made up of the artifacts people construct on the basis of cultural norms. *Nonmaterial culture* comprises the behavior patterns, values, and social relationships of a human group. *Folkways* are types of behavior which have the force of custom but do not necessarily have a moral connotation, while mores attach the ideas of right and wrong to some kinds of behavior. The mores may become sanctified by religion and strengthened by incorporation into law as part of the *stateways*. *Institutions* are organized systems of social relationships which embody common values and procedures and meet basic needs of the society.

A *trait* is the simplest unit of culture; related traits are grouped into *culture complexes*. A *subculture* is the behavior and value system of a group which is a part of the society, but which has certain unique cultural patterns. A *counterculture* is a subculture which is not merely different from, but sharply opposed to, the dominant values of the society.

A culture is an *integrated* system of behavior with its supporting ideas and values. In a highly integrated culture all elements fit harmoniously together. During periods of change, a culture is imperfectly integrated until a new integration is completed. The adoption of Western technology by underdeveloped countries will inevitably bring many other changes in their traditional culture. Such change may take the form of either unplanned *crescive* adaptation or deliberately *enacted* policies.

All societies and all groups assume the superiority of their own culture; this reaction is called *ethnocentrism.* The ideas and customs about which people are ethnocentric vary with social background, but people of all types, liberal and conservatives alike, often display ethnocentrism.

Cultural relativism describes the fact that the function and meaning of a culture trait depend upon the culture in which it operates.

Traits are judged "good" or "bad" according to whether they work efficiently within their own culture.

Every society has an *ideal culture,* including the patterns which are supposed to be practiced, and a *real culture,* including illicit behavior which is formally condemned but widely practiced. Clashes between the two are evaded by rationalization. In some cases, illicit patterns are ways of getting necessary tasks done and thus, even though the mores do not approve the illicit actions, may actually contribute to cultural stability.

Culture both aids and hinders human adjustment. It enables people to survive in an inhospitable physical environment, although in many respects it sustains habits which are physically injurious. We could not live without culture; sometimes it is not easy to live with it.

Questions and projects

1. Which would give the greater understanding of the culture of the Romans—studying the ruins, sculpture, and public works that have been excavated or studying the records of the nonmaterial culture preserved in literature, letters, and legal documents? Why?

2. How do you differentiate between society and culture?

3. What is meant by the statement that, when firmly established, the mores operate automatically? Does this happen in our society?

4. Read the book *The Two Cultures* by C. P. Snow. Have you noticed a difficulty of communication between students with different majors on your campus? Is this comparable to the communication problems outlined by Snow? Can courses in a general education curriculum solve this problem?

5. Apply your knowledge of the integration of culture in evaluating the proposal that our society should return to the "simple life."

6. Is ethnocentrism the opposite of cultural relativism? Explain.

7. Can a liberal be ethnocentric? Why or why not?

8. In what ways does ethnocentrism aid in national survival in the modern world? In what ways does it jeopardize national survival?

9. Read the article by John Diebold, "Management Can Learn from Japan," in *Business Week,* September, 1973, pages 14–19. Would it be desirable to develop the kind of corporate loyalty among Americans which he claims exists among Japanese? Why or why not?

10. Cheating in college is sometimes defended on the ground that it is necessary if a student is to reach the goal of graduation. Is this position defensible in terms of cultural relativism? Why or why not?

11. Are there any respects in which the real campus subculture differs from the ideal campus subculture?

12. In a perfectly integrated culture, would there be any divergence between the real and ideal culture patterns?

13. Read either Lerner, "Respectable Bigotry," in *The American Scholar,* vol. 38, Autumn, 1969, reprinted in M. Friedman, et al., *Overcoming Middle-Class Rage,* 1971, or the article by Gree-

ley, "Intellectuals as an Ethnic Group," *New York Times Magazine,* July 12, 1970, reprinted in Robert K. Yin, *A Race, Creed, Color, or National Origin,* 1973. Defend or attack the view that these articles describe ethnocentric attitudes present among college students and faculty.

14. Can one have opinions and preferences without being ethnocentric? Make a list of several ethnocentric expressions of opinion or judgment. Now make a list of several nonethnocentric statements of opinion or judgment.
15. Select an occupational group and describe the

special behavior which is typical of that occupation.
16. Describe the traits, complexes, attitudes, and values making up a subculture with which you are familiar.
17. Some pre-Civil War thinkers argued that, if left alone, crescive changes in the society would eventually make human slavery outmoded. Would it have been better to have relied on the crescive process than on the enacted change represented in the Emancipation Proclamation? Why or why not? Can this question be answered scientifically, or only speculatively?

Suggested readings

ARMEZ, NANCY L., AND CLARA E. ANTHONY: "Contemporary Negro Humor as Social Satire," *Phylon,* 29:339–436, Winter, 1968. The role of humorists in depicting the incongruity between real and ideal culture.

FREILICH, MORRIS (ED.): *The Meaning of Culture: A Reader in Cultural Anthropology,* Xerox College Publishing, Lexington, Kentucky, 1971. A paperback book of articles on most of the major issues in the interpretation of culture.

KOCHMAN, THOMAS: *Rappin' and Stylin' Out: Communication in Urban Black America,* University of Illinois Press, Urbana, 1972. An analysis of communication among black Americans, including nonverbal communication through gestures and music.

LANGMAN, LAUREN, RICHARD BLOCK, AND INEKE CUNNINGHAM: "Countercultural Values at a Catholic University," *Social Problems,* 20:521–532, Spring, 1973. Description of the diffusion of countercultural values from elite upper-middle-class secular universities to lower-middle-class Catholic universities.

LINTON, RALPH: *The Study of Man: An Introduction,* Appleton-Century-Crofts, Inc., New York, 1936. A classic analysis of the role of culture in human affairs. Chaps. 5, 6, 20, and 25 are especially recommended.

MALMSTROM, JEAN: *Language In Society,* Hayden Book Company, Inc., New York, 1973. A small, easily read paperback which contains many examples of the interaction of language and other aspects of culture.

*MICHENER, JAMES A.: *Return to Paradise,* Random House, Inc., New York, 1950; Bantam Books, 1952, section entitled, "Povenaa's Daughter." A popular writer's hilarious tale of ethnocentric Americans' inability to comprehend the customs of Polynesian society.

MINER, HORACE: "Body Ritual among the Nacirema," *American Anthropologist,* 58:503–507, June, 1956; The Bobbs-Merrill Company, Inc., Indianapolis, reprint S-185. An anthropologist describes the quaint customs and odd values of a well-known modern culture which the student may recognize.

PODHORETZ, NORMAN: "The New Inquisitors," *Commentary,* 55:7–8, April, 1973. A brief analysis of the development and enforcement of ethnocentric attitudes among liberal intellectuals on college campuses.

REED, JOHN SHELTON: *The Enduring South: Subcultural Persistence in Mass Society,* Heath Lexington Books, Lexington, Massachusetts, 1972. A brief and lively sketch of the factors which make for the persistence of a distinctive subculture in the American South.

WILLIAMS, ROBIN M., JR.: *American Society,* Alfred A. Knopf, Inc., New York, 1970, chap. 10, "Institutional Variation and the Evasion of Normative Patterns." A perceptive discussion of the differences between our real and ideal cultures.

Chapter 4 ●The evolution of culture

The cars of the migrant people crawled out of the side roads onto the great cross-country highway, and they took the migrant way to the West. In the daylight they scuttled like bugs to the westward; and as the dark caught them, they clustered like bugs near to shelter and to water. And because they were lonely and perplexed, because they had all come from a place of sadness and worry and defeat, and because they were all going to a new mysterious place, they huddled together; they talked together; they shared their lives, their food, and the things they hoped for in the new country. Thus it might be that one family camped near a spring, and another camped for the spring and for company, and a third because two families had pioneered the place and found it good. And when the sun went down, perhaps twenty families and twenty cars were there.

. . .

Every night a world created, complete with furniture—friends made and enemies established; a world complete with braggarts and with cowards, with quiet men, with humble men, with kindly men. Every night relationships that make a world, established; and every morning the world torn down like a circus.

At first the families were timid in the building and tumbling worlds, but gradually the technique of building worlds became their technique. Then leaders emerged, then laws were made, then codes came into being. And as the worlds moved westward they were more complete and better furnished, for their builders were more experienced in building them.

The families learned what rights must be observed—the right of privacy in the tent; the right to keep the past black hidden in the heart; the right to talk and to listen; the right to refuse help or to accept, to offer help or to decline it; the right of son to court and daughter to be courted; the right of the hungry to be fed; the rights of the pregnant and the sick to transcend all other rights.

And the families learned, although no one told them, what rights are monstrous and must be destroyed: the right to intrude upon privacy, the right to be noisy while the camp slept, the right of seduction or rape, the right of adultery and theft and murder. These rights were crushed, because the little worlds could not exist for even a night with such rights alive.

And as the worlds moved westward, rules became laws, although no one told the families. It is unlawful to foul near the camp; it is unlawful to eat good rich food near one who is hungry, unless he is asked to share.

And with the laws, the punishments—and there were only two—a quick and murderous fight or ostracism; and ostracism was the worst. For if one broke the laws his name and face went with him, and he had no place in any world, no matter where created.

In the worlds, social conduct became fixed and rigid, so that a man must say "Good morning" when asked for it, so that a man might have a willing girl if he stayed with her, if he fathered her children and protected them. But a man might not have one girl one night and another the next, for this would endanger the worlds.

The families moved westward, and the technique of building the worlds improved so that the people could be safe in their worlds; and the form was so fixed that a family acting in the rules knew it was safe in the rules. *(John Steinbeck, The Grapes of Wrath, The Viking Press, Inc., New York, 1939, pp. 264–266.)*

This excerpt from Steinbeck shows how new rules and patterns of behavior develop among people who are forced to grapple with a new set of problems and experiences. The emergence of a subculture embodying definite rules and patterns of behavior among an apparently unorganized horde of migrants illustrates our universal tendency to bring a culturally based order out of what would otherwise be social chaos. In this chapter we are concerned with the emergence of culture, and with the question of whether any definite evolutionary trends can be observed in its development. Since we are a part of the animal world, we start with a view of the differences between ourselves and the other animals, and with an inquiry into the unique aspects of human culture.

The development of culture

Subhuman societies

Many subhuman species have an orderly system of social life. Many bird species mate for a lifetime and (in contrast to humans) are absolutely loyal to their mates. Many species of insects, such as ants and bees, have an elaborate pattern of social life, complete with specialized occupations, lines of authority, and detailed distribution of duties and privileges. But the *subhuman social life is based upon instinct, not upon social learning.* Within a given species of ants, all anthills are very much alike, while human dwellings vary tremendously. For human beings are notably lacking in those inborn patterns of behavior which we call *instincts* in subhuman species. Instead they inherit a set of organic needs, urges, and hungers which we call *drives,* which they must satisfy in some way or other. In their trial-and-error efforts to satisfy their urges, they create culture, with its tremendous variations from society to society. Unable to

rely upon instinct, they must build culture in order to survive.

As animals, human beings are among the larger and more powerful of beasts. Fewer than a dozen other species will ordinarily attack an adult human unless wounded or provoked. Human physical structure and processes are similar to those of other animals and they share many of their diseases. We have certain physical disadvantages. We are far from the strongest of animals; we lack the physical agility of our cousins, the apes; our claws and teeth are puny weapons; and we have no hide, scales, or fur to protect us. We cannot hibernate or adjust organically to great temperature changes.

We also have some advantages. We can digest a wider variety of foods than most other animals. Our eyesight is fairly good at all distances from a few inches to many miles—a characteristic that many animals lack. Alone among the animals, we are well balanced on only two of our feet, freeing the other two for all sorts of mischief. We can oppose the thumb to each finger and are capable of more delicate manipulations than any other animal. No chimpanzee, no matter how brilliant, could perform skillful surgery, for its hands lack dexterity.

Human learning capacity

These advantages would mean little unless human beings had a greater learning capacity. This does not deny that other animals do think, reason, and learn, for their ability is shown by many tests. In some experiments a chimpanzee must figure out that it can get a banana, placed beyond reach, only by fitting together two sticks to make a longer one. In other experiments, where slugs must be put into a slot machine in order to get food, the chimpanzees quickly learn which size or color slugs are valuable, and sort out, hoard, hide, and steal them from one another in a quite human manner. Many such experiments with many species have clearly established that animals *do* learn, and apparently they learn *in the same way* that humans learn; they just do not learn as fast or as much. A famous experiment [Kellogg and Kellogg, 1933] in which a human infant and a chimpanzee infant were raised together and treated alike, showed that they behaved alike in many ways, but that before long the human greatly outdistanced the chimpanzee in learning.

Communication

Animals can learn; they can form interacting groups and have a social life; they can even communicate with one another at a very simple level. These facts lead a few scholars to conclude that some animals have a culture. Several experiments have shown that animal learning is affected by their social setting. For example, Kuo [1931] found that when kittens could watch the mother cat catching rats, 85 percent of them were catching rats themselves by the time they were four months old. Other kittens were raised with rats as companions; none of them killed the type of rats they grew up with and only 16 percent killed any kind of rats. This suggests that animals can learn through example, and that it may be a form of social learning. But if cats have a "rat-killing culture," it is far removed from the hunting complex of the Plains Indians or the English gentry.

The idea of animal culture becomes rather farfetched if we try to imagine Leo the Lion acting in a manner governed by custom, tradition, or sacred ideal. As Myerson observes,

We cannot imagine him, for example, stopping in palpitating pursuit of a tawny female because some Leo the Saint, a hundred lion generations ago, reached the conclusion that burning desire might be satisfied only under very special circumstances. Nor can we visualize this same Leo aching for food yet withholding his mighty paw from a delicacy because that delicacy has been staked off

for another lion or because old lions in a congress a hundred years before decreed private ownership in delicacies and forbade even ravenous hunger to satisfy itself except under strict rule and regulation.

We cannot imagine the young lion contemplating the life of some past Leo the Great and planning his entire career in emulation of the dead hero. . . . We cannot imagine him in agonies of self-condemnation because he has fallen short of an ideal which has been incorporated within him by the teaching and preaching of a thousand years and of countless lions. . . .

He does not foresee his own death, and knows nothing of his own birth. Sex means to him only the satisfaction that an individual of the opposite sex can bring him. It does not mean parenthood, domesticity, respectability, the fulfilling of an ideal, a responsibility, and the becoming part of a great racial sweep. (Abraham Myerson, *Social Psychology,* pp. 3–6, © 1934. Reprinted by permission of Prentice-Hall, Inc., Englewood Cliffs, N.J.

It is fashionable to believe a great deal of nonsense about animal behavior. A faithful dog, gazing intently at its master, inspires all sorts of fanciful notions as to what it is thinking! Dogs are often credited with remarkable homing instincts; yet, for every dog who finds its way home across a continent, the lost-and-found ads list a hundred dogs who cannot find their way home from the next block. Mama Bear is pictured as patiently "teaching" her cubs how to fish, yet we have no evidence that she is consciously trying to teach them anything. Perhaps she is just hungry! Only for the human race is there conclusive evidence of deliberate teaching and intentional communication of ideas.

This may be our greatest advantage—*our ability to communicate our learnings to others.* The chimpanzee may learn how to get the banana, but it has no effective way of communicating its insight to others; each of its brothers and sisters must get the idea for themselves, either through imitation or through their own imagination. Each chimpanzee stands, or rather crouches, on its own feet and must face the world without the advantage of simian learning. The human race stands on the shoulders of its ancestors and brings to problems a great heritage of accumulated wisdom.

Language and symbolic communications. Many animals can exchange feelings through growls, purrs, mating calls, and other sounds. Some animals give off odors or make bodily movements which convey meanings to one another. These sounds and motions are not *language,* for each is largely or entirely an inborn, instinctive response rather than an acquired, symbolic response. There is no evidence that a dog growls or barks because it wants to tell another dog something; perhaps it barks because it feels like barking. As far as we know, no dog has yet developed a barking code (e.g., one short bark for "let's eat," two yips for "after you," etc.). A language is just such a code—*a set of sounds with a particular meaning attached to each sound.* A largely emotional or instinctive set of yips and yells is not a language, even though these sounds do serve to carry some accurate meanings to others of the species. A mother soon learns from her baby's cry whether it is hungry, sick, or angry; but the baby is simply expressing its emotions, not using language. Only when an *artificial* meaning is attached to each sound, so that the sound becomes a symbol—only then do we have language. The idea of "chair" might be represented by any one of thousands of vocal sounds; when the members of a society agree in dependably recognizing one particular vocal sound as meaning "chair," then a *word* has been added to the language. We limit the term *language* to symbolic communication and exclude the exchange of meanings through instinctive cries and sounds as not being true language.

Some highly popular books and magazine articles have coined the term "body language" for the exchange of meanings through gestures and body postures [Fast, 1970; Scheflen, 1973]. Some meanings probably are exchanged in this way. The question has received some scientific study [Ekman and Friesen, 1974], but the current popularizations are largely based upon intuition and guesswork, not upon scientific research. Furthermore, although "body language" may be a form of communication, it is not true *language*, since language is limited to communication through symbols.

Only human beings use symbols; therefore, only human communication reaches beyond the level of exchanging very simple feelings and intentions. With symbolic communication people can exchange detailed directions, share discoveries, organize elaborate activities. Without it, they would quickly revert to the caves and treetops.

Somewhat as speech separates the human race from the animals, the written language is a dividing line between primitive and civilized cultures. Persons in preliterate culture must memorize traditional lore, and those with fine memories are valued as walking libraries. Old people are useful in a society which must rely on human memory to preserve its culture. But the human memory is not limitless. A culture dependent upon human memory and oral tradition must remain fairly simple. The use of writing allows an almost limitless expansion of the culture, since endless bits of lore can be stored away until needed. Techniques and processes of infinite complexity can be recorded in precise detail and endless variety. Even the

Only the human race uses symbols.

illiterate person is affected by living in a literate culture, since his or her entire life is colored by the fact that others can draw upon the storehouse of the written word. The dictum of Pharaoh's court, "Thus it is written; thus it shall be done," is the basis of every civilized society.

Language is so intimately tied up with culture that every new addition to the group's cultural heritage involves additions to the language. In order to know a group one must learn to speak its language. Even special groups within a society, such as hoboes, soldiers, railroad men, or teen-agers have their own vocabularies. Each subculture has its vocabulary. College students are painfully aware that each new field of study forces them to learn many new words and to learn new meanings for many of the old ones.

Language is related to the rest of culture in other ways. Not only does culture produce language, but language helps or hinders the spread of culture. It is difficult to think without language, for one's thoughts are likely to be vague until put into words. One can, perhaps, visualize objects or actions without using words, but ideas require language. Try visualizing ideas such as "goodness," "never," or "necessary" without using words! Sometimes an idea or concept is hard to translate because the language has no words with which to express it. The translation of papal encyclicals into classical Latin is complicated by the lack of Latin terms for modern words like "automation" and "atomic reactor." India's effort to limit the use of English and to employ the traditional Hindustani as the national language is facing similar difficulties. Either a whole new set of expressions must be hastily coined, or Hindustani must absorb words borrowed at a tremendous rate from other languages. Hence the zealous Indian attempt to support Hindustani was followed by a reluctant admission that English might have to be a language of university instruction for the indefinite future [Rao, 1956, pp. 1–12]. An adequate language is the indispensable means of communication through which culture is shared, transmitted and accumulated.

Language is so closely bound to culture that translators must have an understanding of the culture of both societies if they are to translate from one language to the other. The following anecdote is a case in point:

A story is making the rounds these days about some scientists who designed an English-to-Russian translating machine. To test the device they fed in the sentence, "The spirit is willing but the flesh is weak." Back came the translation: "The liquor is good but the food is lousy." (John G. Fuller, "Trade Winds," *Saturday Review,* 45:12, Feb. 17, 1962. Used with permission of the author and *Saturday Review.*

The accumulation of culture

A look at prehistory shows that human beings once lived very much like their animal cousins. Our early human ancestors lived in the open, wore no clothes, raised no crops, domesticated no animals, and used no fire. Archaeological reports indicate that hundreds of thousands of years passed before people learned to cook their food, plant crops, or build shelters. We who have come to expect a "new model" every year find it hard to visualize an era when people made no great change in their habits for perhaps a thousand generations and, like the animals, lived at the mercy of an unfriendly nature.

The human race spent ages in making early discoveries and inventions, but these became the *cultural base* for more rapid discovery and invention in the future. It took several hundred thousand years to invent the wheel; once invented, the wheel might then be used in thousands of other inventions. For this and other reasons, human culture accumulated exceedingly slowly in prehistoric times, more rapidly in historic times, and with breakneck speed in modern times. Our greatest problem today is how to adjust ourselves and our social arrangements to the speed with which our culture is

TABLE 1 IF A MILLION YEARS* OF HUMAN HISTORY WERE COMPRESSED INTO THE LIFETIME OF ONE SEVENTY-YEAR-OLD MAN

1,000,000 years of history	Compressed into one 70-year lifetime
1,000,000 years ago	Pithecanthropus erectus is born.
500,000 years ago	He spends half his lifetime learning to make and use crude stone axes and knives.
50,000 years ago	And most of the next half in improving them.
40,000 years ago	Three years ago he began to use bone and horn tools.
10,000 years ago	Nine months ago the last ice age ended, and he left his cave dwellings.
7,000 years ago	Six or eight months ago he began to make pottery, weave cloth, grow crops, and domesticate animals.
5,000 years ago	About three months ago, he began to cast and use metals and built the Pyramids.
3,000 years ago	Ten weeks ago he invented the spoked wheel and began making glass.
2,000 years ago	Seven weeks ago, Christ was born.
700 years ago	Two weeks ago man finished the Crusades.
200 years ago	Five days ago he crossed the Delaware with Washington.
65 years ago	Yesterday he invented the airplane.
30–35 years ago	This morning he fought World War II.
7–11 years ago	This afternoon he landed on the moon.
In the year 2,000 A.D.	Tonight he will celebrate the arrival of the twenty-first century!

*Or several million years, according to some anthropologists.

changing. The accumulation of culture is treated in greater detail in Chapter 20.

Geographic factors in cultural development

Climate and geography are undoubtedly a factor in cultural development. Extremes of climate or topography are serious obstacles to many kinds of cultural development. Great civilizations do not flourish in the frozen Arctic, the torrid desert, the lofty mountain range or the tangled forest. People can live in these areas and may develop ingenious means of coping with natural forces, but such areas have not produced great cities or highly developed civilizations. On the other hand, the earliest great civilizations known to the world developed in the lowlands of great river basins. When one speaks of ancient Egypt, Mesopotamia, or India, one is talking primarily of the river valleys of the Nile, Euphrates, Tigris, and Indus [Ogburn and Nimkoff, 1964, p. 71]. Only such areas met the requirements for an early civilization: (1) fertile land which could support a dense population, with part of the people free to engage in nonagricultural work, and (2) easy transportation to link together an extensive area.

Within the geographic extremes, however, it is hard to find any definite relationship. The best known attempt is probably that of Ellsworth Huntington, who developed the theory that civilization flourished best in the temperate zones [Huntington, 1924].

The temperate zones of climate do correlate fairly well at present with advanced civilization, but a shift in the time perspective gives a much different picture. The sunny lands of the Middle East were the homes of flourishing civilizations at a time when people in Europe were huddling in caves or tents. In temperate North America, the most advanced tribes were far behind the Mayas of Yucatan and Central America, who built great cities and had developed a culture comparable to that of early Egypt. A look at history reveals that temperate zone areas now flourishing were at one time in a state of cultural stagnation, while splendid civilizations have flourished and then died in warmer climes. Any society is dependent on climate and natural resources; but there is no special type of geographic environment which guarantees human advance, and except for the extremes previously noted, there is no natural environment which dooms human effort to a limited plateau of achievement.

The possession of fertile farm lands or great mineral resources is an obvious advantage. Kuwait has one of the highest per capita incomes in the world, but was a land of poverty until the engineers of the Western world tapped its vast oil resources. Japan, with no mineral wealth and very little fertile farmland, has become a wealthy nation through effective social organization which has made it a workshop for the world. Truly, it seems that lack of natural resources is no insuperable handicap, while bountiful resources are no automatic guarantee of prosperity.

Ogburn and Nimkoff speak of cultural variation within the same physical setting:

. . . there are peoples living in essentially the same climate who have widely different cultures. In the southwestern part of the United States, the Hopi and the Navaho Indians have lived for centuries in the same locality but their cultures are quite different. The houses of the Hopi are built of adobe and may rise several stories like apartment houses. The Navaho live in a single room shaped much like the Eskimo domed snowhouse, but built of branches of trees. The Hopi are agriculturists and harvest crops. The Navaho are nomads and graze sheep. The religion and family life of the two groups are quite different. Since we find vastly different cultures under the same physiographic conditions, we must conclude that climate plays no precipitating or creative role in building the social heritage. (William F. Ogburn and Meyer F. Nimkoff, *A Handbook of Sociology,* Routledge & Kegan Paul, Ltd., London, 1964, p. 77.)

Many norms and institutions which originate in one climate are easily transportable into another climate. "High tea" has accompanied the British all over the world. Cultural tradition is often more important than physical environment in human behavior.

In recent decades, we have been congratulating ourselves on our ability to control our physical environment. Irrigation dams can make the desert bloom, air conditioning can cool the humid tropics, and through central heating, we can work in comfort in midwinter. We can even survive for brief periods in the airless cold of outer space or deep beneath the sea. But such dramatic achievements may be only temporary. Reservoirs silt up, irrigated lands salinate, and the combustible fuels which took millions of years to create may be gone in a few generations. Our capacity to improve our environment has also made it

We congratulate ourselves on our ability to control our physical environment.

possible for us to destroy it. Erosion carries away the soil, pollution destroys rivers, insecticides kill off both the beneficial and the harmful life forms, and noxious gases make air itself a doubtful commodity in our great cities. We have made lakes where nature did not place them, but we have also polluted lakes until some are "dead" bodies of water unfit for either people or fish. And occasionally our most ambitious efforts to improve upon nature turn out to be a monumental blunder and an environmental disaster, as in the case of the Aswan High Dam in Egypt [Sterling, 1971; Van der Schalie, 1974]. We are beginning to learn that the natural environment consists of a series of interrelated ecological systems that we are currently disrupting at a rate which, if continued, will certainly impair the quality of life and probably threaten even our survival. Many species have perished because of changes in their habitat, but humans would be the first species to commit environmental suicide [De Bell, 1970; Klausner, 1971.].

Social evolution

Evolution was one of the exciting ideas of the nineteenth century. While many scholars contributed to evolutionary theory, its most influ-ential sponsor was the naturalist Charles Darwin. After traveling the world and classifying tens of thousands of present life forms and fossil traces of earlier life forms, he developed, in his *Origin of Species* (1859), the theory that the human race had gradually evolved from lower orders of life as a result of progressive adaptation to the environment through the survival of biological forms best adapted to a competitive struggle. The early sociologists were intrigued by the question as to whether an evolutionary pattern could also be discerned in the development of human culture and social life.

Auguste Comte in his *Positive Philosophy* (1851-1854) wrote of three stages through which he believed human thought inevitably moved: the theological, the metaphysical (or philosophical), and finally the positive (or scientific). Herbert Spencer, the sociological "giant" of the latter part of the nineteenth century, was enamored of "social Darwinism." He saw social evolution as a set of stages through which all societies moved from the simple to the complex and from the homogeneous to the heterogeneous. Implicit in the thinking of both Comte and Spencer was an optimism which saw the progress of society unfolding in a way that would gradually end misery and increase human happiness.

The course of two world wars, the appearance of economic depressions, and the rise of dictatorial governments did much to dampen this optimism and to make the idea of social evolution seem like a childish illusion. The cultural relativists denied that one could speak of a "higher" or "lower" type of culture and claimed that every culture was simply one of several possible ways of coping with the environment. The anthropologists denied that the direction of change is always from the simple to the more complex, and pointed out that many primitive tribes had a far more elaborate system of kinship classification than modern families. Even the ultimate triumph of the scientific approach to life over other approaches is doubtful: values remain central to theology, philosophy, and the humanities, and even appear to be creeping back into science. Culture historians such as Spengler and Toynbee deny the existence of any upward lineal progression of culture and claim that societies have moved in cycles in which democracy and dictatorship followed each other in sequence and in which advanced civilizations such as the Roman Empire rose, flowered, and were buried under successive waves of barbarians.

Ideas, however, are hard to kill. The notion of social evolution[1], which in the middle of the twentieth century seemed dead indeed, is very much alive today. One of the factors in its revival is a concern for the future of developing countries which have embarked on the path of industrialization. As developing countries become industrialized, they not only establish technological and economic structures similar to those of the western countries but undergo related changes in religion, government, and the family as a part of this "modernization" [Moore, 1963, pp. 91–92; Levy, 1967, p. 190]. These developments would seem to indicate that social change is not simply a random process and that industrialization does bring about other predictable social changes. For, as we recall, cultures are integrated.

If these nations, whose backgrounds are so different from those of the Western nations, are following a similar course of development, then perhaps there are some broad lines of movement which are part of a universal evolutionary pattern. We are hesitant to speak of these changes as "progress" in the sense of a happier or more just social system, but perhaps we can still speak of progress in terms of mastery over the environment. Thus Lenski suggests that progress be defined as "raising of the upper level of the capacity of human societies to mobilize energy and information in the adaptive process" [Lenski, 1970, p. 70]. Such a definition points out a possible direction to social and cultural change without raising

[1]In our discussion of social evolution we are heavily indebted to Richard P. Appelbaum. *Theories of Social Change,* Markham Publishing Co., Chicago, 1970.

such unanswerable questions as whether the laborer on the factory assembly line is happier than the craftsman in the medieval guild.

Are there common characteristics which all industrial societies share? Although the familial, religious, and governmental institutions of industrial societies may differ considerably, these differences are probably fewer than those of a century ago, while their industrial, commercial, and military institutions show great similarity. All steel mills, for example, must operate in much the same way, and cannot shut down for an afternoon siesta. Thus modern technology brings many common cultural characteristics to any people who embrace modern technology.

All industrial societies share certain common characteristics.

Are there any universal processes or directions of change throughout human societies? Parsons [1971, p. 5] sees several, the first of which is the emergence of stratification (see Chapter 12) and the development of a political organization independent of kinship. In other words, the growth of technology means that someone has to be boss of every operation, and also that authority does not rest upon family connections but upon some other basis of assignment. The next two steps are seen as the appearance of a bureaucracy in which various degrees of authority are institutionalized and the emergence of money and markets which are mechanisms for mobilizing wealth and labor. His final pair of universal processes are more debatable: the acceptance of law which is equally binding on all members of the society and a democratic government which can support a consensus while still expressing an inevitable diversity.

Whether or not Parsons is right in all details is less important than the core of his argument, which is that social arrangements are not accidental or arbitrary but are moving in some definite directions. As societies adopt modern agricultural and industrial technology, they seem inevitably to experience accompanying changes which Smelser summarizes in this manner:

In an emerging nation we may expect profound changes (1) in the *political* sphere as simple tribal or village authority systems give way to systems of suffrage, political parties, representation and civil service bureaucracies; (2) in the *educational* sphere as the society strives to reduce illiteracy and increase economically productive skills; (3) in the *religious* sphere, as secularized belief systems begin to replace traditionalistic religions; (4) in the *familial* sphere as extended kinship units lose their pervasiveness; (5) in the *stratificational* sphere, as geographical and social mobility tend to loosen fixed, ascriptive, hierarchical systems. (Neil J. Smelser, "The Modernization of Social Relations," in Myron Weiner (ed.), *Modernization,* Basic Books, Inc., Publishers, New York, 1966, p. 111.)

Biological and social evolution

Early social evolutionists assumed that the human race completed its biological evolution at some moment in the past, possibly 100,000 years ago, and then began its cultural evolution. We know today that culture has a far longer history—that people were using rude stone tools at least 500,000 years ago, while the age of such items of culture as language, customs, or kinship systems cannot even be estimated. It appears that cultural evolution began before our present level of biological evolution was reached. For instance, the early *hominids,* whose cultural development was extremely limited, had a cranial capacity in the range of 425 to 725 cubic centimeters, comparable to that of the larger apes today. While the beginnings of culture date back to this period, acceleration in cultural progress did not take place until the appearance of Neanderthals about 150,000 years ago. Neanderthals had a cranial capacity similar to that of modern human beings, averaging 1,500 cubic centimeters and ranging between 1,300 and 1,600 cubic centimeters [Lenski, 1970, p. 152]. Thus both biological and cultural change moved together and presumably, are still evolving together.

Through selective breeding, the human race has already produced in nonhuman species "the most rapid evolutionary changes ever recorded" [Creed, 1969, p. 132]. Recent discoveries in genetics suggest the eventual possibility of producing evolutionary changes through direct modification of the genetic pattern, thus giving us great control over heredity, including our own.

We used to assume that people might control their environment but that their heredity was fixed. Thus one who stressed the influence of biological heredity might be regarded as a "racist" because he or she emphasized a type of difference between peoples which seemed beyond human control. By contrast, the "liberal" was one who played down the importance of heredity and interpreted human differences in terms of varied social environments. It is possible that these statements will be reversed. It has proved difficult to change human conduct by manipulating the environment, but we seem to be on the threshold of a day when human beings can make drastic changes in their biological heredity by manipulating the genes. It is conceivable that, in the near future, the hopeful "liberal" may be one who stresses possible changes in biological heredity, while the reactionary "racist" may be one who stresses the extent to which human nature is shaped by an often recalcitrant social environment. Consider, for instance, the import of the following statement on actual and potential progress in the field of genetics:

. . . [is] the breaking of the genetic code, an accomplishment as stunning for its intellectual brilliance, and as important, in all probability, for the history of science as the first discoveries in nuclear physics. The manner in which the genes send out the "messages" that control the development of the organism is now basically understood. A large part of what used to be called "the secret of life" is therefore open for investigation, and presumably for manipulation and redesign. Human cells growing in tissue culture, for example, have been made to undergo inheritable changes when infected by a virus or treated with foreign genetic matter. To take another example, the first week of human fetal life has been reproduced entirely under laboratory conditions: sooner or later, we are told, test-tube babies will materialize.

There is evidence, for example, that the action of the gene for sickle-cell anemia can be suppressed by activating or deactivating other genes to which its functioning is linked. Again, experiments have been performed indicating the possibility of making up for genetic deficiencies by implanting the needed genes. Gene therapy, chemical or surgical, thus appears to be a quite possible, if not immediate, medical procedure. (Charles Frankel, "The Specter of Eugenics," *Commentary*, 57:25–26, March 1974. Reprinted from *Commentary* by permission; copyright © 1974 by the American Jewish Committee.)

Our growing ability to develop culture may be matched by our ability to control the hereditary potential with which we tackle the culture. In the prehistoric period, both our biological capacity and our cultural storehouse were so limited that change was slow and difficult. In the modern era, the accumulation of culture and the prospect of controlling genetic quality set the stage for a period when human beings will have greater possibilities for controlling the world—for good or ill—than have ever before existed.

Conflict versus functionalist theories of evolutionary change

Although many scholars now accept the theory that all industrialized societies eventually develop cultures with certain similarities, controversy rages over the way in which these changes come about. One school of thought holds to

the idea of balance, or equilibrium, and stresses the way that the various parts of society work together [Davis, 1949; Parsons, 1964]. The emphasis on equilibrium does not mean that society is unchanging, but it does imply that a harmonious relationship of different parts of society is the normal situation, and that disharmony or disequilibrium is a temporary phase of a readjustment process. The term *functionalism* is given to the approach which evaluates developments according to whether they promote equilibrium or disequilibrium— whether they stabilize or disorganize a social system. If a particular social change promotes equilibrium, it is seen as functional; if it has no particular effect upon equilibrium, it is nonfunctional; if it disturbs the social equilibrium, it is dysfunctional. Thus, political parties are functional in a democracy, while bombings, assassinations, and vote frauds are dysfunctional, and changes in grammatical usage would probably be considered nonfunctional.

Conflict stimulates the search for new approaches.

It is not easy to foresee the long-term effects of any change. Developments which seem functional from one viewpoint may appear dysfunctional from another. Our interstate highway system, for example, is functional in that it simplifies travel, but dysfunctional in that it has chopped up cities, accelerated urban blight, and undermined the stability of the city. The important point, however, is not that any given change is, on balance, "good" (functional) or "bad" (dysfunctional); the major thesis is that social development comes through successive changes which promote harmonious cooperation among men.

An opposing point of view sees society as characterized by continuous conflict, in which any social change reflects the selfish interests of one party or another [Aron, 1957; Kerr, 1954; Coser, 1956; Dahrendorf, 1959, 1964]. While conflict is often regarded as wasteful and dysfunctional, it also has positive functions (see Chapter 14). Conflict forces the facing of issues and thus leads to their resolution. Conflict between groups promotes cohesion within each of the conflicting groups, stimulates the search for new approaches, and leads to new adaptations. Oftentimes, new ideas are best promoted by new groups, and the conflict which leads to their victory thus promotes social change. An appearance of social harmony is viewed as deceptive, since apparent peace is merely a period when opposing social forces are preparing for renewed battles to challenge the group which momentarily has been able to impose a system beneficial to

itself. Karl Marx, over a century ago, taught that social evolution proceeded through continuous conflict between social classes over ownership of productive wealth [Marx and Engels, 1959, p. 18]. By contrast, Dahrendorf [1964, p. 107] feels that Marx overstressed the importance of property arrangements, and Dahrendorf finds the major source of conflict in the struggle for authority between rival groups. While they argue about the source of conflict, the various conflict theorists agree that social evolution proceeds through the development and resolution of social conflict and, therefore, that the essential starting point for the analysis of social evolution is not cooperation but conflict.

The differences between the functionalist and the conflict approaches are summarized in Table 2. Supporters of neither approach would claim that their set of assumptions holds true without exception, but that their assumptions are more consistently sound than those of their opponents.

The equilibrium (or functional) theorists look at society and emphasize law, treaties, trade, education, welfare provisions, conservation measures and other arrangements through which people work together to build a better life for all. The conflict theorists stress war,

TABLE 2 ASSUMPTIONS OF CONFLICT AND EQUILIBRIUM APPROACHES TO SOCIAL CHANGE

Equilibrium approach	Conflict approach
1. Every society is a relatively persisting configuration of elements.	1. Every society is subject at every moment to social change: social change is ubiquitous.
2. Every society is a well-integrated configuration of elements	2. Every society experiences at every moment social conflict: social conflict is ubiquitous.
3. Every element in a society contributes to its functioning.	3. Every element in a society contributes to its change.
4. Every society rests on the consensus of its members.	4. Every society rests on the constraint of some of its members by others.

Source: Ralf Dahrendorf, "Towards a Theory of Social Conflict," in Amitai Etzioni and Eva Etzioni (eds.), *Social Change,* Basic Books, Inc., Publishers, New York, 1964, p. 103.

riots, repression, revolution and other indications that the world is a jungle in which the battle of group against group is the major social reality. They are not impressed by the cooperative mechanisms and claim that even apparent cooperation is merely a facade of order imposed by coercion of one kind or another.

It is obviously true that society is characterized by both cooperation and conflict (topics we will analyze at greater length in Chapter 14). It follows that society may be analyzed either from the standpoint of the strains which accompany even a cooperative system or from that of the cooperation which is carried on even in the midst of persistent conflict. An overemphasis on common interests may promote a starry-eyed optimism, while a concentration on conflict may lead to a cynical rejection of all types of cooperative association. In summation, both viewpoints are relevant and useful, but neither offers a complete understanding of the human situation.

Summary

The accumulation of culture through the use of language is one of the main features which distinguishes the human race from the lower animals. Other animals may have physical strength and dexterity, but they lack the ability to communicate through language—the use of symbols which is essential if the learning of one generation is to be transmitted to the next.

Geographic factors require human adaptation, but they do not dictate the form which this cultural adaptation will take; they allow for a wide variety of cultural forms. Great cities have usually been the seedbeds of civilization, while cultural development has been more restricted in the isolated rural areas. The claim that the temperate climate favors high cultural attainment may seem to be true at the present day, but historical analysis indicates that tropical climates often gave rise to advanced civilizations while temperate areas were the homes of cavemen.

The idea of social or cultural evolution is regaining support. This is partly explained by the worldwide trend to industrialization, with the necessary changes which this imposes on all aspects of society. Social evolution does not exclude variation or mean that life is inevitably getting better. It does imply that certain universals are found in all industrializing societies. In prehistoric periods, cultural and biological evolution have moved together, with cultural evolution beginning before our present level of biological evolution was attained. Cultural evolution seems to have accelerated after the prehistoric human braincase enlarged. Prospects for the control of the genes indicate that we soon may be in a position to exert some control over biological evolution in the human species. It is clear that cultural and biological change moved together in the past and may continue to do so.

The acceptance of an evolutionary viewpoint still leaves open the question as to how cultural development takes place. The functionalist explanation views society as an organism whose various parts are usually in a state of equilibrium; the conflict theorists view society as a perpetual struggle. According to the functionalist, evolution leads toward greater integration and cooperation; the conflict theorist holds that new forms of social life come about through the effort of antagonistic groups to gain or hold dominance.

Questions and projects

1. Distinguish between symbolic communication among humans and instinctive communication among animals.
2. Do animals have a culture? If your answer is yes, what limits are placed on such a culture?
3. Huntington argues that, since advanced civilization is found in the temperate zone, this type of climate must favor cultural development. What criticism can you make of this thesis?
4. Independent African countries have usually retained the language of the former colonial power for use in the schools. Do you feel that this practice is likely to continue?
5. Do geographic factors determine the nature of cultural development? Can geographic and biological factors be disregarded in making predictions about cultural development?
6. Read the article by Frankel listed in the bibliography. Are the dangers he lists in securing greater control of human heredity serious? What effect would the control of heredity have on social evolution?
7. Can one support the idea of social evolution while doubting that the human race is making ethical progress? Is it possible for us to continue our technical advance without progressing in the application of moral principles?
8. Does social evolution lead to uniformity? If not, what limits does it place on variation?
9. Would Karl Marx have been friendlier to a conflict theory or an equilibrium theory of society? Why?
10. Why is it difficult to classify particular developments as functional or dysfunctional?
11. It may soon become possible to control the genetic makeup of babies, "ordering" whatever combination of characteristics we desire. What conflicts would this create? Would this development be functional or dysfunctional?
12. Read the article "Genetics and Sociology: A Reconsideration" by Bruce Eckland, *American Sociological Review,* 32:173–194, April, 1967. From the viewpoint of this article, what do you think of the prospects of drastically increasing educational achievement?

Suggested readings

*APPELBAUM, RICHARD P.: *Theories of Social Change,* Markham Publishing Co., Chicago, 1970. A concise and yet thorough summary of current sociological thought dealing with evolutionary theory.

DAHRENDORF, RALF: "Conflict Groups, Group Conflicts, and Social Change," in *Class and Class Conflict in Industrial Society,* Stanford University Press, Stanford, Calif., 1959, pp. 202–223. Reprinted in Peter Orleans and Sonya Orleans (eds.), *Social Structure and Social Process,* Allyn and Bacon, Inc., Boston, 1969, pp. 437–452. Examines conflict from the standpoint of its role both in promoting societal integration and in stimulating social change.

DARLINGTON, C. D.: *The Evolution of Man and Society,* Simon & Schuster, Inc., New York, 1970. Presents the viewpoint that similar principles determine both biological and social evolution.

ECKLAND, BRUCE K.: "Genetics and Sociology: A Reconsideration," *American Sociological Review,* 32:173–194, April, 1967. Argues that sociologists have failed to appreciate the importance of genetically transmitted potential and that heredity and culture interact in the evolution of human societies.

ETZIONI, AMITAI: *Genetic Fix,* Macmillan Company, New York, 1973. Sociological analysis of issues involved in "genetic counseling."

FELDMAN, ARNOLD S., AND CHRISTOPHER HURN: "The Experience of Modernization," *Sociometry,* 29:378–395, December, 1966. Describes the cultural changes which take place when traditional societies modernize their procedures.

FRANKEL, CHARLES: "The Specter of Eugenics," *Commentary,* 57:25–33, March, 1974. A philosopher looks at the promise and danger of producing human types on demand by altering the genes.

*HALL, EDWARD T.: *The Silent Language,* Fawcett

Publications, Inc., Greenwich, Conn., 1959. A lively little book on the interaction of language and culture, listing many ways in which meaning is distorted because cultural norms cause the meaning of identical words to vary from one society to another.

LENSKI, GERHARD, AND LENSKI, JEAN: *Human Societies,* 2d. ed., McGraw-Hill Book Company, New York, 1974. An introductory textbook with an evolutionary approach.

LERNER, I. MICHAEL: *Heredity, Evolution, and Society,* W. H. Freeman, San Francisco, 1968. A superbly illustrated treatment of the relationship of genetics to social decisions.

LORENZ, KONRAD Z.: "Morals and Weapons," in *King Solomon's Ring,* Thomas Y. Crowell Company, New York, 1954, pp. 182–199; reprinted in H. LAURENCE ROSS (ED.), *Perspectives on the Social Order,* McGraw-Hill Book Company, 1968, pp. 120–126. Contrasts the instinctive behavior of animals and the cultural behavior of man as a means of limiting in-group warfare.

PARSONS, TALCOTT: "Evolutionary Universals in Society"; ROBERT N. BELLAH: "Religious Evolution"; S. N. EISENSTADT: "Social Change, Differentiation, and Evolution." Three articles on social evolution, in *American Sociological Review,* June, 1954, vol. 29. The articles by Parsons and Eisenstadt also appear in LEWIS A. COSER AND BERNARD ROSENBERG (EDS.), *Sociological Theory: A Book of Readings,* The Macmillan Company, New York, 1969.

*ROSTOW, W. W.: *The Stages of Economic Growth,* Cambridge University Press, London, 1971. A well-known attempt to describe an evolutionary pattern of economic development.

Chapter 5 • Personality and socialization

There are some elements of one's personality and socialization which are shared with all other persons, some which are shared with some other persons, and some which are shared with no other person. What these are and how they operate is the subject of this chapter.

The meaning of personality

Personality is one of those terms which is seldom defined in exactly the same way by any two authorities. All definitions of personality suggest that it represents a tendency for a particular person to act in a somewhat predictable manner which is unique to that person. While some authorities are concerned with inborn predispositions which they credit to each person, others assume that behavior is largely a product of social experience. A quite satisfactory definition is offered by Yinger [1965, p. 141], who sees personality developing from the interaction of both elements: "Personality is the totality of behavior of an individual with a given tendency system interacting with a sequence of situations."

The phrase, "a given tendency system," suggests that the behavior of a person is fairly consistent. He or she acts much the same way day after day. When we remark, "Isn't that just like Ruth," we recognize that Ruth has a behavior "tendency system" that is quite characteristic of her. The phrase, "interacting with a sequence of situations," indicates that behavior is a joint product of a person's behavior tendencies and the behavior situations he or she encounters. To understand personality we need to know how behavior tendency systems develop through the interaction of the biological organism with various kinds of social and cultural experience.

Factors in the development of personality

The factors in personality development are: (1) biological inheritance, (2) physical environment, (3) culture, (4) group experience, and (5) unique experience.

Biological inheritance and personality

A brick house cannot be built of stone or bamboo; but from a pile of bricks, a great variety of houses can be built. Biological inheritance provides the raw materials of personality, and these raw materials can be shaped in a great many different ways.

Unlike many species, the human animal is sexually active throughout the entire year, and this characteristic guarantees the more or less constant association of the sexes. The human infant is born helpless and will survive only if given tender care for many years. Such biological facts provide a basis for human group life. Some species are monogamous by instinct; homo sapiens definitely is not. This is a biological fact which every society must deal with in some manner. Some of the similarities in our personality and culture are due to our common heredity. As far as we know, every human group in the world inherits the same general set of biological needs and capacities. According to Montagu [1958, p. 85], these needs include oxygen, food, liquid, rest, activity, sleep, bowel and bladder elimination, escape from frightening situations, and the avoidance of pain. Our common heredity thus explains some of our similarities in personality, while individual differences in heredity explain some of the individual differences in personality. But *group* differences in personality cannot be attributed to heredity unless there is convincing evidence that the groups differ in average inheritance.

The American Negroes were taken from a number of tribes, mostly in West Africa. Promptly upon arrival, they began absorbing a culture and developing a personality quite different from that of their African kinsmen. Americans of many racial and national origins now share a common culture, and their differences in personality are not closely related to their different ethnic origins. We could cite dozens of examples of a rapid change in culture and personality without any change in heredity. All that we know of heredity suggests that the heredity of a group does not change rapidly enough to account for such changes in group behavior. What heredity does is to provide the set of needs, limitations, and capabilities with which other factors interact in shaping human personality.

In recent years, *ethology* has developed as a new science devoted to "the comparative study of behavior," mainly animal behavior (and not to be confused with *ethnology,* which is a branch of anthropology devoted to the comparative study of cultures). Ethologists believe that they have found biological or genetic bases for much of human behavior. They believe that sociologists have underestimated the importance of biological predispositions in human behavior. A number of popular bestsellers [Ardrey, *The Territorial Imperative,* 1966; Lorenz, *On Aggression,* 1966; Morris, *The Naked Ape,* 1968; Tinbergen, *The Study of Instinct,* 1969; Tiger and Fox, *The Imperial Animal,* 1972] suggest that many aspects of human behavior—such as the tendency to fight, to seize and defend territory, and to seek domination over others—are biologically based. Such theories are appealing, for they provide comforting excuses for much of our nastiness toward one another.

Critics of the ethologists [Alland, 1972; Binford, 1972; Philbeam, 1972] point out that many of the ethologists' observations of animal behavior are conducted in the artificial environment of a zoo or game park, whereas animals in a fully natural environment display quite different behavior characteristics. In ethological literature, human feelings and motives are often attributed to animals, a process known as *anthropomorphism;* yet the truth is that we really know very little about human motives, and still less about those of animals. Ethology may, in time, make substantial additions to our understanding of human behavior, but the popularizations published to date are more successful commercially than scientifically. They are provocative and stimulating, and offer interesting hypotheses, but most reviewers consider their evidence inadequate for their conclusions.

Physical environment
and personality

Some of our earliest manuscripts are attempts to explain human behavior in terms of climate and geography. Sorokin [1928, chap. 3] summarizes the theories of hundreds of writers, from Confucius, Aristotle, and Hippocrates down to the modern geographer Ellsworth Huntington, who have claimed that group differences in behavior are due mainly to differences in climate, topography, and resources. Such theories fit beautifully into an ethnocentric framework, for geography provides a respectable, apparently objective explanation of our national virtues and other peoples' vices.

As shown in Chapter 4, physical environment is a factor of some importance in cultural evolution. It is a factor of less importance in personality, for, whereas physical environment sets many limits upon cultural development, it imposes very few upon personality. Practically any kind of personality can be found in every kind of climate.

True, the physical environment has *some* influence upon personality. The Australian bushmen had a desperate struggle to stay alive, while it took the Samoans only a few minutes a day to gather more food than they could eat. Some regions, even today, can support only a very thinly scattered population, and density of population has some effects upon personality. The Ik (pronounced "eek") of Uganda are slowly starving, following the loss of their traditional hunting lands, and, according to Turnbull [1973], they have become one of the most selfish, grasping peoples on earth, totally lacking in kindness, helpfulness, or compassion, even seizing food from the mouths of their children in the battle to survive. The Qolla of Peru are described by Trotter [1973] as the most violent people on earth, and he attributes this to hypoglycemia arising from dietary deficiencies. Obviously, physical environment has some influence upon personality and behavior. But of the five factors discussed in this chapter, physical environment is least often important—far less often than culture, group experience, or unique experience.

Culture and personality

Some experience is common to all cultures. Everywhere infants are nursed or fed by older persons, live in groups, learn to communicate through language, experience punishments and rewards of some kind, and have some other experiences common to the entire human species. It is also true that each society gives to virtually all its members certain experiences which many other societies do not offer. From the social experience common to virtually all members of a given society, there emerges a characteristic personality configuration which is typical of many members of that society. DuBois [1944, pp. 3–5] has called this the "modal personality" (taken from the statistical term, "mode," referring to that value which appears most frequently in a series). How the modal personality may vary between two different societies is seen in the following contrast.

Some experiences are common to all cultures.

The anxious Dobuan. [Fortune, 1932; Benedict, 1934, chap. 5] The Dobuan child in Melanesia might think twice about coming into this world, if it had any choice in the matter. It enters a family where the only member who is likely to care much about it is its uncle, its mother's brother, to whom it is heir. Its father, who is interested in his own sister's children, usually resents it, for its father must wait until it is weaned before resuming sexual relations with its mother. Often it is also unwanted by its mother, and abortion is common. Little warmth or affection awaits the child in Dobu.

The Dobuan child soon learns that it lives in a world ruled by magic. Nothing happens from natural causes; all phenomena are controlled by witchcraft and sorcery. Illness, accident, and death are evidence that witchcraft has been used against one and call for vengeance from one's kinsmen. Nightmares are interpreted as witchcraft episodes in which the spirit of the sleeper has narrow escapes from hostile spirits. All legendary heroes and villains are still alive as active supernaturals, capable of aid or injury. Crops grow only if one's long hours of magical chants are successful in enticing the yams away from another's garden. Even sexual desire does not arise except in response to another's love magic, which guides one's steps to his or her partner, while one's own love magic accounts for one's successes.

Ill will and treachery are virtues in Dobu, and fear dominates Dobuan life. Every Dobuan lives in constant fear of being poisoned. Food is watchfully guarded while in preparation, and there are few persons indeed with whom a Dobuan will eat. The Dobuan couple spend alternate years in the villages of wife and husband, so that one of them is always a distrusted and humiliated outsider who lives in daily expectation of poisoning or other misadventure. Because of numerous divorces and remarriages, each village shelters men from many different villages, so that none of them can trust either their village hosts or one another. In fact, no one can be fully trusted; men are nervous over their wives' possible witchcraft and fear their mothers-in-law.

To the Dobuans, all success must be secured at the expense of someone else, just as all misfortune is caused by others' malevolent magic. Effective magic is the key to success, and success is measured by accomplishments in theft and seduction. Adultery is virtually universal, and the successful adulterer, like the successful thief, is much admired.

On the surface, social relations in Dobu are cordial and polite although dour and humorless. There is very little quarreling, for to give offense or to make an enemy is dangerous. But friends are also dangerous; a show of friendship may be a prelude to a poisoning or to the collection of materials (hair, fingernails) useful for sorcery.

What kind of personality develops in such a cultural setting? Dobuans are hostile, suspicious, distrustful, jealous, secretive, and deceitful. These are rational reactions, for they live in a world filled with evil, surrounded by enemies, witches, and sorcerers. Eventually, they are certain to be destroyed. Meanwhile they seek to protect themselves by their own magic, but never can they know any sense of comfortable security. A bad nightmare may keep them in bed for days. As measured by Western concepts of mental hygiene, all Dobuans are paranoid to a degree calling for psychotherapy. But simply to call them paranoid would be incorrect, for their fears are justified and not irrational; the dangers they face are genuine, not imaginary. A true paranoid personality *imagines* that other people are threatening him, but in Dobu, other people really *are* out to get him. Thus the culture shapes a personality pattern which is normal *and useful* for that culture.

The cooperative Zuñi. [Benedict, 1934, chap. 4] The Zuñi of New Mexico are a placid people in an emotionally undisturbed world. The child is warmly welcomed, treated with tender fondness, and receives a great deal of loving attention. It is never disciplined or punished, yet becomes a well-behaved member of a society in which crime is rare and quarreling almost unknown.

Cooperation, moderation, and lack of individualism are carried into all Zuñi behavior. Personal possessions are unimportant and readily lent to others. The members of the matrilineal household work together as a group, and the crops are stored in a common storehouse. One works for the good of the group, not for personal glory. (Zuñi children do poorly on competitive examinations in the government schools, for it is impolite to answer any question whose answer may be unknown to one's classmates.)

The magical forces in the Zuñi world are

never malevolent and often helpful. Since the supernaturals have the same tastes as living persons, they need not be feared. Supernatural and magical aid is sought through many long ceremonials, yet the ceremonial dances are never frenzied or orgiastic. Violence or immoderation is distasteful, and even disagreements are settled without open bickering. For example, one wife who became weary of her husband's many amours decided to settle the matter. "So," she said, "I didn't wash his clothes. Then he knew that I knew that everybody knew, and he stopped going with that girl." Without a word the issue was settled [Benedict, 1934, p. 108]. Unlike most Indians, the Zuñi rejected alcohol because it tempts men to immoderate, undignified behavior. They do not use peyote or other drugs, or resort to self-torture or prolonged fasting in an effort to induce ecstasies, visions, or other unusual sensory phenomena. They desire only the normal sensory experience of moderate behavior. The individual Zuñi craves no power or leadership, and the necessary leadership roles must be thrust upon him. Responsibility and power are distributed; the group is the real functioning unit.

The Zuñi have no sense of sin. They have no picture of the universe as a conflict between good and evil, nor any concept of themselves as disgusting or unworthy. Sex is not a series of temptations but part of a happy life. Adultery is mildly disapproved, but is largely a private matter and a probable prelude to a change of husbands. Divorce is simple; the wife simply piles her husband's things outside the pueblo, where he finds them, cries a little, and goes home to his mother. Since the family is matrilineal and matrilocal (descent follows the mother's family line, and family residence is with the mother's family), a divorce and the disappearance of the father does not seriously disrupt the life of the children. Yet divorce is not very common, and serious misconduct is very rare.

The normal personality among the Zuñi stands in stark contrast to that of the Dobuans. Where the Dobuan is suspicious and distrust-

ful, the Zuñi is confident and trusting; where the Dobuan is apprehensive and insecure, the Zuñi is secure and serene. The typical Zuñi has a yielding disposition and is generous, polite, and cooperative. He or she is unthinkingly and habitually conformist, for to be noticeably different is something neither the individual nor the group can tolerate. Apparently this serves to control behavior without the sense of sin and the guilt complexes found in many societies, including our own.

As the two foregoing sketches illustrate, personality differs strikingly from society to society. *Each society develops one or more basic personality types which fit the culture.* The Dobuans do not consciously or intentionally train their children to be hostile and suspicious; yet the atmosphere of constant treachery and fear has this result. Each culture, simply by being what it is, shapes personality to fit the culture. Let us consider some aspects of the culture which affect the process of personality development.

Norms of the culture. From the moment of birth, the child is treated in ways which shape the personality. Each culture provides a set of general influences, which vary endlessly from society to society. As Linton writes,

In some [societies] infants are given the breast whenever they cry for it. In others they are fed on a regular schedule. In some they will be nursed by any woman who happens to be at hand, in others only by their mothers. In some the process of nursing is a leisurely one, accompanied by many caresses and a maximum of sensuous enjoyment for both mother and child. In others it is hurried and perfunctory, the mother regarding it as an interruption of her regular activities and urging the child to finish as rapidly as possible. Some groups wean infants at an early age: others continue nursing for years. . . .

Turning to the more direct effects of culture patterns upon the developing individual, we have an almost infinite range of variations in the degree to which he is consciously trained, discipline or the lack of it and responsibilities imposed upon him. Society may take the child in hand almost from infancy and deliberately train him for his adult status, or it may permit him to run wild until the age of puberty. He may receive corporal punishment for even the smallest offense or never be punished at all. As a child he may have a claim upon the time and attention of all adults with whom he comes in contact or, conversely, all adults may have a claim upon his services. He may be put to work and treated as a responsible contributing member of the family group almost from the moment that he is able to walk and have it constantly impressed upon him that life is real and earnest. Thus in some Madagascar tribes children not only begin to work at an incredibly early age but also enjoy full property rights. I frequently bargained with a child of six for some object which I needed for my collection; although its parents might advise, they would not interfere. On the other hand, the children in a Marquesan village do not work and accept no responsibility. They form a distinct and closely integrated social unit which has few dealings with adults. The boys and girls below the age of puberty are constantly together and often do not go home even to eat or sleep. They go off on all-day expeditions, for which no parental permission is required, catch fish and raid plantations for food, and spend the night in any house they happen to be near at sunset.

Examples of such cultural differences in the treatment of children could be multiplied indefinitely. The important point is that every culture exerts a series of general influences upon the individuals who grow up under it. These influences differ from one culture to another, but they provide a common denominator of experience for all persons belonging to a given society. (Ralph Linton, *The Study of Man,* © 1936, renewed 1964. Reprinted by permission of Prentice-Hall, Inc., Englewood Cliffs, N.J.)

Some of the American literature on psychoanalysis and child development, drawing heavily upon the theories of Freud, has attached great importance to specific child-training practices. Breast feeding, gradual weaning, demand-feeding schedules, and easy and late induction to bowel and bladder training have often been recommended, with the opposite practices being blamed for all sorts of personality difficulties. These recommendations are generally unsupported by any carefully controlled comparative studies, although dramatic case histories may be cited in illustration. One serious effort [Sewell, 1952] to test these recommendations made a comparison of American children who had received differing training practices. This study found that no measurable adult personality differences were associated with any particular child-training practices. Studies of personality development in other cultures have likewise failed to substantiate Freudian theories of the results of specific child-training practices [Eggan, 1943; Dai, 1957]. Apparently, it is the total atmosphere, and not the specific practice, which is important in personality development. Whether a child is breast-fed or bottle-fed is unimportant; what *is* important is whether this feeding is a tender, affectionate moment in a warmly secure world, or a hurried, casual incident in an impersonal, unfeeling, unresponding environment.

Cultural personality types. A society poses one or more personality types which children are urged to copy. Among most of the Plains Indians, the approved personality for the adult male was that of a vigorous, self-reliant, aggressive warrior. Under many circumstances, to take what he wanted from the weak was a virtue; any tendency to overlook insults or to compromise disagreements was a weakness. Since only these personality characteristics were admired and rewarded in males, they were the ones most boys developed.

The most widely approved personality in our culture is probably friendly and sociable, somewhat cooperative yet quite competitive and aggressively individualistic, progressive, yet practical and efficient. Many features of our social life conspire to develop these characteristics within us. We live in a society where sociability has a cash value. Cordiality is taught and cultivated as a necessity in almost any career. The (middle-class) child is trained to make all requests with a "Please," and receive all favors with a smiling "Thank you."

Television commercials, clerks, and salesmen mount an unending barrage of smiling, friendly-sounding appeals. While much of this outward show of friendliness is phony, it nonetheless surrounds one with an atmosphere of sociability which probably leaves some residue. Our society forces people to develop an acute time consciousness, since nearly everything is done on a time schedule. The American Indians' serene unconcern with time was exasperating to whites who had dealings with them, just as the white person's endless fretting and clock watching perplexed and bored the Indian.

Children are urged to copy.

A close relationship between personality and culture should be expected, because in a sense, personality and culture are two aspects of the same thing. As Spiro [1951] has observed, "The development of personality and the acquisition of culture are not different processes, but are one and the same learning process. . . ." In a stable, well-integrated society, personality is an individual aspect of culture, while culture is a collective aspect of personality. This discussion could be prolonged indefinitely; but we have said enough to illustrate the point that every culture surrounds the individual with experiences that develop a normal personality, more or less perfectly reflected by most members of that society.

Subcultures and personality. This picture of a single approved personality type (for each sex and age level) in a society holds fairly true for the simple society with a well-integrated culture. But in a complex society with a number of subcultures, the picture changes. Are there personality differences between the Yankee and the Deep Southerner? Does the sharecropper think and feel as does the urban professional? In a complex society, there may be as many "normal personality types" as there are subcultures.

The United States has many subcultures—racial, religious, ethnic, regional, social-class, perhaps even occupational. The boundary lines are indistinct, and some subcultures are more important than others. For example, the Catholic and Protestant subcultures probably affect less of a member's life than the Jewish subculture, and still less than the Amish subculture. Yet subcultures are real, and we have some justification for speaking of the "urban middle-class personality" or of the "typical salesman." Of course, we must not exaggerate; it is likely that personality similarities within our culture greatly outnumber personality differences between subcultures, and there are individual personality differences within each subculture. But the physician, the minister, the carnival worker, and the migrant fruit picker show some predictable personality differences from one another. Therefore we cannot describe the normal American personality without first naming the subculture we have in mind.

Individual deviation from modal personality. In even the most conformist of societies, there is some individuality in personality. The modal personality merely represents a series of personality traits which are most common among the members of a group, even though comparatively few of them may have developed every one of the traits in the series. Wallace [1952a] used Rorschach tests on a sample of Tuscarora Indians, and concluded that only 37 percent of them showed all twenty-one of the modal personality traits which had been established as characteristic of the Tuscarora. Other similar studies [Wallace, 1952*b*; Kaplan, 1954] show that while a modal personality type characteristic of a society exists, it is not a uniform mold into which all members are perfectly cast. Likewise, in discussing the "typical" personality of nations, tribes, social classes, of occupational, regional, or other social groups, we must remember that the typical personality merely describes a series of personality traits, a *great many* of which are shared by *most* of the members of that group. Each society and each social group allows a certain amount of individual deviation from the modal personality. When this deviation extends beyond what the group or society considers "normal," then that person is considered to be a "deviant." Such deviation will be considered in some detail in Chapter 7.

Socialization and the self

The infant enters this world as a biological organism preoccupied with its own physical comforts. It soon becomes a human being, with a set of attitudes and values, likes and dislikes, goals and purposes, patterns of response, and a deep, abiding concept of the sort of person it is. Every person gets these through a process we call *socialization*—the learning process which turns him or her from an animal into a person with a human personality. Put more formally, socialization is *the process whereby one internalizes the norms of the groups among whom one lives so that a distinct "self" emerges, unique to this individual.*

Group experience

As one's life begins there is no self, for the individual is simply an embryo sharing the life processes of the mother's body. Nor do birth and the severing of the umbilical cord produce any awareness of self. Even the distinctions between the limits of the physical self and the rest of the world are a matter of gradual exploration as the infant discovers that the rattle or the bars on its crib belong to the external world and are not a part of its body, as are its toes and fingers.

The realization of a distinctive personality is an even more complicated process which continues throughout life. The child learns to differentiate between various other people by names—Daddy, Mummy, and Baby. At first, any man is a "daddy" and any woman a "mummy," but eventually the child moves from names which distinguish a status to specific names which identify individuals, including itself. At about the age of two it begins to use "I," which is a sign of definite self-consciousness—that it is becoming aware of itself as a distinct human being [Cooley, 1908; Bain, 1936]. As time passes and social experiences accumulate, the child forms an image of the kind of person he or she is—an image of self. One ingenious way of trying to get some impression of a person's self-image is the "Twenty Questions Test" [Kuhn and McPartland, 1954], in which the informant is asked to write twenty answers, exactly as they come to mind, to the question, "Who am I?" One's formation of the self-image is perhaps the most important single process in personality development.

Social isolates. Seven hundred years ago, Frederick II, Holy Roman Emperor, conducted an experiment to determine what language children would grow up to speak if they had never heard a single spoken word. Would they speak Hebrew—then thought to be the oldest tongue—or Greek, or Latin, or the language of their parents? He instructed foster mothers and nurses to feed and bath the children but under no circumstances to speak or prattle to them. The experiment failed, for every one of the children died. (Cass Canfield, undated promotional letter, Planned Parenthood Federation.)

To some degree, personality is dependent upon physical-growth processes. But personality development is not simply an automatic unfolding of inborn potentials, as is shown by social isolates. Several times each year the newspapers report instances of neglected children who have been chained or locked away from the normal family group. They are always found to be retarded and generally antisocial or unsocial. Without group experience, human personality does not develop. The most dramatic reports are those of so-called feral children, separated from their families and supposedly raised by animals [Singh and Zingg, 1942: Krout, 1942, pp. 106–114]. Social scientists doubt that a child would live for long in care of animals, and suspect that so-called feral children simply had been lost or abandoned by their parents and then discovered by others shortly thereafter [Ogburn, 1959].

It is highly doubtful, then, that allegedly feral children are examples of animal nurture. It does seem evident, however, that children who are emotionally rejected and deprived of normal loving care fail to develop the type of personality we usually consider human. This conclusion is consistent with the findings of a number of experiments in which animals were raised in isolation from their normal groups. Harlow [1961] raised monkeys in isolation, with only a heated terry cloth-covered wire framework as a substitute "mother," from which they received their bottle and to which they clung when frightened. As infants, they seemed satisfied with this substituted "mother," but as adults, they were almost entirely asocial. Many were apathetic and withdrawn; others were hostile and aggressive. None showed the social group behavior of normal adult monkeys. Apparently the substitute mother met the infant's need for affection and security, but was unable to carry the monkey through any further stages of psychosocial development. Other animal experiments show similar failures of isolated animals to develop the behavior normal for their species [Krout, 1942, pp. 102–105]. Both animals and human beings need group experience if they are to develop normally.

Cooley and the looking-glass self. Just how does a person arrive at a notion of the kind of person he or she is? This concept of self is developed through a gradual and complicated process which continues throughout life. The concept is an image that one builds only with the help of others. Suppose a girl is told by her parents and relatives how pretty she looks. If this is repeated often enough, consistently enough, and by enough different people, she eventually comes to feel and act like a beautiful person. But even a pretty girl will feel that she is an ugly duckling if, beginning early in life, her parents act disappointed and apologetic over her and treat her as unattractive. *A person's self-image need bear no relation to the objective facts.* A very ordinary child whose efforts are appreciated and rewarded will develop a feeling of acceptance and self-confidence, while a truly brilliant child whose efforts are frequently defined as failures will usually become obsessed with feelings of incompetence, and its abilities can be practically paralyzed. It is through the responses of others that a child decides whether it is intelligent or stupid, attractive or homely, lovable or unlovable, righteous or sinful, worthy or worthless.

This "self" which is discovered through the reactions of others has been labeled the "looking-glass self" by Cooley [1902, pp. 102–103], who carefully analyzed this aspect of self-discovery. He may, perhaps, have been inspired by the words in Thackeray's *Vanity Fair:* "The world is a looking glass and gives back to every man the reflection of his own face. Frown on it and it will in turn look sourly upon you; laugh at it and with it, and it is a jolly, kind companion."

There are three steps in the process of building the looking-glass self: (1) our perception of how we look to others; (2) our perception of their judgment of how we look; (3) our feelings about these judgments. Suppose that whenever you enter a room and approach a small knot of people conversing together, the members promptly melt away with lame excuses. Would this experience, repeated many times, affect your feelings about yourself? Or if whenever you appear, a conversational group quickly forms around you, how does this attention affect your self-feelings? A wallflower is a person who learned early in life that he or she could not make conversation. How did he or she discover this?

Just as the picture in the mirror gives an image of the physical self, so the perception of the reactions of others gives an image of the social self. We "know," for instance, that we are talented in some respects and less talented in others. This knowledge came to us from the reactions of other persons. The little child whose first crude artistic efforts are sharply criticized soon concludes that it lacks artistic talent, while the child whose first efforts win praise from a considerate parent may build up a belief in its own ability in this field. As the child matures, others will also give a reaction which may differ from that of its parents, for the social looking glass is one which is constantly before us.

Another difference between the functioning of the "looking glass" in early childhood and in later life is that the child may be deeply affected by the response of anyone with whom it comes in intimate contact, whereas the older individual is more discriminating in appraising the importance of the response it receives from various individuals. The baby-sitter's responses affect the child more than they affect the parent. That is, as we mature we develop

reference groups to whom we give special attention [Rosen, 1955a]. A child may base its estimate of its musical talents on the opinions of parents regardless of their musical sophistication; an adult is more likely to give special attention to the opinions of musical experts and ignore the reactions of others. Not only do we become more selective in choosing the reference groups who comprise our social looking glass but we also are selective in the perception of the images which do influence us. We pay more attention to some reactions than to others; or we may misjudge the reactions of others. It may be that the ego-boosting remark which we take at face value is mere flattery; a scolding may have been caused by the boss's headache rather than by our own errors. Thus the looking-glass self which the individual perceives may easily differ from the image others have actually formed of his or her personality. Several research efforts have sought empirical evidence of the correlation between one's *perception* of responses of others and the *actual* judgments they have made of the person. These studies find that there is often a significant variation between the individual's perception of how others picture him (or her) and the views they actually hold. Calvin and Holtzman [1953] found that individuals vary considerably in their ability to perceive accurately the judgments of others about them, and that the less well-adjusted person was less accurate in these perceptions. Another experiment by Mi-

TABLE 3 SELF-CONCEPTION AS RELATED TO PERCEIVED AND ACTUAL GROUP RESPONSE

Characteristic	Number of groups in which subjects' self-conceptions were closer to their perceptions of group response	Number of groups in which subjects' self-conceptions were closer to actual group response
Intelligence	8	2
Self-confidence	9	0(1 tie)
Physical attractiveness	10	0
Likeableness	7	3

Source: S. Frank Miyamoto and Sanford M. Dornbusch, "A Test of Interactionist Hypothesis of Self-Conception," *American Journal of Sociology*, 61:399–403, March, 1956. (The "1 tie" shown in the table means that in one of the ten test groups, the replies were so evenly divided that this group could not be placed in either column.)

yamoto and Dornbusch [1956] found that a subject's self-conception is closer to his perception of a group's impression of him, than to their actual reported impression of him as is shown in Table 3.

In this study of ten groups totaling 195 subjects, the "perception of group response" is each subject's estimate of how the other members of the group rate him according to four characteristics—intelligence, self-confidence, physical attractiveness, and likeableness. The "actual group response" is the rating actually assigned to him by the others in the group. In most of these groups (of fraternity members and classmates who knew each other well) the subjects' self-conceptions were closer to their perceived response than to the actual response of the group to them. Clearly, it is our perception of the responses of others and not their actual responses which shapes our self-image, and these perceptions are often inaccurate.

Mead and the generalized other.   The process of internalizing the attitudes of others has been aptly described by George Herbert Mead [1934, part 3, pp. 140–141] who developed the concept of "the generalized other." This "generalized other" is a composite of the expectations one believes others hold toward him or her.

This person then looks at himself as though he were another person and judges his actions and appearance according to these judgments of his "generalized other." This awareness of the "generalized other" is developed through the processes of "role taking" and "role playing." *Role taking* is an attempt to assume the behavior of a person in another behavior situation or role. (The concept of role will be more fully explained in Chapter 6.) In childrens' play, there is much role taking, as they "play house" ("You be the mama and I'll be the papa and you be the little baby"), play cops and robbers, play with dolls, etc. *Role playing* is acting out the behavior of a role one actually holds (as when the boy and girl *become* papa and mama), whereas in role taking one only pretends to hold the role.

Our self-image is shaped by what we think others think of us.

Mead sees a three-stage process through which one learns to play adult roles. First, there is a preparatory stage (1–3 years) in which the child imitates adult behavior without any real understanding (as when the little girl cuddles her doll, then uses it as a club to strike her brother). Next comes the play stage (3–4 years) when children have some understanding of the behavior, but switch roles erratically. One moment the boy is a builder, piling blocks upon one another, and a moment later he knocks them apart; or at one moment he is a policeman and a moment later an astronaut. Finally comes the game stage (4–5 years and beyond) where role behavior becomes consistent and purposeful, with an ability to sense the role of the other players. To play baseball, each player must internalize his own role as well as the role of all the other players. Thus through child play, one develops an ability to see his or her own behavior in its relation to others, and to sense the reaction of the other persons involved.

It is through this awareness of others' roles, feelings, and values that the *generalized other* takes form in our minds. This generalized other is roughly equated with the standards or values of the community. By repeatedly "taking the role of the generalized other," one develops a concept of self—of the kind of person he or she is—while repeatedly applying the judgments of this generalized other to one's own actions. A failure to develop this capacity to adopt another's point of view (to take the role of another) seems to cripple personality development. Chandler [1970] tested a group of delinquent boys and found them to be several years retarded in their role-taking abilities. After several weeks of an "actor's workshop" in which each boy took all the roles in succession (aggressor, victim, arresting officer, judge), the boys gained several years in their role-taking skills. This supports Mead's theory that role taking is an essential learning process in socialization.

Other scholars have added the concept of the *significant other.* The significant other is the person whose approval we desire and whose direction we accept. As Woelfel and Haller [1971, p. 75] define the concept, "significant others are those persons who exercise major influence over the attitudes of individuals." These might be parents, admired teachers, certain playmates, and perhaps certain popular celebrities. The concept of the significant other and of the reference group have much in common, except that significant others are individuals, while reference groups are groups.

Two very popular terms which reflect one's sense of self are *identity* and *self-respect.* Identity is a sense of being a unique individual, distinct from all others, or of being part of a unique group, differing from other groups in ways which this group values. Thus the "search for identity" among black Americans today involves the effort to establish a "black" cultural heritage, distinct from those elements of "white" culture which blacks have absorbed. The problem in establishing a satisfactory sense of identity is that the individual or group needs to be distinguished by characteristics which carry prestige in the eyes of the generalized other. Often people are assigned an identity on a basis of race, nationality, religion, or occupation, and these characteristics of theirs may carry low prestige in the eyes of those who "count." Hence the person or

group engages in a vigorous (but sometimes futile) struggle to find a more prestigious identity which is more highly respected by others and consequently by themselves [Merrill, 1957]. The feeling of self-respect is also socially determined. One's ability to achieve self-respect is dependent on the perception of how one is rated by others, especially the others whom one considers important. The man or woman whose interpretation of the generalized other leads them to perceive a favorable reaction to their own personality will develop a sense of self-respect. Otherwise they are likely to turn on themselves, lack self-respect, and regard themselves as unworthy and deficient.

Freud and the antisocial self. Our treatment thus far implies a basic harmony between the self and society. In the words of Cooley:

A separate individual is an abstraction unknown to experience. . . . In other words "society" and "individuals" do not denote separate phenomena but are simply collective and distributive aspects of the same thing. . . . And just as there is no society or group that is not a collective view of persons, so there is no individual who may not be regarded as a particular view of social groups. He has no separate existence; through both the hereditary and the social factors in his life a man is bound into the whole of which he is a member, and to consider him apart from it is quite as artificial as to consider society apart from individuals. (Charles Horton Cooley, *The Nature of Human Nature,* Charles Scribner's Sons, New York, 1902, pp. 1–3.)

This concept of the socialized self was challenged by Freud, who saw no identity of self and society. Freud believed that the rational portion of human conduct was like the visible portion of an iceberg, with the larger part of human motivation resting in the unseen, unconscious forces which powerfully affect human conduct. He divided the self into three parts: the id, the superego, and the ego. The *id* is the pool of instinctive and unsocialized desires and impulses, selfish and antisocial; the *superego* is the complex of social ideals and values which one has internalized and which

Freud believed that the larger part of human motivation rests in unseen, unconscious forces.

form the conscience; the *ego* is the conscious and rational part of the self which oversees the restraint of the id by the superego. Since society restricts the expression of aggression, sexual desire, and other impulses, the id is continually at war with the superego. The id is usually repressed, but at times it breaks through in open defiance of the superego, creating a burden of guilt that is difficult for the self to carry. At other times the forces of the id find expression in disguised forms which enable the ego to be unaware of the real underlying reasons for its actions, as when a parent relieves aggression by beating the child, believing that this is "for his own good." Thus Freud finds that the self and society are often opponents, and not merely different expressions of the same phenomena. He asserts,

If civilization imposes such great sacrifices not only on man's sexuality but upon his aggressivity we can understand better why it is hard for him to be happy in that civilization. . . .

We may expect gradually to carry through such alterations in our civilization as will better satisfy our needs and will escape our criticisms. But perhaps we may also familiarize ourselves with the idea that there are difficulties attaching to the nature of civilization which will not yield to any attempt at reform. . . .

In all that follows I adopt the standpoint, therefore, that the inclination to aggression is an original, self-subsisting instinctual disposition in man, and I return to my view that this constitutes the greatest impediment to civilization. (Sigmund Freud, *Civilization and Its Discontents, Standard*

Edition of the Complete Psychological Works of Sigmund Freud, vol. XXI, translated and edited by James Strachey, W. W. Norton, New York, 1961, pp. 115, 122. Reprinted with the permission of Sigmund Freud Copyrights Ltd., The Institute of Psycho-Analysis, and The Hogarth Press, Ltd.)

Freud's theories have inspired bitter controversies, rival "schools," and numerous interpretations and revisions. His concepts represent ways of looking at personality rather than actual entities which can be verified through specific experiments. There is no simple empirical test which can be used to determine whether the superego, ego, and id are the best possible concepts to use in describing the component parts of the human personality. As our understanding of human nature grows, we may expect to develop additional forms of analysis which will relegate Freud's concepts to the status of pioneering ventures rather than ultimate truths. But the fact that theories are subject to revision and modification does not lessen the importance of their contribution. Most social scientists today agree that Freud was probably right in his claim that human motives are largely unconscious and beyond rational control, and do not always harmonize with the needs of an orderly society.

While Cooley and Mead describe the development of the self in somewhat different terms, their theories complement rather than oppose each other. Both contradict Freud in that they see self and society as two aspects of the same reality, while Freud sees self and society in eternal conflict. But all see the self as a social product, shaped and molded by the society.

Multiple groups and socialization. In a complex society, one's group experience is not always consistent and harmonious. All complex societies have many groups and subcultures with differing and sometimes opposing standards. The individual is presented with models of behavior which are rewarded at one time and condemned at another, or approved by some groups and criticized by others. Thus the boy learns that he should be tough and able to "stand up for his rights" and at the same time that he should be orderly, considerate, and respectful. Some people caution the girl that society demands modesty and maidenly reserve, while others show how a bold, provocative approach is rewarded. In a society where the individual participates in a number of groups, often with conflicting standards and values, each must work out some way of dealing with these opposing pressures. Failure to do so is likely to bring personal maladjustment and even mental illness. People may deal with this problem by compartmentalizing their lives, developing a different "self" for each group in which they move. Or they may select a favorite reference group to conform to and have their real life within, rejecting other groups, as in the case below:

"Thirteen arrests." The judge shook his head over my file. "Gang fightings, shootings, burglary, stealing a car . . . I don't know what to make of you. Your parents are hardworking, religious people in pretty good circumstances. Your IQ is extraordinarily high. Why do you do these things?"
I shrugged. What a dumb question. Every boy I knew did these things. Maybe I just did more of them and better. ("A Gang Leader's Redemption," *Life,* Apr.. 28, 1958, pp. 69ff.)

This boy had adopted the standards of a delinquent peer group rather than those of his family. Research studies [Warner and Lunt, 1941, p. 351; Rosen, 1955b] have usually emphasized the power of the peer group to cultivate behavior patterns contrary to those of the family. Not all youth, however, are as firmly wedded to peer-group standards, and not all peer groups are as much in conflict with family or the society. Most youths find their principal extra-family group allegiance in athletic teams, church youth groups, neighborhood clubs, or youth cliques which are in harmony with most of the standards of conventional adult society. A great deal has been written in recent years about the "youth revolt" and the "generation gap." Yet careful surveys show that while there is a strong urge for change among today's young people, they are in fundamental agreement with their parents on basic values more often than they are in disagreement [Yankelovich, 1972; Erskine, 1973].

Why do some youths select peer groups which generally support the socially approved adult values while others choose peer groups which are at war with adult society? The choice seems to be related to self-image. Habitual delinquents are usually those who see themselves as unloved, unworthy, unable, unaccepted, unappreciated; they join with other such deprived youth in a delinquent peer group which reinforces and sanctions their resentful, aggressive behavior. Law-abiding youths see themselves as loved, worthy, able, accepted, appreciated; they join with other such youth in a confirming peer group which reinforces socially approved behavior. Truly, seeing is behaving. How we see ourselves is how we behave.

Unique experience and personality

Why is it that children raised in the same family are so different from one another, even though they have had the same experiences? The point is that they have had the same experiences; they have had social experiences which are similar in some respects and different in others. Each child enters a different family unit. One is the firstborn; he or she is the only child until the arrival of the second, who has an older brother or sister to fight with, and so on. Parents change and do not treat all their children exactly alike. The children enter different peer groups, may have different teachers, and survive different incidents. Identical twins, in addition to having identical heredity, come very close to having the same experience. They enter a family together, often have the same peer groups, and are treated more nearly alike by other people; yet even twins do not share *all* incidents and experiences. *Each person's experience is unique in that nobody else perfectly duplicates it.* A detailed inventory of the daily experiences of the several children in the same family will reveal an impressive number of differences. So each child (excepting identical twins) has a unique biological inheritance, exactly duplicated by no one, and a unique set of life experiences, exactly duplicated by no one.

Furthermore, *experiences do not simply add up; they integrate.* Personality is not built by piling one incident upon another, like a brick wall. The meaning and impact of an experience depends upon the other experiences which have preceded it. When a popular girl is "stood up" by her date, this is not the same experience for her as it is for the wallflower. Psychoanalysis claims that certain incidents in one's experience are crucial because they color one's reaction to all later experience. "Psychological" movies often imply that psychoanalysis consists of probing into one's unconscious and dredging up *the* traumatic experience which caused all the trouble. This is a gross oversimplification. No woman has had her personality blighted *because* papa stomped on her dollie when she was five. But it is possible that such a traumatic episode might become the first of a series of mutual rejection experiences and thus color the meaning of a great many later experiences. This means that each person's experience is an infinitely complicated network of millions of incidents, each gaining its meaning and impact from all those which have preceded it. Small wonder that personality is complex!

Still another factor appears in the selection of roles to play within the family. Children imitate each other a great deal, but they also strive for separate identities. Younger children often reject those activities which their older siblings already do well and seek recognition through other activities. Parents may unwittingly aid this selection process. Mother may say, "Susie is mama's little helper, but I guess Annie is going to be a tomboy," whereupon Susie starts clearing the table while Annie turns a few handsprings. Sometimes a child in a well-behaved family selects the "bad boy" role, and scowls impressively while his parents describe their problem to the visitors. In large families a child may be hard pressed to find a role which has not already been annexed by an older sibling. Thus, in these and many other respects, each person's life experience is unique—unique in that nobody else has had exactly this set of experiences, and unique in that nobody else has the same background of experience upon which each new incident will impinge and from which it will draw its meaning.

Dynamics of the self

As already hinted, personal self-image is a highly active factor in behavior. There is a great deal of research showing how self-image affects task performance. For example, the famous study *Equality of Educational Opportunity* [Coleman, 1966, pp. 319–325] found that the most important variable associated with school learning was the child's self concept and sense of control over its environment—that is, the child's feeling that its efforts would make a difference. Effective teaching in school, plant, or army rests upon building the learner's confidence that one *can* do it! Conversely, the lack of a satisfactory self-image nearly always cripples learning or task performance, and often leads to antisocial or delinquent behavior [Schwartz and Tangri, 1965]. In fact, a great deal of behavior, ranging from mildly annoying habits like bragging and "knowing-it-all" to serious neuroses and delinquencies can be viewed as desperate efforts to repair an intolerable image of the self. Truly, the image of the self lies at the core of one's behavior system.

Summary

Personality is one's total behavior tendency system. Our *heredity* gives us a set of needs and potentialities which other factors may channel and develop; the new science of ethology has developed to study the possible biological or genetic bases for much of human behavior. Our *physical environment* is relatively unimportant in personality development. Our *culture* provides certain fairly uniform experiences for all members of our society. Our *group experience* develops personality similarities within groups and differences between groups; the *unique experience* of each person shapes his or her individuality.

The normal personality differs dramatically from society to society, as is shown by the suspicious, treacherous, insecure Dobuan and the amiable, secure, cooperative Zuñi. Each society develops a normal personality, produced by the total experience of a person raised in the society. Such cultural influences include the norms of the culture, the ideal personality types presented as models, and many other kinds of experience. All these influences tend to develop a *modal personality* type for the society.

The more complex societies may have a number of subcultures, each developing its characteristic personality and reducing the overall uniformity of personality within the culture. Even in the simpler societies, there is no complete uniformity in personality; only a minority of the members share all the traits of the modal personality. In complex societies, the variation in personality is still greater.

Socialization requires group experience, and *social isolates* fail to develop a normal human personality. Socialization is heavily centered upon the development of the concept of *self*. Cooley saw a person forming his or her image of the self—the *looking-glass self*—in the "looking glass" of other peoples' reactions to him, and the person's feelings about those reactions. Mead emphasized *role taking* in child play as the learning process whereby one becomes aware of the feelings of others. Through applying the standards of this *generalized other* to one's own actions, one develops an image of self. Freud saw the self as composed of unsocialized inborn impulses (the *id*) restrained by a socially acquired conscience (the *superego*) while the conscious or rational part of the self (the *ego*) sought to keep a balance between id and superego. Cooley and Mead viewed the self and society as two aspects of the same thing, whereas Freud viewed the self as basically antisocial, with most personality difficulties arising from the clash between the impulses of the self and the restraints of society.

In a complex culture with many kinds of groups, one may have difficulty in developing a satisfactory self-image and an integrated system of behavior. One may resolve this problem by compartmentalizing one's life and acting differently in each group, or by conforming to one group while, if possible, ignoring any others whose standards conflict with those of that one group. Failure to do either may bring confusion and maladjustment. While there are common elements in the experience of all people and even more in the experience of people within a particular society, each person is still unique. Thus each man is socialized in such a way that his personality is at the same time much like that of others in his society and yet unique.

Questions and projects

1. How do we know that personality is not simply the maturing and unfolding of inherited tendencies?
2. What might be some possible differences in social life and human personality if human infants were normally born (and nursed) in litters instead of one at a time?
3. It has been said that a person raised in one culture may learn to act like people in an adopted culture, but will never be able to think and feel like a person of the adopted culture. Do you agree?
4. Suppose the Dobuans were visited by a man who persistently acted in a straightforward, trusting, confident manner. Tell why you believe they would, or would not:
    a. Admire him   *c.* Fear him
    b. Copy him   *d.* Pity him
5. If culture develops similarities in personality within a society, how do we explain personality differences within a society? Are such personality differences greater within a simple or a complex society? Why?
6. How would you explain the fact that groups which have a major socializing influence upon one person may leave another person in the same vicinity unaffected?
7. Can you recall a specific "looking-glass" incident in your experience? Write it up, describing your actions, others' reactions, your perception of their reactions, and your feelings about that perception. How do you think this incident affected you?
8. How is the self a social product?
9. How do games contribute to the development of the self?
10. Do you feel that Freud and Cooley are in basic disagreement on the nature of the self? Explain.
11. How can children in the same family develop such strikingly different personality traits?
12. Explain how a number of types of annoying people—braggart, bully, gossip, Casanova—may be seeking to repair an unsatisfactory self-image.
13. For slavery to be profitable, it was necessary for slaves to *feel* inferior and *feel* fit only to be slaves. How were slaves in the United States made to feel inferior? Why has the self-image of black people in the United States been changing?
14. When the Shell Oil Company planned an office building in Japan, the Japanese objected to the private offices which American executives cherish. They don't like to work alone. What does this show about culture and personality?
15. Write an account of a typical day in your life, listing all the standardizing cultural influences which you have experienced along with nearly every other American, and state how you suspect each has helped to shape your personality.
16. Prepare an analysis of the behavior of "Yank," the fireman in Eugene O'Neill's *The Hairy Ape.* Is his behavior consistent with what this chapter outlines about others and the concept of self?

Suggested readings

*BENEDICT, RUTH: *Patterns of Culture,* Houghton Mifflin Company, Boston, 1961. Shows how each culture develops a behavior and personality which is normal and useful for that society.

BERREMAN, GERALD D.: "Aleut Group Alienation, Mobility and Acculturation," *American Anthropologist,* 66:231–250, April, 1964. A comparison of Aleuts who became alienated from Aleutian culture with those who remain loyal to the Aleut membership group, and comments upon the difficulties of retaining loyalty to an original ethnic group while becoming acculturated to a new one.

*DANZIGER, K. (ED.): *Readings in Child Socialization,* Pergamon Press, New York, 1970. Eleven empirical studies and two theoretical papers on socialization, written for the advanced student.

*ELKIN, FREDERICK, AND GERALD HANDEL: *The Child and Society: The Process of Socialization,* Random House, Inc., New York, 1972. A simply-written description of the socialization process.

EYSENCK, HANS J.: *The Biological Basis of Personality,* Charles C Thomas, Publisher, Springfield, Ill., 1970. A comprehensive, authoritative summation of the evidence on the biological factor in personality.

GARABEDIAN, PETER G.: "Socialization in the Prison Community," *Social Problems,* 2:139–152, Fall, 1963. How "square Johns" learn to become "right guys" according to the definition of prison inmates.

*GOFFMAN, IRVING: *Presentation of Self in Everyday Life,* Social Science Research Center, University of Edinburgh, 1956; Anchor paperback, Doubleday & Company, Inc., Garden City, N.Y., 1959. A detailed picture of how the self emerges through everyday experiences.

HAVIGHURST, ROBERT J., AND ALLISON DAVIS: "A Comparison of the Chicago and Harvard Studies of Social Class Differences in Child Rearing," *American Sociological Review,* 20:438–442, August, 1955. Two separate studies show that cultural influences on personality development differ from one social-class subculture to another, and also differ by region, religion, and ethnic group within the same social class.

KOHN, MELVIN: *Class and Conformity,* Dorsey Press, Homewood, Ill., 1969. A study of class differences in the socialization process and personality development.

KUHN, MANFORD: "Self-attitudes by Age, Sex, and Professional Training," *Sociological Quarterly,* 1:39–55, January, 1960; Bobbs-Merrill Company, Inc., reprint S-156. Exploration of self-attitudes by members of different social categories through use of the Twenty Questions Test.

MAZUR, ALLAN, AND LEON S. ROBERTSON: *Biology and Social Behavior,* The Free Press, New York, 1972. A brief summary of the views of ethologists upon human behavior.

*MEAD, MARGARET, AND MARTHA WOLFENSTEIN (EDS.): *Childhood in Contemporary Cultures,* The University of Chicago Press, Chicago, 1955. A number of studies of patterns of child development in different cultures.

MERRILL, FRANCIS E.: "The Self and the Other: An Emerging Field of Social Problems," *Social Problems,* 4:200–207, January, 1957. An analysis of anxiety over others' image of the self in a society stressing achieved status.

Chapter 6 • Role and status

This excerpt from a popular magazine shows how one of the important roles and statuses in our society is changing. Status is usually defined as the *rank or position of an individual in a group,* or of a group in relation to other groups. (In fact, some sociologists use the term *position* instead of *status.*) *Role* is the *behavior expected of one who holds a certain status.* Children occupy a status usually subordinate to adults' and are expected to show some degree of deference to adult authority. Soldiers occupy a status different from that of civilians, and their role calls for risks and duties which the general populace is not expected to bear. Women have a different status from men (and one which some women are determined to change). Each person may occupy a number of statuses and be expected to perform the roles appropriate to them. In a sense, "status" and "role" are two aspects of the same phenomenon. A status is a set of privileges and duties; a role is the acting out of this set of duties and privileges.

The norms of the culture are learned mainly through learning roles. While a few norms apply to all members of a society, most norms vary according to the statuses we fill, for what is correct for one status is wrong for another. Socialization, the process of learning enough of the folkways and mores to become a part of the society, is largely a process of learning role behavior.

Socialization through role and status

Each person must learn to fill roles as child, student, parent, employee, organization member or officer, members of a particular racial and social class, citizen, resident of a community, and many others. Role learning involves at least two aspects: (1) We must learn to perform the duties and claim the privileges of the role, and (2) we must acquire the attitudes, feelings, and expectations appropriate to the role. Of these two aspects the latter is the more important. Almost anyone (male or female) can fairly quickly learn how to feed, bathe, and diaper a baby; what one does not learn quickly are the attitudes and sentiments which make baby care a satisfying and rewarding activity. One cannot fill a role happily and successfully without having been socialized to accept that role as worthwhile, satisfying, and appropriate.

Imagine the mental state of a young male German Jew, raised in a prosperous, cultivated home, who graduated from medical school just as the Nazi government closed the professions to Jews; at best, he could work only as a menial and live only as an outcast. Or consider the difficulties and discontents of a woman who has been socialized to view the role of housewife as the only really rewarding role for a woman, but who finds herself an unmarried career woman living alone and competing in a man's world.

Role training for most of the important roles begins early in childhood as one starts to form attitudes toward those roles and statuses. Most of the role training is painless and unconscious. Children "play house," play with the toys given them, watch and help mother and father, hear and read stories, listen to family talk and share in the countless incidents of family life. From all this experience, they gradually form a picture of how men and women act, and of how husbands and wives treat each other.

Social roles and personality

The little boy who assumes the role of his father while playing house is aware that he must think and act in a different manner than when he is simply acting out his own role, that of child. At first he may have little understanding of the reasons which underlie his father's actions, but this understanding grows and his "pretend" roles will help prepare him for the time when he actually becomes a father. At a more mature level "pretend" role taking has been a helpful aid in assisting people to understand the reactions of others in a diagnostic and therapeutic technique known as the *psychodrama,* developed by Moreno [1940] and others. A husband, for example, may assume the role of the wife while she assumes his role as they reenact in an unrehearsed dialogue some recent discussion or conflict. As each tries to play the part of the other, voicing the other's complaints and defenses, each may gain greater insight into the other's feelings and reactions.

The concept of role implies a set of expectations both of one's own behavior and of the reciprocal behavior by other people in the situation. Whether a new role is taken on a pretend basis or as a genuine result of acquiring a new status, the person is forced to analyze the attitudes and behavior of himself and of those about him [Turner, 1956]. Obviously the self does not remain unchanged after this kind of experience. The married woman is in a different status from that of the single woman. Her role is different and in many ways she will seem a different person. Occupational roles also produce personality changes, so that there are "reciprocal effects of man on job and job on man" [Kohn and Schooler, 1973]. Certain personality characteristics favor the choosing and playing of certain roles, while these roles, in turn, tend to develop and reinforce the personality characteristics which are appropriate to the role.

Role sets

The term *role set* is used to indicate that a status may have not just a single role, but a number of associated roles which fit together [Merton, 1957a, p. 369]. A wife, for example, is also a daughter, a relative, a neighbor, a citizen, and a sex partner; probably a mother, a hostess, a cook and housekeeper, and a worker: and possibly a churchwoman, P.T.A. member, union member, employer, or civic personage. Thus her role set involves a constellation of related roles, some of which may require drastically different types of adjustment. It is not uncommon for people to fail to operate equally well in all items of their role set. The woman who is a charming office receptionist may be a poor bookkeeper; the attentive father may be a wretched lover; a clergyman who is an eloquent preacher may be a poor administrator. Successful role performance often requires competence in a number of related behaviors. Meanwhile, one may fill several different role sets at the same time. A man may be a business manager, a reservist in the National Guard, and a prominent civic leader, quite an assortment of roles. This multiplicity of roles may make for some role strain, but not necessarily so, for it may also increase one's overall fulfillment and life satisfaction [Sieber, 1974].

Role behavior

While a *role* is the behavior *expected* of one in a particular status, *role behavior* is the *actual* behavior of one who plays a role. Actual role behavior may vary from expected behavior for a number of reasons: differences of interpretation, personality characteristics which alter a role pattern, variations in degree of commitment to a given role, and possible conflict with other roles—all of which combine in such a way that no two individuals play a given role in exactly the same way. Not all soldiers are brave, not all priests are saintly, nor are all professors models of scholarly rectitude. There is enough diversity in role-behavior performance to give variety to human life, yet there is enough uniformity and predictability in role behavior to carry on the work of organizations even though the personnel is constantly changing.

Uniforms, badges, titles, and rituals are aids

in role behavior. They lead the observers to expect and perceive the behavior called for by the role, and encourage the actor to act in accord with role expectations. For example, in an experiment an instructor delivered identical lectures to two class sections, wearing a clerical collar in one and ordinary clothing in the other. He was perceived by students as more "morally committed" when wearing the clerical collar [Coursey, 1973]. Another experiment showed that people are more obedient to a uniformed guard than to a man in a business suit [Bickman, 1974]. Both the patient and the physician feel more comfortable as the physician conducts an intimate physical examination while wearing white coat in a sterile office than if (s)he were wearing bathing trunks at poolside. The appropriate uniforms, badges, titles, equipment, and setting are all aids to role performance.

While much role behavior is the unconscious playing of roles to which one has been socialized, some role behavior is a highly conscious, studied effort to project a desired image of the self. The concept of *dramatic role presentation* refers to a conscious effort to play a role in a manner which will create a desired impression among others. Conduct is regulated not only according to functional role requirements but also according to what the audience expects. Few of us will ever be movie stars, but everyone is an actor with a wide variety of audiences. The children in the home, the neighbors, the office force, other students in a school—all these, and many others, form audiences. As Goffman [1959, 1967] has noted, we put on a presentation of ourselves when the audience is present, acting out roles so that we give a dramatic picture of the self. The debutante making a grand entrance at a party, the policeman controlling traffic, the salesman making a pitch, the father lecturing his children, the tough guy on the playground— everyone at some time and place is essentially an actor putting on a presentation for the sake of the impression he makes on the audience. Persons of both sexes and all ages sometimes lay claim to fictitious sexual adventures in order to give a more "sophisticated" image of themselves. Many business suits creep out of hiding and many haircuts shorten when the corporate recruiters visit the campus in the spring. Even among groups where "naturalness" and lack of affectation are prized, the frayed blue denims and bare feet are no less a studied presentation of self than are the Brooks Brothers suits in the executive dining room.

Ascribed and achieved status

Statuses are of two sorts: those *ascribed* to us by our society, irrespective of individual qualities or efforts, and those we *achieve* through our own efforts [Linton, 1936, chap. 8].

Ascribed status and role

If a society is to function efficiently, people must perform a vast number of daily chores willingly and competently. The simplest way to ensure their performance is to parcel most of the routine work of the society into a series of *ascribed* roles, and socialize people to accept and fill their ascribed roles. Since role training must therefore begin early in childhood, ascribed roles must be assigned according to some criterion which can be known in advance. Sex and age are universally used as a basis of role ascription; race, nationality, social class, and religion are also used in many societies.

Ascription by sex. Although role training may be largely unconscious, it is no less real. As a noted American educator has remarked, "Adults ask little boys what they want to be when they grow up. They ask little girls where they got that pretty dress." No wonder that by adolescence, boys are becoming concerned about careers while girls are preoccupied with baiting the man trap! This is no accident, since a major part of the socialization process consists of learning the separate activities of men and women. The little girl plays with dolls, helps mother in the housework, and is rewarded for being a "little lady," while learning that "tomboy" activities, though possibly tolerated, are not really "ladylike." The boy finds out that dolls are for girls and babies and that no worse fate can befall him than to be a "sissy." Many years of differential training, if consistent, will bring boys and girls to maturity with great differences in their responses, feelings, and preferences.

Every society handles many tasks by making them part of a sex role. Yet most of the sex-linked functions can be performed equally well by either men or women, provided they are socialized to accept the tasks as proper for them. Thus in Pakistan, men are the household servants; in the Philippines, pharmacists are usually women, while men are preferred as secretaries; in the Marquesas, baby tending, cooking, and housekeeping are proper male tasks, while women spend much of their time primping; in many parts of the world the heavy agricultural labor is performed by women.

The definition of masculine and feminine roles is subject to infinite variation, yet every society has an approved pattern which the people are expected to follow. Individuals may be permitted to bypass some parts of the pattern at times, but they risk alienation from the society unless they can identify themselves with the role expected of their sex. A few societies have a recognized status and role for those who do not absorb the expected sex identities. For example, the *nadle* among the Navaho and the *berdache* among the Plains Indians are recognized gender statuses which differ from both male and female sex statuses [Hill, 1935; Lurie, 1953; Voorhies, 1972]. But in most societies, no comfortable status is open to those who do not develop the expected sex-role behavior.

Many of the considerations which presumably underlay our ascribed sex roles are themselves changing today. The assumption of vast innate sex differences in intellect and aptitude has been discredited. Greater dependability and availability of contraception and abortion has weakened the rationale for a "double standard" of sexual behavior. Declining family size means that women spend less time in childbearing and care. The shift from human to machine power means that greater masculine physical strength becomes less important. The Women's Liberation Movement is demanding a wholesale overhaul of sex role ascription (see Chapter 21). No one doubts that men and women will continue to be different in recognizable ways, but current developments are narrowing the differences in their ascribed roles and opening more achieved roles to women.

In the United States, homosexuals (and some sympathizers) have actively campaigned for "gay liberation," and the more brutal penalties for homosexuality have been somewhat relaxed. The American Psychiatric Association in 1973 changed its designation of homosexuality from a "mental disorder" to a "sexual orientation disturbance," a less punishing title [Lyons, 1973]. But the gay liberation movement has not yet succeeded in gaining widespread acceptance of the idea that homosexuality is not a behavior abnormality but rather a normal and healthy alternative life style.

Ascription by age. In no society are children, adults, and the aged treated alike. Age roles vary greatly between societies. American children spend their childhoods in pampered play while Navaho children tend sheep and do weaving at an early age; the aged in prerevolutionary China were honored authority figures as long as they lived, while the American aged are pushed into uselessness and irrelevance. Persons whose behavior is inappropriate for their age status are either laughed at or resented. The teen-ager who claims adult privileges is irritating, while the mature person who acts like a teen-ager is ridiculous.

Sex and age are universally used as bases of status ascription. Other commonly used bases

include social class, race or nationality, ethnic group, and religion. All such ascribed statuses involve roles which can be filled successfully only when one has been socialized to expect and appreciate the role.

We may today have developed a form of quasi-ascription through our trend toward *meritocracy.* A meritocracy is a social system in which status is assigned according to merit, and merit is most commonly measured by scores on standardized tests which control access to educational programs and occupational roles. Whether such tests are classified as means of role ascription or of role achievement depends upon the degree to which the scores are affected by conscious effort after one has passed the stage of early childhood. If one assumes that these scores are reasonably stable for an individual, then the result is a kind of caste system in which test scores, largely dependent upon heredity and early environment, may shape one's entire life. This means that a new type of ascribed status has developed, not directly dependent upon the status of one's ancestors, but perhaps almost as rigid.

Achieved status and role

A social position which is secured through individual choice and competition is known as *achieved status.* Just as each person occupies a number of ascribed statuses, assigned without regard to individual ability or preference, so one occupies a number of achieved statuses which are secured through one's own ability, performance, and possibly good or ill fortune. The difference is aptly stated by Young and Mack:

"Princess" is an ascribed status; where there is a hereditary royalty a girl does not work her way up to being princess. She is *born* a princess, and whether she is pretty or ugly, tall or short, intelligent or stupid, a princess she remains. *Achieved statuses,* on the other hand, are not assigned at birth, but are left open to be filled by the persons who compete more successfully for them. Being male is an ascribed status. It is determined at birth; either you are male or you are not. Being a husband is an achieved status; it does not result automatically from one's being born a male but depends upon a male's own behavior in the future. Negro is an ascribed status. One cannot change his color to white. But policeman is an achieved status. One is not born a policeman; he becomes one through his own talent or choice or action. (Kimball Young and Raymond W. Mack, *Sociology and Social Life,* American Book Company, New York, 1959, pp. 160–161.)

Being married is an achieved status.

In traditional societies most statuses are ascribed, with one's occupation and general social standing determined at birth. Industrialized societies have a greater range of occupations, require a greater mobility of labor, and allow greater scope for the individual to change one's status through one's own efforts. The society stressing achieved status will gain in flexibility and its ability to place people in occupations best suited to their talents. The price it pays for these advantages is seen in the insecurity of those unable to "find themselves" and in the strain of constant adjustment to new roles. Achieved status requires the individual to make choices, not only of occupation but also of friends, organizations, schools, and place of residence. Further, it leads the individual into roles which were not foreseen or desired by one's parents. In the traditional society, where statuses and roles are ascribed, persons are trained from childhood and guided through life by rules of conduct which they have carefully learned in preparation for the roles they are destined to play. In a changing society where they are free to experiment, individuals meet situations far removed from the parental way of life and may have to feel their way awkwardly into unfamiliar roles.

Ascribed and achieved statuses are basically different; yet they interact with each other and may overlap. Thus it is easier for one with the ascribed status of male to reach the achieved status of President of the United States than it is for the one with the ascribed status of female. The achieved status of physician is open to both blacks and whites, but in the United States whites reach it more easily than blacks. General social standing in the community (social-class status) is partly ascribed, reflecting the status of one's parents, and partly achieved through one's own accomplishments. At many points the boundaries between achieved and ascribed status are indistinct; yet the concepts are useful.

Psychic costs of achieved status. The ideal of the society which permits most statuses to be achieved is to place people according to their abilities. To some extent, this effort enables the highly talented to move upward, but it also destroys the alibi of the failures. In a society where most statuses are ascribed, individuals are not expected to improve their lot. Those who receive low rewards and little prestige feel no guilt or shame.

They are taught that their role and status are right and proper. They can take pride in their accomplishments without any need to compare them with those of persons in other statuses. They are freed from the sense of insecurity, the nagging of ambition, or the sting of failure. Socialization is eased because they are not expected to change their status; they have only to learn and accept their social roles.

It is difficult to rationalize low status if hereditary barriers are removed and positions are open to all on the basis of ability. If positions are filled on competitive examinations and if adequate schooling is free to everybody, then the reason for low status must be incompetence, and this is not a comfortable explanation. The low-caste person in India could blame his or her status on the inexorable laws of the universe; the American university student who fails to graduate is hard put to find a similar justification. In self-defense the mediocre generally support the attempt to limit achievement by the imposition of seniority rules, group quotas, veterans' preference, and similar techniques.

Achieved status makes maximum provision for the attainment of roles on the basis of individual ability. It provides a high degree of choice and flexibility at the cost of psychic insecurity for the individual who has limited talents or has unequal opportunity to develop and employ them. The roles which accompany achieved statuses may be difficult to learn and mutually conflicting. In essence the achieved status probably represents both the most efficient use of the human potential and the greatest threat to the individual's peace of mind.

Status inconsistency

Each person holds a number of statuses at the same time, and some of them may be incompatible with the others. This conflict is called by several terms which are used more or less interchangeably by sociologists: *status inconsistency, status incongruity,* and *status discrepancy.* While some sociologists attempt to draw a distinction between these terms, any of them may be used to refer to *any kind of disparity between a person's several statuses.* One status may have more prestige than the others, as in the case of the poverty-stricken nobleman who sells real estate or opens a haberdashery. Or, the statuses may be socially defined as inappropriately linked; for example, when a person has an uncle who is younger than he or she is, or a nephew who is older, age and kinship statuses are inconsistent. Any deviation from customary age relationships is regarded as status inconsistency. A teen-aged President is an impossibility under our Constitution, older people who marry partners young enough to be their children are criticized, and a ribald cynicism awaits the old man who proudly announces the birth of a child.

Another kind of status inconsistency is that in which a person is not accorded the status which (s)he feels is deserved. The new rich may fail to gain acceptance among aristocrats; the honorably discharged veteran, home from Vietnam, has been too young to buy a beer in many states; the Doctor of Chiropractic craves, but is denied, the status of the Doctor of Medicine. Ethnic minorities and women often find that their ascribed status limits both their access to achieved statuses and their rewards if they can surmount the obstacles. The prosperous Jew who cannot join the country club and the brilliant professional woman who is patronized by men are enduring the results of status inconsistency. One whose statuses are consistently low may be able to accept low status, but one who ranks high in some statuses and low in others is likely to feel wronged when judged by the low rather than by the high-ranking statuses [Lenski, 1967, p. 298].

Several studies have been made of the behavior of people with statuses which are generally perceived by others as inconsistent [Lenski, 1954; Mitchell, 1964; Kelly and Chambliss, 1966; Treiman, 1966; Broom and Jones, 1970], but there is no definite agreement upon the kind of behavioral response which can be expected [Hartman, 1974]. Perhaps this is because persons caught in the bind of status inconsistency may pursue either of two mutually contradictory courses of action. Since they are partially excluded from the desired status, they may identify with the lower status group and take upon themselves the attitudes and behavior of this group. They may thus be able to gain leadership in this group and then demand a degree of deference from the rest of society. History tells of many who exacted a tribute as revolutionary leaders which they were denied as would-be members of the establishment. The colonial national in Asia and Africa who obtained a good job but was denied social recognition often became a nationalist leader of the independence movement, just as the Women's Liberation Movement today is almost entirely composed of educated women who reject the docile-housewife role as insulting.

A different reaction to status inconsistency is to deny any linkage to the undesired status, but to identify with the symbols of the desired status even more rigidly than those who have long enjoyed them without question. The new rich, whose humble ancestry or ethnic origin inhibit their social acceptance, often indulge in ostentatious spending to prove their wealth, and may support reactionary politics to prove their ideological identity with the bastions of privilege—a process long noted among Texas oil millionaires. Immigrants who "made good" may change their names to hide ethnic identity and reduce their contacts with those of their own ancestry. One holding inconsistent statuses may seek to reduce stress by identifying with either the lower or the higher aspects of his status characteristics, but one way or another, the situation affects his status definition and role behavior.

Role personality and true personality

If role preparation were entirely adequate, each person would develop a personality which perfectly harmonized with his or her role demands. But imperfections in preparation, plus unpredictability of future role demands, make it certain that many people will develop a personality which differs considerably from the *pattern of personality traits which the role requires*—the *role personality*. For the

ascribed roles and statuses, the divergence may be small enough so that little clash will occur between role personality and true personality. Thus most adult males can fill the male role simply by "being themselves."

For the achieved roles and statuses, which often are not selected until after one's adult personality has already been formed, considerable divergence between role and true personalities is fairly common. For instance, in the role of salesman a man needs to be friendly, extroverted, and perceptive of the reactions of others. Suppose his true personality is shy, withdrawn, contemplative, and insensitive to the reactions of others. Such a person is unlikely to become a salesman or to succeed as one. If he does succeed, he does it by masking his true personality with an outward show of friendliness and a deliberately cultivated attentiveness to the clues to other's reactions. This role playing is not easy to accomplish successfully and may entail a good deal of emotional strain. If the role playing is done successfully over a long period of time, however, the true personality may gradually be modified to come closer to the role personality. Mrs. Eleanor Roosevelt was a rather shy young woman and a hesitant and reluctant public speaker. In her role as wife to a politically ambitious but physically handicapped husband, she forced herself into vigorous political activity and became an eloquent speaker. Apparently she found the role a rewarding one, for long after her husband's death she accepted a diplomatic appointment, remained a tireless world traveler and public speaker, and became perhaps the most remarkable woman of her age. On the other hand, the wives of several men prominent in public life have rejected the role of politician's wife and divorced their husbands.

It is likely that a good deal of success and failure in achieved roles is explained by the degree to which the true personality coincides with the required role personality. Personnel management today is much concerned with this coincidence and uses job analyses, psychological tests, depth interviews, and other devices in an effort to fit people into jobs where there will be little clash between true and role personalities.

Role strain

It would be ideal if each person could fill all roles in a role set with equal ease, but few people are able to do this. *Role strain* refers to *the difficulty people have in meeting their role obligations.* Role strain may arise through inadequate role preparation, role transitional difficulties, role conflict, or role failure.

Inadequate role preparation

The little girl singing lullabies to her doll, the small boy building a model airplane, the single woman filling her hope chest, the apprentice copying the work techniques of the master craftsmen—all these are experiencing a *continuity of socialization* by learning skills and attitudes at one period of life which they can use at another. By continuity in socialization we simply mean that the experiences at each life stage are an effective preparation for the next stage. An example of how continuity in the socialization process provides a smooth transition into the adult role is seen in the child-training practices of the Cheyenne Indians, as described by Benedict.

The essential point of such child training is that the child is from infancy continuously conditioned to responsible social participation while at the same time the tasks that are expected of it are adapted to its capacity . . . . At birth the little boy was presented with a toy bow, and from the time he could run about serviceable bows suited to his stature were specially made for him by the man of the family. Animals and birds were taught him in a graded series beginning with those most easily taken, and as he brought in his first of each species his family duly made a feast of it, accepting his contribution as gravely as the buffalo his father brought. When he finally killed a buffalo, it was only the final step

of his childhood conditioning, not a new adult role with which his childhood experience had been at variance. (Ruth Benedict, "Continuities and Discontinuities in Cultural Conditioning," *Psychiatry,* 1:161–167, May, 1938.)

Such an easy transition from one status to the next is by no means universal. Our culture is characterized by built-in *discontinuities,* which make the socialization experience in one age period of little use in the next. In frontier America, boys and girls learned their adult roles by simply observing and taking part in whatever was going on around them— clearing land, planting crops, caring for babies, and so on. Today there is less opportunity for such continuity. Most adult work is performed away from home, where children cannot watch and share it. Many households offer only a poor opportunity for a child to learn the skills, attitudes, and emotional rewards of housekeeping and parenthood. Children and youths have few important tasks in most households, and much of the child's play activity is not closely related to adult tasks and responsibilities. Another imperfection in our socialization process is that the moral training of boys and girls introduces them mainly to the *formal* rules of social behavior rather than to the informal modifications of these rules which operate in the adult world. In other words, they are taught the ideal, not the real culture. The result is that young people become cynical as they find that the textbook maxims do not work out. The politician does not appear as a public servant who negotiates a livable adjustment between bitter opponents, but as one who compromises on sacred principles; the businessman seems a greedy manipulator rather than an individual struggling to find his place in the market; the clergyman is apparently not one who mediates the ways of God to humanity, but a huckster who fails to live up to the ideals the church proclaims. Thus many young people graduate from a naive idealism directly into a naive cynicism without ever reaching an appreciation of the services of those who work out livable compromises with the unsolved problems of society.

Our culture is characterized by built-in discontinuities.

Some gap between the formal expressions of the mores and the actual adjustments of social life is probably found in all societies. And in all societies, "maturity" involves coming to terms with these inconsistencies in some sort of liveable compromise.

Such discontinuities are also favored by rapid social change, since parents cannot possibly anticipate the type of world their children will face. While the emergence of new inventions is often recognized as a disrupting factor, the changing social climate is equally unpredictable. Thus the parent in Ceylon, who in the 1930s looked on Christianity as the religion of the enlightened and powerful, raised children who sometimes find this religious affiliation a social handicap now that Buddhism has become identified with resurgent nationalism in a newly independent country. Conversely, many an African, trained as a child to respect the traditions of the tribe and the authority of the chief, may grow up to live as an urban worker in a culture where chiefs are powerless and tribal traditions are irrelevant. The American farmer may carefully train his children in the attitudes and techniques appropriate to farming, although it is a predictable certainty

that many of these children are headed for an urban life and work.

Current sex role changes create problems in role preparation. Should little girls be socialized to view motherhood and homemaking as their primary fulfillment, or socialized to believe that such a commitment is a waste of their potential? Should boys be socialized to view the "provider" task as their primary duty, or should they accept an equal willingness to sacrifice career advancement while sharing equally in household and child care duties?

Such examples could be multiplied endlessly. They show how it is impossible to prepare young people for precisely the roles they will play as adults in a changing society. Since adult roles cannot be accurately predicted, socialization and education can be adequate only if they prepare the child to play any of a wide variety of roles. Memorization and rote learning in schools have been replaced, in theory, by efforts to develop abilities in "problem solving" and "adjustment," but how successfully may be debated. Yet the rapidity of change and the uncertainty of future role ascriptions make flexibility and adaptability necessary conditions for survival.

Role transitional difficulties

In many societies there are role transitions—especially in ascribed age roles—which are structured in such a way as to be inevitably difficult. This is because of discontinuities in role preparation—because the learning experiences of one age status do not provide the attitudes and values needed to fill the next role one is expected to assume. In most primitive societies the adolescent period is not marked by any unusual stress. At any given age in most primitive societies, individuals have a clearly defined status and role; they, and everyone else, know exactly what their duties and privileges are. Our society has no clearly defined age statuses, except for the relatively minor legal maturity at twenty-one, which, adding still greater confusion, is now rapidly changing to eighteen. American youth and their parents have no standardized set of duties and privileges to guide them. Parents are uncertain about just how much "maturity" to concede to teenagers, and they bicker endlessly about their choice of companions, the hours they keep, their use of money, the use of the car, and whether they are old enough to marry. Coleman, a distinguished educational sociologist, suggests that in American society, prolonged schooling tends to isolate youth from adults and to shift socialization to the peer group; this, he believes, perpetuates the irresponsibilities of childhood and fails to prepare youth for adult roles [Coleman, 1974].

In most primitive societies adolescents enter a period of training which ends in an elaborate ceremony, in which they may endure ordeals or submit to circumcision, tatooing, or scarification. Such ceremonies, called "rites of passage," establish their status and announce that they are now ready to assume adult responsibilities, and their successful role performance is almost guaranteed. Our closest equivalents are found in such events as confirmation or first Communion, getting a driver's license, holding a full-time job, graduating from high school or college, and getting married. Yet we lack any systematic preparation, or any general agreement upon the age, achievement, or type of ceremony which clearly establishes the transition into adult status.

The transition to middle age is not a happy one in our society, especially for women. Our accent on youth and glamour dooms every woman to feel her desirability slipping away from her. The menopause is a relentless announcement that youth, glamour, and romance are over; instead, she can become "matronly." Plastic surgeons, cosmeticians, and beauticians make fortunes by catering to women's futile efforts to stave off the ravages of time. We suspect that many of the physical and emotional difficulties that sometimes accompany the menopause are due to this painful role transition. And for men, the middle

years are rightfully called the "dangerous age," when they are notoriously prone to reckless romantic adventures.

Old age in many primitive or traditional societies is highly honored, perhaps because in such a society the old are closest to the source of hallowed tradition. Thus in pre-Communist China the grandmother was the reigning female in a multiple-family home, and the grandfather was a patriarch whose whim was close to law. In contemporary industrialized society old age is a nuisance. A rapidly changing society seldom looks to its aged for guidance, for people who were socialized two generations ago are likely to be behind the times. The compulsory retirement-at-age-sixty-five system is an expedient way of discarding the fossils. Three-generation households are scarce, and where they exist the aged are likely to be dutifully tolerated rather than revered as heads of the household. The role of the aged is a retirement in which their income is reduced, their responsibilities withdrawn, and their influence undermined; their main function in life is to divert themselves while waiting to die. The unhappy position of our aged illustrates the fact that a role transition is difficult when the characteristics which one develops in one role may become useless or even troublesome as one moves into the next role.

Among the Plains Indians, the warriors were trained from childhood to become aggressive, hostile, and uncompromising; then upon retirement from warrior to "old man" status, they were expected to be placid peacemakers. This called for an abrupt reversal in personality, and few of them could make the transition gracefully. An equally painful transition is demanded in our society. To be successful in the active adult role, one must develop independence and self-reliance, must learn to find satisfaction in useful work, and in being adviser and protector of the young. As an aged person, one must become dependent and submissive, able to respect oneself with no useful work to do, and must learn to keep advice to oneself while being ignored or patronized by the young. Is it any wonder that many of our old people sicken and die soon after retirement, while many others become bored and fretful? The rapidly developing field of *geriatrics* indicates a serious concern with this problem. But as long as youth suggests activity, adventure, and romance, while age symbolizes uselessness and irrelevance, growing old will continue to be a painful experience.

Role transitions often are also made more difficult through the necessity of *role relinquishment.* To accept a new role, one often must relinquish an old one, along with whatever rewards it carried. The "swinging" single who marries, the alcoholic who must resume responsibilities when (s)he goes "on the wagon," and the business owner who must surrender his power and authority when he turns the business over to his son—these are a few examples of difficult role relinquishment. Just as the Plains Indians found it difficult to relinquish the warrior role, many parents find it difficult to relinquish control over their children. Efforts to "rehabilitate" prostitutes generally fail because "the life" is more exciting than any "straight" jobs which these women can hold. To succeed in "straight" jobs, ghetto youth must forget their street skills and surrender too much personal worth and dignity, as these are measured in the world of ghetto street life.[1] Thus an unwillingness to relinquish the rewards of a current role may prevent the full acceptance of a new role.

Role conflicts

There are at least two kinds of role conflicts: conflicts between roles and conflicts within a single role. Often two or more roles (either independent roles or parts of a role set) may impose conflicting obligations upon a person. The employed wife finds that the demands of her job may conflict with home duties; the married student must reconcile student role

[1]See Institute of Social Research *Newsletter*, University of Michigan, Autumn, 1973.

demands with duties as husband or wife; the police officer must sometimes choose between violating his duty and arresting a friend. Or, within a single role, there may be a structured (built-in) conflict. The military chaplain, preaching a gospel of love, must sustain men in their readiness to kill, a role conflict which many chaplains find disturbing [Burchard, 1963; Zahn, 1969]. Among the younger Catholic clergy, the conflict between the vows of celibacy and the desire for marriage is the greatest source of role strain [Schoenherr and Greeley, 1974]. The "company doctor" in any industry with health hazards dare not find that many workers' illnesses are due to unhealthful working conditions if he wishes to remain a company doctor. In many occupational roles, ranging from repairman to physician, there is a built-in "conflict of interest" in that the obligation to be honest with the customer or patient may conflict with the desire to make money, so that a number of needless repairs to car or body may be made. Very few roles are completely free from structured role conflicts. Difficulties in managing the resulting role strain are often expressed in psychosomatic illnesses or in addiction to alcohol or drugs [Winick, 1961].

There are several common processes which reduce role strain and protect the self from guilt. These include *rationalization, compartmentalization,* and *adjudication.* The first two are not conscious, intentional protective devices; if they were, they would not "work." Only when people are not aware of them will these processes function successfully.

Rationalization is a defense process whereby one redefines a painful situation in terms which are socially and personally acceptable. The classic illustration is that of the man who comes to feel that he is fortunate that he didn't marry that girl who rejected him, or even comes to believe that it was really *he* who rejected her! Rationalization conceals the reality of role conflict, preventing awareness that any conflict exists. Thus our belief in democracy and our denial of equality to women and to black people caused few anxieties as long as we believed that women and blacks were on the intellectual level of children. "All men are created equal," but slaves were not *men,* they were *property.* The Catholic doctrine (which Luther and Calvin also followed) of "just" and "unjust" wars makes it possible for Christians (on both sides) to commit mass murder with a clear conscience. Through rationalization, the situation is defined in such a way that there is no role conflict and therefore no role strain.

Compartmentalization reduces role strain by fencing one's roles off into separate parts of one's life and responding to only one set of role demands at a time. It has been noted that many cruel Nazi concentration camp guards and executioners were kindly, affectionate husbands and fathers. Their work and family roles were entirely separated. The businessman who conspires to violate the antitrust laws in the afternoon and speaks eloquently at a citizen's law-and-order meeting in the evening is not necessarily a hypocrite; he is merely switching roles. Within each role are found the pressures and justifications which make the expected role behavior seem necessary and good. Uniforms, judicial robes, surgical gowns and professional titles are aids in insulating roles from one another. Many people cannot "relax" (that is, cannot step fully outside a role) until they are "out of uniform."

If one is successfully socialized, one develops a wardrobe of role personalities, and slips into one or another as the situation demands. At the office, the woman treats men with a brisk, formal efficiency; at home she is tender, responsive, and "feminine." This process of switching role personalities creates the possibility of emotional strain whenever it is not entirely clear which of several sets of attitudes and guidelines should apply to a particular behavior situation. Many a businessman, faced with the necessity of laying off employees, finds it painful to ignore their human needs and treat them impersonally as "cost factors in production." The dishonesties, deceptions, and exploitations that are a part of many occupational roles are inconsistent with the usual moral and religious training. If the

individual is not fully successful in fencing his or her behavior off into compartments, these cultural contradictions become mental conflicts within the individual. Some psychiatrists hold that such culture conflicts, and the mental conflicts they produce, are major causes of personality disorder.

He develops a wardrobe of role personalities.

Cultural conflicts and inconsistencies are probably found in every culture. In well-integrated cultures, these inconsistencies are so well rationalized, compartmentalized, and fenced off from one another that the individual does not sense them at all. Thus many primitives who treated one another with great tenderness were ruthlessly cruel to outsiders; their humanitarian mores applied only to tribal fellows, while outsiders were considered and treated like any other animals of the forest. By contrast, our belief in a universal God of all humanity makes it harder for us to bomb our enemies with a clear conscience (but we generally manage to, somehow). *Cultural contradictions and multiple roles are upsetting only when they subject the individual to conflicting pressures in a situation that demands a single action.* For example, should the virgin respond to her lover's tender persuasions, or remember what her mother told her? Should the employee, official, or soldier, when given an order which he feels to be dishonest or immoral, follow his conscience or protect his career and his family? When torn between the insistent demands of her aging, senile parents and the needs of her husband and children, what should a wife do? For many role conflicts, there is no satisfactory compromise. When role strain becomes unendurable, neurotic or psychotic behavior may follow.

Adjudication differs from the protective devices just discussed in being conscious and intentional. It is a formal procedure for turning over to a third party a difficult decision on a possible role conflict, thereby relieving the individual of responsibility or guilt. Much of the work of professional associations and the codes of ethics which they develop is devoted to the solution of role conflicts. The American Bar Association often hands down statements which serve as precedents in deciding the duties of attorneys to the court, to their clients, and to themselves. The American Medical Association identifies as "unethical" that role behavior which constitutes a breach of trust either toward the client or toward other physicians. Cynics may argue that such professional associations usually operate to defend the interests of the profession. In many codes of ethics, the clauses protecting the competing members from one another greatly outnumber the statements protecting the clients or customers. Yet members of professions have been barred from the profession for violating the expected role behavior, and the need to justify action before one's peers does place some limitations upon behavior. In any event, a decision on proper role behavior by the professional association or labor union means that the individual is relieved of the duty of making his or her own decision in difficult cases.

Role failure

In a stable, well-integrated society with a high proportion of ascribed roles, most people fill these roles successfully. Most of the roles in any society can be filled by almost any member who has been adequately prepared for them. But in a rapidly changing and less well-integrated society like ours, where we cannot predict all adult roles in advance and where discontinuities limit role preparation, a good deal of role failure is inevitable. Some persons even fail in their ascribed roles of male and female, as in the case of the homosexual, or of the woman with the complex of hostile, resentful, and aggressive attitudes toward men which is called the *masculine-protest* pattern, or of the man who is a woman-hater or who never outgrows his dependence upon mother. Even more persons fail in some of their achieved roles. Some of them fail to achieve the role they court—the boy (or girl) fails to become a physician or executive, or the girl fails to get a husband and become a wife and mother. Others achieve a role but fail to fill it successfully. Many husbands and wives fail as marital partners, and face either the often painful experience of divorce or a lifetime of mutual frustration. Many parents fail to socialize their children successfully. Only a few in any occupation or profession can be spectacularly successful, because for each manager there must be many subordinates. Those who crave the highest levels of excellence in a particular role are usually frustrated. Role failures of many kinds and degrees keep swelling the ranks of unhappy, frustrated people.

The revolt against ascription

All kinds of status ascription are under attack throughout much of the world. "Racial discrimination" is another term for status ascription by race. Racial and ethnic groups are rebelling against subordinate status ascription. There is no universal surge towards racial equality, for in some parts of the world, racial and ethnic persecutions have been rising. But in many areas, racial and ethnic minorities are militantly demanding an end to status ascription by race, and are finding many supporters among the general population. Differences in class status, regardless of whether ascribed or achieved, are under sharp attack as undemocratic and oppressive.

Ascription by age is widely challenged, as young people demand adult privileges and do not give traditional deference to their elders, while old people are angrily rejecting their ascribed role of incipient corpses. Ascribed sex roles are under especially bitter attack. The Women's Liberation Movement is demanding not merely that sex roles be changed but that they be abolished, so that no duties or privileges of any sort are ascribed on a basis of sex.

Most American young women still desire husbands and families, and their career choices follow relatively traditional channels [Gump, 1972]. Yet women's occupational aspirations are clearly expanding, with family background differences largely accounting for traditional or nontraditional preferences [Klemmack and Edwards, 1973]. Even dating behavior is changing; women have been taking the more aggressive role previously reserved for men [Winick, 1968, pp. 18–24]. Ascribed sex roles are undeniably changing, while surveys show that these changes receive very nearly as much verbal support from men as from women [McElroy, 1974].

It is not surprising that many women today object to being identified in terms of marital status alone. When a national magazine describes a family with the words:

Their son is a lawyer in Houston; their daughters Joanie and Claire are both married,

the sexism of this description becomes apparent if we turn it around to read:

Their daughter Joanie raises horses and their daughter Claire is a church worker; their son Joe is married. (See *Time*, April 8, 1974, p. 5.)

To all such sex-role stereotyping, many women take violent exception.[2] But, while the traditional sex-role ascription is clearly doomed, its replacement is unclear. The more extreme spokeswomen for women's liberation seek *androgynous* sex roles. Androgynous sex roles would be as nearly alike as physically possible. Thus there would be *no role ascription based on sex*. Babies would necessarily be born to women (at present), but cared for equally by fathers and mothers. *All* duties and privileges would be equally shared by the sexes under androgynous sex roles.

Are androgynous sex roles possible? No known society has ever had them, but they are at least theoretically possible. Whether they could be achieved and maintained cannot be predicted.

Are androgynous sex roles desirable? There is no real evidence upon which to base an answer. Many mental health professionals believe that clearly differentiated sex identities are necessary for mental health and personality adjustment, but some disagree [Broverman, 1972; Black, 1974; Woodward, 1974]. The present trend is clearly in the direction of androgyny, but it is far from having reached this destination. Whether it *should* is a question sociology cannot answer; whether it *will* is uncertain.

In conclusion, role ascription offers a simple way of dividing the work of society, and facilitates early and successful role preparation. But role ascription is successful only when most people wholeheartedly accept their ascribed roles. Vast numbers of people are today questioning or rejecting them. While it seems doubtful to sociologists that all status and role ascription will cease, many changes in ascription are a certainty.

[2]This creates a problem for textbook authors. Should they "tell it like it is," or "like it ought to be?" The fact *is* that most women are housewives and mothers, that most working women work at traditional women's jobs, and that most working wives are more heavily committed to their marital role than their work role. The author who "tells it like it is" is accused of perpetuating sex-role stereotypes. Yet the feminists are not the only persons who hold firm ideas of how it "ought to be." No matter what the author writes, some will be displeased.

TABLE 4 TOTAL ARRESTS FOR VIOLENT CRIMES, 1960–1973

Crime	Percent increase	
	Males	**Females**
Murder	141	103
Robbery	160	287
Aggravated assault	116	106
Burglary	76	193
Larceny	84	341
Auto theft	59	155
Fraud	50	281
Narcotics	995	1,027

Note: Women are catching up with men in many areas.
Source: *FBI Uniform Crime Reports,* 1973.

Summary

Socialization takes place largely through learning roles. *Social status* is a position in society with consequent privileges and duties; a *role* is the behavior expected of one who occupies a particular status. Even in a single status, people are confronted with a related cluster of roles in what is known as a *role set.* One may assume several role sets at the same time, taking a multiplicity of roles which gives both a potential for strain and for fulfillment. *Role behavior* is the actual behavior of one who plays a role, and is affected by *dramatic role presentation,* in which the individual acts in a deliberate effort to present a desired image to the spectators.

Roles and statuses are of two sorts: those which are *ascribed* to persons according to age, sex, class, race, or some other inherited characteristic, and those which are *achieved* through personal choice or effort. Achieved statuses are often gained at a substantial psychic cost, since the efforts and frustrations may be intense. A *meritocracy* is a form of quasi-ascription, in which a status is open to achievement, but largely inherited characteristics give some persons great advantages in the competition.

When a person's several statuses are inconsistent with one another, this is called *status inconsistency. Role personality* refers to the complex of personality characteristics appropriate for a particular role. Role and personality interact, with individual personality characteristics affecting role choice and role behavior, while the experience of playing a role, in turn, affects the personality.

Role strain refers to the difficulty of meeting role obligations. *Inadequate role preparation* may leave one poorly equipped, mainly in attitudes and values, to appreciate and enjoy the role. Many *role transitions* are difficult, usually because of *discontinuities in socialization,* or because the necessary *role relinquishments* demand that some current satisfactions be sacrificed.

Role conflicts arise from conflicting duties within a single role, or from conflicting demands imposed by different roles. Role conflicts can be managed by *rationalization* in which the situation is redefined in the mind of the actor so that he is aware of no conflict, by *compartmentalization* which enables one to operate within a single role at a time, and by *adjudication* in which a third party makes the decision. *Role failure* is quite common, especially in a changing society.

A sweeping revolt against ascription seeks to reduce or end ascription of nearly all sorts. Feminists, for example, wish to replace sex-role ascription with *androgynous* sex roles. Whether these are possible or desirable are unsettled questions.

Questions and projects

1. Are *role* and *status* two separate concepts or two aspects of the same phenomenon? Explain.
2. What is the function of children's play in socialization? How does play aid in role preparation?
3. Why is it a comparatively easy task to assume one's age roles in most primitive societies? Why do we not have a clearly defined set of age roles?
4. How does our culture make old age a difficult period? Is it a difficult period in all cultures? Analyze our old-age problem in terms of discontinuities. In terms of conflicting roles.
5. Describe the shift from the status and role of a high school student to that of college student in terms of cultural continuities and discontinuities in socialization. From civilian to soldier.
6. In role preparation for most adult roles, which is more important: the attitudes and values which make that role acceptable, or the knowledge and skills necessary to fill the role? Illustrate for the homemaker, schoolteacher, army officer, research scientist, and old-age roles.
7. Is there any conflict between your roles as college student and as son or daughter? If you are a married student, a third (and possibly a fourth) role is added. What possible role conflicts are added?
8. What social costs accompany an emphasis upon achieved status? Ascribed status?
9. In what respects is your present role as college student preparing you for later roles? In what respects is your present role experience irrelevant or even dysfunctional?
10. Are there any respects in which you are already assuming role personalities which differ from your true personality? Are you aware of any stresses which this acting a part produces?
11. What are the pros and cons of a meritocracy, as compared with alternative methods of status ascription or achievement?
12. Describe in some detail a role and status with which you are familiar and which involves a good deal of conflicting pressure within the role. How do persons in that role usually resolve these conflicts?
13. Describe some situation you know about in which a person has been under pressure to fill two or more conflicting roles. How did (s)he resolve the conflict? Would you say the resolution was successful or unsuccessful?
14. If the conventional sex roles of our society are replaced by androgynous sex roles, what will each sex gain? Lose?

Suggested readings

BIDDLE, BRUCE J., AND EDWIN J. THOMAS (EDS.): *Role Theory: Concepts and Research,* John Wiley and Sons, Inc., New York, 1956. A comprehensive collection of statements and research on role theory.

BROVERMAN, INGE K., ET AL.: "Sex-Role Stereotypes: A Current Appraisal," *Journal of Social Issues,* 28, No. 2, pp. 59–78, 1972. A research study showing that clearly defined sex-role stereotypes persist despite unisex appearances.

BURR, WESLEY A.: "Role Transitions: A Reformulation of Theory," *Journal of Marriage and the Family,* 34:407–416, Summer, 1972. A sophisticated theoretical examination of such role transitions as those into parenthood, retirement, and bereavement.

FELDMAN, SAUL D.: "Impediment or Stimulus: Marital Status and Graduate Education," *American Journal of Sociology,* 78:983–994, January, 1973. A study of the role conflict between the wife-graduate student roles, and how divorce has opposite effects on male and female academic progress.

GOFFMAN, ERVING: *Where the Action Is,* Doubleday and Co., Inc., Garden City, N.Y., 1967. A skillful analysis of role behavior.

GOWMAN, ALAN G.: "Blindness and the Role of the Companion," *Social Problems,* 4:68–75, July, 1956. The process through which the companion develops a role relationship satisfactory to the blind person and the changes which occur in the definition of the situation.

*GRACEY, HARRY L.: "Learning the Student Role: Kindergarten as Academic Boot Camp," in Dennis H. Wrong and Harry L. Gracey: *Readings in Introductory Sociology,* (2d ed.), The Macmillan Company, New York, 1972. Shows how the kindergarten teaches children how to fill the role of student.

HUBER, JOAN (ED.): *Changing Women in a Chang-*

ing Society, the January, 1973, issue of the *American Journal of Sociology* (vol. 78, no. 4), entirely devoted to articles on the changing role and status of women.

KOMAROVSKY, MIRRA: "Cultural Contradictions and Sex Roles," *American Journal of Sociology* 52:184–189, November, 1946; The Bobbs-Merrill Company, Inc., Reprint S-150; also, "Cultural Contradictions and Sex Roles: The Masculine Case," *American Journal of Sociology,* 78:873–884, January, 1973. A classic discussion of the role conflicts of the college-educated woman, followed by a later look at male role conflicts.

MACCOBY, ELEANOR EMMONS, AND CAROL NAGY JACK-LIN: "What We Know and Don't Know About Sex Differences," *Psychology Today,* December, 1974, pp. 109–112. A very brief summary of the realities and myths of sex differences.

MCCORD, JOAN, AND WILLIAM MCCORD: "Effects of Parental Role Models on Criminality," *Journal of Social Issues,* 15:66–75, 1958. A study of social worker reports upon the parents of delin-quents, showing that some popular ideas are unsound.

STEINMANN, ANNE: "Lack of Communication between Men and Women," *Marriage and Family Living,* 20:350–352, November, 1958. A role-centered analysis of communication difficulties between the sexes.

WARDWELL, WILLIAM, AND ARTHUR L. WOOD: "Extraprofessional Role of the Lawyer," *American Journal of Sociology,* 61:304–307, January, 1956. A discussion of the community service responsibilities involved in the role of lawyer.

WEITZMAN, LENORE, J., ET AL.: "Sex-Role Socialization in Picture Books for Preschool Children," *American Journal of Sociology,* 77:1125–2250, May, 1972. A study of how children's picture books perpetuate sex-role stereotypes.

WINICK, CHARLES: "Depolarization of Sex," *Annals of the American Academy of Political and Social Science,* 376:18–24, March, 1968. Describes the decreasing distance between masculine and feminine roles.

Chapter 7 • Social control and social deviation

The Hawaiians had long obeyed some of the *Kanawai* [laws]. They had always honored fathers and mothers, and their days had been long upon the land. They had utterly abolished idols before the Longnecks [whites] came.

Theft they had dealt with in a way that had served well enough, though it could scarcely have been pleasing to Jehovah. In the old days if a man took something from one below him in the social scale, it was not stealing; for that which was taken had in reality belonged by virtue of rank to the taker. And if a commoner made off with the calabash or the weapon of a superior, the injured man could go to the thief's house and take back his possession, along with anything else he saw that he wanted.

But when the *haoles* [white traders] came with their bean pots and silver spoons, their monkey wrenches and linen towels, their sawed lumber and their keen-edged axes, this method no longer served. Complaints from foreigners rang unceasingly in the governor's ears. White men did not want to go poking into native huts to find their lost articles. They wanted Boki to haul up the thief and arrange for restitution and punishment.

Gradually the enlightened chiefs saw what they must do. Some of them put their men in irons for proven theft or set them free only to work and pay for what they had stolen. The boy prince Kauikeaouli, when his beloved *kahu* was found accessory to a theft, consented quickly to the man's dismissal. "My *kahu* must go," he declared, "or by and by the foreigners will think that I myself am guilty."

The *haoles* applauded such measures. Here was a Commandment they liked to see enforced.

Then there was the Commandment forbidding murder in a few short words. Once, if a native killed in sudden anger, it was proper for the victim's relatives to avenge the deed, unless the murderer took shelter in a place of refuge. If the guilty man were of equal rank with the victim's avenger, there might be an appeal to the king or the governor or to the chief of the district. The aggrieved one and the accused would then sit cross-legged in the judge's yard and each would eloquently argue his case till the magistrate made his decision.

But these customs failed when Honolulu swarmed with hot-headed sailors, and brown and white alike drank rum and got *huhu* [very angry]. Again, as with theft, the traders wanted stern laws, strictly enforced, so that the riffraff of all nations would think twice before bashing their fellows on the head. They told the chiefs to build a lofty engine of death which would string up a murderer by the neck and leave him hanging limp from a rope's end—a potent reminder to the living to restrain themselves. *(Reprinted by permission of Dodd, Mead & Company from* Grapes of Canaan *by Albertine Loomis, pp. 227-229. Copyright 1951 by Albertine Loomis.)*

The disintegration of the traditional system of law and order when the European traders brought changes and new problems to Hawaii could be duplicated in many other lands. Changes in a society demand changes in its ways of maintaining social order. When the Hawaiian chiefs were shifting from their traditional customs to the jails and gallows suggested by the traders, they were seeking to adjust the techniques of social control to a changed situation—a problem which is a continuous concern of every modern society.

The study of *social control*—the means through which people are led to fill their roles as expected—begins with the study of the social order within which people interact. Consider, for example, the orderly arrangements which underlie the bustling confusion of a great city. Tens of thousands of people take their places and perform their tasks with no apparent direction. Thousands of vehicles butt their way through clogged canyons, missing by inches, but seldom actually colliding. Thousands of kinds of merchandise arrive at the expected places in the expected amounts at the expected times. Ten thousand people whom an individual never sees will labor on this day so that meals will be ready for him when needed, drinking fountains will flow, drains will carry off the wastes, bulbs will blink and glow, traffic will part to let him pass, and various conveniences will meet his other needs. A hundred people may serve him within an hour, perhaps without a word from him to any of them.

This is what is meant by *social order*—a system of people, relationships, and customs operating smoothly to accomplish the work of a society. Unless people know what they may expect from one another, not much will get done. No society, even the simplest, can function successfully unless the behavior of most people can be reliably predicted most of the time. Unless we can depend upon police officers to protect us, workers to go to work on schedule, and motorists to stay on the right side of the road most of the time, there can be no social order. The orderliness of a society rests upon a network of roles according to which each person accepts certain duties toward others and claims certain rights from others. An orderly society can operate only as long as most people reliably fulfill most of their duties toward others and are able successfully to claim most of their rights from others.

How is this network of reciprocal rights and duties kept in force? Sociologists use the term "social control" to describe *all the means and processes whereby a group or a society secures its members' conformity to its expectations.*

Social control and social order

How does a group or a society cause its members to behave in the expected manner? In a number of ways, whose relative importance is difficult to measure.

Social control through socialization

Fromm [1944] has remarked that if a society is to function efficiently, "its members must acquire the kind of character which makes them *want* to act in the way they *have* to act as members of society . . . . They have to *desire* to do what objectively is necessary for them to do."

People are controlled mainly by being socialized so that they fill their roles in the expected way through habit and preference. How did we persuade women to accept the endless drudgery of household and child care? Mainly by socializing them so that they *wanted* husbands and children, and felt cheated without them, and, therefore, did not see these duties as "drudgery." How is man, unlike the male of most other species, persuaded to exchange his freedom for a sense of social responsibility toward the offspring he sires? Mainly by cultivating within him a set of cherished sentiments and yearnings which this troublesome little creature promises to fulfill. As we stated in an earlier chapter, the crucial part of one's role preparation is the development of attitudes and wishes which make the role attractive. Most role failures come, not because one is unable to perform the role's tasks, but because of being trapped in a role one does not really want or enjoy.

Socialization shapes our customs, our wishes, and our habits. Habit and custom are great time savers. They relieve us of the need for countless decisions. If we had to decide whether and how to perform each act—when to arise, whether and how to wash, shave, dress, and so on—few students would get to class at all! The members of a society are schooled in the same customs and tend to develop much the same set of habits. Thus habit and custom are great standardizers of behavior within a group. If all members of a society share similar socialization experiences, they will voluntarily and unthinkingly act in very much the same ways. They will conform to social expectations without any conscious awareness that they are "conforming," or any serious thought of doing otherwise. The desire of two college students to get married arises from motives less academic than a wish to "conform to the nuclear monogamous family pattern," yet such conformity is the result.

Social control through social pressure

In a novel by Sinclair Lewis, George F. Babbitt, a small-town realtor, somehow strays into "radical" notions about government and politics. Soon his business declines, his friends begin to avoid him, and he grows uncomfortably aware that he is becoming an outsider. Lewis describes how Babbitt's associates apply these subtle pressures until, with a sigh of relief, Babbitt scurries back into a comfortable conformity [Lewis, 1922, chaps. 32, 33]. In all human societies, and even in many nonhuman species, this tendency to conform to group pressure and example is evident. Nineteenth-century explorer David Thompson was impressed by the reckless, headlong flight of wild horses, and when his dull, placid packhorse escaped to join the wild horses, it amazed him to see how quickly it assumed their wild temperament "with nostrils distended, mane flying, and tail straight out" [Ryden, 1971, p. 106].

LaPiere [1954] sees social control as primarily a process growing out of the individual's need for status within his or her primary groups. He claims that these groups are most influential when they are small and intimate, when the individual expects to remain in the group for a long time, and when he or she has frequent contacts with them. All authorities agree that our need for acceptance within intimate groups is a most powerful lever for the use of group pressure toward group norms.

The individual experiences this group pressure as a continuous and largely unconscious process. Its operation is illustrated by the life of one of the author's acquaintances. He spent most of his working life as a small farmer in central Michigan; like most of his neighbors, he thought conservatively, voted Republican, and scolded labor unions. During World War II he moved to Detroit and worked in a war plant, joined a union, became a union officer, and voted Democratic. After the war, he retired to a small central Michigan village where he again thought conservatively, voted Republican, and scolded labor unions. He explained these about-faces by claiming that the parties and the unions had changed. He did not realize that it was *he* who had changed. Like most of us, he soon came to share the views of his group associates. This tendency to conform to group attitudes is so compelling that the Catholic church in France found it necessary to abandon its worker-priest program. This was an effort to stem the drift of French workers toward communism by sending out priests who would take ordinary jobs and work beside the workers, meanwhile leading them back to the church. After a ten-year trial, when it became evident that the workers were converting the priests to the Marxian view of the class struggle, the program was curtailed [Brady, 1954].

Our need for acceptance within intimate groups.

Social psychologists [Sherif, 1935; Bovard, 1951] have made a number of classic experiments which show how a person tends to bring personal expressions in line with those of the group. The method in such experiments usually consists of asking the members for individual estimates, attitudes, or observations on a topic, then informing them of the group norm, and finally asking for a new expression from each member. Many of the informants modify their second expression in the direction of the group norm. In a series of ingenious experiments, Asch [1951], Tuddenham [1961], and others have shown that many people will even alter an observation which they *know* to be correct rather than oppose the group. Each subject in these experiments was surrounded by a group which, by secret prearrangement, made factual observations that the subject *knew* to be wrong; yet one-third of these subjects accepted the wrong observation when opposed by a unanimous group opinion to the contrary. Schachter [1951] has also shown experimentally how the member who sharply deviates from group norms in opinion is rejected by the group.

We often notice that a new member of a group is more carefully conformist and more fiercely loyal than the old members. Religious converts and naturalized citizens often show a zeal which puts lifelong members to shame. An experiment by Dittes and Kelley [1956] helps to explain this. They found that among members who equally value their membership in a group, those who feel *least accepted* are the most rigidly conformist to the group's norms. Meticulous conformity is a tool for gaining acceptance and status within a group, while rejection is the price of nonconformity.

It is probable that no other structure even approaches the tremendous controlling power of the group over the individual. Any parent who has tried to counter a teen-ager's argument, "*All* the kids are wearing them!" is fully aware of the controlling power of the group.

Informal primary-group controls. Groups are of two kinds, primary and secondary; these concepts will be analyzed in detail in a later chapter. For our present discussion, it is sufficient to note that primary groups are small, intimate, informal groups, like the family, clique, or play group, while secondary groups are impersonal, formal, and utilitarian, like a labor union, trade association, church congregation, or student body.

Within primary groups, control is informal, spontaneous, and unplanned. The members of the group react to the actions of each member. When a member irritates or annoys the others, they may show their disapproval through ridicule, laughter, criticism, or even ostracism. When a member's behavior is acceptable, a secure and comfortable "belonging" is the usual reward. Many novelists have used the sub-plot in which a character violates the norms of the group in some way, is disciplined by group disapproval, and must earn group acceptance through penitence and renewed conformity (like Sinclair Lewis's Babbitt.)

In most primitive societies, where virtually all groups were primary groups, there was very little serious misconduct. Each person was born into certain kinship groups—for example, a family, a clan, and a tribe. One could not move on to another tribe or clan, for a person divorced from kinship ties had no social existence—that is, no one was obligated to regard and treat him or her as a human being. One who wanted to survive *had* to get along with the groups in which one was enmeshed. Since there was little privacy and no escape, the penalty of serious nonconformity was an intolerable existence. For example, the polar Eskimo institutionalized ridicule and laughter as a social control. The person who violated cultural norms was mercilessly ridiculed. Birket-Smith writes of the Chugach Eskimo:

Once a habitual thief entered a house, and an old woman sitting there began to sing:
>   Analurshe
>   Analurshe
>   Makes me ashamed
>   He was looking at me
>   While I was eating
>   Analurshe
>   Analurshe

He immediately left the house, but the children used to sing the song whenever they saw him. Thus he acquired the nickname Analurshe, i.e., Old Excrements, and after that he stopped stealing. (Kaj Birket-Smith, *Eskimos*, Rhodes, Copenhagen, 1971, p. 173.)

Lowie describes the use of scorn and ridicule by a number of American Indian peoples:

When a Fox Indian boy in Illinois was taught not to steal and never to abuse his wife, his elder did not hold up to him any tangible punishment here or hereafter nor any abstract rule of morality. The clinching argument was, "The people will say many things about you, although you may not know it."

Gossiping sometimes took special forms of ridicule. An Alaskan youth thus reports his experience: "If you do not marry within your village, they joke about you—they joke so much that it makes it disagreeable." The Crow sang songs in mockery of a miser, a bully, or a man who should take back a divorced wife—the acme of disgrace. Certain kinsmen had the privilege of publicly criticizing a man for breaches of etiquette and ethics, and there was nothing he would fear more than to be thus pilloried. This system was developed by the Blackfoot along slightly different lines. "For mild persistent misconduct, a method of formal discipline is sometimes practiced. When the offender has failed to take hints and suggestions, the head men may take formal notice and decide to resort to discipline. Some evening when all are in their tipis, a head man will call out to a neighbor asking if he has observed the conduct of Mr. A. This starts a general conversation between the many tipis, in which all the grotesque and hideous features of Mr. A.'s acts are held up to general ridicule, amid shrieks of laughter, the grilling continuing until far into the night. The mortification of the victim is extreme and usually drives him into a temporary exile or, as formerly, upon the warpath to do desperate deeds."

A primitive man sacrifices half his property lest he be dubbed a miser; he yields his favorite wife if jealousy is against the code; he risks life itself, if that is the way to gain the honor of a public eulogy. That is why savages of the same tribe are not forever cutting one another's throats or ravishing available women, even if they lack written constitutions, jails, a police force, and revealed religion. (From *Are We Civilized?* by Robert H. Lowie, copyright, 1929, by Harcourt, Brace and World, Inc.; copyright, 1957, by Robert H. Lowie. Reprinted by permission of the publisher.)

In many authenticated instances where primitives have violated important norms, they have committed suicide because they could not endure the penalty of group disapproval [Malinowski, 1926, pp. 94–99]. In such a group setting, the penalty for serious nonconformity is so unendurable as to make serious nonconformity quite rare. Likewise in complex cultures, wherever persons are trapped in primary group settings which they cannot easily escape, as in a prison cell or a military unit, this great controlling power of the primary group comes into operation.

In many societies, the group is held responsible for the acts of any of its members. For example, if a Tlingit Indian of the American Northwest murdered a member of another clan, his own clan had to provide for execution a person equal in social status to the murdered victim, while the actual murderer was punished by living with the knowledge that he had caused the execution of a clansman. In our military units, one dirty rifle or messy locker may deprive an entire company of their weekend passes. Such forms of collective punishment may seem unjust, *but they work!* A soldier whose indolence has once caused his company to lose their weekend passes is unlikely to repeat his error—or to be permitted to forget it!

A great deal of "leadership" and "authority" rest upon the skillful manipulation of the group as a control device. Successful schoolteachers, for example, often use the class to maintain discipline; they manipulate the situation so that the child who misbehaves will look ridiculous before the class. But if they allow a situation to develop wherein the misbehaving child appears as a hero or martyr to the class, this control is lost.

Normal people everywhere need and seek the approval of others, especially of the primary group associates upon whom they depend for intimate human response. English workers sometimes punish a fellow worker who has violated group norms by "sending him to Coventry." This means that workers will not speak to him, answer him, look at him, and will act as though he weren't there at all. Such a punishment is generally unendurable. The victim usually either does his penance or quits his job. Thousands of novels, dramas, and operas have elaborated this theme. Most people will give almost anything, even their lives if necessary, to retain this approval and the comforting feeling of belonging to the group that is most important to them. It is the overwhelming need for group approval and response that makes the primary group the most powerful controlling agency known to man.

Secondary-group controls. As we shift from primary- to secondary-group situations, we also shift from informal to more formal social controls. Secondary groups are generally larger, more impersonal, and specialized in purpose. We do not use them to meet our need for intimate human response, but to help us to get certain jobs done. If a secondary group does not meet our needs, we can generally withdraw with no great anguish, for our emotional lives are not deeply involved. To maintain our status in the secondary group is desirable but not a desperate emotional necessity as it is in the primary group. True, it is possible in our society for people to change their primary groups—leave their families, divorce their mates, find new friends—but the process is generally painful. The secondary group is a less compelling control agency than the primary group.

The secondary group is still an effective control. Some of the informal controls still operate in the secondary group. No normal person wants to appear ridiculous at the union meeting, the church worship service, or the chamber of commerce banquet. Such informal controls as ridicule, laughter, gossip, and ostracism operate in secondary-group settings, but generally with a reduced impact. Meanwhile, other more formal controls are characteristic of secondary groups—parliamentary rules of order, official regulations and standardized procedures, propaganda, public relations and "human engineering," promotions and titles, rewards and prizes, formal penalties and punishments, and still others.

These formal controls of the secondary group are most effective when reinforced by a primary group. A prize or decoration is more sweet when an admiring family and an applauding clique of close friends can watch the presentation ceremony. Within the large, impersonal secondary group may be many very closely integrated primary groups, such as squads within an army or work crews within a corporation. These primary groups can either reinforce or undermine the formal secondary-group controls and greatly affect the performance of the secondary group. Much of the human-engineering approach in industry is an effort to use these primary groups to reinforce the controls and the objectives of the corporations [Gross, 1953].

Special language as a social control. An *argot* is a special language of a subculture. It includes specially coined words as well as ordinary words with a special meaning attached. For example, Howard [1974, p. 44] reports that in the ghetto (at that particular moment), to be called "all bad" meant that one had dash, verve, and style, while "bad motherf_____" was a compliment. An argot serves important functions of social control. It promotes communication within the group, since each term is freighted with meaning which only the group members can understand. Argot also excludes outsiders; to enter the group, one must "speak the language." Learning the argot thus not only strengthens the tie between the individual and the group, it also cuts down communication with the world outside. No individuals are entirely cut off from contacts outside the subculture, but as Bernstein [1966] observes, the argot serves to maximize the social barriers between the group and the rest of society.

Language is a way of describing reality, and changes in language may change people's perceptions of reality. A redefinition which ascribes new meanings to familiar words may promote a redefinition of attitudes and relationships. For example, the recent use of the term "welfare rights" has had some success in changing the image of "welfare" from a charity (which the poor gratefully accept in whatever amount offered) to a "right" (for which the recipients may legitimately negotiate, bargain, and battle). Revolutionary and terrorist groups may call themselves an "army" and assume military titles ("field marshal," "chief of staff"). A field marshal over a ten-person "army" may be absurd, but if the media can be persuaded to use these terms, it lends an air of legitimacy to the group and to its demands—as the Symbionese Liberation Army realized. Words do redefine situations.

Control through force

Many primitive societies succeeded in controlling the behavior of individuals through the mores, reinforced by the informal controls of the primary group, so that no formal laws or

---

"Man, that some fine stuff you mackin' on. . . ."

"I hear ya, brother. 'Cept punk over there rankin' my play. Nigger runnin' off at the jibs 'bout his 'new shot' and how it be decked out with lifts and some ole pimp rest and color bar. Chump better cool it, man, 'cause I'm gonna bug his ticket, *for sure!*

(From Edith Folb, "Rappin' in the Black Vernacular," *Human Behavior,* August, 1973, pp. 16–17. Translation: One young man receives a compliment upon his attractive girl friend; he complains that another man is trying to attract the girl by bragging about his new car and its accessories, and may get beaten up for his intrusion.)

---

punishments were necessary. But with larger populations and more complex cultures, formal governments, laws, and punishments are developed. Wherever it becomes possible for the individual to become lost in the crowd, informal controls are inadequate and formal controls are necessary. For example, in a clan of one or two dozen adult kinsfolk, informal food sharing is practical; persons can take what they need and contribute whatever they can catch, while informal group pressures can be trusted to prevent laziness and control greed. But in a village of hundreds of persons, it would be impossible to keep tabs on each person informally; individual laziness and greed would make a system of informal food sharing unworkable. Some *system* of assigning work and distributing rewards becomes necessary. Thus, with larger populations and cultural complexity comes a shift to impersonal secondary-group controls—laws, regulations, councils, and formalized procedures.

When the individual does not wish to follow these regulations, the group tries to compel him or her to do so. In large groups, however, the individual is too anonymous for informal group pressures to be brought to bear. Furthermore, in larger groups with complex cultures, some subcultures that conflict with the culture of the majority are likely to develop. The indi-

TABLE 5 AVERAGE SOCIAL DISTANCE FELT TOWARD VARIOUS DEVIANT GROUPS

Groups (in order of increasing intolerance)	Mean social distance (Range 1 to 7)
Intellectuals	2.0
Ex-mental patients	2.9
Atheists	3.4
Ex-convicts	3.5
Gamblers	3.6
Beatniks	3.9
Alcoholics	4.0
Adulterers	4.1
Political radicals	4.3
Marijuana smokers	4.9
Prostitutes	5.0
Lesbians	5.2
Homosexuals	5.3

Responses of a representative public sample. (A score of 1.0 would show little or no social distance, while a score of 7.0 would show great social distance.)
Source: J. L. Simmons, *Deviants,* Glendessary Press, Berkeley, Calif., 1969, p. 33.

vidual who rejects the conventional regulations of the society may find emotional support from other persons who think and act as he or she does. A few of the many current examples might include the Amish community, the hippie commune, the homosexual subculture, and perhaps the student-and-nonstudent communities adjacent to major universities. Although the participants in any of these subcultures may fondly imagine that they are "free," the person is still subject to group pressures, but these group pressures come from a nonconforming group which insulates the person from the informal group pressures of conventional society. So conventional society sometimes uses force—in the form of laws and formal punishments—to compel a required minimum of conformity. This force is not always successful, but is used in every complex society. Ironically, some of the world figures most widely admired by American nonconformists (Castro, Mao Tse-Tung) are noted for the severity of their punishment of nonconformists in their own countries!

Punishment of deviation

Deviants (except for certain approved types) are disliked in all societies, and as Table 5 shows, American society is no exception. No known society has allowed complete freedom to "do your own thing." All communes which have attempted to grant such license have failed. The only enduring communes have operated under the rule of a charismatic leader or under a system of their own rules and procedures [Roberts, 1971, Ch. 11]. All societies and all groups punish deviants with punishments ranging from nonacceptance and ridicule to every imaginable form of torture, mutilation, imprisonment, and death. Often the punishment has more the flavor of vindictive revenge than of intended control. The deviants sometimes accept punishment with stoical calm, as did the early Christians, and sometimes they protest bitterly over their persecution and oppression, as do today's hippies and radical leftists. The "persecution" theme is a useful promotional tactic which organizers have used for centuries. But although often exaggerated and sometimes provoked, the persecution of deviants is very real in every society.

At the very least, hostile glares and unkind remarks await those who deviate from cultural norms (or the member of a deviant group who deviates from its group norms), but this is hardly "persecution." A denial of civil rights or an unequal enforcement of laws, however, might justifiably be termed "persecution." For example, Hamersma [1970] test-mailed stamped letters addressed to the Young Lords in Chicago, a group of Latin revolutionaries, and found that the letters were frequently delayed, opened, or never delivered. Heussenstamm [1971] found that when a selected group of students added Black Panther decals to their cars and attempted to continue driving in their usual manner, their traffic tickets multiplied astronomically. These are two recent experiments which document the perfectly obvious fact that deviants suffer some forms and degrees of punishment in all societies. The severity of punishment varies with the tolerance level of the society or group in question, and the degree to which a particular deviation seems to threaten cherished values of other people. The several hundred Americans serving long sentences in foreign prisons for first-offense drug violations [Weiner, 1972] now realize that, on balance, American society is probably more tolerant of deviation than many—possibly than most—of the world's major societies.

The punishment of deviants is very real in every society.

Situational determinants of behavior

When laymen see some behavior they do not like, they often attribute it to evil human nature, wicked impulse, weak character, or some other *individual* cause. What separates the sociologist from the layman here is the sociologist's habit of looking for *social* factors in the causation of behavior. True, when one individual or a few people change in character or behavior, the explanations may be purely individual. But when any *large number* of people change their character or behavior in the same way, we look for the probable cause in some change in the social and cultural influences upon behavior.

To a far greater degree than most people recognize, one's behavior in a particular situation is a result of the needs, pressures, and temptations of that situation. There is ample evidence that many people who would not cheat a blind newspaper vendor will cheat the national supermarket if they get a chance to do so; a little cheating on one's income tax is apparently engaged in by practically everybody; war veterans who did not rob their neighbors back home "liberated" many articles from the enemy population; people do things as part of a mob which they would never do as individuals. War atrocities are committed by all armies, including American armies [Taylor, 1970]. Whether a surrendering enemy is shot or taken prisoner depends more upon the circumstances at the moment of surrender than upon the character of the capturing troops [Draper, 1945]. Kinsey's data show that most civilian husbands are faithful to their wives, at least most of the time; but it appears that most overseas military personnel, when long separated from their wives, seized almost any attractive opportunity for infidelity. Labor union officials believe in labor unions—except for their own employees! So when the staff employees of the large unions seek to organize and bargain collectively with their bosses, these union official-bosses seem to react just like any other employers, even crossing picket lines when their office workers go on strike.[1] And when union staff workers go on strike, they act just like any other workers on strike; thus in Michigan, several local chapters of the Michigan Education Association were unable to get the aid of MEA staff negotiators in bargaining with their local school boards because the MEA staff was on strike against the MEA [Cote, 1974]. Argyris [1967] reports that, "As a sociological experiment, two Detroit ministers went to work on an assembly line and soon found themselves cheating on quality, lying to their foremen and swearing at the

[1]See "Pickets Cry 'Scab' at UAW Leaders," *Business Week*, March 20, 1971, p. 31.

machines." Their new work situation carried pressures and frustrations to which they responded like any other workers. Illustrations of how the total behavior situation affects the behavior outcome could be multiplied almost without end. Many are found in Chapter 16, "Collective Behavior."

People tend to obey an authority figure; therefore, guards are dressed in impressive uniforms [Beckman, 1974]. In a widely criticized experiment, Milgram [1974] found that in a university laboratory setting, volunteer research subjects would obey a scientist's orders, even when they believed that their obedience was inflicting excruciating pain upon other subjects involved in the experiment. The atrocities of warfare, often in obedience to orders, become understandable as we study the way the total behavior situation affects behavior.

True, the internalized norms and other personality characteristics one brings to a situation are a factor in one's behavior; sometimes they are the determining factor. A few people are honest in *all* situations; some husbands and wives will be faithful despite *any* temptation. But more often than our folklore admits, a situation prompts the appearance of a characteristic kind of behavior among most of the participants. For example, county fairs are attended mainly by locals, often as family groups, in decently appointed and policed fairgrounds, with the people divided into many small groups and crowds. Behavior in this situation is generally orderly. Rock music festivals are attended mainly by young people with no local ties or family responsibilities, with ready drug availability, and a focal interest and a hypnotic beat to unify them into a crowd. Little wonder that rowdy behavior, petty vandalism, and angry confrontations with local residents often develop.

A major part of social control consists of trying to manipulate the behavior situation, for most people will respond with the kind of behavior the situation encourages. For example, if we wish to discourage littering, sermons on littering are less effective than strategically placed litter barrels; but if these are allowed to overflow and are not emptied regularly, the control effect is destroyed [Finnie, 1974]. Many old-time slums, with their busy street life and their well-populated doorsteps, had less crime than the modern high-rise housing projects which replaced them, whose empty sidewalks and corridors actually invited crime [Jacobs, 1961]. Architectural design is now being reconsidered in view of the discovery that design affects crime rates [Jeffery, 1971]. Thus the deliberate manipulation of "situational determinants of behavior" is one of the principal means of social control. Many other means of social control are described by Lumley [1925] and Landis [1956]—symbols, traditions, myths, legends, threats, intimidations, tortures, and still others—but they would be only an elaboration of the preceding outline.

Social deviation

No society succeeds in getting all its people to behave as expected all the time. The term *deviation* is given to *any failure to conform to customary norms*. Deviation takes many forms. The juvenile delinquent, the hermit, the ascetic, the hippie, the sinner and the saint, the artist starving in a garret and the miser gloating over wealth—all have deviated from the conventional social norms.

We note that deviation requires a social definition of an act as deviant. As Becker [1963, p. 9] notes: ". . . deviance is not a quality of the act the person commits, but rather a consequence of the application by others of rules and sanctions to an offender. The deviant is one to whom that label has successfully been applied; deviant behavior is behavior that people so label."

In a simple society with a single set of norms, deviation is easy to define. In a complex society with many different competing norms, the problem grows more complicated. In a neighborhood where most of the teen-agers are delinquent, and many of the adults repeatedly violate the law, who is the deviant—the delinquent or the nondelinquent? Obviously, deviation needs more detailed definition.

Basic types of deviation

Cultural and psychological deviation. One may deviate from the norm in social behavior, in personality organization, or sometimes in both. Sociology is primarily interested in the *cultural deviant,* who deviates in behavior from the norms of the culture. Psychologists are primarily interested in the *psychological deviant,* who deviates from the norm in personality organization—the psychotic, the neurotic, the paranoid personality, and others. These two categories often converge. Deviant behavior may spring from personality abnormality, and many studies of deviant behavior report evidence of such an association. Radical political behavior is often interpreted as an outlet for emotional hostilities [Ernst and Loth, 1952; Almond, 1954; Hendin, 1971]. The prostitute is often explained as a product of an emotionally deprived childhood, in which she had little opportunity to integrate a secure personality [Greenwald, 1959]; and other sex deviations, along with alcoholism, drug addiction, and compulsive gambling, are often attributed to a personality disorder of some sort.

Personality disorder, however, is far from the sole cause of deviant behavior. Although Hendin reports evidence that student revolutionaries come from a particular kind of unsatisfactory home life, he observes that "psychological forces alone [cannot] explain why students become revolutionaries at a particular time and place in history" [1971, p. 30]. And, while some psychologically abnormal people have a compelling urge to be bad, other psychologically abnormal people have an equally compelling urge to be good. These disturbed people become overconformists. The insecure, compulsive neurotic who *must* do his or her work perfectly, cannot stand disagreements, obeys all the mores, and finds comfort in

meticulously following all the rules and regulations is fulfilling a neurotic need to conform. This shows that cultural and psychological deviation are related, but not in any simple cause-and-effect relationship. The puzzling question of why personality abnormality sometimes leads to deviant behavior and sometimes to conforming behavior is a problem which continues to interest both psychologists and sociologists.

Individual and group deviation. A teen-ager in a "good" neighborhood of stable families and conventional people may reject middle-class norms and become a delinquent. In this case, the individual deviates from the norms of the subculture. He or she is thus an *individual deviant.* In a complex society, however, there may be a number of *deviant subcultures,* whose norms are condemned by the conventional morality of the society. Thus in the deteriorated areas of the city, Cohen [1955] and W. Miller [1958] find a delinquent subculture in which many of the youths participate. For many of them the life of the street gang is the only life that seems real and important. In such neighborhoods, delinquent behavior is as "normal" as law-abiding behavior. When boys and girls from these neighborhoods become delinquent, they are not individually deviant from their subculture; it is their subculture (the group, not the person) that is deviant from the conventional norms of the society. The delinquent episodes are not revolts against the area subculture but are "status-seeking mechanisms within the group" [Short and Strodtbeck, 1965, p. viii].

These delinquents are not individually deviant in the beginning; they are conforming normally to the norms of a deviant subculture. This subculture directs them into patterns which eventually result in many of them becoming individually deviant. As they graduate from the adolescent gang into adult society, their gang experience has placed them at war with conventional society, so that they often become and remain individual deviants.

Deviant groups tend to develop subcultures.

We therefore have <u>two ideal types of deviants: (1) individual deviants who reject the norms which surround them and deviate from their subculture;</u> and (2) group deviants, <u>wherein the individual is a conforming member of a deviant group.</u> In practice, deviant persons are not sharply divided into two such distinct groups. The "ideal type" always is a clearcut expression of an idea, while most real persons fall somewhere between the sharply contrasting images presented by the "ideal types." This is the reason for constructing the ideal types; they clearly express an idea. Meanwhile, we should remember that very few people perfectly fit into an ideal type, but are intermediate; for example, few people are either "dominant" or "submissive"; most people show some of each characteristic.

In the case of deviant persons, many deviants are not perfect examples of either individual or group deviation, but show elements of both. Rarely is an individual deviant *completely* surrounded by conventional groups and influences. If one were, it is unlikely that one would ever deviate at all! But even the most carefully sheltered children hear about crimes and immorality, come across literature their parents would censor, and observe other children violating the norms their parents revere.

In other words, even a highly conventional subculture does not completely isolate the person from deviant patterns which he or she can observe and follow.

Furthermore, deviant persons tend to join with other similar persons into deviant groups. The "bad boys" in the schoolroom tend to form a clique, reinforcing one another's boisterous behavior. Individual hot-rodders, hippies, drug addicts, or homosexuals tend to drift together into groups of deviants. These groups reinforce and sanction the deviation, give the member emotional protection against conformist critics, and possibly help to cultivate new deviants. These groups of deviants tend to develop a private language and a set of rigidly stereotyped behavior norms of their own. In short, they tend to develop subcultures. Thus it becomes hard to say whether the hippie of the 1960s was a deviant nonconformist or a rigidly conforming member of a deviant subculture. In practice, then, the distinction between the individual and the group deviant becomes blurred; yet the theoretical distinction is an important one, as our later discussion will elaborate.

Primary and secondary deviation. The concepts of primary and secondary deviation, proposed by Lemert [1951, pp. 75–76; 1967], help to show how people may become confirmed deviants. <u>*Primary deviation* is the deviant behavior of a person who is conformist in the rest of his or her life organization.</u> The deviant behavior is so trivial, or so generally tolerated, or so successfully concealed that he is not publicly identified as deviant, nor does he consider himself a deviant, but views himself as a "decent person" who has a little secret or eccentricity. Lemert writes that "the deviations remain primary . . . as long as they are rationalized or otherwise dealt with as functions of a socially acceptable role" (1951, p. 75). <u>*Secondary deviation* is that which follows one's public identification as a deviant.</u> Sometimes the discovery of a single deviant act (of rape, incest, homosexuality, lesbianism, burglary, drug use), or even a false accusation, may be enough to "label" one as a deviant (rapist, "dope fiend," etc.). This *labeling process* [Lemert, 1951, p. 77; Becker, 1963, chap. 1] is highly important, for it is often the "point of no return" in the development of a deviant life organization. While engaging in no more than primary deviation, one still maintains a conventional set of statuses and roles, and is subjected mainly to the normal series of conformity-reinforcing group pressures and associations. But being labeled as "deviant" tends to be followed by isolation from these conformity-reinforcing influences. Persons so labeled may be dismissed from their job or disbarred from their profession, ostracized by conventional people, and possibly imprisoned and forever branded as "criminal." They are almost forced into association with other deviants by their exclusion from conventional society. As one becomes dependent upon deviant associations and begins to use deviation as a defense against the conventional society which has branded him, the deviation becomes the central focus of the person's life reorganization.

There is also a self-isolating factor in much secondary deviation. As one continues to repeat a deviant act, one may become increasingly bored and uncomfortable among conventional people, and may voluntarily begin to confine one's associations to other deviants. Thus one moves from primary to secondary deviation.

This progression is not an inexorable process; that is, the deviant is not helplessly swept down a chute from which he or she cannot possibly escape. Instead, as Matza points out [1969], the deviant *has a choice.* At many points in the process of becoming deviant, the person does make an election to continue into deviation. Yet this choice is heavily affected by the societal reaction to the deviation, so that the choice is not entirely free.

It is likely that much of the disorganization and demoralization which often accompany deviation are due to the effects of secondary deviation. For example, it has been widely noted that LSD users are likely to become unmotivated, passive "dropouts." Many members of the hippie subculture report that LSD was the turning point in their change of philosophy and life style [Freedman, 1968]. But these are subjective impressions, and cannot be accepted as conclusive. A ten-year follow-up study of 247 subjects who received multiple doses of LSD under medical supervision found "little evidence that measurable, lasting personality, belief, value, attitude, or behavior changes were produced in the sample as a whole [and that LSD] becomes less attractive with continued use and, in the long-term, is almost always self-limiting" [McGothlin and Arnold, 1971, p. 35]. This suggests that any lasting demotivation and demoralization accompanying LSD usage may be due mainly to the conditions and associations surrounding its use, plus the possible self-selection of unstable persons who became LSD users. In this and many other instances, it is difficult to separate the effects of primary and secondary deviation.

Simmons [1969, pp. 122–124] has pointed out how a great many people experiment with deviation at some moments during their lives. Most of them eventually return to conformity. Labeling, isolation, and secondary deviation all impede this return to conformity and thus help to confirm people in a pattern of deviant life organization.

Culturally approved deviation

Deviant behavior is culturally evaluated. Some deviation is condemned; some is applauded. The wandering holy man of one society is the worthless bum of another; the rugged hero of the raw frontier is the uncouth boor of an urban community. In our society, the genius, the hero, the leader, and the celebrity are among our culturally approved deviants.

There have been many studies of leadership, "great men," and extraordinary achievement. They have failed to isolate any special "qualities" of greatness or factors which are highly associated with extraordinary achievement. Perhaps this is because each field of activity calls for different abilities and personality characteristics, so that the qualities which make for success in one field lead to failure in another. In any event, this topic is more clearly the province of psychology than of sociology.

Sociologists do note that the values of the culture determine whether a particular deviant is praised or pilloried. This is another example of cultural relativism. Some cultures, such as the Zuñi or Hopi, encourage very little deviation of any kind whatever; persons of remarkable individual achievement are rare in such a culture. Other cultures, such as the Haida or Kwakiutl, or the contemporary American culture, encourage individual distinction of certain approved sorts. In such cultures, persons of great achievement are fairly numerous, highly honored, and widely emulated. A culture may thus encourage or discourage great personal achievement, direct it into one channel or another, or even block it completely. What would Einstein have accomplished in a society which had no need to count beyond ten? Beethoven among the American Indians might have added a new drum beat, but he would never have written the Ninth Symphony.

Some people will insist that a genius in any society would still find some way to express his talents through great achievements. Since we cannot reincarnate Einstein for a second try among the Hottentots, such statements cannot be either proved or disproved. But we suspect that when a primitive genius came up with a new idea, it was accepted and used only if it fitted in with the needs and values of the society; otherwise it was generally suppressed, ignored, or ridiculed, and thereby lost and forgotten. Thus the genius in any society is able to make only the kinds of contributions which are welcomed by at least some groups in the society.

Culturally disapproved deviation

Although culturally approved deviation is an important feature of all modern societies, most sociological treatments of deviation focus exclusively upon forms of deviation that are disapproved.

Deviation through physical inability to conform. Those with physical or mental defects may be incapable of normal achievements or normal social behavior. The term *mental defect* refers to limited learning capacity, through either inheritance, brain damage, or some other organic imperfection. It has recently been noted that the diagnosis of mental defects is very difficult and often inaccurate. Sometimes people of normal learning capacity are incorrectly labeled as mentally defective, after which the avenues to normal learning and life adjustment are closed off. Thus incorrect labeling can create mental retardation (Mercer, 1973). The diagnosis and treatment of physical or mental defect lie largely outside the field of sociology. But sociologists are interested in beliefs about mental defects and social policies concerning defectives. The popular belief that all mental defectives multiply like hamsters is incorrect. Birth rates are high only among the "high-grade morons" or borderline defectives; among the more seriously defective, the greater the defect, the lower tends to be the birth rate and the survival rate. Most of the inherited severe mental defects appear among children of normal parents who carry recessive gene defects, so that only a small fraction of severe mental defects could be prevented by sterilizing all mental defectives. Since all true mental defects and most physical defects are incurable at present, social policy is mainly concerned with preparing defectives to be as socially useful as their abilities permit.

Mental illness is a disorganization of behavior rather than a lack of learning capacity. In mental illness, persons who may be within the normal range of learning capacity are unable to perceive and respond to realities in an orderly and rational manner. Their reality perceptions may be so distorted that they imagine people are persecuting them or that they hear strange voices and commands, or they become disoriented and forget where they are and what they are doing. Their self-perceptions may become distorted, so that they become obsessed with their own worthlessness, sinfulness, or incompetence, or perhaps develop delusions of grandeur and power. Their reactions to reality may become confused and erratic, or they may withdraw from reality into an inner world of fantasy.

Some psychiatrists object to the "illness" model, claiming that the mind does not get "sick" and that the diagnosis and treatment of "mental illness" should not be a medical specialty [Szasz, 1961, 1970; Kiester, 1972]. Scheff, a sociologist, claims that "mental illness" is actually a form of "residual deviance," that is, a catch-all term for odd or annoying actions which do not fall into any other convenient behavior category [Scheff, 1963]. Such persons, according to Scheff and others [e.g., Szasz, 1970], are labeled mentally ill and then rewarded for accepting the label and assuming the mentally ill role as expected. Such scholars suggest that mental illness should simply be treated as deviant behavior, possibly by behavior modification techniques [Boisnert, 1974]. But there are others who defend the illness model, holding that mental illness is a genuine illness, not a label tacked on people by a conspiratorial society [Siegler and Osmond, 1974]. Thus the respective roles of medical and social factors in mental illness remain in dispute.

Physical-type theories of deviation. The idea that certain body types are predisposed to certain kinds of behavior is almost as old as human history. A number of scholars, including Lombroso [1912], Kretschmer [1925], Hooton [1939], Von Hentig [1947], and Sheldon [1949] have made studies claiming to find that certain body types are more prone to deviant behavior than others. The most elaborate theory is that of Sheldon, who identifies three basic body types: endomorph (round, soft, fat); mesomorph (muscular, athletic); and ectomorph (thin, bony). For each type, Sheldon describes an elaborate series of personality traits and behavior tendencies. For example, he finds that delinquents and alcoholics are generally mesomorphs. He attributes neurosis largely to one's effort to be different from what one's body type predisposes one to be.

Some cultural conflicts can encourage mental conflicts.

Physical-type theories appear occasionally as "scientific" articles in popular magazines and Sunday papers. They have become quite popular, possibly because they seem to offer a simple, scientific way of classifying people and predicting or explaining their behavior. Social scientists, however, are quite skeptical of the body-type theories [Clinard, 1968, pp. 173–174]. Although these theories are supported by impressive empirical evidence, critics have noted serious errors in method which cast doubts upon their findings. For example, the process of classifying subjects into the several body types included no adequate methodological safeguards against unconscious bias: consequently, a borderline subject may have been placed in whatever body-type class he or she "belonged" in order to support the theory. The subject groups used in most of these studies were composed of institutionalized delinquents, who are not properly representative of all types of delinquents. Furthermore, the control groups of "normal" people were collected so unsystematically that it is doubtful whether they were a representative cross section of people. More carefully controlled research is continuing, and associations between body type and behavior continue to be claimed [Cortez and Gatti, 1970], but no reliable associations have yet been generally accepted by social scientists.

Psychoanalytic theories of deviant behavior. Psychoanalysis is firmly rooted in Freud's concepts of the id, ego, and superego, as described in Chapter 5. Deviant behavior is attributed to conflicts between the id and the ego, or between the id and the superego. Crime, for example, takes place when the superego, the civilized self-control of the individual, is unable to restrain the savage, primitive, destructive impulse of the id [Zilboorg, 1943; Abrahamson, 1944].

Do the id, ego, and superego represent major aspects of the human personality, or are they merely words that psychoanalysts quote to one another? Do death wishes, castration complexes, and Oedipal stages actually exist in the normal personality, or does the psychoanalyst unconsciously plant the expected symptoms in the patient's mind and dig them up in subsequent interviews? We do not definitely know. Psychoanalytic theory is almost totally unsubstantiated by empirical research, while a number of such efforts have been inconclusive or nonconfirmatory. In Chapter 5 we cited Sewell's findings [1952] which cast doubt on psychoanalytic theory about specific child-training practices. Barnes [1952] sought to test the Freudian theory of the successive oral, anal, and phallic levels of psychosexual development and concluded that "the Freudian the-

ory of levels of psychosexual development has not been supported as a whole." In all, comparatively few empirical attempts to test psychoanalytic theory have been made. It would, in fact, be quite difficult to design research that would either establish or disprove the usefulness of such concepts as the id or the ego. But until such research is completed, psychoanalytic theory remains debatable, even though it is widely used in the treatment of behavior disorders. Its clinical success is sometimes cited as proof of psychoanalytic theory; that is, since some of the patients improve under psychoanalytic treatment, the theory must be sound. But such claims for successful treatment are not accompanied by a comparison of these patients with a control group of untreated patients, many of whom improve without treatment. Consequently, we cannot know whether the patients improved because of the treatment or because of other factors.

If, without using psychoanalytic terminology, we merely state that culture often frustrates biological drives, little argument is possible. While the id may be debatable, there is no doubt about the existence of biological drives such as hunger and sex, or of the organic reactions associated with fear and anger. Clearly, too, culture often frustrates these drives and impulses. Our culture, for example, makes no socially approved provision for the sexual drives of those who are unmarried, widowed, or separated. If one gratifies such impulses in defiance of cultural taboos, one is engaging in deviant behavior. If, however, one disposes of the impulse by *repressing* it into the unconscious (to return to psychoanalytic theory), it does not go away, but remains as part of one's unconscious motivation and may still give rise to deviant behavior of some kind. Thus the sex-starved spinster may repress her sex drives into her unconscious, where they remain active, perhaps impelling her to extreme prissiness, to religious fanaticism, to health anxieties, or to some other emotional "cover-ups." Stated in this less tortuous manner, psychoanalytic theory, while still un-proved, becomes a highly plausible explana-tion for some deviant behavior.

Socialization failures and deviation. Every member of a society is frustrated by the clash of his or her biological drives with the taboos of the culture. But not everyone becomes a devi-ant. Why, when most persons conform to the norms of the culture, do some become deviant? There is no convincing evidence that most of these deviants differ significantly from the conformists in their inherited or constitutional behavior impulses. Therefore, *social scien-tists assume that they are deviant because the socialization process has failed in some way to integrate the cultural norms into the individual's personality.* Where the socializa-tion process is successful, the individual adopts the surrounding norms, and the ap-proved goals and values of the culture become emotional needs, while the taboos of the cul-ture become a part of his or her conscience. The individual *internalizes* the norms of the culture so that he or she automatically and mechanically acts in the expected manner most of the time [Scott, 1971]. Many studies of family atmosphere and the attitudes and val-ues of children have reached the same conclu-sion that while "peer groups can influence those attitudes and behavior in later years, they act not as originators, but as reinforcers of the values and behavioral patterns developed earlier in the family" [Mantell, 1974, p. 62]. Where children are socialized in a happy, af-fectionate, conventional family, they usually develop a secure, well-adjusted personality, behave conventionally in most respects, marry successfully, and provide a happy, affection-ate, conventional home for their children, who then repeat the cycle. Where family life is unsatisfactory, children often develop perso-nality difficulties and behavior deviations. The Gluecks [1959], after many years of carefully controlled comparisons of delinquent and non-delinquent youth, predict that juvenile delin-quency is at least a 90 percent probability when the "five highly decisive" factors in fam-ily life are unfavorable: father's discipline (harsh, erratic, unsympathetic); mother's su-pervision (indifferent, unconcerned); father's affection (lacking); mother's affection (cold, indifferent, hostile); cohesiveness of the family (unintegrated, empty of companionship). Where all five of these factors are favorable, they find virtually no serious delinquency.

The exact manner in which one's family life molds personality into conforming or deviant channels shows an endless variety. Some fam-ilies make no conscious effort to transmit the cultural norms to their children, while others try but fail, as is shown in this personal history taken from the authors' files.

As far back as I can remember anything, I can recall those scenes which always ended with my mother's tearful lament, "Why can't you be more like your brother?" while I kept to myself the thought, "Be like that big sissy? Not on your life." He was older and was expected to look after me, which I resented. So anything he counseled against, I promptly did. I think it was emotionally necessary for me not to be or do anything he was or did. He was studious; I avoided school books like they were disease germs. He was neat, orderly, punctual, and methodical: I shunned these weak-nesses. He did exactly what our parents and teach-ers asked; I did nothing they asked. He was a "good boy," and they showed their pride in him on every occasion; they were never proud of me. He and my father were close confidants and compan-ions; my only companions were other "bad boys" from whom my parents made strenuous—and un-successful—efforts to separate me. When I finally stood, dry-eyed, beside my father's casket while my brother sniffled, my only thought was, "Why don't you die too, you stupid square!"

We cannot be certain just why this boy re-jected parental values and standards while his brother was accepting them. One might guess that his parents showed some favoritism and perhaps a lack of sympathetic interest, and made a clumsy use of the older brother as model. Yet a similar family atmosphere had an opposite effect upon another child, as is shown in this case, also taken from the authors' files.

All my life I have been competing with my older brother. From the first I felt that he was better, smarter, and more handsome than I. He was the one whom my parents loved the more, criticized more gently, praised more highly, and proudly showed off before the relatives and guests. I recall that at such moments, I harbored no feelings of resentment, but only feelings of wistful longing that I might also deserve such appreciation. I became very dutiful and obedient, and my intense efforts to do what they wished were sometimes rewarded.

Today, as a middle-aged adult, I feel a good deal of resentment toward them. I suppose that my dedicated efforts to earn their affection are responsible both for my success, which greatly surpasses my brother's, and for my anxieties and tensions, which are considerable. Although both parents have been dead for years, my persistent emotional need to seek approval through perfect performance is both my virtue and my curse. I often wonder what I would be today, had I received the warm acceptance my brother always enjoyed.

These two cases illustrate the fact that *there is no social situation which has uniformly predictable effects upon all persons in that situation*. All attempts to link predictably a particular behavior outcome with a particular type of family experience are doomed to failure. The most we can say is that certain kinds of family experience *usually* produce well-adjusted, conforming people, while family life which is deficient in certain characteristics is more likely to produce poorly adjusted personalities and behavior deviation. The specific deficiencies may be of many sorts—parental neglect or abuse, lack of sympathy and affection, harsh or erratic discipline, lack of family cohesiveness, excessive parental demands and unrealistic standards, or any of a number of other defects which keep the home from being a pleasant, comfortable place. Inadequate parents may fail in at least two general ways:

(1) They may fail to provide a satisfactory model of normal behavior for their children to copy. If the parents are themselves deviant persons, their children have little opportunity to learn the conventional behavior norms. There is a good deal of speculation upon the possibility that much alcoholism, drug addiction, sex deviation, marital inadequacy, and other behavior difficulty may stem from a boy's inability to identify with his weak, ineffectual father, so that the son was never able to form a satisfactory masculine self-image. Feminine difficulties are often attributed in like manner to a girl's unsatisfactory mother-model, or to her father's failure to fill the role of the protective, admiring, appreciative father. Such theories are plausible and widely accepted by behavior therapists.

(2) Parents may strive to present a satisfactory model and to instill the cultural norms in their children, but they may still fail as parents if they are too demanding, too critical, too strict, too erratic, or too unloving. At any rate, a child sometimes develops a strong emotional need to resist parental goals and standards and to shock parents and others by unconventional behavior. A study of American ex-Communists by Ernst and Loth [1952] found that most of them were resentful, somewhat unhappy children of conventional, domineering parents, and had joined the Communist party briefly during young adulthood as a means of emancipation from and revenge upon their parents. Psychiatrists are convinced that some alcoholics are resentful persons who, probably unconsciously, are revenging themselves upon their families by destroying themselves [Fox, 1956; Podalsky, 1960]. A study of unmarried mothers by L. Young [1954] concluded that most of them *wanted* an illegitimate child as a form of revenge, usually upon their mothers. An endless variety of behavior difficulties are often traced to some disturbance in the parent-child relationship. Such conclusions are difficult to prove or disprove, but are widely held by behavioral scientists.

Cultural conflicts and deviation. In a well-integrated culture with a single set of behavior codes and moral values, socialization is smooth and untroubled. Parents express the cultural norms in their words and actions, and these are reinforced by the rest of the society. But in a rapidly changing society, old norms and values are constantly being undermined and replaced by new ones. Thus the matron who, as a girl, was cautioned by her mother to cherish her chastity may today be cautioning her own daughter to be sure to take her pill!

The extreme heterogeneity of American society produces many conflicting norms and values. A variety of immigrant groups have brought differing cultural traditions which are difficult to fuse into a common set of norms. Even the different branches of the Christian faith cannot agree on several questions of morality. Some Protestant groups condemn all alcoholic beverages, dancing, and all kinds of gambling as sinful, while certain other Protestant groups, together with the Catholics, claim that under certain conditions these activities are harmless. The Catholic Church condemns divorce and contraception, while most Protestant bodies will permit them. All American churches teach that one should be generous, sympathetic, and self-sacrificing, but our economic system rewards those who are ruthless, selfish, and grasping. This list of culture conflicts could be extended indefinitely. Many current social critics angrily charge the society with "hypocrisy" and attribute such cultural contradictions to the insincerity and duplicity of others whose hearts are less pure than theirs. They may not realize that such inconsistencies and culture conflicts are found in most societies, and especially in all heterogeneous, changing societies.

What is "hypocrisy?" It is usually defined as pretending to be what one is not; as taking actions which betray one's professed principles. How often do people *knowingly and consciously* betray their principles in their actions? Not very often, for most inconsistencies between professions and actions *are usually so fully rationalized* that the actor is not aware of any inconsistency. For example, the person who praises democracy and freedom while helping chase a new black resident out of the neighborhood sees no inconsistency; he or she is merely exercising the democratic right and duty to "protect" the neighborhood. Thus "hypocrisy" is generally found in the eye of the observer rather than in the heart of the actor. Culture conflicts and inconsistencies create a need for rationalizations and compromises which some persons perceive as hypocrisy and deceit, and this perception undermines and weakens the common set of norms and values upon which social order depends. A fairly high rate of deviation may be an inevitable consequence of having a complex, rapidly changing culture.

Anomie, alienation, and deviation. From such a variety of conflicting norms arises a condition which Durkheim [1897] called *anomie,* a condition of "normlessness." He did not mean that modern societies have no norms; instead they have many sets of norms, with none of them clearly binding upon everybody, so that individuals become "normless." Later sociologists extended the term to include the state of mind in which the person has no firm sense of belonging to anything dependable or stabilizing. As Parsons writes, anomie is

. . . the state where large numbers of individuals are in a serious degree lacking in the kind of integration with stable institutions which is essential to their own personal stability and the smooth functioning of the social system . . . . The typical reaction of the individual is . . . insecurity. (Talcott Parsons, *Essays in Sociological Theory,* The Free Press, New York, 1954, pp. 125,126.)

This approach implies that anomie arises from the confusion and conflict of modern society. People move about too rapidly to be bound to the norms of any particular group and, as a result, have no stable perspective from which to make decisions. In this sense anomie is the result of freedom of choice without the balance assumed to come from stable relationships to church, state, family, or community.

Merton [1938] suggests that anomie comes not from freedom of choice but from the inability of many individuals to follow norms which they are perfectly willing to accept. He sees the major cause of this difficulty as a disharmony between cultural goals and the institutionalized means for reaching them. He notes that while our society encourages *all* its members to aspire to wealth and social position, our approved modes of attaining these goals are so restrictive that only a few have any realistic prospect of reaching them. True, an exceptional poor boy or girl reaches wealth and fame, and these rare exceptions help to preserve the myth of equal opportunity. But poor children with a family background of ignorance and apathy and without valuable "connections" have to struggle for success even if highly talented. If they have only average abilities, they have still less chance of ever reaching the goals which our culture holds before them, unless they violate the rules for seeking them. So Merton concludes:

It is only when a system of cultural values extols, virtually above all else, certain common success-goals for the population at large while the social structure rigorously restricts or completely closes access to approved modes of reaching these goals for a considerable part of the same population, that deviant behavior ensues on a large scale . . . .

The moral mandate to achieve success thus exerts pressure to succeed, by fair means if possible and by foul means if necessary. (Robert K. Merton, "Social Structure and Anomie," in his *Social Theory and Social Structure,* The Free Press, New York, 1957, chap. 3, pp. 146,169.)

The approved path to success in our society lies in education and occupational advancement. To many people, however, education is a frustrating, boring experience which they escape as soon as possible; occupational advancement eludes them, and the idea of saving and investing is not even seriously considered. Since these people still feel entitled to affluence, they proceed to look for other means than those society approves. These deviant routes to legitimate ends may include gambling, swindling, participation in the rackets, or resort to violent crime. When the condition of anomie becomes so widespread that deviancy becomes the rule rather than the exception, then social control may be considered to have completely broken down.

This substitution of illegitimate for legitimate means is only one of several possible reactions to the disparity between universalized goals and restricted methods of obtaining them. A full range of possible responses is given in Merton's typology [1957a, pp. 140–57] illustrated in Table 6. (1) *Conformity* is an acceptance of both the conventional goals and the conventional, institutionalized means of seeking them. (2) *Innovation* is an attempt to attain the conventional goals through unconventional means (including illicit or criminal means). (3) *Ritualism* preserves the institutionalized means, which have become ends in themselves, as the goals are largely ignored or forgotten. The rituals, ceremonies, and routines are followed, but the original meanings or functions have become lost. (4) *Retreatism* abandons both the conventional goals and the institutionalized means for attaining them, as illustrated by most of the advanced alcoholics, drug addicts, hippies, skid-row habitués, hermits, and other "drop-outs." (5) *Rebellion* involves a retreat from the conventional goals and means, with an attempt to institutionalize a new system of goals and means. Revolutionists are an illustration.

Whereas Merton sees deviation growing from one's inability to achieve culturally inspired goals, Riesman [1950] sees deviation growing from the shift to *other-direction* in modern society. In traditional societies, according to Riesman, people are *tradition-directed;* that is, they are guided by a coherent set of traditions which they follow with little deviation. Some centuries ago, Western society became *inner-directed,* with people guided by a conscience which had internalized the rather

TABLE 6 A TYPOLOGY OF MODES OF INDIVIDUAL ADAPTATION

Modes of adaptation	Culture goals	Institutionalized means
I. Conformity	+	+
II. Innovation	+	−
III. Ritualism	−	+
IV. Retreatism	−	−
V. Rebellion	±	±

Note: In the table above (+) signifies "acceptance," (−) signifies "rejection," and (±) signifies "rejection of prevailing values and substitution of new values."
Source: Robert K. Merton, *Social Theory and Social Structure,* The Free Press, New York, 1957, p. 140.

authoritarian indoctrination of family and other groups in a stable community. Today people are becoming increasingly *other-directed,* for the lack of a coherent tradition or a stable community is leaving them with no clear guide to conduct except the judgments of other people. But since modern societies have many groupings, with differing norms, other-direction provides no dependable guide to conduct. The other-directed person is a conformist at heart, and wishes to do what others expect, but has no clear model to follow. Consequently the behavior of the individual often lacks consistency and conforms to no dependable norm. Since it is impossible, in our complex and changing society, to reestablish stable communities, Riesman looks to the development of "autonomous" persons who can order their lives responsibly without being rooted in stable communities or being puppets of their peer groups. Whether this autonomy is possible remains an unanswered question.

McClosky and Schaar [1965] suggest that anomic normlessness may be simply one aspect of a negative and distrustful outlook on life and society. They present evidence that anomie appears, not only among Merton's frustrated failures, but also among the highly successful. They find that persons who score high on anomic scales also show high scores for hostility, anxiety, pessimism, authoritarianism, political cynicism, and other symptoms of alienation.

The concept of *alienation* is more inclusive than anomie, for it includes the components of *powerlessness, normlessness, and social isolation* [Nettler, 1957; Dean, 1961; Sykes, 1964]. The alienated person not only has no fully internalized system of binding norms, but also feels like a powerless, helpless victim of a heedlessly impersonal social system in which he or she has no real place. The alienated person has few group affiliations or institutional loyalties. Alienation is therefore an almost total emotional separation from one's society.

Marxian scholars stress the concept of alienation, holding that capitalist society inevitably alienates its workers and even its intellectuals because of its isolation of workers from control over work policies, work conditions, or managerial decisions [Blauner, 1964; Kon, 1969; Anderson, 1974]. Such alienation weakens the binding power of traditional norms and controls, and thus encourages deviant behavior. Marxian analysts see increasing alienation as a symptom of the approaching end for capitalism. Whether work alienation is actually increasing is difficult to know, for we have no clear historical baselines for comparison. Numerous surveys have shown that most American workers are fairly well satisfied with their jobs, and that the level of job satisfaction has not declined significantly within the past decade [Kahn, 1972; Form, 1973; Quinn, et al., 1974]. A recent comparison of job satisfaction in capitalist United States and socialist Yugoslavia found a higher level of job satisfaction in the United States, and also found that the pattern of work dissatisfaction was quite similar in both countries [Tannenbaum, 1974].

These findings contradict the Marxian assumption of work alienation as a special feature of capitalism.

Significance of deviant behavior

Deviation is relative, not absolute. People are not completely conformist or completely deviant. A completely deviant person would have a hard time staying alive. Even the more spectacular deviants, such as pyromaniacs, revolutionists, or hermits, are generally fairly conventional in some of their activities. And nearly all "normal" people are occasionally deviant. Kinsey [1948, p. 392, 576] has shown how over half our adults could be imprisoned for using techniques of lovemaking which were (and still are) forbidden by the laws of most states. A number of studies have shown that most people have committed a number of major crimes for which they could be prosecuted if all laws were fully enforced [Porterfield, 1946; Wallerstein and Wyle, 1947; Gold, 1970]. It is clear that nearly everyone in our society is deviant to some degree; but some are more frequently and broadly deviant than others, and some conceal their deviant actions more fully than others. To some extent, the recognized deviant is one who does openly what others do secretly.

Deviation from real or ideal culture? Since the real and ideal cultures often diverge, as mentioned in Chapter 3, conformity to one may be deviation from the other. For example, the ideal culture includes the cultural norm of obedience to all laws, yet practically no one obeys all laws.

Where important values are involved in the divergence between what people say (ideal culture) and what they do (real culture), this becomes an important distinction. In each discussion of deviation where this distinction is important, the normative base—real or ideal culture—should be either implied or expressly stated. For example, in any discussion of premarital intercourse or of certain sex "crimes" which are widely practiced by married couples, the normative base should be specified.

Norms of evasion. Whenever the mores or laws forbid something that many people strongly wish to do, *norms of evasion* are likely to appear. These are the patterns through which people indulge their wishes without openly challenging the mores. For example, Roebuck and Spray [1967] show how the cocktail lounge functions to facilitate discreet sexual affairs between high-status married men and unattached young women. More common norms of evasion in our society would include driving a few miles over the speed limit and "padding" one's income tax deductions as much as is "safe."

The fact that a particular norm is often violated does not create a norm of evasion. It is only when there is a *pattern* of violation which is *recognized and sanctioned by one's group* that we have a norm of evasion. Patronizing a bootlegger became a norm of evasion when it became a standard, group-approved way of getting the forbidden alcoholic beverages. In becoming group-sanctioned, the evasion loses its moral censure. Among many groups, success in "fixing" traffic tickets or in seducing women will earn one the admiration of others. Norms of evasion thus are a semi-institutionalized form of deviant behavior.

Sometimes a pattern of deviation is neither sufficiently accepted to be a norm of evasion nor sufficiently condemned to be routinely suppressed. In such situations, the toleration of such deviation may operate as a form of social control. Prostitutes and gamblers may be permitted to operate as long as they provide information to the police. In most prisons, influential prisoners who can insure a quiet and orderly cell block are permitted to commit minor rule infractions [Strange and McCrory, 1974]. Thus the tolerance of some deviation, with the implied threat of withdrawing this privilege and actually enforcing the rules, functions to maintain social control.

Deviation and social change. Deviation is both a threat and a protection to social stability. On the one hand, a society can function efficiently only if there is order and predictability in social life. We must *know,* within reasonable limits, what behavior to expect from others, what they expect of us, and what kind of society our children should be socialized to live in. Deviant behavior threatens this order and predictability. If too many people fail to behave as expected, the culture becomes disorganized and social order collapses. Economic activity may be disrupted, and actual shortages may appear. The mores lose their compelling power, and the society's core of common values shrinks. Individuals feel insecure and confused in a society whose norms have become undependable. Only when most of the people conform to well-established norms most of the time can a society function efficiently.

On the other hand, *deviant behavior is one way of adapting a culture to social change* [Coser, 1962]. No society today can possibly remain static for long. Even the most isolated of the world's societies faces sweeping social changes within the next generation. The population explosion, technological change, and the passing of tribal or folk cultures are requiring the more primitive peoples to learn new norms, while changing technology continues to demand adaptations from the more advanced peoples. But new norms are seldom produced by deliberative assemblies of people who solemnly pronounce the old norms outworn and call for new ones. While the grave deliberations of congresses, religious councils, and professional associations may accelerate or retard the development of new norms, their pronouncements more often serve to legitimate new norms which are well on the way to general acceptance. New norms emerge from the daily behavior of individuals, responding in similar ways to the impact of new social circumstances. The deviant behavior of a few individuals may be the beginnings of a new norm. As more and more people join in the deviant form of behavior, a new norm will eventually be established, and the behavior will cease to be "deviant."

The emergence of new norms is neatly illustrated in the decline of the patriarchal family. In an agrarian society where all the family

The deviant behavior of one generation may become the norm of the next.

worked together under the father's watchful eye, it was easy to maintain male dominance. But changing technology moved the father's job to the shop or office, where he could no longer keep his eye on things; changing technology also began drawing the wife into jobs where she worked apart from her husband and earned her own paycheck. The husband was no longer in a strategic position to assert his male authority, and, bit by bit, it slipped from him. In the nineteenth century, the relatively independent, equalitarian woman with a mind of her own and a habit of firmly voicing it was a deviant; today she is commonplace, and the Women's Liberation Movement demands additional changes of sex status. Thus the deviant behavior of one generation may become the norm of the next.

Deviant behavior thus often represents tomorrow's adaptations in their beginnings. Without any deviant behavior, it would be difficult to adapt a culture to changing needs and circumstances. A changing society therefore needs deviant behavior as the incubator of the new norms it must develop if it is to operate efficiently. The question of *how much* deviation and *what kinds* of deviation a society should tolerate is a perpetual puzzle. It is easy now for most people to agree that the eighteenth-century republicans and the nineteenth-century suffragists were socially useful deviants, while the utopians were harmless and the anarchists were socially destructive. But which of today's deviants will prove tomorrow to have been today's trail blazers—the nudists, hippies, pacifists, marijuana users, commune members, free-lovers, one-worlders, or whom? It is difficult to say.

Not all forms of deviation will fit the above analysis. The behavior of the assassin, the child molester, or the alcoholic rarely contributes to the forging of a useful new social norm. At any particular moment, deviant behavior takes many forms, only a very few of which are destined to become tomorrow's norms. Much deviation is entirely destructive in its personal and social consequences. But *some* deviation is socially useful, as is indicated above. To separate the socially harmful from the socially useful deviations requires an ability to predict the social norms that tomorrow's society will require. Although sociologists cannot forecast future norms with any certainty of accuracy, they may forecast them somewhat more accurately than others who are not professionals in the study of culture and social change.

Summary

A society must have *social order* if it is to function smoothly. A society maintains *social control* over its members in three principal ways. First, it socializes them so that they will want to behave as they should. Second, society imposes *group pressure* upon the individual so that he or she must conform or be punished by the group. This group pressure may be expressed through the informal controls of the primary group—approval and disapproval, praise, scorn, ostracism, etc.; or it may operate through the more formal controls of secondary groups—rules and regulations, standardized procedures, propaganda, rewards, titles, and penalties. Finally, control through *force and punishment* is used where other controls fail. But in many social situations, behavior is more greatly controlled by the needs and pressures of the situation—the *situational determinants of behavior*—than by the character one brings to the situation.

Social deviation arises whenever a person fails to conform to the usual norms of the society. Deviation may be individual, in that a person deviates from the normal behavior of the group; or it may be group deviation, in which the entire group deviates from social norms, so that the individual is a conforming member of a deviant group or subculture. In practice these two types tend to merge, since deviants tend to seek out other deviants and form deviant groups. *Primary deviation* is the deviant behavior of persons who hold conventional statuses and fill conventional roles in most of their behavior, while *secondary deviation* develops when people are publicly labeled as deviant, are to some degree isolated from conventional roles and associations, and use deviation as an "adjustment" to their social isolation. Deviants are also divided into *cultural deviants* and *psychological deviants.* Cultural deviants simply deviate from the expected behavior norms. Psychological deviants are deviant from the norm in their personality integration; in their social behavior they may be either deviant or conformist.

Some forms of deviation are approved—the leader, hero, genius, and saint are often (although not always) honored and revered. Many other forms of deviation are disapproved. Deviation through physical *inability* to conform—often caused by physical or mental defect or illness—is usually viewed with sympathy. The role of social and cultural influences in producing mental illness cannot be exactly measured, but there is widespread agreement that our culture provokes mental conflicts which contribute to mental illness. Where there is no clear physical incapacity to conform, the causes of deviation are debatable.

Physical-type theories of deviation are popular but unproved. Psychoanalytic theories are popular and plausible, but also unproved. Most of the disapproved individual deviation probably stems, at least partly if not entirely, from failures in socialization, so that the norms and values of the culture are imperfectly integrated into the personality of the individual. The family plays the key role in socialization and is the main channel through which the child absorbs the society's norms and values. Unsatisfactory family life is, therefore, a very important factor in disapproved individual deviation. The family, however, is a part of the culture, and unsatisfactory family life is often a reflection of conflicts within the culture. Such conflicts surround cultural norms with uncertainty, and by thus imposing pressures upon individuals, help to produce a state of normlessness called *anomie.* The disharmony between our cultural goals and our means for attaining them encourage anomie and deviation. When anomie is combined with feelings of powerlessness and social isolation, a feeling of *alienation* develops. Marxian scholars assume that alienation is increasing and that this dooms the capitalist system, but this remains undetermined.

Deviation is relative, not absolute, in that most people are deviant to some degree. Whenever a particular pattern of deviation becomes widely followed and excused, it is called a *norm of evasion.* Whenever some aspect of a culture becomes unbearably confining, norms of evasion are likely to appear. In time, these may become the new norms. Thus deviation, while an enemy of social stability, is also a means of introducing the changed norms which become necessary if a changing society is to remain reasonably integrated and efficient.

Questions and projects

1. How does social order depend upon predictability of behavior?
2. Some ancient societies required many human sacrifices. Why did the victims consent to die quietly instead of revolting?
3. Evaluate this statement: "Only weaklings follow the herd. A person with true strength of character will do what is right without being swayed by the group."
4. In the factory a "rate buster" is a worker on piecework who produces and earns so much that management may revise the piece rate downward. How do the other workers treat this person? Is he or she anything like a "course spoiler" in college, who works so hard in a course that the professor begins to expect more from the other students?
5. What do you think of the Tlingit practice of holding the entire group morally responsible for the acts of each member? Does the practice make for effective social control? How widely could we follow it? Is it consistent with our ethos? Does our society have the kind of group structure in which such a practice is workable?
6. Under what circumstances will practically all students cheat? When will very few students cheat? How does this contrast in attitude illustrate "situational determinants of behavior"?
7. In a hippie commune, where each member is "free," what group controls might operate?
8. Why do "backward" or primitive societies have less crime and fewer violations of the mores than "progressive" societies like ours?
9. Distinguish between individual and group deviants. How do these two ideal types tend to merge in practice?
10. What do you think of the suggestion to publish the names of all juvenile delinquents?
11. How does the concept of secondary deviation help interpret the disorganization of the life of drug addicts?
12. Labeling theorists seem to imply that the problem of deviation could be solved by simply not labeling deviants. Would this be practical for any kinds of deviation? Impractical for any kinds?
13. How would you interpret the high crime rate in the ghetto in terms of Merton's theory of cultural goals and institutionalized means? In terms of the Marxian alienation theory?
14. Discuss these propositions: (1) "Norms of eva-

sion are a threat to social stability." (2) "Norms of evasion are a protection to the stability of a society."

15. Read one of the disaster studies such as William Form, et. al., *Community in Disaster,* Harper & Row, Publishers, Incorporated, New York, 1958, Harry E. Moore, *Tornados over Texas,* University of Texas Press, Austin, 1958, or Allen H. Barton, *Communities in Disaster,* Doubleday & Company, Inc., Garden City, N.Y., 1969. Show how social order breaks down and then is restored.

16. Compare and explain the differing success of two families in their effort to insulate their children from the influences of a slum neighborhood, as described in Betty Smith, *A Tree Grows in Brooklyn,* Harper & Row, Publishers, Incorporated, New York, 1943, and James T. Farrell, *A World I Never Made,* Vanguard Press, Inc., New York, 1936.

17. Read Michael E. Brown, "The Condemnation and Persecution of Hippies," *Trans-action,* September, 1969, pp. 33–46. Do you think hippies were truly persecuted, or do you think Brown exaggerated?

Suggested readings

*BECKER, HOWARD S.: *Outsiders: Studies in the Sociology of Deviance,* The Free Press, New York, 1963, 1966. A concise description of how people become deviant, applied particularly to marijuana users and dance musicians.

BELL, ROBERT R: *Social Deviance,* The Dorsey Press, Homewood, Ill., 1971. A textbook with chapters on many kinds of deviance.

BERNSTEIN, BASIL: "Elaborated and Restricted Codes: An Outline," *Sociological Inquiry,* 36:254–261, Spring, 1966. Analysis of the role of language in facilitating communication within the group and simultaneously isolating it from outside contacts.

BROWN, PAULA: "Changes in Ojibwa Social Control," *American Anthropologist,* 54:57–70, January, 1954. Tells how loss of traditional controls and lack of effective replacements left the Ojibwa with an unsolved problem of social control.

BRYAN, JAMES: "Apprenticeships in Prostitution," *Social Problems,* 12:287–297, Winter, 1965. Shows how call girls become socialized into the call girl role.

CLINARD, MARSHALL: *Sociology of Deviant Behavior,* Holt, Rinehart and Winston, Inc., New York, 1974. A comprehensive textbook on deviation.

*DINITZ, SIMON, RUSSEL B. DYNES, AND ALFRED C. CLARK (EDS.): *Deviance: Studies in the Process of Stigmatization and Societal Reaction,* Oxford University Press, Fair Lawn, N. J., 1969. A comprehensive reader with essays and research studies on many kinds of deviance.

KLAPP, ORRIN E.: "The Folk Hero," *Journal of American Folklore,* 62:17–25, January, 1949; and "Hero Worship in America," *American Sociological Review,* 14:53–62, February, 1949. A study of those who deviate through superfulfillment of cultural norms, and a study also of their admirers.

LEMERT, EDWIN H.: *Social Pathology,* McGraw-Hill Book Company, New York, 1951, chaps. 1–3. A classic outline of social deviation.

*MCCAGHY, CHARLES H., JAMES K. SKIPPER, JR., AND MARK LIFTON: *In Their Own Behalf: Voices from the Margin,* Appleton Century Crofts, 1974. A wide variety of deviants tell their own story.

MATZA, DAVID: *Becoming Deviant,* Prentice-Hall, Inc., Englewood Cliffs, N.J., 1969. Argues that the deviant is not helpless, but has a choice at various points in the process of becoming deviant.

MERTON, ROBERT K.: *Social Theory and Social Structure,* rev. ed., The Free Press, New York, 1964, chaps. 3 and 4, "Social Structure and Anomie," and "Continuities in the Theory of Social Structure and Anomie." A classic statement upon anomie and deviation in modern society; chap. 11, "The Self-fulfilling Prophecy," is a description of the self-fulfilling prophecy as a basic process in society.

*RAINWATER, LEE (ED.): *Social Problems: Deviance and Liberty,* Aldine Publishing Co., Chicago, 1974. A collection of both theoretical and descriptive essays on deviation.

SAGARIN, EDWARD: *Odd Man In: Societies of Deviants in America,* Quadrangle Books, Inc., Chicago, 1970. A readable description of a number of organizations which deviants have formed in the United States.

*SCHUR, EDWIN M.: *Labeling Deviant Behavior,* Harper & Row, Publishers, Inc., New York, 1971. A brief discussion of labeling theory.

*SIMMONS, J. L.: *Deviants,* Glendessary Press, Berkeley, Cal., 1969. A brief, simply written paperback describing sympathetically the process of becoming a deviant and the life of deviants.

Three/Social organization

This section describes how society is organized. People are not independent units, like grains of sand on the beach. The members of a society are organized into many kinds of groups, organizations, and relationships. Chapter 8, "Social Groups," describes the kinds of groups which appear in any society—ours in particular. Chapter 9, "Social Institutions," describes how the norms of the culture and the relationships of a society are organized into working systems in order to meet people's needs. Chapter 10, "The Family," is a detailed description of one of these social institutions—probably the most important. Chapter 11, "Formal Organizations," describes the associational structures through which a complex society operates. Chapter 12, "Social Class," describes an extremely important set of status relationships among individuals, and shows how these relationships affect their entire lives. Chapter 13, "Social Mobility," shows how people change their class status.

Chapter 8 •Social groups

Take each of us alone, a man apart from the Cheyenne people who remember the same things and wish for the same things. Take each one of us that way, and you have nothing but a man who cannot respect himself because he is a failure in the white man's way. A man who does not respect himself cannot make a good future. There is no strength in his spirit. Now take all of us together as Cheyenne people. Then our names are not the names of failures. They are the names of great and generous hunters who fed the people, fighters who died for freedom just as white men's heroes died, holy men who filled us with the power of God. Take us together that way and there is a drink for every man in the cup of self-respect, and we will have the strength of spirit to decide what to do and to do it. We will do good things as a tribe that is growing and changing that we cannot do as individual men cut off from their forefathers. *(From an introduction to a Northern Cheyenne land consolidation program, quoted in* Indian Affairs, *Newsletter of the Association on American Indian Affairs, Inc., no. 37, New York, June, 1960.)*

At 24, Steve had a long record of success. Unusually enterprising, he was already making money at the age of 13 by importing and selling Japanese toys at Christmas time. He had done well in college and also in business, so well that he used to spend $300 for his suits and could quit work and go to California with $25,000 in ready money. While there, he decided to experiment with encounter groups at Esalen and soon became absorbed in the movement full time. . . . He later became a group leader, built a cabin in the mountains near by, took occasional acid trips, and wrote in his diary: "This is such a weird place. . . . Somehow I'm still not dead, although for the first time in my life I've begun to look carefully at the possibility." On Feb. 9, 1971, in a craft shop on the grounds at Esalen, Steve picked up a Hawes .357 Magnum revolver and killed himself. *(Adapted from Bruce Maliver,* The Encounter Game, *Stein and Day, New York, 1973, pp. 109–127. Reprinted by permission of the author and his agent, Raines & Raines.)*

Many Americans of Cheyenne ancestry have been able to build successful lives without participating in tribal life, and few persons participating in encounter groups have the disastrous experience of Steve. Some appear to have been helped. It is likely that few groups are entirely positive or entirely negative in their effects on group members, but the effects of the group upon the individual are profound. All people, regardless of race or culture, find personality fulfillment through group life. The infant becomes "human" as it takes its place in the family. As the child moves beyond the family circle, it enters into still other group relationships which will continuously remold its personality until death ends the process.

While "group" is one of the most important concepts in sociology, there is no complete agreement upon a single definition. Such confusion is not because sociologists can't make up their minds! Confusions persist because most concepts (in sociology) are not invented and then put into use; instead, most sociological terms are words which have long been in general use and which sociologists come to use with a particular meaning. Some terms continue to be used with more than one meaning, because to invent an entirely new set of several words to cover the several meanings would be even more confusing.

Consequently, there are several meanings of "group" in the sociological literature. In one usage, the term denotes *any physical collection of people* (e.g., "a group of people were waiting . . ."). In this usage, a group need share nothing beyond physical proximity. Many sociologists would call such a collection of people an *aggregation* or a *collectivity.*

A second meaning is that of *a number of people who share some common characteristic.* Thus, males, college graduates, physicians, old people, millionaires, commuters, and cigarette smokers would each be a group. *Category* would be a more satisfactory term, but sociologists often use "group" where "category" would be more precise, but perhaps would read more clumsily.

Another usage defines a group as *a number of people who share some organized patterns of recurrent interaction.* This would exclude all casual, momentary meetings of people whose interaction has no pattern of organization or repetition, such as the spectators at a traffic accident. This definition would include the family, the friendship clique, organizations like a club or church organization—any kind of collective contact between people who repeatedly interact according to some pattern of customary procedures and relationships.

Another quite common usage (which your authors prefer) is *any number of persons who share a consciousness of membership and of interaction.* By this definition, two persons waiting for a bus would not be a group, but would become a group if they started a conversation, a fight, or any other interaction. A number of people walking down a street would be an *aggregation* or a *collectivity,* not a group, unless something—a street orator, an accident, a suicide—caught their attention and held their interest, converting them into an *audience,* which is one kind of group (see pp. 372–373). A busload of passengers would not ordinarily be a group because they have no consciousness of interaction with each other but simply happen to be in the same place at the same time. It is possible that interaction may develop in the course of the trip and groups may form. When children begin to play together, or boy meets girl, or businessmen discover a common interest in the stock market or the baseball game, groups begin to develop—transient and amorphous though they be. On occasion the entire aggregate may become a group, as in this instance related by Bierstedt.

Subway passengers in New York, for example, are notoriously indifferent to one another. But only the slightest stimulus is needed to transform [them] . . . into a social group. The writer was in a fairly crowded car one evening in the spring when a very young, very tipsy Scandinavian sailor happened to stroll in from the adjoining car. He began to sing aloud in his native language, a gay pleasant song, and the passengers, aroused from their reveries and their newspapers, responded warmly to his effort and began to exchange smiles with one another. With unexpected and indeed, unusual solicitude for subway passengers, several of the men in the car asked the sailor where he wanted to go and made sure that he did not ride past his destination. After he left, the remaining passengers, augmented now by others who were strangers to the episode, returned to their reveries and their newspapers. The spell was broken. What for a few transitory moments had been a social group became once again . . . people with no more in common than their accidental togetherness at the same time and place, enough to give them a consciousness of kind but not enough, without this extra stimulus, to induce them to enter into social relations with one another. (From *The Social Order* by Robert Bierstedt, p. 283. Copyright © 1970 by McGraw-Hill Book Company. Used with permission of McGraw-Hill Book Company.)

The essence of the social group is not physical closeness but a consciousness of joint interaction. The passengers in the subway car were close together, but until the entry of the sailor gave them a common interest, they were not engaged in joint interaction. Other kinds of stimulus incidents may change an aggregation into a group. For example, a rate increase for passenger fares or a threat to discontinue commuter service may change an unstructured aggregation of passengers into an effective, selfconscious group, developing the usual group patterns as they seek to safeguard a privilege which they might lose. This consciousness of interaction depends on many factors and may be present even when there is no personal interaction between individuals. Thus we are members of a national group and think of ourselves as nationals even though we are acquainted with only a tiny fraction of those who make up our nation. Nevertheless, we interact through political campaigns, the payment of taxes, the use of government services, the response to symbols such as the flag and the national anthem, and perhaps most of all through our consciousness that as citizens of one nation we are bound together in a way that distinguishes us from the citizens of other nations. Thus the term "group" covers a wide variety of kinds of human association.

The group and the individual

Our individualistic ethos tempts us to assume that we are in full command of our behavior and blinds us to the degree to which individual behavior is controlled by group experience. This assumption is revealed by the popular reaction to the announcement that some American soldiers held prisoner by the Chi-

nese in the Korean War had collaborated with the enemy. There was a popular disposition to blame individual weaknesses and character defects, but a more scientific inquiry found that the captured soldiers had been demoralized by a systematic attack upon their group loyalties.

Physical hardship, poor food, limited medical attention, and inadequate shelter played a part in weakening the resistance of the American prisoners, but these conditions were not considered sufficiently severe to account for their behavior. Torture and, more frequently, the threat of torture did take place on occasion but affected only a minority of the prisoners. The major means of demoralization used by the Chinese was something more powerful than physical force—*the systematic attack upon group ties,* described by Biderman [1960] and Schein [1960]. Just as "dying is easy for anyone left alone in a concentration camp,"[1] death came easily to prisoners of war who were isolated from their fellows.

The Chinese used such techniques as solitary confinement, isolation of small groups of prisoners, and frequent shifting of personnel to hamper the formation or survival of cohesive groups. More important, they also sought to divide the prisoners in their attitude to each other and to cut off the prisoners from any feeling of effective links with the homeland. Casual information gathered in interviews was used to convince them that all other Americans were informers and that they might as well give in too. If a prisoner resisted what he thought were improper demands from the Chinese, the whole unit was denied food or a chance to sleep until the objector had been forced to come round by his own buddies.

By contrast with the Korean War, the Vietnam conflict produced proportionately fewer examples of "incorrect" behavior among American POWs. This does not mean that all American captives were consistently heroic in resisting improper demands by the North Viet-

[1]An anonymous concentration-camp survivor, quoted in *Life,* Aug. 18, 1958, p. 90.

namese. Confronted by many forms of torture, inadequate diet, casual and sporadic medical care, infrequent mail from home and the possibility of additional punishment by being placed in solitary confinement in cramped quarters, some Americans did make statements which were used in North Vietnam propaganda broadcasts. However, when compared with the Korean experience, there was proportionately less open collaboration, fewer deaths during the time of imprisonment, and a generally higher sense of morale and unity among the POWs.[2]

This change is usually attributed to a system of training instituted after the Korean War which stressed that, above all else, a POW must keep in communication with other POWs and obey the senior American officer at all times. He was no longer a lonely and abandoned individual, but a part of a functioning group. It wasn't easy to do, since the North Vietnamese frequently moved the prisoners, seldom kept them in large groups and tried to restrict communication.

In spite of these difficulties, the Americans (mostly aviation personnel) organized in military style, calling themselves the "Allied Prisoner of War Wing." They organized a command structure which had effective power and could give orders to POWs threatened by their captors. A claim which may be extreme, but which seems to have been borne out by the behavior of many of the men, was made by the ranking officer in the prison compound, known facetiously as the "Hanoi Hilton": "We had a comradeship amongst us, a loyalty, an integrity which may never be found again in any group of men" [Risner, 1973].

The role of the maintenance of communication and group ties in sustaining morale among American POWs is especially striking, since American public opinion was sharply divided about the legitimacy of our war in Vietnam. The North Vietnamese constantly reminded the POWs of this antiwar feeling, but apparently with little effect on POW attitude or behavior.

In this respect the behavior of American POWs in Vietnam is similar to the way the German army survived years of unbroken defeats in World War II. During the war the Allies nursed the hope that "psychological warfare" could undermine the German soldier's faith in his cause and his loyalty to his government and thus impair his fighting morale. Postwar studies [Shils and Janowitz, 1948] have shown that this approach was not very effective. It was rooted in the unsound theory that the soldier is sustained mainly by loyalty to his country and faith in the rightness of its cause, whereas postwar investigations found that he is sustained mainly by his unity with, and loyalty to, the small military units to which he is attached. As long as the soldier's immediate group—the primary group which we shall analyze within a few pages—remained integrated, he continued to resist. Even those who were critical of their "cause" remained effective soldiers because of their group loyalties. Among the comparatively few German deserters, their failure to have become fully absorbed into the primary-group life of the army was far more important than any political or ideological doubts. Long after their cause was clearly lost, most German units of all sizes continued to resist until their supplies were exhausted or they were physically overwhelmed.

Is it only in warfare that the individual develops a sacrificial loyalty and a leonine courage? By no means. We cite research on military groups (even though some may find this displeasing) because they have been more intensively studied than most other kinds of groups, and from this study we have learned something about groups of all kinds. We see how the group is a vital social reality, with profound effect upon the behavior of individuals in all social situations. Cut a man off from all group ties, and in many cases he will soon sicken and die; unite him in group loyalty and his endurance and sacrifice are almost beyond belief.

---

[2]"Korea Lessons Saved POWs," UPI dispatch, Feb. 15, 1973.

Some major group classifications

In-groups and out-groups

There are some groups to which I belong—my family, my church, my clique, my profession, my race, my sex, my nation—any group which I precede with the pronoun, "my." These are *in-groups,* because I feel I belong to them. There are other groups to which I do not belong—other families, cliques, occupations, races, nationalities, religions, the other sex— these are *out-groups,* for I am outside of them.

The least advanced primitive societies live in small, isolated bands which are usually clans of kinsmen. It was kinship which determined the nature of the in-group and the out-group, and when two strangers met, the first thing they had to do was establish relationship. If kinship could be established, then they were friends—both members of the in-group. If no relationship could be established, then in many societies they were enemies and acted accordingly.

Modern society is based upon many ties besides those of kinship, but the establishment and definition of in-groups is equally important to us. People placed in a new social situation will usually make cautious conversational feints to find out whether or not they "belong." When we find ourselves among people who are of our own social class, our religion, our political views, and who are interested in the same types of sports or music, then we may have some assurance that we are in an in-group. Members of the in-group are likely to share certain sentiments, laugh at the same jokes, and define with some unanimity the activities and goals of life. Members of the out-group may share many of the same cultural traits, but do not share whatever is necessary for inclusion in this particular in-group.

In modern society, we find that individuals belong to so many groups that a number of their in-group and out-group relationships may overlap. A member of a senior class will consider that a freshman belongs to an out-group;

In-groups and out-groups.

yet the same senior and freshman may both be members of an athletic team in which they have an in-group relationship to each other. Similarly, men who have an in-group relationship as members of the same church may be in different political parties; women who work together in the PTA may find that they are no longer in the same in-group when plans are made for a party at the country club.

The fact that in-group and out-group classifications cut across many lines does not minimize their intensity; the subtlety of some distinctions makes exclusion even more painful. We may crave membership in a group which excludes us. Thus the "new rich" who have all the surface qualifications for admittance to "society" may still find themselves excluded from the social register. The teen-age boy who hopes desperately for acceptance may find that no clique welcomes him; the housewife may be left out of the coffee klatsch; and the man on a work gang may find himself the butt of ridicule rather than one of a group of comfortable companions. Exclusion from the in-group can be a brutal process. Most primitive societies treated outsiders as part of the animal kingdom; many had no separate words for "enemy" and "stranger," showing that they made no distinction. Not too different was the attitude of the Nazis, who excluded the Jews from the

TABLE 7 RANKING OF ETHNIC GROUPS BY SOCIAL DISTANCE SCORES (S.D.S.) BY MEXICAN-AMERICAN STUDENTS AND "OTHER WHITE" STUDENTS ON A TEXAS COLLEGE CAMPUS IN 1971, AND BY AFRIKAANS-SPEAKING SOUTH AFRICANS IN 1968

Mexican-Americans			"Other Whites"		
Order	Ethnic group	S.D.S.	Order	Ethnic group	S.D.S.
1.	Mexican-Americans	1.08	1.	American (U.S. whites)	1.04
2.	Mexicans	1.09	2.	English	1.15
3.	Spanish	1.12	3.	Canadians	1.19
4.	Americans (U.S. whites)	1.28	4.	Swedish	1.23
5.	Italians	1.38	5.	French	1.27
6.	British	1.39	6.	Norwegians	1.35
7.	Indians (American)	1.57	7.	Hollanders	1.36
8.	Hollanders	1.88	8.	Finns	1.49
9.	Negroes	1.95	9.	Indians (American)	1.60
10.	Germans	1.95	10.	Mexican-Americans	1.75
11.	Jews	2.41	11.	Mexicans	1.95
12.	Chinese	2.44	12.	Negroes	2.13
13.	Japanese	2.54	13.	Chinese/Japanese	2.17
14.	Turks	2.61	14.	Russians	2.33
15.	Russians	2.76	15.	Turks	2.36
16.	Koreans	2.80	16.	Indians (India)	2.45
17.	Indians (India)	2.94	17.	Koreans	2.48

Source: Adapted from Robert L. Brown, "Social Distance Perception as a Function of Mexican-American and Other Ethnic Identity," *Sociology and Social Research*, 57, April, 1973, p. 278, and H. Lever, "Changes in Ethnic Attitude in South Africa," *Sociology and Social Research*, 56, January, 1972, p. 206.

human race. Rudolf Hoess, who commanded the Auschwitz concentration camp in which 700,000 Jews were put to death, characterized this slaughter as "the removal of racial-biological foreign bodies."[3]

In-groups and out-groups are important, then, because they affect behavior. From fellow members of an in-group, we expect recognition, loyalty, and helpfulness. From out-groups, our expectation varies with the kind of out-group. From some out-groups we expect hostility; from others, a more or less friendly competition; from still others, indifference. From the sex out-group we may expect neither hostility nor indifference; yet in our behavior a difference undeniably remains. The twelve-year-old boy who shuns girls grows up to become a romantic lover and spends most of his

life in matrimony. Yet when men and women meet on social occasions they tend to split into one-sex groups, for each sex is bored by many of the conversational interests of the other.

Social distance. We are not equally involved in all our in-groups. One might, for example, be a passionate Democrat and a rather indifferent Rotarian. Nor do we feel equally distant from all our out-groups. A loyal Democrat will feel far closer to the Republicans than to the Communists. Bogardus [1958, 1959] and others [Westie, 1959] have developed the concept *social distance* to measure the *degree of closeness or acceptance we feel* toward other groups. While most often used with reference to racial groups, social distance refers to closeness among groups of all kinds.

Social distance is measured either by direct observation of the relationships which people have with other groups, or more often by questionnaires in which people are asked the relationships in which they would accept or reject

[3]See Rudolf Hoess, *Commandant of Auschwitz*, tr by Constantine Fitzgibbon, The World Publishing Company, Cleveland, 1960, in which Hoess tells with nostalgic pride how efficiently he organized this operation; reviewed in *Time*, Mar. 28, 1960, p. 110.

Afrikaan Speakers		
Order	Ethnic group	S.D.S.
1.	Afrikaans-speaking South Africans	1.16
2.	English-speaking South Africans	1.45
3.	British	2.30
4.	Hollanders	2.47
5.	Germans	2.55
6.	Jews	2.94
7.	Italians	3.86
8.	Greeks	3.94
9.	Portuguese	4.61
10.	Chinese	5.07
11.	Coloreds	5.23
12.	Africans	5.40
13.	Japanese	5.32
14.	Indians	5.71
15.	Russians	5.95

members of certain other groups. In these questionnaires, a number of groups may be listed and the informants asked to check whether they would accept a member of each group as a neighbor, as a fellow worker, as a marriage partner, and so on through a series of relationships.

Table 7 shows a study of social distance reactions of two groups: (1) students in a Texas college classified as Anglo-Americans and as Other Whites, and (2) Afrikaans-speaking South Africans. The lower the score, the more favorable the reaction. A score of 1 indicates complete acceptance in all relationships, a score of 2 indicates indifference rather than acceptance, and higher scores indicate increasing degrees of rejection. By categories, the greatest acceptance was as a fellow worker and the most frequent rejection was as a marriage partner.

By comparison with earlier studies, this test would indicate that social distance in the United States is lessening. The overall score for the

Texas school (Mexican-Americans and Other Whites combined) was 1.43. In 1926, a national sample showed an overall score of 2.14, while in a 1966 study it was 1.92 [Brown, 1973, p. 276]. The similar survey of social distance attitudes in 1968 among White Afrikaans-speaking South Africans came up with a social distance score of 5.40 toward black Africans and an average score for fifteen different ethnic groups of 3.86. A similar test in 1964 showed a slightly lower social distance score of 3.65 [Lever, 1972].

The higher scores for South Africans would presumably indicate a greater polarization of ethnic attitudes both between blacks and whites and between ethnic groups in general than is true in the United States. The increase in social distance scores in South Africa is too small to be statistically significant and might be the result of sampling error, but would at least tend to indicate that there was no decrease in ethnic polarization in the Republic of South Africa during that four-year period. Both the South African and the Texas tests indicate a tendency to accept one's own group as first preference and to indicate high social distance toward groups which seem to be sharply differentiated, either physically or culturally, from one's own. It is also interesting that, except for their own groups and those closely related, the Mexican-American and the "Other White" students showed a high degree of similarity in the social distance rankings they gave to the various ethnic groups. This similarity between the rankings of the two groups illustrates a tendency for the minority group to accept the social definitions of the majority.

The social-distance questionnaires may not accurately measure what people actually would do if a member of another group sought to become a friend or neighbor. The social-distance scale is only an attempt to measure one's feeling of unwillingness to associate equally with a group. What a person will actually do in a situation also depends upon the circumstances of the situation (situational determinants of behavior), which will be illustrated at some length in the chapter on race and ethnic relations.

Reference groups. There are groups which are important to us as models even though we ourselves may not be a part of the group. The opinions of "high society" may be important to the social climber who has not yet made the social register. At times the in-group and the reference group may be the same, as when the teen-ager gives more weight to the opinions of the gang than to those of his or her teachers. Sometimes an out-group is a reference group: American Indians wore war paint to impress their enemies, and little boys (of all ages!) show off to impress girls. A reference group is any group to which we *refer* when making judgments—any group whose value judgments become our value judgments. You will recall that we mentioned the concept of reference group when speaking of the "looking-glass" self, indicating that the young child is interested in the reactions of everyone with whom it is in contact, while the more mature person selects particular groups whose approval—or whose disapproval—he or she especially desires.

Stereotypes. Out-groups are generally perceived in terms of stereotypes. A *stereotype* is *a group-shared image of another group or category of people.* Stereotypes can be positive (the kindly, dedicated family doctor), negative, (the unprincipled, opportunistic politician), or mixed (the dedicated, fussy, sexless old-maid school teacher). Stereotypes are applied indiscriminately to all members of the stereotyped group, without allowance for individual differences. Stereotypes are never entirely untrue, for they must bear *some* resemblance to the characteristics of the persons stereotyped or they would not be recognized. But stereotypes are always distorted, in that they exaggerate and universalize *some* of the characteristics of *some* of the members of the stereotyped group.

Just how stereotypes begin is not known. Once the stereotype has become a part of the culture, it is maintained by *selective percep-*

tion (noting only the confirming incidents or cases and failing to note or remember the exceptions), *selective interpretation* (interpreting observations in terms of the stereotype: e.g., Jews are "pushy" while gentiles are "ambitious"), *selective identification* ("they look like school teachers . . ."), and *selective exception* ("he really doesn't act at all Jewish"). All of these processes involve a reminder of the stereotype, so that even the exceptions and the incorrect identifications serve to feed and sustain the stereotype.

Stereotypes are nonetheless constantly changing. The dowdy old-maid school teacher is so rare today that this particular stereotype is virtually dead. A stereotype dies when confirming illustrations can no longer be found. Unflattering racial and ethnic stereotypes have become unfashionable in the mass media today (and, besides, the offended groups today are prepared to make effective protest against unflattering or inaccurate stereotypes). Racial and ethnic humor has almost entirely disappeared from the stage and screen, while the villain today rarely has any recognizable racial, ethnic, national, religious, or occupational identity.

The stereotyping process is continual. Any long-haired, bearded, blue-denimed youth today is likely to be treated as a hippie, even though relatively few of these youths share the hippie subculture. But the stereotyping process runs both ways, as the following letter from *Playboy* magazine reveals:

I am one who was born too late for the hippie movement. I sympathize with its goals and philosophy, but I've dressed and looked like a straight person all my life and it would be phony for me to change my appearance at this point. One night, a friend and I, wearing jackets and ties and relatively short hair visited a popular hippie coffeehouse in Los Angeles. We'd no sooner sat down than we hear someone loudly say, "There are two narcs in the room." The remarks, for our benefit, got more and more threatening, till we decided, for the sake of peace and love, to leave our expresso unfinished and departed. (John Hawkins, in *Playboy,* December, 1970, p. 18.)

Stereotypes are maintained by selective perception.

Stereotypes are important because people treat members of other groups in terms of the stereotyped views they hold of that group. They interact, at least initially, with the stereotype rather than with the true person. This results in many individual injustices, since only some of the persons in a group fully fit the stereotype. Most important, however, is the tendency for interaction in terms of stereotypes to encourage people to become more like the stereotype. In this sense, the stereotype is an example of a "self-fulfilling prophesy." In Chapter 5, we learned how people tend to become whatever other people seem to think they are (the "looking-glass self"). Thus the stereotype tends to mold group behavior in the direction of the stereotype. It is highly likely, for example, that the "pig" stereotype of the police officer serves to increase police brutality rather than to inspire a sympathetic sensitivity among the police.

Primary and secondary groups

Primary groups are those in which we come to know other people intimately as individual personalities. We do this through social contacts that are *intimate, personal,* and *total* in that they involve many parts of the person's life experience. In the primary group, such as family, clique, or set of close friends, the social relationships tend to be informal and relaxed. The members are interested in one another as persons. They confide hopes and fears, share experiences, gossip agreeably, and fill the need for intimate human companionship. In the *secondary group* the social contacts are *impersonal, segmental,* and *utilitarian.* One is not concerned with the other person as a person, but as a functionary who is filling a role. Personal qualities are not important; performance—only that part, or segment, of the total personality involved in playing a role—is important. The secondary group might be a labor union or a trade association, a country club, or a PTA, or it might be two persons bargaining briefly over a store counter. In any case the group exists to serve a specific, limited purpose involving only a segment of the personalities of the members.

Primary groups persist in a secondary-group dominated world.

The terms "primary" and "secondary" thus describe a type of relationship rather than the relative importance of the group. The primary group may serve objective functions such as the provision of food and clothing, but it is judged by the quality of its human relationships rather than by its efficiency in meeting material needs. The secondary group may function in pleasant surroundings, but its principal purpose is to fulfill a specific function. One does not consider a home "good" just because the house is clean. Primary groups are not judged so much by their "efficiency" in performing some task as by the emotional satisfactions they bring to their members. Thus the quartet of ladies who meet for bridge Tuesday afternoons may play a pretty indifferent bridge game but share a lot of pleasant, gossipy conversation. Tournament and duplicate bridge are another matter. Here, virtual or total strangers meet and play to win. A "good partner" is a skillful player who wastes no time on distracting small talk. The major goal is a winning score (and master points chalked up), not sociability. A good lunch-table clique is one that has fun; a good labor union is one that succeeds in protecting its members' interests. Primary groups are judged by the satisfying human response they supply; secondary groups are judged by their ability to perform a task or achieve a goal. Although secondary groups sometimes also provide pleasant human relationships, sociability is ordinarily not their goal. In brief, *primary groups are relationship-oriented,* whereas *secondary groups are goal-oriented.*

Primary and secondary groups are important because feelings and behavior are different. It is in the primary group that personality is formed. In the primary group one finds intimacy, sympathy, and a comfortable sharing of many interests and activities. In the secondary group one finds an effective mechanism for achieving certain purposes, but often at the price of suppressing one's true feelings. For example, the saleslady must be cheerful and polite, even when she has a splitting headache and the customer is a boor. The concepts are useful because they describe important differences in behavior.

Gemeinschaft and gesellschaft

Somewhat similar to the concepts of primary and secondary groups are the concepts of *Gemeinschaft* and *Gesellschaft,* developed by the German sociologist Ferdinand Tönnies [1887, tr. 1957]. These two terms translate roughly as "community" and "society." The gemeinschaft is a social system in which most relationships are personal or traditional, and often both. A good example is the feudal manor, a small community held together by a combination of personal relationships and status obligations. Although great inequality existed, the lord of the manor was personally known to his subjects, while their duties to him were balanced by his obligation for their welfare. When money was used, economic transactions were governed by the concepts of a just price; more often the people involved simply carried out a network of customary obligations to one another. Written documents were scarce, formal contracts unknown, bargaining rare, and behavior of all types operated in traditional patterns that were known and accepted by all the community. Children had little hope of surpassing their parents and equally little fear of falling behind the parental status. Except for occasional feast days, life was monotonous; but loneliness was rare in a community of lifelong neighbors.

In the gesellschaft, the society of tradition is replaced with the society of contract. In this society neither personal attachment nor traditional rights and duties are important. The relationships between people are determined by bargaining and defined in written agreements. Relatives are separated as people move about and live among strangers. Commonly accepted codes of behavior have less force than rational—or "cold-blooded"—calculation of profit and loss. The gesellschaft flourishes in the modern metropolitan city. Some of the contrasting characteristics of gesellschaft and gemeinschaft relationships are summarized in this table:

GEMEINSCHAFT RELATIONSHIPS	GESELLSCHAFT RELATIONSHIPS
Personal	Impersonal
Informal	Formal, contractual
Traditional	Utilitarian
Sentimental	Realistic, "hard-boiled"
General	Specialized

Modern trend toward secondary-group association

Our sentiments and emotional ties are centered in primary groups, but an accelerating trend toward a gesellschaft society based on secondary groups has been irresistible in the modern era. The small principalities of feudal Europe have given way to national states, and the intimate association of master and workmen in the guild workshop has yielded to the giant corporation employing thousands of people. Population has moved from the country to the city, and lifetime residence in familiar surroundings has become a rarity as approximately one American family in five moves each year.

An industrialized urban society attacks the primary group in at least two ways. First, it increases the relative proportion of secondary-group contacts, as one activity after another is withdrawn from the primary group and assumed as a secondary-group function. Second, the primary-group associations which remain are at the mercy of secondary-group needs. Changes in industry may move the wage earner about, disrupting his local associations. Industrial changes also influence the roles played in the family. A prolonged depression, the result of a maladjustment of secondary relationships, may deprive the father of his earning power and substitute the wife and the relief administrator as symbols of authority. Changes in office and factory work lead to the employment of women, so that the mother has the same kind of career as the father, and both share in the domestic tasks of the home. Changes in the international political scene may take the husband or son out of the family and move him to the other side of the world. The worker's family must adjust itself to whatever working hours the corporation finds most profitable. Negotiations between the international union and the corporation may result in work changes which break up informal primary groups formed on the job. The "little red schoolhouse" where a small group of children

and a teacher formed an intimate primary group lasting for years is succeeded by the consolidated school, drawing hundreds of children from a large area and shifting them about from class to class and teacher to teacher. Scores of similar examples show how primary groupings have become transient and changing units, swept along by the heedlessly changing trends of a gesellschaft society.

Durkheim [1897], in his study of suicide, came to the conclusion that not only high rates of suicide but many other behavior difficulties are explained by the lack of traditional and personal ties in a secondary society, where the individual is engulfed by anomie. Many students of society have followed his lead in regarding the secondary trends of the modern world as an evil force, destructive of the relationships that assured people of membership in a warm and secure society where their tendencies toward crime or despair were curbed by their obligations to a stable and intimate social community.

Contributions of the gesellschaft

While the gesellschaft has brought problems, it has also brought benefits. The most obvious is the efficiency of large-scale impersonal organizations in which sentiment is subordinated to the need to get the job done in the most practical way. The tremendous advances in material comfort and in life expectancy in the modern world would be impossible without the rise of goal-directed secondary organizations, in which the paternal squire has been replaced by the efficiency expert and the production manager.

Nor has the rise of the gesellschaft and the accompanying division of labor had only materialistic advantages. These changes have opened channels of opportunity and specializations of function which, while they fragment society, also open a greater chance to develop individual talents. Much has been written about how modern societies are "oppressive" and "alienating"; yet earlier societies offered far fewer choices and opportunities for self-fulfillment. The contrast between the thousands of occupations in the metropolis and the handful of pursuits in the rural village shows how a society dominated by secondary groups opens the way for specialized careers. This process has gone so far today that not only is the talented individual able to rise from an obscure background but society actively seeks out those whose abilities may be developed along professional, artistic, scientific, or managerial lines.

The secondary group also has a tendency to impose patterns of conformity on its members. In this way it offers a counterbalance to the prejudices or vested interests of the immediate locality. Since its boundaries extend beyond the primary group, it forces a consideration of events from a larger perspective. This difference in attitudes may be seen in the tendency of religious organizations, operating on a national or international scale, to espouse viewpoints which may be unpopular in local congregations. The reaction of the Southern Baptist Churches to the school-integration issue is a case in point. With a membership of white Southerners, most congregations were strongly segregationist in their beliefs and practices. Prominent members, including some pastors, were active in the efforts to keep racial separation in the schools. Nevertheless, when meeting as a national body somewhat removed from the pressures of local groups, the convention of the Southern Baptist Churches voted to *endorse* the 1954 Supreme Court decision for school desegregation [Fey, 1954]. A similar type of reaction to the segregation issue occurred among Roman Catholics in Louisiana. Here the violently segregationist stand of local Catholics contrasted sharply with support for integration by the church as a whole, as voiced by the Archbishop [*America*, 1957].

Lest these be viewed as isolated incidents peculiar to an especially violent racial controversy, we should add that this disparity between national and local views is common in many church groups on many questions. For example, a study [Glock and Ringer, 1956] of the Protestant Episcopal Church showed a wide divergence between statements of the national body and views of members of local congregations on eight out of nine issues. Such a divergence between national and local sentiment is sometimes attributed either to hypocrisy at the local level or to a misrepresentation of the "real" views of the organization at the national level. A more penetrating analysis would emphasize the fact that while the local group and the national organization interact, the national body has concerns which may override local feelings.

It is probable that such divergences reflect a difference between those who are professionally associated with the nationally organized secondary group and those who see their major connection with the local group; in the case of churches, this often means clergy and laity. Thus a 1967 survey found that 86 percent of the laity, but only 35 percent of the clergy, subscribed to a statement that blacks would be better off if they took advantage of available opportunities rather than spending time protesting [Hadden, 1969, p. 141].

This tendency for the national organization to be more universal in its judgments and the local units to be more particularistic—that is, influenced by local concerns and personal attitudes—is not confined to churches and may be observed in the deliberations of business, labor, and political organizations. The emphasis on goals rather than on personal relationships and the need to accommodate a large number of individuals and localities tend toward an outlook which reaches beyond the primary group. Such an outlook is, however, not necessarily more liberal or humanitarian. Communist Russia and Nazi Germany are extreme examples of situations in which the goals of secondary organizations demanded action which violated the local code of human decency. The expulsion of the more well-to-do peasants in Russia from their farms and the large-scale use of concentration camps in Germany were motivated by goals beyond the usual concern of a local community, but they diminished rather than increased the area of human fellowship. Secondary groups may restrain local greed and shatter the bonds of provincialism, or they may let loose a ruthless force which transgresses the traditional mores in pursuit of organizational goals.

Persistence of primary groups

The secondary group has overshadowed but not destroyed the primary group. In fact, the two major primary groups, the clique and the family, appear to be stronger than ever. The clique is a small group of intimates with intense in-group feelings based on common sentiments and interests. It may develop in almost any situation, and nearly every secondary group shelters a large number of cliques which add a highly personal note to an otherwise impersonal organization. As for the family, in spite of a high divorce rate and some experimentation with communal living, most of the world's population still live in families and probably always will. Furthermore, today's family is steadily becoming less directed toward mundane goals and more concerned with human relationships. Yesterday's family was primarily a work crew, sometimes a brutally repressive one; today's family is primarily a companionship group and a perfect example of primary-group persistence.

Primary groups persist in a secondary-group-dominated world because the human need for intimate, sympathetic association is a continuous need. Most people cannot function well unless they belong to a small group of people who really care what happens to them. Wherever people are ripped from family and friends and thrust into large, impersonal, anonymous groups, as in a college dormitory or an army camp, they feel such great need for primary groups that they promptly re-form them.

Primary groups in a secondary setting

If we classified groups according to the extent to which they show primary- or secondary-group traits, the result would be a listing of secondary groups such as the army, the corporation, and the national state, and a list of primary groups such as the family, the clique, and the gang. Proceeding in this fashion, we should then contrast the impersonal goal-directed nature of the large organization with the personal, relationship-oriented focus of smaller intimate groups. Such a separation is often assumed when we attempt to analyze the efficiency of large organizations. If we are interested in the productivity of industrial labor, we might study the goals, techniques, and rewards of the factory and then look at the character and training of the individuals who make up the labor force.

The fallacy of this approach is that it overlooks the extent to which every large organization is a network of small primary groups. A person is not simply a unit in an organization chart designed by top management; he or she is also a member of a smaller informal group with its own structure and its own system of statuses and roles which define the behavior of its members. In the factory the worker finds a place in a group of peers with its own leadership, from which the foreman is usually excluded, since the very position precludes this in-group relationship. Since workers need the approval and support of the clique more than the approval of their supervisors, they respond to the demands of management only as these demands are consistent with their in-group relationships.

New norms cannot be effective unless they are also accepted by the group.

The influence of the primary group is one reason why incentive pay plans giving the worker a bonus for greater output have frequently been ineffective. The logic of such plans is that many workers who fail to exert their maximum efforts will work harder if paid in proportion to the work they do. The major defect in such plans is that their effective operation destroys the unity of primary groups. Rather than a number of equals cooperating together, the work gang would become a number of competing individuals each striving to outdo the others. Aside from the strain of continuous competition, this situation threatens the workers' social relationships. As a defense, factory cliques develop a norm of a "fair day's work." The worker who attempts to ignore this norm is the butt of ridicule, ostracism, and possible violence. Management may employ time and motion study experts to decide a "reasonable" output, but new norms cannot be effective unless they are also accepted by the group [Davis, 1972, pp. 488–490].

While the primary group in the secondary setting can be an obstacle, it can also be a positive aid in the accomplishment of organizational objectives. [Miller and Form, 1964, pp. 282–283]. Gross has examined the way in which informal cliques that cut across formal work assignments may lead to cooperation and smoother functioning of the organization. He finds that the clique may even reinforce the idea of organization loyalty, as one private secretary reveals:

A private secretary is the top of the heap. You need something else beside the ability to type and take shorthand. You've got to feel that you are working for the company and not just for yourself. Now Mildred and Emma [other private secretaries], we see eye to eye on that. Louise—she's a good little stenographer, but she'll never be a secretary. She doesn't fit into our crowd. When we go out for coffee she usually tags along. Then she'll complain about her boss. She can't accept the idea that you don't work for a boss, you work for the company. (Edward Gross, "Some Functional Consequences of Primary Controls in Formal Work Organizations," *American Sociological Review,* 18:372, August, 1953.)

At times the primary groups may even violate the rules of the larger secondary organization in order to get things done. If the formal rules are not always workable in all situations, primary worker groups simply trim some corners—that is, break a few rules—in order to get the work out [Roy, 1955].

Just as we cannot realistically consider the individual apart from society, so we cannot understand secondary and primary groups completely except in relation to each other. In modern society the functions and influence of primary groups have been weakened by a growth of impersonal, goal-directed secondary groups which are assuming an increasingly dominant role. Each of these secondary groups, however, creates a new network of primary groups that provide intimacy and personal response in an otherwise impersonal situation. While these and other primary groups are often destroyed or modified by the impact of secondary groups, the primary groups in turn exert a major influence on the secondary groups. Primary groups may resist the goal-directed efforts of secondary organizations, or they may help to integrate disparate parts of the organization, and provide an emotional security which reinforces the individual's ability to play the roles demanded by his or her status in the secondary group.

Group dynamics

For a long time sociologists were busy trying to convince a skeptical world that the group was real and not simply a collection of individuals. Only recently have sociologists turned their attention to the specific factors which affect the functioning of groups. *Group dynamics is the study of the relationships of group members to one another.* Obviously many possible patterns may occur. A group may be dominated by one or two individuals, or it may involve the participation of all its members; leadership may be democratic or authoritarian, transitory or enduring; the group may stimulate productivity or hold it down; its atmosphere may be relaxed and friendly or tense and charged with hostility; it may forge new approaches to problems or stick to old routines. These and many other patterns have often been observed. The question arises, "What factors produce one or another type of group life and how can these factors be controlled?"

The academic interest of sociologists in expanding the frontiers of knowledge in this area has been stimulated by demands from organizations who want help in solving their problems. Social agencies such as the Boy Scouts and the YMCA and YWCA wish to use leaders more effectively and secure more intensive participation from their members. Governmental bodies hope to make their employees more efficient and more responsive to the needs of the people. The armed forces are constantly revising their policies in the search for the type of organization which will lead to the most effective use of military personnel. Industrial corporations seek knowledge which will help them plan their work groups in a way to minimize friction and to secure the maximum efficiency in their operations. Reformers and revolutionists want to know how to organize and unify the groups whose potential they wish to mobilize.

These practical needs, joined by the intellectual curiosity of scholars, have led to a field of research usually labeled either "group dynamics" or "small-group research." Such research painstakingly records the interaction which actually occurs in group activities, oftentimes using such devices as a conference room in which oneway visibility enables observers to see the interaction and record conversations without being noticed by the participants. The problems to be solved are difficult because groups are affected both by the specific way in which they are organized and also by the general cultural background of their members. In spite of the complexities of the task, however, this type of research is gradually enlarging our understanding of how groups function [Strodtbeck and Hare, 1954; Bales, 1959; Cartwright and Zander, 1960; Mann, Gibbard, and

Hartman, 1967; T. Mills, 1967; Roby, 1968; Luft, 1970; Gibbard, Hartman and Mann, 1974.]

Enthusiasts for small-group research hope that insight into the operation of small groups may lead to an understanding of macro (large) societies. For instance, Freilich [1964] argues that the triangular relationship is not simply a feature of a romantic situation with more than two participants, but is a constant feature of all human groups both large and small. Freilich sees a "natural triad" consisting of one person who is a "high-status authority," another who is a "high-status friend," and a third who is a "low-status subordinate." He sees the struggle in human life as reflecting a constant shift of alliances between two members of the triad against the third. Research studies of this sort increase our understanding of human interaction.

Communication patterns

One of the important problems in any group is communication among its members. Communication is not merely a matter of the language spoken and the types of printed or audiovisual material used to get across messages, even though these are important. Communication is also a matter of the structure of the group and the physical and social proximity of its members. Any group must devise some way for its members to share their information. There are many possible ways of arranging the flow of communication, and possibly not all these patterns have the same effect on the work of the group and the relationship among its members.

The influence of different patterns of communication in a problem-solving group has been listed by Bavelas [1953]. He arranged groups of five men in different communications patterns which may be described as the circle, the chain, the Y, and the wheel. In the circle everyone had an equal chance to communicate with everyone else; in the other patterns the man at the center has maximum communication and the others were restricted. Morale and leadership turned out to be closely related to centrality of position. Member satisfaction with the situation was greatest in the circle, where no one man emerged as a leader. In the wheel, where the man in the center became the leader, production was greater but group satisfaction less. As an offset to its lower production, the circle was found to adapt more quickly to new tasks than the other patterns.

Effective communication promotes the individual's satisfaction with the group and enables him to express himself freely and to receive the impressions of others. A centralizing of communication focuses the attention of group members on specific topics and promotes a concentration of effort. The implications for the organization of school classrooms and industrial work plans depend on whether the major emphasis is on routine productivity or on developing flexibility and achieving satisfaction in the group situation. Research on the lecture versus the discussion method of college instruction, for instance, reports that students memorize as much even in very large groups with the lecture method (analogous to the wheel pattern) but that they have greater stimulus to do their own thinking in the discussion method (analogous to the circle pattern) [Bloom, 1954, pp. 37–38]. These are a few examples of how small-group research can help in solving practical problems.

Therapeutic and encounter groups

Alcoholics Anonymous organizes the emotional support of the group in the effort to help an alcoholic control the urge to drink. The Synanon Houses use similar group-therapy techniques for drug addicts; Weight Watchers helps people to lose weight; even cigarette smokers are trying the therapeutic group approach. There are also a number of groups organized to help the members live with a difficult affliction—relatives of alcoholics or drug addicts, relatives of mental patients, re-leased mental-hospital patients, homosexuals, dwarfs, blind people, the recently handicapped, and others [Sagarin, 1970]. This tendency for people who share an affliction to band together for understanding and mutual support in either overcoming or accepting it is a quite recent development.

Another relatively new form of group experience is the *encounter group,* broadly defined to include "all sensitivity, meditative, body, consciousness-expanding, and other current encounter experiences which take place in more than dyadic [two-person] groups" [Burton, 1969, p. 8n]. The objective of an encounter group may be educational, directed mainly at increased emotional and attitudinal learnings; or it may be therapeutic, seeking to help members understand themselves and interact more comfortably with others. But while the therapeutic groups mentioned above will unite in one group a number of persons sharing the same affliction, a single encounter group may include people with all sorts of problems.

The encounter-group movement is quite new, its theory is poorly developed, and its definitions and vocabulary are not established. The term "encounter group" thus covers a wide variety of kinds of group experience. The widely used term "T-group," an abbreviation for "training group," covers the entire range of manipulated group experience for the purpose of learning outcomes [Egan, 1970, p. 10]. The *sensitivity training* group is an educational encounter group which attempts to structure the communication within a group to maximize exchanges of meanings and attitudinal changes. It originated among educators seeking ways to stimulate learning [Golembiewski and Blumberg, 1970]. It later developed to include an effort to increase mutual understanding between hostile groups, such as management and labor, police and youth, blacks and whites, through a blunt, honest verbal confrontation in which each voiced attitudes and "gripes" at the "gut level" and presumably gained insights in the process [Bouma, 1969, pp. 149–153]. Such confrontations may increase sympathetic mutual understanding if skillfully conducted; otherwise they can easily confirm prejudices and intensify hostilities.

There is a highly-publicized commercialized encounter-group movement whose objective is primarily the improvement of personal adjustment. An estimated six million customers are attending encounter-group sessions organized by over a hundred centers in the United States [Maliver, 1971, 1973], patterned after the original provided by the Esalen Institute in California [Schutz, 1967]. Under more-or-less trained leaders, a number of people, usually strangers, will assemble, strip themselves of names, titles, social and professional statuses, all ordinary amenities and civilities, and sometimes clothing, so that they can cast aside all sham, pretense, and defense, and interact with complete "honesty." A series of exercises and "games" may be played to heighten contact and response. Touching, holding, caressing, and embracing is encouraged or demanded, but this is not expected to be erotic or to lead to sexual intercourse. Uninhibited verbal and physical interchange is encouraged, with occasional episodes of screaming or fighting. Such encounter sessions may be brief, but often are "marathon" sessions lasting twenty-four hours, a weekend, or even longer [Bach, 1966;

Shepard and Lee, 1970]. These experiences are expected to increase insights into one's self, to relieve one of anxieties and "hang-ups," and to aid one in relating to others.

Several questions about the functioning of encounter groups are still the subject of debate. One is whether or not participants should be screened so that individuals who might be emotionally damaged by the stress involved in the encounter process could be kept out of such groups. A somewhat similar question is whether especially skilled leaders are required for such groups to function effectively. Finally, there are questions as to the extent to which significant good or harm may come from encounter-group experiences.

One of the most carefully designed research projects to date—a study of encounter groups involving Stanford University students—[Lieberman, Yalom and Miles, 1973, p. 107] found that approximately equal proportions of the participants were helped by the encounter experience, showed no effects, or were harmed. While they concluded that "over-all encounter groups showed a modest positive impact," they also found that over 9 percent of the participants suffered "significant psychological injury" [Lieberman et al., p. 174]. Since encounter groups may have some tendency to select those with severe problems, these negative findings do not necessarily indicate harmful effects of the group experience itself, but they certainly raise serious questions.

On the other hand, Carl Rogers, who has long been a leader in the encounter group movement, reports of his experiences:

In all of the eight thousand persons engaged in these groups to date, there has been no psychological breakdown of any kind during the weekends. There have been, much later, two instances of a psychic break by participants in the program. It is a question whether this is more than would normally occur in any equal number of the population over the same period of time. (Carl R. Rogers, *Carl Rogers on Encounter Groups,* Harper & Row, Publishers, Inc., Evanston, Ill., 1970, p. 155.)

Commercialized encounter-group movement.

The role of the leader is a matter of continual controversy. Supposedly, it is the group interaction rather than the leader's direction which leads to the elimination of emotional blocks. On the other hand, the leader may be expected to "set the stage" for intense group interaction, to help the group to endure periods of stress or frustration, and to recognize personality changes taking place among individuals.

In spite of the supposed importance of the leader—or "group facilitator," a sometimes preferred label—there is much doubt about the nature of the leader's contribution. Group leaders are not necessarily more aware than ordinary members of changes taking place in the participant's self-concept or even of the types of patterns which are considered part of group development [Lieberman et al., 1973 p. 72]. Even Rogers, who evidently has much faith in the ability and potential contribution of "group facilitators," admits that leaderless groups seem to function in about the same way as those with a supposedly qualified leader [Rogers, 1970, p. 8].

Most group leaders have no professional training other than some experience at encounter centers. Persons with professional training in the behavioral sciences are not preferred as group leaders because they are said to be "too intellectual and remote." Most psychiatrists and other behavioral scientists are highly critical of any form of group therapy conducted by untrained and unsupervised laymen. When a patient's psychological defenses are stripped away and the psyche laid bare, with guilts, anxieties, and repressed impulses exposed (as they are in psychiatric treatment), the therapist must know how to handle what he or she has "dug up" if the patient is to be helped rather than shattered. Orthodox behavioral scientists are highly critical, but it has not been established whether nonprofessionally conducted encounter groups are a useful therapy [Burton, 1969; Egan, 1970] or a highly profitable racket [Rakstis, 1970; Maliver, 1971, 1973; Malcolm, 1973].

The most ardent advocates of intensive group experience believe that it may have a variety of instrumental uses. Thus, the T-group may be an effective way of bringing employees to recognize ways in which their personal behavior, though well intended, handicaps their cooperation with other people; therapy groups may enable members to shake off an addiction or even to cope with the symptoms of mental or physical illness; and encounter groups may bring greater emotional liberation to people inhibited by the greater restraints of more conventional groups.

It may be that the proponents of group experience have attempted to claim too much and that their critics have been overly demanding. Even though the T-groups do not always produce efficient executives, the therapy groups do not inevitably solve the personal hangups of their members, or encounter groups do not always lead to long term liberation, there may still be value in these forms of intensive group experience. Undoubtedly, some individuals have achieved major changes in their outlook and behavior through intensive group encounter, while others have been left relatively unchanged. However, direct therapy is not all that such groups have to offer. One of the major values from such experience is that lonely people can be exposed to the stimulus of group interaction, and in our impersonal society, this is no mean achievement. The comment of one writer on encounter groups would probably apply in some degree to all forms of intensive experience:

With a far more limited context, groups can be freed to pursue modest goals like helping friends to talk straighter, confront problems more directly, be open to feelings and work on a sense of community. Compared to the claims on earlier handbills, this agenda may seem paltry. Compared to what's in fact available, in or out of the human potential movement, such fare is a feast. (Ralph Keyes, "Love and Fun and Therapy Together," *Human Behavior,* September, 1973, p. 71.)

Summary

Both strength and weakness are largely the result of the manner in which a person is integrated into a network of groups. A fundamental distinction is that between *out-groups* and *in-groups*—a distinction which has been measured by the use of the concept of *social distance*. *Reference groups* are those which we accept as models and as guides for our judgments and actions. *Stereotypes* are distorted impressions of the characteristics of out-groups which have become widely accepted in a society. Emotional conditioning is largely the result of *primary-group* contacts, but our society is increasingly affected by the growth of *secondary-group* relationships. While many groups may be easily characterized as either primary or secondary, the two types of influence interact, each influencing the other.

Since the industrial revolution, the trend has been from the traditional *gemeinschaft* toward the *gesellschaft*. This has meant a loss of intimacy and security, which has been countered to some extent by the growth of new primary groups within a secondary-group setting.

Group dynamics studies interaction within groups, both to gain understanding and to solve organizational problems.

Both group forms such as the *triad* and various types of communication patterns have been studied extensively. *T-groups* (training groups) are used to sensitize people to interpersonal factors affecting cooperative group relations. *Therapy groups* of many kinds bring support and possibly understanding to troubled people. *Encounter groups* seek to bring greater personal liberation to people inhibited by the restraints of conventional living. Controversy surrounds both the techniques most useful in such groups and the extent to which they produce constructive changes in group members. It may be that the major value of these organized intensive group experiences is simply to provide social interaction to lonely people living in an impersonal type of society.

Questions and projects

1. Why do sociologists have so many different definitions for the term *group?*
2. Comment on this statement: "A group is made up of individuals; and the characteristics of a group are the sum of the characteristics of its members."
3. Is courage an individual character trait or a response to group influences?
4. What differences are found in the in-group–out-group distinction in primitive and modern societies?
5. Why are primary and secondary groups important? In-groups and out-groups?
6. To what extent would you expect social distance to be related to geographical distance?
7. College is often an introduction to the complexities of secondary-group relationships. Is this experience worthwhile for a young woman whose major interests are centered in the primary-group relationships of family life?
8. Why was the morale of most American POWs in Vietnam able to survive both the hardships of

capture and the propaganda stressing the divided nature of American public opinion about the conflict?
9. Is there a sociological explanation of how decent, clean-cut American young men could have been guilty of atrocities in Vietnam?
10. The early Christians were sometimes crowded into large prison cells and later marched into the Colosseum to be crucified or fed to the lions before thousands of spectators. They could have saved themselves by denying their faith, but few did so. Why?
11. How does a stereotype become a "self-fulfilling prophecy"?
12. In a recent experiment, conventionally groomed college students passing out peace literature in an airport were politely treated, while hippie-type students, behaving identically, were often abused, insulted, or jostled. Explain this in sociological terminology.
13. What do you think is the real reason the leaders of encounter groups so often are persons without

professional training in the behavioral sciences?
14. How do you explain the fact that some observers feel encounter groups can function without trained leaders?

Suggested readings

APPLEY, DEE G., AND ALVIN E. WINDER: *T-Groups and Therapy Groups in a Changing Society,* Jossey-Bass, San Francisco, 1973. A scholarly reference book presenting a research-based analysis of the theoretical foundations and operating methodologies of these two types of groups.

ATHANASIOU, ROBERT: "French and American Sexuality," *Psychology Today,* July, 1972, pp. 53–56ff. Exposes the falsehood of the stereotype that French mores are less sexually restrictive than the American. A sample of French and American persons was found to be highly similar in their sexual conduct and attitudes, with the Americans usually on the permissive side when a significant difference existed.

BALES, ROBERT F.: "How People Interact in Conferences," *Scientific American,* 192:31–35, March, 1955. A popular description of social interaction in the conference.

BECKER, TAMAR: "Black Africans and Black Americans on an American Campus: The African View," *Sociology and Social Research,* 56, January, 1972, pp. 202–211. A discussion of tension between two groups with a common physical appearance but different cultural backgrounds.

*EGAN, GERARD: *Encounter: Group Processes for Interpersonal Growth,* Wadsworth Publishing Company, Belmont, Calif., 1970. A balanced general description of the encounter group movement.

GIBBARD, GRAHAM S., JOHN J. HARTMAN, AND RICHARD D. MANN (EDS.): *Analysis of Groups,* Jossey-Bass, San Francisco, 1974. A series of articles on various aspects of the intensive group experience. The treatment covers T-groups, therapy groups, and encounter groups.

*HOWARD, JANE: *Please Touch,* Dell Publishing Company, reprinted by McGraw-Hill Book Company, New York, 1971. A popular, insightful treatment of many types of sensitivity training groups.

HUNT, CHESTER L., AND LUIS L. LACAR: "Social Distance and American Policy," *Sociology and Social Research,* 57, July, 1974, pp. 495–509. Description of social distance in the Philippines, where Americans are still one of the most accepted groups.

JACOBS, JAMES R.: "Street Gangs Behind Bars," *Social Problems,* 21: 395–410, 1974. An analysis of the results when the incarceration of a large number of gang members enabled them to take over the informal group structure of a prison.

KEYES, RALPH LOVE: "Fun and Therapy Together," *Human Behavior,* September, 1973, pp. 67–72. A brief, readable article on the problems and possibilities of encounter groups.

MILLS, THEODORE: *The Sociology of Small Groups,* Prentice-Hall, Inc., Englewood Cliffs, N.J., 1970. A brief but comprehensive account of basic small-group research.

VOLKMAN, RITA, AND DONALD R. CRESSEY: "Differential Association and the Rehabilitation of Drug Addicts," *American Journal of Sociology,* 69: 129–142, September, 1963. Describes the principles and operation of a therapeutic group, Synanon.

WARRINER, CHARLES K.: "Groups Are Real: A Reaffirmation," *American Sociological Review,* 21:549–554, October, 1956; reprinted in Milton Barron, *Contemporary Sociology,* Dodd, Mead & Company, Inc., New York, 1964, pp. 120–127. Shows how the nature of the group is not completely represented by the individuals who compose its membership.

Chapter 9 ● Social institutions

A few months ago, the Kimbanguist Church (officially called the Church of Jesus Christ on Earth through the Prophet Simon Kimbangu) was approved for full membership in the World Council of Churches; membership is close to three million, mostly in the Democratic Republic of the Congo.

The Bakongo founder and preacher, Simon Kimbangu, was around 32 years old in 1921 when he spoke of having visions and dreams commanding him to go preach and pray for the healing of the sick. He was at first reluctant, but fearing a visionary threat of death, he began his ministry. Soon thousands flocked around for the services, especially for his prayers for healing. The crowds grew so large that Kimbangu had to appoint "apostles" to help him. The huge gatherings drew the attention of the Belgian authorities, Roman Catholic and Protestant leaders. Arrests of Kimbangu and hundreds of his followers were quickly made and sentences were handed down without proper hearings from military tribunals whose records are not to be found. Thus the total ministry of Simon Kimbangu was less than six months.

He died in prison in Lubumbashi in 1951.

The sad history of Kimbangu exemplified to Congolese the message of salvation of him who lived to do good but died on the cross.

His followers went underground and into exile, surviving, with difficulty, various types of repression and discrimination. With the coming of independence in the Congo, the Kimbanguists gained acceptance as a legitimate religious movement and came to be regarded as an acceptable, even though exotic, form of Christianity. After their legitimacy was accepted, the Kimbanguists turned to works of social improvement. Community projects of social benefits and of agriculture are often undertaken. Fisheries and experimental chemically fertilized fields of manioc are being tried in hope of producing more and better food. Skilled workmen give after-work hours to the construction of school buildings.

The Kimbanguist Church has not become a crystallized organization with a huge body of traditional doctrines. Kimbanguists are still studying the nature and meaning of baptism and the Lord's Supper, hoping to follow the implications of this study in the work ahead. They do have some rigid moral requirements such as the prohibition of polygamy and of the use of alcohol and tobacco. *(Adapted from Haldor E. Heimer, "Kimbanguists in the Congo," World Call, 51, March, 1970, pp. 16–17. Reprinted by permission of The Disciple.)*

Within a few decades, the Kimbanguists changed from an excitable, esoteric, and outlawed cult surrounding a charismatic leader into an accepted religious denomination. This transition illustrates the process of emergent institutionalization. The statement that "the Kimbanguist Church has not become a crystallized organization with a huge body of traditional doctrines" would indicate that the process of institutionalization is not yet completed. But the emergence of formal leadership, the development of a fairly consistent pattern of worship, the establishment of moral rules, the interest in community social welfare projects, and the acceptance by an international council of religious bodies are all signs that the process of institutionalization is well under way.

What is institutionalization and what are institutions? Perhaps the first thing to say is that the sociological usage is a bit different from the common parlance. An institution is not the building where certain activities take place; nor is it a particular group of people. Rather, an institution is an organization of mores to achieve some goal or activity that people feel is important. Institutions are the structured processes through which groups and individuals strive to carry on their activities. Bierstedt [1970, p. 321] puts it this way: "An institution in short . . . is a definite, formal and regular way of doing something." However, agreement on the definition of "institution" is not complete even among sociologists. Thus Broom and Selznik [1973, p. 232] include both process and group: "In the language of sociology an institution may be a group or a social practice, the Republican Party or the secret ballot."

The authors of this text like to avoid, as much as possible, attributing multiple meanings to the same word. Therefore, we restrict "institution" to mean an organized set of beliefs and practices and use "association" for the group which embodies these beliefs

and practices. Thus, as its activities become systematic and predictable, a church undergoes "institutionalization," but the particular church, viewed as a group of people, is an "association." The beliefs and practices form the institution, while a group of people is an association carrying on institutionally related activities.

All definitions of institutions imply both a set of behavior norms and a system of social relationships through which these norms are practiced. Let us suggest a formal definition which clearly includes both ideas: *An institution is an organized system of social relationships which embodies certain common values and procedures and meets certain basic needs of the society.* In this definition, "common values" refers to shared ideas and goals; the "common procedures" are the standardized behavior patterns the group follows; and the "system of relationships" is the network of roles and statuses through which this behavior is carried out. Thus the family includes a set of common values (about love, children, family life), a set of common procedures (dating, child care, family routines), and a network of roles and statuses (husband, wife, baby, teen-aged child, fiancé), which form the system of social relationships through which family life is carried out. Five important basic institutions in complex societies are the familial, religious, governmental, economic, and educational institutions. Today, the values and procedures of science are so important and so highly standardized that some would add the "scientific institutions" to the list. The activities involved in social work or medical care have become so definitely patterned that we might speak of either of these systems of behavior as institutions. In referring to the Middle Ages one could speak of chivalry and knighthood as aspects of the institution of feudalism.

While they are separate concepts, institutions and associations are not entirely separate from each other. An institution is a set of relationships and a system of behavior, and

An institution embodies certain common values and procedures.

these require *people.* Although the institution itself consists of relationships and norms, it is people who fill these relationships and practice these norms.

Students reciting in a classroom are carrying out the norms and practices of education. Likewise, voters casting their ballots are manifesting the behavior institutionalized in government, and worshippers singing hymns are following the practices of institutionalized religion. Such examples could be multiplied indefinitely and simply indicate that it is people who carry out the institutionalized social processes. In order to carry out institutionalized behavior, people often organize themselves into associations.

Some of these associations are almost synonymous with a particular institution. Thus when we think of religion, we speak of the church, and when we think of education, we think of schools. This is only partly accurate, for some religious behavior occurs outside of churches and much education is conducted outside of the school setting. Further, each major association has many satellite associations which also carry on institutionalized behavior. The church has its organized local congregations, Sunday schools, clubs, and groups of many kinds, carrying out the work of the church; the school has its PTA, alumni association, athletic association; the state has

its political organizations, voters' leagues, taxpayers' associations, and organized pressure groups. Institutions and associations are very much interrelated; yet the concepts are distinct and should not be confused. Religion is a social institution; the First Methodist Church on Main Street is an association. *The* corporation is a social institution; the First National Bank and the Ford Motor Company are associations. Education is a social institution; Harvard University and the PTA are associations.

The development of institutions

The process of institutionalization

Institutions emerge as the largely unplanned products of social living. People grope for practical ways of meeting their needs; they find some workable patterns which harden through repetition into standardized customs. As time passes, these patterns acquire a body of supporting folklore which justifies and sanctions them. The custom of "dating" developed as a means of mate selection. Banks gradually developed as the need for storing, transferring, borrowing, and lending money gave rise to a series of practices for accomplishing these purposes. From time to time, men might gather to codify and give legal endorsement to these practices as they continued to develop and change. In such manner, institutions arise.

Institutionalization consists of the establishment of definite norms which assign status positions and role functions in connection with such behavior. A norm is a group expectation of behavior. Institutionalization involves the replacement of spontaneous or experimental behavior with behavior which is expected, patterned, regular, and predictable. Thus the pre-institutional phase of a religious movement brings forth spontaneous ecstatic and often confused behavior as the followers of the new leader respond to his dynamic appeal. Every day is an adventure, and every religious meeting is an unpredictable sequence of emotional events in which no one is able to predict what he or she will do. As the institutionalized church emerges, the participants acquire definite roles, and their activities begin to follow a routine pattern. Some people are simply worshipers; others assume specialized roles such as choir member, clergyman, teacher, usher, secretary, janitor, and so on. Novelty and excitement fade as procedures come to be governed by definite norms, and the behavior of each participant becomes standardized and predictable. Thus, when we say that the Kimbanguist church is in the process of emergent institutionalization, we do not mean that this church is becoming an institution, but that the activities carried on in the church are becoming routine and predictable, and the relationships of various types of members definitely patterned. It is these activities and relationships which comprise the institution and not the church as an organization.

A tavern brawl is noninstitutionalized behavior; a professional boxing match is institutionalized. A set of social relationships has become institutionalized when (1) a regular system of statuses and roles has been developed, and (2) this system of status and role expectations has been generally accepted in the society. Dating in American society meets both of these qualifications. A rather clearly defined set of courtship roles has emerged, in which the duties and privileges of each party are defined (he generally asks, she accepts, he usually pays, etc.), and safeguarded with some limitations or restraints intended to prevent complications; thus dating became part of our marriage and family institutions.

When we say that dating has become institutionalized, we mean that it is generally accepted by the society as a necessary and proper activity whereby young people mature emotionally and eventually find agreeable partners. Many societies have also institutionalized premarital sexual intercourse, making it a normal and expected part of the activities leading to marriage. Although premarital intercourse is fairly common in American society, it has not been institutionalized. Present trends, which include providing contraceptives to the unmarried and allowing coed dorms or all-night visitation privileges, may be leading to the institutionalization of premarital intercourse, meaning that it may become an accepted and safeguarded pattern of behavior.

Individual roles in institutional behavior

Not all roles are institutionalized. The "bad boy" and "mother's little helper" roles in the family are noninstitutionalized roles, while son and daughter are institutionalized roles. An institutionalized role is a set of behavior expectations that leaves little room for personal eccentricity. All judges act a good deal alike when on the bench, however much they differ at other times. Every Methodist minister and every Catholic priest finds that his duties and privileges are quite precisely defined by his institutional role; to deviate from his expected role in any way is hazardous. Even presidents and kings, apparently so powerful, are in fact most highly circumscribed in their freedom of action. If they fail to operate within the role expectations of the institution, they generally lose their influence.

An interesting example of the persistence of institutional roles is seen in the transition of the English coal mines from private to public ownership [Koening, 1948]. Under private ownership the miners were supervised by the "boss," an agent of the private capitalists who owned the mines. Acting in this role, the boss sought to get the greatest production at the least possible cost. When the government took over the mines, some of the miners thought the new ownership meant the end of annoying rules and regulations. The boss, however, was still with them. Although now an agent of the state, he still had the job of making the nationalized mines produce the greatest possible amount of coal at the lowest possible cost. Ownership and sometimes personnel had changed, but the system of roles which had grown up in response to institutional needs remained pretty much the same.

This lack of change in the role of the supervisor in the coal mines under nationalization is not an isolated example; similar experiences occur in other institutional settings. Occasionally a man contrasts the smooth and efficient way in which his secretary anticipates his needs in the office with the rather demanding attitude of his wife at home. Sometimes a discontented husband divorces the wife and marries the secretary, only to find that when the secretary assumes the role of wife, she begins to act like a wife! Many an employee who is promoted to a supervisory role tries to retain his comradeship with his former crew; this rarely succeeds, for the new role inevitably alters his relationship to the old buddies whom he now bosses.

It is true that individual personality differences do affect institutional behavior to some degree. One foreman is grouchy and another is cheerful; one professor is stimulating and another is dull. But the range of individual variation is limited and is greatly overshadowed by role requirements. The conflicts that arise within an association are sometimes due to clashes of personality but more often to the clash of institutional roles. The foreman and the inspector clash because the foreman must keep production going while the inspector keeps finding defects that must be corrected. The salesman is frustrated when the credit manager refuses to extend more credit to a slow-paying customer. The university professor's wish to stimulate intellectual controversy on the campus may clash with the dean's or president's wish to avoid off-campus criticism.

Many such clashes are inherent in the interrelation of institutional roles with an association. With some modification, Gertrude Stein's famous statement, "A rose is a rose is a rose," may be applied to institutional roles. A wife is always a wife; a husband is always a husband; and a supervisor is always a supervisor. The difference made by individual personalities in institutional roles is comparable to the difference between a mediocre and a highly talented actor in a dramatic production. The highly talented actor realizes more fully the potentialities of the part he is playing, but at the same time his expression must be channeled within the limitations of the role. Organizations function most smoothly when they can attract competent personnel, and sometimes they are handicapped by personnel unequal to the roles assigned them. Regardless of differences in personnel, however, the persistence of role requirements will require some degree of uniformity in the conduct of those who carry out a particular institutional role.

Institutional traits

While each institution has its peculiarities, each institution is also like all others in some respects. If institutions are to function, ways must be found to assign responsibility to different functionaries, formulate standards of behavior, maintain the loyalty of participants, and develop methods of dealing with other institutions. Since these are common problems, it is not surprising that similar techniques may develop in institutions with very different goals.

Cultural symbols

All institutions acquire symbols which serve as a shorthand reminder of the institution. The citizen is reminded of his allegiance to the government by the flag, to religion by a crucifix, crescent, or star of David, to the family by a wedding ring, to education by the school colors or animal totem (mascot), and to the system of economic controls by brand names and trademarks. Music also has symbolic meanings. National anthems, school songs, religious hymns, and the singing "commercials" all use the art of melody to strengthen institutional ties. Buildings may become institutional symbols, so that it is hard to think of home without a house, religion without a church edifice, education without a school building, or government without the government house or king's palace.

Codes of behavior

The people involved in the activities of institutions must be prepared to carry out their appropriate roles. These roles are often expressed in formal codes, such as the oath of allegiance to the country, the marriage vows, the medical profession's oath of Hippocrates, and the codes of ethics of several other groups. As we saw in Chapter 7, these institutionally defined roles are an important part of social control.

A formal code of behavior, however impressive, is no guarantee of proper role performance. Husbands and wives may prove unfaithful to marital vows; citizens who fervently repeat the oath of allegiance may commit treason; and church members who have sworn fidelity to their religion may lapse into indifference. If the affirmation of a verbal or written code is the climax to a long process of attitude formation and role preparation, it may be observed; if not, and if there are no swift and sure punishments for violation, the code may be quietly ignored.

A formal code is only a part of the total behavior that makes up an institutional role. Much of the behavior in any role—parent, soldier, priest, professor, politician—consists of an elaborate body of informal traditions, expectations, and routines which one absorbs only through long observation and experience with the role. Children who have never lived in a harmonious family setting are likely to have difficulty in ever filling the roles of parent and husband or wife. They have had no good chance to observe these roles in successful operation or to absorb the attitudes needed for successful role performance. Like roles of all kinds, institutional roles can be filled most successfully by those who have fully learned the proper role attitudes and behavior.

Institutional functions

Society is so complex and its forces so interrelated that it is impossible to foresee all consequences of a particular action. Institutions have *manifest* functions which are easy to recognize as part of the professed objectives of the institution, and *latent* functions which are unintended and may be unrecognized, or, if recognized, regarded as byproducts [Merton, 1957b, pp. 19–84].

Latent functions

Persons with important institutional roles often fail to realize the latent effects of the activities they promote. Henry Ford, the founder of the company that bears his name, is a case in point. He cordially detested labor unions, big cities, mass credit, and installment buying; yet through his promotion of the assembly line and mass production he probably did more than any other one man to stimulate these very developments. The latent functions of an institution may support the professed objectives, or be irrelevant, or even lead to consequences quite damaging to the norms of the institution. For instance, every institution has norms which favor heavy expenditures on impressive symbols. Religion encourages the building of cathedrals, education is symbolized by impressive school buildings, government by the splendor of the palace, and business by the company jet airplane. It is expected that such symbols will impress people with the importance and power of associations carrying on institutional activities and thereby generate continued support. The latent function may be quite different. Rather than being impressed, people may become resentful and decide that the symbols represent exploitation. Taxpayers may resist school-building levies, worshippers may feel that the soaring buildings and rich vestments are unbecoming in the worship of the Christ who lived a life of poverty, unruly subjects may burn the king's palace, and consumers may blame high prices on corporate luxuries. While the manifest function of expensive symbols is to promote loyalty to institutional goals and associations, the latent function may be to stimulate criticism and resentment. The manifest function of Western health institutions has been to reduce illness, premature death and human misery; the latent function has been to promote a population explosion and massive famine in the underdeveloped countries. There are, therefore, many instances in which the latent functions might more accurately be termed "latent dysfunctions," since they sometimes tend to undermine and weaken the institution or to impede the attainment of its manifest functions.

Manifest functions

Institutional norms and practices will not survive unless related associations are able to carry on two types of manifest functions: (1) the pursuit of their objectives in a world which is often indifferent or hostile to these objectives and (2) the preservation of their own internal cohesion so that they may survive. When an association fails in either of these manifest functions, the institutionalized norms and processes will either be revised or abandoned. The family, for instance, is concerned both with raising its children and with maintaining harmony and loyalty among its members so that it does not dissolve in the divorce courts. The national state must serve its citizens and protect its boundaries and, at the same time, escape the peril of revolution or conquest. The church which seeks to convert outsiders and increase its influence must also hold the loyalty of its members and enhance their feeling of satisfaction with the institution.

The interrelations of institutions

No institution exists in a vacuum. The preceding sections of this chapter show that one cannot understand a social institution unless one studies its relationships with the rest of the culture. Religion, government, business, education, and the family all exist in a constant state of mutual interaction. Business conditions affect the number of people who feel able to marry; the marriage and birth rates affect the demand for goods. Education creates attitudes which influence the acceptance or rejection of religious dogma; religion, in turn, may either exalt scholarship because it reveals the truths of God or denounce scientific inquiry because it threatens the faith. Businessmen, educators, clergymen, and the functionaries of all other institutions seek to influence the ideals and practices of government, since governmental action may make the difference between success and failure in their institutional enterprises.

The interrelationship of institutions explains why associations which express institutional ideals and carry on institutionalized practices are seldom able to control their members' behavior in a manner fully consistent with institutional ideals. Schools may offer a standard curriculum to all children, but the reaction of students depends on many factors outside the control of educators. Children from a home which offers stimulating conversation and challenging reading materials are more apt to acquire intellectual interests than are children in homes where comic books and confession magazines are the reading fare and where television replaces conversation. Churches profess high ethical ideals, but their members often feel obligated to compromise these ideals in their adjustment to business, politics, or the process of securing a mate. Patriotism glorifies self-sacrifice and a devotion to the welfare of the state that conflict with many individual wishes and obligations.

The need to harmonize the roles which associations with different institutional commitments seek to impose on the same individuals has often led to a deliberate effort to arrange institutional alliances. Our nineteenth-century alliance between business and government made it possible for business to pursue maximum profits with government assistance instead of governmental restraint. A state church ensures that religion and government will support, rather than oppose or undermine, each other. Education has such a profound influence on the rest of the society that persons influenced primarily by other institutional considerations attempt to capture it by controlling the schools. Business and labor associations attempt to influence the schools by propaganda in the guise of free "educational" materials; politicians investigate them to be sure they conform to the current standards of nationalism; and some churches operate schools of their own in an effort to guarantee that education will support religious indoctrination.

Many work roles pose a conflict between career loyalty and family loyalty on the part of their functionaries. Business concerns try to secure "corporation wives" who will cheerfully adjust their family concerns to harmonize with the demands the corporation makes on its executives. The army discourages marriages for privates and tries, by providing living quarters, to enable the upper-rank officers to adjust their family life to the needs of military service. The most thorough effort to control family influence is seen in the Roman Catholic Church, which strives to free its priesthood entirely from family entanglements through the requirement of celibacy.

All institutions must adapt to a changing society.

All institutions face the necessity of continuous adaptation to a changing society. Changes in one institution compel changes in other institutions. Since family patterns change, the state sets up a system of social security. As workers drift from farm to factory, the church must revise its language, its procedures, and possibly its doctrines in order to remain "relevant" to the needs of an urbanized, industrialized society. No institution can avoid affecting other institutions or being affected by them.

Institutional autonomy

The fact that institutions are interdependent does not mean that the defenders of any institution willingly surrender ideological or structural control. Rather, the goal is to preserve their freedom to act within the norms and practices of a specific institution while at the same time seeking to influence, if not to dominate, the people committed primarily to other institutions. In all the basic institutions, patterns of behavior have developed which are intended to maintain some degree of independence and to prevent dominance by persons associated with other institutions.

Unlike some other societies, past and present, American society has not encouraged the complete domination of any institution by another. It has fostered the separation of church and state, a rejection of widespread government ownership of industry, the preservation of private business enterprise, and a somewhat uncertain tradition of academic freedom for educational enterprises. These methods of assuring institutional autonomy are not completely accepted, and associations primarily committed to each institution make a continued effort to increase their influence upon other social institutions. For example, business organizations object to adverse criticism from the churches; the churches try to get religious instruction into the schools; and so it goes. While distinctive attitudes and goals do develop in institutionally related associations, their members carry into one institutional arrangement the attitudes formed in another, and the social order is the stage for a continual interplay adjustment, and competition among different institutionally related groups.

Dual function of the intellectuals

In all complex societies, social institutions are the objects of constant comment by the intellectuals. An intellectual is one who, regardless of education or occupation, devotes himself or herself seriously to the analysis of ideas. Their power is indirect. Intellectuals are seldom "in control" of anything, but they are influential since their writings affect the thinking of those who are in authority [Kadushin, 1974].

Intellectuals are often found in "wordy" occupations such as religion, teaching, journalism, and the law. However, many persons in these occupations are not seriously concerned with examining ideas, but operate in a routine fashion, while some persons in less verbal fields develop a general intellectual concern. An example of such a person would be Eric Hoffer [1951], a longshoreman who became a well-known social commentator. What makes one an intellectual is not occupation or education, but one's attitude towards ideas: ". . . he lives for ideas—which means he has a sense of dedication to the life of the mind which is very much like a religious commitment" [Hofstadter, 1964, p. 27].

The importance of ideology in sustaining loyalty to institutional norms leads all institutions to develop mixed attitudes of appreciation and fear toward those who are able to manipulate ideas. Intellectuals are needed to perform the vital service of explaining social developments in terms harmonious with institutional norms. Communist intellectuals, for instance, have the task of showing how all recent history really fulfills the predictions of Marx and Lenin, although this task requires a spectacular distortion of the facts. China's 1966 campaign to destroy the influence of the intellectuals reflected Mao Tse-Tung's fear that the intellectuals were wavering in their support of the revolutionary regime [Bloodworth, 1966].

The intellectual cannot be fully trusted, because the training that equips the intellectual to defend the ideology may also enable this person to analyze its deficiencies. He or she may even develop a rival ideology more satisfying to the demands of the time. It is the intellectuals who promote revolutions and lead the attack upon entrenched institutions. Conversely, it is the intellectuals who are called upon to defend institutions under attack.

No institution can avoid the constant need to justify its basic beliefs and practices. All institutions are sustained by intellectuals who are able to interpret the social situation in terms harmonious with the institutional ideology. The difficulties of the intellectual come from the fact that devotion to the institution may be subordinated to a concern for the truth. Conflict is minimized when the two types of interest converge, as was illustrated by Adam Smith's argument that the pursuit of private gain by businessmen served the public good. But modern economists and environmental ecologists have come under criticism when their research led them to the conclusion that, under modern conditions, the public good may require some limits upon the quest for private gain [Helfrich, 1970].

Sometimes the intellectual is alternately praised and condemned during his lifetime, as were Plato, Galileo, Luther, Trotsky, and many others. In his youth, Milovan Djilas interpreted communism as the main hope for achieving social justice. His writings were widely quoted, and he became Vice-President of Yugoslavia. On more mature reflection he wrote a book describing communism as a new form of human exploitation [1957]; its publication resulted in his being imprisoned by the same authorities who had praised his previous works.

Recently, the basic features of American liberal democracy have come under heavy attack from intellectual critics, of whom Herbert Marcuse [1969a] may be the most influential, while being vigorously defended by other intellectuals such as Sidney Hook [1969a; 1969b]. Intellectuals are often difficult for the institutional supporters to work with, since the intellectual who is a defender of the faith today may become a critic tomorrow. Nevertheless, no institution in the modern world escapes the constant appraisal of intellectual critics, and no features of the institution can long survive without some degree of intellectual support.

It is easy to see why Communist countries are constantly vacillating between freedom and greater restraints upon their intellectuals. The intellectual who is best able to defend established institutions is a person acknowledged to be devoted to the truth regardless of institutional commitments. Such a person is both helpful and dangerous to the welfare of the institution—helpful because his support gains respect for established institutions, dangerous because his search for truth may lead him to conclusions which provide ammunition

A PARTIAL LIST OF THE TRAITS OF MAJOR AMERICAN SOCIAL INSTITUTIONS

Family	Religion	Government	Business	Education
ATTITUDES AND BEHAVIOR PATTERNS				
Affection	Reverence	Loyalty	Efficiency	Love of knowledge
Loyalty	Loyalty	Obedience	Thrift	Class attendance
Responsibility	Worship	Subordination	Shrewdness	Studying
Respect	Generosity	Cooperation	Profit making	"Cramming"
SYMBOLIC CULTURE TRAITS				
Marriage ring	Cross	Flag	Trademark	School colors
Wedding veil	Ikon	Seal	Patent sign	Mascot
Coat of arms	Shrine	Mascot	Slogan	School song
"Our Song"	Hymn	Anthem	Singing commercial	Seal
UTILITARIAN CULTURE TRAITS				
House	Church building	Public buildings	Shop, factory	Classrooms
Apartment	Church equipment	Public works	Store, office	Library
Furnishings	Literature	Office equipment	Office equipment	Stadium
Car	Liturgical supplies	Blanks and forms	Blanks and forms	Books
CODE OF ORAL OR WRITTEN SPECIFICATIONS				
Marriage license	Creed	Charter	Contracts	Accreditation
Will	Church law	Constitution	Licenses	Rules
Geneology	Sacred books	Treaties	Franchises	Curricula
Marriage law	Taboos	Laws	Articles of incorporation	Graduation requirements
IDEOLOGIES				
Romantic love	Thomism	Nationalism	Laissez faire	Academic freedom
"Togetherness"	Liberalism	States rights	Managerial responsibility	Progressive education
Familism	Fundamentalism	Democracy	Free enterprise	Three "r"s
Individualism	Neo-orthodoxy	Republicanism	Rights of labor	Classicism

Source: Adapted from table "Nucleated Social Institutions" in F. Stuart Chapin, *Contemporary American Institutions*, Harper & Row, Publishers, Inc., New York, 1935, p. 16.

for institutional critics while weakening the convictions of its supporters. This dual role creates a problem of discipline for the society and a problem of conflicting loyalties for the intellectual.

Institutional structures

Because the family is so basic to all social life, Chapter 10 is devoted to it. Space does not permit an equal treatment of each of the other basic institutions, but the following brief sketches of religious, educational, economic, and governmental institutions may provide a clearer idea of institutional structure and function. Often these structures and functions can best be seen in related associations which are "institutionalized."

Religious institutions

Manifest functions of religion

Functions of religion cluster about three types of concerns: a pattern of beliefs called *doctrines,* which concern the nature of the relationship of man to the ultimate reality in the universe; *rituals* which symbolize these doctrines and keep people aware of their significance; and a series of *behavior norms* consistent with the doctrines. The work of explaining and defending the doctrines, carrying out the rituals, and reinforcing the desired behavior norms leads to a complex pattern of worship, teaching, evangelism, exhortation, and philanthropic works requiring a considerable investment of money and personnel.

A perennial question is whether the churches will be as viable in the future as they have been in the past. In most parts of Europe, the proportion of people who attend religious services has decreased steadily since 1900 [Tomassan, 1971, p. 112]. In the United States, trends have been mixed. From 1940 to 1962, there was a marked increase, both proportion-

ate and absolute, in church affiliation, which rose from 49 percent in 1940 to 64.4 percent in 1962 [S. Lipset, 1959; *Yearbook American and Canadian Churches, 1964*, p. 279]. Since 1962, growth has leveled off; in 1973, the total membership in religious organizations was virtually static, although population continued to increase [*Yearbook of American and Canadian Churches, 1974*]. Reports abound of a continued interest in religious issues, especially the bizarre and the occult, but the extent to which religious interests will continue to be expressed through churches is still an open question. For the present, though, American churches still attract large numbers of people, and this may continue indefinitely.

Latent functions of religion

Few Americans will object to the manifest functions of religion—the worship of God and instruction in religious ideology and moral behavior. Some of the latent functions of the churches, however, bring consequences which often surprise even the faithful, while they may stimulate either approval or opposition from those who do not consider themselves very religious.

Christian missions in colonial areas have often served to stimulate nationalistic feeling. This was not the intention of the missionaries, who, though not mainly concerned with government, usually considered Western rule essential to the progress of an underdeveloped area. Rather than a direct goal, the stimulus of nationalistic feeling was a latent result of the training received in mission schools and the need to treat potential converts with some measure of equality. The manifest function was simply to produce Christians, but the latent function has often been to train nationalist leaders who became bitter enemies of colonial rule.

The Christian emphasis on monogamous marriage has some latent consequences quite the opposite of the desires of churchmen. In

Protestant countries, where divorce is usually relatively easy to obtain, the desire to have a change of mates leads to a high divorce rate. In Catholic countries, divorce is usually either prohibited or made quite difficult. The consequence of the Catholic restriction of divorce is a considerable number of more or less permanent extramarital relationships. Many among the lower classes react to the prohibition of divorce by setting up households without legal marriage and shifting mates when they wish. Most of the middle- and upper-class people are properly married, but a discontented husband may establish a relationship with a mistress which the wife is powerless to prevent, since divorce is either completely outlawed or religiously taboo. Thus both the Protestant and the Catholic approach to ideal family life have latent consequences which modify the monogamous character of the family.

One of the most often cited latent effects of religion is the relation between the "Protestant ethic" and the "spirit of capitalism." Protestant leaders of the Reformation had no desire to erect the spiritual foundations for a capitalistic society and often denounced capitalistic trends in their day. Yet the industrial revolution and the growth of large-scale business concerns was much more rapid in predominantly Protestant than in largely Catholic areas, and in mixed areas Protestants were much the more active in business development. This circumstance helps explain the economic depression in France which followed the revocation of religious tolerance and the expulsion of the Huguenots. The phrase "as rich as a Huguenot" became a popular stereotype, and the expulsion of the Protestants slowed down French industry while accelerating business development in the countries where they settled as refugees.

The Protestant ethic made religious virtues of individualism, frugal living, thrift, and the glorification of work—practices which obviously favored the accumulation of wealth. These practices are usually attributed to the Protestant emphasis on individual responsibility rather than churchly sacraments, to the interpretation of worldly success as a sign that one was predestined for salvation, and to the reaction against the symbols of wealth which had been accumulated by the traditional church. None of these Protestant practices orginated in a deliberate desire to encourage commerce, and perhaps for that reason, their effect was all the more potent. The classic presentation of this theory is found in Max Weber, *The Protestant Ethic and the Spirit of Capitalism.* While most social scientists accept Weber's theory as a plausible hypothesis, some disagree [Fanfani, 1955, and Samuelson, 1961].

Catholics today are increasingly accepting the values of a business society, whereas the power of the Protestant ethic has been weakened by installment buying and the general emphasis on leisure, recreation, and luxury in an affluent society. A few decades ago it was fashionable among Protestant leaders to glorify business activity, but in more recent years capitalism has come under heavy criticism, and modern Protestants are uncertain whether their identification with business development is a virtue to be proclaimed or a mistaken emphasis to be corrected.

Some research indicates that, regardless of the situation in the early days of the Industrial Revolution, religious affiliation bears little relation to economic ideology in twentieth-century America [Greeley, 1964; G. Bouma, 1970]. On the other hand, a Detroit survey found that the Protestant ethic was still viable. This survey indicated a greater commitment to work, thrift, and individualism among Protestants than among Catholics and also a more rapid social mobility [Lenski, 1961]. A replication of the study at a later date confirmed the findings on work attitudes but did not support the other Protestant-Catholic differences in the earlier survey [Lenski, 1971; Schuman, 1971]. A 1971 report of a sample of Protestant and Catholic men in a Midwestern American city indicated some evidence that the Protestant ethic was still viable. No difference in education was found between Catholics and Protestants, but Protestants had reached a higher income and occupational status [Crowley, 1971]. Other studies indicate a higher economic level among Catholics [Glenn and Hyland, 1967; Bode, 1970]. It may be that the Protestant ethic still has some influence, but it seems evident that whatever Catholic-Protestant differences still exist are rapidly diminishing.

Another latent function of religious institutions in some societies is the promotion of sociability. In their worship and educational activities, as well as in the celebration of special occasions, churches draw people together. They provide companionship and "wholesome" recreation, along with courtship opportunities and training in leadership. Religious holidays in the United States are comparatively prosaic (with the possible exception of New Orleans' Mardi Gras), but in many societies they involve the whole community in elaborate pageantry. Among primitive societies it is common for religious holidays to be the occasion for orgies, when the customary restrictions on heavy drinking and sexual license are temporarily lifted. It often seems that one of the major functions of religious institutions is to draw people out of their isolation and to break the daily routine with distinctive celebrations.

Interrelation of religion and society

History records a constant struggle between the associations representing different institutions. In this struggle, the churches have developed four different modes of organization, each of which has had some success in guaranteeing the autonomy of religious associations, although each involves some concessions. The most prominent is the state church known as the *ecclesia,* which accepts state support and, in return, sanctions the basic cultural practices of the society. In a somewhat vestigial form, the state church survives in Britain and in the Scandinavian countries. In a much more vigorous form, it could be seen in Spain under Franco, in Italy, in Saudi Arabia, and in Tibet before the Communist regime.

The *sect* and the *cult* are at opposite poles from the ecclesia. Both of these may be greatly at odds with the general society, and their membership is usually small. Both of them have, in essence, abandoned any attempt to control activities influenced by other social institutions. The cult has little concern with governmental, educational, or economic activities. It stresses ecstatic emotional experience of its members and asks only that the larger society tolerate what is often regarded as weird behavior.

The sect is concerned about all aspects of life and is insistent that its members follow its doctrines without deviation. Its mores may differ greatly from those of the general society. It may be pacifist in a warlike state, collectivist in an individualized economy, and austere in an affluent society. However, the sect makes no serious attempt to sway the general society and asks only the right to live apart in separate enclaves. It sometimes secures toleration because it is regarded as too small to be threatening. For instance, a government which would not tolerate widespread pacifist attitudes can ignore a few Quakers or Mennonites without seriously reducing its military power.

The fourth category, the *denomination,* is a large group but one with less than a majority of the nation's citizens. It is usually supported by private gifts rather than government subsidy and, since it is still a minority, it does not feel as much pressure to accept all majority social norms as does the ecclesia. Thus, at least until recently, Methodists deviated from the majority in their criticism of drinking and gambling, and Catholics differed in their opposition to birth control. On the other hand, the denomination is too large to prevent deviation among its members, whose behavior tends to follow the general social practices. Yet the denomination attempts to influence the behavior of both its own members and the general society while simultaneously resisting institutional influences at variance with its behavioral norms. The idea of the separation of church and state is accepted in theory, but many arguments about its application occur in practice.

Classification of a religious group as ecclesia, cult, sect, or denomination does not imply any value judgment concerning its validity or prestige. Rather the classification is an indication of a difference in type of emphasis and in pattern of relationship to the general society. There are, however, no churches which are "pure" types, and the classification is a continuum with degrees of difference rather than a dichotomy with absolute contrasts. Since no single church claims a majority of Americans, it is probably correct to say that the United States does not have an ecclesia and that all the larger groups are denominations.

Educational institutions

In early and primitive societies, no schools were necessary. Children learned what they needed to know by watching and taking part in whatever was going on. Education, along with everything else, was handled by the family or the clan. Schools became necessary when cultural complexity created a need for specialized knowledge and skill which could not easily be acquired by the watch-help method.

The complexity of modern life has not diminished the importance of the teaching functions of the family, but it has added the need for many types of instruction which require specialized educational agencies. In the early days of American life even elementary education in the "three Rs" was far from universal. Today, graduation from high school is regarded as a desirable minimum preparation, while higher education grows steadily more common. Nor is education ended in youth, since changes in science and technology may require retraining at any stage in one's working life. Education beyond literacy was, at one time, necessary only in the professions such as the ministry, law, and medicine, and as a sort of ornamental

gloss for the rich. Today, advanced education is regarded as a necessity for a large portion of the population.

Manifest functions of education

Whether it is basic general education or training in specific skills, the primary manifest function of education in American society is to prepare people for occupational roles. Practically all occupational roles require basic literacy, while many also demand some type of specialized training. The cybernetics revolution with computer controlled machines is rapidly cutting the demand for unskilled labor, while the market for professionals, semiprofessionals, and technicians is rapidly expanding.

The list of other manifest functions of education is quite extensive: preserving the culture by passing it on from one generation to the next; encouraging democratic participation by teaching verbal skills and developing the person's ability to think rationally and independently; enriching life by enabling the student to expand his or her intellectual and aesthetic horizons; improving personal adjustment through personal counseling and such courses as applied psychology, sex education, family living, drug abuse; improving the health of the nation's youth by providing physical exercise and courses in hygiene; producing patriotic citizens through lessons illustrating the country's glory; and finally, "building character." Some of these manifest functions may not actually be fulfilled, but they are nonetheless *intended* functions of the educational system. In fact, the manifest functions of the school have multiplied to such an extent that we often seem to assume that education can solve all the problems of society.

There is some fear that the school's concern with a great many other matters may be eroding its ability to develop basic intellectual skills. Officials of the Educational Testing Service report that the average scores attained by college applicants have been dropping steadily for a decade. Scores dropped from 478 on the verbal test and 502 on the mathematical test in the 1962–1963 school year to 445 on the verbal portion and 481 on the mathematical in the 1973–1974 school year. One explanation is that the lower scores simply reflect the fact that college enrollment is less selective now than in earlier years, but another explanation is that elementary and high schools may be less successful in teaching verbal and mathematical skills [Maeroff, 1973].

Latent functions of education

Education also has latent functions, which include keeping youth off the labor market, weakening the control of parents, promoting the Americanization of immigrants, and altering the class system.

To a great extent, the complaints about the schools are a reaction to these latent functions. Keeping youth off the labor market may be attractive to labor unions, but it appears in a different light to farmers who need seasonal workers or to those remaining industrialists who rely on cheap and unskilled labor. Parents want their children to achieve higher status through education but are distressed when their children learn about ideas that conflict with parental norms; immigrant parents who wish children to cling to the practices and customs of a foreign culture have mixed feelings about the Americanization of the school. Altering the class system by enabling youth from low-income families to get the education needed for higher-status positions likewise meets with a mixed response. Some laud this as a step toward a better society; others fear the increase of competition or fear a shortage of workers who will be content with low-status jobs. Some, however, argue that the school actually perpetuates class inequalities [Rist, 1970; Greer, 1972], making the exact latent function on class structure a matter of debate. The American school system is now engaged in

probably the most bitter controversy in its history—over whether its latent functions should include the promotion of racial integration. (Some would maintain that this is a manifest function.)

Educational autonomy

The beliefs of educators are as varied as the beliefs of Americans in general and educators at all levels often argue vehemently with each other. Some educators lead highly conventional lives; others might be classed as swinging or "emancipated." Many educators are ardent churchgoers, some are agnostic and a few are atheists. Some educators are radical critics of the economic system, others would like to repeal most of the social legislation of the last forty years. Some educators supported the Vietnam war, others were bitterly opposed.

Although educators are divided on social issues and life styles, they do have two points in common. One is that their role in the classroom and sometimes in publication and public address brings them into the public eye and exposes them to possible criticism. Another is that, regardless of their differences on other matters, educators have a rationale of their own and are restive when leaders of other institutional associations attempt to exert control over the schools. The rationale of the educator is that schools exist to disseminate the truth as it is discovered by each academic discipline. Usually this search for truth does not have revolutionary implications, but it frequently issues forth in a form somewhat different from that preferred by those primarily committed to other institutional associations. Further, the very process of intellectual inquiry is upsetting to those who have made an absolute commitment to institutional goals and accompanying ideologies. Hence the schools are often under suspicion of undermining the faith of citizens and are closely watched by representatives of other institutionally related associations.

The ideology used to safeguard the autonomy of educational associations is *academic freedom.* This means that schools are to be run by their own authorities rather than being directly subservient to other institutions, and that professors are free to conduct research, publish, and teach their findings without fear of reprisal if the results of research should prove unpopular.

From the point of view of educators, academic freedom is the passport to their search for truth wherever it may lead. From the viewpoint of society, this means of assuring educational autonomy may at times prove embarrassing to other institutional associations whose leaders feel that they have not received the proper support from the school. Its merits lie in the assurance that both students and the general public will receive what actually is the truth as the professor understands it, rather than some position to which the professor is forced to subscribe because of pressure.

In recent years, academic freedom has come under fire from militant students who want the university to be an agency of social reconstruction. Such students have firm ideas about the type of social change they wish to see, and they view the university, not as a place of intellectual inquiry, but as an arena in which their forces may be mobilized. In their view, the good professor is one whose teaching is *relevant*—that is, whose teaching materials and ideas are designed so as to cultivate support for the radical students' social-policy objectives. Any reluctance to attack the established institutions makes the professor a sure target for the militant students, in much the same way that Nazi students ran liberal professors off the campus in the days of Adolf Hitler in Germany. Since academic tenure supports academic freedom by making it difficult to discharge unpopular professors, tenure thus is also under attack by militant students, who, like the archreactionaries on the political right, tend to work for a university in which teaching supports their own ideologies.

In the 1970s still further attacks on academic tenure have been made as campus enrollments have ceased to grow and, in some cases, dwindled. Administrators are criticizing tenure as a device which "freezes in" an existing faculty and makes it difficult to launch new programs with the appropriate personnel. Ethnic minorities are also critical, regarding tenure as a device to protect the positions of the majority ethnic group against the demands of the minority. To the educator, tenure is seen as an indispensable means of protecting the autonomy the educational profession requires to give effective service. To critics, tenure often appears as a device to protect an ideological position, frustrate educational change, or resist the economic demands of outsiders. In the long run, minority educators will find that tenure serves their interests as well as those of the majority, and educational administrators will realize the need of a tenure system to protect the schools against the complaints of ideological critics. In the short run, though, these advantages are not always apparent, and tenure—and all other devices to assure educational autonomy—are under heavy assault.

Another threat to control of the schools by educators is a byproduct of increased federal aid to education. Federal aid to education has been accompanied by demands that the schools adhere to federal standards as promulgated by officials of the Department of Health, Education and Welfare [Seabury, 1972]. Such demands mean that the individual schools have lost a portion of their control over personnel and curriculum to an agency of another institution—that of government. Reflecting on such trends, the head of the New York City Teachers' Union recalls the time when federal aid for the schools was being debated and notes:

. . . the basic conflict was between "liberals" and "conservatives" over the issue of whether federal aid would lead to federal control of schools. Liberals generally argued that federal aid would not lead to such control or, to the extent that the federal power of the purse was exerted, it would be used to promote beneficial national educational objectives that would supplant local and discriminatory interests. As we look back at that debate from the standpoint of 1974, it would seem that the old conservatives were not far off base (Shanker, 1974).

Governmental and economic institutions

While it would be possible to look at governmental and economic institutions separately, they are so closely intertwined that it seems most efficient to look at them together. Government does have other concerns besides economic activity, but fostering or carrying on the production of goods and services is such an important function of modern governments that governmental and economic policy are always closely related regardless of whether the prevailing ideology is socialist or capitalist.

Development of governmental-economic institutions

When human society gained a subsistence by gathering nuts and herbs, there was little need for either trade or government. The extended family provided all the coordination needed at this stage of activity. Trade developed when a need was felt for an orderly and dependable way of obtaining resources controlled by another group. Economic institutions emerged as people organized a division of labor and recognized private claims to property. The domestication of animals, the establishment of settled agriculture with claims to land, and the eventual development of industries all led to the development of economic and governmental systems of various degrees of complexity. In recent years, the specialization of labor has reached a point where over 30,000 different occupational titles are listed in the government publication, *Alphabetical Index of Occupations in the United States*, and an economic

system has developed in which virtually no one subsists by his own efforts alone. The functions of government have grown so greatly that more than 30 percent of the national income is expended by the several levels of government in the United States.

Even modern business makes use of tradition, ritual, and sentiment.

Governmental-economic institutions are more than standardized ways of doing things. As with all institutions, they also include supporting ideas, sentiments, traditions, and values. Canoe building among the Polynesians, the walrus hunt among the Eskimos, rice planting in the wet rice culture of Southeast Asia—all these involve ascribed roles, traditions, and elaborate rituals. These rituals bring the blessing of the gods on the undertaking and also solidify the cooperation of humans. Government is supported by a panoply of flag waving, martial music, impressive buildings, and the stirring sentiment of patriotism. Even modern business makes use of tradition, ritual, and sentiment. The singing commercial, stories of the charismatic business leaders, gifts to charity and public services, the recognition banquet for retiring employees—all these combine to make the business system take on the appearance of a warm-blooded collection of human beings rather than simply a cold economic machine.

Governmental-economic institutional patterns

In Chapter 4 we noted that the evolution of a money economy and of social stratification have been suggested as two of the inevitable developments in social evolution. This is another way of saying that modern economies require a medium of exchange more flexible than barter, so a monetary and credit system has developed. A modern economy also requires the coordination of the labor of many specialized functionaries and the enforcement of the rules whereby they operate. One function of social stratification is to furnish a system of leaders and followers which provides the coordination of labor.

Three different types of governmental-economic systems have emerged, each of which handles the problem of economic coordination differently.

Mixed economy. This type of system may take either a capitalist or a socialist label, but these labels make little difference in the way the institutions function. Whether the society in point is the allegedly capitalist one of the United States or the allegedly socialist one of Sweden, the relation between government and the economy is similar in kind and differs somewhat in degree. In either case, a large part of the society's economic activity is carried on by businessmen whose activities are dictated largely by what seems to be the best way to make profits. In each country, however, some enterprises are operated by the government. Similarly, government control of the supply of both credit and money does much to influence economic activity in each country, while variations in government expenditures also affect the level of business. Finally, both countries operate as welfare states in which the provision of both a minimum income and a large number of services such as housing, education and medical care is a government responsibility. Sweden has a higher level of taxation and for many years has provided a more complete range of such services, but the United States is now moving in the Swedish direction of greater welfare expenditures and consequently higher taxes. Socialist parties in Sweden and other Scandinavian countries have had trouble in elections in recent years and there is evidence that many Swedes have begun to question whether the benefits received from government outweigh the cost of taxation, which gives 40 percent of the Gross National Product to the government, and the inconvenience of many regulations [Ross, 1974]. Since the United States has a constantly mounting demand for greater welfare expenditures, it may be that the two countries are converging toward a similar pattern. Such a pattern would imply a slowing down in the growth of activities of the welfare state in Sweden and an acceleration of these activities in the United States, thus blurring the former contrast between the two countries.

Communist societies. The term "democratic" is used in communist societies to describe a system in which people have no effective means of control but in which a one-party dictatorship claims to rule in their behalf. Agriculture is often organized in collective farms which usually draw bitter opposition from the farmers, with agricultural output lagging in communist countries. Overall coordination of the economy, including the level of prices and wages and the kind of goods produced, is determined by central planning agencies. In recent years, communist countries in Europe have reverted partially to a capitalist model where each industry makes more of its own business decisions and is expected to make a "profit" in its operations. These profits are retained by the government to be used as the government thinks best. Yugoslavia is the communist country which allows the individual enterprise the greatest degree of independence in operation. While there are variations between countries, some type of communist system operates in the Soviet Union, the satellite Eastern European countries, Laos, Vietnam, China and

Cuba. Communism in the Soviet Union did produce some degree of economic development, but whether economic advance there was more or less rapid than it might have been under a capitalist system is still under dispute.

Communism typically gains power in poor, underdeveloped countries with an archaic social system and constitutes the form of their effort to modernize themselves [Kiernan, 1972, p. 35]. It is, however, by no means certain that Communism offers the most rapid route of economic improvement for underdeveloped countries. Most of the recently independent nations have rejected the Communist pattern in favor of a mixed economy. A few of these nations, such as Singapore, have reached a high degree of prosperity with a mixed economic system which is more heavily capitalist than collectivist.

Fascist societies. A fascist society is ruled by a one-party dictatorship organized by a charismatic leader. The people have practically no voice in governmental affairs and find their satisfaction in the glorious strength of the nation. Military power and conquest were major features of Hitler's Germany and Mussolini's Italy, but Franco's Spain and Peron's Argentina operated without military expansionism. Private ownership of business is tolerated, but the businessman is given limited freedom and is subject to detailed state direction. Welfare benefits are provided by the state and are as high as the stage of industrial development and the needs of the military will allow. All private interests are subordinated to the state. Labor unions become agencies for imposing state policy upon workers, while churches are either forced to support the regime or find their activities severely restricted. Fascism develops in countries with a relatively advanced economy and some democratic experience. Such countries may "turn fascist" when they have been unable to reconcile their social tensions or to solve their social problems democratically [Ebenstein, 1973].

Fascism, communism, and mixed economies compared. All three of these governmental-economic systems are oriented to increased productivity. The mixed economies provide more scope to individual initiative, while communism and fascism limit individual freedom sharply and depend upon centralized government agencies for planning economic goals and activities. Insofar as they are industrialized, there tends to be a restriction of extreme wealth and a raising of the standards of the lower income level. Yet in all three types of societies, inequalities in income persist. In the communist society, inequalities in income stem from unequal wage and salary scales which allow a professional or managerial person to earn several times as much as a common laborer (see discussion on page 257), while in the fascist society and in the mixed economies, property ownership and inheritance lead to great differences in income. Most of the developing countries have not yet settled neatly into any of these patterns, and the trend in these countries seems to be toward a one-party or military dictatorship in government with a mixture of governmental enterprise and private business in the economy.

Latent functions of governmental-economic institutions. The manifest functions of all three systems—communist, fascist, and mixed economy—are to maintain order, achieve consensus, and maximize economic production. No society is completely successful in any of these functions. The totalitarian communist or fascist societies seem most successful in maintaining order, at least temporarily, while the mixed economies have the best record in reaching a consensus which still allows expression of minority opinion, and they have also achieved the greatest success in economic production.

An analysis of the three types of societies indicates a high degree of similarity in their latent functions. One latent function of all modern governmental-economic institutions is the destruction of traditional culture. Customary forms of land tenure, religious belief, family organization, residential location, and many other established patterns of social life undergo change as industrialism develops. Social mobility is encouraged, one consequence of which is increased anomie and alienation.

Another latent function is the acceleration of ecological deterioration. Unless expensive and complicated precautions are taken, every increase in production leads to an increase in environmental destruction. Sometimes capitalists are blamed for this on the grounds that they are unwilling to let concern for ecological balance interfere with profits. However, the Soviet Union, without any capitalists except the state, has the same problem. Basically, the difficulty is that any system is reluctant to pay the costs of preventing pollution. A major reduction in pollution would probably require increases in production costs and in taxes, with a consequent drop in the standard of living, and will certainly require a halt in the world's population explosion. Neither communists nor capitalists will find it easy to carry pollution-reduction policies into effect.

Culture and government

Political scientists suggest that the success or failure of democratic governments depends largely on the compatibility of the democratic process with the culture of the country. It is futile for a country to adopt a constitution which provides for elected officials unless the attitudes of the people enable them to support a democratic regime. Attitudes of this kind have been given the name *the civic culture* [Almond and Verba, 1963]. The civic culture is described as a fusion of attitudes directly supporting participation in the political structure combined with other attitudes, such as trust in other people and a general disposition toward social cooperation and involvement. An unwillingness to participate in elections or political discussion renders a democratic system meaningless. But participation is not enough. If people lack trust in each other and in the

government processes, then political participation leads to insoluble conflict. We then say that the group has been "politicized," meaning that it has substituted political partisanship for a real effort to solve issues. In many countries, such "politicization" has led to disgust with the democratic process and the rise of dictatorial regimes.

Almond and Verba have analyzed Italy, Mexico, Germany, the United States, and Great Britain in terms of the prevalence of the civic culture. Italy was found to lack both trust and a pattern of participation. In Mexico a lack of mutual trust was also apparent, but government had become a symbol of Mexican hopes and aspirations and thereby secured the consensus needed for functioning. Germany was seen as a country in which attitudes favoring political participation were not well developed, and a lack of trust was manifested in bitter hostility between members of different political parties. Americans were seen as people with a highly developed sense of political participation and general trust, but with a fairly high suspicion of administrative agencies. Great Britain is described as the country which best approximates the civic culture. Political participation is highly developed, and Britons combine a general trust in the system with intense loyalty to their political parties [Almond and Verba, 1963, pp. 402–469].

Whether the presence or absence of the civic culture is an adequate explanation as to why democracy flourishes in some countries and falters or fails to survive in others may be debatable. One premise seems fairly certain: for any set of practices to flourish in a society, they must be integrated with the rest of the culture.

Summary

Social institutions are organized systems of social relationships which embody certain common values and procedures and meet certain basic needs of the society. Institutions develop gradually from the social life of a people. When certain activities have become the standardized, routinized, expected, and approved means of accomplishing important goals, this behavior has been *institutionalized.* An *institutionalized* role is one which has been standardized, approved, and expected, and is normally filled in a quite predictable manner, regardless of the person filling it. Each institution includes a cluster of *institutional traits* (codes of behavior, attitudes, values, symbols, rituals, ideologies), *manifest functions* (those functions which it is intended or believed to perform), and *latent functions* (those results which are unintended and unplanned).

Leaders of institutionally related associations (schools, churches, businesses, etc.) normally seek for some degree of *institutional autonomy,* or independence from other institutions. Struggles over institutional autonomy have led to such church-state arrangements as the *sect, denomination,* and *ecclesia,* and to the development of the concept of *academic freedom* in educational institutions. Institutions are *interrelated,* so that changes in one institution affect the others in a continuous cause-and-effect relationship.

The analysis of particular institutions illustrates these characteristics of institutions. The latent functions of religious institutions may subvert their formal norms, as in rules resulting in family living outside of formal marriage. Latent functions of educational institutions, such as the promotion of social mobility or racial integration, may involve the schools in severe conflict, while latent functions of the governmental-economic institutions may lead to ecological destruction. In modern times, governmental institutions have overshadowed the others. In communist countries the government officials have direct control of the economy; in fascist countries they dominate it indirectly; and in the mixed economies the governmental and business leaders share societal control. The leaders in each institutionally related association seek both to preserve their institutional autonomy and to extend their influence over other institutions. Studies of government and culture suggest that the values and attitudes of a culture determine the kind of governmental institutions which will develop. Attitudes favorable to the support of a democratic form of government are known as the *civic culture.*

Questions and projects

1. What are five basic social institutions found in all complex societies? How does an institution differ from an association?
2. What is meant by the process of institutionalization? Is art an institution? Recreation? The United Nations? Marriage? Birth control? Science?
3. Do you think the increased rate of divorce in the family institution is related to changes in our economic institutions? If so, how?
4. Is it possible that a church could be an ecclesia in one country and a denomination in another? Can you think of an example?
5. What is the meaning of the statement that Weber's interpretation of the Protestant ethic refutes the Marxian emphasis on the primacy of economic factors in the interrelationship of institutions?
6. Are there any reasons why a person who is anxious to promote radical social change should defend the academic freedom of faculty who oppose radical social change?
7. Has the community college been institutionalized in terms of the role behavior expected of students, faculty, and administrators? How about the "free universities" that have appeared on or near the campus?
8. Read either the book, **Kids and Cops: A Study in Mutual Hostility* by Donald G. Bouma (Eerdmans Publishing Co., Grand Rapids, Mich., 1969), or the journal article by Donald G. Bouma and Donald G. Williams, "Police-School Liaison: An Evaluation of Programs," *Intellect,* November, 1972, pp. 119–122. Evaluate the police-school liaison program in terms of institu-

tional interrelationships. Does the program allow the police to dominate education or is it mutually helpful to both education and police?

9. The Socialist Worker's Party in the United States, a small group with no hope of winning an election, is bitterly critical of other parties that have missed the true path of Marxian socialism and is very proud of its own steadfast devotion to basic principles. What type of religious group does it resemble? What kind of motivation keeps parties of this type alive?

10. Make a comparison of the Communist Party and the Christian church(es) as institutionally related associations. (William Ebenstein, *Today's*

Isms, Prentice-Hall, Inc., Englewood Cliffs, N.J., 1973, chap. 1, is a good source on the Communist Party.) For each, identify its sacred writing, saints and martyrs, absolute truths, symbols, codes of behavior, manifest and latent functions, claims upon members, and recent examples of disorganization and reorganization.

11. From the Suggested Readings compare the articles by Sidney Hook with the one listed for Herbert Marcuse; or compare Berger with Neuhaus in *Movement and Revolution.* In each case, one defends present institutions while the other calls for revolution. Which do you think makes the more convincing case? Why?

Suggested readings

ABRECHT, MILTON C.: "Art as a Social Institution," *American Sociological Review,* 33:383–390, June, 1968. Presents art as a social institution, but one which does not follow exactly the type of format usually characterizing other institutions.

BENNETT, WILLIAM S., JR., AND R. FRANK FALK: *New Careers and Urban Schools*, Holt, Rinehart and Winston, Inc., New York, 1970. Describes the institutionalization of the role of teacher aide.

*BERGER, PETER L., AND RICHARD J. NEUHAUS: *Movement and Revolution,* Doubleday & Company, Inc., Garden City, N.J., 1970. Berger argues the case for the viability of the present structure of American society, while Neuhaus urges the need for revolution.

BROOKOVER, WILBUR L. AND EDSEL L. ERICKSON: *Society, Schools and Learning,* Michigan State University Press, 1973; *Susan Budd: *Sociologists and Religion,* The Macmillan Company, London, 1971; *Neil J. Smelser: *The Sociology of Economic Life,* Prentice-Hall, Inc., Englewood Cliffs, N.J., 1963. Brief sociological descriptions of these basic institutions.

COSER, LEWIS A.: *Greedy Institutions: Patterns of Undivided Commitment,* The Free Press, New York, 1974. Institutionally related associations sometimes fight the trend toward multiple loyalties by demanding the complete dedication of people involved. Examples include the eunuchs who performed tasks for rulers, the activist in the Communist Party, the Catholic priesthood,

the domestic servant, or the housewife who subordinates all nonhousehold interests. A readable book revealing total institutional commitment.

EDWARDS, HARRY: "Sport as a Social Institution," chap. 5 of *The Sociology of Sport*, Dorsey Press, Homewood, Ill., 1973. A semipopular presentation of institutionalized aspects of sport.

*HADDEN, JEFFREY K.: *Religion in Radical Transition,* Society Books, Chicago, 1973. Articles from *Trans-action* magazine (now renamed *Society*) on the current state of religion in the United States and elsewhere.

HAMMOND, JOHN L.: "Revival Religion and Anti-Slavery Politics," *American Sociological Review,* 39:174–186, April, 1974. Reveals the association between religious revivals and anti-slavery sentiment, illustrating the institutional interaction between religion, government, and economics.

*HOFSTADTER, RICHARD: *Anti-Intellectualism in American Life,* Alfred A. Knopf Co., New York, 1963. A stimulating discussion of the love-hate relationship between intellectuals and American social institutions.

HOOK, SIDNEY: "Real Crisis on the Campus," *Reader's Digest,* August, 1969, pp. 41–45; "War against the Democratic Process," *Atlantic,* Apr., 1969, pp. 45–49. Two brief articles defending American liberal democratic institutions.

HUNT, CHESTER L.: *Social Aspects of Economic Development,* McGraw-Hill Book Company, New

York, 1966. A brief, simply written analysis of the interrelationship of economic patterns with other institutions in developing countries.

MARCUSE, HERBERT: "Student Protest Is Nonviolent Next to the Society Itself," *New York Times Magazine,* May 4, 1969, p. 137. A short statement of Marcuse's indictment of American society.

MERTON, ROBERT K.: "Manifest and Latent Functions: Toward the Codification of Functional Analysis in Sociology," *Social Theory and Social Structure,* The Free Press, New York, 1968, pp. 19–84; reprinted in Merton, Robert K., *On Theoretical Sociology,* The Free Press, New York, 1967, pp. 73–138. A discussion of latent and manifest functions of institutions.

TURNER, JONATHAN H.: *Patterns of Social Organization: A Survey of Social Institutions,* McGraw-Hill Book Company, New York, 1972. A systematic treatment of the main institutions of American society, including kinship, economy, education, law, government and religion, and of their interaction with one another.

Chapter 10 ● The family

It happened one morning when Johnny [an American ex-GI] came to work and found Maggi, Kim Sing, Povenaaa, and three other men rolling dice. Teuru [Johnny's native girl] stood nearby, watching the game with interest, advising Maggi, "You better try harder! You need three more sixes!"

"What's the game?" Johnny asked.

"Dice," Teuru said.

"I can see that. What's it about?"

Teuru blushed and looked away, so Johnny asked Povenaaa. "Don't bother me now," the excited man cried. Suddenly there were shouts of triumph and Maggi swore the Chinaman had cheated, but Kim Sing grinned happily and picked up the dice.

"The damned Chinaman gets the baby," Povenaaa spat.

"Gets what?" Johnny asked.

"The baby."

"Whose baby?"

"Teuru's."

"I didn't know Teuru had a baby."

"She doesn't . . . yet."

"You mean . . . my baby?" Johnny fell back with his mouth gaping. Then he yelled. "Hey! What's this about my baby?"

"He won it," Maggi said disconsolately.

Grabbing Teuru the American cried, "What are they talking about?"

"When it's born," Teuru said. "All the people in Raiatea would like to have it. So we rolled dice."

"But it's your own baby!" he stormed.

"Sure," she said. "But I can't keep it. I'm not married."

"Your own flesh and blood!"

"What's he mean?" Teuru asked Maggi.

Johnny Roe looked beseechingly at the fat woman and asked, "Would you give away your own baby? Would you give away Major?"

The crowd in the vanilla shed burst into laughter and Johnny demanded to know the joke. "It's Major!" Povenaaa roared, punching Johnny in the ribs. "Major's not her baby. She's Hedy's."

"You mean that Hedy. . . . "

"Of course," Maggi explained. "Hedy had to go to Tahiti for a good time before settling down. So she gave me Major."

Johnny Roe had heard enough. He stormed off and bought two bottles of gin, and when Teuru found him he had returned to his Montparnasse days except that now he blubbered, "Our baby! You raffled off our baby with a pair of dice!"

He kept this up for a whole day and Teuru became afraid that it was the start of another epic binge, so she broke the gin bottles and said, "All girls give away their first babies. How else could they get married?"

Johnny sat upright, suddenly sobered. "What do you mean, married?"

"What man in Raiatea would want a girl who couldn't have babies?"

"You mean . . . the men don't care?"

"Very much! Since people find I'm to have a baby, several men who never noticed me before have asked when you were going away."

"What happens then?" Johnny asked suspiciously.

"Then I get married."

Johnny fell back on his pillow and moaned, "It's indecent. By God, it's indecent." *(James A. Michener,* Return to Paradise. *Reprinted by permission of Random House, Inc., and William Morris Agency, Inc., on behalf of author. Copyright © 1951 by James A. Michener.)*

Family patterns show a fascinating variation from society to society, and persons from one society who become involved in the family patterns of a different society generally react in a predictably ethnocentric manner. Why, if the family is so important, have we been unable to find and agree upon some ideal pattern of family life which best serves human needs?

In the most primitive societies, the family is the only institution. Among the polar Eskimos, there were no other institutions—no chiefs or formal laws, no priests or medicine men, no specialized occupations. Within the family all the business of living was fulfilled. In other words, they had no physical or social needs that called for an institutional structure other than that provided by their family.

As a culture grows more complex, its institutional structures become more elaborate. The family is an adequate structure for handling the economic production and consumption of primitive hunters and farmers. But what happens when they develop trade with neighboring or distant tribes? Before long the group includes traders, shippers, and other specialists whose work is no longer a part of the family life of the society. Later, specialized craftsmen begin to produce trade goods, giving rise to further occupational differentiation. Economic institutions exist whenever economic functions are performed in routine ways by specialists, operating outside their family roles and functions.

In the most primitive societies, order is maintained with no formal laws, police, or courts. The only authority known in many simple societies is family authority; that is, certain family members have certain authority over others. With increasing tribal size and growing cultural complexity, more formal political organization is needed. Family heads are joined into tribal councils, tribes combine into confederations, and bureaucracies begin to develop. Warfare, in both primitive and modern societies, is a powerful stimulus to political organization, for only through political organization can an aroused rabble be mobilized for an effective military effort. In like manner, religious and educational institutions develop as professional functionaries, following standardized procedures, withdraw from the family certain activities which are too complicated for the family to handle well.

The family, then, is the basic social institution, from which the others have grown as increasing cultural complexity made them necessary. A study of the family will tell us something about the family and about institutions in general.

Structure of the family

Like all institutions, the family is a system of accepted norms and procedures for getting some important jobs done. The family is defined as a *kinship grouping which provides for the rearing of children and for certain other human needs.* If a society is to survive, people must find some workable and dependable ways of pairing off, conceiving and raising children, caring for the ill and aged, and carrying out certain other functions. These family functions vary considerably from society to society, while the family forms for fulfilling these functions vary even more greatly. In fact, if one were to list every possible way of organizing family life, a search of anthropological literature would probably reveal that each form of organization was the accepted pattern in at least one society. With only a few exceptions, where family patterns are concerned, everything is right some place.

Composition of the family group

When we speak of the family, we ordinarily think of a husband and wife, their children, and occasionally an extra relative. Since this

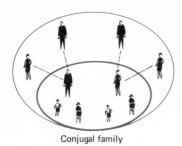

Conjugal family

The basic family unit consists of husband and wife and their children, with a fringe of relatives.

Consanguine family (matrilocal)

The basic family unit consists of a group of sisters and brothers, and the sisters' children, with a fringe of spouses. (In the less common patrilocal form, it is the children of the brothers who complete the family.)

Figure 1. Conjugal and consanguine family types.

family is based upon the marital or "conjugal" relationship, it has been called the conjugal family. Today, however, it is most often referred to as the *nuclear family.* The *consanguine family* is founded not upon the conjugal relationship of husband and wife but upon the blood relationship of a large number of kinspersons. The consanguine family is an extended clan of blood relatives together with their mates and children. The term *extended family* is often used to refer to the nuclear family plus any other kin with whom important relationships are maintained. While Americans use the extended family for family reunions and other ceremonial purposes, most of the routine family functions proceed on a nuclear family basis. Our folklore warns against in-laws and urges the couple to set up a household of their own. This is known as *neolocal* marriage, as distinct from *patrilocal* marriage, where the married couple live with the husband's family, and

from *matrilocal* marriage, where the couple live with the wife's family. Our laws require a husband to maintain his wife in a home apart from other relatives if she insists, and she sometimes does. Our laws require parents to support their own minor children, but impose only slight obligation to care for their parents, and no obligation to care for brothers and sisters, cousins, uncles and aunts, nephews and nieces, or other relatives.

The consanguine family has a very different atmosphere. Whereas the conjugal family has a married couple at its core, surrounded by a fringe of blood relatives, the consanguine family has a group of brothers and sisters at its core, surrounded by a fringe of husbands and wives. In most instances of the consanguine family, a married person remains primarily attached to his or her parental family and remains a semioutsider in the spouse's family. This has important consequences. One's principal responsibilities are toward the family into which one was born, not the family into which one has married. Thus a woman may depend not upon her husband but upon her brothers for protection and help in raising her children. Her husband does not escape, however, for he is saddled with his sister's children. [For descriptions of the consanguine family, see Linton, 1936, chap. 10; Murdock, 1949, chap. 3.]

In such a family, affection and responsibility are widely diffused among a fairly large group of people. Children are the joint responsibility of the entire family, and a child develops a relationship with its aunts very like that with its mother. It is surrounded by many adults, any of whom may momentarily act as parents toward it. The family tends to turn out personalities with less individuality than ours, since each child has more nearly the same socialization experience. Such a family protects the individual against misfortune. If a child's mother dies or is neglectful, good substitutes are at hand. The consanguine family offers little opportunity for individuality and little danger of loneliness or neglect.

Obviously the consanguine family is not

Where family patterns are concerned, almost everything is right someplace.

practical everywhere. Where both the family of birth and the family of marriage are in the same village, it is easy to be with one's mate while fulfilling obligations to one's parental family. If they are in different villages, a strain is imposed. In a highly mobile, individualized, specialized society like ours, the consanguine family would be unworkable. But for the Tanala of Madagascar, whose farm work required a cooperative team of a half dozen or more adult males, the consanguine family was ideal [Linton, 1936, chap. 12].

Forms of marriage

The path to marriage is lined with a variety of impediments, requirements, preliminaries, and ceremonials which would be downright discouraging—were not the objective so attractive. Rare is the society in which it is usual for a couple quietly to pair off and start playing house. While this happens with some frequency in contemporary American society, it is not the approved and expected (and therefore not the institutionalized) arrangement. Marriage is too important for such casual arrangements. Marriage is *the approved social pattern whereby two or more persons establish a family.* It involves not only the conceiving and rearing of children (who are sometimes conceived as an institutionalized preliminary to marriage), but also a host of other obligations

and privileges affecting a good many people. Every society has, therefore, developed a pattern for guiding these marriages.

In this matter of guidance our ethnocentrism is likely to be evident. To us it is monstrous that parents should arrange and compel the marriage of two persons who may never even have met. How do they know whether they will love each other? Why are not their wishes consulted? Our reaction illustrates the usual error of ethnocentrism—assuming that people with another culture will think and feel as we should think and feel if transplanted into their situation. It overlooks the fact that most people wish and feel only what their society trains them to wish and feel. We think of marriage as a romantic adventure with a person we have come to love. The girl in classical China, about to enter an arranged marriage with a stranger, eagerly anticipated her marriage as a desirable status and a comfortable companionship with a man she would come to love, because he had been wisely chosen by her parents. Each society has viewed the other with an ethnocentric pity; we pitied their young people for their lack of freedom; they pitied our young people for their lack of parental assistance. In neither case did the young people themselves feel any need for pity. Today, of course, the Chinese family has changed rapidly and painfully in the Peoples' Republic [Levy, 1949, Chandrasekhar, 1959; Yang, 1959; Huang, 1961; Leslie, 1973, pp. 113–118].

Endogamy and exogamy. Every society limits choice in marriage by requiring that one choose a mate outside some specified group. This is called *exogamy.* In our society the prohibition applies only to close blood relatives; one may not marry a brother or sister, first cousin, or certain other close relatives. Many societies extend the circle of prohibited kin to forbid marriage within the clan, the village, or sometimes even the tribe.

Most societies also require that mates be chosen within some specified group. This is called *endogamy.* Clan, village, and tribal endogamy are quite common among primitive societies. In our society, racial endogamy was required by law in many states until the U.S. Supreme Court held all such laws unconstitutional in 1967, but custom and social pressure continue to discourage racial intermarriage throughout our society. With varying degrees of pressure, we also encourage religious endogamy and class endogamy in our country.

Every society practices both exogamy and endogamy, as it specifies the limits of group closeness (exogamy) and the limits of group distance (endogamy) within which mates must be found. Sometimes between these two limits there is little room for hunting! The Aranda of Central Australia have a complicated marital pattern known to anthropologists as an "eight-class system with exogamy and indirect patrilineal descent." To skip the detailed explanations, this means that a man can marry only a woman from a particular group within the proper subsection of the opposite half of his tribe [Murdock, 1936, pp. 27–30]. In a number of societies, a formula such as this makes an actual choice unnecessary, for only one person may be in the permissible category for a boy or girl to marry. If there is none at all, then the couple who are supposed to become parents-in-law normally adopt a marriageable boy or girl from another family with a surplus. After all, an institution is a structure for meeting human needs, and it usually does so in one fashion or another.

Marital choice. The process of arranging a marriage shows a fascinating range of possibilities. As shown above, some societies follow a formula whereby the children of certain socially designated kinsmen marry each other, so that the individual choices may be unnecessary. Where actual choices are necessary, they may be made in many ways. The couples can do their own choosing, sometimes with parental guidance or parental veto. The parents can arrange the marriage, with or without considering the couple's wishes. A wife may be purchased, or perhaps a complicated series of gifts are exchanged between families. Wife capture is not unknown. Each of these patterns is the standard way of arranging marriages in some of the world's societies. All of them work—within the society in which they exist—and are supported by the surrounding values and practices of the culture. Wife capture worked very well for the Tasmanians, who practiced village exogamy and were not greatly concerned over the differences between one woman and all the others. For our society, it would be less practical. This illustrates the concept of cultural relativity—a pattern which works well in one cultural setting might work badly in another. As Peters shows [1971], parental engagement of three-year-old girls to teenaged boys works out very well for the Shirishana of Brazil, while any attempt to impose the Western concepts of marriage would undermine Shirishana stability and invite chaos.

Monogamy and polygamy. To all properly ethnocentric Americans, there is only one decent and civilized form of marriage—*monogamy*—one man to one woman (at a time). Yet a majority of the world's societies have practiced *polygamy,* allowing a plurality of mates. There are three theoretical forms of polygamy. One is *group marriage,* in which several men and several women are all in a marriage relationship with one another. While this is an intriguing theoretical possibility, there is no authentic instance of a society in which group marriage has been fully institutionalized, with the possible exception, at one time, of the Marquesans. A very rare form is *polyandry,* where several husbands share a single wife. The Todas of Southern India provide one of our few examples. Here, as in most other cases, polyandry was fraternal, meaning that when a woman married a man, she automatically became wife to all of his brothers, and they all lived together with little jealousy or discord. Toda polyandry becomes understandable when one learns that it accompanied female infanticide and a shortage of women [Murdock, 1936, pp. 120–121; Queen et al., 1974, chap. 2]. Only where some situation has created a shortage of women is polyandry likely to be found [Unni, 1958]. But the scattered handful of societies which practice polyandry serve to show how a practice which seems to us to be contrary to human nature can still be the accepted and preferred pattern for people who are socialized to expect it. The usual form of polygamy is *polygyny*—a plurality of wives, not usually sisters and generally acquired at different times during one's life.

Mention of polygyny will arouse a predictably ethnocentric response from most Americans. They conjure up images of female degradation and helpless enslavement, and rise to impressive heights of moral indignation at such heathen brutishness (or possibly of harem delights as pictured in Hollywood's mass-produced daydreams). The facts are otherwise. It would be difficult to show that women have generally had a more satisfactory status in monogamous than in polygamous societies. Even in polygynous societies, most of the marriages are monogamous. It is generally only the more successful and powerful men who can afford or attract more than one wife. In many polygynous societies, the second wife fills the status function of the second Cadillac in our society. Far from feeling resentful, the first wife often urges her husband to take more wives, over whom she generally reigns as queen bee. Polygyny in operation takes many forms in different societies, all of them far removed from the imagination of the normal ethnocentric American.

Divorce. What is to be done when a married couple can't stand each other? Although most societies make some provision for divorce, some make it very difficult or perhaps give the privilege of divorce only to the men. Some make divorce very simple. Among the Hopi, divorce is rather rare but very uncomplicated. The husband merely packs up and leaves, or in his absence his wife tells him to get lost by pitching his things outside the door.

The social and family structure of many societies makes divorce a fairly painless and harmless operation. In many societies where there is no great emphasis upon romantic love and no intense individual love attachments, divorce entails no great heartbreak. Where the consanguine family surrounds the child with a protective clan of kin and designates the mother's brother as the responsible male in a child's life, the loss of a child's biological father is hardly noticed. The meaning of divorce depends upon how it relates to other aspects of the institution of the family. In our society, with its strong accent upon individual love attachments within an isolated nuclear family unit, a divorce may complete the collapse of the emotional world for both child and adult.

Other variations in family structure. We could extend the list of "odd" family patterns indefinitely. Some societies, like ours, encourage an informal camaraderie between brother and sister; among others, such as the Nama Hottentots, brother and sister are expected to treat each other with great formality and respect, may not address each other directly, or even be alone together. Such *avoidances* are found in many societies. Mother-in-law avoidance is very common; the Crow husband may not look at or speak to his mother-in-law, or even use a word which appears in her name. In many societies, avoidance taboos demand extreme decorum toward certain relatives, while *privileged relationships* permit special familiarities with certain other relatives. Thus the Crow, who must act with great decorum toward his sister, mother-in-law, son-in-law, and his wife's brother's wife, is socially expected to show great familiarity toward his sister-in-law, joke with her, and engage in various immodesties. Among the Nama Hottentots, brother-sister incest is the worst of all offenses, but cross-cousins[1] enjoy a "joking relationship" which includes loose talk, horseplay, and sexu-

---

[1]*Cross-cousins* are the children of a brother and sister with their respective mates; where the related parents are of the same sex, as in the case of two brothers or two sisters, the cousins are called parallel cousins.

al intimacy. All this is merely to say that the family includes a varying number of people whose relationship to one another is defined differently in different societies.

Is there any sense in all this, or is the family an irrational jumble of odd notions and historical accidents? Two things we should remember. First, many different patterns will "work," as long as all members of the society accept them. Wife purchase, wife capture, or wives-for-the-asking—any one of these patterns works out acceptably, provided the people view it as the proper way to stake out a mate. Thousands of societies have been in existence at some time or other. It is not surprising that most of the possible ways of organizing human relationships have been tried out sometime, somewhere. Many of them have survived, showing that people are highly adaptable animals, capable of being trained to find their satisfactions in a remarkable variety of ways.

Second, we invoke the concept of cultural relativism and repeat that how a custom works depends upon how it relates to the rest of its cultural setting. Where wife purchase exists, the transaction is not merely a way of arranging marriages but a central feature of the entire economic and social system. The consanguine family exists in certain societies because it is an efficient *economic* unit in such societies, and not just because it is nice to have the family together [Sahlins, 1957; Nimkoff and Middleton, 1960]. Societies which are today becoming industrialized and commercialized are also replacing the consanguine with the nuclear family, which better meets the needs of a mobile, individualized society [Leslie, 1973, pp. 243–246]. As we stated in an earlier chapter, institutions are interrelated.

Functions of the family

The family in any society is an institutional structure which develops through a society's efforts to get certain tasks done. What are the tasks commonly performed through the family?

The sexual regulation function

The family is the principal institution through which societies organize and regulate the satisfaction of sexual desires. Most societies provide some alternative sexual outlets. With varying degrees of indulgence, each society also tolerates some sex behavior in violation of its norms. In other words, there is in all societies some deviation of the real culture from the ideal culture in sexual behavior. But all societies expect that most sexual intercourse will occur between persons whom their institutional norms define as legitimately accessible to each other. These norms sometimes allow for considerable sexual variety; yet no society is entirely promiscuous. In every society there are mores which forbid certain persons access to one another. What may look to us like promiscuity is more likely to be a complicated system of sexual permissions and taboos which we do not fully understand.

A clear majority of the world's societies allow young persons to experiment with sexual intercourse before marrying [Murdock, 1949, 1950]. Many societies think the idea of virgin marriage is absurd. Yet in such societies, this premarital sex experience is viewed as a preparation for marriage, not as a recreational pastime. Sometimes its principal purpose is to determine fertility; a girl who conceives shows her readiness for marriage. Most of these societies have not merely *allowed* premarital sexual behavior; they have *institutionalized* it. They have defined it as a proper and useful activity and have developed a supporting set of institutional arrangements which make it safe and harmless. Since there is full social approval, there is no fear, shame, or disgrace. The family structure and living arrangements in such societies are generally of a sort where one more baby is no special inconvenience or burden. Premarital sex experience can be a useful and harmless preparation for marriage in a society which has institutionalized it. Ours has not, but may be in the process of beginning to do so today.

The reproductive function

Every society depends primarily upon the family for the business of producing children. Other arrangements are theoretically possible, and many societies arrange to accept children produced outside a marriage relationship. But no society has established a set of norms for providing children except as part of a family.

The socialization function

All societies depend primarily upon the family for the socialization of children into adults who can function successfully in that society. Thinkers from Plato to Huxley [1932, 1958] have speculated about other arrangements, and dozens of experiments in communal child rearing have been attempted and abandoned. After the Russian Revolution, the Soviet Union experimented with raising children in institutions, hoping to free their mothers for labor and to rear the children more "scientifically." But Russia never practiced this idea very widely, soon gave it up, and then did everything possible to strengthen the family [Alt and Alt, 1959]. In the Soviet Union today, school and family cooperate closely to socialize children for conformity, obedience, and altruism [Bronfenbrenner, 1970]. In modern Israel, children in the kibbutz (cooperative farm) are raised in communal cottages and cared for by nursery workers while the other women work elsewhere in the kibbutz. Parents are normally with their children for a couple hours a day and all day on Saturday. This communal rearing seems to work very successfully in the kibbutz [Bettelheim, 1964, 1969; Leon, 1970], al-though some critics disagree [Spiro, 1958]. Yet only a few of the Israeli children ever lived in the kibbutz, and the proportion is declining as the founders pass away and the youth find the kibbutz dull. To paraphrase an American ballad, "How you gonna keep 'em on the kibbutz, after they've seen Tel Aviv?" In Israel today, the family is reclaiming functions from the kibbutz [Talmon, 1972], and the family survives as the standard institution for looking after children. The family is the child's first primary group, and this is where the child's personality development begins. By the time it is old enough to enter primary groupings outside the family, the basic foundations of its personality are already firmly laid. The kind of person it will be is already profoundly influenced. For example, Mantell [1974] compared the early family backgrounds of a sample of Green Berets (an elite volunteer unit in the Vietnam War, noted for its ruthlessness) with a matched sample of war resisters, finding many significant differences.

One of the many ways in which the family socializes the child is through providing models for the child to copy. The boy learns to be a man, a husband, and a father mainly through having lived in a family headed by a man, a husband, and a father. Some socialization difficulties are encountered where such a model is missing and the boy must rely upon the second-hand models he sees in other families or among other relatives [Biller, 1960; Santrock, 1970; Hartnagel, 1970]. There is no fully satisfactory substitute for a mother and a father, although they need not be the biological parents.

The importance of the family in the socialization process becomes clear when its impact is compared with that of other influences. For example, Mayeske [1973] studied the roles of racial-ethnic group, social class, and quality of school attended as causes of different rates of learning in children. He found that none of these was nearly as important as the presence or absence of a family atmosphere which encouraged learning aspirations and study habits. Numerous such studies have established the family as the primary determinant of child socialization.

Socialization in the multiproblem family. A multiproblem family is one with a depressing assortment of problems and inadequacies. It is usually poverty-stricken and conflict-ridden, is often fatherless, and is beset by other problems such as unemployment and irregular work habits, alcoholism, drug addiction, illegitimacy, dependency, delinquency, and physical and mental illness. Such families fail to fulfill *any* of the family functions adequately, and thus socialize their children to continue the pattern of inadequacy and dependency. Malnutrition permanently blights their physical and intellectual growth, and contributes to their school failure [Birch and Gussow, 1970]. Every slum, rural or urban, white or black, throngs with the "drifters"—children of disorganized lower-class families—who are deprived of love and affection, alienated from society, purposeless, and hopeless [Pavenstedt, 1967].

The affectional function

Whatever else people need, they need intimate human response. Psychiatric opinion holds that probably the greatest single cause of emotional difficulties, behavior problems, and even of physical illness, is *lack of love,* that is, lack of a warm, affectionate relationship with a small circle of intimate associates [Fromm, 1956; Schindler, 1954, chap. 10; Hayanagi, 1968]. A mountain of data shows that the serious delinquent is typically a child whom nobody cares very much about. Infants who get good physical care but are not cuddled, fondled, and loved are likely to develop a condition medically known as *marasmus* (from a Greek word meaning "wasting away"). They lose weight, fret and whimper listlessly, and sometimes even die [Ribble, 1943, chap. 1; Evans, 1972]. Several studies have shown how children in the sterilized but impersonal atmosphere of hospitals or foundling homes will suffer in emotional development and often show startlingly high rates of illness and death [Spitz, 1945]. Lack of affection actually damages an infant's ability to survive.

The evidence is overwhelming that our need for companionship and intimate, affectionate human response is vitally important to us. Indeed, this is probably our strongest social need—far more necessary than, for example, sex. Many celibates are leading happy, healthy, and useful lives, but a person who has never been loved is seldom happy, healthy, or useful.

Most societies rely almost entirely upon the family for affectionate response. The companionship need is filled partly by the family and partly by other groupings. Many primitive societies had organizations and clubs somewhat like modern lodges and fraternities, filling much the same functions. Yet even these were often organized on a kinship basis and were, therefore, another aspect of the family.

The status function

In entering a family one inherits a string of statuses. One is ascribed several statuses within the family—age, sex, birth order, and others. The family also serves as a basis for ascribing several social statuses—as, for example, a white, urban, middle-class Catholic. In any society with a class system, the class status of a child's family largely determines the opportunities and rewards open to it and the expectations through which others may inspire or discourage it. Class status can be changed through some combination of luck and personal efforts, as is described in Chapter 13, "Social Mobility." But each child *starts out* with the class status of its family, and this initial placement probably has greater effect upon achievement and reward than any other single factor. The assignment to a class may seem unfair; yet it is inevitable. The family cannot avoid preparing the child for a class status similar to its own, for the very process of living and growing up in such a family is preparation for its class status. The child normally absorbs from its family a set of interests, values, and life habits which make it easy to continue in the class status of its family and somewhat difficult for it to achieve a higher class status.

The protective function

In all societies the family offers some degree of physical, economic, and psychological protection to its members. In many societies any attack upon a person is an attack upon its entire family, with all members bound to defend it or to revenge the injury. In many societies guilt and shame are equally shared by all family members. In most primitive societies the family is an extended food-sharing unit which starves or fattens together; as long as one's relatives have food, one has no fear of hunger. And in many primitive societies, as in ours, very few persons outside one's family really care what happens to the individual.

The economic function

As stated earlier, the family is the basic economic unit in most primitive societies. Its members work together as a team and share jointly in their produce. In some societies the clan is the basic unit for working and sharing, but more often the family performs the function. This situation, however, is now changing, as will be seen in the following section.

The changing American family

The family is a prime example of the interrelatedness of institutions, for the changes in the family mirror the changes in the other institutions with which it dovetails. For example, in most hunting societies the men are clearly dominant over women, who make inferior hunters because of their limited strength and incessant child bearing. But as the economic base shifts from the hunt to the garden, women's role in the family grows somewhat more influential, for women can and do perform most of the hoe agriculture. As the plow replaces the hoe, male dominance again tends to grow, for plowing generally calls for the greater strength of the male. Thus there is some relation between one's power within the family and the importance of his or her economic contribution. Other examples of interrelatedness will follow.

Changing family structure

The size of the American family has decreased. It is no secret that the twelve-child families of the last century are rare today. The birthrate in the Western world began falling about a century ago. It reached a low during the Great Depression of the 1930s, when in the United States it fell to 16.6 births per thousand in 1933, rose to 26.6 in 1947, and fell to 14.9 by 1973. Today's "smaller family," however, does not mean that all families are proportionally smaller. As Figure 2 shows, small families are about as common as they were a half century ago, but very large families are increasingly rare. As birth control becomes increasingly available to the poor and uneducated, this trend away from the very large family will probably continue.

Why has overall family size declined in the Western world? Contraceptive devices have provided the means but not the motive. Contraceptives are not the cause of smaller families any more than ropes are the cause of suicides. The motives for desiring smaller families carry us into many other aspects of the culture. The shift from an illiterate agricultural society to a literate, specialized, industrialized society has changed children from an economic asset into an expensive burden. Shifts in patterns of

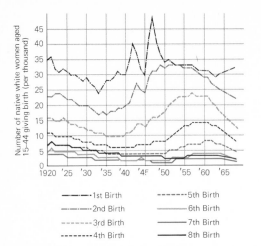

Figure 2. Family size in the United States since 1920. (Source: *Vital Statistics of the United States*, 1964, vol. 1, *Natality*, U.S. Department of Health, Education, and Welfare, pp. 1–11; *Statistical Abstract of the United States*, 1973, p. 56.)

recreation, in aspirations for education and social mobility, and changing concepts of individual rights have all united to curb indiscriminate child bearing. At present, the traditional idea that raising a large family is a noble service to society is rapidly being replaced by the idea that bearing many children is an act of irresponsible self-indulgence. There is also a growing recognition, which is fully supported by research evidence [Michel and Feyrabend, 1969], that excessive fertility is damaging to marital happiness. Thus changing technology, changing economics, and changing values are all involved in the change in family size.

The status of divorce has changed. Divorce is the object of much agonized dismay by Americans who cannot accept divorce as an integral part of the modern American family system. Divorce is not necessarily a symptom of moral decay or social instability. The average Anamatian peasant married three times and usually had some outside love affairs, without producing any dire consequences [Freilich and

Coser, 1972]. To invoke again the concept of cultural relativity, whether divorce is a disruptive crisis or a useful adjustment depends upon the culture.

A society can secure a very low divorce rate in at least five ways. First, it can deemphasize love. In many societies marriage is a working partnership, but not a romantic adventure as well. If less is expected of marriage, more marriages will be "successful." Second, it can separate love from marriage. A number of societies have a series of men's clubs for companionship, and allow men a wide freedom to prowl in search of sex adventure. Here again, less is demanded of the marriage. Third, the society can socialize its members to be so much alike in personality and expectation that practically all marriages will work out successfully. The stable, well-integrated society generally succeeds in accomplishing this leveling; our society does not. Fourth, familism may be so encompassing that divorce is intolerable. In other words, so many of one's necessities, privileges, and satisfactions may be connected to the marital and family ties that to sever the marital tie is to cancel nearly all the claims and privileges which make life tolerable. This was approximately true in early America, where divorce was legally simple but not very practical. Finally, divorce can be legally forbidden, or made so difficult that most unhappily married couples are unable or unwilling to seek divorce as a solution. Our society has actually done none of these things. It socializes people so that they differ more and more greatly in personality and expectation, gives them values which lead them to expect a great deal of marriage and to demand a high level of love satisfaction in marriage, and provides no approved outlet for their frustrated marital needs when they fail. All this makes a fairly high rate of marital failure and divorce an inescapable part of our modern family structure. The American divorce rate has risen until, in 1973, there was slightly over one divorce for each three marriages performed. (Note that this is one to three *marriages,* not one out of three *persons.*) From being a rare example of moral disgrace, divorce has become a fairly common, more-or-less respectable way of dealing with an intolerable marriage.

Where children are involved, a divorce creates a broken home. But while divorce has been creating more broken homes, falling death rates have reduced the number of homes broken by the death of parents. When both causes of broken homes are combined, we find that we now have proportionately fewer broken homes than formerly [Landis, 1970, p. 6]. The proportion of children who reach adulthood under the care of their own parents is higher today than in the "good old days" when families were supposed to be stable. This suggests that the popular practice of blaming rising delinquency and other problems on broken homes is not supported by the facts.

The division of labor and authority has changed. The traditional American family was highly patriarchal. But today, according to one major student of the family,

The dominant, child-frightening Victorian paterfamilias has turned into the embattled husband-father of today . . . struggling to maintain his self-image in the face of an aggressive wife-mother and a powerful adolescent peer group—needing, but often denied, the love of his family. (E. E. LeMasters, "The Passing of the Dominant Husband-Father," *Impact of Science Upon Society,* 21:21, January, 1971.)

When women began earning paychecks, they began to gain power. This illustrates the "resource theory," which states that family authority is held by those who "bring home the bacon" [Blood and Wolfe, 1960; Fox, 1973]. Even among groups whose family is often said to be patriarchal, such as Catholics, immigrants, or farmers, investigation shows that "the patriarchal family is dead" [Blood and Wolfe, 1960, p. 29]. In their investigation of 909 Detroit-area marriages, Blood and Wolfe found that power or domination of decision making was about equally divided between white husbands and wives [p. 35]. Black middle-class families resemble white middle-class families, but among black lower-class families, there is considerable research evidence that the wife is the more dominant [Lincoln, 1965; Moynihan, 1965b; Aldous, 1969; Blood and Wolfe, 1969; Kephart, 1972, pp. 252–254]. There are, however, some research studies which contest the "black matriarchy" thesis [Hyman and Reed, 1969; Mack, 1971; Babchuck and Ballweg, 1972; Hays and Mindel, 1973; Myers, 1975]. These critics maintain that an extended kin network among lower-class black families provides male models and male support where the father is absent. At present, the "black matriarchy" issue is unsettled [Bracey et al., 1971].

Although female-headed families are three-and-a-half times as prevalent among blacks as among whites, the majority of all female-headed families are white. A "function-by-function" comparison of female-headed families with intact families will suggest that the intact families have many advantages. For example, the economic advantage is clear, for female-headed families are disproportionately poor and on welfare. Other male kin may be helpful in some ways, but they appear to be an imperfect substitute for the husband-father.

They differ more and more greatly in personality and expectation.

The "quiet revolution" in women's employment. Perhaps the greatest change of all has been the increase in "working wives." Women workers

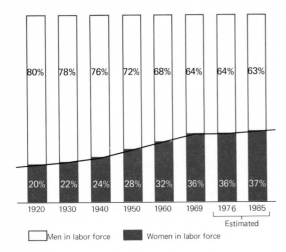

80%	78%	76%	72%	68%	64%	64%	63%
20%	22%	24%	28%	32%	36%	36%	37%
1920	1930	1940	1950	1960	1969	1976	1985

Estimated

☐ Men in labor force   ■ Women in labor force

Figure 3. Women in the labor force, United States, 1920–1985. (Source: Department of Labor, Bureau of Labor Statistics.)

today make up over one-third of our labor force. One-half of all women between eighteen and sixty-four years of age are in the labor force at any single moment, and five-sixths (83 percent) of these are married and living with their husbands. Nine out of ten married women work for some part of their married lives. Of all women workers, two-fifths (39 percent) have children under eighteen, and one-eighth (14 percent) have children under six years old. About one-third of all mothers with children under eighteen are employed, and about 4 million preschool children have working mothers. [All above data from Women's Bureau, 1972.] From these figures, the "normal" life pattern of the American woman emerges. Typically, she begins working before marriage, works until her children arrive, takes off a few years, then returns sometime after her children get into school. Obviously, it has become normal for the American wife to work for a major part of her lifetime.

Historically, a woman who worked was living evidence that she had no husband able and willing to support her. A survey of 140 married women workers in 1908 found that only six husbands held jobs above the grade of unskilled laborer [Bureau of Labor Statistics, 1916, pp. 163–164]. The working wife, once a lower-class phenomenon, is increasingly common among the prosperous middle classes. There is no reason to believe that this trend will be reversed. The "American standard of living" now assumes two incomes. As the "normal" standard of living increasingly becomes insupportable on a single income, the pressure upon the nonworking wife to get a job is difficult to resist. The majority of the readers of this textbook will be either working wives or the husbands of working wives for a major portion of their married lives. Are working wives happier than housewives? Evidence on this question is mixed, but it is clear that the wife is happier if she works from choice rather than from necessity [Orden and Bradburn, 1969].

This quiet revolution has transformed the household division of labor. The work time of housewives has *not* been reduced by laborsaving devices; today's housewives work as many hours as those of a half-century ago [Hall and Schroeder, 1970]. The time once spent in hand-washing clothes and homecanning is now spent in putting in order a daily avalanche of toys, books, magazines, and hobby gear, chauffeuring children, attending the PTA, and doing other tasks which grandmother did not do. Obviously, when the wife works, *something has to give.* Some of the housekeeping niceties may be sacrificed, and some tasks may be commercialized (sending out the laundry, buying prepared foods), but the working wife still works longer than the housewife by an average of about ten hours a week. A recent study of time-use in twelve European and American countries [Converse, 1972] found that this ten-hour figure held true within a very small variation for all of the twelve countries studied. Husbands and children, on the average, assume only a modest share of household tasks when wives work, and the husband's attitude toward the wife's employment is crucial in making the necessary adjustments

[Arnott, 1972]. Women today, however, are beginning to reject the idea that they should do all the housework while holding a job. Many of the male readers of this text will (if they have not already done so) eventually learn whether their masculinity will dissolve in dishwater!

Changing family functions

Structure and function are two aspects of the same thing. Changes in one are both cause and effect of changes in the other. What changes in function accompany the changes in family structure?

The economic functions have changed most greatly. A century ago the American family was a unit of economic production, united by shared work on the farm. Today only one-nineteenth of our families are farmers, and even the farm family is not the self-sufficient unit of the past. Except on the farm, the family is no longer the basic unit of economic production; this has shifted to the shop, the factory, the office. The family is no longer united by shared work, for its members work separately. Instead, the family is a unit of economic *consumption,* united by companionship, affection, and recreation.

The sexual-regulation functions have diminished. Although most sexual intercourse is still marital, the proportion has probably fallen below the 90 percent figure claimed by Kinsey in 1948 [p. 588]. Research studies show no great change in premarital sexual behavior between 1948 and 1965, but after 1965 females began catching up (or down?) to the male figure of about three out of four being sexually experienced before marriage [Robinson et al., 1972]. A recent survey finds well over 90 percent of college students approving of sexual intercourse among persons who are engaged, in love, or with "strong affection," while over two-thirds even approve of intercourse among those who are "not particularly affectionate"

[Perlman, 1974]. Many other studies [Schmidt and Sigursch, 1972; Zelnik and Kantner, 1972; Hunt, 1974] all point to the same conclusion: virgin marriage has become relatively uncommon and seems likely virtually to disappear in the near future. Whether this is a "sexual revolution" as some scholars proclaim [Skolnik, 1973, pp. 410–413] or whether it is only another of many historical swings between permissiveness and restrictiveness [Hindus, 1971; Shorter, 1971] is not yet apparent.

There is, however, no recent historical parallel for the rapid growth of "nonmarital cohabitation," less elegantly called "shacking up." The U.S. Census listed 34,000 people living in nonmarital cohabitation in 1960 (probably an underestimate) and 286,000 in 1970; the figure has almost certainly risen since then. Studies on several college campuses show that nonmarital cohabitation has become quite common on many campuses, where it is viewed as an acceptable living pattern by most of the students [Macklin, 1974]. Yet this cohabitation is not "trial marriage," for most of these couples have no definite marital intentions and no strong commitment to each other, but simply view nonmarital cohabitation as an extension of "going steady" [Macklin, 1974]. Nonmarital cohabitation is also increasing among aged Social Security recipients, who seek to avoid the income loss that marriage would bring. Thus the "sexual regulation" function of the family is being trimmed at both ends.

The reproduction function has declined in importance. True, birth rates are much lower than a century ago, but if one considers only the size of the *surviving* family, then the family reproductive function is not so greatly changed. A few centuries ago, one-half to three-fourths of the children died in infancy or childhood; today over 96 percent reach adulthood. Today's average American family of three surviving children (3.2, to be exact) is not far from what it has been through most of Western history. At present, the birth rate in the United States (when adjusted for age distribution) is falling, and probably will fall still farther. A further decline in family size, aside from its ecological implications, may be expected to increase family harmony. There is solid research evidence that the smaller families are less stressful, more comfortable, and "most satisfactory to spouses, parents, and children" [Nye et al., 1970], and are happier and better adjusted [Hurley and Palonen, 1967; Schooler, 1972]. Even when other variables are controlled (such as income, education, and occupation), children in smaller families are more healthy, creative, and intelligent [Lieberman, 1970]. But if small families are good for children, having no children seems to be good for adults. As shown in Figure 4, the happiest adult categories were those with no children at all. Marriage, but not parenthood, is associated with superior contentment.

The socialization function claims increased attention. The family remains the principal socializing agency, although the school and the peer group unquestionably fill important socializing functions. Other social agencies are occasionally called in for guidance. The major change has been in our *attention* to the socialization function. An earlier generation knew little about "personality development"; today nearly every literate parent knows about Dr. Spock [1945, 1957, 1974]. We know something today of the role of emotional development in school progress, career success, physical well-being, and practically all other aspects of the good life. Our great-grandparents worried about smallpox and cholera; we worry about sibling jealousies and peer-group adjustment.

How has the quiet revolution affected the socialization function? Does the child suffer when mother takes a job? There have been several dozen studies of this question [reviewed by Stoltz, 1960; Herzog, 1960; Nye and Hoffman, 1963; Schooler, 1972]. The earlier studies failed to control for such variables as social class or family composition. As a result, the working-mother sample had a higher pro-

portion of poor, uneducated slum dwellers, widows, and divorcées than the nonworking-mother sample. Such poorly controlled studies seemed to show that children suffered when mother worked. Later studies compared children of working mothers with children of *otherwise comparable* nonworking mothers. Although not entirely conclusive, these studies do not show any general tendency for children to suffer when the mother is employed. The Gluecks [1959] compared 500 delinquents with 500 nondelinquents, carefully matched for social class, age, ethnic-racial derivation, and intelligence. They found no difference between the delinquency rates of the children of non-working and those of regularly employed mothers, while children of irregularly employed mothers had a higher delinquency rate. They attributed this higher delinquency rate to the fact that the irregularly employed mother more often had an unstable husband with poor work habits; they suspected that the mother herself was more often unstable and, consequently, was a poor mother whether working or not.

Whereas the Gluecks studied working-class mothers, Nye [1958] studied middle-class mothers and found greater delinquency among the children of working mothers. On the other hand, several studies [Nye, 1952, 1969; Douvan, 1963] find that part-time employment of the mother seems to be beneficial to the adolescent child. One study concludes that maternal employment is beneficial to sons but not to daughters [Farley, 1968]. Although the evidence is somewhat mixed, it is clear that *whether* the mother works is not very important, while the *kind* of mother she is and the kind of home she and the father provide are the important variables [Hoffman, 1963].

The affectional and companionship functions have gained in relative importance. The primary community, the small group of neighbors who knew one another well and had much in common, has disappeared from the lives of most Americans. Urbanization and specialization have destroyed it. In an increasingly heed-

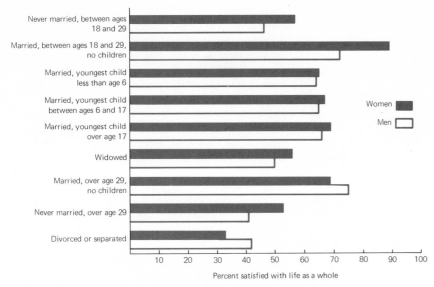

Figure 4. Life satisfaction of women and men at stages of the life cycle. (Source: Published by the Institute of Social Research, University of Michigan; reprinted by permission of the *ISR Newsletter.*)

less, impersonal, and ruthless world, the immediate family becomes the bulwark of emotional support. A man may be insulted by his boss, patronized by his colleagues, and ignored by his neighbors, but at home he can be King Solomon to his wife and Hercules to his children! Herein lies one of the greatest functions and strengths of the family.

The importance of the affectional and companionship functions are further magnified by the expansion of the *postparental period.* In earlier generations, relatively few parents lived very long beyond the maturing of their children. In 1870, as shown in Figure 5, fewer than half the American fathers and mothers were still living when their youngest child married. By 1960, this median length of the postparental period had grown from nothing at all to sixteen years for women and fourteen years for men, and was still lengthening. A fairly long postparental period, as a *normal* rather than an exceptional life stage, is a very recent development. The bucolic literature

about loving grandparents and venerable great-grandparents gives little hint of how rare they really were. The modern appearance of the postparental stage of the life cycle means that most couples now reach that point where there is no urgent necessity for them to remain together—unless shared affections and companionship make it seem worthwhile.

The status-definition function continues. Many families continue to prepare children to retain the class status of the family; a considerable fraction seek to prepare their children for social mobility. They do this mainly by trying to give children the kind of ambitions, attitudes, and habits which prompt them to struggle for a higher class status and to fill it successfully. This is called *anticipatory socialization,* for it is an effort to socialize children for a class status which it is hoped they will someday achieve. At best, this effort is only partly successful. The child may acquire the ambitions and work habits which prompt it to struggle

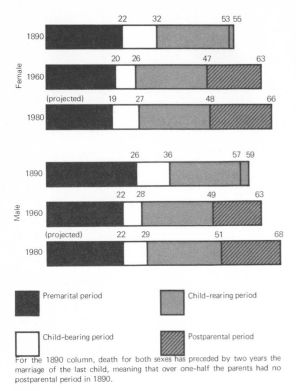

	Premarital period		Child-rearing period
	Child-bearing period		Postparental period

For the 1890 column, death for both sexes has preceded by two years the marriage of the last child, meaning that over one-half the parents had no postparental period in 1890.

Figure 5. The new postparental stage in the American family. Shown are median ages at marriage, end of child-bearing period, marriage of last child, and at death, United States, 1890–1980. (Source: Adapted from Gerald R. Leslie, *The Family in Social Context*, Oxford University Press, 1973, p. 263.)

successfully for upward mobility, but no family can fully succeed in socializing a child for a way of life not practiced by that family.

The protective functions have declined. The traditional family in Western society performed most of the functions of organized social work today—nursed the sick, gave haven to the handicapped and shelter to the aged. Today, we have a medical technology which only specialists and hospitals can handle. Today's urban household is an impractical place in which to care for many kinds of handicapped people. Family care of the aged was a practical

arrangement when the aging couple stayed on the farm, joined by a married child and mate. The parents could retire gradually, shifting to less strenuous tasks, but remaining useful and appreciated. This pattern is available today to only a tiny minority, and many elderly couples feel—and are—useless and unappreciated in the homes of their children. Our rapid rate of social change and social mobility also means that many tensions may develop when three generations live under one roof. So for a variety of reasons—most of which have nothing to do with selfishness or personal irresponsibility—many of the protective functions of the traditional family have been shifted to other institutions.

The evolution of the family

The American family has largely completed the transition "from institution to companionate" [Burgess and Locke, 1953]—from a family wherein the role of each person was rigidly fixed by tradition and enforced by law, custom, and social pressure to a family wherein the roles and tasks are arranged according to the wishes of the members. It is united not by work and external pressures but by shared interests and affections. It shows a far greater variety, since no uniform set of marriage roles and duties are impressed upon all without regard for individual preferences and aptitudes. Such a family has a far greater potential for personality development and individual fulfillment

The companionate family has a regard for individual preferences and aptitudes.

than the traditional pattern. This potential, though not always realized, influences the form our family is taking.

There are several developments which reveal the stresses in the modern American family.

The generation gap

Although disagreements between parents and children are as old as history, the current "generation gap" arises from the modern invention of "adolescence." At most times and places in history, children began to assume adult roles at about the time of puberty. Today's young people must wait an added five to fifteen years while they presumably prepare themselves for these adult roles. During this waiting period, young people often become impatient, critical, and dissatisfied [Bryan and Horton, 1974, pp. 24–27]. In fact, the chasm sometimes seems to be so unbridgeable that Margaret Mead proposes that it can be spanned only when parents consent to sit at the feet of their children and learn the facts of life [Mead, 1970]. But there is considerable evidence that the generation gap is in large part a myth [Brunswick, 1970; Meisels and Canter, 1971; Fengler and Wood, 1972; Kandel and Lesser, 1972; Rigby, 1974]. In studies of the views of parents and their own children, it has been found that the actual generation gap is greater than estimated by parents but less than imagined by children [Walsh, 1970; Bengtson and Kuypers, 1971; Freeman, 1972]. Although attitude divergence within families is quite common, divergence between the collective attitudes of the parent and youth generations is relatively small [Connell, 1972]. Thus the generation gap is relatively small, but the "education gap" is far larger. College youth diverge from noncollege youth far more widely in their attitudes than either group diverges from their own parents [Seligman, 1969; Brunswick, 1970]. Furthermore, since only about one-third of today's college students

have college-educated parents, any student-parent attitude comparison is more greatly a measure of education gap than of generation gap. Some degree of generation gap is inevitable in a rapidly changing society, but our modest generation gap today seems unlikely to threaten the family as an institution.

The commune

One alternative life-style is the commune. Many communes are little more than a temporary living arrangement of college students or other young people trying to live cheaply, but many others involve a rejection of both the conventional family and of the entire competition-success-consumption system of values. These are often called "countercultural communes."

The commune is not exactly new, for American history is dotted with dozens of communal experiments [Burton, 1939; Bestor, 1950, 1970; Halloway, 1951; Kanter, 1972; Veysey, 1974]. Only a few lasted as long as a generation, and nearly all are gone today. The present communal movement is more widespread and varied than the earlier American experiments, and it is possible that some may survive. Numbering possibly as many as several thousand, communes are of many kinds—political, religious, vegetarian, hippie, artistic, revolutionary, and still others. Some are highly structured, with detailed rules and procedures; many are almost totally unstructured, with each person "doing his own thing." Organization may be authoritarian or democratic, but in either case is generally informal. Leadership is often charismatic, with one strong personality dominating the others. Some highly structured communes are hard-working, and some forbid nonmarital sex and drug use. Many communes, following the counterculture, emphasize voluntarism and immediate gratification, and allow easy access to sex and drugs, although orgiastic promiscuity is rare. Some communards work hard, especially at subsistence farming, with work informally organized and surrounded with a festive and playful atmosphere. In most communes work for cash income is sporadic, voluntary, and unorganized, and the main source of cash income in many communes is welfare. Most communes are highly unstable, with "members" drifting in and out rapidly and the group soon dissolving. Very few last more than a few months. Most of the descriptive accounts of communes are journalistic [Davidson, 1970; Hedgepeth, 1970; Houriet, 1971; Fairfield, 1972; Kinkade, 1974], although some scholarly accounts are appearing [Roberts, 1971; Zablocki, 1971; Kanter, 1972; Rigby, 1974; Veysey, 1974].

The commune's admirers see the isolated nuclear family as psychologically inadequate and emotionally barren, and pervaded by a sterile materialism. They see the commune as a means of regaining the security and emotional health of the consanguine family. But, aside from a handful of religious communes, very few communes last long enough to be more than a way-station. Communes which are not unified by a strong sense of purpose soon split up. Most countercultural communes attempt to unite "free" individuals, guided only by "love," but sociologists know of no instance where group life has endured on this "free" basis. In all enduring communes, such as the Hutterites or the kibbutz, the individual is tightly bound by group norms. It is doubtful whether any commune of "free" individuals can endure. Communes may continue to provide stopovers for some young people, but offer no serious competition to the family.

Women's liberation

When Susan Swanger won the Rensselaer Polytechnic Institute's annual award for excellence in math and science, her prize was a tie tack! It is against such presumptions that the Women's Liberation Movement is in full revolt. Numerous studies have shown that women's career accomplishments are far below those of men. The higher the job level, the fewer the women. Many surveys have shown that women are paid less than men doing identical work with identical credentials. And in recent decades, women have been losing rather than gaining in occupational status and income [Knudson, 1969]. Some of this achievement differential is due to overt sex discrimination, and some is due to several other factors which may constitute more subtle forms of discrimination. For example, one explanation for the lower earnings of wives may lie in the fact that geographic moves, made to advance the husband's career, are often damaging to the wife's career [Long, 1974]. Women's career interruptions for child bearing and child care are a major impediment to their career advancement. But possibly the greatest factor in women's lesser career advancement to date is their lesser motivation. Recent research shows that both men *and women* tend to evaluate women according to their husband's status and to ignore the wife's own accomplishments [Felson and Knoke, 1974]. Traditionally, a man's success as a person has been measured primarily by his career accomplishments, while a woman's success as a person has been measured by her "feminine" accomplishments as sex object, wife, mother, homemaker, and hostess. Spectacular career attainments may even detract from a woman's image. Career attainments are rewarded in men and penalized in women. Feminists view this as crippling and unjust. Their demand for employment equality is now recognized in the Civil Rights Act of 1964, which forbids sex (and race) discrimination in hiring, promotion and pay. Numerous "affirmative action" programs are now bringing employment closer to reality.

More subtle than employment discrimination, however, is the differential socialization which prepares men to assume dominant roles, but persuades women to imagine they are more "contented" and "fulfilled" in playing whatever subordinate roles men expect them to assume.

TABLE 8 WOMEN COLLEGE SENIORS: NEW CAREER ORIENTATIONS AND ROLE PERCEPTIONS*
(IN PERCENT)

	College H		College D	
	1968	**1972**	**1968**	**1972**
Long-run career preference				
Life centered on home and family	45	18	33	17
An academic, business, or professional life	40	58	33	53
15-year career goal				
Housewife with children	43	22	49	16
Career, marriage, children	37	50	35	62
Career, no children†	3	9	2	5
Uncertain	3	16	14	16

*Data shown for two colleges are illustrative of trends found in all colleges surveyed.
†With or without marriage.
Source: Kenneth M. Wilson, "Today's Women Students: New Outlooks, Options," *Findings* (quarterly newsletter of the Educational Testing Service), Vol. 1, No. 4, 1974, p. 6. Copyright 1974 by Educational Testing Service, Princeton, N.J. 08540.

The Women's Liberation Movement, therefore, maintains that both sexes should be socialized to expect equal rights and duties as respecting career, child care, and household responsibilities. When the young couple has children, why should it automatically be the wife who interrupts her career to baby-tend? Twenty-four-hour day-care centers, part-time jobs for both parents, and full equality in all kinds of educational and occupational opportunity are among Women's Liberation demands. But even this would be insufficient, because many other subtle forms of discrimination are under attack—the language use of masculine gender to refer to all of peoplekind; the soft, yielding image of "femininity"; the "playmate" image of women as sexual toys; the double standard of declining sexual desirability with advancing age [I. Bell, 1970]—these are only some of the features of our society which Women's Liberation would like to change [Roszak and Roszak, 1970; Carden, 1973; Rossi, 1973]. Among the more extreme feminists are some who call for the complete abolition of the family and a total revolution in sex roles [Firestone, 1970; Greer, 1971; Martin and Lyon, 1972].

How attainable are the goals of Women's Liberation? Anthropologist Michael Harris [1975, p. 61] states flatly that "Male supremacy is on the way out. It was just a phase in the evolution of culture." Sociologist Stephen Goldberg, in a book entitled *The Inevitability of Patriarchy* [1973], states with equal firmness that men have always been and always will be the dominant sex in all societies. Anthropologists generally agree that in all known societies, child care has been primarily a female responsibility. Women's other work has been of the kinds which fit in with her child-care responsibilities—work which is close to the home, is relatively monotonous, does not demand close concentration, is not dangerous, and can be carried on despite frequent interruptions [Brown, 1970]. In demanding a completely *equal* involvement of both sexes in child care and household duties, with fully *equal* freedom of choice for work of all kinds, Women's Liberation is proposing a revolutionary departure from the experience of all known societies throughout history. While this proposal will not immediately be achieved, current trends are in its direction. The eventual consequences upon the society will be substantial, but not exactly predictable, since we have no experience upon which to base a prediction.

Will "liberation" increase women's happiness and contentment? Reports from Latin America suggest that their "unliberated" wives are more contented than our partly liberated women [Pescatello, 1973]. There are no satisfactory comparisons of the happiness levels of "liberated" and "traditional" wives in our society. And such a comparison would tell little about prospective happiness levels in the changed society the feminists desire. But present trends indicate that, although we do not know whether women's liberation will increase human happiness, we may soon find out.

Children's liberation

While not broadly enough based to be a "movement," there has arisen the suggestion that children, too, need to be liberated. It is claimed that the conventional family is oppressive because it denies children control over their lives, and in some cases subjects them to crippling physical and emotional abuse. Advocates of children's liberation assert that children should have all the rights of adults as soon as they wish to claim them—to work, own property, make contracts, direct their own education, live where they wish, have sex, receive their own welfare checks, and to drink, smoke, eat, and live as they wish [Adams et al., 1972; Farson, 1974; Holt, 1974]. Thus the status of adolescence and later childhood would be virtually abolished, and children would move directly into adult roles, as, indeed, they have done in many societies throughout history.

There is little doubt that our long postponement of adult roles creates many difficulties. Much of our juvenile delinquency consists of acts which are legal when done by adults. Many social scientists recommend that children and youth should spend less time in the classroom and more time in the shop, store, and office, where the real work of the world goes on [Coleman, 1972]. Wherever practical, the "look, listen, and wait" phase should be tempered by active involvement in meaningful activities. A number of recent changes, such as lowering the voting age, lowering the age for purchase of alcoholic beverages, and granting greater legal rights to schoolchildren and juvenile offenders, are a recognition of this idea.

The proposal to abolish childhood dependency, however, springs from the romantic illusion that in earlier days, children were more "free" than they are today. Early induction into adult tasks does not necessarily denote "freedom," as many nineteenth-century child laborers in mines and factories could attest. And in some primitive societies where children had little adult direction, a uniform moral code and strong primary group controls left few choices open to the individual.

Early childhood induction into adult roles and responsibilities is characteristic only of very simple cultures with highly uniform, undifferentiated adult roles. As cultures grow more complex and adult work roles more differentiated and specialized, longer preparatory periods become common. It is sociologically naïve to imagine that this historic trend can be ignored or overturned.

The future of the family

Predictions of the imminent death of the family are almost as old as history. Thus, books like *The Death of the Family* [Cooper, 1970] are blazing a trail down a well-traveled highway. Critics picture the nuclear monogamous family as an oppressive trap where people endure "holy deadlock" while their emotional growth withers and their personalities sour [Cadwallader, 1966; Casler, 1974, ch. 5]. As corrections for the "failure" of the traditional family, such "alternative family forms" as nonmarital cohabitation, group marriage, open marriage (extramarital affairs permitted to each), swinging (mutual temporary sex exchanges without emotional commitment), and bisexual and homosexual cohabitation are proposed.

These "innovations" (most of which have been tried and discarded repeatedly in the past) are welcomed by a considerable amount of "missionary research," that is, research which is more noted for its promotional enthusiasm than for its objectivity [DeLora and DeLora, 1975; Sussman, 1973; Skolnik and Skolnik, 1974].

While it is true that there is now one divorce to every three marriages, it is also true that five out of six persons[2] remain in their first marriage until separated by death [Leslie, 1973, p. 58], and well over half of these persons consider themselves to be happily married. No other intimate human relationship in our society shows such endurance—certainly not the revolving-door communes and the "intimate life-styles" about which some scholars write effusively. Even as they hail these alternatives to the family, there is evidence that experimentation with them may have passed its peak. By 1974 the "sex clubs" were closing, swinging was declining, the "open marriage" fad was fading, and pollster Daniel Yankelovich was reporting that the campus view of marriage as obsolete had peaked in 1971 and had since receded [*Time,* Nov. 25, 1974, pp. 100–101].

A return to Victorian sex behavior is not anticipated, but the "sexual revolution" of the past decade is making less enduring changes in the family than were feared by its critics or hoped for by its defenders. The present trend is unmistakably unisex, with sex-linked behavior differences of all kinds diminishing [Winick, 1969; Heisel, 1970]. One study suggests that whereas wives (as homemakers) and husbands (as workers) have each had one job, today the wife has two jobs (homemaker and worker) while the husband has one, but that in the future both husband and wife will have two [Young and Willmot, 1973]. While a few sociologists doubt that the family has a future

[2]According to a Bureau of the Census study in 1967. The odds have changed somewhat since then, but not enough to alter the fact that most people remain married to their first mate throughout life.

[Keller, 1971], most sociologists disagree. It is noteworthy that in the Israeli kibbutz, after more than a generation of successful communal living, including a deliberate effort to abolish the family as a functional unit, the recent trend has been toward increasing the functional significance of the family [Shepher, 1969; Talmon, 1972]. All evidence thus indicates that the family, however often its death may be listed in the obituaries, is nonetheless here to stay. The really important question is not, "Will the family endure?" but, "How will it be changed?" Two major family theorists have recently predicted that the next few decades will see a return to a more highly structured, less permissive family than that of today [Vincent, 1972; Zimmerman, 1972]. Once again, the "wave of the future" may turn out to have been only a ripple. Change and adaptation, rather than replacement by some startling alternative, seems to be the future of the family.

The present trend is unmistakably unisex.

Summary

The family is the basic social institution. It varies greatly in form. The Western family is normally *conjugal,* composed of husband, wife, and children. But in many societies the family unit is *consanguine,* a much larger group of blood relatives with a fringe of spouses. All societies practice *endogamy,* requiring selection of mates within some specified groups, as well as *exogamy,* requiring that one go outside certain groups for selection. Although most marriages are *monogamous,* many societies permit *polygamy,* generally *polygyny,* wherein it is the husband who has more than one mate at a time. Most societies provide for divorce, with wide variance in grounds and procedures. The fascinating variety of family forms shows how basic human needs can be satisfactorily met under a great variety of institutional arrangements. In all societies the family performs certain functions—regulates sex relations, provides for reproduction, socializes children, offers affection and companionship, defines status, protects its members, and serves as a working and sharing team.

The present American family is in the midst of sweeping changes. It is a little smaller than a century ago. Divorce has become common and almost respectable. Male authority has declined, and the division of labor has changed since it has now become normal for the wife to hold a job during a considerable part of her married life. This development has aroused many alarms over the welfare of children, but the evidence suggests that these alarms are largely unjustified.

The sex-regulatory, reproductive, and status-definition functions of the family have probably been the least affected by recent social changes. In economic function, the production activities of the family have been largely absorbed by separate economic institutions, leaving the family mainly a unit of economic consumption. The protective functions have been largely shifted to other institutions. The socialization and affectional functions of the family have gained greatly in relative importance, both because of changes in other institutions and because of our increased knowledge about our personal and social needs. Probably these trends will continue, and tomorrow's family in America will be more equalitarian, probably still smaller than today, and oriented toward companionship and family recreation. Some people suspect that the generation gap, the commune, or the demands of Women's Liberation may destroy the family. But the generation gap is in substantial part a myth. The commune is notably unstable, and while the demands of Women's Liberation would greatly change the family, it is not certain that they would weaken it. They might even strengthen it.

A number of "alternatives" to the family have been proposed, and seriously discussed by some scholars, but most of these seem unlikely to have much lasting impact upon the family.

Questions and projects

1. Why is the family found in all societies? Would it be possible, with modern technology, to dispense with the family?
2. Why do American parents today play only a limited role in guiding the courtship choices of their children? Would it be desirable for them to play a larger role in determining marriage choices?
3. In a society such as the Trobriand, where a man has no special duties or particular affection for his own children, how can he possibly take a truly "fatherly" concern for his sister's children?
4. We use the term "uncle" for the brothers of our father or mother. Among the Todas the term "father" includes not only one's father but all of one's uncles. What is the importance of such variations in terminology? Some societies have no word for "illegitimate." What does the omission mean?
5. How do recent and current family changes illustrate the interrelationship of institutions?
6. Test-tube fertilization and incubator gestation of

human beings may soon become feasible. Do you think women will ever prefer this to natural childbirth?

7. What do you consider the pros and cons of the current trend toward unisex roles?

8. In what ways does some research exaggerate the generation gap?

9. Is the commune likely to replace the family as the customary living arrangement? Why or why not?

10. What are some personality traits that make for conflict between marriage partners? Would these traits also create trouble in a commune, group marriage, or nonmarital cohabitation?

11. The text states that there is one divorce to each three marriages, but that about five out of six persons remain married to their first mates throughout life. How can both be true?

12. Defend each of these positions: (1) "Divorce is a necessary and useful institution for a society like ours." (2) "Divorce is cause and evidence of family breakdown, and should be avoided."

13. Discuss these two propositions: (1) "The proper socialization of the child requires the intimate, continuous, affectionate supervision that only a full-time mother can give." (2) "An uninterrupted mother-child contact encourages an exces-

sive dependence; the child develops most healthfully when cared for by several warmly responsive adults."

14. Discuss these two propositions: (1) "The American family is badly disorganized by the sweeping social changes of the past century." (2) "The American family is reorganizing itself to meet changing human needs in a changing society."

15. Prepare a statement of the reasons why you believe you will, or will not: (1) be a working wife, if you are female, or (2) have a working wife, if you are male. Then identify each reason as to whether it is a value judgment—a statement of what you like or dislike—or whether it is a statement of social forces and trends which may affect your decision.

16. Read John P. Marquand's *H. M. Pulham, Esq.,* Little, Brown and Company, Boston, 1941. How does the Pulham family prepare Harry for his sex role and class status, and generally socialize him to act in the expected manner?

17. Read Hans Ruesch, *Top of the World,* Harper, Row, New York, 1950; Pocket Books, 1951. A novel about Eskimo life. Evaluate the Eskimo family as an institutional structure for meeting the needs of people in a particular environment.

Suggested readings

BERNARD, JESSIE: *The Future of Motherhood,* Dial Press, New York, 1974. A distinguished sociologist analyzes the changing motherhood function.

*BLOOD, ROBERT O., JR., AND DONALD M. WOLFE: *Husbands and Wives,* 2d ed., The Free Press, New York, 1965. A research study presenting evidence contradicting many widely held notions about the American family.

BRODERICK, CARLFRED B.: "Man and Woman: A Consumer's Guide to Contemporary Pairing Patterns Including Marriage," *Human Behavior,* July/ August, 1972, pp. 8–15. A concise summary of differing patterns of marriage and the issues involved in each.

DOTEN, DANA: *The Art of Bundling,* Holt, Rinehart and Winston, Inc., New York, 1938. An entertaining account of the rise and fall of a quaint

American custom, showing how it related to the other institutions of the period.

FOLSOM, JOSEPH K.: *The Family,* John Wiley & Sons, Inc., New York, 1934, 1943, chap. 1, "The Family Pattern." An interesting parallel-column comparison of the American and Trobriand family patterns.

*LEMASTERS, E. E.: *Parents in Modern America,* Dorsey Press, Homewood, Ill., 1970. A sociological analysis of the parental role.

*LINTON, RALPH: *The Study of Man,* Appleton-Century-Crofts, New York, 1936, chap. 10, "The Family," chap. 11, "Marriage," and chap. 12, "Social Units Determined by Blood." An anthropologist's description of various forms of marriage and family life.

*QUEEN, STUART A., ROBERT W. HABENSTEIN, AND JOHN B. ADAMS: *The Family in Various Cul-*

tures, 4th ed., J. B. Lippincott Co., Philadelphia, 1974. Readable descriptions of the family in a dozen societies, ancient and modern.

*ROBERTS, RON E.: *The New Communes*, Prentice-Hall, Inc., Englewood Cliffs, N.J., 1971. A brief analysis of historic and current communes.

*ROSSI, ALICE S. (ED.): *The Feminist Papers: From Adams to DeBeauvoir*, Columbia University Press, New York, 1973. A collection of early and modern papers on feminism, with perceptive commentary by Rossi.

VEYSEY, LAURENCE: "Individualism Busts the Commune Boom," *Psychology Today*, December, 1974, pp. 73–78. A brief, semipopular treatment of the conflict between individualism and communal living.

YOUNG, KIMBALL: *Isn't One Wife Enough? The Story of Mormon Polygamy*, Holt, Rinehart and Winston, Inc., New York, 1954. A readable analysis, by a Mormon sociologist, of the only serious attempt at polygamy in America.

*ZABLOCKI, BENJAMIN: *The Joyful Community*, Penguin Books, Baltimore, Md., 1972. A detailed description and analysis of a successful commune, now in its third generation.

ZASTROW, CHARLES H.: "Dramatic Changes Foreseen in the American Family of Tomorrow," *International Journal of Sociology of the Family*, 3:93–101, March 1973. An attempt to forecast the coming changes in the family.

Chapter 11 • Formal organizations

My analysis of hundreds of cases of occupational competence led me on to formulate *The Peter Principle:*
IN A HIERARCHY EVERY EMPLOYEE TENDS TO RISE TO HIS LEVEL OF INCOMPETENCE
A New Science!

Having formulated the Principle, I discovered that I had inadvertently founded a new science, hierarchiology, the study of hierarchies.

The term "hierarchy" was originally used to describe the system of church government by priests graded into ranks. The contemporary meaning includes any organization whose members or employees are arranged in order of rank, grade, or class.

Hierarchiology, although a relatively recent discipline, appears to have great applicability to the fields of public and private administration.

This Means You!

My principle is the key to an understanding of all hierarchal systems, and therefore to an understanding of the whole structure of civilization. A few eccentrics try to avoid getting involved with hierarchies, but everyone in business, industry, trade-unionism, politics, government, the armed forces, religion, and education is so involved. All of them are controlled by the Peter Principle.

Many of them, to be sure, may win a promotion or two, moving from one level of competence to a higher level of competence. But competence in that new position qualifies them for still another promotion. For each individual, for *you,* for *me,* the final promotion is from a level of competence to a level of incompetence.

So, given enough time—and assuming the existence of enough ranks in hierarchy—each employee rises to, and remains at, his level of incompetence. Peter's Corollary states: *In time, every post tends to be occupied by an employee who is incompetent to carry out his duties.*
Who Turns the Wheels?

You will rarely find, of course, a system in which *every* employee has reached his level of incompetence. In most instances, something is being done to further the ostensible purposes for which the hierarchy exists.

Work is accomplished by those employees who have not yet reached their level of incompetence. (Reprinted by permission of William Morrow & Co., Inc., and Souvenir Press, Ltd., from The Peter Principle *by Dr. Laurence J. Peter and Raymond Hull. Copyright © 1969 by William Morrow & Co., Inc.)*

I n this popular essay, Professor Peter has written, with tongue in cheek, on the tendency for incompetence to emerge in bureaucracies. The suggestion has been made by women's liberationists that organizations keep operating because female secretaries fail to get promoted to their level of incompetence. The processes of promotion and the effect on organization functioning are a part of what we call "bureaucratic" behavior. Bureaucratic behavior is important, but it is only one of the many aspects of formal organization which interest sociologists. What are formal organizations and what is their importance?

Definition of formal organizations. Formal organizations are related to social organization as the parts are related to the whole. Social organization is that network of relationships between individuals and groups which binds them into a society. Formal organizations are one aspect of social organization. They are distinguished from small, informal organizations such as friendship groups or work teams, and from social institutions such as religion or the family.

The friendship clique is an informal organization generally arising casually and operating according to no set rules to pursue some vaguely defined companionship goals. The formal organization is created deliberately and operates according to definite rules to pursue one or more specific goals. Blau and Scott offer a definition of a formal organization as "any social unit which has been deliberately organized for the explicit purpose of reaching a specific goal" [Blau and Scott, 1962, p. 5].

Informal organizations are *organized* groups, for all human groups have structure. But informal organizations have no *formal* organizational structure. They have leaders and followers, procedures and taboos, but there are no written rules, titles, or elective offices. Often the informal organizations are primary groups, while formal organizations are secondary groups. Like all secondary groups, formal organizations are segmental, utilitarian, and goal-oriented; but they may have primary groups or friendship cliques among their members. Formal organizations appear when a group becomes too large to organize its affairs informally.

Formal organizations differ from social institutions in that formal organizations are *associations of people* while institutions are *systems of norms and values*. However, as we pointed out in Chapter 9, many of the institutionally related activities are carried out by associations, and these are often formal organizations.

Formal organizations appear when a group becomes too large to organize its affairs informally.

While the formal organization has membership requirements and rules which differentiate it from the rest of society, it nonetheless interacts with the rest of the society [Katz and Kahn, 1966, pp. 14–29]. The formal organization's activities stimulate a response in the society which, in turn, is fed back to the formal organization and modifies its operations. The automobile manufacturing corporations, for example, have profoundly affected American life; yet public pressure has forced some very unwelcome changes upon them. Unpopular models like the Edsel have been dropped, smaller cars have been marketed in response to consumer demand, and costly changes are reluctantly being made to increase safety and reduce pollution. The Roman Catholic Church has been a powerful influence in Western civilization, but current trends in scientific thought and social organization are profoundly changing the Church. Although the formal organization is a separate entity, it is heavily involved in interaction with the rest of the society.

One prominent sociologist, Talcott Parsons, classifies the types of formal organizations under four headings: (1) economic production, (2) political power, (3) societal integration, and (4) pattern maintenance [Parsons, 1960, pp. 45–46]. Economic-production organizations carry on activities which add value to products or provide services (corporations, cooperatives). Political-power organizations are those which influence the allocation and operation of political power (political parties, organized pressure groups). Integrative organizations seek to maintain the order and unity of society through the resolution of conflicts (bar associations, arbitration panels, ethics committees). Pattern-maintenance organizations are those which offer channels of cultural transmission—that is, which pass on cultural patterns from generation to generation—such as schools and churches.

Parsons' list is incomplete, for he omits what is possibly the most rapidly growing type of formal organization—that devoted to play—for example, the American Contract Bridge Association, the Antique Automobile Club of America, and thousands of local and regional organizations such as archers, bird watchers, and snowmobilists. Even organizations devoted to play still need some formal structure. Regardless of organizational focus, the coordination of their activities makes some degree of formal organization necessary for all large organizations.

Voluntary associations

Voluntary associations have been termed a third sector [Levitt, 1973] since they are not exactly private, in the sense of referring to individuals, nor are they a part of government. They are formal organizations directed toward some definite function which supposedly one enters by a voluntary decision rather than by ascription (as in the case of being born a citizen of a country). Churches are not usually classified as voluntary associations, although they may be fully voluntary for some people, and satellite organizations usually are classified as voluntary associations. Similarly, labor unions are often excluded on the grounds that membership usually is not entirely a matter of personal choice.

In the typical voluntary association, most or all of the members are spare-time volunteers, sometimes with a small core of paid full-time professionals to handle the routines. There are many local voluntary organizations—church organizations, PTA, recreational clubs, neighborhood associations and others—which have volunteer officers, a minimum constitution (if anyone can find it), and bylaws or procedures which are highly "flexible" and sometimes forgotten or ignored. In such organizations, the informal aspects greatly overshadow the "formal organization" aspects, as the association operates vaguely and loosely according to Robert's *Rules of Order*. Where membership is fairly small, with a general consensus upon simple goals, such informal operation is highly efficient. It completes desired tasks with a minimum of bureaucratic fuss. Where membership is large or geographically scattered and when goals or policies are controversial, a more formal and rigid organization develops. A large association with a scattered membership, such as the National Rifle Association or Rotary International, must have a bureaucracy with a paid professional staff that conducts routines and an elected board of directors that determines policies. In practice, however, the function of the board of directors is generally to approve the policies which the professional staff has developed and "sold" to the board. While the membership theoretically controls the organization, the actual control is by a small clique of officers and professionals in fulfillment of Michel's "iron law of oligarchy," which is discussed later in this chapter.

Voluntary associations have long been prominent in the United States, as indicated in the following statement made in the early nineteenth century by a foreign observer:

Americans of all ages, all conditions, and all dispositions constantly form associations. They have not only commercial and manufacturing companies, in which all take part, but associations of a thousand other kinds, religious, moral, serious, futile, general or restricted, enormous or diminutive. The Americans make associations to give entertainments, to found seminaries, to build inns, to construct churches, to diffuse books, to send missionaries to the antipodes; in this manner they found hospitals, prisons, and schools. If it is proposed to inculcate some truth or to foster some feeling by the encouragement of a great example, they form a society. Wherever at the head of some new undertaking you see the government in France, or a man of rank in England, in the United States you will be sure to find an association. (Alexis de Tocqueville, *Democracy in America,* II, 106, edited by J. P. Mayer and Max Lerner, Harper & Row, Publishers, Inc., New York, 1966.)

Functions of voluntary associations

An outlet for individual interests. The major appeal of the voluntary association lies in its ability to provide a means of satisfying the proclivities of a number of citizens even though their interest is not shared by the total society. A few men who like to play golf can band together and provide a country club even though the city council may be cool to the use of tax money for adult playgrounds. In the days when our government feared to support birth control, it was still possible for individuals to promote family limitation by establishing Planned Parenthood Associations as voluntary associations. Lane [1962, p. 143] maintains that a variety of voluntary associations provide a type of "cultural pluralism," in which varied interests may be supported within the same society. Whatever the purpose, the voluntary association has the supreme merit of enabling a minority of the people to take some action toward realizing their aims without being held back by a hostile or indifferent majority.

A testing ground for social programs. The voluntary association can develop a program and so demonstrate its value that it is ultimately taken over by the church or the state. The Sunday school began as an individual project by Robert Raikes, then was promoted through the London Sunday School Society, and is now an organic part of most Protestant churches.

Planned parenthood programs, once too controversial for tax support, are today supported, in part, by federal grants. Most of the welfare functions of the modern state were born in voluntary associations which saw a social need, pioneered a program, and educated the public to the point where government was expected to assume the responsibility.

A channel of purposive social action. The voluntary association enables the private citizen to share in the making of major social decisions. Many observers feel that this is a vital part of the democratic process. One sociologist observed:

More specifically, the hypothesis is that the voluntary associations have three important functions in supporting political democracy in the United States: (1) They *distribute power over social life* among a very large proportion of the citizenry, instead of allowing it to be concentrated in the elected representatives alone, so that the United States has a little of the character of the ancient Greek democratic city-state, as well as of the modern European centralized republic. (2) The voluntary associations *provide a sense of satisfaction with modern democratic processes* because they help the ordinary citizen to see how the processes function in limited circumstances, of direct interest to himself, rather than as they grind away in a distant, impersonal, and incomprehensible fashion. (3) The voluntary associations provide a social *mechanism for continually instituting social changes,* so that the United States is a society in flux, constantly seeking (not always successfully, but seeking nevertheless) to solve long-standing problems and to satisfy new needs of groups of citizens as these needs arise. (Arnold Rose, *Theory and Method in the Social Sciences,* The University of Minnesota Press, Minneapolis, 1954, p. 52.)

Participants in voluntary associations

Although voluntary associations provide a means for individuals to increase their social power by banding together, this is more true of some types of people than of others. The middle and upper classes are more likely than the lower classes to enter voluntary associations. Smith and Freedman [1972, p. 154] summarize the situation as follows: "All of the work on the topic points to a single direction. Low socio-economic status . . . is highly correlated with low rates of participation and even lower rates of leadership positions in organizations."

An exception to the foregoing statement appears in an analysis of black-white participation in the United States. In spite of the much larger lower-class proportion of the black population, blacks are more active in voluntary associations than whites [Williams et al., 1973]. The suggestion has been made that such black participation may be a "compensation" for the disabilities of minority status, but this explanation falters when one considers the low rate of participation in voluntary associations by Mexican-Americans. No convincing explanation of the high rate of black participation has been developed, but evidently, poverty does not deter organized sociability as much among blacks as it does among whites.

In recent years, the "War on Poverty" sought to stimulate the organization of poor people in voluntary associations. The effort was not very successful, as most of the poor never became involved [Moynihan, 1969]. Among those who did participate, the "least poor" were most represented and black participation was greater than white [Curtis and Zurcher, 1971].

Voluntary associations are important in all industrialized countries, and to a lesser extent are found in other areas as well, but in no other major country are they as numerous and influential as in the United States and Canada. Many European countries in the past have been suspicious of voluntary associations, feeling that they might represent a conspiracy against the state or the church. Even today the increase in voluntary associations in Europe has been mostly along the lines of cooperatives, church-sponsored societies, political parties, and labor unions. The notion that active participation in strictly voluntary single-purpose groups is both an obligation and an opportunity of the citizen is still primarily an American idea, not widely shared by the rest of the world [J. Curtis, 1971].[1]

Organizational structures

Almost by definition, organizations have structure. The *normative structure* is the cluster of norms—of expectations, rules, and procedures—written or unwritten, formal or informal. The *personnel structure* is the network of persons, roles, and statuses through which the activities of the organization are carried out. Both the normative and the personnel structures can be either closely or loosely organized.

Some organizations are *closely structured,* that is, authority is highly centralized and procedures are highly standardized with little autonomy for either local groups or individuals. Other *loosely structured* organizations have less centralization and allow more freedom of action. In the closely structured organization, roles are rigidly defined, even to the prescription of specific rules for most situations; in the loosely structured organization, the roles are less defined and may be adjusted by the individual or local group as the occasion warrants.

Associations with a similar ideology may differ in structure. The Catholic Church is closely structured, with a strong central au-

[1]Kenneth Little ("The Role of Voluntary Associations in West African Urbanization," *American Anthropologist,* 59:579–596, August, 1957) states that the West African cities may be an exception, with many associations, often based on tribal or kinship lines, involving many people and functioning to provide sociability and mutual aid as well as social control. More typical of the developing areas is the situation reported by Floyd Dotson ("A Note on Participation in Voluntary Associations in a Mexican City," *American Sociological Review,* 18:380–386, August, 1953) in a study of Guadalajara, the second largest city of Mexico, where he found voluntary organization was rudimentary and participation far less widespread than in American cities of comparable size. Similarly, Delbert C. Miller (*International Community Power Structure: Comparative Studies of Four World Cities,* Indiana University Press, Bloomington, 1970) in a study of community power in Seattle, Bristol, Lima, and Cordoba found that voluntary associations were most influential in Seattle.

thority, elaborate organization, and detailed rules and procedures. The Baptist Church is very loosely structured. Baptist congregations are highly autonomous; they select and dismiss their own ministers, run their own affairs, and are very loosely tied together into a denominational organization. Likewise the Communists and Socialists both base their ideology on the writings of Karl Marx. Yet the Communist party is a closely structured organization, whereas the Socialist parties operate in a loosely structured system which somewhat resembles the congregationally organized Protestant churches.

Which is more effective—the closely structured or the loosely structured organization? This depends upon the size of the organization and the nature of its activities. A large army must be fairly closely structured; a smaller military unit can be quite loosely structured. Under some circumstances, loosely structured guerrilla units are the more effective, as in the defeat of the carefully organized troops of General Braddock by a less orderly collection of French and Indians, or the failure of magnificently equipped American and South Vietnamese troops to defeat poorly equipped Vietcong guerrillas. Churches and political parties apparently can be effective with varying degrees of close or loose structuring. Any intrinsic superiority of one over the other is difficult to prove. The loosely structured organization is apt to pride itself on freedom, tolerance, and individual responsibility while being criticized for inconsistency, laxness, and ideological deviations. The closely structured unit prides itself on the purity and consistency of its ideology and the close integration of its component parts, while it is criticized as dogmatic, intolerant, and heedless of local problems far removed from the central office.

Formal and informal structures

In the armed forces a table-of-organization chart shows the exact rank and duties of every category of personnel. The recruit soon learns that he must "go through channels," that is, take up his business with the appropriate officer, without going over his head to any of this officer's superiors. In a short time, however, the perceptive soldier will learn that the organization chart does not really tell how the army operates. He will find that sometimes a sergeant or secretary has more to do with decision making than the commanding officer. As he continues in an army career he will, if successful, learn that there is a "shadow" table of organization, different for every unit and not printed in any headquarters, which he must learn in order to get things done. This shadow table is a list of the men who have "influence." Sometimes they are the men named in the official organization chart, sometimes not; but the individual who can discern the real pattern of power will find adjustment easy in the armed forces, whereas the man who relies on the official table of organization will experience bewildering delays and frustrations.

The individual who can discern the real pattern of power will find adjustment easy.

A crucial distinction must obviously be made between *authority* and *influence*. Authority is an official right to make and enforce decisions; influence is the ability to affect the actions of *oligarchy - rule of a group or organization by a small clique of self-perpetuating leaders.*

others apart from any authority to do so. Authority stems from rank; influence rests largely upon personal attributes. Authority is based upon the status one holds; influence is based upon the esteem one receives. Professors have authority to make assignments and assign grades; they may have much or little influence upon their students, depending upon how students feel about them. An admired institutional officer will have both authority and influence; an unpopular officer has authority but little influence; a competent, popular subordinate may have much influence even though he has little authority. The interactions of authority and influence in the upper levels of government is perceptively described in Halberstam's *The Best and the Brightest* [1972] and in the several novels of C. P. Snow.

This informal structure grows partly from the personality differences among individuals and partly from the fact that no system of roles is completely successful in meeting all the needs of the organization. In order to get things done, one may prefer to go outside regular channels and use the informal structure of the organization. This procedure is sometimes risky and must be handled skillfully if it is not to backfire; yet it is very common. Without informal structures and procedures, many things would not get done quickly or efficiently.

The tendency toward oligarchy

Prior to the nineteenth century most groups were organized under an authoritarian leadership in the belief that a few wise and experienced men, preferably of noble birth, could give more able direction than a mass of ordinary people. The nineteenth century saw the rise of numerous associations devoted to a different principle: democratic control through the decisions of the rank-and-file membership. Even these avowedly democratic associations, however, found that control tended to drift into the hands of a few leaders. This tendency was usually explained either as the action of power-hungry officials who had deliberately distorted the democratic goals of the group, or as a proof that ordinary men had not yet acquired enough education and experience to run an organization democratically.

About sixty-five years ago a European social scientist, Robert Michels, studied this persistence of authoritarian tendencies in an organization which considered itself the enemy of all dictatorial power, the German Social Democratic party. He concluded that the dominance of a small number of leaders was not due either to the immaturity of the membership or the lust for power of the leaders; rather it was the result of patterns which were inevitable in any organization. In his words: "It is organization which gives birth to the dominion of the elected over the electors, of the mandatories over the mandators, of the delegates over the delegators. Who says organization says oligarch" [Michels, 1949, p. 41]. He called this the "iron law of oligarchy."

Oligarchy tends to develop in all formal organizations, of whatever type or size. Even rather small organizations, such as a local PTA or church "couples club," tend to be run by a rather small clique. Oligarchy flows directly from the pattern of participation of the ordinary member of the group. He or she usually attends meetings irregularly if at all; is poorly informed about the problems of the organization; and lacks the means of uniting with other members to exercise real control. Under these circumstances a few able persons who are willing to give time and attention to the task can easily assume control. They do not "seize" it; control is dumped in their laps by the members who do not want to bother themselves.

Unless it is spectacularly inept, a bureaucratic oligarchy can quite easily perpetuate itself in office. A successful membership revolt is likely only when there is a division among the oligarchs, with rival factions bidding for membership support. A successful revolt installs new oligarchs who generally operate much like the ones they replace.

An exception to oligarchical rule

The "iron law of oligarchy" simply expresses the tendency for all groups to fall under an oligarchical form of control. Is this necessarily true of all organizations, or is it simply the easiest of several patterns which an organization may follow? An illuminating example is found in a study [Lipset et al., 1956] of the internal control of the International Typographical Union. This union attracted attention because, unlike other unions and unlike most voluntary associations of any kind, the ordinary members were active in union affairs, and union officers found themselves constantly under the scrutiny of an effective opposition. Certain unusual features of the International Typographical Union seem to be related to its democratic structure, which includes: (1) a two-party system; (2) strong local units, large enough to influence the international union yet small enough for personal influence to operate within the local; (3) a network of social clubs which reinforce primary-group relations among printers and indirectly stimulate an interest in and acquaintance with union affairs; (4) union officers with salaries at about the same level as the earnings of working printers.

These features appear to meet certain problems that prevent many organizations from operating in a democratic manner. The two-party system means that the member who is unhappy with the union leadership has a channel at hand through which to express grievances and to press for a change. Every civics student hears that the two-party system is essential to democratic government, but in private associations it is usually condemned as "factional," with the result that there is usually no effective means of organizing opposition to the officeholders who are in power.

Oligarchy usually arises from the indifference of most of the membership, allowing authority to drift into the hands of those who are willing to devote their time to the organiza-tion. But occasionally oligarchy is attained by deliberate manipulation of the membership by successful oligarchs. The United Mine Workers Union for many years was run by an oligarchy which successfully resisted efforts at membership control. The national officers did this by granting votes to pensioners who no longer paid dues but were dependent upon national officers for pensions, by placing nineteen out of twenty-three local unions under national office control and replacing locally elected officers with nationally appointed local officers, by use of organizational funds to support the political power of national officers, and (according to opponents within the union) by fraud [O'Hanlon, 1971, pp. 78–83]. It was only when criminal activities brought government prosecution that this oligarchy was displaced.

Nature of bureaucracy

Role of the bureaucrat

When human ingenuity first tackled projects which demanded an organizing of human activity beyond what family and clan organization could provide, bureaucrats first appeared. Some feel that perhaps the ancient irrigation and flood-control projects first gave rise to the need for a disciplined and organized division of labor [Wittfogel, 1957]. Bureaucrats are never very popular. Most people regard themselves, rightly or wrongly, as productive workers and look with suspicion upon the bureaucrat who "does no real work" but just organizes and records the work of others.

A bureaucracy is a pyramid of personnel who conduct rationally the work of a large organization. Thompson [1961, pp. 13–17], drawing mainly on the work of Max Weber, presents the main characteristics of bureaucracy as (1) *specialization,* to assign each task to an expert; (2) *merit appointment and job tenure,* to ensure competent personnel; (3) *formalistic impersonality,* to see that a set of formal

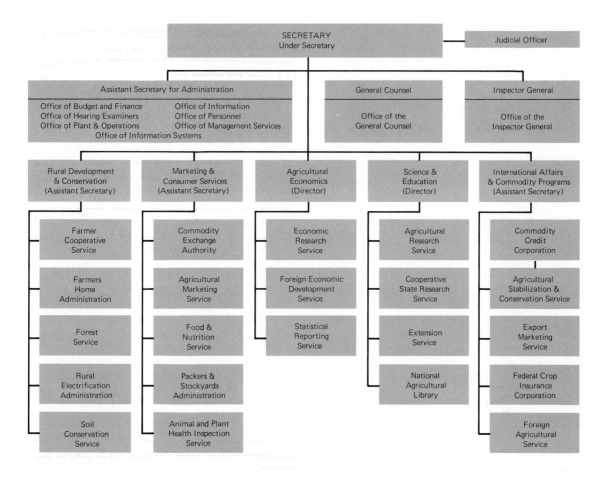

Department of Agriculture organization chart. Many government agencies and industrial corporations have even more elaborate organizational charts. Which office would you ask help from if you were a farmer interested in producing beef for an export market? Would it be Packers & Stockyard Administration? The Foreign Development Service? The Extension Service? The Export Marketing Service? All of these? Or some other office? Does this chart give you an insight into what is meant by "the complexity of modern organizations"? (Source: *U.S. Government Organization Manual, 1972–1973*, National Archives and Research Service, General Services Administration, Washington, D.C., 1974, p. 90.)

procedures is carried out impartially; and (4) a *chain of command*, to define each person's authority and responsibility.

Bureaucracy inevitably develops in all large organizations—government departments, churches, universities, voluntary associations, and private business concerns. Suppose, for example, a business concern has an office force of three persons. They can divide the work casually and informally, and each can get from the supply closet whatever office supplies are needed. Suppose the office force grows to 3,000. Now an orderly division of work and authority is necessary to get the work done; a set of formal policies is needed to keep the supplies in order, along with a system of inventory control and requisitions to keep supplies in stock and to prevent pilferage. Bureaucracy thus has at least three roots: the needs for efficiency, for uniformity, and for prevention of corruption.

Civil service as a bureaucratic model

While bureaucrats conducted routine government operations in ancient Egypt, Rome, and China, the great modern expansion of the civil service is due both to the expansion of government functions and to a new concept of the nature of the state. The state is no longer the property of either an hereditary ruler or a successful politician but becomes the servant of the people. As such it performs many functions which it did not assume in an earlier era. If governmental employees are not just loyal henchmen claiming their just rewards, then a system must be devised to obtain people who will assume their responsibilities in an impartial and capable manner. To gain this type of employee, civil service rules carefully define qualifications, duties, authority and compensation. Civil service employees ordinarily make decisions, not to please the political ruler or to gratify their own prejudices, but according to definite rules. Their income is not based on either their ability to gather taxes or the generosity of the ruler; they receive a salary according to their rank in the governmental organization. Their tenure is usually for life, and they may be promoted on the basis of seniority or proved competence; they can be dismissed only for wrongdoing or lack of efficiency.

The civil service system is designed to secure uniformity of administration by employees who have a special competence for the particular task to which they are assigned. The fact that it is still subject to criticism, even though it has largely succeeded in reaching the objectives for which it was established, reveals some of the problems of bureaucratic operation [Levitt, 1973].

The criticism of civil service may be summarized as (1) creation of an invidious status, (2) rigidity of performance, (3) division of responsibility and excessive clerical routine, (4) bifurcation of allegiance [Cohen, 1965, pp. 14–16; Merton, 1949a, pp. 151–160].

To some extent these tendencies may be alleviated by changes in the structure, but they appear in all bureaucracies and are probably impossible to eliminate.

An *invidious status* is one which automatically tends to create ill will, resentment, or animosity. It arises from the fact that although the bureaucratic employee is supposed to be the servant of the public, he is often in a position of making decisions that vitally affect the welfare of the citizen. The clerk who informs a jobless man that he is ineligible for unemployment benefits or tells a homeowner that his tax assessment has been raised is probably acting according to regulations, but he is in the position of handing down a distasteful decision to the citizen who is nominally one of his employers. It is easy for the bureaucrat to defend himself by citing the regulations and his duties as a public official, but this Olympian detachment may simply infuriate the citizen who already believes himself the victim of an unfair decision.

Rigidity of performance characterizes the actions of personnel who must follow a set of rules. When conditions unforeseen by the rules arise, the bureaucrat may be unable to act constructively because the regulations permit no exceptions. An amusing example of the bureaucrat's habit of blindly following the rules occurred when the cold wave of 1962 brought freezing temperatures to many Southern cities which had not had a freeze in decades. In at least one city the street department proceeded with its regular street-sprinkling schedule. The water promptly froze, bringing traffic to a standstill. After all, the regulations provided for daily sprinkling and a good official follows the rules.

It is often alleged that bureaucrats develop a habit of blindly following regulations, with an emotional incapacity to see any further than the rule book. Much bitter satire has been directed at the myopic bureaucrat with nose in the rule book and guided by all the initiative and imagination of an oyster. While many entertaining confirmations of bureaucratic rigidity can be collected, there is evidence that rigidity of performance is a characteristic of the bureaucratic system, not of the bureaucrats themselves. A careful comparison of bureaucrats with other personnel in nonbureaucratic positions concludes that "there is a small but consistent tendency for men who work in bureaucratic positions to be more intellectually flexible, more open to new experience, and more self-directed in their values than are men who work in nonbureaucratic organizations" [Kohn, 1971, p. 461]. However, the bureaucrat's effort to be flexible may lead him or her into concessions to clients at the cost of organization objectives. For example, U.S. Employment Service offices have sometimes sought to follow employers' preferences in referring job applicants, but this "flexibility" often resulted in favoring the white applicants the employers preferred and thus defeating the agency's pledge of nondiscrimination [Cohen, 1965]. Thus, rigidity of performance is not so much a product of blindly habituated bureaucrats as it is a product of the necessary rules of procedure by which any large organization must operate.

The disadvantages of rigidity are recognized by governmental administrators, and they try to reduce rigidity by giving more discretion to subordinate officials as well as by leaving some positions free to be filled by appointees selected without regard to the usual civil service regulations. But the granting of a great deal of discretionary authority to officials increases favoritism and corruption, and this in turn leads to a new set of regulations. Rigidity remains a problem, and the bureaucrat usually has difficulty in coping with a situation not clearly defined by regulations.

Division of responsibility is another irritating aspect of bureaucracy. In order to be sure that a uniform policy is followed and all individuals are treated equally, it may be neces-sary to build up an elaborate file and to consult several officials at different levels of the hierarchy. The citizen often feels that he is getting the "runaround" as he tries to find some official whom he can pin down to a decision. If this difficulty is minimized by decentralization to give subordinate officials more power, then the bureau faces the danger of criticism because of favoritism and inconsistent decisions.

Bifurcation of allegiance is perhaps the most deep-rooted of the objections to any bureaucracy, civil service or otherwise. Bifurcation means a splitting off in two divergent paths. In the bureaucracy, this may take the form of a split between service to the clientele and adherence to the norms and procedures characteristic of the bureaucratic structure. Supposedly the bureaucracy exists to serve its clientele, and procedures are developed with service in mind. Actually the procedures sometimes become an end in themselves. For example, the prison and the mental hospital have the goal of rehabilitating inmates or patients. But in each institution an employee culture develops, oriented toward controlling the inmates or patients in the easiest way, which sabotages the formal goals of the prison or hospital [Dunham and Weinberg, 1960]. Every bureaucracy offers similar examples of means becoming ends. An office may go through the motions without ever actually solving a problem. A bureaucrat may handle a citizen's complaint by filing a report, or by referring him to Mr. X. The official who follows this path may feel that he or she has done all that could be expected according to the rules; but the public is dissatisfied because its needs have not been met. Efforts to punish an official are usually fruitless when he can prove that he has followed the letter of the regulations. Again, a greater amount of freedom for the official, though it would enable him to meet problems more realistically, would destroy uniformity in treatment and invite corruption.

A number of these dysfunctional tendencies in bureaucracy are summed up in the concept of _bureaupathology_, a word apparently coined by Thompson [1961, chap. 8]. All large impersonal organizations produce a great many tensions among their personnel. Anxieties and frustrations over promotions, criticisms, failures, lack of recognition, unwelcome demands of others, and conflicting pressures of many sorts all combine to produce great stress in the individual. He or she often responds in ways which reduce tension but sabotage the goals of the organization. The insecure employee plays it safe by concentrating on report filing and record keeping. Buck passing and responsibility ducking are ways of keeping one's record "clean." Bureaupathic behavior is oriented to personal needs rather than to institutional goals. Since it arises from the anxiety and insecurity created by all large organizations, it is a problem in organizational theory, not in psychopathology.

Reactions to bureaucracy

The tendency for bureaucracies to accumulate rules and procedures is well known. In fact, many bureaucracies become so entangled in red tape that their daily work can be accomplished only by violating or evading some of the rules. Employees can stage a limited form of strike—a "work slowdown"—by simply abandoning their shortcuts and following the rule book. In this way the employees of the British Post Office slowed the mails to a crawl during a dispute in 1962 [*Time,* Jan. 19, 1962, p. 35].

The difficulties of bureaucratic organization lead to attempts both to improve it and to revolt against it. The formal study of administration with a careful analysis of bureaucratic forms and functions is an attempt to make the bureaucracy an efficient instrument for meeting organizational needs. Training programs for businessmen, educators, public officials, and clergymen all stress courses in "administration" (a more popular term for bureaucratic procedures). Since bureaucracy is both a necessary and an annoying feature of all modern societies, efforts to improve bureaucracy are continuous and only partly successful.

Bureaucracies tend to accumulate rules and procedures.

Revolts against bureaucracy take many forms. In government they may be seen in the persistence of "machine politics." The political machine is sometimes regarded as an effort to outflank the bureaucracy, since the citizen who is frustrated by the bureaucracy may be cared for by a political boss who gives preferential treatment in return for votes. The boss may be less honest than the bureaucrat but more skillful in primary-group relations. While he ignores red tape and violates rules, he gets things done.

Discontent with bureaucratic rule appears among the members or clients of all kinds of formal organizations. The elaborate ecclesiastical structure of the major denominations is often threatened by irregular clergy or by less formal churches which provide religious solace to those who distrust the formalized organization. The elaborately organized business may be undercut by a smaller competitor which can more swiftly pursue profitable opportunities. Schools find themselves confronted with taxpayers' revolts which are due in part to a feeling of helplessness of the average citizen in dealing with educational administration. Labor-union leaders often find their control is jeopardized by wildcat strikes in which the rank and file take action that the official union leaders would rather suppress. Student discontent with the bureaucratic characteristics of the university is claimed to be a significant factor in campus protests [Otten, 1970].

Various kinds of "direct action" seek to force modifications in bureaucratic action and have brought a type of voluntary group action which is noisy, abrasive and intolerant of bureaucratic delay:

. . . parents roll baby carriages into the streets to keep bulldozers from cutting new highways through their neighborhoods . . . professional women strike and march for women's rights . . . penitentiary inmates go on hunger strikes. White collar professionals and managers join in boycotts against gun manufacturers and non-union lettuce farmers . . . suburban housewives march against escalating meat prices. Blue collar workers demonstrate against busing their children across town. (Theodore Levitt: *The Third Sector: New Tactics for a Responsive Society,* Amacom, New York, 1973, pp. 73–74.)

Whether or not they win, such tactics produce an "adversary society" [Levitt, 1973, p. 72] which exacts a high cost in terms of the loss of trust and of increased disorder. The ombudsman, an office developed in Sweden in 1913 [Gellhorn, 1967, p. 194], has been adopted by corporations, governments, and universities as an orderly way of securing redress against a bureaucracy. The ombudsman usually has the power to investigate complaints and can often compel a reversal of an official decision. While he or she may prove to be a real protector of the humble citizen, there are latent effects of the office which are a bit different in character. For instance, supervisors may be less concerned with correcting alleged injustices themselves in the belief that the ombudsman can take care of any trouble. Also, the fear of being called to account for any kind of irregularity may make officials even more bureaucratic and inflexible in the effort to prove that they have followed all regulations to the letter. Whatever the ultimate effect of the growing acceptance of the ombudsman, there is no doubt that the existence of the office is one of many efforts to make bureaucracy humane as well as efficient. Yet

there is no easy answer to the problems of bureaucratic abuse. The uniform and impersonal character of bureaucracies is the basis for their usefulness; yet these same qualities sometimes make bureaucracies unable to respond to unique human needs.

Freedom versus compliance

Possibly the crucial problem of formal organization is to secure compliance with basic policies without stifling individual freedom. If the organization becomes a vast bureaucratic machine with a few people at the top giving orders while the others are mere robots following standardized routines, the results are fatal both to organizational success and to individual development. The world is not so simple that a handbook of rules can anticipate every situation, and any organization in which initiative is stifled will soon be so out of touch with the real world that its function will be impaired. Similarly, people are more than clerks or machines, and an organization will suffer if its personnel are deprived of any real voice in the decision-making processes. The formal organization seeks a high degree of compliance with at least the spirit of its announced goals; but if this conformity is purchased at the cost of stifled initiative and blunted thought, the cost to the organization is great.

Communications problems

In Chapter 8, we noted that the form of the communication chain makes a difference in the type of response. Morale is higher and communication more frequent in the circle with no designated leader, and lowest in the wheel where the person at the hub acts as director. This is also true of hierarchical versus egalitarian patterns. A system in which superiors give orders to subordinates is more likely to secure a uniformity of response, but also tends to dampen initiative and to repress feedback which might reveal problems. This is the reason why organizations often find a great deal of communication flowing from the top down and very little from the bottom up. A free flow of ideas which will stimulate suggestions, expose errors, and relieve anxiety through shared responsibility, will also make it difficult to agree on one master plan or uniform solution. What is gained in stimulation to increased creativity must be balanced against possible loss in coordination of activity.

Patterns of communication which stimulate the flow of ideas are a stimulus to creativity, but other attitudes which encourage the acceptance of innovations are also important [Strother, 1969, pp. 7–16]. For instance, there is always a very real risk that an innovation may be impractical. Thus an organization which fosters creativity must also be willing to accept risk and uncertainty. Further, most innovations are disruptive and expensive in the short run while the "bugs are being worked out." A creative organization requires a long-term perspective in which short-term costs are considered less important than future gains.

Professional versus bureaucratic competence

All formal organizations need the expertise provided by professionals.[2] Economists, sociologists, biologists, and a host of others are employed by governments, business, labor unions, political parties, and even churches, as well as by many other organizations. As organizations become larger, more centralized, and more bureaucratic, the "professionalization" of personnel tends to increase [Montagna, 1968, pp. 138–145].[3] The professional differs from the

[2]In this section we are indebted to Peter M. Blau and W. Richard Scott, *Formal Organizations,* Chandler Publishing Company, San Francisco, 1962, pp. 242–250, and to Victor A. Thompson, *Bureaucracy and Innovation,* University of Alabama Press, Tuscaloosa, 1969, pp. 69–70, 104–106.
[3]For a stimulating analysis of the efforts of a wide variety of occupations, ranging from librarians to funeral directors, to seek the status of a profession, see Harold L. Wilensky ("The Professionalization of Everyone?") *American Journal of Sociology,* 70:137–158, September, 1964.

other bureaucratic officials in frame of reference. The bureaucrat looks to the rules and the policies of the organization to provide a justification for decisions, while the professional is guided by the norms of his or her profession and by the opinions of professional colleagues who may be entirely outside the organization.

The professional employee of an organization is thus often torn between the rules of the bureaucracy and the standards of the profession. University professors have a similar problem of whether their first commitment is to their university or to their discipline. Those who seek national recognition among their fellow physicists, historians, or sociologists are called the "cosmopolitans," and those who look mainly to their own university for recognition are called the "locals" by one observer [Gouldner, 1957, p. 282]. The "local" has greater dedication to his or her particular college or university but somewhat less concern with academic colleagues outside the school, while the "cosmopolitan" is intensely concerned with the affairs of the international academic society, but may feel little loyalty to the college in which he or she is employed. Both types of professors are needed, but their goals and values are so different that the effort to coordinate their activities often leads to difficult conflicts.

Other kinds of professionals employed by the university may also experience role conflicts. Does the university psychiatrist owe primary loyalty to his patient, observing the strict confidentiality of the physician-patient role model? Or is loyalty due to the administrators to whom he or she should reveal anything about the student that the administrators wish to know [Szasz, 1967]? Should the college physician or someone else make the decision whether the health service should dispense contraceptives or arrange abortions for unmarried students? Such questions are not fully answered by existing codes of ethics of the professions.

Some authorities feel that the increasing professionalization of society is making the hierarchical bureaucratic forms of organization obsolete. Instead of an organization developed from the top with fairly rigid policies based upon rank or seniority, they envision a number of temporary task forces representing different professional skills; these task forces would be organized and reorganized for the needs of specific problems. The executives and managers in such a setup would not be decision makers, but would be liaison people who had learned enough technical jargon to be able to communicate between groups and thus achieve coordination [Toffler, 1970, pp. 128–129]. To date, no large-scale organization has been able to operate without a bureaucratic structure, but the very fact that alternatives are being considered points to the seriousness of the problem and the need to devise better methods for combining professional expertise with bureaucratic coordination.

Centralized control versus local initiative

The ideal pattern of a formal organization is one which has a group of experts at the top to decide general policies, and local functionaries to adapt them to specific situations. Actually, the organization has difficulty avoiding the twin dangers of (1) subversion of the central directives by local employees, or (2) their mechanical implementation in a way which fails to take varying conditions into account. A strict hierarchical supervision is likely to leave subordinate employees with so little freedom that innovation is stifled, while a more relaxed policy may mean that there is little resemblance between policies determined in the central office and practices in the field.

Some business concerns have sought to avoid this dilemma by the "horizontal" plan of organization which gives branch managers almost complete autonomy as long as they produce the desired results. Service agencies have found that reports enable the supervisor to react to lower-level communication rather than simply carry out orders from above. Sometimes a completely impersonal mecha-

nism such as an assembly line determines operations so completely that there is little room for supervisory decision.

However, we do not mean to imply that top-level direction is always restrictive and the local representative always advances human freedom. In our discussion of secondary groups in Chapter 8, we noted that the top-level decision making (as represented by central headquarters) is often more universalistic in character and more removed from local prejudice than is the naive grass-roots reaction. The kings of Spain, for instance, usually planned humane policies toward the South American Indians, but the policies were frustrated by the king's inability to control the actions of distant personnel in his colonial administration. High-level policy changes are often frustrated by grass-roots personnel because they conflict with what the field personnel have been trained and rewarded for doing. Such difficulties are revealed by the following item:

Agriculture Secretary Hardin has announced a dramatic new policy on pesticides. Henceforth USDA [United States Department of Agriculture] "will encourage those means of pest control which provide the least potential hazard to man, his animals, wildlife, and other components of the natural environment." But will such a policy statement redefine reality for Entomologist Durkin, County Agent Woodburn, and their colleagues across the land? It is not a difficult question to answer.

The Agriculture Establishment has been committed to the use of hard pesticides at all levels of government, but especially at the local level. Commitments may be slowly changing in Washington but out in mid-America, where the 6,170 county agents and the 4,281 Extension specialists perform their "education" duties, little has changed.

They are committed by 20 years experience—their life's work, really—to a certain point of view. Secretary Hardin can restate policy all he wants to from Washington, and President Nixon can reorganize anything he likes. At the local level nothing's going to change because the same people are going to be doing the job, and they're not equipped to do it any other way than the way they're doing it now. (Peter Montague and Katherine Montague, "The Great Caterpillar War and the Ecopolitics of Pesticides," *Audubon*, January, 1971, p. 58. Copyright © 1971 by Peter Montague.)

The problems of balancing freedom and order, efficiency and justice, uniformity and flexibility, stability and receptivity to change—these problems are inherent in the nature of all large-scale organizations. Policies that are repressive or freedom-expanding may originate at either level. To maintain some tolerable balance is an enduring task of bureaucracy.

Organizational responsiveness

There are two ways in which organizations are kept responsive to current needs. One is by constant reform and reorganization; the other is by the disappearance of old organizations and the birth of new ones. The birth or death of organizations is a frequent event. Voluntary associations are created and disappear with baffling speed. New business concerns are constantly being formed, and many of them quickly go into bankruptcy. Nation-states come and go; over thirty have been formed in Africa in the last twenty years, and in other parts of the world, nations such as Serbia and Montenegro have been absorbed into larger political units. Most churches survive for a long time, but many have merged in recent years. Some, such as the Shakers, lose their adherents and disappear, while the growth of such groups as the Mormons, Christian Scientists and Jehovah's Witnesses testifies to the possibility of developing new religious organizations.

Some organizations are able to make internal changes which prolong their life expectancy. Business concerns hire outside consultants to evaluate the company and make recommendations for changes which the management might be reluctant to introduce on its own. Governmental units are reorganized, as when a city changes from a mayor-council to a city-manager form of rule. Churches allow new leaders to develop different approaches. A case in point is the way the Jesuits, founded by Ignatius Loyola, reinvigorated the Roman Catholic Church after the Protestant Reformation. Rigid bureaucracies, in the long run, are less powerful than they appear, and either the organization finds a way to adapt to change or it dies.

Summary

Formal organizations are relatively enduring, deliberately organized groups operating according to a set of rules in pursuit of certain goals. These goals may encompass economic production, the pursuit of power, the integration of social organization through the resolution of conflict, the maintenance of patterns through the transmission of culture, and the enjoyment of various forms of play. *Voluntary associations,* which are especially numerous in the United States, provide people with an outlet for individual interests, a testing ground for action programs, and a channel for purposive social action. Active involvement in voluntary associations is more likely with middle-class people than lower-class people, although, in the United States, blacks seem to be more organizationally committed than whites.

Formal organizations may be either *closely or loosely structured.* The *informal structure* of a formal organization is an important aspect of organizational structure and may operate either to complement or to frustrate the formal chain of command. A *tendency toward oligarchy,* the rule of an organization by a small governing group, is a universal tendency; but an occasional organization remains truly democratic.

Bureaucracy is an administrative personnel which is specialized, appointed on merit, impersonal, and directed by a chain of command. While much criticized and ridiculed, bureaucracy is necessary and inevitable in all large organizations, arising from the need for efficiency, uniformity, and prevention of corruption. *Bureaupathology* is a name given to the defects of bureaucracy, including invidious status distinctions, rigidity, excessive red tape, and bifurcation of allegiance. Reactions to bureaupathology include efforts to improve bureaucracy through analysis and training and to curb it by militant "protest" activity. In recent years, several organizations have utilized ombudsmen to provide their members relief from discriminatory treatment by officials.

The dilemma of *freedom versus compliance* is a major problem for all large organizations, which need both the initiative and high morale of personnel who have some freedom of action and yet must obtain personnel compliance with organizational policy. Bureaupathology may make an organization insensitive to pressing human concerns, but ultimately, it either recognizes and tries to meet these concerns or dies.

Questions and projects

1. Emerson made the statement, "An institution is the lengthened shadow of one man." As the terms are defined in this book, was he talking about institutions or formal organizations? Defend your answer.
2. Does your school have an ombudsman? What arguments do you see for and against establishing such a position?
3. "Turn the rascals out" is a frequent battle cry in politics. Comment on the effectiveness of this procedure as a means of changing role behavior of officials and bureaucrats. As a means of changing political institutions.
4. Is it correct to say that modern labor unions are a latent effect of changes in business enterprise brought about by the industrial revolution?
5. Read and compare *The Demonics of Bureaucracy* by Harry Cohen and *The Dynamics of Bureaucracy* by Peter Blau (see Suggested Readings). Among other things, these men differ on the effect of requiring detailed reports from bureau employees. Which do you think is most nearly right?
6. Why does dissatisfaction arise with bureaucratic developments? What is the major obstacle in eliminating bureaucratic features which cause resentment?

7. Can you cite any examples of bureaupathic behavior in any bureaucracy with which you are familiar? By college students? By professors?
8. What is the meaning of the "iron law of oligarchy"? Does it operate in campus politics? Do you think that the formation of opposition parties in campus politics increases participation?
9. Read and compare Lawrence F. Peter and Raymond Hull's *The Peter Principle* with C. Northcote Parkinson's *Parkinson's Law and Other Studies in Administration* (Houghton Mifflin Co., Boston, 1957). Are there any means by which the problems treated in these books can be ameliorated?
10. Read and compare two fictional or biographical presentations of organizational roles in James Gould Cozzens, *Guard of Honor* (army officer); A. J. Cronin, *The Keys to the Kingdom* (Catholic priest); Pearl S. Buck, *Fighting Angel: Portrait of a Soul* (missionary); Sara Lucille Jenkins, *Lost Lamp* (Protestant minister); Theodore Morrison, *Stones of the House* (college president); James Hilton, *Good-bye, Mr. Chips* (old schoolmaster); Cameron Hawley, *Executive Suite* (business executive); Fortune (editors of), *The Executive Life* (business executive).

Suggested readings

*BLAU, PETER M.: *The Dynamics of Bureaucracy,* University of Chicago Press, Chicago, 1973. Reports on the dysfunction of detailed reports in a government agency. His analysis is challenged by Cohen, who worked in a similar agency.

BOGART, DODD H., AND HAVENS C. TIPPS: "The Threat From Species O," *The Futurist,* April 7, 1973, pp. 63–65. Two sociologists ponder the hypothesis that formal organization constitutes a "Species O," which threatens to dominate the world. A science-fiction-type treatment of a serious topic.

COHEN, HARRY: *The Demonics of Bureaucracy,* Iowa State University Press, Ames, Iowa, 1965. A participant observer report by a sociologist who worked in a governmental bureaucracy. Unlike many critics, he feels that the particular bureau he studied was too flexible in its disregard of directives from the central office.

GRUSKY, OSCAR, AND GEORGE A. MILLER (EDS.): *The Sociology of Organization: Basic Studies,* The Free Press, New York, 1970. A comprehensive reader on formal organizations.

*PETER, LAURENCE J., AND RAYMOND HULL: *The Peter Principle,* William Morrow & Company, Inc., New York, 1969. A humorous yet serious discussion of the manner in which reaching the level of incompetency becomes an organization trait.

ROSE, JERRY D.: "The Attribution of Responsibility for Organizational Failure," *Sociology and Social Research,* 53: 323–332, April, 1969. A study of how the careers of baseball managers are damaged by having managed losing teams, while baseball pitchers playing with losing teams apparently experience no harmful results to their careers.

*ROSENGREN, WILLIAM R., AND MARK LEFTON: *Organizations and Clients,* Charles E. Merrill Books, Inc., Columbus, Ohio, 1970. An analysis of organizations from the viewpoint of the clients they serve.

SMITH, CONSTANCE, AND ANNE FREEDMAN: *Voluntary Associations: Perspectives on the Literature,* Harvard University Press, Cambridge, Mass., 1972. A comprehensive and readable summary of research on all aspects of voluntary associations.

THOMPSON, VICTOR A.: *Modern Organization,* Alfred A. Knopf, Inc., New York, 1961, chap. 8, "Bureaupathology." An incisive analysis of some dysfunctional aspects of bureaucracy.

TIGER, LIONEL: "Bureaucracy and Charisma in Ghana," *Journal of Asian and African Studies,* 1: 13–26. January, 1966. A study of a struggle between a charismatic president and a well-entrenched civil service.

WILSON, THOMAS P.: "Patterns of Management and Adaption to Organizational Roles: A Study of Prison Inmates," *American Journal of Sociology,* 74: 146–157, September, 1968. A study finding that prisoners who participate in decision making have better relations with peers and superiors than those who simply take orders.

Chapter 12 • Social class

It was no easy life, this, under the feudal system; but it worked and has been called a social hierarchy of "confusion roughly organized". . . . The villein was bound to remain in the manor all his life and could not even marry without consent. Also, he could be bought, or won, by another lord, complete with family. . . . All the same, feudalism was not thought of as slavery. It was a pyramidal society, with each man tied to his superior up the social scale and eventually to the king. An exact counterpart of it could be seen in the servants' halls of Victorian houses, where a tweeny dared not cross swords with a parlourmaid and a footman could be brought before the master of the house for insolence to the butler. . . .

The hierarchy of feudalism was expressed in dress very firmly. The trimming of ordinary folks' tunics and surcoats was of rabbit; more exalted personages could wear squirrel; only royalty and the loftier nobility were entitled to ermine; and there was a law that forbade the lower orders to wear any cloth but russet, thus leaving the fine cambrics, the silks and brocades and damasks in brilliant colours and fine workmanship for those who could show them off to advantage. But the basic designs differed little. Both men and women wore long girdled tunics, cloaks with cowls over small round caps (or kerchiefs for women), and sandals or shoes of soft kid leather. An elaborately trimmed red tunic would cost twenty pounds—ten times the annual wages of a laborer or artisan, whose russet wool cost six or seven shillings, his shoes sixpence; but he could support himself and his family from the produce of his acres and from the occasional sale of a fat pig for five pence. And since he worked all day every day except Sunday and those church feast days that were marked by canon law he had little need for any clothes except the durable and drab. *(A. F. Scott, "Life in a Feudal Manor,"* British History Illustrated, *August, 1974, pp. 54–55. Used with permission of* British History Illustrated.*)*

Feudalism, with its knights, castles and elaborate code of dress and behavior for each rank of society, seems far away from us. Our society has no titles for those of different social strata, and the new styles quickly pass from the rich to the masses. Nevertheless, our society is marked by social class lines which define our social ranks as truly as different styles of clothing separated the serf from the noble in the days of King Arthur and his Round Table. What is this "social class" and how does it affect our behavior?

Aristotle observed two millennia ago that populations tended to be divided into three groups: the very rich, the very poor, and those in between. For Karl Marx the principal social classes were the wage workers (the proletariat) and the capitalists (the bourgeoisie), with a middle group (the petty bourgeoisie) which was on the way out. Adam Smith divided society into those who lived on the rent of land, the wages of labor, and the profits of trade. Thorstein Veblen divided society into the workers who struggle for subsistence and a leisure class which has become so wealthy that its main concern is a "conspicuous consumption" which proves how far this group has risen above the common herd. Franklin D. Roosevelt in 1937 gave a vivid description of lower-class life when he said in his inaugural address, January 20, 1937, "I see one third of the nation ill-housed, ill-clad, and ill-nourished." All these descriptions of social class imply that money separates people into different groupings.

Are there social classes?

Although the concept of social class has long been used by sociologists, some sociologists feel that it is not a useful concept [Faris, 1954; Nisbet, 1959; Lasswell, 1965]. They state that there are no definite boundaries or dividing lines for social classes, that persons placed in one class according to one measure belong in another class according to another, and that, consequently, the members of a "class" differ from one another too greatly for the concept of class to be valid.

The following pages will show why, despite the above objections, your authors believe that social class *is* a valid and useful concept.

What is social class?

Is social class purely a matter of money? If so, the rich gangster would out-rank the minister, nurse, or professor. While money is a factor, social class is not directly measured by one's bank account. A social class may be defined as a *stratum of people of similar position in the social status continuum*. The social position

of the janitor is not the same as that of the college president; a student will not greet them in exactly the same manner. Most of us are deferential toward those whose social position we believe to be above ours, and are condescending to those whom we consider socially below us. These processes of snubbing and kowtowing, of trying to claw one's way in or of shouldering out the person who doesn't "belong"—these provide the inexhaustible material for hundreds of novels, plays, movies, and television scripts.

The members of a social class view one another as social equals, while holding themselves to be socially superior to some others and socially inferior to still others. In placing a person in the proper social class, one asks such questions as: "To whose dinner party will they be asked as social equals?" or "For whose daughter will their son be an 'acceptable' escort?" The members of a particular social class often have about the same amount of money; but what is much more important is that they have much the same attitudes, values, and way of life.

How many classes are there? This question is hard to answer. Classes are not sharply defined status groupings like the different ranks in an army. Social status varies along a continuum, a gradual slope from top to bottom, rather than a series of steps. As "youth," "middle age," and "old age" are points along an age continuum, social classes may be viewed as points along a status continuum. Consequently, the number of social classes is not fixed, nor do any definite boundaries and sharp status intervals separate them. Instead, persons are found at all status levels from top to bottom, just as persons are found at all weights and heights, with no abrupt gaps in the series.

Such a series can be broken up into any convenient number of "classes." Earlier students of social class broke up the status continuum into three classes—upper, middle, and lower. Later students found this division unsatisfactory for many communities, because it placed persons in the same class even when they were much too far apart to treat one another as equals. Later students have often used a sixfold classification by breaking each of these three classes into an upper and a lower section. The top, or *upper-upper class,* is composed of the wealthy old families, who have long been socially prominent and who have had money long enough for people to have forgotten when and how they got it. The *lower-uppers* may have as much money but have not had it as long, and their family has not long been socially prominent. The *upper-middle* class includes most of the successful business and professional persons, generally of "good" family background and comfortable income. The *lower-middle* class takes in the clerks, other white-collar workers and semiprofessionals, and possibly some of the supervisors and top craftspeople. The *upper-lower* class consists mainly of the steadily employed workers, and is often described as the "working class" by those who feel uncomfortable about applying the term, "lower," to responsible workers [Miller and Riessman, 1961]. The *lower-lower* class includes the irregularly employed, the unemployable, migrant laborers, and those living more or less permanently on public assistance.

This sixfold classification, used by Warner and associates [1941, 1942] in studying an old New England town, is probably fairly typical of the large and medium-size cities in the more settled parts of the country. In the rapidly growing Western regions, "old family" may be less important. In smaller towns, the class system is less complex. In studying a small city in the Midwest, Hollingshead [1949] used a fivefold classification in which the two upper classes were combined into one. In a small rural community, West [1945] found no agreement among the residents upon the number of classes, although the status range probably would correspond to the bottom half of the six-class system of an urban society. Lynch [1959], studying the class system of an impoverished agricultural community in the Philippines, found only two classes—the self-sustaining and the destitute.

The number of social classes, therefore, varies from place to place; possibly it also varies with the observer's appraisal of the number of social strata whose members have the same general status. When we speak of, for example, the middle class, we do not refer to a group of people who are clearly set off from others by a definite status interval; we refer to a group of people who cluster around a midpoint in a status scale and who view and treat one another as social equals. The fact that the terms have no distinct boundaries does not keep the terms from being useful concepts and research tools. Social class is a significant social reality, not just a theoretical construct, for people *do* classify others as equals, superiors, and inferiors. Whenever people define certain other people as social equals and treat them differently from those who are not so defined, their behavior creates social classes.

Genesis of social classes

All complex societies have some system of stratification which unequally ranks people. The extent and kind of inequality varies tremendously, but there are always some accepted standards by which people distinguish their peers from their inferiors. This is true in Communist countries which deplore class divisions and in capitalist countries which may justify them; it is true in both democracies and autocracies and in agricultural as well as industrial societies. The only possible exception is in the most primitive food-gathering societies where people live by collecting such foods as fruits, nuts, roots, and berries. Here there is little possibility of any division of labor and hence little possibility of rank which may lead to group differentiation.

As soon as the society develops enough complexity to require coordination, the basis is formed for the development of social classes. Some people will be in charge of the work of other people, and their authority will inevitably be reflected in privileges which they try to pass on to their descendants. Warner describes the process in the following terms:

For example, among primitive peoples simple fishing expeditions may be organized so that the men who fish and handle each boat are under the direction of one leader. The efforts of each boat are directed by the leader and, in turn, each boat is integrated into the total enterprise by the leader's taking orders from his superior. The same situation prevails in a modern factory. Small plants with a small working force and simple problems possess a limited hierarchy, perhaps no more than an owner who bosses all the workers. But a large industrial enterprise with complex activities and problems, like General Motors, needs an elaborate hierarchy of supervision. The same holds true for political, religious, educational, and other social institutions; the more complex the group and the more diverse the functions and activities, the more elaborate the status system is likely to be. (W. Lloyd Warner, with Marchia Meeker and Kenneth Eells, *Social Class in America,* Harper & Row Publishers, Inc., New York, 1960, pp. 8–9.)

Although social class includes many features besides occupation, it is fundamentally based on the division of labor. A complex society requires many workers with varying degrees of skills and many coordinators with varying realms of authority. Prestige and power attach to the higher-ranked occupations and in turn enable the persons in these occupations to confer advantages on their descendants. Thus a group of people arise whose hereditary privileges are greater than are those of people who have descended from less highly regarded ranks.

An agricultural society with only two or three categories of responsibility may have a completely rigid system of stratification in which the gulf between nobles and commoners is never bridged. An industrial society is apt to have a far greater variety of occupations with greater ease of movement from one level to another, but distinct levels still remain. Social class, then, grows out of the system of division

of labor, and the ease of movement from one level to another depends upon the complexity and flexibility of the occupational structure of the society. Class mobility within a society is a highly complicated topic and is considered in some detail in the following chapter.

People do classify others as equals, superiors, and inferiors.

Social classes as subcultures

It is, after all, this division into working class and business class that constitutes the outstanding cleavage in Middletown. The mere fact of being born upon one or the other side of the watershed roughly formed by these two groups is the most significant single cultural factor tending to influence what one does all day long throughout one's life; whom one marries; when one gets up in the morning; whether one belongs to the Holy Roller or Presbyterian church; or drives a Ford or a Buick; whether or not one's daughter makes the desirable high school Violet Club; or one's wife meets with the Sew We Do Club or with the Art Student's League; whether one belongs to the Odd Fellows or to the Masonic Shrine; and so on indefinitely throughout the daily comings and goings of a Middletown man, woman, or child. (Robert S. Lynd and Helen H. Lynd, *Middletown,* Harcourt, Brace & World, Inc., 1929. Copyright 1929, by Harcourt, Brace & World, Inc, renewed © 1957 by Robert S. Lynd and Helen H. Lynd. Reprinted by permission of Harcourt Brace Jovanovich, Inc., and Constable Publishers.)

Each social class is a system of behavior, a set of values, and a way of life. While some overlapping and some exceptions occur, it remains true that the average middle-class child has a socialization vastly different from that of the average lower-class child. Let us take just one aspect of socialization—those experiences which shape ambition, education, and work habits—and see how they differ between two social-class worlds.

Typical upper-middle-class children live in a class subculture where they are surrounded by educated, cultivated persons who speak the English language correctly most of the time, enjoy classical music, buy and read books, travel, and entertain graciously. They are surrounded by people who are ambitious, who go to work even when they don't feel like it and who struggle to make their mark in the world. They are acquainted with the successes of ancestors, relatives and friends, and it is normal for them simply to assume that, like them, they are going to amount to something in the world.

When they go to school, scrubbed and expectant, they find a teacher whose dress, speech, manner, and conduct norms are much like those they already know. They are met by a series of familiar objects—picture books, chalkboard, and others—and introduced into a series of activities with which they are already familiar. The teacher finds them appealing and responsive children, while they find school a comfortable and exciting place. When the teacher says: "Study hard so you can do well and become a success some day," this exhortation makes sense. Their parents echo these words; meanwhile, they see people like themselves—older brothers and sisters, relatives, family acquaintances—who actually are completing educations and moving on into promising careers. For them, to grow up means to complete an advanced education and launch a career.

Lower-lower-class children live in a class subculture where scarcely anyone has a steady job for very long. To be laid off and go on welfare is a normal experience, carrying little sense of shame or failure. They live in a world where one can spend weekends in drinking, gambling and sexual exploration and miss work on Monday without sacrificing the respect of friends or neighbors. In their world, meals are haphazard and irregular; many people sleep three or four to a bed; and a well-modulated speaking voice would be lost amid the neighborhood clatter.

These children go to school often unwashed and unfed, and meet a person unlike anyone in their social world. The teacher's speech and manner are unfamiliar, and when they act in ways that are acceptable and useful in their social world, they are punished. The classroom materials and activities are unfamiliar. The teacher, who usually comes from a sheltered middle-class world, is likely to decide that they are sullen and unresponsive children, while they soon conclude that school is an unhappy prison. They learn little. The school soon abandons any serious effort to teach, brands them as "discipline problems," and concentrates upon keeping them quiet so that the other children can learn. When the teacher says, "Study hard so you can do well and become a success some day," the words make no sense. They receive little reinforcement from parents, who may give lip service to educational goals but seldom persuade the children that school and learning are very important. More important, the children see almost no one *like themselves*, no one in their own world, who actually *is* using school as a stepping stone to a career. In their world, the flashy cars and flashy companions are possessed by those who picked a lucky number, or got into the rackets, or found an "angle." Thus the school fails to motivate. For the lower-lower-class children, "growing up" means to drop out of school, get a car, and escape from the supervision of teachers and parents. The horizon of ambition seldom extends beyond the next weekend. Work habits are casual and irregular. Soon they marry and provide for their children a life which duplicates the experiences of their own socialization. Thus the class system operates to prepare most children for a class status similar to that of their parents.

Such differences in class behavior are found in virtually every activity of life—food habits, personal care, discipline and child care, reading tastes, conversational interests, vocabulary and diction, religious behavior, sleeping arrangements, sex life. Even the procedures followed in making love, according to Kinsey [1948, pp. 355–357], show important class differences. This is what we mean in speaking of class subcultures—that a great many of the normal life experiences of people in one class differ from those of people in another class. It is true that there are no sharply defined boundaries. From top to bottom, one kind of behavior shades gradually off into another; for example, vocabulary gradually becomes less genteel and diction less precise as we descend the class continuum (see Figure 6). But if we pick several points along this continuum for comparison, then the class differences are easy to see.

Figure 6. Class stratification of pronunciation. (Source: Slightly modified from William Labov, "Stages in the Acquisition of Standard English," in Roger W. Shur, ed., "Social Dialects and Language Learning." Copyright © 1965 by the National Council of Teachers of English. Reprinted with permission.)

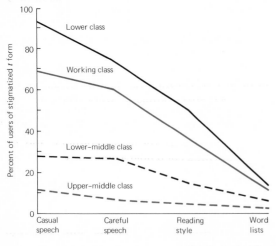

The pronunciation of *th* as in *thing, through, three,* in New York City. Shown in percentages of stigmatized form *t* versus prestige form *th,* by social class and context.

The culture of poverty

In the last decade it has been increasingly fashionable to refer to a culture of poverty [Lewis, 1959, 1966a, 1966b]. What this implies is that the poor form a subculture in which, as a result of their common experiences, they have developed certain attitudes and behavior patterns which have been transmitted from parent to child. These include the matricentric family, the casual resort to physical aggression, a disdain of thrift, and an apathetic attitude toward "getting ahead." The concept has been criticized [Roach and Gursslin, 1967; Glazer, 1971] on the grounds that it does not apply to such groups of the poor as the aged and the ill and that it may not apply equally to all ethnic groups. Further, the behavior patterns may not be so much norms or ideals as simply a pragmatic adjustment to what appear to be unalterable circumstances. On opinion surveys, poor people often express attitudes similar to those of the middle class, illustrating the concept of "value stretch" [Rodman, 1963; Fave, 1974]. The ideals are those of the general society, but the expectations are lower since the poor have learned to expect defeat. The "stretch" involves expressing ambitious aims in life, but settling for lower—and supposedly more realistic—accomplishments.

Whether all poverty-stricken groups perfectly fit the Lewis "culture of poverty" pattern can be debated, but there is no question that distinct behavior patterns characterize those who are poor. To a highly significant degree, social classes are different cultural worlds.

Determinants of social class

What places one in a particular social class? Is it birth, money, occupation, or what? The answer to each question is "Yes," for all these attributes are involved.

Wealth and income. Money is necessary for upper-class position; yet one's class position is not directly proportional to one's income. An airline pilot has less status than a college professor at half the income; a clergyman may outrank a prizefighter at fifty times his income.

To understand the place of money in class determination, we must remember that a _social class is basically a way of life._ It takes a good deal of money to live as upper-class people live. Yet no amount of money will gain _immediate_ upper-class status. The "new rich" have the money, but they lack the way of life of the upper-class person. They can buy the house, cars, and clothes, and hire a decorator to select the proper furnishings, books, and paintings. It takes a little longer to learn the formal manners of the upper class, but some careful observation, plus intensive study of Emily Post or Amy Vanderbilt, will probably suffice. But to acquire the attitudes and feelings and habitual responses of the upper-class person takes far longer. Unless one is born and socialized in an upper-class subculture, one is almost certain to make occasional slips which betray plebeian origin. Novels and plays abound with social climbers who never quite "make it" because they occasionally use the wrong word or reflect the wrong attitude and thereby betray their humble origin. Most of the "new rich" are no more than marginal members of the upper class during their lifetimes.

Their children, however, have a better chance, and for their grandchildren, a secure upper-class status is practically assured. Money, _over a period of time,_ usually gains upper-class status. People who get money begin to live like upper-class people. By the time their grandchildren mature, they are becoming "old family," while the grandchildren have fully absorbed upper-class behavior. Thus the two requisites of upper-class status are fulfilled.

Money has other subtle overtones. Inherited money confers greater status than earned money, for inherited wealth shows family background. Income from investments also suggests family background. Income from genteel professions is better than wages; money from speculating on stocks is better than money from gambling on horses. The

Figure 7. Poverty in the United States: Persons below the poverty level, 1959 to 1972 (millions). The poverty level for a nonfarm family of four was $4,275 in 1972. (Source: _Social and Economic Status of the Black Population in the United States,_ Series p-23, No. 46, Bureau of the Census, Washington, D.C., 1972, p. 28.)

nature and source of one's income carry suggestions as to one's family background and probable way of life.

Money one used to have is almost as good as money one has now. The "real" aristocracy of the South, for example, no longer has great wealth, partly because its class values prevented it from engaging in the grubby scrabbling which eventually created the oil millionaires and the industrial magnates. Yet the impoverished aristocrats can still retain upper-class status as long as they have enough money to eke out an upper-class pattern of living, even though it is somewhat frayed around the edges.

Money, then, is an important determinant of social class, partly because of the way of life it permits or enforces, and partly because of what it suggests about one's family background and way of life.

Occupation. Occupation is another determinant of class status. As soon as people developed specialized kinds of work, they also got the idea that some kinds of work were more honorable than others. In a primitive society, the spear maker, the canoe builder and the medicine man each hold a definite social status because of his work. Classical China honored the scholar and despised the warrior; Nazi Germany reversed the formula. Table 9 gives a prestige ranking of some occupations in the United States, according to one national-opinion survey.

Just why one occupation _should_ carry greater prestige than another is a question

TABLE 9 DISTRIBUTIONS OF PRESTIGE RATINGS, UNITED STATES

Occupation	Rank	Occupation	Rank
U.S. Supreme Court justice	1	Official of an international labor union	37
Physician	2	Electrician	39
Scientist	3.5	County agricultural agent	39
State governor	5.5	Trained machinist	41.5
College professor	8	Farm owner and operator	44
U.S. representative in Congress	8	Undertaker	44
Lawyer	11	Policeman	47
Dentist	14	Reporter on a daily newspaper	48
Architect	14	Insurance agent	51.5
Minister	17.5	Carpenter	53
Civil engineer	21.5	Mail carrier	57
Airline pilot	21.5	Plumber	59
Banker	24.5	Barber	62.5
Instructor in public schools	27.5	Machine operator in a factory	62.5
Captain in the regular army	27.5	Clerk in a store	68
Accountant for a large business	29.5	Singer in a nightclub	74
Owner of a factory that employs about 100 people	31.5	Taxi driver	80.5
Building contractor	31.5	Farmhand	83
Musician in a symphony orchestra	34.5	Garbage collector	88
Author of novels	34.5	Shoe shiner	90

Source: Adapted from Robert W. Hodge et al., "Occupational Prestige in the United States, 1925–1963," *American Journal of Sociology*, 70:290–292, November, 1964. The situation may have changed since this study was conducted, but unfortunately, studies of this sort are not conducted every year.

which has long fascinated social theorists. The high-prestige occupations generally receive the higher incomes; yet there are many exceptions. A popular night-club singer may earn as much in a week as a Supreme Court justice earns in a year. The relatively low-paid clergy, diplomats, and college professors rank far above the higher-paid airline pilots and building contractors, and have about equal ranking with the far wealthier physicians and lawyers. The high-ranking occupations generally require advanced education, but again the correlation is far from perfect. The importance of the work is an unsatisfactory test, for how can we say that the work of the farm hand or police officer is less valuable to society than the lawyer or corporation director? In fact, it has been

suggested that the low-ranking garbage collector may be the most essential of all workers in an urban civilization!

Obviously, the prestige ranking of occupations cannot be easily explained on a purely rational basis; yet it can hardly be an accident that all contemporary complex cultures have developed much the same hierarchy of occupational status. A survey of data from many countries by Inkeles [1960] finds that a particular occupation has about the same status rating in all urbanized, industrialized societies. Apparently the industrial system fosters certain attitudes, perceptions, and status relationships wherever it develops. In all societies, industrial or preindustrial, we see that persons tend to be assigned a class status according to their occupation, and that people will find those occupations open to them which are appropriate to their present class status.

Occupation is an exceedingly important aspect of social class because so many other facets of life are connected with occupation. If we know a person's occupation, we can make some guesses about the person's amount and kind of education, standard of living, associates, the hours he or she keeps and the daily routines of his or her family life. We can even make some guesses about this person's reading tastes and recreational interests, standard of moral conduct, and this person's religious affiliations. In other words, each occupation is part of a way of life that differs considerably from that which accompanies certain other occupations. It is one's total way of life that ultimately determines to which class one belongs. Occupation is one of the best clues to one's way of life, and therefore to one's social-class membership [Haug, 1972, p. 431].

The underdeveloped countries have a class structure which reflects a society that has limited use for professional, white-collar, or highly skilled workers and hence has a small middle class and a very large lower class. This pattern is changing as these countries become industrialized. Mexico, for instance, is a nation which is making rapid strides in this direction, and has had consequent changes in social-class distribution. The *popular* category (Mexican term for lower class) comprised only 40 percent of the population in 1960 as compared with 90 percent in 1890 [Cline, 1963].

Education. Social class and education interact in at least two ways. First, to get a higher education one needs money plus motivation. Lack of money is less of a barrier than it used to be, now that scholarships and student loans are so widely available; yet relatively few students complete college without some financial aid from their families. Even if it is no more than free room, board and laundry for all or part of the year, this is a considerable help. Upper-class youths already have money for the finest schools; they also have family tradition

TABLE 10 AN ESTIMATE OF INCOME AND SOCIAL CLASS

Class	Percentage of U.S. population	Income boundaries per year
RICH (Upper-upper)	1	Over $50,000
AFFLUENT (lower-upper)	8	$25,000–$50,000
PROSPEROUS (upper-middle)	26	$15,000–$25,000
AVERAGE (lower-middle)	26	$10,000–$15,000
BELOW PAR (upper-lower)	24	$5,000–$10,000
POOR (lower-lower)	15	Under $5,000

Based on data in "Money Income in 1973 of Families and Persons in the United States," *Current Population Reports*, Series P-60, Bureau of the Census, Department of Commerce, Washington, D.C., January, 1975, Table A, p. 1. Classifications adapted from Sylvia Porter: "Rich, Poor and Between," *Your Money's Worth*, syndicated news column, Publishers House Syndicate, February 1, 1974. This is an admittedly rough estimate which should be used with caution because inflation may make the figures out of date.

and social encouragement. For the upper-class or upper-middle-class high school youth, the question is, "What college are you going to?"; lower-middle-class and perhaps upper-lower-class youths ask one another, "What will you do after graduation?"; lower-lower-class youths are more likely to ask, "How soon can I quit school?" Second, one's amount and kind of education affects the class rank secured. Education is one of the main levers of the ambitious. Higher education not only brings occupational skills; it also brings changes in tastes, interests, goals, etiquette, speech—in one's total way of life.

Although a wealthy family background is a necessity for secure upper-class status, education may substitute for family background at the intermediate class levels. The middle classes are so large and move around so much that it is impossible to know the family background of each individual. Newcomers to a locality are likely to be accepted into whichever of the middle or lower classes their behavior fits them. Education, occupation, and expended income are three fairly visible clues, and with these are associated most of the other behavior characteristics which make one "belong."

Social scientists make great use of these three criteria—education, occupation, and income—in dividing people into social-class levels for research purposes. As we have already explained, these are fairly useful clues to the total way of life distinguishing social classes. Furthermore, these criteria are fairly easy to objectify. It would, for example, be difficult to use "crude or cultivated speech" as a test of class rank in a research study, because speech, though easy to notice, is hard to measure.[1] Finally, the data on education, occupation, and income are available from the census reports, broken down by "census tracts," or areas of a few blocks each. Suppose a sociologist wishes to compare death rates, or polio rates, or average family size, or practically anything, as it varies among social classes. Using census data on occupation, education, and average income of the different census tracts within the community, it is easy to locate an upper-class tract, a middle-class tract, and a lower-class tract for comparison. While social class involves more than these three criteria, they are adequate to identify social classes for most research purposes.[2]

Self-identification and class consciousness. Most sociologists consider social class a reality even if people are not fully aware of it. Ameri-

can democratic beliefs emphasize equality and tend to inhibit a frank recognition of class lines. People will deny that there are social classes in their community, yet state this denial in terms which reveal that classes really do exist. Lantz cites one of many such statements by the residents of a small town:

You see, this no-class idea makes it a good place to live. The Company houses are called "Silk Stocking Row" but I would feel as good with the mining superintendent's wife as I would with anybody else. You see, this is a melting pot. Our people, you see, all came from foreign countries. Why, my grandparents came from England. You see, I belong to the DAR. I can trace my family tree all the way back through the Revolutionary War into England. I take a great deal of pride in this. Why, I can trace my ancestry back to a captain who was a friend of Washington's in the Revolutionary War. (Herman R. Lantz, *People of Coal Town,* Columbia University Press, New York, 1958, p. 216.)

A Polish sociologist, Ossowski, indicates that "Social structure in the United States is sometimes interpreted as a continuum of social positions without class divisions" [Ossowski, 1956]. This statement is based on the fact that Europe retains highly self-conscious class feelings, which may be interpreted as a survival from the rigid classifications of feudalism. In the United States, the founding fathers rejected the establishment of a hereditary nobility, while Americans have always cherished the idea that, regardless of station in life, all persons were basically equal. ("The inconsistent treatment of slaves was rationalized for over two centuries by defining slaves as "property," not "persons.")

Probably this emphasis on basic equality is the reason that fewer Americans regard themselves as "lower-class" than might be indicated by the indices of income, occupation, and education. Acceptance of the term "lower-class" seemed to be degrading and insulting. Yet Americans do recognize social classes, and when people are given a chance to choose the more neutral category of "working class" rather than "lower-class," they do so in about the same proportion as are placed in the lower

---

[1]For a discussion of speech as an indication of social class, see William Labov, "The Effect of Social Mobility of Linguistic Behavior," *Sociological Inquiry,* 36:186–203, Spring, 1966.

[2]See Joseph A. Kahl and James A. Davis, "A Comparison of Indexes of Socioeconomic Status," *American Sociological Review,* 20:317–325, June, 1955, for a defense of the view that occupation is the best overall measure of class position or Marie Haug, "Social-Class Measurement: A Methodological Critique," in Gerald W. Thielbar and Saul D. Feldman, *Issues in Social Inequality,* Little, Brown, and Co., Boston, 1972, pp. 429–449. For a claim that a composite "index of status characteristics" is a better measure see John L. Haer, "Predictive Utility of Five Indices of Social Stratification," *American Sociological Review,* 22:541–546, October, 1957.

class in the classifications constructed by social scientists [Hodges and Trieman, 1968].

Is one's class membership, then, determined by the feeling that one belongs in a particular class, or by the facts of occupation, education, and income? Largely by the latter, for they determine one's overall way of life. Yet the *feeling* of class identification is of some importance, for one tends to copy the behavior norms of the class with which one identifies. Eulau [1956] found that those informants who placed themselves in a class in which they did not objectively belong shared the political attitudes of the class they claimed rather than those of the class in which they belonged. Self-identification with a social class has some effect upon behavior, whether one actually is a member of that class or not.

Status symbols. One of the rewards of higher social status is to be recognized as a member of a superior stratum. Since the rich and well born have the same physical appearance as others, they need some means of insuring that their position is recognized. In the past, this has been found through the *status symbol,* which can be any desirable trait or object whose supply is sharply limited [Blumberg, 1974, p. 481], such as Cadillacs, mink coats, private swimming pools, and diamonds. Such items were valued as much for their status shouting as for their utility or beauty. However, current trends indicate that the day of the status symbol may be about over.

Part of the reason for the decline in status symbols is the rise in the absolute level of income, which has made these symbols available to a larger sector of the population. Over 80 percent of American families own automobiles and nearly a third own two or more. By sacrificing other items or by using a secondhand car, it is fairly easy to get even the most expensive model. Genuine jewelry and furs may be beyond the reach of many people, but imitations which can be identified only by experts make items of this type available to a wide sector of the population. Concern for ecology has also made some

status symbols less acceptable. Does a big car indicate success or simply a callous indifference to the shortage of gasoline and air pollution? There has also been a change in fashion which often appears to have the rich copying the poor—a change indicated by a 40 percent drop in the sale of men's suits during the sixties and an increase of 400 percent in the sale of denim [*Statistical Abstract of the United States,* 1972, p. 721].

Today the rich often appear to be copying the poor.

Even intangible symbols are no longer as effective as formerly. Golf is played by the assembly line worker as well as by the professional. Television brings a wide variety of cultural fare into all American homes. Programs may be selected along the lines of social class, but this can easily be varied by anyone concerned about cultural snob appeal. A great majority of youth have graduated from high school and so many from college that educational credentials have less and less status value. The homogenizing effects of American social mobility are weakening both the material and the nonmaterial status symbols.

The final thrust (which may be a temporary swing of the pendulum) is an abandonment of the quest for status symbols by many of those best able to pursue it. Blumberg describes this tendency:

What has happened is that the status seekers have become the anti-status seekers. Not only in standards of fashion, but in personal grooming (e.g., long hair), in speech (the black vocabulary), in music (country, folk, rock), in film (the alienated youth films of the 1960's and the black films of the 1970's), in drama (e.g., *Jesus Christ Superstar*) and political *Weltanschauung,* there has been in the last decade more percolating up from the bottom than trickling down from the top. (Blumberg, 1974, p. 494)

Size of each social class

Earlier studies agreed that, in a six-class ranking scale, the two lower classes include slightly over half the population [Warner and Lunt, 1941; Centers, 1949]. The trends in Table 11 for traits associated with lower-class groups and the income estimated in Table 10 would seem to indicate that the lower classes are decreasing in size and the middle and upper classes increasing. Hence, it seems reasonable to assume that the two lower classes now represent less than half of the population. Changing technology is destroying lower-class jobs and creating middle-class jobs. Looking at Table 11, you will notice that educational, occupational, and income data all tell the same story. A majority of the population has now finished high school, as contrasted to only about a third in 1947; the proportion in semi-skilled and unskilled jobs has dropped, as has the proportion of the population classed as living in poverty. The only index related to poverty to show an increase is that indicating a rising proportion of one-parent, female-headed families. Almost every kind of middle-class job is expanding as the changes in economic life continually demand more technical and professional personnel. Furthermore, as technology changes the content of jobs, their status also changes. Historically, most factory jobs were dirty, filled by people who were comparatively unskilled and low paid. Today a growing fraction of factory jobs are clean, calling for highly trained and well-paid workers. Such workers seem likely to move into the middle class.

Measurement of classes is complicated by the fact that there are several criteria of membership in a given class and many families do not show *all* the characteristics of any one class level. For example, the "ideal type" lower-lower-class family would live in an urban slum or rural shack; one or more adult members would drink quite heavily, and the male family head would not be consistently in the household; the family would have little education or interest in education; and its low income would be derived partly from intermittent unskilled labor and partly from welfare sources. Probably comparatively few lower-lower-class families meet all of these conditions. While class differences are real, the boundaries and membership of each class cannot be clearly fixed.

Blue-collar and white-collar class status

Frequently the decisive dividing line between the middle class and the lower class has been whether the occupation was manual or non-manual. In recent years, there has been so much of a convergence of manual and non-manual income levels that some authorities doubt that this is still a measure of social class. Two English sociologists [Goldthorpe and Lockwood, 1963, p. 133] have coined the word "embourgeoisment" to indicate that the working class is gradually taking on a middle-class (bourgeoisie) type of outlook. This viewpoint is supported by figures like those in Table 12 which show that average incomes of craftsmen and foremen are higher than those of clerical workers and female sales workers. On the other hand, the income of operatives (a category largely comprised of semiskilled and unskilled factory workers) is considerably lower for men, although women operatives and salespersons have similar incomes. Looking at a variety of personal and social attitudes, De

TABLE 11 HOW LARGE IS OUR LOWER CLASS? PROPORTION OF UNITED STATES POPULATION IN SELECTED EDUCATIONAL, OCCUPATIONAL, AND INCOME CATEGORIES

Type of individual or group	Year	Approximate % of population	Year	Approximate % of population
Adults (18 or over) in labor force who did not complete high school	1947	67.0	1972	41.8
Adults in civilian labor force in "semiskilled" and unskilled positions	1950	49.6	1973	39.6
Adults with 4 grades of education or less	1947	11.0	1972	4.6
Family units with income below low-income level (In 1972 the poverty line was $4,275 for an urban family of four.)	1960	18.9	1972	9.3
Household units reporting female head	1950	9.2	1973	12.1
Adult illiterates	1947	2.7	1969	1.0

Source: Manpower Report to the President, U. S. Department of Labor, March, 1969, p. 226. *Statistical Abstract of United States*, 1973, Monthly Labor Review, 93, July, 1970, p. 100. *The Social and Economic Status of Blacks in the United States 1972*, Series P-23, No. 46; Bureau of the Census, Washington, D.C., July, 1973.

Fronzo [1973] found wide differences between white-collar and blue-collar workers in Indianapolis, but these differences largely disappeared when education was equal for the two groups. The figures by categories conceal some rather wide differences within each group, and one would suspect that embourgeoisment would be quite evident among the most highly paid blue-collar workers, such as printers, electricians, plumbers, and automobile factory workers.

Since embourgeoisment of blue-collar workers implies that the growing middle-class tendency is making the idea of class struggle obsolete, it is attacked by Marxian sociologists. One of the most avowedly Marxian of these, Charles H. Anderson, says that neither white-collar or blue-collar workers can be considered middle-class. Rather, both are in the same class—the working class. "The proletarianization of white-collar workers, including the professional strata, is the dominant fact . . . rather than the embourgeoisment of the blue-collar worker" [Anderson, 1974, p. 168]. In other words, he argues that blue-collar and white-collar workers are coming closer together, but this means that white-collar workers are becoming part of the working class rather than blue-collar workers becoming middle class.

Anderson believes that the "proletarianization" of the white-collar worker is an outcome of the lack of opportunity in American society. However, it is possible to argue that the ease of movement from blue-collar to white-collar oc-

TABLE 12 ANNUAL INCOMES OF BLUE- AND WHITE-COLLAR WORKERS, 1972

	Sales workers	Clerical	Craftsmen and foremen	Operatives
Male	$11,610	$9,716	$10,413	$8,747
Female	4,445	6,054	5,545	5,004

Source: *Statistical Abstract of the United States*, 1974, p. 361.

A convergence of manual and nonmanual income levels.

cupations and the improvement of conditions for blue-collar workers are the factors really responsible for whatever white-collar proletarianization exists. Hamilton [1966] found that 52 percent of a sample of American clerks identified themselves as working class. He found this especially true of those who had come from blue-collar families who, since they found no gain in income, retained their working-class self-identification. Whether one looks at the embourgeoisment of the blue-collar worker or the proletarianization of the white-collar worker, it is becoming clear that the old distinction between manual and non-manual work is losing at least part of its meaning. Lenski [1966, p. 362] does point out, however, that clerks still have better mobility prospects than manual workers for moving into managerial, professional, or entrepreneurial posts. Since people guide themselves at least partly by their expectations, this difference in mobility prospects may be enough of a distinction to prevent a complete merging of blue-collar and white-collar social attitudes.

The significance of social classes

Determining life opportunities

From before one is born until one is dead, opportunities and rewards are affected by class position. Poor nutrition for the mother may affect the health and vigor of the fetus before birth, while total living conditions thereafter continue the advantages or handicaps of class position. One study of the relation between education (taken as a rough index of social class) and mortality reveals this in grim detail [Kitagawa and Hauser, 1967]; men between twenty-five and sixty-four with less than five years of education had a mortality index 49 percent higher than that of men with some college. For some women the difference was even greater, being 98 percent higher for those with less than five years of education than for college alumni. Figure 8 indicates that the least-educated group had nearly twice as many days of restricted activity due to illness or accident as the highest-educated group. The lower-class person is not only likely to die prematurely, but will also endure more days of illness during his or her comparatively short lifetime.

In mental health, the class differential is equally striking. Over two dozen studies have been made, all showing that the lower class has more mental illness than the higher classes [Hollingshead and Redlich, 1953, 1958; Miller and Mishler, 1959; Rushing, 1969]. In education, there may not be any great disparity in facilities. The poor in the cities may attend schools with more adequately paid teachers and better equipment than the middle-class students in smaller towns. Also federal and state aid have greatly benefited the schools attended by the very poor. The difficulty is that the students themselves have a major impact on the effectiveness of the school. General attitudes and the strength of achievement motivation are even more important than the caliber of the teachers and the lavishness of educational equipment [Coleman, 1966].

In the case of lower-class students, motivation toward effort in school is weakened by the general frustration of friends and family. School requires a commitment toward a long-term payoff. The attitudes of the lower-class students are likely to be slanted toward short-run rewards. These attitudes are produced by a neighborhood characterized by crowded housing and irregular family life and by people whose grasp on jobs, health, and housing is tenuous and short-term. The rigor of education must be endured now, while the rewards come at a later date, but the lower-class student is conditioned to rely on the short-term payoff.

One psychologist, Julia Vane, has found that performance on intelligence scores (often associated with race) is related to social class. She studied an all-white sample in Britain and Ireland and found that children from white-collar families, on the average, had higher IQ scores than children from blue-collar families. This was true on all parts of the test, but the difference was greatest in vocabulary, indicating support for the belief that blue-collar families tend to have a limited amount of verbal interaction [Vane, 1973].

When lower-class youth come to seek jobs, they lack the education, the work habits, and the poise or bearing to command a job with a promising future. The lower-class occupations, such as farm laborer or unskilled laborer, carry low wages, irregular employment, and few welfare or "fringe" benefits. Often they involve high accident danger or health hazard; yet this class can afford only the poorest living conditions and the least medical care.

In wartime, the lower-class youth is more likely to be rejected by the draft because of physical or mental handicaps, but he is less likely to be deferred for either occupational or educational reasons. If entering the armed forces, he is less likely to qualify as a specialist, which might place him in a relatively safe position, and more likely to wind up in combat. Exact statistics on class-related factors are difficult to get, and these statements are based on data on the proportion of men from various educational levels and on the experience of blacks. It is felt that education is a rough index of social class and that the black experience is more a result of black overrepresentation in the lower class than of strictly racial factors. The educational data indicate that (see Figure 9), in the middle of the Vietnam War, the proportion actually serving whose educational

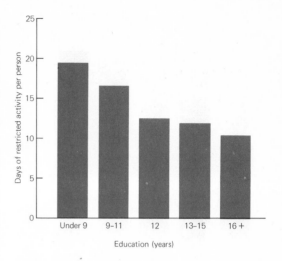

Figure 8. Disability by socioeconomic level (United States noninstitutionalized civilian population, 1969, ages 17–64). (Source: Unpublished data from the National Center for Health Statistics. Cited in *Statistical Bulletin*, Metropolitan Life Insurance Company, June, 1972.)

level varied from high school dropout to college graduate was about the same; the proportion of those with eight grades or less was low; and that of those who had attended graduate school was lowest of all [*National Advisory Commission on Selective Service*, p. 23]. Blacks were less likely to serve in the army at all, since nearly 50 percent were rejected for physical or mental disabilities, compared to about 25 percent of whites. Thus, in 1964, only 37.3 percent of the black youth aged twenty-six to twenty-nine had been inducted, as compared to 61.1 percent of white youth. On the other hand, 22.8 percent of combat troops were black, although they made up only 11 percent of all troop personnel in Vietnam [*National Advisory Commission on Selective Service*, 1967, pp. 22–26]. In summary, then, lower-class youth were more likely to be excused completely from military service, but if drafted, were more likely to be assigned to hazardous combat duty.

Happiness and social class. Perhaps the whole syndrome is summed up in an article by Paul

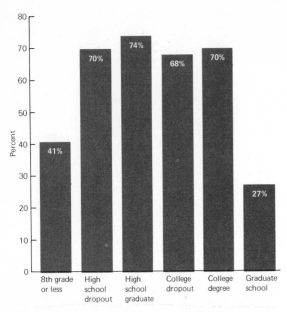

Figure 9. Percentage of men in military service, by educational level (aged 27–34 in 1964). (Source: *Military Service in American Life Since World War II: An Overview,* National Opinion Research Center, 1966. Cited in National Advisory Commission on Selective Service, *In Pursuit of Equity: Who Serves When Not All Serve?,* p. 23)

Cameron [1974] which finds that happiness itself is somewhat class-bound. Cameron and his colleagues asked a large sample of people to indicate their feelings of happiness or unhappiness. They found that happiness did not vary by the presence or absence of physical handicaps or of mental retardation. Neither was it affected by age, for the old are happy about as often as the young. Of all the factors he studied, social class seemed to have the strongest relationship to euphoric feelings. In a summary of several such studies, Easterlin [1973] found that the proportion reporting themselves as "very happy" rose steadily from 25 percent in the lowest income group to 50 percent for those with incomes of over $15,000. On the other hand, the relation between income and happiness doesn't indicate that if a country is wealthier, its citizens will be happier. Easterlin's analysis shows that the

population of the United States was no happier in 1970 than in 1940, although real income was 60 percent higher in 1970. Likewise, comparisons on an international basis show that citizens of wealthier, industrialized countries are no happier than those of poorer, less developed countries. The relation is not with absolute income, but between income and perceived need. Within a given society, although there is some variation by social class, there is also some degree of consensus among most people as to the extent of "real needs." The more prosperous people in that society are better able to meet perceived needs and thus more likely to be happy than those who are less prosperous. However, as a whole society becomes more prosperous, the standard of "need" rises, and an income considered adequate in a less prosperous era may seem grossly inadequate in relation to new expectations. Thus it is relative advantage rather than absolute amount of money which makes for happiness.

Even relative advantage has some drawbacks among those who receive the advantage by inheritance rather than by achievement. Readers of this book who have not had the luck to be born in prosperous families may take comfort in having a better chance of escaping "dysgradia." This malady is a constellation of ills, including severe anomie and depression. According to Wixen, who made a study entitled *Children of the Rich* [1973], dysgradia arises when middle-class values of work and family life which have been strongly held by the older generation make no sense to their children. Life has been so easy for the rich children, and their sense of security is so great, that they sometimes see no need for hard work either as a means of rising in the world or as a way of making good on their obligations to others. Not being able to participate in the satisfaction of step-by-step advancement, they fall prey to boredom.

Not all children from wealthy homes suffer from dysgradia, since some gain a satisfaction from validating inherited status by their own achievement and others have internalized a sense of duty to society known as *noblesse oblige.* Either wealth or poverty may have adverse effects on personal adjustment, and the most favorable circumstance appears to be one of modest advance which gives a feeling of success without removing the prod of still unsatisfied ambition.

Assigning social responsibilities and privileges

A lot of unpleasant work must be done in any society, and someone must be persuaded to do it. Occasionally special rewards may be used—honor for the warrior, or wealth and fame for the prizefighter, for example. But each complex society relies mainly upon the class system to compel someone to do the drudgery. A combination of cultural background, educational limitation, and job discrimination all work together to make the lower-class person unable to compete for the better jobs; as a result, only the poorer jobs are left. The result, though it may be entirely unintentional, is no less real. Social class gets the grubby work of the world done by excluding part of the people from the nicer jobs.

The lower class also functions as a storehouse for surplus unskilled labor. Our economy requires a good deal of seasonal or irregular labor, especially in farm labor and construction projects. Those who are not continuously needed are "stored" in the lower class, where the class subculture makes it possible to survive periods of unemployment and go on relief without guilt or sense of failure. The lethargy, lack of ambition, and willingness to accept squalor which middle-class people criticize so self-righteously are, in fact, the *necessary and useful* life adjustments of the lower class. Such attributes are necessary to the mental health and sanity of our "stand-by" unskilled labor supply.

Other social classes also provide distinctive subcultures that prepare class members for specialized functions in society. The upper class need not "make a living" or struggle for status, but may feel impelled to justify its status and income through some form of public service. The Roosevelts, Rockefellers, Kenne-

TWO PATTERNS OF CHILD REARING: THOSE CONDUCIVE TO EDUCATIONAL ACHIEVEMENT AND THOSE CHARACTERISTIC OF LOW-INCOME FAMILIES

Conducive to achievement	Low income
1. Child given freedom within consistent limits to explore and experiment.	1. Limited freedom for exploration (partly imposed by crowded and dangerous aspects of environment).
2. Wide range of parent-guided experiences, offering visual, auditory, kinesthetic, and tactile stimulation.	2. Constricted lives led by parents: fear and distrust of the unknown.
3. Goal commitment and belief in long range success potential.	3. Fatalistic, apathetic attitudes.
4. Gradual training for and value placed on independence.	4. Tendency for abrupt transition to independence: parents tend to "lose control" of children at early age.
5. Educational-occupational success of parents; models as continuing "learners" themselves.	5. Tendency to educational-occupational failure; reliance on personal versus skill attributes of vocational success.
6. Reliance on objective evidence.	6. Magical, rigid thinking.
7. Much verbal communication.	7. Little verbal communication.

Source: Adapted from Catherine S. Chilman, "Child Rearing and Family Relationship Patterns of the Very Poor," *Welfare in Review,* 3:10, January, 1965.

dys, and many others are examples. Such patricians very often promote social policies which are of the most direct benefit to the lower classes. Their political success shows that the masses will accept the leadership of a wealthy elite who are able to rise above their own narrow class interests.

There is a lot of unpleasant work.

A most vulnerable aspect of upper-class claims to social usefulness is the existence of a group who become "jet-set" types and devote their time and money to expensive dissipation in an endless search for novelty to stimulate jaded senses dulled by little responsibility and much indulgence. Persons of this type may be a minority of the upper class, but they are very conspicuous in an era of mass communication, and the envy and resentment they arouse is a major obstacle to the acceptance of the legitimacy of an upper class by the rest of society.

Vigorous controversy has developed in sociological circles over the question of whether social-class stratification is useful as an efficient means of role allocation. Some claim that society requires a variety of occupational roles, and that one's social-class background gives one the attitudes desirable for occupational function. The following is a typical statement of this viewpoint:

Social inequality is an unconsciously evolved device by which societies insure that the most important positions are filled by the most qualified persons. Hence every society, no matter how simple or complex, must differentiate persons in terms of both prestige and esteem, and must therefore possess a certain amount of institutionalized inequali-

ty. (Kingsley Davis and Wilbert Moore, "Some Principles of Stratification," *American Sociological Review,* 10:242–249, April, 1945. Reprinted by permission of the authors and the *American Sociological Review*.)

This position has been sharply criticized on the grounds that social-class conditioning and role ascription may make it difficult for the individual to make the best use of his or her potential abilities. The brilliant person from a lower-class background may have neither the objective opportunities to prepare for an important career nor the value system which will encourage pursuing long years of education apprenticeship. Conversely the upper-class moron may be kept from useful service by family privilege and may lack completely the attitudes which enable unskilled laborers to adjust to their occupational roles. These and other criticisms have been made by Tumin [1957], who suggests that social class may be dysfunctional, i.e., it hinders social adjustment, whereas a better system of allocating occupational roles could be devised.

This is another form of the argument over ascribed versus achieved roles. A plausible summation is suggested by Gordon [1958, pp. 166–173], who points out that, while an equalitarian society might be ideal, such a society has never existed. Some system of differential reward always develops, and parents do seek to transmit their advantages to their children. The resulting class system has a major influence in the allocation of occupational roles. It is not a perfect system, but is seriously wasteful of talent only when a "closed" system develops which does not allow people to cross class lines. This is a topic we will take up in more detail in the following chapter, "Social Mobility."

Cultivating class ethnocentrism

There is an anecdote of a private tutor in a wealthy family who sought to teach his pupil about the life of the poor. Then the little rich girl wrote a story about the poor, beginning:

"Once upon a time there was a very poor family. Everybody was poor. The Papa was poor, the Mama was poor, the children were poor, the cook was poor, the maid was poor, the butler was poor, the gardener was poor—Everybody was poor."

Members of one class cannot help judging members of other classes in terms of their own class expectations and values. The middle class scorns upper-class snobbishness, but strives desperately to raise its own children in a "good" neighborhood. People at every class level tend to see those above themselves as effete, snobbish, and pretentious, and those beneath as either disgusting or pathetic, as either good-for-nothing or "awfully pushy." At all intermediate status levels, people tend to attribute their own status to personal achievement, the status of those above to luck, and that of those beneath them to inability and laziness. Miller suggests that, of all forms of ethnocentrism, class ethnocentrism is one of the most difficult to restrain:

It is considerably easier to manifest "tolerance" for the ways of the Zulu, Navaho, or Burmese than to achieve emotional acceptance of features of lower-class culture in our own society; in the former case it is relatively easy to recognize that disapproved or exotic behavior is a direct product of the group's culture and to accept such behavior on the grounds that it is "their way" of doing things, a way which is different from ours. In the case of lower-class culture, however, there is an almost automatic tendency to view certain customary behaviors in terms of right and wrong and to explain them as blameworthy deviations from accepted moral standards rather than as products of a deep-rooted cultural tradition. It is not too difficult to view the device of polygamous marriage and the mother-centered household among the Zulus as one alternative arrangement for meeting the problem of marriage and childrearing; it is much harder to see the practice of serial mating and the female-based household in our own society as social forms which may constitute a practical or effective adaptation to the milieu in which they are found. . . .

The basic values and emphases of lower-class culture produced a vast army of woodsmen, construction workers, cattlemen, Indian fighters, frontier women, and many others without whose labors

our country would never have achieved its present strength. . . . (Walter B. Miller, "Implications of Urban Lower Class Culture for Social Work," *Social Service Review,* 33:232–234, September, 1959. Copyright, 1959, by The University of Chicago.)

Defining the conventional morality

The social classes do not merely differ in etiquette; they also differ in moral judgments. The term "loyal worker" has one meaning in the union hall, another at the chamber of commerce. Kinsey [1948, pp. 375–379] has shown how sex mores differ between the classes. The lower-class emphasis is upon naturalness, not upon chastity; thus premarital sex experience is viewed rather tolerantly, since it is "natural"; but the lower classes strongly condemn as degenerate and "unnatural" the adolescent masturbation which the middle classes view more tolerantly, or the elaborate love play which the middle-class marriage manuals recommend. On almost every point of moral conduct, class-typed mores differ.

Middle-class mores, however, tend to become the conventional mores. The church, the school, and the welfare and "uplift" agencies are middle-class institutions, staffed and run by middle-class persons, and dedicated to the cultivation of middle-class values. Political candidates must be models of middle-class virtue; stupidity is forgivable, but not immorality. The laws are written by middle-class legislators and enforce middle-class values. Thus the middle-class mores tend to become the official or conventional morality of the society.

This tendency creates certain strains for lower-class persons. They often find that behavior which is normal and acceptable in their class subculture is condemned and punished when they step outside this subculture, as they must do at school and in nearly all their dealings with persons in positions of authority. A good deal of resentment and class antagonism accumulates among the lower classes, which feel that they are constantly being prodded, scolded, and "pushed around" by middle- and upper-class people.

In the "permissive" atmosphere of today, the lower-class person is likely to find the middle-class model somewhat confusing. The casual dress, and casual sex relations and drug usage which are part of the current "youth image" bear a deceptive and misleading similarity to lower-class clothing and behavior traits. The youth revolt against middle-class ambition may well be a passing phase for middle-class youth, but one cruelly deceptive to the lower-class youth who seeks to rise in class status. The differences between classes still exist, and the blurring of distinctions presents an added hazard to lower-class youth who aspire to move into the middle class.

On the other hand, it may also be argued that the ambitious blue-collar youth who disdains the permissiveness and world weariness of many middle-class youth has thereby a better chance for upward mobility. This may lead to a "bluing of society" in the sense that the children of blue-collar parents displace those of white-collar parents in the struggle for upper-class status [Berger and Berger, 1971].

Explaining many other group differences

Many other kinds of group differences—racial, religious, regional—are really class differences. For example, almost any black-white comparison will prove to be very flattering to whites. Blacks have proportionately more crimes, more venereal disease, more illegitimate births, more drunkenness, more desertions, more broken families, and proportionately more people on relief. If, however, social class levels are held constant, these differences between racial groups greatly decrease [Banfield, 1974, pp. 79–87]. For example, the overall black birth rate is higher than the white, but if women with less than a high school education are omitted, the black birth rate is less than the white [Whelpton and Campbell, 1966, pp. 342–348]. Similarly, differences in school dropout rates almost disappear if one restricts the comparison to children

of white-collar parents [Colemen, 1966, pp. 454–456].

Variations in the class composition of religious groups affect comparisons between them. One would expect Baptists and Catholics to have a higher rate of juvenile delinquency than Episcopalians and Congregationalists simply because juvenile delinquency usually is more frequent in lower-social-class groups. For the same reasons, exclusive residential suburbs of Long Island will have lower death rates than slum districts in New York City. Therefore, whenever data for two groups are compared, the critical observer will always wonder, "Are these groups comparable in class composition?" If not, some very misleading conclusions may be drawn.

Shaping life-adjustment patterns

The way people handle life situations varies with social class, as is illustrated in the following incident, reported to one of the authors by a perceptive student.

I was in a small two-man garage on a Saturday morning, making small talk with the proprietor as he worked on my car. He pointed to another car parked nearby. "How much do you think that car is worth?" he asked. I studied it a moment, and ventured, "Oh, perhaps $300." "I bought it a few minutes ago for $150," he remarked. "Now, I wonder why a fellow would sell his car so cheaply," I mused. He paused a moment, and said, "Oh, . . . you wouldn't understand." Suddenly I did understand. The proprietor was thinking "You, in your sheltered middle-class world of careful plans, long-term goals, and wisely rationed puritan pleasures, are unable to understand how a fellow would turn his car into quick cash to gratify a pressing impulse. Perhaps his eye is on something he can't wait to buy, or he needs money to finance a big weekend or to gain a new girl friend's gratitude. In his world, these may be more important than protecting his capital investment."

Social class affects the way people deal with virtually every aspect of reality. As space forbids examining them all, let us describe just two areas of life in which class background appears to produce contradictory tendencies: political attitudes, in which the lower classes appear to be more liberal (some would say "radical") and social attitudes, in which the lower classes appear to be more conservative. (The terms "liberal" and "conservative" are here used to describe differing degrees of receptivity to social change.)

Social class and political attitudes. If social class influences the basic outlook of people, we should expect people to support the party and candidates closest to their class interests. Several surveys [Centers, 1949, chap. 5] seem to confirm this expectation in showing that the lower classes are more favorable toward government welfare benefits and services and government regulation of business than are the other classes. Since 1936 the electorate has divided quite sharply along class lines for many years, and, "every cross-section political survey ever conducted shows the inevitable pattern of low-income people being dominantly Democratic and upper-income people being Republican" [Harris, 1957]. In the 1956 campaign, the list of those who contributed over $5,000 to either political party numbered 269 Republican and 56 Democratic contributors [*New York Times,* Feb. 3, 1957, p. 52]. In 1952 and 1956, the immense personal appeal of Eisenhower made deep inroads into the normally Democratic labor vote: yet these voters did not change their *party* preference and continued voting Democratic for other offices. In 1964, Johnson captured many middle-class and upper-class voters, but they returned to their usual voting habits in 1966.

Yet it would be a great oversimplification to indicate that there was a consistent division by social class in American politics. In 1968, for instance, George Wallace, running as the American Independent Party candidate, captured a significant portion of blue-collar voters. In 1972, the greatest enthusiasm for George McGovern, the Democratic candidate, came from middle-class intellectuals, while a good many lower-class voters turned to Nixon, whom they perceived as being friendlier to their standard of values.

The emergence of a popular leader in either party, the rise of third parties and the appeal of issues which cut across class lines are among the factors which may change traditional social-class political alignments. In spite of a differential class support, both major American parties attempt a "consensus" type of appeal which reaches across class lines. In many industrialized countries, the link between class status and voting behavior is stronger than in the United States. In a study of British voting behavior, Lenski [1970, p. 362] found that the spread between lower-class and upper- and middle-class support for a particular party was 33 percent, as compared with 18 percent for the United States. This means that British voters divided along class lines in voting nearly twice as faithfully as American voters.

Social class and social attitudes. The lower class tends to be liberal on economic questions but conservative in many other social attitudes. In recent years, there has been considerable evidence that strong opposition to student unrest and black militancy has come from the white working class. Apparently, many of the working class feel hard pressed themselves and view middle- and upper-class liberals as advocating measures which take money from the working class to give to the "undeserving poor" [Ransford, 1972]. On the other hand, opinion surveys on attitude toward the Vietnam War show that the least favored part of the working class was less "hawkish" (prowar) than the rest of the population [Wright, 1972]. However, this lack of enthusiasm for the war may reflect less a liberal humanitarianism than it does the response of a stratum of the population which has little concern with any affairs beyond its immediate neighborhood.

The lower class appears reluctant to accept new ideas and practices and is suspicious of the innovators. Changes in health practices, food usage, religious doctrines, family life, or educational procedures are likely to find their strongest opposition among lower-class groups. Their limited education, reading habits, and associations isolate the lower class from a knowledge of the reasons for these changes, and this ignorance, together with their class position, makes them suspicious of the middle- and upper-class "experts" and "do-gooders" who promote the changes.

Social class largely determines which parts of the culture one will experience.

A case in point is an experiment in the use of the Salk vaccine for the prevention of poliomyelitis [Deasy, 1956]. The experiment occurred in a suburban area near Washington, D.C., where a large-scale trial program of the vaccine was attempted before it was released for use in general. Parents were notified of the opportunity in a letter from the school asking permission to give a free vaccination to the child. A follow-up survey disclosed that proportionately twice as many parents of upper and middle socioeconomic status gave permission, as is shown in Table 13. The reasons for lower-class refusal were explored. Fewer of the lower-class mothers had read about the program in the newspapers or discussed it with

friends, and more of them expressed worries over its possible dangers. Lower-class participation was inhibited by lack of confidence in scientific experts, a greater fear of the new and untried, and a tendency to be unconcerned about actions whose results would not materialize until a future date.

A cross-cultural confirmation of lower-class conservatism comes from a survey of the response of English housewives to a program of free dental care under the government health system. Table 14 reveals a considerable lower-class resistance to this type of dental care even when it is free of charge.

Many other examples of lower-class conservatism could be cited. "Contemporary" design in art and home furnishings is first found in the shops catering to the wealthy and later vulgarized for the lower-class tastes. The lower class is last to feel the trend toward the democratic family, permissive child-training practices, and birth control procedures [Downs, 1970, p. 27; McNall, 1974, p. 147]. It does not follow that *all* social changes filter downward from the top, but a pattern of lower-class conservatism does seem to apply to many activities and interests.

Social class and social participation. Social class largely determines which parts of the culture one will experience—opera, country club, and cotillion, or jukebox, tavern, and brawl. This is illustrated by class differences in degree of social participation. In general, the lower the social class, the fewer are the associations and social relations of the individual. Lower-class people belong to fewer organizations of any kind—clubs, civic groups, or even churches—than do middle and upper-class people [Stone, 1960; Hyman and Wright, 1971]. We might assume that this lack of organized sociability is compensated by more numerous informal contacts, but we find that these also diminish as we go down the class continuum. Lower-class people have fewer acquaintances, fewer friends, gossip with and about fewer other people, and do less informal visiting [Hodges, 1964, p. 12].

TABLE 13 PERCENT OF RESPONDENTS WHO GAVE CONSENT FOR THEIR CHILD TO PARTICIPATE IN POLIOMYELITIS VACCINE TRIAL

| | Socioeconomic status | | |
	Highest (N-42) percent	Middle (N-44) percent	Lowest (N-44) percent
Gave consent	86	84	43
Did not give consent	14	16	57
Total	100	100	100

Source: Leila Calhoun Deasy, "Socio-economic Status and Participation in the Poliomyelitis Vaccine Trial," *American Sociological Review*, 21:185–191, April, 1956. Reprinted by permission of the author and the *American Sociological Review*.

Expenditure patterns. An obvious difference between the lower and upper classes is that those with less money spend a higher proportion of their income for subsistence. Thus lower-class families spend a bigger part of their income for food and shelter than do the middle and upper classes. If the lower class has a simpler diet than wealthier groups, it is from necessity rather than choice. Indeed, one measure of the spread of affluence to a greater proportion of American society is the doubling of meat consumption in twenty years' time—from 62.2 pounds per capita in 1952 to 117 pounds in 1972 [*U.S. News and World Report,* July 10, 1972].

There are some differences in consumption which reflect present-time valuation and lack of future planning more than they do differences in income. This is strikingly brought out by the results of one current form of archaeology—digging in garbage dumps. University of Arizona archaeologists felt that examination of garbage would give a reliable indication of consumption habits in the city of Tucson, and systematically examined samples of household garbage [Rathje, 1974]. In accord with previous studies, lower-income households consumed a higher proportion of beef, with middle-class households eating more of the less expensive pork and chicken. Lower-income households also consumed the largest quantities of liquor. Surprisingly, however, the

lower-income households showed less total waste of food and more consumption of vitamins and child education products. The heavier expenditure for beef and liquor is consistent with a lower-class preference for immediate satisfaction; the lesser waste indicates the effect of economic pressure and the purchase of smaller, more manageable items; and the use of vitamins and child education materials demonstrates that advertising, at least to some extent, reaches across class lines.

The future of social classes: from "proletariat" to "status seekers"

Karl Marx, in the volumes entitled *Das Kapital* and in the *Communist Manifesto,* probably did more to emphasize the importance of social class than any other thinker in history. In the Marxian view, conflict between social classes has been continuous since the dawn of history, and the rise and fall of various social classes offer the key to the understanding of history. Prior to the industrial revolution, the top social class was a landed aristocracy which owned great estates by virtue of inheritance and noble rank. This class was forced to share top status with the manufacturers, traders, and financiers, whose wealth and prestige were greatly increased by the expansion of business since

TABLE 14 CLASS ATTITUDES TO FILLING PERMANENT TEETH

| | Class as measured by job and dwelling | |
Responses to filling permanent teeth	Clerical, private housing	Unskilled, public housing
For	91.0%	53.0%
Against	6.3	40.3
Don't know	2.7	6.7
Total	100.0	100.0
	n = 140	140

Source: Stewart Dickson, "Class Attitudes to Dental Treatment," *British Journal of Sociology*, 19:207, June, 1968.

the time of the industrial revolution. Marx prophesied that the ultimate struggle would take place between the proletariat (wage workers) and the bourgeoisie (capitalists) and would end in the inevitable triumph of the proletariat, who would in turn establish a classless society under the banner of communism. This interpretation of history gave to communists a sort of "messianic hope" which enabled them to believe that, in spite of present obstacles, history was on their side and their final triumph was certain. For many years discussion of social class centered on the validity of the Marxian analysis.

The current opinion among social scientists is that Marx was only partly correct and that the class struggle is not proceeding on the lines he predicted. Marx predicted, for example, that classes would grow farther apart as industrialization advanced. Hence the lower class would become more conscious of its distinct interests and more hostile to the upper class, while the middle classes would gradually be pushed down into the proletariat. Actually the exact opposite seems to have taken place; classes are coming closer together both in possessions and in attitudes. The middle class is stronger than ever in Western societies, and the lower class is gaining a stake in the society which Marx wanted them to overthrow. Marx had predicted that communism would follow industrialization and that the most advanced countries would be ripe for communism under the influence of revolutionary urban wage earners. Since the writing of Marx, communism has spread in many places, but not in the manner that Marx predicted. The industrial countries have not developed Communist parties strong enough to take over the government (both Russia and China were primarily agricultural at the time of their Communist revolutions in 1917 and 1949), and expansion has come either through Chinese or Russian military conquests or by movements in agricultural areas led by the urban intellectuals with the support of a landlord-hating peasant population.

Skepticism about the Marxian prediction of an eventual classless society has also been strengthened by the difficulties of eliminating social class in Communist-controlled countries. The Soviet Union made an early attempt to abolish class privileges and insure equal opportunities to those of humble social origin. But it is clear that by the 1950s, the Communist party officers, factory managers, government officials, professional men, scientists and artists in the Soviet Union formed a distinct self-perpetuating social class with special privileges and a distinct style of life with appropriate attitudes [Inkeles, 1950; Feldmesser, 1953]. A strong statement on the development of social-class lines in Communist society comes from the pen of Milovan Djilas, formerly vice-president of Tito's government in Yugoslavia, who was later thrown into prison for making statements such as this:

The establishment of the ownership of the new class was evidenced in the changes in the psychology, the way of life, and the material position of its members, depending on the position they held in the hierarchical ladder. Country homes, the best housing, furniture, and similar things were acquired; special quarters and exclusive rest homes were established for the highest bureaucracy, for the elite of the new class. The party secretary and the chief of the secret police in some places not only became the highest authorities but obtained the best housing, automobiles, and similar evidences of privilege. Those beneath them were eligible for comparable privileges depending upon their position in the hierarchy. . . . More than anything else, the essential aspect of contemporary Communism is the new class of owners and exploiters. (Milovan Djilas, *The New Class*, Praeger Publishers, Inc., New York, 1957, pp. 57–58.)

Far from achieving a classless society, the Communists have set in power a new class, based on the possession of nearly absolute power, which is even more rigid in its composition and more differentiated from the masses in its privileges than the upper class of capitalist societies. The dreams of the new freedom have given way to a regimentation more rigid than the old slavery. Judged by its creed, Communist society is the enemy of class privilege; judged by its results, it is class privilege's newest and strongest bastion. Some idea of the range of inequality in the Soviet Union is provided by Table 15, which gives earnings in the steel industry, but this table greatly underestimates the range of income, since it does not include the highest-paid scientists or party officials and omits such extremely important fringe benefits as bonuses, free housing, official cars, and other favors enjoyed by the Soviet officials. The importance of such "fringe benefits" may be indicated by practices followed in the compensation of Soviet factory managers: "Traditionally a plant manager has received for plan fulfillment a bonus which ranges from 20 percent to 100 percent of his monthly salary" [Leeman, 1970, p. 434]. In institutions of higher learning, compensation varies from 105 rubles a month for an assistant without an academic degree to a high of 600 rubles for a rector or dean of an institution with 3,500 or more students [Smirenko, 1972, p. 156]. Writing of an effort to reduce income disparities, Yanowitch [1963] estimated that the top 10 percent of the Soviet population receives an income averaging six or seven times as high as the bottom 10 percent, a disparity not much different from that in the United States.

Joseph Stalin, long-time ruler of the U.S.S.R., stated the Soviet view in terms similar to the Davis-Moore defense of the functional character of a class system (see p. 250) in saying: "The consequence of wage equalization is that the unskilled worker lacks the incentive to become a skilled worker . . . We cannot tolerate a situation where a rolling mill hand in a steel mill earns no more than a sweeper . . . where a locomotive driver earns only as much as a copying clerk" [quoted in Daniels, 1965, p. 26]. Soviet economists continue to defend wage inequalities, saying, "Wage differentials continue to be an important instrument of economic development policy. They help to safeguard priorities, to ensure

TABLE 15 REMUNERATION IN THE SOVIET STEEL INDUSTRY

	1959*	1965
Director of scientific institute	600	600
Director of steel plant	400	400
Elevator operator, janitor, watchman	55	60
Typist, secretary	41	60

*Rubles per month
Source: Murray Yanowitch, "The Soviet Income Revolution," *Slavic Review*, 22:693, December, 1963. (1965 figures are a projection of earlier plans.) More recent data would be desirable, but very few such statistics are published by the Soviet Union.

the desirable geographical and sectoral division of labour and to stimulate the workers to perform more efficiently and to attain additional qualifications and higher skill levels" [Jalnine, 1972, p. 202]. The Soviet regime thus continues to use compensation plans similar to those of Western societies, in which substantial inequality is taken for granted.

Success versus equality

In non-Communist societies the possibilities of a Marxian-style class struggle for the control of society seem to be diminishing, but we are becoming increasingly aware of class struggle of a different type—the pursuit of status. Several years ago, this struggle was depicted in a semipopular book by the sociology popularizer Vance Packard [*The Status Seekers*, 1959]. The theme of his book was that American workers had rejected the idea of a classless society, but sought increased mobility for themselves; in other words, not a flat level, but a better chance to move ahead. However, the idea of equality has a perennial ethical appeal even though no advanced society has found it practical. In recent years, an increasing number of Americans, drawn mainly from the ranks of the more affluent, do seek a more egalitarian society. They argue that the goal is not just to eliminate dire poverty but to secure a larger proportionate share for the bottom 20 percent of the population [Miller and Roby, 1970, pp. 3–20]. Still others disdain interest in material goods and are recruits for a counter-cultural life-style in which a voluntary type of poverty is at least a temporary requirement for participation. So far, the countercultural drop-outs are a visible but powerless minority, yet their existence is a challenge to the prevailing economic values.

The advocates of greater equality sometimes ignore the progress already made toward a diminution of the extreme differentials of the past. They neglect the very complex question of how equality can be defined in the case of people with different needs, and they cheerful-ly accept the enormous abridgement of free-dom required to prevent any of us from acquir-ing more money than any of the rest of us.

In recent history, the income of all classes of people has grown through increases in produc-tion caused by the exertions of ambitious per-sons free to become as unequal as their perfor-mance made possible. "Equality" has recently become a sacred word in our culture, but per-haps the main reason why we shrink from directing our entire society to this end is indi-cated in a recent analysis of who would be affected by a more rigorous leveling policy:

. . . most people who, when they think of the "top five per cent or the top 20 per cent" promptly have visions of the Great Gatsbys or the Rockefellers or at least the executives of major corporations . . . may very well, without knowing it, be thinking of themselves. The "top five per cent" consists of all households with incomes over $30,000 a year. The "top 20 per cent" consists of all households with incomes of over $20,000 a year. Most of the "rich" people are people who, in the ordinary course of events, are regarded as "middle class"—our doctor, our dentist, our lawyer, our accountant, our chil-dren's professors, perhaps ourselves. Politicians who start out with "taxing the rich" end up with a middle-class tax revolt on their hands. (Irving Kristol, "Taxes, Poverty and Equality," *Public Interest*, 37, Fall, 1974, p. 7.)

Changes in relative class status

One reason for lack of revolutionary fervor among workers is that many of the changes that Marx, Debs, and others worked for have now taken place without revolution. Such com-monplace arrangements as legalized collective bargaining through labor unions, minimum wage laws, old-age pensions and vacations with pay, which would have been considered fantastic dreams in the 1920s, are now taken for granted by most industrial workers. The result is that those who have usually been placed in the lower class now have many of the privileges of the middle class. In fact, this "top 20 percent" includes a number of "working class" families in which both husband and wife are employed.

The essence of the Marxian appeal for class warfare was the belief that with the passing of time the rich would become increasingly wealthy and the poor increasingly miserable. This is not exactly what has been happening.

Figure 10. Who gets richer in the United States? Shown is the percentage of national personal income, before taxes, received by each income fifth, 1910–1972. (Source: Adapted from data presented in Gabriel Kolko, *Wealth and Power in America*, Frederick A. Praeger, Inc., New York, 1962, p. 14; *Statistical Abstract of the United States*, 1973, p. 330.)

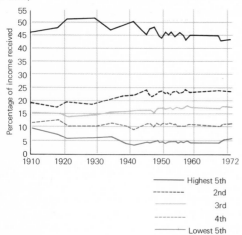

Highest 5th
2nd
3rd
4th
Lowest 5th

All income levels have shared in the increasing productivity of our society, all have gained in absolute standards, and the middle groups have obtained a slight increase in their proportionate share. As shown in Figure 10, the share of our national income received by the top fifth has decreased significantly, the middle-income receiver's share has grown, and the share of the poorest fifth has remained about the same.

There is a good deal of argument as to the relative effect of taxation and government benefits on the net income of various income groups. In general, sales taxes and social security taxes take a larger percentage of the income of the low-income groups, even though they may escape the income tax altogether. Conversely, the wealthy pay a smaller proportionate (although greater absolute) amount in sales taxes and, while they pay more in income tax, this burden is reduced by many "loopholes." The poor receive obvious benefits from welfare payments, but the wealthier groups are the ones who benefit most by government support of airports, universities and yacht basins and by subsidies to business and agriculture. Trying to get reliable estimates is an accountant's nightmare, since the needed data are hard to secure. The subsidies of the rich to the poor are probably greater than the subsidies of the poor to the rich (see Table 16), but this has not been exactly determined. The following anecdote, related by a friend of one of the authors, is a case in point

As my host guided his 55-foot yacht toward its slip, he applauded the decision of a [Florida] city commission to cancel an urban renewal project, largely federally financed, which would benefit mainly the city's Negro slum area. As he expanded on the "taint" of federal funds to solve "local" problems, he tuned in on a weather report from a federally operated weather station, waved at the captain of a federally operated coast guard vessel which stood ready to rescue him if he got into trouble, carefully noted the position of the federally placed bouys and channel markers, nosed down a channel dredged with federal funds, and entered a marina financed

TABLE 16 THE IMPACT OF ALL TAXES AND TRANSFERS IS GENERALLY PROGRESSIVE

In these income brackets	The net effect on income is this . . . [Percent increase or decrease]	. . . since welfare and Social Security payments add this to income [Percent]	. . . while taxes take these amounts [Percent]
Under $2,000	+56.5%	106.5%	50.0%
2,000–4,000	+13.9	48.5	34.6
4,000–6,000	−11.4	19.6	31.0
6,000–8,000	−21.5	8.6	30.1
8,000–10,000	−23.7	5.5	29.2
10,000–15,000	−25.9	3.9	29.8
15,000–25,000	−27.0	3.0	30.0
25,000–50,000	−30.7	2.1	32.8
Over 50,000	−44.7	0.4	45.0
Average	−24.6	6.9	31.6

Note: all figures for 1968

Data: Roger Herriot & Herman Miller, Census Bureau.
Source: Reprinted from the Aug. 12, 1972, issue of *Business Week* by special permission.
© 1972 by McGraw-Hill, Inc.

partly from federal funds and tied up to a federally subsidized dock, concluding his lecture on the evils of government welfare programs with the sage observation, "We coddle people too much. People should stand on their own feet and pay their own way."

Although class privileges and obligations differ, all classes make useful contributions to society, and all types of class environments produce individuals who are problems to themselves and to society. Whether a class system is the best means of assigning different social functions is probably a question of only academic interest, since all modern societies follow the system. Ethical interest focuses on two questions: First, should the privileges and responsibilities of different classes be modified in the direction of minimizing differences between them? And second, can, or should we promote the opportunities for individuals to change their class levels? Most societies are now more or less seriously committed to a program of curtailing upper-class privileges and improving levels of living for the lower class. The possibilities of individual movement between classes will be explored in a later chapter on social mobility.

Summary

Social classes arise from the consequences which follow from a division of labor. A social class is made up of people of similar social status who regard one another as social equals. Each class is a subculture, with a set of attitudes, beliefs, values, and behavior norms which differ from those of other classes. Expression by lower-class people of values similar to those held by the middle class is explained by the "value stretch" theory. Social class is based on total social and economic position in the community, including wealth and income, occupation, education, self-identification, hereditary prestige, group participation, and recognition by others. Class lines are not clearly drawn but represent points along a continuum of social status. The exact size and membership of a given class is difficult to establish.

Social class is an important social reality. Social class largely determines one's life opportunities and colors one's personality development. Social class assigns privileges and responsibilities to individuals and thereby helps to get necessary work accomplished. Social-class subcultures breed a highly subtle and tenacious class ethnocentrism, which prevents classes from fully understanding one another. It is mainly the standards of the middle class that are written into law and sanctioned by the conventional morality. Many differences ordinarily assigned to race, religion, ethnic group, or to some other kind of group difference, are actually class differences; confusion arises from the fact that racial, religious, and other groups may be unevenly distributed along the class continuum. Social class lines have not been eliminated in socialist societies and do not depend on the existence of capitalism.

Social class molds the life-adjustment patterns of the individuals; the lower class tends to be liberal in political action connected with economic benefits and conservative in accepting other social changes, while the opposite tends to be true of the upper class. This is partly explained by the fact that the lower the class level, the more limited tends to be the participation of the individual in social and community life.

Many class linked differences in attitude flow from the present-time preference of the lower class.

Current scientific interest in class has shifted from the Marxian theory of class warfare to the struggle for individual social mobility and a lessening of the amount of inequality between classes. Current technological, economic, and governmental changes are increasing the relative size of the middle classes and bringing us closer to a middle-class society.

Questions and projects

1. Has the elimination of private capital led to an equality of incomes in the Soviet Union? If not, how would you explain a continuing inequality in a socialist state?
2. Is there a culture of poverty? Can you explain the recent decrease in the number of the poor by a change in their culture?
3. How can social classes really be subcultures when children of all class levels attend school together?
4. Given unlimited money, to what degree could a government or a community provide children with complete "equality of opportunity"?
5. Is there a relation between the problems of health and education and the attitudes engendered by lower-class life? Explain.
6. How does class affect political attitudes? When a college student switches from the father's political party, is it because of increased knowledge, youthful rebellion, or social mobility? Outline each possibility.
7. When a college student from a wealthy family takes a summer job working in a factory, how much does he or she learn from the "working class"?
8. What is meant by the "messianic hope" of Marx-

ism? Have recent developments supported the Marxian theory of social class?
9. Do you feel that social-class stratification is harmful or beneficial to society as a whole? Why?
10. Is the United States primarily a middle-class country? Defend your answer.
11. Make a chart of officers in your senior high school class (or some other organization you know well). From which social-class level does each come? Are the officers proportionately representative of the social class present in the organization? Do members from different social classes view the group in the same way? Wherein, and why, do they differ?
12. Read and analyze the treatment of social class in one of the following novels: *Kitty Foyle* by Christopher Morley, *Marjorie Morningstar* by Herman Wouk, *Studs Lonigan* by James T. Farrell, *The Forge* by Thomas S. Stribling, *Mansfield Park* by Jane Austen, *The Age of Innocence* by Edith S. Wharton, *Fraternity* by John Galsworthy, *Tobacco Road* by Erskine Caldwell, *Hunky* by Thomas R. Williamson, *Babbitt* by Sinclair Lewis, *So Little Time* or *B. F.'s Daughter* by John P. Marquand.

Suggested readings

ANDERSON, CHARLES H.: *The Political Economy of Social Class,* Prentice-Hall, Inc., Englewood Cliffs, N.J., 1974. A Swedish sociologist makes a Marxian analysis of American society.

*BAALI, FUAD, AND CLIFTON D. BRYANT (EDS.): *Introductory Sociology: Selected Readings for the College Scene,* Rand McNally & Company, Chicago, 1970. This collection of interesting readings has several articles dealing with aspects of social class which affect the campus. These include: IRA L. REISS, "Social Class and Campus Dating": DELBERT C. MILLER, "Town and Gown: The Social Status of a University Town"; RICHARD FLACKS, "The Liberated Generation: An Ex-

ploration of the Roots of Student Protest"; J. ROSS ESHLEMAN and CHESTER L. HUNT, "Social Class Influences on Family Adjustment Patterns of Married College Students."

BLUMBERG, PAUL: "The Decline and Fall of the Status Symbol: Some Thoughts on Status in A Post-Industrial Society," *Social Problems,* 21:480–498, April, 1974. Points out that the spread of luxury goods to a larger portion of American society makes it difficult to distinguish social classes by visible material possessions.

BRUNSWICK, ANN F.: "What Generation Gap: A Comparison of Some Generational Differences among Blacks and Whites," *Social Problems,* 17: 358–370, Winter, 1970. An indirect commentary on social-class influence, since it finds that differences in education are as influential in determining attitudes as differences in age.

COLEMAN, RICHARD P., AND BERNICE L. NEUGARTEN: *Social Status in the City,* Jossey-Bass, Inc., Publishers, San Francisco, 1971. A lucid analysis of the social-class structure of Kansas City, Missouri.

CUTLER, RICHARD L.: *The Liberal Middle Class: Maker of Radicals,* Arlington House, New Rochelle, N.Y., 1973. An analysis of factors promoting the growth of radicalism on university campuses.

HAMILTON, RICHARD F.: "The Marginal Middle Class: A Reconsideration," *American Sociological Review,* 31:192–199, April, 1966. A discussion of the class status of white-collar employees.

HOLLANDER, PAUL: *Soviet and American Society: A Comparison,* Oxford University Press, New York, 1973. A Hungarian sociologist goes beyond ideology to delineate social class processes in each society.

KRISTOL, IRVING: "Taxes, Poverty and Equality," *The Public Interest,* 37:1–28, Fall, 1974. A critical discussion of the idea that the tax burden of other classes can be eased by abolishing tax loopholes and thereby soaking the rich. Kristol's analysis indicates that tax loopholes benefit primarily the middle class and that really effective use of the tax system to secure greater equality would hit hardest the person who regards himself as "an average citizen."

*MILLER, S. M., AND PAMELA A. ROBY: *The Future of Inequality,* Basic Books, Inc., Publishers, New York, 1970. Argues the viewpoint that the notion of poverty as any fixed level of living is out of date and the current problem is not only to raise absolute levels, but also the relative position of the bottom 20 percent of the population.

MITCHELL, ROBERT EDWARD: "Class-linked Conflict in Liberalism-Conservatism," *Social Problems,* 13: 418–427, Spring, 1966. A research study of contrasts in social-class attitudes on the national and local levels as seen in Berkeley, California.

*SHOSTAK, ARTHUR B., AND WILLIAM GOMBERG: *New Perspectives on Poverty,* Prentice-Hall, Inc., Englewood Cliffs, N.J., 1965. A series of articles devoted to the culture of poverty and to methods by which the lower class might absorb some elements of middle-class standards.

WARNER, W. LLOYD, AND PAUL S. LUNT: *The Social Life of a Modern Community,* Yale University Press, New Haven, Conn., 1941, chap. 7, "Profiles of a Yankee City." A long chapter, reading like a novel, in which the attitudes and behavior of the different classes are dramatized.

*WINTER, J. ALAN (ED.): *The Poor: A Culture of Poverty or a Poverty of Culture?* Wm. B. Eerdmans Publishing Co., Grand Rapids, Mich., 1970. A collection of essays debating the idea of the culture of poverty.

Chapter 13 • Social mobility

George Foreman, in his time, only 25 years, has played many parts. Once . . . a mentally depressed young street drifter, a junior-high-school dropout who wandered through one of the oldest established permanent urban ghettos in the South, popping pills, getting drunk on cheap wine and staying one jump ahead of a mainline heroin shot. Then he became the perfect picture of the Great American Dream Machine's end product. More or less on a whim, he enrolled in the Job Corps and started working his way toward a secure future by the sweat of his back.

George Foreman stopped drinking entirely and found joy, happiness and fulfillment in athletics. . . . When he won a gold medal, he pulled an American flag from his pocket and paraded around the ring waving it.

The gesture came so close to a dramatic black-power demonstration on the winners' platform at Mexico City by two sprinters, John Carlos and Tommie Smith, that there were accusations that Foreman was an Uncle Tom at best and an outright traitor to the civil-rights struggle at worst. He received nearly a thousand pieces of hate mail. . . .

Then in January, 1973, he defeated Joe Frazier to become champion. *(Wells Trombly, "Champ," New York Times Magazine, Mar. 24, 1974, p. 18. © 1974 by The New York Times Company. Reprinted by permission)*

This brief sketch of George Foreman, onetime heavyweight champion of the world, illustrates several aspects of social mobility. His aimless drifting as a school dropout is all too typical of lower-class youth, who see no connection between their longings and the drudgery of the schoolroom. His transformation in the Job Corps is a prize success story of this government agency's effort to upgrade the so-called hard-core unemployed youth. His expression of loyalty to the American system is one that would be duplicated by many who, without his success, still share his faith in the opportunities the system provides. Professional boxing, Foreman's route to success, is one field where the minorities form a majority. There are models of success to copy, and there is little fear of discrimination. Thus the prize ring has been a mobility ladder for the disadvantaged—first the Irish, then the Italians, and now the blacks and the Puerto Ricans. As each minority group moved upward, its youth relinquished the prize ring to a new disadvantaged minority.

Nature of social mobility

Social mobility may be defined as the act of moving from one social status to another. Social mobility makes the inequality of social class tolerable and, in the view of some, even justifiable. If social mobility is high, even though individuals have unequal social origins, all may believe that they are equal in having a chance of reaching a higher social-class position. If social mobility is low, then it is clear that most people are frozen into the status of their ancestors.

The opening sketch is one of several incidents which, like the Horatio Alger novels of an earlier generation, have helped to sustain the belief that America is a land of boundless opportunity where all positions are open to the ambitious. This belief is often derided by skeptics, but there is much in the American experience to support it. As Senator Edmund Muskie, a one-time candidate for the vice-presidency and the son of a Polish immigrant named Marciszewski, says of his father:

He had landed here with only five years of formal education, the ability to work as a tailor and not much else. One year before he died, his son became the first of Polish ancestry to be elected governor of any state. Now this may not justify the American system to you, but I am sure it did for him. (Edmund Muskie, *Journeys,* Doubleday and Company, Garden City, N.Y., 1972, pp. 46–47.)

If desirable social statuses are actually available to all who make an effort to reach them, there will probably be little agitation for absolute social equality. If, however, the channels of social mobility are so clogged that a great many are doomed to failure, then a demand for complete equality for all is more likely. The balance of this chapter will be devoted to an analysis of how social mobility occurs, its frequency, and the factors which may accelerate or retard movement from one social stratum to another.

Individual and group mobility

Mobility applies to both groups and individuals. For instance, the success of the Kennedy family is an example of individual social mobility, while the Irish Catholics' march from the slum to the suburb illustrates group mobility. The two kinds of mobility very often go together. A disadvantaged group may produce an occasional celebrity, but the higher the status of the group, the greater the number of high achievers.

Group upward mobility may either reflect the hard work and wise planning of individuals who make up the group or it may be a largely accidental result of circumstances. The rapid ascent of Japanese-Americans since 1945 is an example of the former, while the latter may be seen in the current prosperity of Appalachian coal miners, described in the following newspaper story:

Even the miner is more flush than usual. Some teachers have quit the security of the schools for the higher wages of mining. Wages run anywhere from $50 to $100 a day for a miner who gets some overtime. A high school graduate can start out earning $6 an hour in the mines, if he's willing to take a hard and often dangerous job. . . .

Some mountain observers take pleasure in seeing a change in what has been perceived as the political and economic "inferiority" of mountain people to those living in lowland sections.

"It makes me laugh," said one Hazard [Kentucky] businessman. "These people always laughed at our ignorance and poverty down in Bourbon County. Now our old mountain boys are buying up those bluegrass farms. Serves 'em right." (Bryce Nelson: "East Kentucky Riding High on Big Coal Boom," *The Los Angeles Times,* Nov. 16, 1974.)

Downward social mobility

Economic expansion and technological changes which produce a demand for more high-level personnel are not the only sources of opportunity for the upwardly mobile person. Upper-level vacancies are also created by the downwardly mobile. Social mobility runs in both directions, and some people fail to maintain the social-class rank into which they were _born_. A typical example may be seen in the following report supplied by a student of one of the authors:

Peter Wilson's father was a successful small-town lawyer who lived modestly but comfortably and was a pillar of small-town respectability. Peter was always a "different" child, obstinate and selfish; his parents indulged his whims and excused his shortcomings. Peter flunked out of two colleges in prompt succession and evaded two shotgun marriages as quietly as his father's legal skill could arrange. At this point his father gave up hope and moved to another locale.

For several years Peter clung to the edges of the lower-middle class. He held a succession of lower-middle-class jobs—cashier in a garage, inspector in a furniture factory, timekeeper on a construction project—but never held them for long. Nor did he ever get a very good job, for he lacked both education and dependability. Also, he never looked clean, and every suit he wore promptly assumed a slept-in look.

He finally drifted into a semiskilled factory job which he has now held for over a dozen years. He earns average wages, buys the food for the family, and spends the rest of his wages and most of his time with his cronies who work at the same factory. His father is still paying the rent, and his wife does housework to pay for other family needs.

The older sons have finished high school and hold semiskilled jobs. Both have married daughters of unskilled or semiskilled workers. The third generation now appears firmly fixed in the upper-lower or "working" class.

The extent of downward individual mobility is one of the tests of an open class society. If practically all people remain firmly fixed in the social-class rank of their parents, then we have a closed class society in which ascription (in this case, parental position) accounts for more than achievement. However, if many people drop, while many others rise, then we can assume that inherited advantages and handicaps are not great enough to keep achievement from being a major determinant of social class position.

Even a casual look at American society shows the advantage of those born in middle-

TABLE 17 UPWARD AND DOWNWARD OCCUPATIONAL MOBILITY IN THE UNITED STATES

Occupation in 1962	Percent who have:		
	Moved up	Moved down	Not changed
Professionals	85.5	0.0	14.5
Managers	84.9	6.4	8.7
Clerks	77.7	17.8	4.5
Factory laborers	40.1	54.0	5.9
Farmers	2.9	15.1	82.0
Farm laborers	0.0	85.5	14.5

Note: From a national survey based on a sample of 20,700 males showing proportions of persons in each occupation who have moved up, moved down, or stayed at the same occupational level as their fathers.
Source: Adapted from Peter M. Blau and Otis Dudley Duncan, _The American Occupational Structure_, John Wiley & Sons, Inc., New York, 1967, table 2.8, p. 39.

or upper-class families. They have at least a modest amount of capital to help them get a start in life; they have influential friends and relatives who can help them and successful models they can imitate; they usually benefit from adequate nutrition and medical care, along with the best schooling available. Lower-class children usually lack some, or even all, of these assets.

As any parent can testify, children do not always seize their opportunities. Are the advantages of middle-class background strong enough to offset the effects of a lack of ability or ambition? You will notice, in Table 17 above, that there is considerable downward mobility in America. One of the most elaborate studies of inequality has been made by Jencks [1972]. Although Jencks is an outspoken critic of class inequalities in American life, he recognizes that middle-class parents, and sometimes upper-class parents, cannot protect their offspring from downward social mobility.

Nonetheless, our strongest overall impression is that there does not seem to be _any_ mechanism available to most upper-middle-class parents for maintaining their children's privileged economic position. Insofar as incomes are relative rather than absolute, most upper-middle-class children simply end up worse off than their parents. Among men born into the most affluent fifth of the population, for example, we estimate that less than half will be part of this same elite when they grow up. Of course, it is also true that very few will be in the bottom fifth. Rich parents can at least guarantee their children that much. Yet if we follow families over several generations, even this will not hold true. Affluent families often have at least one relatively indigent grandparent in the background, and poor families, unless they are black or relatively recent immigrants, have often had at least one prosperous grandparent. This is particularly true of maternal grandparents, since affluent families seem to have a harder time guaranteeing their daughters a good marriage than guaranteeing their sons a good job. (From *Inequality: A Reassessment of the Effect of Family and Schooling in America,* by Christopher Jencks et al., © 1972 by Basic Books, Inc., Publishers, New York.)

Mobility and social structure

While "caste" and "closed-class system" mean approximately the same things, the concept of open and closed classes is more useful than the concept of caste, because it can be used as a measure of the amount of mobility in different societies. If a society has many individuals who came from lowly homes and rose to high positions, along with others who fell from the high status of their parents, then we say there is a high degree of social mobility and an approximation of the open-class society. A society in which only a few rise or fall from their parental status is closer to the caste system.

A fairly open class system seems to be typical of most industrialized countries and one would assume that the rapid changes coming with industrialization also promote the chances of new occupational roles. Using the transition from manual to nonmanual occupations as a measure of social mobility, Lenski estimates that in industrialized countries approximately 30 percent have made this transition as shown in Table 18.

Ethnic and religious factors in mobility

While rates of upward mobility are similar in various industrialized societies, as seen in Table 18, the rate tends to vary sharply among ethno-religious groups within the country. One group may forge ahead very rapidly, another may move more slowly, and still others seem to be stuck at the bottom. These are not permanently fixed, for the comparative ranking of ethno-religious groups may alter over a period of time.

Table 19 illustrates the relationship between ethnic background and occupation in Canada. This table indicates the differential participation in various occupations by ethnic group. The English have twice the expected number of professional and financial posts in proportion to the size of the English population, while the French have about half the expected number of such posts. Scandinavians, who are mostly immigrants attracted to Canada by the prospect of cheap land, have ten times the expected number of farmers, while largely urbanized Jews have less than one-eleventh of their expected number of farmers.

Most religious groups are highly conscious of how they differ from other groups in religious

TABLE 18 UPWARD MOBILITY IN INDUSTRIALIZED COUNTRIES

Country	Percent moving from manual to nonmanual occupations
United States	34
Sweden	32
Great Britain	31
Denmark	30
Norway	30
France	29
West Germany	25
Japan	25
Italy	22

Source: Gerhard E. Lenski, *Power and Privilege*, McGraw-Hill Book Company, 1966, p. 411 (Data drawn from various studies).

TABLE 19 ETHNIC REPRESENTATION IN OCCUPATIONAL CATEGORIES IN CANADA

	British	French	Ger-man	Italian	Jew-ish	Dutch	Scandi-navian	East Euro-pean	Other Euro-pean	Asian	Indian and Eskimo	Total male labor force
Professional and financial	+2.0	−1.9	−1.8	− 5.2	+ 7.4	− .9	− 1.9	−1.2	−1.1	+ 1.7	− 7.5	8.6
Clerical	+1.3	− .2	−1.8	− 3.2	− .1	− 1.7	− 2.4	−1.7	−2.0	− 1.5	− 5.9	6.9
Personal service	− .9	− .2	− .7	+ 2.9	− 2.4	− .5	− 1.1	+ .9	+5.1	+19.1	+ 1.3	4.3
Primary and unskilled	−2.3	+2.8	−2.1	+11.5	− 8.9	− 2.0	− .2	−0.0	+1.8	− 3.6	+34.7	10.0
Agriculture	−1.5	−1.4	+8.8	− 9.5	−11.7	+10.3	+10.6	+6.9	+ .6	− 6.5	+ 6.9	12.2
All others	+1.4	+ .9	−2.4	+ 3.5	+15.7	− 5.2	− 5.0	−4.9	−4.4	− 9.1	−29.5	58.0
Total	0.0	0.0	0.0	0.0	0.0	0.0	0.0	0.0	0.0	0.0	0.0	100.0

*A +2.0 sign indicates that the ethnic group has twice as much as its proportionate share of a given occupation, whereas a −2.0 sign indicates that the ethnic group has only one-half as much as its expected occupational quota, considering the ethnic group's size in proportion to the total population.
Source: Adapted from presentation in John Porter, *The Vertical Mosaic*, University of Toronto Press, Toronto, Canada, 1965, p. 87.

doctrines and in practices, but are less aware that they also differ in social class, nationality, racial, and religious background. In these respects, the Protestant denominations not only differ from Catholics and Jews, but also from each other.

Churches may be concentrated in a section of the country, as with the Southern Baptists, or in a specific nationality, as in the case of the Swedish Lutherans. Many of their members may be upper-class, as with Presbyterians and Episcopalians, or many may be lower-class, as in the Church of the Nazarene. Catholic churches also vary in the nationality background of their members—for example, Polish in Buffalo, Italian in New Haven, and Mexican in Texas. Like Protestant congregations, a particular Catholic parish may be drawn primarily from the elite upper class, the middle class, the lower class, or some combination of these.

The behavioral effect of religious teaching is not always obvious, and it may be that many religious groups with a primarily lower-class membership are actually teaching middle-class behavior. As one example, Johnson [1961] suggests that this is true of the "Holiness Sects" (highly emotional expressive churches, mostly lower class in membership).

Although the emotional intensity of their services is unappreciated by middle-class people, their values are conducive to upward mobility. They emphasize ascetic norms to an extreme degree:

Members of Holiness sects are forbidden to consume alcoholic beverages, to dance, to gamble, to play cards, to "smoke, dip or chew" tobacco. They may not attend places of "worldly amusement" such as plays, movies, fairs, ball games or pool rooms. They may not engage in mixed bathing, women may not use makeup or wear short skirts, short sleeves, short hair or ornamental jewelry. Profanity is forbidden and strict Sabbath observance is enjoined. Obligations, including debts, must be faithfully discharged. (Benton Johnson: "Do Holiness Sects Socialize in Dominant Values?", *Social Forces*, 39:315, May, 1961.)

Few middle-class Americans subscribe to rules such as these, but most middle-class Americans are even more at odds with the impulsive, present-oriented behavior often attributed to the lower class. People practicing ascetic self-denial learn to control emotional responses, to be concerned about their reputations and to save money. Such practices build up capital and improve employability, thus favoring a move to middle-class status.

Social mobility and deferred gratification

So many aspects of life are determined by one's attitude toward social mobility that certain mobility-oriented attitudes have been grouped under the term *deferred gratification pattern* (abbreviated, DGP). This is simply the pattern of postponing immediate satisfactions in order to gain some later goal. You readers who are now studying this textbook, instead of playing poker or "goofing off," are practicing the DGP. The DGP may be described as a series of behavior tendencies of one who realizes that social mobility, either upward or downward, is a real probability. Consequently, this person's attitudes and actions are guided by their supposed effect on the chances for upward social mobility.

A deferment of present satisfactions.

In this type of planning, any activity today is viewed from the question of its consequences for tomorrow. Marriage may be postponed until one has finished school and secured a job. Education is considered neither a luxury nor a bore but an investment in future prospects. Thrift will lay the basis for eventual economic power, and emotional control will permit eventual emotional satisfaction. Time is used for self-improvement instead of aimless relaxation. A good description of this pattern has been given by Schneider and Lysgaard.

Deferred gratification evidently refers to postponement of gratifications or satisfactions. . . . It may be contended that it does indeed fall into a *pattern,* characteristic of the so-called "middle-class," members of which tend to delay achievement of economic independence through a relatively elaborate process of education, tend to defer sexual gratification through intercourse, show a relatively marked tendency to save money, and the like. . . . [An] important point is the *normative* character of the deferred gratification pattern. Middle-class persons feel that they *should* save, postpone, and renounce a variety of gratifications. There are very probably also normative elements in the "lower-class" pattern of non-deferment. Thus, Whyte notes that one of the important divergences between the social mobility pattern and the corner-boy activity pattern in Cornerville appears in matters involving expenditure of money. The college boys save money for educational purposes or to launch business or professional careers. But the corner boys must share their money with others and avoid middle-class thrift. Should a corner boy have money and his friend not have it, he is expected to spend for both. The corner boy may be thrifty, but, if so, he cannot hope to hold a high position in the corner gang. (Louis Schneider and Sverre Lysgaard, "The Deferred Gratification Pattern: A Preliminary Study," *American Sociological Review,* 18:142–149, April, 1953. Used with permission of the authors and the *American Sociological Review.)*

Aspects of the DGP sometimes appear in a discussion of concepts with a different label. For instance, in a study of the desire for occupational self-direction, Kohn and Schooler [1969, p. 677] state: "The conditions of life at higher social class levels foster a view of self and society that is conducive to believing in the possibilities of rational action toward purposive goals. . . . Conditions of occupational life at lower social class levels foster a narrowly circumscribed conception of self and society."

A reverse illustration may be drawn from the

lower-class tendency to bridge the gap between the ideal and the real by a *value stretch*. As developed by Rodman [1963], the value of stretch has two basic tenets: (1) the range of behavior considered compatible with a given value is wider; and (2) commitment to attaining these values is weaker. This means that the lower class has developed ways of verbalizing middle-class values and goals without actually practicing the DGP. The value stretch means, for example, that in the matter of limiting family size, the "small family ideal" might be perceived as four children, instead of the two children considered ideal by middle-class people. Likewise, if difficulties arise, the lower-class person is not blamed for failing to attain the ideal even while continuing to give verbal assent [Haney et al., 1973].

Value stretch offers an explanation for the fact that an equal verbal acceptance of middle-class goals and values is not always accompanied by an equal effort to attain them. As Jencks points out: "Some will choose curriculums that lead nowhere, because such curriculums involve less work, in the short run. Some will eschew college, because they dislike the idea of spending four more years reading books. Some will avoid high status jobs because they are afraid of responsibility or even of success" [Jencks, 1972, p. 37].

Much of the vitality of early Americans may have come from their ability to adopt the DGP. Thus a study of this early American period remarks of the colonial American farmers, artisans, and tradesmen: "They were neither so unfortunate as to be imbued with a sense of hopelessness nor so privileged as to be satisfied with their present status. They possessed just enough to whet their appetites for more and to feel confident of their power to attain it" [Perry, 1944, p. 298].

The middle class has the most to gain by practicing the DGP. The upper class has little need to defer gratifications, for it needs only to retain a position already gained. It is sometimes argued that the rejection of the DGP by the lower class is functional because life is so hard and mobility so unlikely that trying to act on the basis of future goals would be futile. One may well ask, though, in view of the numbers of the lower class who *have* moved above the poverty line—more than three million families in a period of less than fifteen years—if the situation is really so hopeless that planning for the future is futile. The Cuban refugees to the United States are a case in point. Many of them were lower-class in their incomes and jobs, but middle-class in their life outlook. This did not enable very many to enter directly into middle-class occupations in the United States. Those who had been professionals in Cuba usually found that their credentials as professionals were not acceptable in the United States, while former businessmen lacked the money and connections for establishing new businesses. Persons who had been physicians or nurses in Cuba might be hospital orderlies in the United States. Lawyers and accountants might be tending bars, waiting in restaurants, or doing routine factory work. Housewives who had been served by maids in Cuba might be working as domestic servants themselves. Children who had been at the head of the class in Cuban schools found themselves faced with a heavy language handicap in American schools.

While their middle-class background did not enable many Cubans to avoid entering American economic life at a lower-class level, it did enable them to make the best of the situation they faced and to minimize the problems often found in lower-class circles. Thus reports of Cuban adjustment tell of a low crime rate, good school work by the children, low unemployment, increased home ownership, and generally high morale. After little more than a decade, there is also evidence of rapid mobility into middle- or even upper-class status [*Nation's Business*, 1972, pp. 78–80]. Although the Cuban refugees had neither material wealth nor acceptable occupational credentials, they did have ambition, a willingness to work, and a future-time outlook (DGP), and these worked in their favor.

Mobility and the counterculture

The life-style of the counterculture is a total rejection of middle-class values, of the DGP, of status mobility, and of the traditional work ethic. The communard in the commune may occasionally work very hard at making hand-made furniture or growing an organic garden, but totally rejects the idea of work to accumulate possessions, new clothes, or to gain social status, or because one "ought" to work [Andrews, 1970]. The values of the counterculture elevate immediate satisfactions over future concerns, feeling over reason, "freedom" over obligation, and a euphoric state of consciousness (often drug induced) as the ideal condition of existence. All this is puzzling to middle-class parents whose children disdain the opportunities their parents struggled and sacrificed to provide. Lower-class people are often angry and hostile toward youths who reject the opportunities they never had.

The countercultural youth felt that material rewards could always be reclaimed easily if desired. By the mid-seventies, economic difficulties had weakened the self-assurance of middle-class youth and the countercultural movement had declined in numbers and influence. The future trends of counterculture popularity are uncertain, but whatever the fate of this movement, its appearance certainly indicates there is no inevitable relationship between adherence to any value system and a particular social class origin.

The process of social mobility

Techniques of social climbing

For the boy who wishes to elevate his social-class status, the prime essential is an education and an occupation which fit his class ambitions. For the girl, either a prestige occupation or a higher-status husband are needed for upward mobility. As already indicated, education, occupation, and income are the main factors which, operating over a period of time, will lift one's class status. There are, however, many ways for a skillful climber to speed up the mobility process.

Change in standard of living. It is not enough merely to get and spend more money, for what one buys is more important than the amount one spends. To gain acceptance at a new status level, one must assume a material standard of living appropriate to that level. This means moving to an appropriate neighborhood, decorating one's house in an appropriate manner, driving a car which is neither too humble nor too ostentatious, and so on. The outward appearances must fit. After one is solidly established, one may ignore some of the appearances, especially at the upper-class level. The person whose secure upper-class status is beyond question can afford to drive a nondescript car and dress with a casual unconcern for fashion. But those who are on the way up must be careful about conformity to the pattern.

Cultivation of class-typed behavior. The mobility-oriented person will not be fully accepted into a higher class until he or she has absorbed the behavior patterns of that class well enough to follow them without glaring errors over a considerable period of time. The time can be shortened by deliberate effort. An aspirant can study books on etiquette, read the magazines on home decoration, and consciously watch and copy the manners of those whose acceptance is desired. Patterns of dress, vocabulary and diction, recreational activities, reading interests—these can be overhauled and polished. The children can be given music and dancing lessons, and be sent to carefully chosen private schools and summer camps. It is true that not all aspects of a class subculture can be acquired through deliberate study and conscious imitation, but such efforts can speed up the process of acceptance.

Manipulation of associations. If opportunities for social climbing were removed, many church organizations, civic associations, welfare societies, and other local associations would suffer a calamitous loss of membership. For how is the mobile person to meet and cultivate those who are a notch higher in social status?

The most useful device for social climbing is the association whose membership overlaps two or more class levels. Mobile persons cultivate the highest-status members of an organization. Then they use these friendships as levers to get into other higher-status organizations in which these friends are also members. Thus they climb, dropping out of the lower-status organizations as they gain admission to those of higher status [Meeker, 1949, pp. 130–148; Chambers, 1954, pp. 384–406]. The mobile Catholic can move to a better part of town, and thus transfer from a parish of lower-class members to a more aristocratic parish. The mobile Protestant may do likewise, or may even switch to another denomination in which middle- or upper-class members are more numerous—from Church of God to Methodist, or from Methodist to Presbyterian. Church and welfare organizations are always in need of voluntary workers. A determined climber can easily find some whose members are worth cultivating. The informal clique, though perhaps harder to get into, is extremely useful because of its intimacy.

This, then, is the standard technique of the successful climber—to cultivate the upper-status members of one's cliques and associations, and use them to gain entrée into status groups in which one is not yet accepted. It takes a good deal of finesse to play this game. One must be socially perceptive, must learn quickly, and probably must have a certain amount of charm. Those who can play the game successfully achieve rapid mobility.

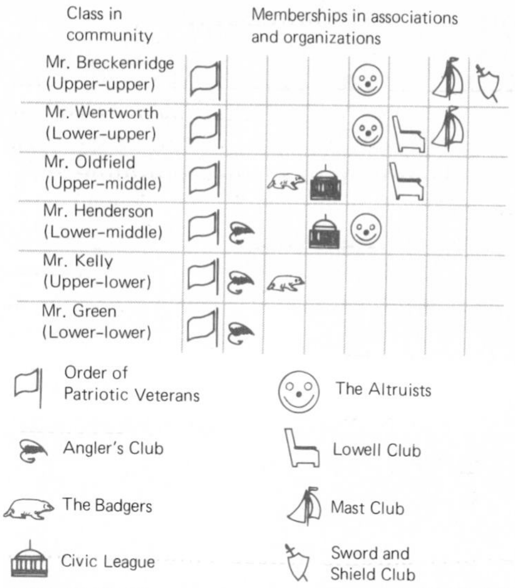

Marriage. People on the way up must be careful whom they marry. At the very least, they must choose a mate whose social finesse and learning abilities will not be a drag. At best, a "good" marriage is a priceless asset. By marry-

Class in community	Memberships in associations and organizations
Mr. Breckenridge (Upper-upper)	
Mr. Wentworth (Lower-upper)	
Mr. Oldfield (Upper-middle)	
Mr. Henderson (Lower-middle)	
Mr. Kelly (Upper-lower)	
Mr. Green (Lower-lower)	

Order of Patriotic Veterans   The Altruists

Angler's Club   Lowell Club

The Badgers   Mast Club

Civic League   Sword and Shield Club

The community is a network of associations or organizations whose membership may include persons at different class levels. Thus the organization helps persons to make social contacts across class lines. For the skillful manipulator, these associations are ladders of upward mobility, but few will climb more than one rung during a single lifetime.

Figure 11. The community is a network of overlapping associations. (Source: Adapted from descriptive materials in W. Lloyd Warner and Paul S. Lunt, *The Social Life of a Modern Community,* Yale University Press, New Haven, 1941, chap. 7.)

ing into a family a notch or two above his, an ambitious man gets a better opportunity to use his talents. He may get financial backing to complete an education or launch a business; he gets good connections and valuable introductions; he gets a wife who already fully understands the class culture he must absorb; he gets a powerful motive to "succeed" and prove himself worthy of his wife's confidence in him. A girl who "marries up" is not automatically accepted into her husband's social class, especially if the jump up has been a long one. Such marriages, however, are very rare. The upper-class college boy may romance the tavern maid, but he rarely marries her. Interclass marriages are generally between persons at adjacent class levels. Where the wife has the social finesse and learning ability to absorb the class culture quickly, she is likely to be accepted into her husband's social class with little difficulty.

When a woman "marries down," does she lose her class status? That depends upon him. If he soon gains the education, occupation, and income, and absorbs the class culture of her class level, he generally becomes accepted at her class level. But if he retains lower-status education, occupation, income, and behavior, she is likely to find that her old associates are forgetting her.

Mobility channels

In even the most restrictive of societies, there are usually some accepted ways to move ahead. Traditional Latin American and European countries were largely closed-class societies. A poor boy might occasionally move ahead in the church or in the army, but his prospects were poor because the church and the army were the common destination of younger sons of aristocrats, whom primogeniture prevented from inheriting any of the family lands. In Spain, to become a rich and famous bullfighter is every poor boy's dream. Some competitive sports (professional boxing, football, baseball, basketball, but *not* polo, tennis, or golf) have usually been open to talented youth regardless of ethnic or social-class status and have usually been neglected by men from the upper classes.

Modern society has two main routes of mobility—business entrepreneurship and bureaucratic promotion. One might either gain promotion within an organization or establish one's own business and profit thereby. For either process, education was considered a source of skills which might lead to success. In recent years, government has sought to raise the status of whole sectors of the population through such measures as "affirmative action," the War on Poverty, and increased welfare payments. Let us see how business opera-

tion and paid employment have fared as mobility channels, and how the whole process has been affected by increased education and by special government measures to aid lower-class people.

Occupational opportunities. The prospects for social mobility depend upon the total number of openings in higher-status occupations and upon the barriers to their attainment by the lowly born. The need for an increasing number of individuals in higher-status occupations depends on changes in society which create more upper-class jobs and on the extent to which the upper-class parents produce enough children to fill these places. The need for personnel in high-status occupations in the United States has been growing, as shown in Figure 12. Meanwhile the high-income groups have had until recently a birth rate too low to replace themselves. This makes room for a good deal of upward occupational mobility.

Oddly enough, the very success of mobility aspirations in the past threatens to cut the rate of social mobility in the future. The reason for this is that we have been getting ahead so fast that American society no longer has a large reservoir of people at the bottom of the heap who can move ahead. Mobility has consisted largely in moving from lower-status to higher-status occupations, but the proportion of workers in lower-status occupations continues to shrink. In 1970, only 8.67 percent of the male workers under 35 were in laboring and farm occupations, compared to 13.27 percent in 1962 [Hauser and Featherman, 1973, p. 305]. Certain categories of lower-status workers, such as household servants, have almost entirely disappeared. What has usually been thought of as the bottom is becoming so narrow that it can't shrink much more without reaching absolute zero. In many other countries, mechanization is still displacing farm and unskilled work, but in the United States, this source of mobility has drawn to a close.

Although upward mobility from the very bottom may be ending there is still a good bit of movement within intermediate occupations and from middle- to higher-ranking activities. The direction of this movement can be seen from Figure 12. Business entrepreneurship affords a significant number of persons an opportunity to strike out on their own and possibly escape the ladderlike ordeal of organizational promotion. However, the decline in the proportion of the self-employed would indicate that this route of social mobility is available to a decreasing number. On the other hand, the proportion of higher-status employment opportunities appears to be increasing. The development of automation is decreasing the demand for unskilled and semiskilled workers and for fine craftsmen, and is at the same time calling for a greater number of technicians capable of maintaining and coordinating complicated automatic machinery. This development is opening up a still larger number of higher-status positions, while still further decreasing the openings for the person who has little education or training. There will be a rapidly growing number of openings for specialists of many sorts and for technicians with at least a high school or junior college education plus specialized technical training. The net result of these changes would seem to be some increase in mobility, with the United States probably a more nearly open-class society today than it has been for a long time. In fact, a relatively open-class system seems to characterize all of the modern industrial societies. Studies of mobility in a number of European countries find that mobility patterns are remarkably alike in all, both capitalist and communist [Lipset, 1972].

One measure of mass social mobility is the extent to which Americans have been able to move above the poverty level of living. This level is defined as the minimum amount required by a nonfarm family of four. In 1959, 7.9 million families were below the poverty level of $2,973; by 1972, when the poverty dividing line had risen to $4,275, the families below this level had fallen to 4.9 million. [Bureau of the Census, 1972, p. 29]. Even this

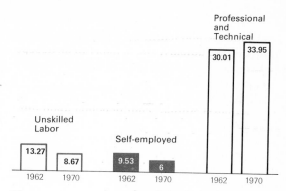

Figure 12. Some occupational mobility changes, 1962–1970. (Source: Adapted from March, 1962, OCG survey and March, 1970, "Current Population Survey," cited in Robert M. Hauser and David L. Featherman, "Trends in Occupational Mobility," *American Sociological Review*, 38:3, p. 305. Used with permission of *American Sociological Review* and the authors.)

number of families living in poverty in the world's wealthiest country is far too many, but it represents a shift of three million families out of the "poverty" category in thirteen years, making it one of the more important historical instances of mass social mobility.

Some increase in mobility.

Governmental programs to promote mobility. It is arguable to what extent the upward movement from poverty is due to the expansion of industry in response to market conditions and to what extent it results from deliberate government policy. Obviously, the two interact, and it is difficult to say which has been the more important. Certainly, the expansion of industry creates a greater demand for labor and improved chances for mobility. However, such programs as "affirmative action," the War on Poverty, and increased welfare payments were designed both to help individuals rise from the bottom and to improve the situation of those still at the bottom. These programs pressured employers to give special consideration to women and to lower-status ethnic groups, offered job-related training to the poor and uneducated and, in many cases, made payments which raised those on welfare above the poverty line.

Statistics from the War on Poverty activities are rather scanty, and their meaning is far from clear. Numbers of poor people who had received training were hired, but how many might have been hired in any event and trained by the employer? Similarly, employers report hiring or promoting people as a result of the pressure of affirmative action programs. The question remains whether many of these same people might have been hired or promoted in the normal course of events to meet the employer's need for labor. Probably the answer is that such programs can work only when the demand for labor is increasing, but that they may stimulate the acceptance by employers of workers who had not previously been seriously considered as part of the skilled labor force.

The mobility effect of welfare payments is even more difficult to unravel. For one thing, there is a great variety of welfare programs, and these vary from state to state. Thus the average Aid to Families of Dependent Children (AFDC) payment for a family of four varies from $51 a month in Mississippi to $340 in New York [*Social Administration Bulletin,* Aug. 1974, p. 3]. In addition, most welfare families benefit from more than one type of payment. Thus the AFDC family may also receive food stamps, rent supplements, medical care, scholarships, school lunches, etc. It was estimated that, by 1971, four states had established welfare payments high enough to

lift families above the poverty level [ibid]. This statement does not include "payments for special needs," which sometimes are quite substantial. Even at best, welfare families have a difficult time, and an approach to adequacy should be a cause for rejoicing rather than complaint. The difficulty is that a fairly adequate welfare program may be one which discourages social mobility if it causes people to rely upon welfare rather than upon work.

A recent study of a congressional committee found that some women in female-headed households can get more on welfare than they can by working. The study found, for instance, that in 1972, a woman with a family benefiting from five or more programs could collect a tax-free income of $426 a month against a taxable income of $371 a month earned by the average employed woman in the same neighborhood [*Business Week,* 1973]. Under such circumstances, people might easily prefer the secure but limited welfare grants to insecure and even more limited earnings, even though the earnings might eventually grow to a substantial amount. Decisions of this type handicap the society both by the cost of welfare payments and by taking people out of the labor force. They also handicap individuals by detouring them from the opportunities of employment and thereby from a chance to be in the mainstream of economic opportunity.

Our welfare programs are survivals of the day when welfare meant subsistence relief payments barely enough to keep people alive. As yet, we have not been able to devise a system which provides "adequate" welfare without affording an incentive to avoid employment. It is sometimes argued that work is so attractive that people will prefer it under any circumstances, but studies have shown that either unemployment compensation [Munts and Garfinkel, 1974] or a guaranteed welfare income tend to diminish the motivation to work. This was shown in an experiment designed to test whether the Nixon proposal for a guaranteed family income would result in a decreased tendency to work. One set of families (the experimental) was told that their incomes would not be allowed to fall below a certain level and that they would be allowed to keep part of what they earned in addition to welfare payments. They were compared to a control group of families which did not have these income guaranties. Although the differences were not large, there was some evidence of a decreased tendency to work among the experimental group. This is expressed as follows in a summary of the report:

There was, overall, some small average disincentive responses around the break-even level with increasing and accelerating disincentives for husbands whose wages and potential earning power were further and further below the average . . . . Wives in families participating in the negative income tax plans did less work than wives in the control groups, but the source of work reduction was almost entirely concentrated among white wives; black and Spanish wives showed no experimental disincentive. (Felicity Skidmore, "Appendix D: Abstracts of Research Papers in Volumes I–III of Final Report," in *Operations, Surveys, and Administration,* Edited by Jerilyn Fair and David Kershaw, from *The Final Report of the New Jersey Graduated Work Incentive Experiment.)* Institute for Research on Poverty, University of Wisconsin, Madison, 1973.

Changes have been made in the scheme of welfare payments to allow recipients to keep a portion of their earnings, but these changes are difficult to implement. Welfare reformers have three choices, none of which is satisfactory. (1) If welfare payments are kept below the amount of the lowest wage earner's income, then they fall below the prevailing ideal of adequacy. (2) If the payments meet minimum standards of adequacy and recipients are still permitted to keep a portion of earnings, then their total compensation is high compared to lower-paid (or even medium-paid) workers who are not receiving welfare. (3) If welfare payments are reduced by the amount of earnings, then there is little incentive for recipients to accept employment. In the meantime, welfare has an ambiguous effect on social mobility, since it aids mobility by maintaining and even raising the standard of living, but reduces mobility by keeping people out of gainful employment.

Upgrading of occupations. Although large-scale manufacturing may offer the poor person few chances for promotion from within, the multiplication of the service industries—sales and service, retail trade, recreation, resort industry, and many others—do offer opportunities to persons with talent and ambition, even though they may lack college degrees.

In some occupations, the status of the occupation itself has changed. Farming has historically included a very few upper-class planters or plantation owners, a moderate number of fairly prosperous middle-status farm owners, and a large number of marginal farmers and tenant farmers of low income and low status. Today we have fewer farmers, but the average farm is larger and more prosperous, its owner is better educated, and his status and living standards compare more favorably with those of urban residents. Between 1940 and 1969 the number of tenant-operated farms declined from 39 to 13 percent of all farms [*Statistical Abstract of the United States,* 1973, p. 586]. The ex-tenant farmers have moved to town or city [Smith, 1969]. Those who remain farmers today are likely to have higher status and income than farmers a generation ago, while many of those who have left the farm have found a job of higher status than the one they left. Other occupations have shown a similar change in the nature or grade of work involved and the status of the occupation.

Education and mobility

Education is often considered to be a prime means of social mobility, yet it is doubtful that it should be considered a channel in the same sense as entrepreneurship or bureaucratic jobs. This is because education does not provide a route to social advancement as much as it does the ability to take advantage of routes already in existence. Education may provide the know-how which is valuable in a business or profession, but it does not automatically provide the opportunity to use these skills. Without these, education is of little economic value. In other words, the unemployed Ph.D. is just as poor as the unemployed illiterate, and his or her job possibilities may be fewer.

Since the positions requiring educational credentials are often among the more highly paid and have been rapidly increasing in recent years, it is often, but not always, true that the earnings of the highly educated are above average. In 1971, 37 percent of the white males with a college education had an income of over $15,000 a year and only 5 percent were under $3,000. Of those with seven years education or less, only 1.4 percent had incomes of over $15,000 [*World Almanac,* 1974, p. 312]. These figures indicate the tendency of the highly educated to have better incomes, but they also indicate that a few of the less educated do very well financially and some of the better educated fare very poorly. This, by the way, is borne out in an analysis of multimillionaires, which found that five out of six of a group who had made an average of over 200 million since World War II were high school or college dropouts [Alsop, 1965]. The late H. L. Hunt, an oil billionaire with a fifth-grade education, may not be typical of the rich, but his career does indicate that lack of education is not an insuperable obstacle to gaining great wealth. While it is true that school dropouts usually fare less well in the job market, most of this can be attributed to factors other than lack of formal education (such as class, race, ability, personal maladjustments, delinquency history, etc.) [Hansen, 1970; Bachman, 1972].

Positions requiring the most education are not always highly paid. Some students reading this book may have siblings who dropped out of school and are earning more than a college graduate can expect in the first job. One example of this: the 1969 census found that black men under the age of thirty-five employed as public school teachers earned an average of $8,253 a year, compared to $8,271 for black men in the same age bracket employed as bus drivers [Bureau of the Census, July, 1973, p. 52]. Jencks also questions the value of prolonged education, saying, "For working-class whites, blacks and women, dropping out often seems to be the most economically rational decision." He adds the opinion that ". . . equalizing everyone's educational attainment would have virtually no effect on income inequality" [1972, p. 224].

It is sometimes assumed that, since the average income correlates positively with the amount of education, the way to improve the overall economic position of a total society, or of a depressed group within the society, is to increase the educational facilities. This is true only if there is a simultaneous expansion of economic opportunities using greater amounts of education. An increased proportion of high school graduates does not necessarily mean occupational advancement. Between 1952 and 1965, the percentage of unskilled factory workers having twelve years of education increased from 13.8 percent to 23.9 percent, proving that more education does not always lead to a better job [Johnston and Hamel, 1966].

Nor is it necessarily true that upgrading educational requirements leads to better performance of a given type of work. Berg [1969], in a study of routine assembly line jobs, found that higher education was dysfunctional for this type of employment. Among the more highly educated workers, efficiency was less and absenteeism and turnover greater.

Developing countries seeking a quick way to improve their economy often contrast their schools with the levels of education in industrialized countries. Since industrialized countries have more schools, it seems obvious that more schools will produce industrialization. Unfortunately, this is a case of reversing the order of cause and effect. It was not education that produced industrialization, but industrialization which stimulated education. As Table 20 indicates, there is no necessary relation between the amount of education and the amount of industrialization. Many a poor country has spent a large part of its resources on education without realizing any great advance in economic development.

In view of this criticism of education as a mobility vehicle, does it have any mobility function at all? Yes, in at least two ways. One is that education is the gateway to the professions. A professional career is not always the most rewarding, and many a professional makes less money than his or her father earned as a businessman. On the other hand, professions are high in prestige, at least average or better in income, and have provided mobility opportunities for many people. Further, the scarcity of professional schools, the cost of such education, and the rigors of a demanding curriculum all operate to discourage enough persons so that most professions maintain a rather favorable supply-and-demand situation. Thus the education which provides professional credentials gives some assurance of a prestigious and moderately remunerative career.

A second way in which education aids mobility lies in the modern promotion process from laborer to management. In another era an intelligent worker who had mastered mechanical skills might be steadily promoted through supervisory levels until he reached a position in top management; or if these roads were blocked, he might use his mechanical skills to start a shop of his own. Today's workers find that supervisory positions above the level of foreman are usually filled by college-trained specialists, and that routine assembly-line work does not provide mechanical skills which may be used elsewhere; in fact, it usually provides no mechanical skill at all. This situation represents a "break in the skill hierarchy," meaning that one may move from unskilled to skilled labor and eventually become a foreman, but that beyond that point lie barriers which are difficult to pass without the proper educational qualifications. Thus we have not one occupational ladder, but two: One stops with foreman; the other begins with a col-

TABLE 20 RELATION OF LITERACY TO INDUSTRIALIZATION

More literate than industrial		Less literate than industrial	
Bulgaria	Panama	Egypt	Libya
Colombia	Philippines	India	Malaya
Costa Rica	Poland	Indonesia	Nepal
Ecuador	Rumania	Iran	Union of South Africa
Finland	Thailand	Iraq	

Source: Hilda Hertz Golden: "Literacy and Social Change in Underdeveloped Countries," *Rural Sociology*, 20:3, March, 1955.

lege diploma and a job in the "executive-development program" and ends with the presidency. To leap from the top rung of the first to the bottom rung of the second is rarely possible.

The break in the skill hierarchy has largely destroyed the stock-boy-to-president route, and education has largely taken its place in large corporations. Thus education is more necessary to occupational mobility than before, but education is also more readily available than ever before in the United States. Scholarships and other institutionalized aids to talented youth are available in considerable number, while the community college explosion has made higher education available to many who cannot afford the cost of a residential college.

It has often been charged that poor children were seriously handicapped in elementary school and in high school. It was maintained that either the schools available to poor children were of low quality, or that the teachers discriminated against lower-class children. Current research is challenging these assumptions. The Coleman report [Coleman, 1966] for instance, not only found no disparity in the facilities of schools attended by black and white children, but also found that superior facilities were not related to higher educational achievement. Another research study examined the idea that the teachers' preconceptions influenced grades, but failed to confirm this theory. In this study, teachers were advised that an experimental group of children would show unusual gains in language and mathematical skills. The preliminary reports claimed an association, but follow-up studies showed that neither the students' achievement nor the teachers' evaluations had been influenced by these predictions [Dusek and O'Connell, 1973; O'Connell et al., 1974].

Jencks remarks that only a few lower-class children behave in ways the schools cannot tolerate, and suggests that the popular notion of the middle-class character of school life is questionable. He finds that the superior performance of middle-class children is not based on their liking of school, but on the greater stress their parents place on educational success [Jencks, 1972, pp. 139–140]. Mayeske [1973] also finds that a family atmosphere which rewards learning aspirations and encourages good study habits has a far greater effect upon pupil learning than the quality of the school attended. Milner [1972] agrees with Jencks that nothing which the school does can have much effect upon poverty or inequality. While there are some scholars who maintain that lower-class children suffer severe discrimination in school opportunities [Rist, 1973], the burden of evidence does not support that charge.

How about higher education? How much has the expansion of higher education enabled poor persons to gain a college degree and thereby counteract the break in the skills hierarchy?

As Jencks comments: "It is hard to say to what extent the selectivity (by social class) of higher education represents a denial of equal opportunity and to what extent it results from variation in people's appetite for education" [Jencks, 1972, p. 19]. Statistics indicate that children from high-socioeconomic-status families who are in the highest fourth of ability distribution have about 1.5 times the probability of post-high-school education of students of equal ability from homes of low socioeconomic status [Sewell, 1971, p. 795]. This would seem to indicate that children from wealthy homes have an edge in education. There are other class-related factors, however, one of which is that the level of aspiration is lower among youth from low-income families [Sewell, Haller and Straus, 1957]. Poor youth, even those of high ability, are less likely to aspire to a college degree than youth from wealthier homes; but if their ambitions have been aroused, they have a chance of getting the needed education. Certainly, many able American youth from low-income families do go on to higher education, and the proportion is much higher than in the Soviet Union, for instance, where the proportion of children of the lowest class attending a university is only one-sixteenth that of the children of the most favored group [Katz, 1974].

These observations on the possibility of lower-class youth pursuing higher education are borne out by the fact that the proportion of youth completing a college education had doubled between the 1920s and the 1970s, moving from 10 to 20 percent of the youth population [Jencks, 1972, p. 19]. One would assume that the increased availability of higher education is more than enough to make up for road blocks in lower-class mobility caused by the break in the skill hierarchy.

Overall outlook for mobility channels. Some channels of mobility have diminished. Individually operated businesses occupy a decreased proportion of the total work force. The break in the skills hierarchy has blocked the stockroom boy-to-manager route: free land has long since ceased to exist; a wide variety of jobs, which at one time were open to all, now require educational credentials. Welfare programs may slow mobility by keeping people out of the labor force. Increased education does not necessarily mean increased social mobility, since it may simply mean that requirements have been raised for essentially low-status jobs.

On the other hand, low-status, unskilled occupations continue to decrease and higher-status occupations to increase, thus affording more mobility opportunities. Demands for service workers afford new and moderately profitable careers to many. Government programs have sought to improve mobility-related skills, to persuade employers to hire members of depressed groups, and to make transfer payments via welfare grants. Education by itself may not be a mobility channel, but it has enabled people to cope with increased educational requirements. Statistics reveal a fall in the numbers in poverty and a continuing high rate of upward occupational mobility, indicating that, at this time, the factors encouraging upward mobility outweigh those against it.

Costs and gains of mobility

The idea that social mobility is good is part of our democratic ethos. We argue that a closed-class society thwarts the fulfillment of individual personality and deprives society of the contributions of many talented people.

While social mobility offers society the ability to fill its occupational niches with the most able people and offers the individual a chance to attain his or her life goal, it also involves certain costs. A mobile society is one which arouses expectations it is seldom able to fulfil, thereby creating dissatisfaction and unhappiness. On the other hand, a traditional society in which one is born into one's appointed place arouses few hopes and few frustrations (as long as this traditional social structure remains intact). The benefits of social mobility are inextricably mixed with its costs, since when one breaks the bonds which hold him back, he also cuts the protective web which keeps him from sinking still lower. An open-class society may be desirable from the viewpoint of both society and the individual, but it still has some penalties.

These penalties include the fear of falling in status, as in downward mobility; the strain of new role learnings in occupational promotions; the disruption of primary group relationships as one moves upward and onward. One who is passed over for promotion may envy the security of a less mobile society. Parents and children may become strangers due to changes in social attitudes and geographic location consequent on success. Occasionally, offered promotions are declined because of a fear of the burden of new responsibilities. Even marriages may be threatened when spouses are not equally interested in mobility. One mate resents the implied insult of being prodded, polished, and improved; the other resents the apparent lack of cooperation. Some studies have even found that a high rate of mental illness may accompany either upward or downward mobility [Ellis, 1952; Hollingshead, et al., 1954; Turner and Wagenfeld, 1967]. In any case, the "middle-class convert" will experience a shift of attitudes and associations which will probably be even more drastic than that involved in the process of religious conversion or of changed citizenship.

Occasionally a worker declines an offered promotion.

Yet there is considerable evidence that those who occupy the top occupational positions are healthier and happier than others. Tropman [1971] finds that probabilities of holding high occupational rank are highest for men in continuing successful marriages, are intermediate for remarried widowers or divorcees, and are lowest for the unmarried, divorced, and separated. A Metropolitan Insurance Company study found that the death rate among top business executives was only 64 percent of that for the rest of the white male population of similar ages [*Statistical Bulletin*, Feb. 1, 1974]. But these studies are open to two criticisms. They do not study *mobility* because they do not separate those who moved up into their high rank from those who merely retained the rank into which they were born. Nor do these studies take account of the selective factor, in that those who are healthy and happily married are most likely to be promoted. Almost *any* employed group will show health levels above national averages, since persons in poor physical or emotional health tend to become unemployed.

Studies which compare mobile with stationary occupants of the upper ranks are not fully consistent. Typical of many studies is one reported by Hacker [1962], which shows a 50 percent higher rate of heart symptoms among a group of young executives of working-class background as compared with a control group of young executives of middle-class origin. But a detailed survey of recent research by Jackson and Curtis [1972] concluded that, after controlling for various other intervening variables, no convincing evidence remained to show that upward mobility was particularly stressful. Thus the question of stresses and costs of upward mobility is not fully settled. A number of studies have also reported that downward mobility is associated with many unpleasant accompaniments, such as poor health, marital discord, and feelings of alienation and social distance; but, once again, cause and effect are not identified. Such unpleasant developments could be either a cause or an effect of downward mobility. For both the individual and the society, the costs and benefits of mobility and the open-class society are open to debate.

Mobility and equality

For years, America was regarded as the land of equality because of the possibility of a "rags to riches" mobility. Recently this concept has been challenged by various writers [Jencks, 1972; Rawls, 1971] who insist that what matters is not equality of opportunity but equality of results. In other words, a just society is not the one in which people have an equal chance in the race for social status, but one in which they cross the finish line together.

There is a legend that the great Russian singer Feodor Chaliapin was informed by the revolutionary government that he might continue at the Moscow Opera, but would receive the same pay as the stagehands. He replied, "Very well, but then I'll work as a stagehand." This anecdote reveals one of the difficulties of enforcing absolute equality. Inequality has generally been regarded as providing an incentive for arduous and risky exertion by offering compensating prizes. If the easy jobs pay as much as the more difficult and the unskilled as much as the skilled, why should one work so hard?

The attainment of equality poses many difficulties. For example, the many kinds of help given by parents to children is a major source of inequality. Is it desirable, or even possible, to end these types of parental assistance? All indications are that people are unequal in talents, aspirations, motivation, and character traits. To maintain equality of reward would require a great deal of regimentation, involving far greater government control than Americans have ever known. Could such control be maintained without a brutal and bloody totalitarianism? The controls and regimentation needed to maintain equality in a prosperous, developed society might reduce total productivity so greatly that incomes could be equalized only at a relatively low level, with most of the people poorer than before. No advanced society has sought to attain equality of reward, so we have no past experience to appraise. It is a possibility that a cooperative dedication to the "common good," such as is encouraged in Communist countries as a major value, might bring high levels of both equality and productivity, but as yet, this has not been demonstrated. Even the more recently Communized countries, such as China and Cuba, still glowing with revolutionary fervor and founder zeal, have found that work motivation is highly dependent upon individual financial incentives [Lelyfeld, 1974; Morgan, 1974].

It is common for critics of American life to charge that our present situation represents some kind of fall from a Golden Age. In the past, the United States was allegedly a land of tremendous opportunity with an absence of social-class constraints, a relative equality of income and property, and an easy chance for all to get ahead. Supposedly, class divisions today have become sharper, the ownership of wealth more steeply concentrated, income more unequal, and the chance for the poor to get ahead nearly nonexistent.

The difficulty with these charges is that none

of them are true. Even forgetting the fact that 20 percent of the population of colonial America were slaves, the distribution of property and income was far more unequal than it is today [Pessen, 1971]. Since that time, we have seen a steady shrinkage in the size of the most poverty-stricken part of the population and an actual increase in the proportion of people going from the bottom to the top [Lipset, 1972]. Rather than social-class barriers becoming stronger, they are so weak that families have difficulty in passing on their status to their children. There is nearly as much difference in the occupational status of brothers as in that of random individuals. On an occupational-status scale measuring from zero to 96, the difference between brothers was 23 points, whereas the difference between random individuals was 28

TABLE 21 THE CHANGING DISTRIBUTION OF U.S. NATIONAL INCOME, 1948–1974 (Division of National Income Between Employees and Other Categories of Income Receivers)

Category	Percent of national income received		
	1948	1964	1974
Employee compensation			
Wages and salaries	60.4	64.4	65.7
Supplements*	2.6	6.2	9.2
Total employee compensation	63.0	70.6	74.9
Entrepreneurial and capital income:			
Proprietors' income			
Farm operators	7.8	2.3	2.8
Business and professional	10.1	7.8	5.4
Rental income of persons	3.6	3.5	2.3
Net interest	0.8	3.0	5.4
Corporate profits†	14.7	12.8	9.3
Total entrepreneurial and capital	37.0	29.4	25.1
Total income national	100.0	100.0	100.0

*Includes employer's contributions for social insurance, employee's pensions, and health and welfare funds.
†Includes inventory valuation adjustments.
This presentation does not accurately reflect the changing average incomes of individuals within these categories, due to changing size of the categories, but reveals only the changing division of national income between various categories of income receivers.
Source: 1948: Computed from Table 1.10 of *The National Income and Product Accounts of the United States*, 1929–1965. 1964: Computed from Table 1.10 of *U.S. National Income and Product Accounts*, 1964–1969. 1974: Computed from million-dollar worksheet underlying Table 6 of the national income and product tables published in the February, 1975, *Survey of Current Business*.

points [Jencks, 1972, pp. 178–179]. As strong as the props of privilege may seem, they are unable to prevent downward social mobility, and as formidable as the handicaps of the poor may appear, they do not constitute insurmountable barriers. Individual variations in ability, training, and motivation make a difference in social mobility even within the same family.

Often it is assumed that the degree of inequality in income in a society is determined by political decisions, with capitalist regimes fostering inequality and socialist governments securing equality. Research indicates, however, that the greatest difference is between developed and underdeveloped countries, with the developed (industrialized) having the least inequality [Lenski, 1966, p. 313]. Among industrialized countries, both inequality and social mobility seem to be about the same, including even the Soviet Union [Kristol, 1972, p. 461]. A specific study directed to comparing the type of government and the distribution of income in thirty-six countries found no consistent relationship [Jackman, 1974].

The distribution of wealth may be more unequal than the distribution of income. Socialist countries often give tremendous privileges to favored individuals, but they do not permit the accumulation of personal fortunes on the scale of those owned by millionaires in Western countries. Thus the occupational distribution of income in socialist and capitalist countries may be similar, but capitalist countries do allow greater inequality in the ownership of wealth.

Trends in social mobility vary, but in the last period for which we have U.S. data, 1962 to 1970, more sons of fathers with a manual occupation moved into nonmanual occupations than was true in most preceding periods [Hauser and Featherman, 1973]. Neither in the United States nor in any other society do we have absolute equality of income and wealth. Nor do we have perfect social mobility in which the able poor always move to the top and the wealthy incompetents unfailingly drop to the bottom in every generation. Whether either perfect equality or perfect mobility would lead to a better society may be doubtful, but this is not the main issue. The important question is whether existing trends toward social mobility are leading to a productive society with both opportunity and freedom for the average person. Currently, the indications are clear that American society offers more chance for mobility than ever before.

The fact that today most people prefer mobility to equality is no assurance that this will always be true. Utopias, theoretically perfect but usually tyrannical in practice, have a powerful attraction which neither logic nor experience can always expunge. If we ever experience a time when the aspirations of most people are seriously frustrated, then the masses may join the philosophers in a demand for a completely egalitarian society. Such a society would probably not be compatible with either freedom or high productivity, but it would remove disparities of fortune and thus eliminate the resentment that arises when some of us do better than the rest of us.

Summary

Social mobility refers to movement up or down in social status. This usually involves a change in occupation. Differential reproduction rates and expanding industry offer a continuous chance for occupational advancement and social mobility; they are probably at least as great in the United States now as in earlier years. Some European countries also have considerable social mobility; in others the rate has been held down by the fact that a slower trend toward industrialization leaves a larger part of the population in rural areas. The underdeveloped countries are entering a period of industrialization which increases social mobility, but the amount of mobility in these countries is still less than in more industrialized areas. Mobility in the United States has been hampered by the imposition of rigid educational requirements for many higher-level jobs but has been accelerated by the rapid growth in the number graduating from high school and college. Education is not a direct channel for mobility, but it may prepare people to take advantage of changes in the occupational structure. Government welfare programs retard mobility by deterring people from potentially rewarding work careers, but increase mobility by assisting the less fortunate and reducing poverty.

Both societies and ethnic groups vary in the number of channels of mobility open to their members. Channels may be restricted by the limited technological development of the society, discrimination against an ethnic or social-class group, failure of perception, and lack of development of the necessary personal qualities.

A society in which people are ranked strictly according to individual ability and performance is known as an *open-class* society; one in which status is theoretically based strictly on heredity is known as a *closed-class* or *caste* society. No class system is entirely open or closed. Modern industrial societies tend toward the open-class system; traditional agricultural societies may develop caste systems which restrict social mobility. Ethnic and religious membership to a certain extent still affects class position. Black-white relationships in the United States are often cited as a caste situation, although the attacks on segregation in recent years make racial differences more clearly a matter of class than of caste barriers and class background is today a greater handicap to the impoverished black, Puerto-Rican, or American Indian than is skin color.

While a change in occupation is the crucial step in social mobility, the process may be speeded by: (1) revising one's standard of living, (2) cultivating class-typed modes of behavior, (3) manipulating associational memberships, or (4) a strategic marriage.

Upward mobility is aided by a time perspective, most often found in the middle class, known as the *deferred gratification pattern.* The lower class, along with the middle-class hippie, tends to reject this pattern in favor of immediate gratification, whereas the upper class has a continuing status security that makes the deferment of gratification seem unnecessary. Mobility brings new opportunities and greater outlets for potential ability, but it also brings emotional strains and threatens patterns of friendship, residence, and family ties.

Recent research questions the harmful effects of mobility and points to evidence that life adjustment may be correlated with occupational success. Mobility may be regarded as a substitute for equality since the chance to get ahead may lessen resentment at an unequal status. Since people are unequal in ability, an open-class society will not lead to an absolute leveling of differences and there is an emerging demand for government to order an absolute equality of income. Such an imposed equality might reduce prosperity by lowering economic incentives and threaten freedom through the amount of government regulation required. A high rate of mobility is characteristic of industrial societies and mobility in the United States is at least as high as in previous periods.

Questions and projects

1. Why is it that persons at the very top of the status ladder often spend less freely and put up less "front" than many persons who are a level or two beneath them?

2. What advantages and disadvantages does a closed-class system hold for a society? For the individual? Do you know of any deliberate attempts to decrease competition for status in the United States?

3. What advantages and disadvantages does an

open-class system hold for a society? For the individual? What makes absolute equality of opportunity impossible?

4. Do you consider yourself to be highly mobility-oriented? What factors do you think explain your own mobility orientation?

5. It is often said that the hippies can always drop back into middle-class roles if they wish. Is this true?

6. Assume that higher education should become completely free of all costs and that all jobs were filled strictly on merit without regard to family connections. Would you expect the same proportion of lower- and middle-class youth to reach high-status positions? Why or why not?

7. Why do upward-mobile persons usually drift away from their relatives and old friends? Is the tendency due to snobbishness?

8. Is marriage while in college an aid or a threat to the student's prospects for social mobility? Will social mobility become a threat to the marriage?

9. Read *A Tree Grows in Brooklyn,* by Betty Smith. What factors account for Francie's rejection of the slum subculture and her desire to escape it? Did she escape through luck or through her own efforts?

10. Analyze a pledge list in a fraternity or sorority in terms of those you would label socially mobile as contrasted to those who are simply maintaining the family status. Describe any contrasts between the personality traits of the socially mobile and the stationary pledges.

11. Describe the groups in your community characterized by the most rapid and least rapid rate of upward mobility. On the basis of present trends in both of these groups, attempt to predict their relative position fifty years hence.

12. Among the journal articles in the Suggested Readings, read and compare the one by Seymour Martin Lipset or by Irving Kristol with the one by Milton Mankoff. Do you find Mankoff's viewpoint as persuasive as the others? Why or why not?

Suggested readings

BERG, IVAR: "Rich Man's Qualifications for Poor Men's Jobs," *Transaction,* 6:45–50, March, 1968. Stresses the fact that increased popular education may simply lead to increased demand for educational credentials without helping either the individual or the employer.

GLENN, NORVAL D., ANDREAIN ROSS, AND JUDY CORDER TULLY: "Patterns of Intergenerational Mobility of Females Through Marriage," *American Sociological Review,* 39:683–699, October, 1974. A research study finding that females are more mobile (both up and down) than males, and that female upward mobility through marriage is less than male upward mobility through occupation.

GREELEY, ANDREW: "American Catholics—Making It or Losing It," *The Public Interest,* 8:26–37, Summer, 1972. Analysis of Catholics in terms of assimilation and social mobility.

HAUSER, ROBERT M., AND DAVID L. FEATHERMAN: "Trends in the Occupational Mobility of U.S. Men, 1962–1970," *American Sociological Review,* 38:302–310, June, 1973. A careful survey

which finds that the rate of mobility is being maintained.

JENCKS, CHRISTOPHER, ET AL: *Inequality: A Reassessment of the Effect of Family and Schooling in America,* Basic Books, New York, 1972. A provocative book whose candid treatment of myths about the effects of education will be interesting even to those who reject its basic premise that equality should be enforced by government edict.

KRISTOL, IRVING: "About Equality," *Commentary,* 54:41–47, November, 1972. An article which emphasizes the human and economic costs of government action to obtain absolute economic equality.

LIPSET, SEYMOUR MARTIN: "Social Mobility and Equal Opportunity," *The Public Interest,* 29:90–108, Fall, 1972. Presentation of the United States as a society of opportunity.

MANKOFF, MILTON: "Toward Socialism: Reassessing Inequality," *Social Policy,* 4:20–31, March–April, 1974. A critical view of social stratification in the United States and a demand for government intervention to guarantee equality of compensation.

SCHACTER, GUSTAV C. AND EDWIN L. DALE, JR.: *The Economist Looks at Society,* Xerox, Lexington, Ky., 1973. A treatment of a number of social problems, including poverty, from the economist's viewpoint. An excellent example of the integration of economics and sociology.

SCHNEIDER, LOUIS, AND SVERRE LYSGAARD: "The Deferred Gratification Pattern: A Preliminary Study," *American Sociological Review,* 18:142–149, April, 1953; The Bobbs-Merrill Company. Inc., Indianapolis, reprint S-250. The classic statement of the DGP.

SILVERBERG, JAMES: *Social Mobility in the Caste System in India,* Mouton, The Hague, 1968. A series of reports on the adjustment of the caste system to economic changes.

SMELSER, NEIL, AND SEYMOUR MARTIN LIPSET (EDS.): *Social Structure and Mobility in Economic Development,* Aldine Publishing Company, Chicago, 1966. A series of papers dealing with the mutual interaction between social mobility and economic development.

*SOROKIN, PITIRIM: *Social and Cultural Mobility,* Harper & Row, Publishers, Inc., New York, 1927. A monumental study of social mobility in a variety of social systems and time periods.

STRAUS, MURRAY A.: "Deferred Gratification, Social Class and the Achievement Syndrome," *American Sociological Review,* 27:326–335, June, 1962. A study of the relationship between social class and acceptance of the deferred-gratification pattern.

WARNER, W. LLOYD, AND PAUL S. LUNT: *The Social Life of a Modern Community,* Yale University Press, New Haven, Conn., 1941. Description of social class and social mobility in a New England factory town. Chap. 7, "Profiles of Yankee City," is especially recommended.

Four/Social interaction

Part Four describes some of the characteristic ways in which people treat one another. Chapter 14, "Social Processes," describes some fairly standardized types of interaction which appear in some form in most societies. Chapter 15, "Social Power," delineates the types of power and its use by different social groups. Chapter 16, "Race and Ethnic Relations," shows how facts and feelings about race enter into people's treatment of one another. Chapter 17, "Collective Behavior in Mass Society," analyzes a variety of forms of behavior in which the element of group encouragement and protection is especially important.

Chapter 14 •Social processes

The effect of residence in a hospital manifests itself by a fairly well-defined clinical picture. A striking feature is the failure to gain properly, despite the ingestion of diets which are entirely adequate for growth in the home. Infants in hospitals sleep less than others and they rarely smile or babble spontaneously. They are listless and apathetic and look unhappy. The appetite is indifferent and food is accepted without enthusiasm. The stools tend to be frequent and, in sharp contrast with infants cared for in the home, it is unusual for 24 hours to pass without an evacuation. Respiratory infections which last only a day or two in the home are prolonged and may persist for weeks or months. Return to the home results in defervescence (disappearance of fever) within a few days and a prompt and striking gain in weight. *(Ruth M. Bakwin and Harry Bakwin,* Psychologic Care During Infancy and Childhood, *Appleton-Century-Crofts, Inc., New York, 1942, p. 295.)*

In the contrast between the infants' response to the hospital and to the home environments, we have an example of primary versus secondary group cooperation. Cooperation in all its various forms is one of the social processes. What are social processes and what is their importance?

The nature of social processes

The term "social processes" refers to *repetitive interaction patterns of behavior which are commonly found in social life*. One of the most extensive treatments of social process is found in Park and Burgess, *Introduction to the Science of Sociology* [1921]. This highly influential textbook of an earlier period is primarily devoted to the classification and analysis of social processes. In recent decades sociologists have become less interested in social processes and more interested in the intensive analysis of behavior in specific institutional and cultural settings. Yet it still remains important for the student to be aware of the major social processes to be found in all groups and all societies. The most frequent classification of the major social processes is in terms of *cooperation, competition, conflict, accommodation, assimilation, and amalgamation.* These social processes apply to both individuals and groups. We also include two other social processes which apply only to groups— *boundary maintenance and systemic linkage.*

Social processes and value judgments

In the first part of the twentieth century, scholars engaged in heated arguments over the relative importance of cooperation and competition in the natural world. Those who said that competition was the law of the universe often quoted Darwin's statement that evolution had been determined by a struggle for existence in which the strongest survived while the weaker were eliminated. Taking the name of "Social Darwinists," they argued that human life was also perfected by struggle and that philanthropy worked against the perfection of the race by allowing the unfit to survive [Simpson, 1959]. This theory was in turn attacked by Kropotkin [1925] in his book *Mutual Aid.* Kropotkin used the works of Kessler as his rationale for arguing that even the animal world was not one of unlimited conflict and that if humans were looking for biological analogies, they could find significant examples of cooperation in the realm of nature.

I obviously do not deny the struggle for existence, but I maintain that the progressive development of the animal kingdom, and especially of mankind, is favored much more by mutual support than by mutual struggle. . . . All organic beings have two essential needs: that of nutrition and of propagating the species. The former brings them to a struggle and mutual extermination, while the needs of maintaining the species bring them to approach one another and to support one another. But I am inclined to think that in the evolution of the organic world—in the progressive modification of organic beings—mutual support among individuals plays a much more important part than mutual struggle. (Statement of Kessler in *Memoirs of the St. Petersburg Society of Naturalists,* cited in Peter Kropotkin, *Mutual Aid,* Alfred A. Knopf, Inc., New York, 1925, p. 16. Used with permission of the publisher, William Heinemann, Ltd.)

Kropotkin added that while struggle exists between species, within species the dominant social process is cooperation, as is seen in flocks of birds, herds of buffalo, colonies of ants, and other group formations in the animal world. Hence he argued that those species which have survived are precisely those which have developed the process of mutual aid to the highest degree.

Today the philosophical argument about the relative merits of cooperation and conflict has somewhat subsided. Few people are interested in abstract arguments about the superiority of the cooperative or the competitive way of life. But today all face the difficulties of cooperation in a society dominated by secondary groups and the perils of conflict in an age threatened by atomic destruction. The new problems have renewed our interest in the sociological analysis of these topics. In fact, one recently founded magazine bears the title, *Journal of Conflict Resolution.*

Cooperation

Cooperation is derived from two Latin words, *co* meaning *together* and *operari* meaning *to work.* Cooperation may be found in groups as small as the dyad (group of two persons) and as large as the United Nations. Forms of cooperative endeavor in primitive societies are usually traditional and are acted out without any conscious design. Trobriand Islanders do not "decide" to fish cooperatively; they just go fishing as their fathers always did. The more technologically advanced cultures often include elaborate plans for deliberate cooperative activities. Cooperation implies a regard for the wishes of other people and is often regarded as unselfish, but people may also find that their selfish goals are best served by working together.

Deliberate primary-group cooperation

Cooperation by members of small groups is so common in every society that the life history of most individuals may be written largely in terms of their attempts to become a part of such groups and to adjust to the demands of cooperative group life. Even the most ardent individualist will find that much of life's satisfaction arises from the give and take in the family, recreation groups, and work groups. The need for cooperation in these activities is so much taken for granted that we sometimes forget that the enjoyment of a stable group experience depends largely upon one's ability to enter comfortably into cooperative relationships. The person who cannot cooperate easily and successfully is likely to be isolated and perhaps maladjusted.

The selection at the opening of the chapter compared the growth of infants in a hospital and at home. From the viewpoint of diet and sanitation, the hospital provided a near-perfect environment, while most homes are somewhat deficient in these respects. Yet the infants flourished better in the home. In sociological terms, this indicates that the effectiveness of interpersonal stimuli in a cooperative primary group is sometimes more important than the technical efficiency often found in impersonal secondary group associations. And, in addition to being emotionally more satisfying, primary-group cooperation is often technically more

Deliberate primary-group cooperation.

efficient. Zander's research [1974] shows that there are many work situations in which peo-

ple work better as team members than as individuals, and will work harder for group success than for individual achievement.

Not only is primary-group cooperation important in itself, but it is closely related to secondary-group cooperation. Most large organizations are networks of smaller primary groups in which cooperation functions on a face-to-face basis involving many highly personal relationships.

Deliberate secondary-group cooperation

When we think of cooperation, we often have in mind the kind engaged in deliberately by secondary groups. Consumer and producer cooperatives are an example. Consumer cooperatives are organizations of consumers which operate wholesale and retail stores. Producers' cooperatives are most frequently used in the marketing of agricultural produce. Groups of farmers hope to eliminate the profits made by commercial middlemen through establishing their own warehouses and selling channels. Neither consumer nor producer cooperatives try to "undersell" other business concerns; they do business at competitive prices, then distribute profits (usually called "patronage dividends") among the members in proportion to their purchases from, or sales to, the cooperative.

As is true of all types of social interaction, the success of cooperatives seems to depend to a great degree on the culture of the area. Cooperatives have flourished in the United States wherever Scandinavian immigrants were numerous [Kercher et al., 1941; Heino, 1971]. Oddly enough, the most fertile ground for cooperatives seems to be a society in which there has already been a strong development of private business. In these areas cooperatives have often survived both capitalist competition and governmental discouragement. Cooperatives in underdeveloped areas have had great difficulty despite the fact that they have often received governmental help [Hart, 1955]. In these areas the conduct of business is totally outside the experience of most of the people, and the middleman is usually an alien who is barred from participation in cooperative activity. As a result, even when the cooperative has had a government subsidy, it often has failed through corruption, mismanagement, or inability to repay loans. Cooperatives can succeed without governmental encouragement, but they rarely succeed unless the culture has familiarized the people with the practices essential to carrying on economic life in a market economy. This may explain why recent efforts to promote consumer cooperatives among ghetto poor and college students have not been very successful.

These "co-ops" are but one of many forms of large-scale cooperative activity. The desire of people to work together for common goals is expressed through governments, fraternal bodies, religious organizations, and a host of special-interest groups. Such cooperation not only involves many people in the local community but also extends to a network of organized cooperative activity involving state, regional, national, and international relationships. Problems in such cooperation include decisions as to the geographical extent of cooperation, obtaining a consensus on the ends to be pursued and the means of reaching them, conflicts with other cooperative groups, and the inevitable difficulty of reconciling the conflicting claims of labor and capital or, in this case, of the employees of co-ops who want high wages and the producers or consumers who wish to get the services of the co-op as cheaply as possible.

Another type of cooperative adjustment has been the development of regional units such as the Federal Reserve Banks, now organized in twelve regions cutting across state lines. Our need for organized cooperation across national lines has led to the organization of the United Nations, and determining the proper roles to be followed by the constituent members of that body is a major problem of our time.

Impersonal and symbiotic cooperation

The world of nature is sometimes pictured as a world of conflict. Yet the concept of universal strife is contradicted by animals who hunt in packs, by insects who work together to maintain colonies, and even by the cooperation of dissimilar organisms.

Darwin, in his description of the nexus between cats and next year's clover crop, provided the now classic illustration of the network of vital linkages which bind different organisms together. Humblebees alone, his observations disclosed, visit the red clover; other bees and insects cannot reach the nectar. But the number of humble-bees in an area depends in a great measure on the number of field mice, since these latter invade the nests of humble-bees and rob them of their food stores. Cats, in turn, are the natural enemies of mice and hence control their numbers. In areas adjacent to villages the nests of humble-bees were found to be more numerous than elsewhere owing no doubt to the number of cats there. An increase in the cat population, it may be inferred, is followed by a decrease in the number of mice thus permitting an increase in humble-bees and, consequently, a more widespread fertilization of red clover. Creatures that, to all outward appearances, are "remote in the scale of nature" are found to be linked together in a chain of relations. The deeper the analysis of the "web of life" is pushed the more meaningless becomes a word as "independent." (Amos H. Hawley, *Human Ecology, a Theory of Community Structure,* The Ronald Press Company, New York, 1950, pp. 33–34. The reference to Darwin is from *The Origin of Species.*)

This cooperative interdependence of different species or orders upon one another is known in biology as *symbiosis.* Symbiotic relationships are not planned or deliberately established; they grow, as though by accident, from the efforts of organisms to survive. A great part of human cooperation may be said to be on the symbiotic level since it unites people in a mutual interdependence although they may have made no deliberate choice to cooperate. The marketplace draws people into a network of cooperation even though each wishes only to buy or sell for personal needs. The farmer, for instance, produces for the market which gives the greatest net profit, but in this process the farmer cooperates with many people about whom he neither knows nor cares. Most of our economic life is organized on the principle of pursuing self-interest by selling one's labor or goods at the highest price obtainable. Although the goal is self-interest, the effect is to maintain a network of cooperative relationships in which people work to furnish goods and services desired by other people.

Even the dislocations of economic life may be viewed as furthering cooperation. If no one will buy a person's labor or products, their refusal encourages one to shift into some type of labor or product that people will buy. The process is so painful that such market interferences as price supports, subsidies, and unemployment insurance have become common. Nevertheless, Western society may be said to rely to a great extent on mutual aid, which is no less effective because it is motivated by individualistic concerns. The main ideological controversies are not between those who reject cooperation and those who exalt it, but between the proponents of differing types of cooperation. The classical economists believed that the most effective integration of efforts would be ensured by a laissez-faire policy allowing people to be governed entirely by their pursuit of self-interest in the marketplace. Others advocate various forms of deliberate cooperation, ranging from the consumers' cooperative to the enforced overall planning of the Soviet Union. Americans have generally followed the laissez-faire principle but have modified it by many types of cooperation undertaken deliberately either through government or through private associations.

Competition

Competition is the struggle for possession of rewards which are in limited supply—money, goods, status, power, love—anything. It may be formally defined as *the process of seeking to obtain a reward by surpassing all rivals*. It is based on the inexorable fact that not all people can ever satisfy all their desires. It flourishes even in circumstances of abundance; rivalry is still keen for top jobs during periods of full employment. Regardless of the sex ratio, we find in many societies a bitter contest within each sex for the attentions of certain partners. Competition may be personal, as when two rivals contest for election to office; or it may be impersonal, as in a civil service examination in which the contestants are not even aware of one another's identity. Whether personal or impersonal, competition is conducted according to standards which focus attention on the surpassing rather than on the elimination of rivals.

One of the current controversies is whether "affirmative action" programs, designed to increase the employment and educational opportunities of women and minority ethnic groups, decrease or increase competition. To the extent that they stimulate aspirations or persuade employers and schools to consider a larger field of applicants, they increase competition. On the other hand, if they substitute group quotas for decisions on the merits of individuals, they are restricting the competitive process [Seabury, 1972].

It often seems that American business is upholding competitive practices which are under attack from other quarters. This, however, is only one side of the story. American business also seems to be in a flight from competition even as it praises its virtues. The antitrust laws represent an effort to keep competition effective when many business people would rather modify or eliminate it. Monopoly, division of markets, price fixing, and "fair trade" laws are techniques for reducing business competition. In some instances these practices are fought by government, in others they are supported. In transportation and in such public utilities as light and telephone service, government regulation restricts competition by setting rates and assigning territories.

Competition: a culturally patterned process

While competition is present to some degree in all societies, it differs greatly in degree from society to society. The fiercely competitive Kwakiutl and the relatively noncompetitive Zuñi offer a striking contrast. The Kwakiutl work very hard to accumulate wealth which is used primarily to establish status rather than to provide material comfort. The competition for status reaches its height at the famous "potlatch," in which the chiefs and leading families vie with each other to see how much they can give away or destroy [Murdock, 1936, pp. 242–248]. A family may spend a lifetime accumulating wealth, then bankrupt themselves in a single potlatch, thereby establishing the social status of their children. Members of a family who persisted in keeping their wealth would be criticized for their unwillingness to "do anything" for their children. The Zuni, on the other hand, disdain any emphasis on the accumulation of wealth or the demonstration of individual skill. Most wealth is owned by the entire community, and it is bad form to demonstrate individual superiority of any kind. Thus the Zuñi child does not grow up believing that one should make the most money, get the highest grades, or run the fastest race.

Even such strong encouragement of competition as is found among the Kwakiutl does not mean that cooperation is completely absent. As the anthropologist Margaret Mead points out:

Nevertheless, no society is exclusively competitive or exclusively cooperative. The very existence of highly competitive groups implies cooperation within the groups. Both competitive and cooperative habits must exist within the society. There is furious competition among the Kwakiutl at the one stratum of society—among the ranking chiefs—but within the household of each chief cooperation is mandatory for the amassing of the wealth that is distributed or destroyed. (Margaret Mead, *Cooperation and Conflict among Primitive Peoples,* McGraw-Hill Book Company, New York, 1937, p. 360. Used with permission of Peter Smith Publishers.)

Far from being two mutually distinct processes, competition and cooperation overlap in various ways, while both may go on simultaneously, as is true of the group whose members cooperate with one another while the group competes with another group.

Competition in American society

In its competitive emphasis, the United States is probably closer to the Kwakiutl than to the Zuñi; yet this competition is sharply limited by many factors. Enactment of minimum wage laws works toward a situation in which people are not competing for a bare existence, and a growing emphasis on seniority as a basis of promotion means that many occupational goals cannot be reached by direct competitive efforts. In fact, the following description of the control of the competitive impulse in an American factory setting comes close to the Zuñi practice:

Worker: "There's another thing; you know the fellows give the fast workers the raspberry all the time. Work hard, try to do your best, and they don't appreciate it at all. They don't seem to figure that they are gaining anything by it. It's not only the wiremen, the soldermen don't like it either. . . . The fellows who loaf along are liked better than anybody else. Some of them take pride in turning out as little work as they can and making the boss think they're turning out a whole lot. They think it's smart. I think a lot of them have the idea that if you work fast the rate will be cut. That would mean that they would have to work faster for the same money. I've never seen our rate cut yet, so I don't know whether it would happen or not. I have heard that it has happened in some cases though . . ." (F. J. Roethlisberger and William J. Dickson, *Management and the Worker,* Harvard University Press, Cambridge, Mass., 1939, p. 418.)

Such practices modify but still do not eliminate the generally competitive pattern of American life. Athletics, politics, and business offer many competitive spectacles such as the World Series, the national presidential campaigns, and the struggle of the "independents" against the giants of the automobile industry. Americans are encouraged to "make good," and neither the advantage of wealthy parents nor the drawback of being reared on the wrong side of the tracks completely absolves them from the pressure to get into the race for success. Americans cannot rely on matchmaking parents to find a mate, and the sexual competition does not entirely cease when they are married since other persons are still potential rivals. Even religion, often held to be the integrating force in society, functions on a competitive basis as numerous denominations compete for converts. In spite of efforts to moderate or limit the struggle, the average American is enmeshed in competitive activities from the time his or her mother purchases the layette until one is buried in an expensive casket under an impressive headstone.

Effects of competition

Competition functions as one method of allocating scarce rewards. Other methods are possible. We might ration goods on some basis such as need, age, or social status. We might distribute scarce goods by lottery, or even divide them equally among all people. But each of these methods creates difficulties. Needs are highly debatable; any system of priorities will be disputed, for no group is likely to feel that another group is more deserving. Equal rewards to people who are unequal in needs, effort, or ability are certain to be disputed. Competition may be an imperfect rationing device, but it works and it eliminates a lot of arguments.

Another effect of competition is to shape the attitudes of competitors. When persons or groups compete, they normally develop unfriendly and unfavorable attitudes toward one another. Experiments have shown that when the situation is devised so that persons or groups cooperate in pursuit of a common goal, friendly attitudes are encouraged. When they meet under conditions which they consider competitive and frustrating, unfavorable attitudes and unflattering stereotypes appear [Sherif, 1958]. It has often been observed that when racial or religious groups compete, racial and religious prejudices appear and flourish [Berry, 1965, pp. 304–309]. Competition and cooperation differ sharply in the social attitudes they foster in the individual.

Competition is widely praised as a means of ensuring that each person will be stimulated to greatest achievement. This belief was confirmed some years ago by many studies which show that wherever competition is culturally encouraged, it usually increases productivity although it sometimes lowers the quality [Murphy et al., 1937, pp. 476–495]. This generalization seems to apply to organizations as well as to individuals. It is often noted that while the competition of many different religious denominations in the United States may have produced many sects and congregations too small to support their programs efficiently, this competition has also promoted a greater alertness and aggressiveness in American religious institutions. Visitors to Europe often comment on Europe's impressive but empty churches, and evidence shows that Americans attend church and participate in church activities in far higher proportion than do Europeans [Isambert, 1964; Gustaffson, 1965]. In universities, too, competition seems beneficial. A careful study of medical education concludes that competition has stimulated scientific productivity [Ben-David, 1960]. This study compares the universities of France and England, where university education was highly centralized, with those of Germany, where the development of independent regional universities led to an intense competition for scientific prestige, favoring the rapid development of new discoveries. This finding is consistent with the experience of the Russians, who found that competition between factories has increased production even though all the factories are part of the total Communist system. The Soviet Union has resurrected the profit system as a stimulus to productive efficiency, although the profits are not distributed to stockholders as they are in a capitalist system.

The stimulus of competition is, however, limited in at least three respects. First, people may decline to compete. Since competition requires that some must lose while all remain somewhat anxious and insecure, people try to protect themselves from its rigors. Business develops monopolistic practices, sets prices, and engages in collusive bidding; unions set work quotas, enforce promotion through seniority, and limit union membership; farmers want price protection; teachers want seniority salary schedules; practically every group promotes many competition-limiting arrangements.

Furthermore, many persons simply withdraw from competition whenever they lose too regularly. In singing the praises of competition, many people overlook the important fact that although competition stimulates those who win fairly often, it discourages those who nearly always lose. The slow learner in the classroom, the athletic "dub" on the playground, the adolescent who fails to draw the interest of the opposite sex—such persons usually quit trying, for the pain of repeated failure becomes unendurable. They withdraw from competition in these areas, having decided that the activity isn't worthwhile. There is even experimental evidence that repeated failures not only dampen one's willingness to compete, but may even impair one's actual ability to compete [Hurlock, 1927; Winslow, 1944; Vaughn, 1956]. It appears that repeated failures will fill people with such a sense of incompetence and such an overwhelming expectation of failure that they are unable to use their abilities to good advantage. Success or failure become self-perpetuating. There is ample experimental evidence that feelings of self-confidence and expectations of success will improve performance [Schwartz and Tangri, 1965; Coleman, 1966, pp. 319–325]. Even the expectations of other people have been found to affect one's ability to perform well [Rosenthal and Jacobson, 1968; Rist, 1970]. It is not surprising that repeated failures destroy both the willingness and the ability to compete. It

may be that for every genius whom competition has stimulated to great achievement, there are a hundred or a thousand shiftless failures whom competition has demoralized.

A second limitation is that competition seems to be stimulating in only some kinds of activity. Where the task is simple and routine, competition is followed by the greatest gains in output; as the task becomes more intricate and the quality of work more important, competition is less helpful. In intellectual tasks, not only is the production of the cooperative group greater, but their work is of higher quality than that of the group whose members are competing with one another [Deutsch, 1949].

Competition in intellectual work may have mixed results. Competition between scientists may lead to secrecy and an overlapping of effort, but it also means there is a greater chance that some scientist will make an important discovery. Large-scale cooperative research might be both stimulating and economical, but it runs the risk that in working together under direction instead of individually, some potentially valuable field of inquiry may be overlooked [Hagstrom, 1974].

A third limitation upon competition is its tendency to turn into conflict. To accede peacefully while a coveted reward is claimed by a more skillful competitor is not easy, and the rules of competition are often breached by a resort to conflict.

Conflict

The conflict process is little praised but widely practiced. It develops whenever a person or group seeks to gain a reward not by surpassing other competitors, but by preventing them from effectively competing. It is formally defined as the process of *seeking to obtain rewards by eliminating or weakening the competitors.* A murder or beating, a threat, a law passed to injure a competing group, a "gentleman's agreement" to exclude Jewish or black home buyers—these are a few of many conflict devices. In its most extreme form, conflict leads to the total annihilation of opponents as when the Romans destroyed Carthage and exterminated its inhabitants, or as when American settlers exterminated many tribes of American Indians. In less violent forms, conflict may be directed toward displacing an opponent from effective competition by getting him or her fired, getting the building inspector to condemn his or her place of business, smearing his or her reputation, or any one of many devices people use to get their competitors out of the way.

Group interest rather than personal relationships determines conflict alignments.

In recent years intellectual competition between differing schools of thought has been replaced by conflict on many university campuses. Strikes have been declared, buildings occupied, administrators held hostage, and bombs thrown in an effort to force acquiescence to the protestor's point of view. There are even a few instances where professors have led students in shouting down a campus speaker or where academic conferences were paralyzed by a faction's refusal to allow scheduled speakers to be heard [Podhoretz, 1973]. This tendency to replace brain power with lung power is one more illustration of the tendency for competition to turn into conflict.

Conflict between individuals may involve intense personal animosities, while group conflict, the type of greatest interest to sociologists, is highly impersonal. By this we mean that group loyalties and needs take precedence over individual feelings. Failure to understand this distinction often leads to the mistaken assumption that peace between nations is simply the result of good feeling between the individuals who compose the nations. Many Norwegians were shocked to see that some German children whom they cared for as refugees after World War I repaid their generosity by returning as German conquerors in World War II. Actually the apparent ingratitude should not have been a surprise since the German invasion of Norway was the result of conflict between nations in which individual feelings were irrelevant. Group interests rather than personal relationships determine conflict alignments, as is shown by the speed with which our German and Japanese enemies in World War II became our allies when the "cold war" with the Soviet Union began, and by the waning of American support for Israel after the Arab nations declared an oil embargo in 1973. Friendships across boundary lines may help to promote joint activities, but it is a mistake to regard personal relationships as the solution to problems of world peace. Individuals usually find their role in group conflict by reference to the groups to which they belong. When conflict breaks out—a war, a strike, a boycott, a legislative battle—the individual either fights for his or her group or is branded as a traitor. In such a situation, feelings about friends on the other side have less weight than obligations to group.

The cumulative nature of conflict

Once begun, the conflict process is hard to stop. Since each aggressive act inspires a still more hostile retaliation, the conflict process tends to grow more bitter as it proceeds. Grievances are told and retold within each group and hostile attitudes are intensified. Each group develops a set of moral sanctions which justify a chain of even more savage retaliations.

The atrocities in conflict are often mistakenly attributed to the sadism or brutality of the individuals who commit them. Yet most of the atrocities in group conflict are committed by ordinary people in an extraordinary situation. The conflict process often places people in roles where they *must* be brutal. Steinbeck's *The Moon is Down* [1942] pictures an intelligent, humane German commander of forces occupying a Norwegian town, who is forced into brutal acts of reprisal to keep the town under control. In guerrilla warfare, where it is often difficult to tell enemies from noncombatants, as in Vietnam, the temptation is to shoot anyone who *might* be an enemy. Under some battle conditions prisoners who can't be cared for must be slaughtered. In an earlier era of labor-management warfare, the union would not allow strikebreakers to "lose" the strike for them, while management would not allow strikers to close down the plant. Each, in fulfilling his role, was forced into acts of brutality and violence.

But the extremes of conflict cannot be understood unless we recognize that the individual, committing the most indescribable acts of brutality, is supported by the group. The act is seen, not as wanton inhumanity, but as a moral necessity. During the range wars of the American West, the cattlemen who harassed, threatened, burned out, and in some cases murdered the settlers did not see themselves as greedy tyrants, withholding land from its legal claimants; they saw themselves as embattled patriots who had fought Indians, drought, and plague to build up a country and a way of life which a horde of greedy scum and conniving politicians wished to steal from them [Dale, 1930, chap. 9; Wellman, 1939, chaps. 35 and 36; Smith, 1967; Michener, 1974, chap. 10]. To understand why normal people can commit atrocities in conflict, we must understand how the group provides the sense of righteousness which sanctions such actions.

Conflict defines issues

Until the Supreme Court outlawed racial segregation in the public schools, there was much talk about brotherhood but no real decision as to whether black people were to have equal rights in American society. Since the Supreme Court decision, conflict has developed in many formerly peaceful areas and has increased the social distance between whites and blacks. The issue can no longer be buried under platitudinous talk; conflict forces us to face issues and make decisions. The immediate effect of the conflict unleashed by the court decision may have been to shatter many peaceful relationships. The long-run effect, sociologists suspect, will be to reduce both discrimination and prejudice and eventually increase cooperative relationships between whites and blacks in our society.

In this respect group conflict may be compared to the effect of fever in the human body—costly and dangerous, but calling attention to deep-seated tensions which must be relieved if health is to be maintained. Just as the treatment of fever goes beyond symptoms to the cause of the difficulty, so the effective handling of conflict goes beyond merely maintaining order and seeks to treat the basic disturbance. Any tendency to ignore controversial issues or to paper over differences might be compared to the tendency to ignore such symptoms of ill health.

Conflict forces a facing of social issues and polarizes our attitudes towards them. The moderates are pushed, distrusted, and attacked by both sides and eventually forced to make a choice. The end result of the conflict is that the issues are resolved, at least for a time, in a fairly definite manner. The fact that the moderate is forced to take a definite position means that one must assume responsibility instead of simply standing on the sidelines and deploring violence. At the end of the Middle Ages when people were being slaughtered because of religious differences, the moderates who piously deplored fanaticism were driven to a definite program—the separation of church and state—so that religious differences might be tolerated. In present racial controversies the moderate is pushed into active support of integration because of a commitment to orderly legal processes. One sociologist cites an example arising from the school desegregation conflict in Little Rock, Arkansas:

A distinguished religious leader from that community said to me this summer, "You know, while it was bad, maybe it was not a total loss. There is much more intelligent understanding of the responsibilities of citizenship now. People of the moderate or middle group have come to realize that they do not have the privilege of sitting on the sidelines and letting the radicals at the two ends determine the outcomes. They had to learn that ultimately they had to get in there and get their hands dirty with the problem. They had to see that they were being made the testing place for the whole South, and that when the chips were down they had to choose between the law and chaos. "Maybe," he said, "we had to learn that, and it took the crisis to teach it to us." (Dan W. Dodson, "The Creative Role of Conflict Re-examined," *Journal of Intergroup Relations*, 1:5–12, Winter, 1959–1960.)

The disintegrative effects of conflict

Conflict disrupts social unity. Conflict is a highly disturbing way of settling issues. Strikes may idle thousands of people and acres of costly machinery; marital conflicts wreck many families; racial and religious conflicts may prevent communities from facing their problems in a united spirit. As the ultimate example, atomic war now threatens the total destruction of humanity. Even when conflict achieves a new equilibrium, the price may be very great. The Thirty Years' War, 1618 to 1648, established the principle of religious toleration among German states, but it also reduced the German population by at least one-third, and much of the cultivated land became wilderness.

Internal conflict disrupts group unity. Conflict within a group makes it hard for members to agree on group goals or to cooperate in pursuit

of them. At any moment, in several of our states, one of the major political parties is split into warring factions, giving the other party a fine chance to win the next election. It was often claimed that France fell to Germany so easily in 1940 because the French people were so divided into conflicting factions that they were unable to unite against the enemy. Hitler confidently expected that the United States, with its heterogeneous population, would also be so riven with internal conflicts as to be unable to wage a united battle. This was one of his more costly misjudgments!

The integrative effects of conflict

Internal conflicts are sometimes ultimately integrative. A limited amount of internal conflict may indirectly contribute to group interaction. Interests and viewpoints within a group shift from time to time; new policies and new leadership may be needed. An occasional contest within a group may keep its leadership alert and its policies up to date, whereas a suppression of internal conflicts may allow disastrous lags and explosive discontents to accumulate. Coser analyzes the role of conflict in promoting unity as follows:

In loosely structured groups and open societies, conflict, which aims at a resolution of tension between antagonists, is likely to have stabilizing and integrative functions for the relationship. By permitting immediate and direct expression of rival claims, such social systems are able to readjust their structures by eliminating the sources of dissatisfaction. The multiple conflicts which they experience may serve to eliminate the causes for dissociation and to reestablish unity. These systems avail themselves, through the toleration and institutionalization of conflict, of an important stabilizing mechanism. (Lewis A. Coser, *The Functions of Social Conflict*, The Free Press of Glencoe, Ill., Chicago, 1956, p. 153.)

External conflict tends to integrate the group. Conflict with another group provides the members with an external outlet for their hostilities and resentments, and thus siphons off a lot of internal tensions. For example, the Protestant-Catholic conflicts in Northern Ireland have reduced the "generation gap" between adolescents and adults [Jenvey, 1972]. Internal dissension is a common reason for promoting external conflicts, which will integrate the group [Kriesberg, 1973, pp. 258–260]. External conflict compels each group member either to cooperate loyally or to get out. Simmel, a very perceptive early analyst of social conflict, defines the alternatives in these words:

If a political party which unifies many different directions of interest is pushed into a decisive and one-sided position of conflict, an occasion for secession results. In such situations, there are only two alternatives—either to forget internal counter currents or to bring them to unadulterated expression by expelling certain members. . . . The group in a state of peace can permit antagonistic members within it to live with one another in an undecided situation because each of them can go his own way and avoid collisions. A state of conflict, however, pulls the members so tightly together and subjects them to such a uniform impulse that they must completely get along with or completely repel one another. This is the reason why war with the outside is sometimes the last chance for a state ridden with inner antagonisms to overcome these antagonisms, or else to break up definitely. (Georg Simmel, *Conflict,* tr. by Reinhard Bendix, The Free Press of Glencoe, Ill., Chicago, 1955, pp. 92–93. Used with permission of the Macmillan Company.)

External conflict also unifies the group through the imposition and acceptance of tighter controls than are normally accepted. The nation at war allows its business life to be completely directed toward national objectives in a way that would be unendurable in time of peace. The labor union gives "no-strike" pledges and accepts work rules which it would resist in peacetime. All groups tend to build bureaucratic structures and to centralize authority when faced by the need to organize resistance to an enemy.

While external conflict separates a group

from its enemies, it also promotes federations or alliances with other groups. The phrase, "politics makes strange bedfellows," expresses the tendency to seek out allies in times of conflict even though they might be unacceptable in time of peace.

Effects of conflict

INTEGRATIVE EFFECTS

Defines issues
Leads to a resolution of issues
Increases group cohesion
Leads to alliances with other groups
Keeps groups alert to members' interests

DISINTEGRATIVE EFFECTS

Increases bitterness
Leads to destruction and bloodshed
Leads to intergroup tension
Disrupts normal channels of cooperation
Diverts members' attention from group objectives

Conflict sometimes settles issues. Our disdain for communism did not keep us from being effective allies with Russia in World War II; when the cold war developed, our rapid rapprochement with Germany and Japan showed that alliance is based on mutual interest, not mutual affection. Wars and threats of war have unquestionably encouraged the growth of

Internal conflict disrupts group unity.

political states and governmental institutions from the earliest tribal alliance to the United Nations. War forces a nation into coordinated activity, stimulates inventions, and inspires heroic sacrifices. Wars have settled issues: Through war the Italian peninsula became a unified nation; the Mexican War ended controversy over American colonization of the Southwest; World War II appears to have ended efforts for territorial expansion of Japan and Germany. By settling issues, wars often clear the way for cooperative action. Conflict thus performs an associative as well as a divisive function and may be considered in some ways an integrative factor in social life.

Conflict as the basic social process—functionalist versus conflict theory. Some social theorists see conflict as the *basic* social process. A number of earlier theorists—Marx, Novicow, Gumplowitz, Ratzenhofer, and others [Sorokin, 1928, pp. 314–316, 480–487, 523–549, 643] saw society in terms of incessant social conflict. After several decades of neglect, conflict theory has again risen to prominence in social thought (see Chapter 4, pages 76–78). Modern conflict theorists, most of them following Marxian theory, see society not as a network of cooperating groups but as a battlefield of conflicting groups and classes [Kerr, 1954; Dahrendorf, 1964; Coser, 1968; Howard, 1970a].

Orthodox "functionalist" sociologists perceive society as a network of cooperating groups, sharing many common interests and united by a consensus upon certain basic values. Conflict sociologists see society as a constant battle between conflicting groups and classes with opposing interests which are imperfectly papered over by a contrived and deceptive "consensus" upon basic values. That is, the lower classes are deluded into imagining that their interests and values are not in conflict with those of the dominant classes. Functionalists see the normal state of society as one of relative cooperative harmony which occasionally breaks down into conflict. Conflict theorists see the normal state of society as one of continuous conflict between groups and classes, while the interludes of calm are simply periods during which the dominant class gets its way with no effective opposition. Conflict theory is currently quite fashionable in sociology (and other social sciences), and some textbooks are currently written with a conflict approach [Anderson, 1971; Lejeune, 1973].

Considerable research in recent years has used the conflict approach. For example, a study of Italian peasant communities [Lopreato and Salzman, 1968] argues that it is a mistake to assume that the prevailing pattern is one of harmony. Rather than studying these communities according to a consensus model emphasizing social integration, attachment to the soil, personal contentment, and restraint, Lopreato and Salzman argue that one could just as well use a conflict model emphasizing social conflict, dislike of the land, and jealousies and resentments between individuals. They see conflict—sometimes open and active and sometimes hidden and temporarily dormant—as a normal aspect of social interaction.

It should be noted that the theorists who see conflict as the basic social process are not necessarily either "right" or "wrong". Theirs is simply one of the possible ways of viewing society and social change. Just as international relations can be viewed either as a state of war interrupted by intervals of peace or as a state of peace interrupted by intervals of war, so can society be viewed either as in a condition of cooperation which occasionally erupts into conflict or as in a condition of conflict which occasionally is quiescent. It is not yet clear whether the conflict approach is destined to become the dominant frame of reference in sociology, or will remain only one of several viewpoints.

Alternatives to conflict

The conflict process may fulfill useful functions, but at so great a cost that people often seek to avoid it. Conflict is often avoided through some form of three other processes, *accommodation, assimilation,* and *amalgamation*.

Accommodation

It really threw me when my folks got a divorce right after I was graduated. I never thought much about my parents' love life; I guess I just took them for granted. Our home always seemed to me about like most others. At graduation, they came and beamed, gave me graduation gifts, met my friends, and all that. Then Dad took me aside and said that he and Mom were calling it quits. He said that they had bugged each other for years but had stuck it out to give me a proper home. Now that I would be on my own, they were going to separate.

Looking back on it now, I can remember little things that they let slip, but at the time I never noticed anything. They kept it pretty well covered up.

The above story, adapted from a student's life history in the authors' files, is an example of accommodation, a *process of developing temporary working agreements between conflicting individuals or groups.* It develops when persons or groups find it necessary to work together despite their hostilities and differences. Accommodation may be short-lived, or it may persist for centuries. No real settlement of issues is reached; each group retains its own goals and viewpoints, but arrives at an "agreement to disagree" without fighting and perhaps to resume peaceful interaction. It is what Sumner [1907] called "antagonistic cooperation." The accommodation process obviously affects people's attitudes and behavior. Accommodation takes a number of forms. Some are deliberately planned and formally negotiated; others arise as unplanned products of group interaction.

Displacement. Displacement is the process of suspending one conflict by replacing it with another. A classic example is the use of war or the threat of war to end internal conflicts and bring national unity. It is a standard stratagem of dictators and not unknown among democracies.

Finding a scapegoat is a favorite displacement technique. The term refers to an ancient Hebrew ceremony in which the sins of the people were symbolically heaped upon a goat which was driven into the wilderness. Unpopular minorities often become scapegoats. Anti-Semitism has long been used to deflect criticism and to unite conflicting groups in blaming Jews for all the ills of the society. In the newly independent countries, all the nation's problems may be blamed upon the remaining "colonial influences." The true powers and actions of the scapegoat are of little consequence; what matters is that a ruling group may be able to avert a possible attack upon itself by diverting popular hostility to the scapegoat.

Institutionalized release of hostility. In many societies there are some institutionalized provisions for release of hostilities and tensions. Some primitive tribes regulated combat in a manner designed to express aggression, maintain "honor," and yet avoid destructive warfare. Warner [1931] describes an elaborate pattern of ritualistic warfare wherein Murngin tribes in Australia went through involved ceremonial combat in which, though nobody actually got hurt, a lot of hostility could be worked off. Then these rituals closed with a joint ceremonial dance expressing the renewed union and solidarity of the tribes. The Royal Copenhagen Porcelain Works, instead of junking the imperfect pieces, takes them to the Tivoli amusement park, where it collects a fee from people who are willing to pay for the privilege of smashing the rejects. It seems that "busting things up" serves to release hostility and tension.

Perhaps our spectator sports, especially the contact sports like football, hockey, boxing, and wrestling would be examples of opportunities for the institutionalized release of hostility in our society. Ceremonials and feast days, orgies and religious experiences of various kinds may also serve to release tensions or provide catharsis for hostilities and thus ease the pressures toward conflict. Karl Marx was quite correct in holding that believers in a biblical devil, heaven, and Christian forgiveness would be slow to join in class warfare.

Superordination. In some families one member totally and ruthlessly dominates the others. Some group conflicts end in the total defeat and submission of one group to the other. A war may "end" with the defeated people continuing resistance through guerrilla warfare, assassination, sabotage, and noncooperation, thus continuing the conflict. Or they may accept defeat, submit, and make the best of it, as did Germany and Japan after World War II.

Superordination is likely to be accepted only when the parties are so unequal in power that resistance seems useless or impossible. When the subordinate group gains more power, the superordinate group must either relax its rule or risk a revolt. As Germany and Japan recovered from wartime devastation, the United States relaxed its rule rather than face growing resistance, while Russia's stern rule over conquered peoples provoked revolts in East Berlin, Hungary, and Poland, and seething resentment throughout her "colonies."

Conflict between two parties may sometimes be ended by their forced submission to a third party. History is crowded with instances. After Athens and Sparta had exhausted themselves, Macedonia conquered both. Only English rule brought peace between the Scottish clans. Most empires grew by picking off neighbors who were fighting among themselves.

Today the collapse of empires and the end of colonial rule in many areas is followed by the reappearance of local conflicts. The Near East peoples resumed ancient conflicts after the disintegration of the Ottoman (Turkish) Empire. Revolts, conflicts, and tribal war have plagued many African states since their independence. It is uncertain how soon stable na-

tional governments will be possible for such areas.

Compromise. When all the parties are powerful enough so that none of them relish the prospect of conflict, they may compromise their differences. Compromise is a form of accommodation in which each party accepts less than its full goal in order to avoid or end conflict. Each normally makes concessions according to its relative power, with the more powerful party making the fewer concessions.

Since a compromise leaves all parties somewhat dissatisfied, the compromise agreements are likely to be honored only so long as the respective power balance remains unchanged. As soon as either group gains in respective power, it is likely to press for a revision of the compromise, threatening renewed conflict if its demands are refused. During prosperous times, when the employer can scarcely fill the orders, the union will press for a more favorable contract; during a recession, when orders are fewer and stockrooms are full, the employer seizes the strategic moment to seek the revisions desired. Politics may be seen as a continual round of shifting power positions and changing compromises. Politicians are often accused of dishonesty because of their compromising; yet without such compromises between the conflicting demands of many voting groups, democracy would become chaos.

Frequently the conflict has been so bitter and feelings so hostile that the parties are unable to reach a compromise. Several third-party techniques are often helpful in breaking such deadlocks.

Third-party roles in compromise. The techniques of conciliation, mediation, and arbitration use the services of a third party to help reach a settlement [Kriesberg, 1973, pp. 214–216, 226–231]. Mediation and conciliation are essentially the same, with the third party encouraging the disputants to keep talking, suggesting solutions, and using persuasion. In arbitration, a third party hears their arguments and makes a decision, knowing that the contestants have already agreed to accept it. The third party may offer suggestions which the disputants could not offer without losing face, and may be able to find new approaches to end a deadlock. Even if given the power of arbitration, success depends mainly on the arbitrator's ability to gauge the relative power positions and suggest settlements fairly close to what might be obtained through all-out conflict [Kriesberg, 1973, pp. 223–226].

Toleration. In some conflicts victory is either impossible or unbearably costly, and compromise is unendurable; some values may be too deeply cherished to compromise. In these circumstances the participants sometimes discover that agreement may not be absolutely necessary. In toleration, people accept each other's right to differ without demanding a settlement. Toleration is an agreement to disagree peaceably. Religious conflict is a classic example of this situation. In Europe at the time of the Reformation, both Protestants and Catholics were positive that they had the "true" version of the Christian faith which should be accepted by all. Neither group was willing to compromise, and in spite of severe conflict, neither group could destroy the other. Adjustment has been made on the basis of toleration; each church ceases to persecute other churches while continuing to hold that these other churches are in error.

Why was religious toleration so long in developing? Partly because toleration requires a frame of mind in which people are willing to grant others the right to be different; ethnocentrism is the enemy of toleration. Furthermore, toleration is possible only for those matters on which agreement is not absolutely necessary. As long as church and state were combined, rejection of the established church automatically became treason to the state; not until their separation could one worship as one pleased and still be a loyal citizen. Catholic and Protestant neighbors may disagree on many religious questions without the disagreement

impairing their interaction as neighbors, friends, or workers. If they intermarry, some religious differences may still be open to toleration, but their interaction as husband and wife will absolutely require agreement upon a number of other issues. Our rather wide use of toleration today depends not only upon a considerable readiness to tolerate differences but also upon a social structure in which many areas of peaceful interaction are available to groups which are in wide and bitter disagreement in other matters.

Assimilation. Whenever groups meet, some mutual interchange or diffusion of culture takes place. Even groups who strenuously seek to prevent such diffusion, such as the modern Amish or the ancient Hebrews, do not fully succeed in protecting their culture from all cultural interchange. The Old Testament is filled with exhortations to avoid contact with the "heathen" peoples, and the consequences of failure to heed this warning, as in the story of Samson.

This process of *mutual cultural diffusion through which persons and groups come to share a common culture* is called *assimilation.* It is always a two-way process with each group contributing varying proportions of the eventual blend, depending upon respective group size, prestige, and other factors.

The assimilation process is nicely illustrated in the Americanization of our European immigrants. Arriving in great numbers between 1850 and 1913, many of them settled in immigrant colonies in the Northern cities. Within these "ethnic colonies"—Little Italy, Little Poland, and so on—they practiced much of their native European culture while absorbing some of the American culture. The immigrant parents often sought to transmit their European culture to their children, while the children generally sought to become American as rapidly as possible. These children very often rejected the "old world" patterns as bluntly and emphatically as possible. This conflict often caused parental anguish, family disorganization, and loss of parental control, so that many second-generation immigrants became confused, rebellious, and delinquent. As the third generation matured, the assimilation difficulties generally subsided; Americanization became fairly complete, and the ethnic colony disappeared as the descendants scattered over city and suburb [Thomas and Znaniecki, 1927].

The third and following generations are now secure, and can afford to remember their ethnic history. Thus there is a "third-generation return," in which these fully assimilated Americans recall with pride their ethnic heritage and join in recording and preserving some parts of it [Hansen, 1952; Bender and Kagiwada, 1968].

Assimilation reduces group conflicts by blending differing groups into larger, culturally homogeneous groups. The bitter riots against the Irish and the discriminations against the Scandinavians in the United States [Higham, 1955] have disappeared as assimilation has erased the group differences and blurred the sense of separate group identity. Anything which binds people into a larger group will tend to reduce rivalry and conflict between them. This is strikingly illustrated by an experiment which involved the formation of different groupings at a summer camp [Sherif and Sherif, 1953]. The boys were all from the same community and were similar in religion, social-class status, age, and national background. For the first experimental period ("integrative") they were treated as a single group, and they showed no signs of incipient social conflict. In the second experimental ("segregative") period they were divided into two groups who were housed separately and encouraged to develop separate programs of activities. The groups took the names of "Red Devils" and "Bull Dogs." Group antagonisms quickly developed, and physical violence between the groups reached the point where it had to be suppressed by the adult leaders.

This experiment is often taken to indicate that conflict tends to develop whenever group identity is recognizable. Perhaps a better interpretation is that conflict and separation are likely whenever differences are emphasized. Japanese-Americans, by contrast, are a group which have become highly assimilated although physical differences are easily recognizable. Their acceptance of American middle-class values and their dispersion away from ethnic enclaves have operated to make their cultural similarity to other Americans more important than their physical differences.

Cultural assimilation removes many of the stimuli for conflict even when recognizable physical differences are present. Conversely, as in the case of Catholics and Protestants in Northern Ireland, physical similarity will not insure peace when groups cherish deep-seated cultural antagonisms exacerbated by present clashes of economic and political interests [Holden, 1969; Elmen, 1971].

Marginality. The concept of *marginality* was first developed by Park in the course of his study of the assimilation process. He defined the *marginal man* as "a cultural hybrid, a man living and sharing intimately in the cultural life and traditions of two distinct peoples. . . . He was a man on the margin of two cultures and two societies . . ." [1928, p. 892]. The second-generation immigrant is the classic example, described in detail in Stonequist's *The Marginal Man* [1937]. In 1940, Cuber suggested extending the term to cover any people "who occupy a peripheral role between any two differentiated but largely exclusive institutions, culture complexes or other cultural segments" [1940, p. 58]. Shibutani further defined the concept in 1961 in saying that "some men are marginal in that they stand on the border between two or more social worlds, but are not accepted as full participants in either" [1961, p. 275]. A great many people—the immigrant, those who are rapidly mobile in status, the children of overseas American personnel, the children born of a racial or ethnic intermarriage, the converts to (or from) a dogmatic religious faith—are to some degree marginal.

Marginality generally carries feelings of confusion and anxiety, greater possibilities of deviation from group norms, and perhaps an "identity crisis" for the individual. In a society with numerous subcultures, practically everyone is a core member of some subcultures while marginal to some others [Arnold, 1970]. Marginality in any kind or degree is a measure of incomplete assimilation.

Amalgamation.

Amalgamation is the biological interbreeding of two groups until they have become one. Thus ended the conflicts of the Anglo-Saxons with the Norman invaders of England. When it is a limited and disapproved interbreeding between racial groups, it is called *miscegenation,* a value-laden word implying an improper mixing of genes. Whenever racial or ethnic groups meet, some degree of "miscegenation" nearly always follows, often with painful consequences for the persons born from these unions. An incomplete amalgamation generally creates a status system where status is measured by blood "purity" as in Central America and parts of South America, where descent carries status value. When amalgamation becomes wholesale, the separate groups and their attendant group conflicts soon disappear.

Boundary maintenance

The importance of assimilation and amalgamation rests primarily in their elimination of boundary lines as two groups, formerly distinct, assume a common identity. Such boundary lines are a major aspect of social life, and we devote a great deal of energy to their establishment, maintenance, and modification. Questions such as the following are concerned with boundaries: Can a true believer attend services in another church? Can a college athlete play semiprofessional baseball during the summer? Should foreign students be allowed to pursue an occupation in the United States? Should women be admitted to the "men's club"? Should students be admitted or allowed to vote in the departmental faculty meeting? Should women be ordained ministers? Is racial integration really desirable?

Sometimes existing boundary devices may be challenged.

Any answer to these and similar questions will either enlarge or restrict the membership of specific social groups and hence is a "boundary line" type of issue. National states indicate their territorial boundaries by markers, fences, and other evidence of the extent of their claims. Social groups without territorial limits face the necessity of establishing some type of social boundary lines which will separate their members from the rest of the society. For many groups a language, dialect, or specialized argot serves as a boundary which separates the members from outsiders: "If he doesn't speak our language, he certainly can't be one of us." Uniforms are also a device for separating members of one group from the rest of society, a practice found among clergy, police officers, nurses, and soldiers, among others. Sometimes formal identifying insignia such as the Indian caste marks are utilized. Frequently there is no overt indication of group membership, and only a subtle sense of "belonging," related to group standards of conduct, is all that separates the in-group from the outsiders.

Groups need not only to establish definite boundaries but also to convince their members that the boundaries are important. Ethnocentrism usually develops and assists in this task by reassuring us about the virtue of our group and the shortcomings of others. Intense nationalistic indoctrination may build a patriotism which says that any weakening of national sovereignty through international agreements would be fatal. Or a religious body may seek to convince its members that it is the only true church. On a less formal basis, small suburbs may support a myth about the vices and high taxes of the big city as compared with the virtue and low cost of the suburb—a myth which has increasingly little basis in fact.

Loyalty to group boundaries is supported by sanctions which reward those loyal to the group, punish members who deviate from group boundary norms, and keep out those the group wishes to exclude. Rewards may include access to employment through union membership, the prestige of membership in an exclusive club, the congenial companionship of a friendship clique, and many others. Punishments, or negative sanctions, consist largely of the denial of the rewards of group membership. One cannot hold certain jobs without joining the union; one who persists in bringing "inappropriate" guests to the club may be asked to resign; a friend who betrays confidences soon receives none.

People wishing to hurdle the boundaries into a group often seek to lower the boundaries, while those already safely inside are intent upon maintaining them. Unions whose apprenticeships have been open only to sons and relatives of members have bitterly resisted pressure to open apprenticeships to blacks [Good, 1972]. The power of exclusion is one of the rewards of group membership. By keeping others out, we assert our own superior status as social arbiters and emphasize the gulf which separates us from those of less esteem. Whatever the basis used for acceptance or rejection, it quickly becomes a trait which distinguishes one group from another. Those rejected by the dominant group establish their own sense of identity and utilize their own epithets to stigmatize those who have excluded them. Thus to the gentile the Jew is a "kike" or a "yid," but the Jew may retaliate by referring to gentiles as "goy" or "shkotzim" or may use uncomplimentary phrases like "shicker as a goy" (drunk as a gentile). Such epithets set boundaries, since they convey a notion of relative status as well as of difference.

Social boundary lines are constantly shifting and often complex. Is a factory worker with a home in the suburbs lower class or middle class? If a man leaves Judaism for Presbyterianism, is he still regarded as Jewish? Is the Filipino a Westerner or an Asiatic? Is the black army officer defined in terms of military rank or racial status? These and countless similar boundary definitions are constantly being reformulated as groups strive to increase their rewards, avoid penalties, and place themselves in a favorable position. Sometimes boundary determination is accomplished through formal means, as in the case of naturalization requirements or initiation ceremonies. In other cases there is a more informal process of acceptance and rejection which indicates group boundary lines in terms which are definite even though not defined in written documents. Sometimes the existing boundary maintenance devices may be challenged. Many current radicals consider it "oppressive" to demand the cultivation of middle-class speech and conduct norms as the price of admission into the middle class [Kampf, 1970]. Boundary maintenance devices may change, but boundary establishment and modification is a continuous social process [Mack, 1965].

Systemic linkage

Just as nations need both territorial limits and international trade, so other groups which require boundaries also need some type of linkage with the rest of society. The absence of boundaries means that the group is swamped by the larger society, but the absence of relationship with other groups leads to isolation, stultification, lack of growth, and the attempt to perform functions for which the group itself is not fitted. Even bitterly hostile primitive tribes have sometimes recognized this fact by instituting a system of "silent barter" with their enemies. Since personal relationships were too bitter, no face-to-face contact took place, but each group would leave trade articles at a mutually understood spot and pick up the articles left by the other tribe.

Systemic linkage is defined by Loomis [1961, p. 16] as "the process whereby the elements of at least two social systems come to be articulated so that in some ways and on some occasions they may be viewed as a single system." Even the Amish, a relatively isolated group, are linked to the rest of society by education, agricultural marketing, and the payment of taxes. For other groups the linkages are usually far more numerous. The rural village is linked to the urban metropolis by the market economy, by an educational system which sends teachers into the community and takes advanced students out, by churches and lodges which maintain contact with parent organizations, and by many other links. Like the Amish, some groups try to reduce systemic linkage to the minimum because they see in it a threat to boundary maintenance. Other groups promote such linkage deliberately, such as the church which belongs to an ecumenical organization, the labor union which sends a lobbyist to the capital, and the chamber of commerce which looks for new markets for local industries. The methods vary, but even as groups seek to protect their separate identity by boundary maintenance, they are also impelled to seek links by which they can establish a relationship to the rest of society.

Boundary maintenance and systemic linkage use all the other social processes we have described and in this sense are in a different category. They are included in this chapter because the operation of conflict, cooperation, accommodation, assimilation, and amalgamation always influences both the boundaries which separate us and the links by which we are connected to others.

Summary

Earlier scholars argued over the inherent superiority of competition, cooperation, or conflict; sociologists today study the manner in which these and other social processes contribute to social life. These processes are found in all societies, although there is great variation in emphasis. *Cooperation* may be personal or impersonal, deliberate or symbiotic in character. Primary groups demand highly personalized cooperation; secondary-group cooperation is found in many organized social groups as well as in a network of economic relationships which use the motive of individual gain to draw men into essentially cooperative activities.

Competition serves the function of allocating scarce rewards among the competitors. It has the additional function of stimulating both individual and group activity in a manner to increase the total productivity of the competitors, but it also discourages the further efforts of those who regularly fail. Experimental studies show that both cooperation and competition are related to the values of the culture. When the culture legitimizes competition, a competitive system often, but not always, increases the rate of productive activity while quality of work often suffers. Competition is unstable and frequently yields either to cooperation or to conflict.

Conflict develops when attention shifts from the contest itself to an effort to eliminate rivals. Group conflict may take place even when the members of the groups involved lack any personal animosity toward members of the opposing factions. Social conflict is frequently costly and disruptive, but it also has integrative functions. Conflict helps to define issues and bring about a new equilibrium of contending forces. Conflict between groups promotes unity within each group as members unite against the common enemy, and group conflict may lead to expanding alliances with other groups. Some sociologists see conflict as the basic social process and the normal state of society, and see other processes as devices to obscure the reality of conflict.

Conflict may be ended in several ways. Conflicts may be *displaced* and the aggression directed at a new enemy. Conflicts may sometimes be ended or avoided through an *institutionalized release* of hostilities and aggressions through mock combat, festival and orgy, and other emotional outlets. Conflicts may be relieved, at least temporarily, through *accommodation,* which takes several forms. *Superordination* consists in establishing uncontested rule over a weaker group. *Compromise* involves a limited surrender by all groups in order to end or avoid conflict. *Conciliators, mediators,* and *arbitrators* often aid in arranging compromises. Where compromise is unacceptable yet agreement not absolutely necessary, groups may use *toleration* as an alternative to conflict. Finally, when two groups have become *assimilated,* so that they share a common culture and common goals, they normally disappear as separate groups unless some visible identification remains as a focus for conflict. *Marginality* applies to individuals who participate to some extent in two contrasting groups or cultures without being completely identified with either. *Amalgamation* is a biological fusion between two groups resulting in the elimination of distinctive physical characteristics.

Boundary maintenance is the process of preserving lines of distinction between groups and applies to every action which marks one either "in" or "out" of a specific group. *Systemic linkage* denotes the process by which groups avoid isolation while maintaining their separate identities.

Questions and projects

1. Are cooperation, competition, and conflict natural, instinctive, or automatic human responses, or must they be culturally acquired?
2. Why do you think the consumer cooperative has had such limited success in the United States? Will it succeed among the urban poor?
3. What examples of impersonal or symbiotic cooperation can be observed on the campus?
4. Discuss this proposition: "It is human nature to want more than others; competition is therefore firmly rooted in human instinct."
5. Under what conditions is competition an encouragement? When does it inhibit effort?
6. Why does competition often turn into conflict? Does social conflict always involve physical violence?
7. To what extent do friendly personal relations and mutual understanding serve to prevent conflict?
8. How is knowledge of the effects of conflict upon group solidarity sometimes used in international relations? In labor-management relations?
9. When homesteaders invaded the land of the cattlemen, conflict developed. Was there any practical possibility of avoiding that conflict?
10. Do decent and humane people ever take part in atrocities? Why? How would most Americans, had they been socialized in Germany, have felt about the massacre of the Jews?
11. Why is accommodation always an unstable arrangement? What happens when the power balance shifts?
12. Why could toleration not have been used to avoid the Civil War, the cold war, or present racial conflicts?
13. What would be the problems or difficulties in solving the present racial crisis by amalgamation?
14. What boundary lines are maintained between those associated with a college and other resi-

dents of the local community? What types of systemic linkage exist between them?

15. What effect will the modernization of the garb of Roman Catholic nuns have on their group cohesion? Would the same comments apply to distinctive uniforms for students in girls' schools?

16. Find an example of a major disagreement on the campus or in a community. Trace the history of this controversy to the achievement of some accommodation pattern which resolved the cri-

sis. What type of accommodation developed?

17. Take an issue, such as tariffs, disarmament, racism, or sexism, and analyze the extent to which there is a clear-cut "class interest conflict" on that issue; that is, to what extent do the members of the "capitalist class" share a common interest position, in opposition to that held by virtually all members of the "working class"? To what extent does the alignment according to shared interests cut across class lines?

Suggested readings

ALCOCK, JAMES E.: "Cooperation, Competition and the Effects of Time Pressure in Canada and India," *Journal of Conflict Resolution*, 18:171–178, June, 1974. Western and Eastern time perspectives in relation to social processes.

BENDER, EUGENE L., AND GEORGE KAGIWADA: "Hansen's Law of Third-generation Return and the Study of American Religio-Ethnic Groups," *Phylon*, 29:360–370, Winter, 1960. Describes the tendency of the third generation to rediscover pride and interest in the ancestral culture.

BERRY, BREWTON: *Race and Ethnic Relations*, Houghton Mifflin Company, Boston, 1965. A very readable textbook in race relations using a social-process approach and with a good treatment of amalgamation and assimilation.

BOGARDUS, EMORY S.: "The Long Trail of Cooperation," *Sociology and Social Research*, 31:54–62, September 1946. A natural history of the process of cooperation.

*COSER, LEWIS A.: *The Functions of Social Conflict*, The Free Press of Glencoe, Ill., Chicago, 1956. A study of the conflict process by a sociologist who believes it has functional values.

*GORDON, MILTON M.: *Assimilation in American Life*, Oxford University Press, Fair Lawn, N.J., 1964. A sociological analysis of recent trends in the assimilation process together with a typography of various categories of assimilation.

HAGSTROM, WARREN O.: "Competition in Science," *American Sociological Review*, 39:1–19, Febru-

ary, 1974. Discusses the functional and dysfunctional aspects of competition as a means of encouraging scientific discoveries.

KRIESBERG, LOUIS: *The Sociology of Social Conflict*, Prentice-Hall, Inc., Englewood Cliffs, N.J., 1973. A non-Marxian analysis of the conflict process.

MACK, RAYMOND W.: "The Components of Social Conflict," *Social Problems*, 12:388–397, Spring, 1965. An eloquent statement from a sociologist who holds that conflict arises inevitably from the nature of social life, while boundary maintenance is a continuous social process.

MICHENER, JAMES A.: *Centennial*, Random House, New York, 1974, chap. 10, "A Smell of Sheep." A fictional account of the conflict between Western cattlemen and sheepmen, dramatically showing how the conflict process cultivates in-group solidarity and out-group dehumanization.

PARK, ROBERT E., AND H. A. MILLER: *Old World Traits Transplanted*, Harper & Brothers, New York, 1921. A classic treatment of the assimilation process.

SEABURY, PAUL: "H.E.W. and the Universities," *Commentary*, 54:38–44, February, 1972. An analysis of "affirmative action" programs in the universities.

*SIMMEL, GEORG: *Conflict*, tr. by REINHARD BENDIX, The Free Press of Glencoe, Ill., Chicago, 1955. A pioneer German sociologist's classic treatment of the functional nature of conflict.

Chapter 15 • Social power

With an average probability approaching one, I can induce each of ten students to come to class for an examination on a Friday afternoon when they would otherwise prefer to make off for New York or Northampton. With its existing resources and techniques, the New Haven Police Department can prevent about half the students who park along the streets near my office from staying beyond the legal time limit. Which of us has the more power? *(Robert A. Dahl, "The Concept of Power,"* Science News, *2:206, July, 1957.)*

Professor Dahl's question was designed to illustrate the difficulty of comparing different types of power. Just what is power and how is it expressed?

The nature of social power

Although social power has been variously defined by Goldhamer and Shils [1939], Weber [1946], Bierstedt [1950], Simmel [1959], Parsons [1963], Olsen [1970] and others, all definitions carry the idea that *power is the ability to affect the behavior of others*.

Power is often viewed as an ability to control others for the benefit of the power holder. But power is sometimes exercised altruistically, as in promoting the Community Chest Drive. Sometimes power is viewed as a "zero-sum game" in which what one gains, another loses. It may be debated whether there is only a fixed amount of power to be divided up and whether the power gains of some must always reduce the power of others, even though this may be a common outcome. For example, the organization of a neighborhood council, even though it may reduce somewhat the freedom of action of some groups or agencies, may nonetheless add a new dimension of power to the community and thus create a net addition to the total supply of power.

Power may be viewed either as a means of getting things done or as a device which allows individuals or groups to exploit others. Both of these views have some degree of validity. Even arrangements which work for the general welfare aid some people more than others, and there is a constant struggle over who gets how much of any desirable goods or services. On the other hand, without the power to coordinate human activity, all of us would be reduced to a cave-man existence.

When one is studying power, it is important not to forget both of these possibilities. Power may be studied from the standpoint of how it is *distributed*. With at least equal validity, however, power may be analyzed as a facility, coordinating people for mutual benefit [Parsons, 1960, pp. 201–222].

Regardless of the standpoint of analysis, it is important to know how power is manifested. Invariably, power is found to have at least one of three components: force, authority, and influence.

Force is the *use or threat of physical coercion.* Political states usually attempt to gain a monopoly of all important means of coercion for the police and the army, but usually they do not succeed. Examples of forms of coercion outside the state monopoly include invading armies, revolutionary violence, the ability of organized crime to prevent victims and witnesses from making complaints or giving testimony, or the ability of bullying gangs to terrorize citizens or even other school children.

Authority is *an established right to make decisions and order the actions of others.* Sociologists have discussed the various types of authority. Weber, for example [1946, pp. 196–252], sees three main types of authority: (1) *bureaucratic authority,* resting on formal office or rank (general, foreman, civil service officer); (2) *traditionalist authority,* resting on a belief in sacred norms and traditions which one must obey (husband, father, prince, priest); and (3) *charismatic authority,* the authority of an extraordinary person who is obeyed because of charisma—his or her image of remarkable wisdom, saintliness, or invincibility (Christ, Joan of Arc, Napoleon, Franklin D. Roosevelt, Hitler). Authority and force are sometimes combined, as in a police force, army, or prison.

Influence is *the ability to affect the decisions and actions of others beyond any authority to do so.* Professors have authority to command certain work assignments and to assign grades; they have no authority to compel students to accept their opinions, but possibly they can influence students to do so. Influence rests partly upon respect, prestige, and affection and partly upon one's control over "facilities" which affect others. A newspaper publisher can be a valuable friend or a dangerous enemy; the corporation executive, school superintendent, or high-ranking officer can speed or slow down one's promotions; a member of the local aristocracy has "contacts" which can open many doors for a favored protégé. Great influence generally rests upon some combination of engaging personal qualities and a position from which one can affect the destiny of other people.

Authority and influence interact in reinforcing the position of the powerful; or one may undercut the other in reducing a person's power. Brim [1954] found that mothers who attributed high prestige to the role of doctors were more likely to follow the doctor's advice. Strodtbeck [1951] studied authority roles in the family by setting up situations in which the members have a difference of opinion and by then recording the interaction. He found that Navajo wives won 46 arguments to their husbands' 34, while Mormon wives lost 29 to 42. These figures show the differing roles of authority and influence of wives in these two subcultures.

Social power is easier to define than to measure. Sociologists have used three different models in an attempt to locate and measure social power [Rossi, 1957]. First, there is *potential power*—the power which is assumed to go with certain positions or situations in the community or the society. This is the "power elite" thesis of C. Wright Mills [1956]. The mayor presumably has more power than the city-hall janitor, and the chamber of commerce more than the teacher's club. Second, there is *reputed power*—the power ascribed to certain persons and groups by those who know the community [Form and Sauer, 1960; Preston, 1969]. Reputed power is determined by asking the question, "Who really runs things in this town?" of a number of people who know the town well. Finally, there is *decisional power,* as shown by observation of the decision-making process in operation [Fox, 1969; Bouma, 1970]. Observation of a power struggle as it takes place, with a detailed account of who did what and when, may reveal who is really in control of the situation.

Power has many degrees and forms, ranging from the tantrums of the small child to the armed mobilization of a great nation. This chapter will explore social power of five sorts: that of powerful individuals who are said to form an elite, of organized groups, of unorganized masses, of disruptive protest, and of law.

Power of the elite

The power elite is composed of men whose positions enable them to transcend the ordinary environments of ordinary men and women; they are in positions to make decisions having major consequences. . . . For they are in command of the major hierarchies and organizations of modern society. They rule the big corporations. They run the machinery of the state and claim its prerogatives. They direct the military establishment. They occupy the strategic command posts of the social structure in which are now centered the effective means of the power and the wealth and the celebrity which they enjoy. (C. Wright Mills, *The Power Elite,* Oxford University Press, Fair Lawn, N.J., 1956, pp. 3–4.)

Every complex society has a quite small number of persons who are believed to have great power. Such a controlling group is called an *elite.* Membership in the elite is often inherited, but in some societies it may be acquired. Its bases vary. In ancient China, the elite was headed by the scholars who were experts in the Confucian classics, plus the large landowners and military leaders. In medieval Europe the elite was composed of the higher clergy and the landowning nobility. After the industrial revolution these elite were increasingly displaced by the business entrepreneurs whose rapidly growing wealth gained them entree into the elite group. In the Soviet Union, where the possessions of the landlords and the businessmen were confiscated and the clergy largely deprived of influence, a new elite has arisen composed of the artists, intellectuals, engineers, scientists, and top officials and administrators. In England when one speaks of "the Establishment," one refers to a few thousand persons of wealth and influence, mostly of noble or gentle birth, and educated mainly at Eton or Harrow and at Oxford or Cambridge. In the United States, "the Establishment" refers to the conventional society with all of its maintenance personnel (officials, legislators, judges, police, school administrators, and others who keep conventional society in operation).

The wealthy as an elite

One of the best-known efforts to describe an American elite is Ferdinand Lundberg's study [1937] of *America's 60 Families,* followed by *The Rich and the Super Rich* [1968]. Lundberg assumed that wealth brings power, usually exercised indirectly. While members of the sixty wealthiest families occasionally occupy important posts, most of their influence is wielded through their ability to appoint and control those who actually fill the offices. This power of the purse places business managers, politicians, college presidents, and bishops under the sway of the holders of great wealth. Corporations are controlled through the ownership of stock; contributions and benefactions keep the foundations, churches, and universities under control. Occasionally the great families quarrel, but through intermarriage and close social contact they usually develop a common viewpoint and act as a more or less unified group. Thus, according to Lundberg, wealth rules.

This picture, which may have been approximately true at the end of the nineteenth century, is almost certainly less true today. Great wealth today is often invested in many scattered investments and administered by professional experts rather than by the owners themselves. Political parties and philanthropic organizations are steadily growing less dependent upon a few large contributors as they cultivate a mass of small contributors.

A study of American wealth some years ago by *Fortune* magazine located 155 Americans worth $50 million or more, and estimated that there were about another hundred whom it failed to locate [Smith, 1957]. As one indication that these persons were powerful, this study noted that Philadelphia pursued a vigorous program of urban renewal while Boston for a time continued to decay; they attributed this contrast to a difference in attitude on the part of the two cities' millionaires. No doubt wealthy persons have disproportionate power, but the exact degree of this power is not easy to determine.

The knowledge elite

According to some scholars, there is a *knowledge elite*—a few dozen economists, political scientists, historians, sociologists, and free-lance intellectuals who are widely read by the decision makers in the United States [Kadushin, 1971]. Occasionally, they also reach a mass audience and exert a real influence upon events. An example of how much influence one knowledgeable person may have is seen in the changes adopted by the automobile industry after the publication of Ralph Nader's popular book *Unsafe at Any Speed* [1965]. A few irrefutable facts, effectively presented, led to a new federal law, with a new federal agency; and forced one of America's major industries to make substantial concessions. At this writing, he is bringing the same pressure to bear on government by subjecting the work of government bureaus to critical examination by a research staff known as "Nader's Raiders." One obscure young attorney, John Banzhaf, by getting his facts together and taking advantage of existing laws and rulings, forced the television industry to devote millions of dollars of free time to anticigarette messages. Beginning with no finances, authority, or influence, he worked "within the system" to effect significant change [Johnson, 1969; Page, 1970]. Individuals or groups who have the capacity to make effective factual analyses and to make strategic use of laws, rulings, courts, and publicity, can wield a very real power in society. Strategies are outlined in books such as Johnson's *How to Talk Back to Your Television Set* [1970]. The success with which a comparative handful of intellectuals aroused the nation to concern over the environment is an illustration that knowledge is power.

The executive elite

Another theory of the American elite concludes that strategic position is the prime source of power [Burnham, 1941; Mills, 1956; Domhoff, 1967, 1970]. According to this view, the structure of our society is based on a complex division of labor which must be coordinated by a corps of expert managers. These highly paid executives are responsible for the smooth functioning of wealth-producing organizations, but they are not usually the principal owners of the enterprise they manage. Similarly, although they are responsible for supervising the services of scientists and technicians, they are not usually scientists themselves. Their skill lies in mastering the handling of organizations which channel the contributions of many different types of individuals toward a common goal. So strategic is their position that

With a few exceptions, executive skill is transferrable.

they often control the groups of which they are the nominal servants. Thus the typical great corporation is managed by a group of executives who own only a tiny fraction of the corporation's stock. While theoretically controlled by the stockholders who elect them, the managers tend in practice to become a self-perpetuating group whose actual control is unchallenged by stockholders as long as the flow of dividends is uninterrupted. Likewise, the most successful university president or foundation director is one who is able to "handle" the board of directors.

Executive skills are regarded as relatively independent of the context in which they operate; very different organizations may require the same type of coordination. With a few exceptions, executive skill is transferrable. The same individual may rotate among responsible positions in military, political, industrial, or educational organizations. Governments often "draft" corporate executives for top executive posts, and business recruits many of its executives from government or university people. These executives associate together, move from one field to another, and generally select their own successors.

The executive elite have undoubted authority in the detailed control of their enterprises, while their influence is buttressed both by their strategic position and by personality traits which have caused them to be respected. Their power, however, is restricted by limitations on their right to determine policy and the requirement that they operate within institutional norms. The "rubber stamp" board of trustees may quickly dump an executive when a business starts to lose money, a school arouses public criticism, or a church suffers a fall in membership.

Mills viewed the corporation as either the base from which the executive elite originate or the goal toward which they are moving. He felt that their power meant that society becomes dominated by men primarily committed to a view of life expressed by a prominent executive in the immortal words, "What's good for General Motors is good for the country."[1]

[1]C. Wright Mills, *The Power Elite,* Oxford University Press, Fair Lawn, N.J., 1956, p. 168. For the context of Charles Wilson's statement, see "Conflict of Interest," *Time,* Jan. 16, 1953, p. 70.

Mills made a strong case for the theory that executives who have had similar training, association, and outlook are often found in positions which involve decision making. There is no doubt that a professional managerial class has developed in the United States. But many social scientists argue that the case for a ruling elite with a virtual monopoly of social power has not been proved [Rossi, 1956; Reissman, 1956; Dahl, 1958; Bell, 1958; Lowry, 1965, pp. xviii, xix; Miller, 1970, pp. 202, 275, 276].

Is there a conspiratorial power elite?

There are at least three fairly well defined views on this question. The pluralists reject the idea that there is any one cohesive group controlling American life [Dahl, 1961; Arnold Rose, 1967]. Following the lead of Merton [1949b], they see power as *polymorphic* (literally, "having many forms"), with "different persons exercising decision-making powers for each separate issue" [Ferrell et al., 1973]. Thus a variety of different groups compete and share power. None of these groups consistently comes out the winner, and major social decisions are the result of compromise, competing influences, and the force of circumstances.

The two other schools of thought see American social decision making dominated by cohesive quasi-conspiratorial groups, but differ about who these groups are. The right wingers [Smoot, 1962; McBirnie, 1968; Schlafly, 1968; Efron, 1971, 1974, 1975; Buchanan, 1975] see the power elite as radical intellectuals who have infiltrated the government, the schools, and the communications media. By their control of the press, radio and TV, they determine the information which reaches the people. Likewise, by occupying key government posts, they make the decisions which sell out American individualism to a leftist internationalism. It is "they" who were responsible for the "loss" of China to the Communists in 1948, for the doubling of welfare payments in the sixties, and for the court decisions increasing the rights of alleged criminals versus the police. But some leftist critics [Domhoff, 1970; Anderson, 1974] are equally sure that a core of top-level academics, generals, government officials, and corporation executives dominate the society in behalf of big business. It is "they" who maintain an unequal distribution of income, and it is "they" who keep the country at war or on the brink of war in behalf of the "military-industrial complex."

A governmental action which fulfills the demands of either the left or the right is cited in support of the idea of a conspiratorial controlling elite. Actions which do not seem to be clearly dictated by group interest are seen as "moderate accommodation." These accommodations simply prove how sly and deceitful the power elites are, since occasionally they even let measures go through which might appear against their self-interest. Thus, according to leftists, the welfare system is supported by the rich as a device for "regulating the poor" and preserving the capitalist system [Piven and Cloward, 1971]. Any given act of government can be interpreted by either the leftist or the rightist critics to prove that the United States is dominated by a power elite.

Much of the argument is more a matter of definition than of dispute over the facts. To the left-wing critic, the fact that a minority of corporation directors hold seats on the boards of several corporations [Dye, De Clercq and Pickering, 1973] is proof of interlocking control by a small group. To the pluralist, the facts that most corporate directors sit on only one corporate board and that union pension funds are themselves large stockholders, prove that control is diversified even within the business community. Likewise, to the right-wing critic, a left-wing conspiracy is evident in the fact that some editors, TV commentators, professors, clergy and government officials express a "suspicious" similarity of viewpoint. The pluralist notes that there is also disagreement among these opinion makers, and explains any apparent consensus among them as a result of a rational reaction to common problems.

Can the power elite and pluralist views of power be reconciled? First, while there are few, if any, "conspiracies" and most important maneuvers are conducted in the open, there is group action. Citizens with common interests do meet, talk together, and plan appropriate steps. Sometimes they get the changes they desire. More often, they encounter opposition and must make compromises. Second, some people are acknowledged to be experts in the management of organizations or in creating a public image. Whether born poor or rich, such people are soon affluent. They tend to gravitate to people like themselves in both formal and informal association and often come to think very much alike. Finally, while many people spend their careers in a single occupation, there is some movement of personnel between institutions. This is most marked in civil government since many officials have had earlier careers in industry, education, or the military.

As Arnold Rose pointed out [1967], the fact that there is occasional agreement among important individuals or that people rotate between industry and government does not prove that the United States is run by a conspiratorial clique. Allegedly powerful individuals and groups often disagree sharply on policy. New individuals and groups rise from obscurity to challenge present reputed power holders. Powerful vested interests may be forced to yield on labor or welfare legislation, which costs them money and curtails their freedom of action. The military-industrial complex may see policies changed by popular opposition and armament factories closed by an economy-minded government. In brief, it is only by the use of selective examples that one can see any monopoly of power in American society.

If it is hard to prove American life is dominated either by right-wing capitalists or by left-wing intellectuals, does it follow that there is no consistent direction in American life at all? Is one forced to choose between either the right- or left-wing conspiracy theorists or the pluralists who see only chaos, conflict, and competition?

The emergent American consensus. Looking at American history in the twentieth century, one does see a kind of consensus emerging, even though it is a consensus within which there is room for frequent and sometimes bitter conflict. It is manifested in at least three areas: the welfare state, participation in international cooperation, and reliance upon profit-making business. Welfare programs were not produced so much by the machinations of socialist intellectuals as by the need to find security in a fast-changing, impersonal industrial society. International alliances, and the conflicts they often produce, are not so much the work of a military-industrial complex as they are the result of the need to cooperate with other nations in a world in which no nation can stand alone. Finally, it is not because the opinion makers have sold out to greedy business people that businesses are allowed—yes, even encouraged—to make profits; rather, profits are allowed because experience has convinced most people that profit-making business is an essential element of a productive type of economic system.

Earlier in the chapter we contrasted the concept of power as the distribution of a scarce resource with the concept of power as a means of facilitating social cooperation. The scholar who takes the distributive view will probably see any degree of consensus as indicating that a power elite is manipulating society for selfish purposes. Those who view power as a means of facilitating cooperation will more likely see some degree of consensus as both natural and desirable among people reared in a common culture and facing common problems.

If American society could be run conspiratorially by closed groups, it would be so rigid that it would have little chance of making the many adjustments required by a rapidly changing world. On the other hand, if there were no consensus among thoughtful people, the drift toward chaos or civil war would be equally disastrous. America is not run by a unified and consistent power elite of either the left or the right, nor is it the victim of confusion and chaos. To the degree that common goals develop from the interaction of competing groups, it is because there is a measure of agreement in all strata of society. This agreement includes such ideas as the following: That the state, through welfare measures, should relieve distress; that America's interests require international participation; and that needed adjustments in economic life are often most quickly brought about through the mechanism of profit motivation. As long as this consensus remains, it will dictate the limits of political change. If and when the consensus disappears, it is unlikely that the machinations of any "power elite" can prevent consequent changes in government policy.

The community influentials

One approach to reputed power is through an attempt to locate the "community influentials."[2] The usual technique is to select a group of people presumed to be well acquainted with a community and ask them for a list of the persons who are influential in that community. The people on the list are then interviewed in an attempt to narrow the field to a small number who appear to have the greatest power in community decision making. The final list is loaded with corporation executives, wealthy individuals of established social standing who are active in civic affairs, and lawyers associated with business interests. In the studies made to date, virtually everyone listed as a "community influential" is male. Politicians are seldom mentioned unless they are also

[2] The major pioneer work in this field is Floyd Hunter, *Community Power Structure*, The University of North Carolina Press, Chapel Hill, 1953. A brief summary and analysis of these studies is found in Richard A. Schermerhorn, *Society and Power*, Random House, Inc., New York, 1961, pp. 88–92. A comparison of international elites is found in Delbert C. Miller, *International Community Power Structures: Comparative Studies of Four World Cities*, Indiana University Press, Bloomington, 1970. A general review of the role of elites in decision making is the focus of a series of articles edited by Terry N. Clark, *Community Structure and Decision-making: Comparative Analysis*, Chandler Publishing Co., San Francisco, 1968.

prominent in business. Other professionals such as physicians, ministers, and educators form a tiny fraction of the total number of leaders and are usually classified toward the bottom of the list on a ranking of comparative influence. Labor leaders, mentioned in some communities and ignored in others, never form a substantial proportion of the community influentials.

The community influentials are thought to be the top of a power pyramid which determines whether any given project will receive community support. In some communities the survey evidence suggests that the fate of all major community proposals depends on the reaction of the same small group of influentials. Other communities may contain several power pyramids, including different individuals who are effective in different areas. The support of one group might be vital for a hospital-fund drive, of another group for passing a school-bond issue, and of still another group for the success of an urban redevelopment program [McKee, 1953; Kahn, 1970].

Community power appears to be exercised through determining the policies of community organizations. Organizational activity is a time-consuming process, and influentials often feel they have to struggle in order to limit their community participation so that they will have some time available for attention to their own business. The following description of the community participation of an "influential" in Lansing, Michigan is similar to that found in other cities:

On the average he now belongs to more than thirteen organizations: 3.9 business organizations, 2.4 professional organizations, 2.9 civic and welfare organizations, 0.8 service organizations and 3.5 social organizations. He has held the top appointive or elected offices in almost all of the organizations in which he has become actively involved. Almost all of the leaders belong to a common core of organizations: the Chamber of Commerce, Rotary, Country Club, a leading church, and the Community Chest. (William H. Form and Warren L. Sauer, *Community Influentials in a Middle-sized City,*

Institute for Community Development, Michigan State University, East Lansing, Mich., 1960, p. 4.)

One study of a community of 50,000 people found eight men who held office in three or more important organizations and who were well acquainted with each other [Perrucci and Pilisuk, 1970]. Such men would seem to have an obvious ability to influence organizational action and were regarded by important people in the town as being the core of the leadership group.

The actual leadership offices in voluntary organizations are more likely to be held by those who are in the process of reaching the status of "community influentials" than by those who have already arrived. The established leader is apt to operate by remote control through junior executives who perform the endless chores of office holding. The established influential, however, keeps in touch with developments and may take over when some type of emergency seems to demand top-level leadership. His advice is sought on matters considered important, and even when not holding organizational office he is able to exercise a veto power on projects he considers of doubtful merit. New programs have a good chance of success when the influentials lend their support. Fund-raising drives usually get a major portion of their total from small contributors, but influentials add the large gifts that make the difference between success and partial failure, while their endorsement sets a good example of civic virtue.

With occasional exceptions, the community influentials are seldom office holders in local government and consider this kind of activity not very attractive. The influentials recognize the importance of government but dread the prospect of controversies that may be "bad for business" and shrink from direct involvement in "dirty" politics [Hunter, 1953, pp. 151–170; Form and Sauer, 1960, p. 11; Miller, 1970, p. 197]. The community influentials are interested in seeing that government provides the services needed by business without either burdensome regulation or excessive taxation. In addition, as civic leaders they feel that good schools, reliable police protection, efficient public health services, and adequate sewage and water resources help to maintain a community which can attract both customers and employees.

In spite of their limited political participation, community influentials affect the policies of government through campaign contributions and through maintaining a liaison with office holders. When the community influentials are agreed among themselves, they can usually persuade local government and community groups to act as they wish, although many decisions vital to the local community, such as the closing or opening of a factory, may be decided by those beyond the control of anyone in the locality. Yet the community influentials appear to be more powerful in some types of situations than in others. In some cases organized groups appear to be powerful only when their aims are supported by the community elite. In other cases the balance is reversed, and the community elite are helpless unless organized groups are firmly in agreement. Rossi summarizes this situation in the following statement:

Who has power over whom? Perhaps the clearest distinction here is between the two areas of community life—local government and the voluntary community associations. For local government officials who are ultimately brought before the bar of public opinion on election days, the leaders of solidary [highly unified] groups normally on their side carry the most weight. Insofar as wealth and the mass media are seen as potential influencers of public opinion they too are powerful. Within the voluntary community associations which depend largely on the bounty of large contributors, wealth and its control play the major role.

Another distinction must be drawn as to types of issues. An issue which divides the community (or which potentially might divide the community) can be moved to a decision point only by solidary groups. I have in mind in this connection such issues as integration in public housing or public schools. Projects which can be achieved without striking deeply at the gains of one particular group are perhaps best moved by the elite of wealth and status. Thus the best way to get a hospital drive underway is to get together a group of prominent citizens, but the best way to get an FEPC [Fair Employment Practices Commission] ordinance is to prove that some significant part of the electorate is for it. (Peter H. Rossi, "Theory, Research and Practice in Community Organization," in Charles R. Adrian, Peter H. Rossi, Robert A. Dahl, and Lloyd Rodwin, *Social Science and Community Action,* Institute for Community Development, Michigan State University, East Lansing, Mich., 1960, p. 13.)

Organizational power

The struggle for power often appears to be largely a contest between organizations. The John Birch Society attempts to elect conservative candidates to public office, while the Americans for Democratic Action supports liberals. The AFL-CIO calls for a higher minimum wage, and the National Chamber of Commerce assails high wages as the cause of inflation. The National Organization of Women battles the Right to Life organization over the issue of voluntary abortion. These and many other items in the daily press suggest that the power of highly organized groups is checked by the opposition of other groups.

Sources of organizational power

Wealth, numbers, and specialized facilities. The obvious advantage of organization is that it brings together the efforts of a large number of people along with a great deal of wealth. When an organization represents millions of veterans, church members, unionized workers, business people, farmers, or any other group, it has at least a potential claim to speak for a considerable fraction of the population. An organization can accumulate a large treasury from the dues and small contributions of many members. By joining together, even the poor and unknown may gain some of the attributes of power often attributed to the elite, as seen in the recent appearance of the National Welfare Rights Organization and its local chapters.

The specialized facilities of the organization also increase its influence. The individual, far from any seat of government, may make his or her views known through the activities of the organizational lobbyist, who is constantly in contact with those who make government decisions. The special magazines or pamphlets put out by the organization help to keep the membership informed, while newspaper advertisements and radio and television programs carry the organization's program to the general public.

Coordinated membership response. The major source of organizational power lies in the ability to enable many people to take *planned, concerted action* to affect social decisions. In a democracy this action may be accomplished by organizing blocs of voters who will cast their ballots in a way designed to assist organizational objectives. Even a small group may have some political influence if it will vote as a bloc. Many elections are decided by small margins, and a shift of 1 or 2 percent in votes may mean the difference between victory and defeat. If a comparatively small group can organize a united bloc of voters, it may be effective.

Organizations often launch a campaign in which each member is urged to write, wire, or see his congressman. A flood of several thousand individually worded letters from constituents has a sobering effect upon the most daring congressman. The American Medical Association has occasionally sought to have each congressman approached by his or her own personal physician in support of the association's legislative objectives. The effectiveness of such efforts is hard to determine. Apparently, if a measure is earnestly sought by a small but determined group, and if no active or organized opposition appears, its passage is generally assured. Where there is organized opposition, a more prolonged power contest usually follows.

Factors affecting group power

Cohesiveness and action orientation. Solidary groups which can unite their members in a given program have a great advantage over loosely structured organizations which must seek agreement through an education and discussion process and may seldom be able to count on a concerted response from their members.

Large religious groups, veterans' organizations, and political parties usually include individuals with a wide variety of views. Members do not consider themselves bound by the actions of governing bodies of such groups and may ignore or even oppose official views of the organization. By contrast, small organizations in which the leadership can make decisions binding on the members may have an influence greater than their size would indicate. This is borne out in a rather striking fashion by the success of real estate boards in determining the action of municipal government, even though realtors are very seldom included in the lists of "community influentials." The typical board of realtors requires its members to list all properties for sale, splitting the commission between the firm making the listing and the firm completing the sale. The board of realtors also receives a proportion of the commissions on listed property, which gives it a source of income apart from its membership assessments. The board normally has an executive committee with power to make policy decisions binding on all the members. A recalcitrant member can be suspended, which means that he or she is not allowed to make any sales from the board list during the suspension, although other firms may sell off this person's listings.

Such an organization has power much greater than its limited size and the intermediate social status of its members would indicate. In several cities the board of realtors, although seldom regarded as a power organization or pressure group, has been highly effective in influencing community decision making. In one Midwestern city of about 250,000 population the board of realtors first defeated a school-bond issue which was supported in a spirited campaign by a great many of the civic organizations; then two years later the board reversed its stand and helped carry to victory a bond issue larger than the one originally rejected. In a public housing campaign in this city, the board of realtors persuaded the voters to reverse a unanimous city commission by referendum although the housing proposal adopted by the commission had the support of both political parties, both daily newspapers, the council of churches, and many social welfare organizations, labor unions, and leading citizens [Bouma, 1962a, 1962b]. A nearby city repeated this experience on two different occasions and in almost identical detail [Bouma, 1962c; 1970]. While other power factors are also involved, the board of realtors is a prime example of the power potential of small, cohesive, disciplined organizations.

Perceived role as a power factor. The members of an organization have an image of what kinds of activities are proper for the organization, and this image limits the areas in which it can exercise power. Labor union members will usually support their leadership in wage negotiations even to the point of costly strikes, but have repeatedly shown that their union leaders cannot dictate their voting behavior [Marshall, 1961]. If union leaders could really "deliver" the votes of the membership, their political power would be enormously increased. Most church members expect the church to "stay out of politics," and occasional church efforts to control voting behavior have generally failed. A good example was found in Puerto Rico in 1960, where Archbishop Davis attacked the incumbent administration on birth control and other issues and organized a Catholic party in opposition. Puerto Rico is about 85 percent Catholic, and the church leaders threatened to excommunicate anyone supporting the administration; yet the administration was overwhelmingly reelected while the Catholic party got less than 10 percent of the votes [*U.S. News and World Report,* 1960].

For many years teachers' organizations were handicapped in seeking salary increases because their members' perception of the role of a professional organization kept them from threatening to strike [Stiehm, 1961]. In recent years the members' perceived role of their organization has changed and teachers' organizations are using conventional strike tactics in seeking economic gains. There were periods before the widespread adoption of collective bargaining, notably in the middle sixties, when teachers made large gains in real income. Whether the use of strike tactics has actually enabled teachers to secure gains they would not have obtained otherwise is debatable, but there is no doubt that the perceived role of teachers' organizations limited their choice of tactics.

Perceived role.

The power of an organization is also limited by the role assigned to it by the community. To many people the chamber of commerce is an organization dedicated to community welfare, while labor unions are considered selfish and "too powerful." The chamber of commerce is expected to speak out on taxes and other political issues, but the unions are scolded for doing the same thing. Businessmen in government are applauded; labor officials in government are feared; women in important government posts are too rare to have any clear-cut image.

Many consider it proper for medical associations to resist outside pressures for changes in medical practice but think it arrogant for teachers' organizations to resist outside pressures for changes in teaching methods. Thus the public's perceived role of an organization or group limits its social power by determining the public support its actions will receive.

Organizational alliances. Some of the advantages of large size may be won if several smaller groups join in united action. This alliance is simplified when the organizations involved are led by interlocking directorates. Many of the directors of corporations and community organizations also hold several other directorships in other corporations or organizations. Today the board of directors of the City National Bank hold a director's meeting, tomorrow three of them meet again at the community chest luncheon, and the next day one is elected to the official board of the First Methodist Church, and so on. Thus an overlapping network of membership links the organizations together, making for easy cooperation and vesting control of many organizations in a very small group of persons (see Table 22).

An alliance between entirely separate groups may be forged when their interests converge. The socialized-medicine controversies of recent years have found the American Medical Association allied with the Chamber of Commerce, the National Association of Manufacturers, the American Farm Bureau Federation, and many other organizations in opposing certain medical-care proposals, while many labor unions, public health and welfare organizations, and social-work organizations have been united in support. An alliance between farm organizations and business organizations some years ago helped to persuade many state legislatures to pass "right to work" laws which outlaw the closed shop. Labor organizations have sometimes attempted to form an alliance with farm organizations, but without much success. Farm organizations seem to feel a

TABLE 22 AUTHORITATIVE POSITIONS EVER HELD BY INDIVIDUALS CURRENTLY OCCUPYING TOP INSTITUTIONAL POSITIONS

	Indus- try	Comm. and util.	Bank- ing	Insur- ance	Law	Civic assoc.	Founda- tions	Govt.	Educa- tion	Wealth	Pol. Finance	Mili- tary
Average number of authoritative positions ever held	9.9	12.2	10.7	11.6	9.0	11.7	11.1	7.1	10.9	11.5	12.3	0.9
Average number of authoritative positions ever held in each sector:												
Industry	4.0	4.5	4.1	2.8	1.5	2.2	2.0	0.7	2.3	3.5	3.0	0.1
Banking	1.1	1.6	1.7	1.7	0.7	1.0	1.0	0.3	1.0	1.0	0.9	0.1
Insurance	0.4	0.8	0.5	1.4	0.2	0.2	0.2	0.0	0.3	0.3	0.2	0.1
Law	0.2	0.2	0.1	0.3	1.4	0.4	0.3	0.4	0.3	0.0	0.2	0.0
Civic assoc.	1.6	2.2	2.0	2.1	2.3	3.0	2.6	1.1	2.3	2.8	2.8	0.1
Foundations	0.5	0.6	0.7	0.6	0.7	0.8	1.7	1.4	1.0	1.5	0.8	0.0
Education	1.0	1.2	1.0	1.5	0.9	1.4	1.6	1.0	2.0	0.9	0.9	0.3
Average number of public service positions ever held	1.0	1.0	0.6	1.4	1.3	2.6	1.7	3.1	1.7	1.5	3.5	0.6

Source: Thomas R. Dye, Eugene R. DeClercq, and John W. Pickering, "Institutional Elites," *Social Science Quarterly*, 54:23, June, 1973. Used with permission of the authors and the publisher.

greater convergence of interest with business than with labor, especially as farming itself is becoming more commercialized. Some student leftists have romantic dreams of a student-worker alliance, but a more improbable alliance is difficult to imagine.

Countervailing power. The opposite tendency of organized groups—to oppose each other rather than to cooperate—has been given the name of *countervailing power* [Galbraith, 1952]. This theory states that the exercise of great power by one organized group soon inspires an opposing power. Other groups may organize for effective opposition, or they may persuade the government to intervene. In the past, large-scale business enterprise eventually resulted in the appearance of the large labor union, and exploitation of farmers by milling interests and other middlemen produced the farm cooperatives. Large buyers such as chain stores limit the power of large manufacturers to set prices, while in turn the voluntary chains (associations of independently owned stores) enable the independent retailer to compete with the chain stores. Thus the power of one economic group is balanced by the power of another and none can entirely dominate the economy. While the concept of countervailance is most often applied to economic groups, this game of reciprocal checkmate tends to be true of all groups in society. The tendency of great power to inspire the organization of opposing power usually keeps any one group from gaining complete control in a democratic society. In a dictatorship, countervailance cannot freely operate.

Coercion and disruption. Not all decisions are reached through the political processes of debate and persuasion. Groups are likely to resort to coercion, either when their political system is unresponsive to majority opinion, or when a particular group lacks majority support and refuses to accept the majority decision.

 Forceful coercion is normally a monopoly of government, but it is also used by other groups.

Fascist and communist governments have normally become established after a determined, ruthless minority party bullied and shot its way into power. Political kidnappings are a recent device for revolutionary parties to coerce the release of prisoners or payment of ransom.

 Nonviolent coercion has a long history [Gregg, 1966; Hare and Blumberg, 1968]. It consists of nonviolent ways of making a policy so costly and painful to others that they will change it. The use of *economic coercion* through strikes, lockouts, and boycotts is far from new, but still common. Another common technique is for a protesting group to place itself in a position where the dominant group must either make a concession or take violent action against the protestors. This technique is variously called *nonresistance, passive resistance,* or *nonviolent resistance.* The object is to arouse public sympathies and to shame the dominant party into making concessions. In the late 1950s and early 1960s, groups of blacks entered segregated restaurants, parks, and other public accommodations, waited patiently for service and submitted peacefully to verbal assault and arrest [Maybee, 1961; Peck, 1962]. This emotionally moving spectacle helped change public attitudes and led to desegregation of public facilities. The technique of nonresistance, passive resistance, or nonviolent resistance is the historic weapon of the underdog, for it can be used by the totally powerless. Its use by American blacks has declined as they developed a greater sense of "black power."

 Civil disobedience is the open and public defiance of the law because of conscience or moral belief [Smith, 1968; Cohen, 1969]. It is a technique of nonviolent coercion, resting on the powerful appeal of the spectacle of people who are willing to suffer for a moral belief. Punishment is therefore willingly accepted rather than evaded, in order to publicize and dramatize their belief that the law is immoral. This technique can be highly effective in some situations, but requires great self-discipline lest its practitioners turn to violence.

Disruption is a form of coercion which is highly variable in both means and goals. It includes many ways of interrupting and paralyzing the normal day-to-day activities of a social system. Sometimes the goal is to force acceptance of the protester's demands; sometimes it is to dramatize a general atmosphere of protest; sometimes the motive appears to be the exhilarating experience itself with the goals either nonexistent or inconsequential. Offices may be thronged and closed, university classes disrupted, speakers heckled or shouted down, deans and college presidents held hostage, and buildings seized and occasionally bombed or burned. Off campus, streets may be "trashed," buildings damaged, and stores looted [Sharp, 1974; Woodward, 1974]. Disruptions remain nonviolent only if no one attempts to restrain the disrupters or if everyone ignores them and proceeds with normal activities. Very often the disruption escalates into violence, as at Kent State and elsewhere [President's Commission on Campus Unrest, 1970].

Disruption is a technique whereby a small group can gain a great deal of attention without the arduous work, discipline, or patience which building a reform movement would entail. It especially appeals to the malevolent, the immature, and the irresponsible, and in some instances, has few roots beyond egoistic destructiveness. It is a denial of democratic processes and of the rights of majority rule. But whenever a minority feels that its legitimate grievances are not being "listened to," i.e., dealt with fairly by the majority, and that all legitimate channels of redress are blocked, disruption is likely [Gans, 1969].

The term *demonstration* is often used to refer to any of the forms of persuasion, coercion, or disruption. At least one prominent sociologist believes that demonstrations have become a permanent feature of the American political system [Etzioni, 1971]. Many of these demonstrations are certain to be violent. Proponents of violence claim that this is an inherent part of the American tradition. They cite the American Revolution, lynchings and vigilante law in the Old West, the Civil War, and the Ku Klux Klan as evidence [National Commission on the Causes and Prevention of Violence, 1969; Rubenstein, 1970]. Defenders of the democratic process view American history as a gradual evolution from violent disruption to orderly settlement of disputes through democratic means and cite the successful attainment of many basic reforms as evidence. Examples would include the egalitarian division of Western lands under the Homestead Act, the coming of the welfare state, the rapid, recent changes in the status of black people, and the rapid arousal to action to protect the environment.

There appear to be some periods or situations in which violence succeeds more often than nonviolence. Gamson [1975] studied fifty-three American groups and movements which promoted various social changes between 1800 and 1945. He claims that those which gained their goals were generally the ones that used violence (or, more correctly, had violence thrust upon them through police or mob attack), while all the nonviolent victims of attack failed to achieve their goals. But violence is a dangerous weapon. Victories may leave a legacy of bitterness which makes future victories more difficult. Majorities may arise against violence in a wave of law-and-order repression that results in minority groups becoming more powerless than ever.

Social power of unorganized masses

Mass man in mass society

In the folk society the individual lives in a world of rather small, highly integrated local groups whose behavior is closely governed by custom and tradition. In the mass society one's life is increasingly dominated by large, impersonal, secondary groups. Social change is rapid, and custom and tradition provide no sure guide to behavior.

Under ancient despotisms, decisions were made by a few leaders, but these decisions were based upon a traditional morality and custom which the masses could understand and support. The actions of the ancient despot reflected the social values learned in the family and the church and reinforced by the general moral consensus of the community. Today the masses no longer live in a traditional society and are no longer embedded in a protective coating of time-honored customs and institutions. Instead, our "masses" live in an era in which change is the norm, in which older customs cannot be trusted, and in which changes that they have no part in bringing about may transform their lives for better or for worse. They live in communities of people like themselves, as isolated fragments of a varied and complex world. Lacking an opportunity for understanding, they inevitably substitute stereotyped images for social analysis and fads for tradition. In these circumstances the mass media become primarily a route of escape rather than enlightenment.

The student should recall that in describing groups the text distinguished between gemeinschaft and gesellschaft relationships. The gemeinschaft social relationships were of a personal, traditional type that applied to the entire society. The gesellschaft scrapped tradition in favor of a realistic (hard-boiled), impersonal, and highly specialized approach to various aspects of life. While the gesellschaft frees society from older restraints, it also cuts the roots of traditional culture and transforms individuals into masses, helplessly and unknowingly swept along by current fads and fancies.

The expression of mass power

From this discussion of mass society, it might appear that the masses are totally powerless to affect their destiny. Individually, possibly yes. But collectively, no! The unorganized masses can exert a decisive power over social developments through several avenues.

The power of mass markets. In a democratic society the masses exert influence through their choices of what goods to buy, what papers to read, what television programs to watch, and so on. This power is not unlimited, for the consumer is susceptible to some degree of manipulation, as motivation research has demonstrated [Packard, 1957; Dichter, 1971]. But in a competitive market economy such as ours, the consumer's preferences are rarely disregarded for very long. Courting the consumer's favor may produce a gaudy vulgarity in product design and shoddy escapism in television programs, but it unquestionably attests to the power of the mass market.

Mass veto power through noncooperation. Some decisions can become effective only through mass cooperation. Public health programs, mass-immunization campaigns, and voluntary blood banks are successful only if a great many people cooperate. The American civil-defense effort limped through over a decade of monumental public indifference. Government can compel the installation of auto seat belts, but cannot compel the people to use them. Wherever a decision cannot be effective without mass cooperation, the veto power of the masses must be considered.

Direct political power of masses. In a democracy the ultimate power of the masses rests in their franchise to "throw the rascals out." Sometimes, it is true, this power is empty because both candidates hold the same values and serve the same interests. But whenever there is widespread mass discontent with the way things are going in a democracy, some party or candidate will appeal to this discontent, focus it on certain issues, and propose changes. Deep mass discontent almost guarantees change; either a new party pledged to change replaces the old, or the old party introduces changes as the price of continued power. The elite cannot always veto changes sought by the masses. The reforms of Roosevelt's New Deal era, established over the opposition of most of the elite, attest to the power of the skillfully focused discontent of the masses.

These comments about political figures who reflect mass discontent apply much more to democracies than to other forms of government. In 1974, fewer than 25 of the 138 United Nations member governments had come to power through democratic elections [Augustus, 1974]. It may be that the desire to escape mass influence is a major factor in the establishment of nondemocratic governments.

While the elite often cannot veto changes sought by the masses, the reverse is not true. Mass opposition frequently makes elite leadership ineffective. A large number of poorly educated, lower-class people seem to be chronically suspicious of government, suspicious of science and intellectuals, and resentful of the dominant role of the elite. When some issue such as an unfamiliar health plan or a school bond election offers a focus for discontent, they unhesitatingly bury the decision makers in a flood of opposition votes [Thompson and Horton, 1960; Rosenthal and Crain, 1966].

Important as the power of veto may be, it does not altogether dispel the picture of the lowest income group of society as one which is essentially without the power to affect decisions concerning it. Alinsky [1965] argued that the poor can utilize power and must be able to do so if their position is to be ameliorated. He contended that the deliberate organization of the poor, stressing whatever grievances are most keenly felt, can lead to positive action. Through demonstrations, boycotts, and bloc voting, the poor can become one of the pressure groups in the community. He believed that as they achieve power, they can prevent exploitation, formulate positive programs for their own welfare, and replace a helpless apathy with a sense of being able to control their environment. Although Alinsky-type programs seem to have been effective in some localities, there is disagreement concerning their value. Some hold that organizing efforts of this type simply hamper cooperation between different groups without leading to effective participation by the poor. One critic notes that despite

Alinsky's dedicated and sagacious efforts to organize the poor, it was mainly the relatively prosperous and well-educated that he succeeded in mobilizing, while failing to develop real leaders from among the truly poor [Bailey, 1973]. Possibly the poor can be better served by organizations including members of all classes than by organizations of their own. Efforts to involve the poor in policy making and administration of the poverty programs of the late 1960s were not very successful for a variety of reasons, including lack of participation by the poor and the opposition of local political structures [Kramer, 1969; Moynihan, 1969; Brill, 1971; Helfgot, 1974]. Even a highly sympathetic portrayal of one of Alinsky's favorite projects, The Woodlawn Organization (TWO), admits that TWO could neither maintain a persistent adversary stand nor solve unaided the problem of neighborhood decay [Fish, 1973].

In the past, the comments on the poor as being relatively isolated from the instruments of power applied almost equally to blacks. As recently as 1965, a Chicago survey showed that blacks had only 5 percent of the political positions in Chicago, although comprising over one-fourth of the population. In the private sector they fared even worse, since a survey of leading positions in business, labor unions, voluntary organizations, and universities gave blacks only 2 percent of the offices [Baron et al., 1968, p. 144]. This low participation in the power structure supports other findings that individuals whose sense of grievance is combined with a feeling of powerlessness are most inclined to endorse violence [Ransford, 1968, p. 197].

In the 1970s, black representation in the power structure has increased in Chicago and throughout the nation. Any group in society which is glaringly short of its proportionate number of power leaders is likely to develop feelings of helplessness and resentment. A continued expansion of the number of blacks in power positions is an essential aspect of effective black integration in American life.

Who, then, holds the reins of power in our

society? No single group, for power is of several kinds and is diffused among many groups. The paradox of power in the twentieth century is that although our society is largely controlled by highly organized groups dominated by an elite leadership, this leadership may be blocked by the action of normally unorganized and apathetic masses whose basic attitudes toward life are often sharply different from those of the influentials who normally set the pace. Even this pace-setting function of the elite is restricted by the need to draw in the participation of the masses as consumers, workers, and participants in large-scale programs affecting public health and welfare. The gloomy predictions of a society doomed to mediocrity by the power of the most ignorant have not been altogether borne out, but no student of social power can ignore the role of those who seldom sit in the seats of the mighty.

The sociology of law

Law as legitimized power

Power may be either legitimate, that is, socially sanctioned, or illegitimate. The power of the underworld crime syndicates [Cressey, 1969] is very real and very great, although not legitimate. Neither law nor our approved value system authorizes the acts of crime syndicates. Power is legitimate when it is sanctioned by society, and legal authority represents the formal legitimization of power. Most sociologists seem to agree with Roscoe Pound's definition of law as "social control through the systematic application of the force of politically organized society."[3] But this force is not always applied directly, in the form of the club-wielding policeman. As Hertzler [1961, p. 421] comments, ". . . the law in effect structures the power (superordinate-subordinate) relationships in the society; it maintains the status quo and protects the various strata against

[3]Roscoe Pound, in George Gurvitch and Wilbert E. Moore, *Twentieth Century Sociology*, Philosophical Library, Inc., New York, 1945, p. 300.

each other, both in governmental and nongovernmental organizations and relationships."

The law "structures power relationships" by stating who may do what to whom. Before the passing of the National Labor Relations Act in 1935, employers were legally entitled to fire and blacklist employees who joined unions. This law established workers' legal right to join unions and prohibited employers from penalizing workers for union activity. While this law was not fully enforced in all areas, it greatly aided unions in organizing workers and was largely responsible for the great growth of union power from 1935 to 1945. By 1947, union power had grown enough to disturb many people. The somewhat restrictive Taft-Hartley Act was passed, and many state legislatures passed "right to work" laws which outlawed the closed shop. These laws hampered unions' organizing efforts and slowed the growth of union membership. In this way law "structures the power relationships" of a society and legitimizes the power of those whose power has the society's sanctions.

Individual rights do not exist in a vacuum and are viable only when protected in the courts. The Legal Services Division of the Office of Economic Opportunity provided free attorneys who gave the poor person protection from arbitrary action by public officials and swindles by private exploiters similar to that enjoyed by the middle-class citizen. These "poverty program" lawyers also filed many "class action" suits seeking a judicial modification of some business practices, government policy, or welfare ruling [Greene, 1970]. A number of restrictive welfare regulations and procedures were overturned and some business practices ruled illegal. Later court decisions have made it more difficult to bring class action suits, but for a time, they were a potent weapon.

Judicial activism, in recent years, has enabled the courts to make decisions in areas where the citizens have not specifically spoken [Bishop, 1974]. For instance, no legislature decreed that busing would be used for school integration or that abortion would be permitted throughout the nation. The tendency of the courts to extend vaguely worded constitutional provisions into specific rules has greatly enlarged judicial power. In the first part of the century, judges extended the interpretation of constitutional guarantees to nullify social legislation; today they are using this technique to expand the legal basis for social reform. In one era, their actions had a conservative tinge, and in another, they are generally regarded as liberal. In either case, the effect is to expand the power of the courts versus other agencies of social control.

Some critics insist that, despite occasional lapses into liberalism, the legal system operates primarily to protect the interests of the power elite [Quinney, 1970]. This view assumes that there is a power elite, which, as shown earlier, is a debatable assumption. It is undeniable that the law expresses a society's concept of justice and defines this in ways which support the existing social structure, whether it be communist or capitalist. But in democratic societies, law also reflects the divergence of interests and groups in the society, and law changes as these change.

Law as expression of the mores

As was stated in our chapter on social control, law is a means of enforcing the mores in a complex, secondary-group society where informal group controls are less effective. Some laws are morally neutral and merely seek to establish a dependable procedure for doing something, such as, for example, writing an enforceable contract. But a great many laws deal with right and wrong behavior as determined by the values and experience of the society.

When a law expresses the moral consensus of the society, it will be effectively enforced. Comparatively few people in our society are murdered or forcibly raped. It is true that many murderers and rapists go unpunished, but their

acquittal is largely due to the technical difficulties of legally establishing guilt "beyond a reasonable doubt." A law is effectively enforced when violations are comparatively infrequent and known violators may reasonably expect to be punished.

When a law is backed by no firm moral consensus, effective enforcement is less likely. The classic illustration is the Eighteenth Amendment, which prohibited the manufacture, sale, or transportation of alcoholic beverages in the United States. Whether this law reflected the mores of the majority of citizens at that time has been debated. Certainly there was no moral consensus. Many people considered good liquor a part of the good life and soon located a source of supply. Laws against gambling and prostitution are other examples of poorly enforced laws which are supported by no clear moral consensus. Perhaps the best current example of often unenforced laws are those forbidding marijuana use, which have been termed "The New Prohibition" [Kaplan, 1970].

Law often creates "crimes without victims" [Schur, 1965], meaning that the only persons injured, if any, are the ones who commit the act. Many of the laws regulating drug use and sex acts are of this sort. Many such laws are under attack as either unenforceable or as an unjust intrusion of the state into private behavior. When enforcement is attempted, the results are often more destructive to society than the crimes themselves [Haddon, 1969]. One writer suggests that it would be equally rational to punish obesity, which kills more people than drugs or murderers [Geis, 1968].

It is sometimes stated that a law *cannot* be enforced unless backed by a clear moral consensus. This generalization is not necessarily true, for it overlooks the great variation in the types of situations in which laws may be applied. Laws regulating gambling can be enforced only through the detailed supervision of the individual actions of a large number of people. On the other hand, laws requiring a handful of manufacturers to install safety equipment in automobiles can be enforced with comparative ease. Even though a law may have majority support, if this majority is apathetic and if enforcement requires tremendous individual supervision, the prospects for its enforcement are doubtful at best. But when the people supporting the law are keenly interested in its enforcement and when this can be done through inspection at a limited number of checkpoints, then even laws which do not rest on a clear consensus may be effective. And even when an individual is unconvinced of the justice of legislation, law can prevent him or her from carrying an attitude into action.

Law as molder of the mores

In a changing society the mores are constantly changing. Law is one of the forces which change the mores. The law states the approved moral code and makes social policy; thus it functions as an educator [Andenaes, 1971]. It is not always necessary to wait for a moral consensus before passing a law; the enactment and enforcement of the law help to create a moral consensus. Child labor laws and compulsory school attendance laws were passed at a time when there was by no means a moral consensus to support them. A considerable fraction of the people sharply disagreed. But important pressure groups, including labor unions and some business groups, found it to their economic advantage to support these laws. Today virtually all are agreed that full-time child labor is bad and that compulsory school attendance is good. Law had helped to create a moral consensus where none existed. Law is powerless to change the mores of an entire people, or to reverse the direction of changes. But where the mores are conflicting, laws can mold conduct and eventually the mores. Laws can impose the behavior patterns of certain groups upon other groups in the society. Law is unenforceable if it is greatly in advance of, or greatly behind, the trends of change in the society, but law can somewhat

Law can prevent one from carrying an attitude into action.

accelerate or retard those changes in the mores which other changes in the society are encouraging.

Summary

Power is the ability to control the actions of others. It includes *force,* the use or threat of physical coercion; *authority,* a recognized right to give orders to others, and *influence,* an ability to affect others' actions apart from authority. Influence rests both upon personal qualities and upon one's control over rewards which others desire.

The *power elite* includes those with great wealth, the top executives in business and other institutions, and the community influentials. To right wingers, the power elite are those in the communications area who may disseminate their views to a wide audience. Two contrasting views see the United States as: (1) ruled by a power elite, which may be perceived as either right-wing or left-wing, or (2) as a pluralist society in which decisions are reached through conflict. An alternative view is that the direction of policy is due to a convergence of views among the well-informed.

Organizations wield great power, which stems from their ability to mobilize the wealth and specialized skills of a great many people in a coordinated program of action. The degree of an organization's power is affected by its size, its cohesiveness, its role as perceived by members and outsiders, its alliances with other organizations, and countervailing opposition from other organizations and groups.

Coercion and *disruption* have become techniques of minority groups seeking policy change in the United States. Coercion may be *forceful* or *nonviolent. Nonviolent coercion* includes *civil disobedience* and several techniques variously known as *nonresistance, passive resistance,* or *nonviolent resistance. Disruption* is often used by very small groups to seek concessions from the majority. All of these can be loosely included in the term *demonstration,* a fairly common and possibly permanent feature of our political life. Demonstrations are dangerous weapons which sometimes gain victories but which often debase democratic processes and may conceivably provoke a repressive reaction.

Unorganized masses possess a great and often unused power, especially in democratic societies. People may be individually powerless in mass society; yet as masses they may be collectively decisive. Mass power is expressed through the mass market, which determines what products, designs, and entertainment forms shall predominate; it is expressed in the mass veto of elite decisions through mass noncooperation; it is expressed directly through the voting power of the masses, who thus determine which social policies shall prevail.

Law is a major instrument of social power, for law legitimizes the use of force by certain groups for certain ends. Most laws are an expression of the moral consensus of the society. The power of lower-class citizens has been enlarged by provision of free legal services. Judicial activism has enlarged the power of the courts and enabled them to institute policies not specifically approved by legislation.

Law also molds the mores of a society. Law institutionalizes the mores of certain groups and imposes these mores upon the remainder of society. The power of the law to change the mores is not unlimited. Law cannot change mores or behavior in a direction opposed to the other forces of change in the society. Law can accelerate or retard changes in mores or behavior in the direction in which they are already moving in response to other changes and pressures in the society. The effects of the law are indirect; by changing behavior and restructuring the contacts between groups, attitudes and mores are eventually modified. Law both expresses and makes social policy; it is both a conservative and a creative force in society.

Questions and projects

1. Distinguish between force, influence, and authority. Which is most characteristic of the dean of women in a college? Of a greatly admired university professor? Of an ex-President of the United States?

2. Is there a "power elite" among the student body on your campus? If so, upon what positions or characteristics is it based? Are there some reputed power structures which have little real power? Would these differ from campus to campus?

3. In your institution, what persons or groups do you believe would dominate the decision making in each of these issues: whether to drop intercollegiate athletics; whether to add a school of engineering to the institution; whether to dismiss a popular professor who has become "controversial"; whether to approve a student government charter sought by student leaders? Having formulated your answers, now answer the question: Who do you think really runs your institution?

4. Why is an effective alliance between radical students and workers highly unlikely?

5. Why does violence appeal to some campus militants? Is violence a legitimate activity on the campus?

6. Very often the policy statements of the official spokesman for organized groups are not carried into action. What are some reasons for this inaction?

7. Must power be organized? Are there any ways for unorganized masses to express real power? Of all power expression in our society, how much is carried out by organizations?

8. What is meant by the statement that "law structures the power relationships" of a society? Can you think of any recent changes in power relationships which have been brought about (at least in part) by law?

9. What is the normal relationship between law and the mores in civilized societies? Is it ever possible to enforce a law which is not backed by a firm moral consensus?

10. Make a brief study of campus influentials by the *reputed-power* approach. Query a few faculty members to see whether they perceive the campus power system in the same way as the students.

11. Are there any groups in America which have been gaining power in recent years? Losing power? Why?

12. In Marvin E. Olsen, *Power in Societies* (see Suggested Readings), read the selection by Mills, pp. 241–261, and by Bell and Parson, pp. 262–278. Which do you find most convincing, the viewpoint of Mills or of his critics? Why?

13. In G. William Domhoff, *The Higher Circles: The Governing Class in America,* Random House, New York, 1970, read pp. 281–308, in which he discusses charges that America is ruled by a left-wing group of intellectuals. Does he dispose satisfactorily of these charges? Are the charges more credible that America is ruled by a group of managers who manipulate social policy in favor of the wealthy?

14. Read Joseph W. Bishop, Jr., "Lawyers at the Bar," *Commentary,* 58:48–53, August, 1974. Is judicial activism an extension or a restriction of democratic political processes? Make out a case for either view.

Suggested readings

AIKEN, MICHAEL, AND PAUL E. MOTT: *The Structure of Community Power,* Random House, Inc., New York, 1970. A series of readings drawn from research articles on the bases of social power in a community.

BISHOP, JOSEPH W., JR.: "Lawyers at the Bar," *Commentary,* 58:48–53, August, 1974. A discussion of the tendency toward judicial activism and its impact on the democratic process.

BOUMA, DONALD H.: "Issue-Analysis Approach to Community Power: A Case Study of Realtors in Kalamazoo," *The American Journal of Economics and Sociology,* 29:241–252, July, 1970. An analysis of the power of a cohesive organization, with some reflections on the issue-oriented versus the reputational approach to organizational and individual power.

CLOWARD, RICHARD A., AND FRANCES FOX PIVEN: *The Politics of Turmoil: Essays on Poverty, Race and the Urban Crisis,* Pantheon Books, New York, 1974. A series of essays primarily directed at efforts to involve the urban poor in power relationships.

*COLEMAN, JAMES S.: *Community Conflict,* The Free Press of Glencoe, Inc., New York, 1957. A brief, readable analysis of power conflicts in the community.

*ETZIONI, AMITAI: *Demonstration Democracy,* Gordon and Breach Science Publishers, Inc., New York, 1971. An analysis of a series of demonstrations and of their current role in political life.

FISH, JOHN HALL: *Black Power/White Control: The Study of the Woodlawn Organization in Chicago,* Princeton University Press, Princeton, N.J., 1973. A description of an attempt to apply the Alinsky tactics of organizing the poor by stressing their grievances which also highlights black and white interaction in a power context.

*HACKER, ANDREW: "Power To Do What?" in IRVING LOUIS HOROWITZ, *The New Sociology,* Oxford University Press, Fair Lawn, New Jersey, 1964, pp. 134–147. Comments on the limits of the power of the managerial elite.

KAHN, SI: *How People Get Power: Organizing Oppressed Communities for Action,* McGraw-Hill Book Company, New York, 1970. An author with extensive community-organization experience outlines strategies to use in helping poor people gain power.

LINDQUIST, JOHN D., AND ROBERT I. BLACKBURN: "Middlegrove: The Locus of Campus Power at a State University," *American Association of University Professors Bulletin,* 60:367–378, December, 1974. An attempt to determine who really holds the power on the campus.

MILLER, DELBERT C.: *International Community Power Structures: Comparative Studies of Four World Cities,* Indiana University Press, Bloomington, 1970. Report of an investigation of the composition and effectiveness of community power elites in Seattle, Bristol, Lima, and Cordoba.

*MILLS, C. WRIGHT: *The Power Elite,* Oxford University Press, Fair Lawn, New Jersey, 1956. The development of the thesis that our society is run by a small group of power wielders. See also the critical review by DANIEL BELL, "The Power Elite—Reconsidered," *American Journal of Sociology,* 64:238–250, November, 1958.

*MOYNIHAN, DANIEL P.: *Maximum Feasible Misunderstanding: Community Action in the War on Poverty,* The Free Press, New York, 1969. An analysis of the difficulties which arose when the poverty programs of the federal government tried to provide for "maximum feasible participation" of the poor.

*OLSEN, MARVIN E.: *Power in Societies,* The Macmillan Co., New York, 1970. A book of readings which presents many of the classic statements on this topic.

WOODWARD, C. VANN: "What Became of the 1960's?", *New Republic,* 171:18–25, Nov. 9, 1974. Analysis of disruptive demonstrations on the campus during the 1960s.

Chapter 16 •Race and ethnic relations

The most sought-after employee in the U.S. today is a black, Spanish-surnamed female engineer. Several thousand federal contractors would fight to hire her, if only they could find her.

That tells the story of "affirmative action," circa 1975. Five years ago, the government began to enforce its order that federal contractors would have to employ minority workers if they wanted to keep their contracts. Three years ago it did the same for women workers. Now, a *Business Week* survey indicates, the process is well under way, and most contractors have steadily increased their percentages of both.

Down the road, recession layoffs could raise the issue of whether minorities and women should be retained regardless of seniority. But right now, contractors face what Walter A. Haas, Jr., chairman of Levi Strauss & Co., calls the natural "second generation" of affirmative action problems: heavy pressure to move minorities and women into professional and managerial slots. Among these groups, engineers are scarce, and the race to nab them resembles a gold rush. *(Reprinted from the Jan. 27, 1975, issue of* Business Week *with special permission.* © *1975 by McGraw-Hill, Inc.)*

Probably no change in recent years epitomizes the changes in race relations as sharply as the development of government programs of "affirmative action." Not only has discrimination been banned, but correcting the effects of past discrimination has become a major government commitment. This does not mean that either sexual or racial status (and this chapter is primarily concerned with the latter) has ceased to be important.

Racial and ethnic relations are a worldwide concern. One study concludes that only twelve countries in the world are "essentially homogeneous," while another survey finds thirty-four countries containing "subordinate" minorities of over one million people [Deedy, 1975, p. 3]. The United States is not on this list, meaning that there are thirty-four countries which treat sizable minorities less well than does the United States. Much of the world is still separated by what Giddings, an early American sociologist [1913, p. 17], called a "consciousness of kind." People who are "like us" we welcome; those who are "different" we often reject. The basis of similarity is some feeling of group identity, which may be based upon nationality, religious affiliation, economic status, language usage, or regional habitat, as well as race. Of all these criteria, race is one of those most widely used as a basis for group identity, and often "race relations" is considered a subject by itself.

Those who are different we often reject.

The concept of race

"Race" is a troublesome concept, for it has no generally agreed meaning. In popular usage, "race" may mean all of humanity (the "human race"), a nationality (the "German race"), or even a group which is mixed in nearly all respects but socially designated as different (the "Jewish race"). Almost any kind of category of people may be called a "race."

Even social scientists have not fully agreed in defining the term [Bloom, 1972]. Some have defined a race as a group of people separated from other groups by a distinctive combination of physical characteristics. As will be seen later, this poses certain difficulties because of intermixing, overlapping, and the gradual shading of physical characteristics (e.g., skin color) along a continuum without definite separations. Therefore, a "race" is not a biologically distinct grouping of people, yet many people think and act as though it were. Race is a socially significant reality, for people attach great importance to one's assumed racial identity. The scientist's fondness for neat scientific precision must be tempered by the need to deal with a tremendously important social reality. Perhaps an acceptable definition might read: A race is a group of people somewhat different from other groups in its combination of inherited physical characteristics, but race is also substantially determined by popular social definition.

The contemporary view of race

Scientists seek to classify races as groups of people with distinctive combinations of physical traits that set them off from other groups. Skin color is the principal trait used in classifying races, although hair color, hair texture, amount of body hair, eye fold, shape of nose and lips, head contour, and body build are also used.

How many races are there? No objectively correct number can be given. Whether there are three, six, or fifty races depends upon which physical features we consider significant and upon the degree of similarity in physical appearance we demand of the members of a race. Dobzhansky comments on this confusion:

Boyd has recognized five, and Coon, Garn, and Birdsell nine or thirty or thirty-two races. Does it follow that some of these classifications are necessarily wrong? No, all may be right; it should always be kept in mind that while race differences are objectively ascertainable facts, the number of races we choose to recognize is a matter of convenience. (Theodosius Dobzhansky, *Mankind Evolving: The Evolution of the Human Species,* Yale University Press, New Haven, Conn., 1962, p. 266.)

It is conventional to divide the human species into three main racial stocks—the Mongoloid (yellow and brown), the Negroid (black), and the Caucasoid (white). Most groups can be placed in one of these three categories, as is shown in Figure 13. This figure also shows that the racial placement of some groups is uncertain because their physical characteristics overlap. For example, the Asian Indians have Mongoloid skin color but Caucasoid facial features; the Ainu of Northern Japan have Caucasoid skin color and hair with Mongoloid facial features. A further complication arises from the fact that the races have been busily interbreeding for thousands of years so that nearly all racial groups are considerably intermixed. Some groups, like the Jews, are not properly racial at all yet form a definite social entity and are often treated as though they were a race.

Physical anthropologists in searching for an objective basis for racial classification are now placing emphasis on genetic composition as indicated by blood types. Currently, there is an attempt to combine bloodtype data with more easily observable differences such as color, stature, hair form, nasal index, etc. Dobzhansky [1962], for instance, has suggested a tentative classification of thirty-four racial groups which he hopes is neither so broad that it obscures vital differences nor so numerous that it is unwieldy. Such research and attempts at sound classifications may be expected to provide much useful information about the various branches of Homo sapiens. The student should remember, however, that at the present time there is no generally accepted pattern of classification and that whenever one sees comment on "racial" differences, it is necessary to know what groups are involved. In the following sections of this chapter "racial" usually refers to "Negroid" and "Caucasian" and to members of these races found in the North American continent.

At this point a comment on terminology is in order. There is a common tendency to refer to Americans with "Negroid" ancestry as *blacks* rather than as *Negroes*. There really is not much linguistic difference, since *Negro* is a Spanish word meaning black. In this textbook, we have generally used the term *black,* except when reproducing quotations and statistical or historical materials.

The scientific view of race differences

It is clear that the races differ in some inherited physical characteristics. May they also vary in their inborn intellectual and emotional characteristics? This is a reasonable logical possibility. Is it a fact?

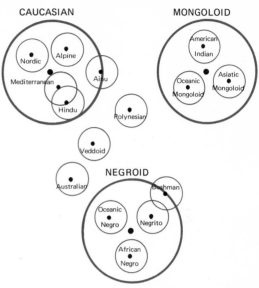

Distance between the centers of circles indicates the closeness of relationship. For example, Kroeber shows both the Polynesians and the Australians (native) as outside all three major racial stocks but shows the Australians as closer to the Negroid races than are the Polynesians.

Figure 13. The human races. (Source: A. L. Kroeber, *Anthropology,* Harcourt, Brace and World, Inc., 1948, p. 10.)

Physical race differences are unimportant

Physically, all races are approximately alike in every important characteristic. With a few exceptions (such as that a dark skin is useful under tropical sun), the differences are ornamental, not functionally important. The physical differences within the human species are very modest compared with the differences within many species—dogs or horses, for example.

Most scientists today are agreed that all races are of one species, the product of a single evolution.[1] and all races are about equally "close" to the other animals. For example, the

[1]For a dissenting view which advocates the theory of a multiple origin of races see C. S. Coon, *The Origin of Races,* Alfred A. Knopf, Inc., New York, 1962. For a critique of Coon's approach, see T. Dobzhansky, "The Origin of Races," *Scientific American,* 208: 169–172, 1963.

blacks more closely resemble the apes in hair color, nose form, and facial slant; but the whites more closely resemble the apes in lip form, hair texture, and amount of body hair.

Intellectual and emotional race differences are hard to measure

Intellectual and emotional characteristics cannot be measured directly but must be inferred from some kind of performance. Here a difficulty arises. Many things can affect performance—native ability, experience, motivation, self-confidence, physical health, testing situation, and still others. The importance of any one of these factors can be measured accurately only if all others are held absolutely constant. How can comparative racial ability be measured? Only by comparing the performance of two racial groups where all these other factors are held constant. Does the evidence usually offered meet this test? Two kinds of evidence of racial inequality are usually offered: differential racial achievement and intelligence-test scores.

Differential racial achievements. If all races have equal innate abilities, why have they not made equal achievements? This question is deceptively ethnocentric. It really asks, "If they are as smart as we are, why don't they do what we do as well as we do it?" Meanwhile, another people may be asking the same question about us. Obviously, if we define achievement purely in terms of our culture's values, we cannot lose. As with the discussion about the superiority of the temperate climate, the proof for superiority of racial achievement is only convincing when one ignores changes over a time span. Suppose achievement is defined as the building of a great civilization. Does this identify the superior races? Superior at what moment in history? By this test, the superior "races" 5,000 years ago would be the Egyptians and the Semitic peoples of Asia Minor; 3,000 years ago, these plus the Indians and the Chinese; 2,500 years ago, the Greeks and the Persians; 2,000 years ago, the Romans; and so it goes. Why, then, did the Nordic whites spend four-fifths of human history hovering about campfires and wiping their greasy fingers on their thighs? The cultural-achievement test of racial superiority works out most nicely if it is confined to the last thousand years of history.

But, one may ask, when have the blacks built a great civilization? Doesn't their lack of creativity show inferiority? It is true that the blacks built no very impressive civilization in the tropical jungles or arid grasslands where many of the blacks lived. Neither did anybody else. But in other parts of black Africa, great trading cities arose which by the fourteenth century were the equal of any of the cities of Europe [Davidson, 1964, 1966]. Later, the history of African civilizations was forgotten or intentionally buried, after the slave trade began to hasten their destruction.

The leading early civilizations were river-valley civilizations. Not until the development of modern technology was it possible to plant civilization in the tropical jungle, where its permanence is still uncertain. The great early civilizations arose in Egypt, Asia Minor, and southern Asia. Some of their builders were, at least in part, Caucasian; others were entirely Mongolian. But all of them built great civilizations when the northern Europeans were illiterate stone-age savages.

Cultural achievement is a product of many variables—geography and climate, contacts with other peoples, dominant values of the culture, the level of preexisting technology, and, possibly, racial ability. Since we know no satisfactory way to hold these other variables constant, we have no scientific way to measure the factor of racial ability in cultural achievement.

A different sort of cultural achievement is a group's success in absorbing and using an advanced culture with which it comes into contact. By this test, the Nordic whites came off rather poorly. Falling heir to Roman civilization, they kicked it to pieces and sat on the remnants for hundreds of years. The nonwhite races of the world today, by comparison, are doing rather well.

Intelligence test findings. For over sixty years, we have been attempting to measure the ability of various groups through intelligence testing. Such tests are practically unanimous in showing that disadvantaged groups make lower scores than the groups which have been more successful. Sociologists tend to discount any significance of these results as demonstrations of innate racial abilities because it seems evident that environmental conditions play a major role in influencing test performance.

The first test scores to be prominently noted were the Army Alpha tests used to screen recruits in World War I. The average scores of whites were higher than those of blacks. Two qualifications, however, are important: Many individual blacks had higher scores than many individual whites; and when the scores were broken down by states, blacks in the top three Northern states had higher average scores than whites in the bottom three Southern states—as is shown in Table 23.

A probable explanation is that the Northern black groups came from a more favorable environment, and that this advantage was reflected in their performance on intelligence tests. The average white man in these Southern states at the turn of the century lived a poverty-stricken life in an area with poor schools and little social stimulation of any kind. The Northern blacks, although subject to many types of discrimination, probably had better schools and a more intellectually stimulating environment than many of the Southern whites.

Not only are there some exceptional cases in which black scores exceed white, but there are many variations within the white groups. Among the earlier intelligence-test studies, almost all heavily Catholic groups made rather low average scores [Klineberg, 1944, p. 35]. Does this mean that Catholics have less native

TABLE 23 INTELLIGENCE TEST SCORES OF SOUTHERN WHITES AND NORTHERN BLACK MEN, BY STATES: ARMY RECRUITS, WORLD WAR I

Whites		Negroes	
State	**Median score**	**State**	**Median score**
Mississippi	41.25	New York	45.02
Kentucky	41.50	Illinois	47.35
Arkansas	41.55	Ohio	49.50

Source: Otto Klineberg, "What Psychological Tests Show," in Bernhard J. Stern and Allain Locke (eds.), *When Peoples Meet*, Progressive Education Association, New York, 1942, p. 449.

intelligence than Protestants? The heavily Catholic groups tested at that time were from urban slum areas, densely populated by immigrants of southern European background; thus, their children were a disadvantaged group. The lowest test scores of all have been made by the isolated mountain people of the Southern highlands. [Hirsch, 1928] who are entirely Protestant, and are the most nearly pure Anglo-Saxons in the country. It is clear that we cannot predict a group's test score from its religion or racial origin, but we can make a quite accurate prediction of a group's intelligence-test score if we know its cultural environment.

These conclusions have been challenged quite sharply by Jensen [1968, 1969, 1973], Eysenck [1971], Herrnstein [1973] and others. Jensen disputes many of the environmentalist explanations and states that blacks come out even poorer on "culturally fair" tests than on verbal tests which might be assumed to have a vocabulary hazard. He interprets what he regards as the failure of compensatory education (special schooling designed to improve the performance of low-achieving students) as due to a disregard of hereditary differences between students. He writes with appropriate scientific caution, stating that hereditary racial differences in ability have been neither proven nor disproven and recognizing that group tests tell nothing about particular individuals; yet he concludes that "it is not an unreasonable hypothesis that genetic factors are strongly implicated in the average Negro-White intelligence difference" [1969, p. 82]. He does not deny that environment has some effect, but estimates that heredity is probably responsible for 80 percent of the difference between IQ scores. A storm of criticism greeted Jensen's report and he has been a constant center of controversy.

Some of the consequences of inferring ability from intelligence tests can be seen in the results of a "readiness for learning test" administered in Dallas, Texas (Table 24). On the one hand, this test demonstrates that there is no warrant for a blanket racial categorization as inferior or superior, since 26 percent of the blacks, those in the "above average" and "average" groupings, ranked ahead of the 31 percent of the whites in the "below average" grouping. Yet if students were grouped by ability, as is often done, three-fourths of the black students would have been in the bottom group. This means that the use of intelligence tests may be seen as a means of resegregating the schools after formal racial segregation has been abolished.

Emotions run high on this question because of the implication that if any differences in average innate racial ability are conceded, this might justify racial discrimination. We should note that two questions are involved: (1) are there any genetically based, hereditary, innate racial differences in ability? (2) are any such differences, if they exist, great enough to justify differential treatment for different races? The first of these questions has no indisputable answer, for most scientists are agreed that while such differences are possible, none have

TABLE 24 READINESS FOR LEARNING AMONG DALLAS FIRST-GRADE PUPILS

Percent	Negro	White
In below-average grouping	74	31
In average grouping	18	32
In above-average grouping	8	37

Source: A. D. Albright, "What are Standards?" *Southern School News*, June, 1958, p. 1.

yet been established. Jensen admits that extremely unfavorable conditions may depress performance on the IQ tests to a considerable degree. Some indication of what this might mean is given by an experiment in which the children of mothers with an IQ of less than 70 (100 is the average score on the Sanford Binet test, and 70 is considered quite low) were given intensive training. Children aged three or four months were "exposed to mental stimulation of a wide variety for several hours each day under a one-to-one ratio with trained adults" until they reached the age of two [Strickland, 1973, p. 154]. From the age of two the program continued in small groups. When these children were compared with a control group of children of apparently similar heredity, the results were quite remarkable. At forty-two months of age, they "measured an average of 33 I.Q. points higher than the control group with some of them registering I.Q.s as high as 135" [Strickland, 1973, p. 158].

This experiment does not prove either that there is no hereditary component in intelligence or that Jensen has overestimated its size. Further, a program as expensive as this in terms of manpower could never be applied to very many children. What the experiment does indicate is that many children, who apparently have a very limited heredity, can be greatly improved with ideal training. This would imply that we may have exaggerated the extent to which members of any group are bound by hereditary limitations. Relatively few persons have parents as limited as did these children, and if children as limited as these can improve, there would seem to be an even better chance for children whose parents are closer to the norm. It may be true that heredity provides upper limits beyond which intelligence cannot grow, but neither Jensen nor others have *proved* what these limits are.

Significance of group ability differences. If innate racial differences exist, are they large enough to justify differential treatment for racial groups? In this respect, we note that even if Jensen's conclusion of an average eleven-point IQ difference between whites and blacks when socioeconomic levels are approximately equal [Jensen, 1968, p. 81] were to be accepted *as an innate, genetic* difference, this is no greater than the average IQ difference between different children in the same family. Furthermore, an eleven-point difference in *average* scores for the two racial groups would still leave many persons in the "inferior" group well above the average for the "superior" group, and many individuals in the "superior" group would rank below the average for the "inferior" group.

Within the family, children of different IQ levels may be given equal treatment even though parents try to provide training appropriate to different abilities and interests. Society does not have to pour all its citizens into a common mold and can adjust education and work to varying interests and talents. Variations in IQ level or other measures of talent may exist, but average group differences do not justify allocating opportunities on a racial basis.

It is also possible that any genetic differences between groups may be impermanent. The discovery of the genetic alphabet by Nirenberg and Korana [Science News, Jan. 11, 1969] and other imminent genetic discoveries open the possibility that we may before long find it easier to alter our genetic characteristics than to change out social environment. It is conceivable that people in the future will be less involved in arguments over genetic differences than in actually changing genetic inheritance and social environment in ways which may make current racial concepts obsolete. (See comments on this topic on pages 75–76).

Group differences in behavior are learned

Sometimes the "all men are alike" theme is distorted into a caricature of the facts. It is true that all groups appear to be alike in most of their inherited capacities. It is also true that groups differ greatly in their learned behavior. This learned behavior includes the presence or lack of the deferred gratification pattern, conventional or rowdy conduct, family responsibility or irresponsibility, and a host of other reactions. Difficult behavior may be due to adverse social conditions, but is nonetheless difficult. Variations in average learned behavior account for many of the problems of group interaction. For instance, white resistance to school integration arises, in considerable part, from the fact that genuine school integration (racial balance) would expose many middle-class white children to the conduct norms and academic achievement levels of lower-class minority children.

How should we interpret such facts? To some, they serve as an excuse for a continued denial of equal opportunity. The more perceptive observer sees that these unflattering facts are the *products* of unequal opportunity and will persist as long as opportunities and rewards are unequal.

The social scientist recognizes that many *very real* group differences exist in personality, behavior, and achievement. There is no convincing evidence that any of these differences are rooted in anything inborn; in fact, the evidence strongly indicates that all or nearly all *major group differences in personality, behavior, and achievement are entirely learned;* they are rooted not in heredity, but in group tradition, opportunity, and reward. The supposedly impartial observer notes that minorities have a more unfavorable record than the dominant group in many kinds of social pathology, and so acquiesces in a system whereby minorities have inferior housing, more limited schooling, and more restricted job opportunities, thus producing the very results originally predicted. Why, then, have blacks excelled in music, dancing, and athletics? Not because of any special ability, but because these fields have been more open to blacks. Why do Jews pursue trade and avoid farming? For over a thousand years, trade was the only occupation gentiles would let them engage in. If scientists wish to understand special behavior traits of any group, they do not study the group's heredity; they study the conditions under which the group has lived and worked and interacted with other groups throughout its history.

Even agreement on the extent to which scholars should use an environmental or a hereditarian perspective does not necessarily bring unity. Table 25 indicates the different words used to describe similar environmental conditions. The reality described is pretty much the same, but the emotional impact of "disadvantaged" is certainly not the same as that of "dispossessed." The more neutral term has the implication of a handicap placed by fate upon a given group, while "dispossessed" implies victimization of one group and exploitation by another. The first label indicates a problem to be alleviated by social engineering; the second, guilt by one party and suffering by another, for which the appropriate action is revolution by the victim or restitution by the erstwhile exploiter. Very often a scholar's choice of vocabulary reveals his or her minority- or majority-group affiliation. However, sometimes there is agreement across ethnic lines. Further, as we shall see in the next section, sometimes those within the same group differ as to how problems are to be handled.

Minority response to pathology

What is the minority response to the problem of high crime rates and low educational achievement? Because of space limitations, our analysis concentrates upon blacks, but it also applies, to a greater or lesser degree, to Mexican-Americans, Puerto Ricans, and American Indians.

School and law observance problems are so glaringly obvious that it is impossible to deny their existence. One may argue as to their extent or attach blame to white society, but

TABLE 25 PERSPECTIVES

Majority	Minority
Disadvantaged	Dispossessed
Handicapped	Penalized
Economic deprivation	Economic subjugation
Culturally deprived	Culturally oppressed
Unequal	Disequalized

Source: Chuck Stone, "The Psychology of Whiteness vs. The Politics of Blackness: An Educational Power Struggle," *Educational Researcher*, 1:6, January, 1972, p. 6.

few people will deny that high crime rates and low school achievement are real problems. This leaves at least three possible alternatives: (1) to attack the measures (of crime and school achievement) as unjust and call for a change in rules of the game to diminish present stigma; (2) to call for black efforts to reduce crime and to increase school achievement; (3) to call for the aid of white Americans in the form of a domestic Marshall Plan, named after the American rehabilitation efforts which brought prosperity back to Western Europe after World War II. This last idea was brilliantly expounded by the late Whitney Young of the Urban League, who called for a crash program involving the expenditure of billions of dollars to solve the ills, not only of blacks, but of all Americans handicapped by poverty [Young, 1964]. Although never officially adopted as government policy, it influenced the expansion of welfare and educational programs which were a part of the "War on Poverty" created in the 1960s, some parts of which are still surviving. The results to date show a massive gain in black social mobility—discussed later in this chapter—with, however, many problems still remaining.

High crime rates. Homicide is around ten times as prevalent among blacks as among whites, and burglary over three times as high while blacks make up about a third of all prisoners, though comprising only about a ninth of the total U.S. population [Wolfgang and Cohen, 1970, pp. 32–33].

One reaction is to charge the courts and police with unfairness and label black criminals as victims of an unjust legal system. This sentiment is expressed in a comparatively restrained way by a black lawyer who states ". . . in an institutional sense in almost all instances the law functions in a discriminatory and unfair manner when blacks (and poor people) are involved" [Burns, 1970, p. 228]. Is this true? Numerous studies using data collected before 1960 report convincing evidence of race discrimination in law enforcement, but more recent studies find very little such evidence [Hindeland, 1969], suggesting that this form of racial injustice has declined. A slightly different accusation is that black crime is produced by an unjust social system. In the words of Eldridge Cleaver: "the blacks . . . cry out 'POLICE BRUTALITY!' The police are the armed guardians of the social order. The blacks are the chief victims of the social order. A conflict of interests exists therefore between the blacks and the police" [Cleaver, 1967, pp. 132–134].

Others in the black community do not see the black criminal as a symbol of social protest but as a menace to the black race. They know that most of the victims are black (see Table 26) and that the black criminal, more than anyone else, has brought terror and violence to the black community. Typical of their response is the action of 200 black ministers in Chicago, who noted that crime had gotten so bad that residents were afraid to leave home after dark and who pledged their cooperation with law enforcement agencies [Weintraub, 1972]. A similar sentiment was expressed by black leaders in a middle-sized Northern city after a young black boy had been killed by a burglar:

Because we are so aware of the depressing conditions under which blacks have been forced to survive and the glaring inadequacies of the criminal justice system in mistreatment of blacks accused, many have been reluctant in the past to support or even appear to work in cooperation with our law enforcement agencies . . .

We recognize that we have reached the apex of crime in the black community and throughout the city.

Therefore:

1. We urge that any information that would lead to the apprehension of the murderer of Todd Ozier should be reported to the law enforcement authorities. . . .

3. It should be evident to everyone that none of us are immune from crime and if effective prevention is to take place, it will be through the shared and collective efforts of the community. (Blaine Lam: "Black Officials Ask Total Effort to Combat Crime," *Kalamazoo Gazette,* Oct. 30, 1974, p. 1.)

Educational achievement. This is not identical with the number of years of schooling completed, in which blacks have made a rapid advance. The proportion of black males finishing high school rose from 38 percent to 64 percent between 1960 and 1972, while the proportion of blacks attending college nearly doubled between 1967 and 1972 [Bureau of the Census, 1973, pp. 62–63]. The gap in the total years of schooling for blacks and whites is fast closing, but in educational achievement, as

TABLE 26 WHO SUFFERS MOST FROM CRIME? Racial and Income Differences Among Victims of Serious Personal and Property Crimes, Per 100,000 Population

Type of crime	Income under $6,000		Income $6,000 or more	
	White	Negro	White	Negro
Against person	402	748	244	262
Against property	1,829	1,927	1,765	3,024

Source: NORC survey cited in Philip H. Ennis: *Criminal Victimization*, President's Commission on Law Enforcement and Administration of Justice, U.S. Government Printing Office, Washington, D.C., 1967. Reprinted in David G. Bromley and Charles F. Longino, Jr. (eds.), *White Racism and Black Americans*, Schenckman Publishing Company, Cambridge, Mass., 1972.

measured by standardized tests, there are still major disparities. In terms of mental age or grade-level performance, the average black child is a year behind the average white child at the start of school and three years behind at the age of eighteen [Jencks, 1972, p. 81].

As in the case of crime, blacks take two almost completely different approaches. One is to charge that the tests are culturally biased toward white middle-class values and thus are irrelevant to black youth. Another approach is to work energetically to raise the level of achievement on these tests by black children. These viewpoints are vividly represented in a controversy between William Raspberry, columnist for the *Washington Post,* and Barbara Sizemore, superintendent of schools in Washington, D.C.

The controversy was triggered by a decline in the reading scores of sixth-grade students in the Washington, D.C. schools, In 1971, they were reading at slightly above the national urban norm for sixth grade, but, by 1974, were reading at a grade level of 5.2. Mrs. Sizemore's explanation, in large part, was that the tests were culturally biased. Raspberry pointed out that whatever defects the tests have, cultural bias can hardly explain a deterioration in one city as compared to others. He adds:

. . . when they [tests] tell you that you're not doing as well as others or as well as you used to do, you've got a couple of choices: you can either attack the tests themselves or you can change what you are doing. It's not necessarily Supt. Sizemore's fault that things are getting worse. But it would have been reassuring if, at the time the tests were released, she had told us where the problem was or that she intended in short order to find out. What we got instead was some disappointing talk about 'cultural bias.'" (William Raspberry: "Reading, Math and 'Cultural Bias,'" *Washington Post,* Oct. 26, 1974.)

The differences between Raspberry and Sizemore typify a major split between two groups of black intellectuals. Mrs. Sizemore represents a group with a major concern for com-

munity control and black identity, who want freedom from what they regard as white standards as well as freedom from direct white supervision. Raspberry is concerned about black social mobility, feels that educational achievement is essential to this, and wants the school to place a major emphasis on enabling black children to meet the standards prevailing in the total community. In essence, their clash is between a drive for success in an integrated society and the construction of what is, at least partially, a separate black society free from white competition. These two issues—crime and educational achievement—are samples of the many problems upon which black leaders are divided as to goals and procedures.

Patterns of ethnic relationships

We often hear people speak of the "Jewish race" or the "German race." These peoples are not races in the usual scientific use of the term; yet they are often thought of and treated as races. Sociologists use the term *ethnic group* to refer to any kind of group, racial or otherwise, which is socially differentiated to an important degree and has developed its own subculture. In other words, an ethnic group is one recognized by society and by itself as a definite group. Although the distinction is associated with a particular set of ancestors, its identifying marks may be language, religion, relationship to a geographic locale, nationality, physical appearance, or any combination of these. The term is properly applied whenever the group differences are considered socially significant enough to set off the group clearly from others. Thus in the United States the name "Catholic" by itself would not be considered an ethnic label, but "French Canadian Catholic" would call up an image of a group with a definite character both in its own eyes and in those of the rest of society. Although we find some pattern of ethnic arrangements in every complex society, we find also a great variety in the way different groups have arranged to live together. We shall look at these patterns under four headings: segregation and discrimination, amalgamation, individual rights, and group rights.

Segregation and discrimination

The essence of this pattern is that society is run for the benefit of one ethnic group. It is carried to its ultimate end when it is decided that there is no place for competing groups and these are eliminated. This was attempted in Germany between 1933 and 1945 by the slaughter of the Jews, and in Uganda in 1973 by the expulsion of the Indians.

Usually the coexistence of different ethnic groups is tolerated but on an unequal basis. *Segregation* is a device to restrict interethnic contact to those forms which the dominant group finds convenient. It includes a ban on intermarriage, along with separate schools and separate facilities of most kinds. The subordinate group, however, is allowed (or more accurately, required) to work for the dominant group. There may be very close and intimate associations, as with house servants and nursemaids, but these are determined by the dominant group and carry no suggestion of equality.

Discrimination means literally treating *equal people unequally.* It means that people in the subordinate ethnic group have unequal access to the desirable jobs, receive less pay for the same work than those in the dominant group, and receive inferior government services and benefits. At this writing, segregation and discrimination are the pattern in the Union of South Africa, where Africans have no participation in the national government and receive wages only a fraction of those paid to whites. This pattern was required by law for many years in the Southern part of the United States. It also existed to a considerable degree, but without legal sanction, in the Northern states. Since World War II, it has been attacked by legislation, court decisions, and the volun-

tary actions of many groups. The current picture is spotty, with discrimination ended (or even reversed) in some activities or fields of employment while it survives in others.

Amalgamation

While assimilation refers to a blending of two cultures, *amalgamation* means a biological interbreeding of two peoples of distinct physical appearance until they become one stock. Although distinct physical types have seldom entirely disappeared, enough interbreeding has taken place so that it is difficult to find any large group of individuals who form a "pure" racial type, if, indeed, there ever have been any. England has practiced amalgamation on a grand scale. The Saxon invasion of the sixth century soon produced the Anglo-Saxon type, to be blended again with the Normans in the eleventh century. Hawaii includes the descendants of the original inhabitants of the islands, plus a large number of Caucasian settlers, Chinese, Japanese, Filipinos, and Koreans. All these have intermarried quite freely, the highest rates being in groups which have more males than females.

In the United States mainland, the conditions of slavery favored the amalgamation of white and black. Although intermarriage was illegal in the Southern states, concubinage was widespread. Sexual access by white males to black females was usually regarded as one of the privileges of the caste system. The system emphasized the dominant position of the white male, since he was in a position to possess black females at will and to prohibit such relationships between black males and white females. Mere association with white females, however willing, would subject a black male to charges of rape, and hundreds of black men have been lynched or legally executed on this charge. No white man has been lynched for a similar offense against a black woman, and only in recent years have white men been legally prosecuted for raping black women.

Amalgamation in the United States has greatly declined during the past century, for a variety of reasons: the end of slavery, the decline of the plantation, the diminishing number of white households with black servants, the rising status of blacks, a growing mutual disapproval of interracial sex contacts, and possibly the spread of contraception. But while extramarital amalgamation has declined, has interethnic marriage increased?

Recent data indicate that in at least two ethnic groups there has been an increase in intermarriage. The intermarriage rate between Jews and gentiles has showed a spectacular increase in the last decade, indicating that the tradition of Jewish endogamy, once very strong, is now greatly weakened (see Figure 14). Black and white intermarriage has also shown an increase (see Table 27), but the total still comprises less than 1 percent of all marriages involving blacks. It is difficult to decide whether the increase is a minor fluctuation or a definite trend toward more interracial marriage.

Among both blacks and Jews, men are more likely to outmarry than women. Among exogamous blacks, men outnumber women by a ratio of 1.7 to 1; among Jews, the ratio is 2.7 to 1 [ratios calculated on data in Cohen, 1974, and Heer, 1974]. Among Jews, women presumably are still more oriented to the endogamous family. This is borne out by an attitude survey of college students [Cavan, 1971, p.

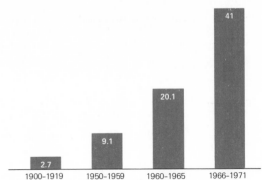

Figure 14. Trends in Jewish intermarriage as a percentage of all marriages involving Jews. (Source: National Jewish Population Survey from Leland B. Cohen, *Jewish Intermarriage: An Analysis of the National Jewish Population Study,* mimeographed paper, August, 1974.)

165] which indicated that 47 percent of Jewish males had no objections to marrying out, as contrasted to only 34 percent of Jewish females. This somewhat more tolerant attitude of Jewish men, coupled with the greater male ability to initiate sexual contacts, may explain the greater male representation in Jewish intermarriages.

The lesser participation of the black woman in intermarriage is a consequence of the sexual interpretation of black liberation. In the days of slavery and even more in the discriminatory period which followed, black women were often considered a natural illicit sexual outlet for white men, while black men were threatened with death if they consorted with white women [Myrdal, 1944, p. 57]. Thus for black women, association with white men had the stigma of oppression. Today the situation is changed. Black men see association with white women as an evidence of their liberation. Similarly, white men fear charges of exploitation if they date black women, while white women see interracial dating as an evidence of liberalism. The result is not only a lesser interracial marriage rate for black women, but an antagonism between black women and white women on many a college campus [Napper, 1973].

In spite of a growing social acceptance, in-

The Saxon invasion of the sixth century soon produced the Anglo-Saxon type.

TABLE 27 NUMBER OF BLACK-WHITE MARRIAGES BY TYPE AND REGION, UNITED STATES, 1960 AND 1970

	1960	1970	Percentage change since 1960
United States: Total	51,409	64,789	+ 26.0
Husband black, wife white	25,496	41,223	+ 61.7
Husband white, wife black	25,913	23,566	− 9.1

Source: U.S. census data. Table arranged by David M. Heer: "The Prevalence of Black–White Marriage in the United States, 1960 and 1970," *Journal of Marriage and the Family,* 36 May, 1974, p. 247. Copyright © 1974 by National Council on Family Relations. Reprinted by permission.

terracial marriage is still an unusual occurrence. Some of the difficulty is indicated by the divorce rates for interracial couples married in 1960, which were higher than for either all-black or all-white marriages [Heer, 1974, p. 250].

Whether there will eventually be a complete blending of the races is by no means certain. Some years ago, it was estimated that 21 percent of the Americans classified as white have some black ancestry, while nearly three-fourths of blacks have some white ancestry [Stuckert, 1958, Burma, 1946]. Legal equality, along with increased contact between members of different races, may bring a high rate of intermarriage. It is possible, however, that our great-grandchildren may be bound by our preferences in mate selection about as tightly as we are bound by those of our great-grandfathers. So many factors are involved that it is extremely difficult to predict future intermarriage trends.

Individual rights

In the Soviet Union a book has been published about the United States entitled, *Land Without Nationality Rights* [1966]. It correctly notes that, unlike the Soviet Union, the United States does not guarantee the legal protection and nurture of ethnic cultures. Ethnic art, language, religion, and literature have to stand or fall on the basis of voluntary individual action. For the most part, ethnic cultural institutions have either disappeared or been transformed into American patterns, which critics refer to as "Anglo-conformity." Assimilation has followed as immigrants found that the society guaranteed their rights as individuals but left their cultures without protection. The "melting pot" has not worked completely, but current commentators probably exaggerate its weaknesses:

. . . the truth is that the American melting pot, on the whole, worked remarkably well. After all, if we assume that there are about 40 million white ethnics, 20 million blacks, and 10 million Spanish-Americans, that leaves 130 million people in America who have no affiliation with any particular ethnic group and little consciousness of their ethnic origins. Among them are millions of former Polish-Americans, Irish-Americans, Italian-Americans, and German-Americans who for a variety of reasons decided to become integrated into the American environment and to shed any ties they had with their respective ethnic communities (Mark M. Krug: "White Ethnic Studies: Prospects and Pitfalls," *Phi Delta Kappan,* 53: 323, January, 1972.)

For many years the big social question was whether white Americans were willing to grant black Americans the same individual rights as other Americans. Culturally, blacks certainly qualified as assimilated Americans, since they had lost practically all traces of their African background. Since black culture was primarily based on lower-class status and on residence in the rural South, it was a distinctive brand of American culture, but still definitely American. However, unlike the Europeans, blacks could be recognized by physical appearance, regardless of clothing or language usage, thereby facilitating enforcement of discriminatory patterns. Also, unlike Europeans, blacks were governed by laws restricting their

TABLE 28 BLACK AND WHITE PROGRESS IN THE UNITED STATES

Category	Year	Blacks	Whites
Percent below low income level ($4,275 in 1972)	1959, 1972	59 32	18 9
Median for man of blue-collar income	1960, 1970	$3,993 $7,772	$5,877 $9,175
Increase in median income of blue-collar workers	1960– 1970	$3,675	$3,298
Median black income as percent of white income	1965, 1972	54 59	
Percent with family income $10,000 and over (1971 dollars)	1947, 1960, 1971	4 10 30	11 24 42
Percent 20–29 years old with 4 years high school	1960, 1972	40 65	65 83
Percent 25–34 years old with 4 years college	1959, 1972	4 7.9	10.3 18.8
Number of black elected officials	1964, 1974	103 2991	

Source: Based on data reported in *The Negroes in the United States: Their Economic and Social Situation*, U.S. Department of Labor Bulletin 1511, June, 1966; Charles E. Silberman, "Negro Economic Gains Impressive but Precarious," *Fortune*, 82:74–78, July, 1970; U.S. Census Bureau, Current Population Report, Series P-23, No. 66, 1973.

activities. There were laws passed by many states (not all Southern) requiring various forms of segregation. In 1944, Gunnar Myrdal, an eminent Swedish economist, surveyed the American scene and found the status of blacks to be the big contradiction in American political practice, since blacks had been excluded from the general principle that all Americans as individuals had equal rights. His analysis was that the United States either had to scrap its claim to being a democracy or admit blacks to the same individual rights guaranteed other Americans [Myrdal, 1944, p. 1021].

The attack on segregation and discrimination, sketched in an earlier section, may be viewed as the extension to American blacks of the system of individual rights. It brought formal equality of opportunity, greatly enhanced social mobility, and stimulated new aspirations. Opportunity was enhanced not only by the substantial elimination of both legal and informal barriers, but also by a host of measures designed to help blacks make up for the

handicaps of a previous era. The extent of social mobility may be seen in Table 28. Some of the changes include a substantial drop in the number of families below the low-income level and more than a sevenfold increase in the proportion of affluent families ($10,000 or better in 1971 prices) since 1947. Most comparisons still favor whites, but there are exceptions. For instance in the Northwestern part of the United States in 1972, young black families with husbands and wives both working made 105 percent of the white average. In the same area, black women college graduates under the age of thirty-five made 108 percent of the income of white women college graduates [Bureau of the Census, 1973, pp. 24–25]. Some of the areas where blacks are underrepresented showed impressive gains. The black proportion of elected public officials is only one-half of 1 percent of the total, but has increased twenty-nine times since 1964. The proportion of college students doubled between 1959 and 1973, when the proportion of blacks who had finished high school equaled the 1960 white proportion of high school graduates. Between 1960 and 1970, the median income of black blue-collar workers showed a larger dollar increase than that of blue-collar whites.

The median black family income was only 59 percent of the white family income in 1972. This is a slight rise from 54 percent in 1965 and indicates that blacks have shared in general prosperity and have increased slightly their share in the national income. That the figure is still low is partly explained by lower incomes in the South and by the large number of female-headed households.

Business recessions fall disproportionately upon black workers who have built up little seniority, and upon recently established black businesses [Lubin, 1975]. It is very possible, however, that the recession losses of the mid-1970s will prove to be only a temporary interruption in the long-term trend toward greater equality of economic opportunity in the United States. In recent years, black Americans have set a record of social mobility which may be unequaled by any other group in so short a period of time. It demonstrates the ability of blacks to handle greater responsibilities when opportunities are opened. It might well be a matter of black pride, but a magazine article detailing these accomplishments [Wattenberg and Scammon, 1973] came under bitter attack. Why should those who have long resented inferences of inferiority resist recognition of this evidence of achievement? Perhaps the answer lies in a theory of minoritarian and majoritarian perspectives developed by a British sociologist [Banton, 1967, pp. 316–318]. The majoritarian has a relativist view and appraises the minority's status in terms of the progress it has made since an earlier period. The minoritarian takes an absolutist view and appraises the progress in terms of the distance from perfection. In other words, one sees the glass as half empty; the other, as half full.

One worry of those taking the minoritarian perspective is that whites will feel no problems remain and become reluctant to support pro-

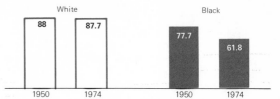

Figure 15. Percent of two-parent families. Figures take into account single parents of either sex, although most single-parent families have a female head. (Source: *The Social and Economic Status of the Black Population of the United States*, Bureau of the Census, Series 1-23, No. 46, U.S. Government Printing Office, Washington, D.C., 1973, p. 68.)

grams for black advance. Despite gains which have been made, nearly a third of black families still live in poverty. Despite evidence that many younger blacks compete with whites on equal terms, the overall black family income is still only about three-fifths of the white family income. A vigorous start has been made, but unless special programs continue, the black mobility advance may grind to a halt.

There is also fear that the diminution of black poverty may have progressed about as far as seems likely in present circumstances. This means that, rather than continual improvement, there is a hard core of distress which will persist even if civil rights programs continue to be vigorously carried out. About two-thirds of the black families in poverty in 1973 were headed by females [Bureau of the Census, 1973, p. 21]. In 1973, 35 percent of all black families were headed by females, which represents twice the proportion in 1950. For white families, the comparable figures are 8.6 percent female-headed in 1950 and 9.6 percent in 1973. [Ibid, p. 68].

There was resentment at the Moynihan report [Moynihan, 1965], which placed much of the responsibility for black poverty on family structure. Critics emphasized the fact that the majority of blacks live in two-parent families and that many female-headed families are aided by male relatives [Hill, 1972]. However, it is impossible to deny that when a woman, whether black or white, is supporting a family on only her own income, she is laboring under a heavy handicap. The most disturbing aspect of this increase in black female-headed families is that it came at a time of economic advance when it should have been easier to maintain a two-parent family. As long as family instability leads to a large number of one-parent families, it seems probable that there will be a significant amount of hardship in the black community even in times of general economic improvement.

In addition to economic problems, there are other issues which concern not only blacks, but also other racial minorities and some groups of European ancestry. One of these issues is the development and maintenance of a distinctive ethnic culture. Some would hope to solve economic and cultural problems through an expansion of the emphasis on the individual rights of all citizens. Others are attracted to a different pattern: the direct guarantee of group rights.

Group Rights

In the United States, the assumption has been that all immigrants would be eventually "Americanized" and assimilated to a modified code of Anglo-conformity. In much of the rest of the world, national governments have taken it for granted that ethnic differences would persist and should be protected. In Yugoslavia for instance, the government provides instruction in the mother tongue of any nationality when there are enough students to justify either a school or class [*Official Gazette,* 1960]. In Switzerland, there is no official language, and four different tongues have equal status. In Canada, public schools are required to offer instruction in both French and English. Such examples could be multiplied indefinitely. The point is simply that government need not promote assimilation to a common culture, but can support ethnic differences. Some governments are actually more protective of the rights of ethnic groups than they are of individuals. We will consider three methods of protecting group rights: separatism, cultural pluralism, and affirmative action (including busing).

Separatism. Subordinate ethnic groups have often supported independence movements in an effort to withdraw completely from political involvement with another ethnic group. Many Third World spokesmen say that American racial minorities are essentially colonies and should separate from the rule of the majority. A United Nations commission declared in 1972 that Puerto Rico was a colony. An occasional Chicano leader calls for the formation of a separate nation "on land that once belonged to us" [*Newsweek,* June 22, 1970, p. 27]. The Republic of New Africa dreams of a nation carved out of five Southern states. The Black Muslims indulge in a rhetoric which might be considered separatist, but their activities are directed toward building up black-controlled institutions within the American society.

To date, most members of American minority groups have considered a separatist program neither desirable nor practical. In Puerto Rico a few weeks after the U.N. colonial declaration, the Independence party secured the support of less than 4 percent of the voters. [*Time,* Nov. 27, 1972]. Few Mexican-Americans give any indication of following the separatist spokesmen, and few blacks support the Republic of New Africa. In fact, even one area that did separate from the United States, the Philippines, has had a flourishing statehood party whose program was that the Philippines should rejoin the United States as the fifty-first state! [*Newsweek,* July 24, 1972, p. 50].

The general rejection of separation from the American political system does not mean that all minority people see assimilation as the only path. Cultural pluralism has an attraction for many.

Cultural pluralism. Cultural pluralism is a form of accommodation in which ethnic groups retain their distinct cultural differences and traditions, while cooperating peacefully and relatively equally in political, economic, and social life. The standard example of cultural pluralism is Switzerland, a country which maintains a high degree of national unity although it has no national language and is religiously divided. In Switzerland, Protestants and Catholics have been able to live agreeably under the same government, while speaking German, French, or Italian. Since Swiss citizens do not feel that either their religious loyalty or their ethnic identification is threatened by other Swiss, they are free to give a complete allegiance to the Swiss nation as a common government which allows for the tolerance of distinctly different cultural groups. Canada, with the division between the French and the English, and Belgium, with a division between the French- and the Flemish-speaking population, are other examples of cultural pluralism (not, however, without some ethnic conflict). The different groups which make up a pluralistic society in these nations frequently engage in a struggle for influence, but the essential idea is that national patriotism does not require cultural uniformity, and that differences of nationality, religion, language, or even race do not preclude loyalty to a common national government.

Our religious divisions are one area of intergroup relations wherein some observers [Herberg, 1960] believe cultural pluralism is an essential and valuable feature of American life. But it may be that cultural pluralism is only a transitional stage. Gordon [1964, pp. 243–245] argues that one has to accept and have pride in the group of origin before one is ready to accept assimilation into the larger society. Thus immigrants and their children may gain a sense of security and identity when encouraged to talk about the contributions which their ethnic cultures have made to American society. Similarly, black students may profit from knowing that Africa has been an historic crossroads of civilization, not merely the locale of primitive tribes.

A number of trends among black Americans are in the direction of cultural pluralism. These include the struggle for community control of schools, retail stores, police, and social agencies in black neighborhoods; a rejection of white participation in some civil rights organizations; the efforts of black cultural nationalists to foster and maintain a distinct black subculture and the organization of black studies programs. These movements are based on a dual fear that integration either may not be complete enough to provide blacks with opportunity, or that it will require blacks to trade their identity for that of the "white middle class" image [Hamilton, 1972].

Cultural pluralism has an obvious appeal along with some disadvantages. It appeals to race pride, to freedom from alleged exploitation by white civil functionaries, teachers or merchants, and to freedom from constant white competition and/or domination. It also has the attraction of self-help and the spirit of "doing your own thing." These are powerful motives which have called forth a deep emotional response in many blacks, especially the young.

There are also drawbacks. These are found in the danger that a black enclave will be a place of limited opportunity and that emphasis on the black control of black neighborhoods will lead to an exclusion of blacks from other areas of society. The best political prospects are that blacks, like Senator Edward Brooks (Mass.) will be accepted as leaders of all the people; the best business opportunities are not ghetto grocery stores, but national corporations; the highest-quality universities are cosmopolitan rather than ethnic. In brief, the rewards of participation in a society beyond black control appear greater than those obtained within the limits of the black community. Some black leaders feel that either separatism or cultural pluralism is a step backward for blacks. For instance, Roy Wilkins of the National Association for the Advancement of Colored People states:

There are individuals (millions of them) and organized forces in the nation itching to respond to the disruptive clamor of Negroes themselves for separation. One day it will be separate, all-black studies centers. The next it will be not only a quota system on jobs, but one on the types of jobs in separate black buildings under black bosses. Then it will be separate (and inferior) schools and residential areas (like South Africa) and the completely separated elective offices so that the impact of a black bloc within a white party will be nil. If Negro youth will think beyond their understandable frustration . . . they will surely realize that they must not commit suicide by opening Pandora's box of racial separatism. (Roy Wilkins, *Des Moines Register and Tribune,* Mar. 30, 1969. Copyright 1975, Des Moines Register and Tribune Company.)

Many sociologists fear that black separatism would leave black people in neglected, poverty-ridden enclaves and that reduced contacts with whites would intensify and perpetuate prejudices and would set back the cause of equal opportunities and rewards for the races [Pettigrew, 1971].

Affirmative action. This is a movement which shifts the emphasis from the individual to the group. Earlier laws against discrimination prohibited employers from discriminating against any individual because of race, creed, color, or country of origin. Such laws enabled many competent individual minority persons to find employment, but did not greatly increase the proportion of a minority group in any employment or educational category. They required the employer to consider each applicant on merit, but did not imply that a particular percentage of any minority group should be hired.

Affirmative action is "result oriented" specification which requires employers to subscribe to a "goal" for the employment of minorities and women. Affirmative action was begun primarily for racial minorities, but now extends to women, to the aged, to youth, and in some jurisdictions, to veterans, to the handicapped, and to homosexuals [Human Rights Information Service, 1974; Martin, 1974]. This would seem to be a *reductio ad absurdum* which tries to embrace nearly everyone except the nonveteran, able-bodied, middle-aged white male.

Affirmative action spokesmen steadfastly deny that the "goals" are really quotas, since employers may be excused for failing to reach a goal if they can prove they have made "good faith efforts." Such good faith efforts include not only attempts to find minority applicants but also often a reduction in qualifications. It is not enough for employers to prove that they judge qualifications impartially; they must also prove that the qualifications are absolutely essential to performance of the job in question. Further, qualifications required of the minority cannot be greater than the lowest required of any majority-group employee in a similar position. In addition, judges have issued absolute orders requiring employers to hire a proportion of minority personnel to make up for past inequities [Seabury, 1972; U.S. Commission on Civil Rights, February, 1973; Seligman, 1973].

It makes a good deal of difference whether affirmative action is regarded as a temporary device or a permanent part of the social order. As a temporary device, it is successful in overcoming resistance to the full use of minorities and women. As a permanent feature, it marks a sharp shift from individual to group rights. The question is no longer whether one has been treated properly as an individual, but whether the group has had its share. This assumes that each ethnic group will have the same proportion of people with the same range of competencies seeking jobs in the same fields. There is a corollary to this view and that is that, if some groups have too few people in a given type of job, other groups have too many. In other words, reverse discrimination sets in, and highly qualified people from an ethnic group with an overage will be denied jobs to make places for less qualified people from underrepresented groups. These features are less serious if affirmative action is a temporary arrangement which is to be discarded when there is evidence that opportunities are open to all.

There are beginning to be so many vested interests that legislative action is difficult. However, the program may break down from the sheer difficulty of enforcement, or the courts may decide that it is an unconstitutional denial of equal protection under the law. In any event, if affirmative action continues for long, it will mark a major departure from the principle that American law is concerned with individuals rather than groups.

The busing controversy. Affirmative action was begun because laws against discrimination did not bring about an ethnically balanced work force in every industry. Busing for desegregation developed because the end of legal (de jure) segregation did not bring perfect racial balance to all the schools. Both of these devices abandon the effort to protect individuals against discrimination and assert that, regardless of individual rights and wrongs, there must be a proper group ratio.

Before the Supreme Court decision against segregation in 1954, there were laws demanding all-white and all-black schools in several states. The court decided that school assignment according to race was incompatible with the American legal system. Other systems of pupil assignment had been based on proximity to the school building or the need for a specific educational program. It soon became apparent that residential segregation was so extensive that few schools would be integrated if the neighborhood school practice continued. Integration was held to have been beneficial in improving black academic performance [Colemen, 1966] and in improving racial understanding. Therefore, children deprived of integrated schooling for whatever reason were held to be suffering, and busing was the answer.

Busing, to date, has not been a happy experience. There has been more resistance than was expected, and the anticipated benefits have not materialized. Most sociological research indicates that black academic performance has not improved and that racial tensions have increased [Armor, 1972; Schellenberg and Halteman, 1974].

The difficulty seems to be that inducing integration by extraordinary means does not have the same effect as removing barriers to allow "natural" integration to proceed. Successful voluntary school integration involved a small minority of black youngsters, probably mostly middle-class, whose families had voluntarily moved into largely white neighborhoods. The black children moving from an integrated residential base into integrated schoolrooms responded well to the higher achievement levels of the integrated schools.

Integration through busing has been a different type of experience. Busing brought lower-class black children involuntarily into a school setting in which they were often a large group, since in many American cities, 33 to 90 percent of the public school children are black. Rather than both white and black children accommodating to common achievement norms, they tended to move into separate hostile camps with intense suspicion among both races. This stimulated a still greater white flight from the city (and also of middle-class blacks) so that even with busing, very large geographic areas would have to be included to bring about racial balance.

The advocates of busing have urged that the preservation of the neighborhood school concept was simply a shield for school segregation since neighborhoods were obviously becoming increasingly segregated. A recent study of the potential for residential integration indicates this may be changing [Hermalin and Farley, 1973]. This study finds that both racial attitudes and income distribution favor a greater move of blacks to the suburbs and that the black concentration in the central city may be about to change. Such a prediction is, of course, hardly a certainty, but if correct, it would indicate that the nation has been engaged in a traumatic battle over busing to accomplish a type of integration which would have come painlessly in the course of years without this type of intervention.

An overview. Amalgamation is apparently increasing, but many generations would be required for amalgamation to bring any great reduction in ethnic differences. In the meantime, we must adjust to the coexistence of several ethnic groups. Discrimination and segregation have been common both in the United States and elsewhere, but have recently been declining in the United States while increasing in several African states. Those who reject ethnic discrimination may turn either to an emphasis on individual rights or to group balance. Group balance may come by separation so that there is only one ethnic group in a geographic area. It may come through a regime of cultural pluralism, which assumes that ethnic differences are permanent and guarantees each group cultural expression. Finally, it may be sought by measures such as affirmative action and busing for school segregation, which seek an almost mechanical method of securing proportionate ethnic ratios in all social activities. Throughout its history, the United States has emphasized individual rights and open competition. For many years, this individualistic emphasis was marred by racial discrimination; now it is threatened by group-oriented measures to guarantee equal ethnic ratios. Whether or not a society can be maintained free of ethnic preferences, where individuals are judged on their merits regardless of race or sex, is a major question.

Separatism and territorially based minorities

Most examples of cultural pluralism are found in countries where each ethnic group is concentrated in a particular territory. In Canada the French are centered in Quebec; in each of the fifteen republics of the Soviet Union, a single ethnic group is generally dominant; most of the cantons of the Swiss Confederation are composed principally of one of three nationalities—German, French, or Italian. But in the United States, each immigrant group was generally scattered rather than concentrated in a single region, and this favored assimilation and integration rather than cultural pluralism. The two major ethnic groups in the

United States which do have somewhat of a territorial base—the American Indians and the Mexican-Americans—have shown considerable resistance to assimilation.

The American Indians. In agriculture at least, the Europeans assimilated Indian culture rather than the reverse. Much of the success of the European colonization was due to the colonists' adoption of the planting of corn, potatoes, tobacco, peanuts, cocoa, rubber, and several other crops. But conflict soon developed, and the colonists adopted a policy of genocide which exterminated most of the coastal and Eastern woodlands tribes. After genocide became unfashionable, the surviving Indians were herded onto reservations provided by treaties, all of which the whites eventually violated. This policy of isolation on reservations foundered on the difficulty of finding any land so worthless that no whites wanted it. Repeated white invasions of reservation lands would be followed by the inevitable succession of incidents, "massacres," and finally an army campaign such as at the Little Bighorn, where Custer earned his ignominious reward. Even in those instances where the Indians had successfully assimilated white culture, the white society's relentless land hunger destroyed this adjustment. For example, the Cherokees of northern Georgia had a stable agriculture, had developed a written language and conducted a publications program, and eagerly adopted new technology. But rumors of gold whetted white appetites, and President Jackson, violating solemn treaty obligations and in open disregard of a decision of the United States Supreme Court, ordered the army to move the Cherokees to Oklahoma along the notorious "trail of tears," where 4,000 of them perished. Even after their arrival in Oklahoma, where they again tried to build a modern society, the Cherokees were yet again frustrated by white land hunger [Wilkins, 1971]. This sordid story, repeated in many variations, constitutes the history of our "generosity" to the Indians [Debo, 1970; Deloria, 1970]. Of the 138 million acres which Indians held by treaty in 1887, only 52 million acres remained by 1934; and to retain even this requires a constant battle against efforts to "free" the Indians from their remaining land [Wax, 1971, p. 54].

Insofar as the whites had a program for Indians, other than pushing them out of the way, it was a policy of disrupting communal tribal life and encouraging cultural assimilation, sometimes with cash payments for loss of lands. Some who received these payments had as little as one-fourth Indian ancestry and had lost any real connection with tribal life. But even the payments to genuine tribal members brought no benefits beyond a momentary splurge. Accustomed to a cooperative tribal life, they individually lacked the land base, the economic opportunities, and the managerial experience to use these payments as capital to finance their economic self-improvement.

The overall results of Indian policy have been dismal: a failure to assimilate the Indians and to integrate them into American cultural and economic life, but a considerable success in breaking down their traditional tribal life, leaving many of them anomic and demoralized. While many Indians have left the reservations, most of these live in squalid urban slums. Assimilation has largely failed for two reasons: (1) it demanded that the Indians stop being Indians and sacrifice their tribal culture; but (2) while demanding that the Indians become assimilated, the whites often blocked their successful assimilation by resisting the kind of cooperative communal ventures which might have proven profitable, while discriminating against Indians in many ways which parallel the discrimination against blacks. Some Indians have indeed become integrated into the mainstream of American life and achieved middle-class status, but many more have reached only a sort of half-way assimilation which combines the worst of both worlds.

In 1934 anthropologist John Collier became Commissioner of Indian Affairs and reversed the historic policy of encouraging tribes to disband and assimilate. He proposed that the Indians be assisted to survive as tribal units and preserve their tribal culture [Wax, 1971, p. 57]. Government policy since then has vacillated between "termination" (disbanding and enforced assimilation, usually with disastrous results), "preservation" (halfheartedly promoted and usually frustrated by local Indian Service personnel), and "relocation" in cities with federal help (with mixed results, depending upon whose evaluation is accepted) [Deloria, 1970]. Recently a spirit of militant activism has arisen, somewhat similar to the Black Power movement among black Americans, urging that Indians reject "Euroconformity" and preserve Indian language, crafts, and religion, and demanding that Indians control their own schools and economic life [Steiner, 1968, pp. 268–289; Wax, 1971, p. 176].

The Indians are also divided between the "traditionalists," who wish to preserve tribal life and customs, and the "progressives," who promote assimilation and industrial development. As much recent conflict has occurred between rival groups of Indians as between Indians and whites. The often criticized Bureau of Indian Affairs, for instance, has over two-thirds Indian employees [Patterson, 1973, p. 52]. The highly publicized "Battle of Wounded Knee" at Custer, South Dakota, in 1973 was an effort by a dissident group of Indians to break the power of an elected chief.

Some Indians have found the white world a bewildering and brutal place; others have found success and a good life, and are inclined to think that all Indians should assimilate. The tension between the assimilated and the nonassimilated is illustrated in the plaint of an Indian who has become a successful lawyer and author:

The long trail to integration from a self-imposed exile is winding and rocky. To travel it and to arrive safely at the other end an Indian must have stamina, confidence, perseverance and determination. He has to learn to blow away the taunts of the buckskin and feather fakers, and to disregard their biting comments. He has to learn to select his own value system from the two cultures on either side of him. His heartstrings will be pulled taut by the cries of despair of the Indians left on the periphery of poverty and the rich life, and if he doesn't heed them they will quickly become cries of vilification and disgust, of traitor and brown-skinned white man, for those are the love cries of his fellow red-men. (W. I. C. Wuttunee, "The Long Trail to Integration," *Kalamazoo College Review*, 35, No. 3, (1972), p. 19.

Whatever past sins the federal government may be charged with, it can hardly be accused of neglect or rigidity at the present time. It has tried almost every suggestion made for dealing with the Indians, and continual experimentation seems to be the only predictable future policy. In 1973, federal appropriations for various services to Indians amounted to approximately 1.5 billion dollars, or almost $1,800 per Indian [Patterson, 1973, p. 54]. Medical, educational, housing, and economic opportunity programs have been steadily upgraded. Many Indians are adjusting successfully either on or off the reservation; however, many other Indians are bogged down in poverty or alcoholism, and the Indian suicide rate is estimated at ten times the American average [Muskrat, 1973, p. 46]. Some Indian tribes have escaped the general demoralization affecting tribal societies, but even these have severe problems. A few Indian tribes, such as the Hopi, have strictly controlled outside contacts and have succeeded both in preserving their own culture and in maintaining a viable economy at a modest subsistence level; others have lost most of their culture and live a life of poverty and apathy on the fringes of white society. And even the Hopi face the possible destruction of their economic base through the pumping out of the ground-water supply of the Black Mesa by coal-mining operators, who use several million gallons of water each day to carry the coal slurry through the pipelines to power plants that provide the white society's electricity [Ashton, 1971].

No matter how worthless land seemed when it was made a reservation, whites will eventually discover that it has valuable resources. This discovery often marks the death of Indian

It is unlikely that the future will see all American Indians moving in a uniform direction.

tribal life. Even if adequate compensation is paid, the economy is uprooted and tribal solidarity threatened. Payment for water does not enable Indians to irrigate their land, and royalties for coal mining do not provide grazing space. Thus what might be seen by whites as progress often marks the end of a tribal economy.

It is unlikely that the future will see all American Indians moving in a uniform direction. Certainly, few assimilated Indians are going to return to the reservation, nor are most tribes going to disappear. Cultural pluralism will be seen in the tribal societies and integration in the assimilation of Indians in American cities. At present many Indians, on the reservation and in the city alike, live in squalor and degradation. Hopefully, the many government programs in operation will eventually allow a viable choice of either assimilation or cultural pluralism, according to the preference of individual Indians. Only when this stage is reached can Americans feel they have made proper retribution for the massive wrongs done to the first Americans. Meanwhile, recent studies are showing that, contrary to the popular image of the Indians as a broken people, uniformly demoralized by feelings of worthlessness and powerlessness, many American Indians today feel a growing sense of personal worth and are hopeful for the future [Trimble, 1974].

The Mexican-Americans. About 70,000 Mexican-Americans, a mixture of Spanish and Indian stocks, were added to the American population as a result of the war with Mexico. These Mexicans were already established in village communities before the "Anglos" arrived, bringing with them a strong sense of racial, religious, and cultural ethnocentrism which expressed itself in a condescension and contempt for everything Mexican. These circumstances produced little Anglo pressure for assimilation, and little Anglo opposition to the retention of the ancestral Mexican culture. While some cultural interchange followed, the eventual accommodation was a cultural pluralism in which cross-cultural contacts were minimal. Natural increase and immigration have increased the Mexican-American population to slightly over five million in 1970, heavily concentrated in the Southwest, where migrants can join existing communities and where proximity to Mexico permits easy visiting.

While much of the traditional Mexican culture survived, the agricultural land base was soon destroyed as the Mexicans lost most of their land to the Anglos. The ancient Spanish land grants, sometimes lost and often accompanied by incomplete records of intervening title changes, were promptly set aside by Anglo courts, presided over by Anglo judges interpreting newly enacted Anglo land laws before Anglo juries. Again, patterns of discrimination arose with the usual dreary consequences. Today, the Mexican-Americans are heavily concentrated in the unskilled jobs with low pay and frequent unemployment.

The Roman Catholic Church, useful as an assimilation bridge and mobility ladder for many European immigrants, has played no such role for the Mexican-Americans, who found themselves in parishes which were almost exclusively Mexican, for very few Anglos in the Southwest were Catholics. Thus land deprivation, discrimination, language barriers, and isolation from equal-status contacts kept most Mexican-Americans poor and unassimilated despite an official policy of promoting assimilation.

It is commonly believed that those of Spanish-speaking background in the United States are more resistant to the use of English than were other nationalities. All immigrants valued their own national language, and the gradual loss of the ancestral language by the younger generation has been one of the most traumatic aspects of Americanization. Until recently, though, the general assumption has been that English was the basic American language and that those desiring full participation in American society had to become English-speaking. In the case of Spanish, this assumption has been weakened in two areas: education and voting. Many states have required voters to be literate in English, but New York State has included literacy in Spanish as an acceptable voting qualification. New Mexico, where many of Mexican ancestry were descendants of pre-annexation settlers, has been officially bilingual since it became a state in 1912. In 1965, a federal appropriation supported the establishment of bilingual education in Spanish and English. While primarily concerned with students from Spanish-speaking homes, it also provided that both Anglo and Spanish-background children should participate and that the school should hire a number of teachers for whom Spanish was a native language. Not only is language instruction itself bilingual, but other subject matter instruction as well.

The reasoning is that such bilingual instruction will enhance the school progress of the children from Spanish-speaking homes. Not only are they expected to do better academic work if there is a more gradual exposure to English, but also the fact that Spanish is officially recognized makes the school less "foreign." Further, since they will have an advantage in Spanish over Anglo children, this should boost their self-image. Likewise, Anglo children should gain a greater understanding and respect for Mexican-American students. As one school superintendent said: ". . . the district tries to create an atmosphere in the classroom where the children who come to us from the dominant culture, speaking the dominant language . . . recognize that here this little kid [Mexican-American] has got something that he [Anglo] doesn't have and that he ought to be interested in getting what this kid can teach him" [U.S. Commission on Civil Rights, 1970, p. 29].

While bilingual education may promote intergroup understanding, there is a definite fear that it may retard the ultimate acquisition of English. This is based on studies which show that bilingual instruction usually leads to less competency in either language and that learning is not as great when subjects are taught in the weaker language [McNamara, 1966, 1967]. As one writer summarizes the situation, ". . . it is good for American society to have many truly bilingual individuals. However, nobody is quite sure whether it is good for the *individual* to be bilingual" [Moore and Cueller, 1970, p. 124].

There is some controversy over these points, and it may be deemed worthwhile to trade some loss in other academic achievement for familiarity with two languages. In any event, the concessions made to Spanish are a definite break with past American practice and mark a move in the direction of cultural pluralism.

While some Mexican-Americans have achieved education and prosperity, far more of them feel powerless and alienated. Today many are rejecting assimilation and integration in favor of separatism and militant protest. The term *chicano* is sometimes applied to all Mexican-Americans and sometimes only to the activist ones, while *chicanismo* is a protest against the "cultural genocide" which they feel has robbed them of a proper appreciation of their Mexican heritage [Moore and Cueller, 1970, p. 149–156]. They stress group social values over individual achievement and recommend confrontation and disruption when ordinary political action fails. While "race" is perhaps an inaccurate term to apply to Mexicans, there is much rhetoric of race pride and of *la raza,* a term which refers to Mexican cultural heritage rather than to biological origin. Under chicano impetus, it is possible that any tendencies toward continuing assimilation may be reversed, and that a territorial ethnic base coupled with a militant ideology may produce a viable and enduring parallel society among the Mexican-Americans.

As with Indians, there is no unanimity on these matters among Mexican-Americans. Some Mexican-Americans who have made progress in the wider society are distressed by separatist tendencies. They even resent a "problem" approach toward Mexican-American adjustment. In the analysis of an investigator for the U.S. Civil Rights Commission, "They felt uncomfortable about the Commission's hearing because in their eyes it would merely tend to continue the polarization of Anglos and Mexican-Americans at a time when they thought it was disappearing" [U.S. Commission on Civil Rights, 1970, p. 3].

The large-scale movement of Mexicans into the United States as permanent immigrants, especially outside of the Southwest, is comparatively new. It is possible that observers have exaggerated their difficulties and underestimated the facility with which they can move into the American mainstream. One bit of evidence relating to social mobility comes from a recent survey of Racine, Wisconsin, which found that not only had Mexican-Americans increased their family incomes in the years between 1960 and 1970, but they had made greater proportional improvement than either white or black Americans in the same city [Shannon and Kim, 1974, p. 105].

It is also possible that the reluctance to learn English has been overstressed. In relatively isolated areas, Spanish remains dominant, but in mixed communities, it is rapidly declining. For instance, a survey of school districts in California showed that only 20 percent of the Mexican-American children needed an "English as Second Language" program. Similarly, a survey of Los Angeles showed that only a minority of Mexican-American families used Spanish exclusively in the home [Moore and Cueller, 1970, pp. 122–123]. At present, the voice of the militant Chicano separatist is loud in the land, but it is hard to know whether this indicates a move toward cultural pluralism or whether it is a last gasp of protest before Mexican-Americans follow the assimilative path taken by other nationalities.

Factors determining ethnic patterns

Ethnic relationships are subject to change because ethnic groups are continually engaged in the types of interaction described in the chapter on social processes. This interaction is constant, but the circumstances and the relative power of different groups are in a constant state of change. For instance, individuals from different ethnic groups are in a continuous state of competition, but the competition changes when a stable rural society enters a period of industrialization. Two major factors influence ethnic interaction. One is deliberate, planned change in the structure of society, which is called *enacted* change, and the other is the gradual movement of society, unplanned and nondirected, which is called *crescive* change. "Crescive" is defined in the dictionary as "increasing" or "growing" and implies change that develops out of the existing order without conscious design.

Enacted change

Occasionally governments or other social institutions decree certain patterns of relationships which have a far-reaching effect. The legalization of slavery is one such enacted measure

which set the relative status of ethnic groups in extremely rigid form.

The legal definition of slaves in the United States as "property," while they were legally "persons" in Central and South America, had great effects on their status. Central and South American slaves had certain rights guaranteed by law (to marry, hold property, buy their freedom, and others), but since property has no rights against its owners, slaves in the United States had no legal rights whatever [Silberman, 1964, chap. 4].

The acceptance of the idea of caste in Hindu religion is another type of enactment with persistent consequences. In the United States, the decision that the public lands would be reserved for homesteaders in 160-acre units prevented the rise of an agrarian landlord-tenant system in the West. Similarly the passing of a restrictive immigration act cut down support for cultural pluralism by limiting the number of immigrants to a number which could be assimilated with relative ease. After the Civil War, the "Jim Crow" laws of the Southern states made racial segregation legally mandatory in that area.

Currently, one of the leading types of enacted change is represented by the civil rights laws passed by the national Congress as well as by many of the individual states. These laws prohibit many types of racial segregation and discrimination. Civil rights laws have made many changes in American society, but no one would claim that they are completely effective. The limits of their effectiveness are very largely set by crescive changes which may work either for or against the aims of the law.

Crescive change

Most change in our society is not enacted by any legislature or the board of trustees of any organization but comes about without deliberate planning. Such unplanned, unintended changes are called *crescive*. No plan or decree is responsible for urbanization. No deliberative group brought forth the cotton gin which created a demand for cheap labor, or the mechanical cotton picker which later made this kind of cheap labor unnecessary. Nor did any legislative body produce the shift in scientific opinion which made a racist interpretation of human conduct untenable.

These examples and many more indicate that crescive development may either accelerate or retard enacted programs of change in ethnic relations. This does not mean that ethnic relations are determined by the unconscious processes of history which man is powerless to control. Rather it means that to be effective without great cost and disruption enacted change must be in harmony with the relevant trends in society. If industrial changes are in process, we must consider how these changes will affect the present and prospective situation of members of ethnic groups. If population is moving from the farm to the city and we desire residential integration, then positive steps must be taken to make the central city more attractive to the majority and also to enable racial minorities to enter the suburbs. If limited education or unstable family life prevent the minority from acquiring the skills and attitudes needed for social mobility, then steps can be taken to stabilize family life and improve the schools. In other words, effective enacted change must do more than simply endorse a desirable pattern of ethnic relationships. It must either relate the enacted change to crescive development or seek to change the course of this development.

Prospects for the future

Since sociologists always look for generalizations, there have been efforts to find general trends in ethnic relations which may illuminate particular situations. Several attempts have been made to develop an ethnic relations cycle [Bogardus, 1930; Brown, 1934; Park, 1949; Glick, 1955]. One which seems somewhat applicable to present situations has been proposed by Greeley [1969, pp. 31–37]. He suggests six phases: (1) culture shock, (2) organization and emergent self-consciousness, (3) assimilation of the elite, (4) militancy, (5) self-hatred and anti-militancy, and (6) emerging adjustment. Let us take a brief look at these phases and see what is involved.

Phase one—cultural shock. The first contact with a new country or with an alien people is usually disturbing. The newcomers are insecure, the old landmarks are gone, and they fear that no one will recognize their worth. They cling to their old culture, but find this both changing and under attack. Their mood is often one of fear, mixed with some hope, and their main concern is how to survive.

Phase two—organization and emerging self-consciousness. The initial feeling of strangeness is gone and the first adjustment has been made. Economic circumstances are difficult, but a few members of the group have begun to climb out of the unskilled worker category. It is a time of organization: churches, sometimes schools, fraternal societies, and other essentially ethnic organizations are formed. Political leaders develop who bargain with the power structure for concessions to the group.

Phase three—assimilation of the elite. Many members of the group are in the lower middle class as shopkeepers, city employees, unionized workers, and clerks. Some of the youth go on to college, usually with the expectation of becoming school teachers. A few of the most talented individuals gain recognition outside ethnic circles. This recognition brings problems of social adjustment, since few of their group are found in elite circles. Their ethnic background becomes an embarrassment from which they must escape by recognition of talents not bound by ethnic dimensions.

Phase four—militancy. Now many of the group are fully middle class, and some edge toward the top stratum. This is a time when the ethnic group asserts its self-sufficiency. Since it has built a solid middle-class culture, it sees little need for the larger society. The group tends to duplicate everything found in the larger society; partially to protect its members from contamination and partially to demonstrate its power. Greeley [1969, p. 33] suggests that the formation of numerous Catholic social agencies, professional organizations, hospitals, learned societies, etc. is a prime example of this tendency. At the same time, the group compensates for earlier rejection by boldly asserting its political and economic power. Once scorned as alien, it now asserts that it represents genuine national patriotism.

Phase five—self-hatred and antimilitancy. Now large numbers of youth have gone to college and form a substantial part of the professional class. They are not so much embarrassed by their ethnic identity as by reminders of the crude behavior their group engaged in at previous phases. Self-hatred emerges in the form of a devastating criticism of all efforts to keep alive the ancestral culture. Yet they do not propose to abandon the ethnic group, but reform it. As Greeley [1969, p. 35] expresses it: "There are intense demands for drastic and immediate modernization—demands which cannot possibly be met—and intense ambivalence toward the ethnic group. The self critics cannot live with their ethnic background and they cannot live without it."

Phase six—emerging adjustment. Now a generation arrives on the scene which, in a significant proportion, is upper-middle-class and secure therein. It is not embarrassed by its ethnic identity and has trouble understanding the self-hatred of the previous generation. Neither is it interested in an aggressive posture in defense of ethnic rights. Indeed, it sees no reason why ethnicity cannot be combined with participation in the larger society. It may develop a nostalgia which encourages an interest in ethnic literature or trips back to the homeland. As a final indication that it has arrived, it

begins to wonder why groups which are not so far along are so belligerent.

Where do various ethnic groups belong in this cycle? Greeley [1969, pp. 35–36] suggests that blacks are just entering phase four and that Poles and Italians are moving beyond it. Irish and German Catholics are in phase five and starting to enter phase six, while many Jews are in phase six. American Indians would probably be placed in phases one and two, for the most part. Mexican-Americans would be found in phases two and three, with some entering phase four. Japanese-Americans might be placed in phases four and five. WASP (white Anglo-Saxon Protestants) would have to be placed in phase six if the cycle is to have any meaning at all.

Interpretations of ethnic behavior in such a cycle have some limitations. One is that the cycle may correspond more closely to the experience of European Catholic immigrants than to groups which are racially distinct. It appears that the Catholic and Jewish drive for separate organizations was stronger than that of other groups. Further, the politicization of our society may enable some of the ethnic groups in stages two, three, and four to force government to provide ethnically distinctive institutions rather than creating ethnic voluntary associations (black studies programs in universities and bilingual instruction in the elementary schools are examples).

The move from stage to stage is not automatic, and Greeley [1969, p. 36] indicates that regression to an earlier stage is always a possibility. If a group is attacked after it has "arrived," it may become defensive and move back to an earlier phase. Greeley suggests that white Protestants may be more long-suffering than others, since they did not have to claw their way up in so difficult a fashion in the first place. Some WASPs are starting to assume a more defensive literary posture [Schrag, 1971], but otherwise his prognosis seems accurate in this respect.

Such a cyclic theory assumes that groups will be neither completely successful nor completely blocked at any stage of the cycle. If they are completely blocked, attitudes may become so rigid that there is little change from generation to generation. If the revolt against the larger society in stages two, three, and four were fully successful, it would result in a rupture of relationships through secession, partition, or independence, thus creating an entirely new situation. If the attack on ancestral ethnicity in phase five were ruthlessly carried out, very little of the ethnic tradition would be left. The cyclic pattern is most likely to operate if only partial success in each phase enables the group both to gain some confidence in its own power and to learn that its own survival requires some kind of cooperation with the society beyond its own ethnic boundaries. If cyclic theory is used as a mechanical type of predictor, it will be misleading. If, however, it is used as a stimulus to analysis, it will help us to realize that tomorrow an ethnic group may lose interest in attitudes about which it feels very strongly today. The realization that ethnic demands are constantly shifting should make it easier for all of us to adjust to change without engaging in fratricidal conflict.

Summary

A *race* is defined either as a group of people who share common physical characteristics or as a group whose boundaries are set by social definition, with no common agreement on usage. Race differences are biologically trivial, but culturally important. All races have the same range of abilities, but scientific investigation has not conclusively demonstrated whether the same distribution exists. If hereditary racial differences do exist, they are small compared to the differences within races.

The scope of the chapter is broadened by the use of the term *ethnic,* which includes not only racial groups but also other groups of common ancestry whose link is religion, language, nationality, territorial origin, or a combination of

one or more of these. Different ethnic groups often exist within the same national boundaries. Perspectives on interpretation of behavior tend to vary with minority or majority ethnic identity.

Minority adjustment is marked by problems such as relatively low school achievement and high crime rates. The minority response to these problems may be to (1) challenge the validity of measures used to indicate the size of problems, such as achievement tests or crime rates, (2) sponsor programs for the disadvantaged of all groups, or (3) stimulate greater minority achievement.

Ethnic relationships may be organized to promote segregation and discrimination, to allow amalgamation, to support the rights of individuals, or to protect group rights. Segregation and discrimination were prevalent in the United States until the civil rights movement and are still dominant in some African countries. This pattern assumes that ethnic distinctions are permanent and that ethnic groups are unequal. Amalgamation may be increasing, but even if current trends continue, it will be generations before separate ethnic identities are substantially weakened. The emphasis on individual rights is the opposite of segregation and discrimination. Under this pattern, individuals were to be treated on their own merits without regard to ethnic identity. This emphasis in the United States has been accompanied by rapid black social mobility. A focus on group rights assumes that it is not enough to protect individual rights, but that the ethnic group must be guaranteed equality of achievement with other groups.

Separatism is the most extreme group rights pattern. It may take the form either of independence or of as isolated an existence as possible within the nation. Cultural pluralism combines the maintenance of ethnic identity and culture with loyalty to the nation. Measures such as affirmative action and busing for integration represent a governmental effort to guarantee that all ethnic groups are equally represented in all phases of the nation's life.

Both of these measures involve a shift from a concern for individual opportunity to a claim for proportionate group ratios.

Cultural pluralism has flourished best in groups related to a particular territory; in the United States, these groups are Indians and Mexican-Americans. Among Indians, cultural pluralism is seen in the effort to maintain tribal groups and related cultures. The United States has not maintained any consistent policy toward Indians, and Indians themselves are divided between cultural pluralism and integration in the larger society. Among Mexican-Americans, cultural pluralism is seen in the attachment to the Spanish language. Concessions to the unique position of Spanish have been made in literacy regulations and in bilingual education. Some Mexican-Americans take a militant stand in resistance to Anglo conformity; others are being assimilated in the dominant culture.

Factors affecting the course of ethnic relations include *enacted* change set in motion by deliberate decision of organized groups and *crescive* changes, which occur through the unplanned growth and development of society.

Cycles of ethnic relationships may indicate future trends. Greeley's six-phase cycle includes: (1) cultural shock, (2) organization and emerging self-consciousness, (3) assimilation of the elite, (4) militancy, (5) self-hatred and antimilitancy, and (6) emerging adjustment. No group will follow an exact replication of the cycle, but most will approximate it. An awareness of cyclical trends helps us to understand that positions which are held tenaciously in one period may be modified or abandoned in another.

Questions and projects

1. Why is the term "ethnic" used in preference to "race" throughout most of this discussion?
2. What are the arguments for and against bilingual education? Is it more helpful for Spanish-speaking students or for Anglos?
3. The United States government has supported a program for relocating American Indians from their reservations to cities. What are the arguments for and against such a program?
4. In terms of Greeley's ethnic relations cycles, what actions are likely to be taken in the near future by blacks? By Indians?
5. Which occupational group has done more to change the pattern of ethnic relations— engineers or government officials?
6. Distinguish between segregation and cultural pluralism.
7. If all ethnic discrimination were ended, would all groups produce equal proportions of highly successful men and women?
8. The first reports of the reaction of the American armed forces to integration were favorable from all concerned. Now there are increasing reports of black discontent and conflict in the army. How would you account for this development?
9. Why are there fewer marriages between white men and black women than between black men and white women? What is the sex ratio in interracial dating on your campus?
10. What is the interrelationship between enacted and crescive change in promoting changes in ethnic relationships?
11. If there are dormitories at your institution, how are black and white students housed? Separate dormitories, separate dormitory sections, or integrated? Are roommates assigned at random, or are blacks paired as roomates? What can be said for or against each arrangement?
12. Read the article by Paul Seabury, "HEW and the Universities," *Commentary*, February, 1972, pp. 38–44, also found in Robert K. Yin: *Race, Creed, Color, or National Origin*, F. E. Peacock, Itaska, Ill., 1973, pp. 243–252. Does your school have an affirmative action program? Would the criticisms that Seabury made apply to it? Compare the Seabury article with James P. Comer, "The Case for Black Quotas," *Ebony*, September, 1974, p. 146.

13. Read Godfrey Hodgson, "Do Schools Make a Difference?", *The Atlantic Monthly*, 231:35–46, March, 1973. What are the implications of this article for a program of busing for integration?

14. Read G. Napper, *Blacker Than Thou*, Eerdmans Publishing Co., Grand Rapids, Mich., 1972. Is the picture it gives of interracial dating and of relations between white and black women true of your campus?

Suggested readings

ARMOR, DAVID J.: "The Evidence on Busing," *The Public Interest*, 7:90–126, Summer, 1972. Armor examines several instances of busing for integration and finds no evidence that it has increased black school achievement or improved race relations. His views are attacked by several critics in the Winter, 1973, issue of *The Public Interest*.

BANKS, JAMES A., AND JEAN D. GRAMBS: *Black Self-Concept*, McGraw-Hill Book Co., New York, 1972. A series of articles dealing with socialization, motivation, and self-concept.

BOORSTIN, DANIEL J.: *The Sociology of the Absurd*, Simon & Schuster, Inc., New York, 1970. A book which, in humorous vein, pushes the principle of merit by ethnicity to the limits of ultimate absurdity.

*DAVIDSON, BASIL: *Old Africa Rediscovered: The Story of Africa's Forgotten Past*, Victor Gollancz, Ltd., London, 1965; or *The Lost Cities of Africa*, Little Brown and Co., 1959. Readable accounts of ancient African civilizations, which neither consign the continent to barbarism nor erect a romantic facade on a basis of dubious historical evidence.

Ethnic Groups in American Life series, by Prentice-Hall, Inc., each volume devoted to one of America's ethnic groups: CHARLES H. ANDERSON, *White Protestant Americans: From National Origins to Religious Groups*, 1970; JOSEPH P. FITZPATRICK, *Puerto Rican Americans: The Meaning of Migration to the Mainland*, 1971; HARRY H. L. KITANO, *Japanese Americans: The Evolution of a Subculture*, 1961; JOAN W. MOORE, WITH ALFREDO CUELLAR, *Mexican Americans*, 1970; MURRAY W. WAX, *American Indians: Unity and Diversity*, 1971; HELENA Z. LOPATA, *Polish Americans*, in press; CHARLES C. MOSKOS, JR., *Greek Americans*, in press.

*GLAZER, NATHAN, AND DANIEL P. MOYNIHAN: *Beyond the Melting Pot*, Harvard University Press, Cambridge, Mass., 1970. A description of the interaction of ethnic groups in New York City.

HEER, DAVID M.: "The Prevalence of Black-White Marriage in the United States, 1960 and 1970," *Journal of Marriage and the Family*, 36:246–258, May, 1974. A thorough analysis of current intermarriage trends.

HUNT, CHESTER L., AND LEWIS WALKER: *Ethnic Dynamics: Patterns of Intergroup Relations in Various Societies*, The Dorsey Press, Homewood, Ill., 1974. A book which applies an analysis based on sociological patterns to ethnic relationships in fourteen different countries.

JENSEN, ARTHUR, R.: *Educability and Group Differences*, Harper & Row, Publishers, Inc., New York, 1973. Jensen's view of the role of genetics and environment in determining the response to education.

LOEHLIN, JOHN, GARDNER LINDZEY, AND J. N. SPUHLER, *Race Differences in Intelligence*, W. H. Freeman and Co., San Francisco, 1975. A comprehensive review of the existing evidence.

MONTAGU, ASHLEY: *Man's Most Dangerous Myth: The Fallacy of Race*, 5th ed., Oxford University Press, New York, 1974. An anthropologist's attack upon racism and its costs.

RASPBERRY, WILLIAM: "Busing—Is It Worth The Ride?", *Readers Digest*, 105:141–2, September, 1974. A black columnist points up reasons why busing for integration is both arbitrary and counterproductive.

SENNA, CARL: *The Fallacy of I.Q.*, The Third Press, New York, 1973. Although definitely intended as a rejoinder to Jensen, this book has a series of well-balanced articles on heredity and intelligence.

*SOWELL, THOMAS: *Black Education: Myths and Tragedies*, David McKay, New York, 1973. A black professor of economics describes how guilt-ridden white faculty and militant blacks combined to rob black students of worthwhile education.

U.S. COMMISSION ON CIVIL RIGHTS: *Civil Rights Digest,* 6, Fall, 1973. This issue is entirely devoted to American Indians. Along with a summary of some current problems, it includes a description of government programs for Indians.

WATTENBERG, BEN J., AND RICHARD M. SCANNON: "Black Progress and Liberal Rhetoric," *Commentary,* 55:35–44, April, 1973. One of many articles which celebrates the growth of the black middle class.

Chapter 17 ● Collective behavior in mass society

At 11:35 on the night of Dec. 19, 1973, Johnny Carson began his opening monologue, a collection of gags that are sometimes almost as funny as the newspaper clips that inspire them. On this day, Carson's writers had read the remarks of a Wisconsin congressman named Harold Froehlich, who said that the Federal Government had fallen behind in getting bids to supply toilet tissue.

"The United States may face a serious shortage of toilet tissue within a few months," the congressman had said.

And so Carson said to America, "You know what else is disappearing from the supermarket shelves? Toilet paper. There's an acute shortage of *toilet* paper in the United States."

Then he swung at a phantom golf ball while 20 million people jumped out of bed and dashed to their shelves. They were people who recently had run out of gas and meat and onions too, so they were keenly shortage conditioned, and the next morning all of them sallied forth to hoard. By noon of Dec. 20, some Americans owned enough toilet paper to welcome the first man back from Mars. *(Ralph Schoenstein, "It Was Just a Joke, Folks." Reprinted with permission from TV Guide ® Magazine. Copyright © 1974 by Triangle Publications, Inc., Radnor, Pa.)*

Large-scale cultural forces, rather than the designers, are in control of fashion changes. . . . To the extent that a double standard has prevailed by which women can be arrested for exposing their breasts in public, while men suffer no such restrictions, toplessness is a liberationist issue. Hence, I do not expect the taboo on female breast exposure to be maintained much longer. *(Reprinted with permission from What Goes Up, May Stay Up by Marvin Harris, Natural History Magazine, January, 1973. Copyright © The American Museum of Natural History, 1973.)*

Brad Tufts made no speeches, no personal appearances, but still garnered enough write-in votes to win a recent primary election for student body president at San Diego State University. Candidacy was experiment by members of a class called Advertising Campaigns. Class flooded campus with Brad Tufts posters, T-shirts, bumperstickers. "We set out to see if formally educated students would vote for a candidate solely on basis of advertising image," says Asst. Prof. Jack Haberstroh. Brad Tufts is two years old. (Behavior Today, May 1, 1972, p. 3. Copyright © Ziff-Davis Publishing Company. All rights reserved.)

These anecdotes touch upon three topics—rumor, fashion, and public opinion—which fall within the field of collective behavior. This is not an easy field to study scientifically. Riots and panics do not often occur under the calm gaze of a visiting sociologist. Deliberately to provoke one, however studious our intent, would put us in jail. Besides, just how would a sociologist conduct an interview in the midst of a mob or panic? We are limited to eyewitness accounts by observers and participants, to police records, newspaper accounts, and other scattered data. Seldom can we locate a statistically adequate sample of participants for systematic study. A number of ingenious attempts have been made to duplicate crowd conditions of behavior in a laboratory for purposes of research, but relatively few types of crowd behavior can be so reproduced. Even with these limitations we have a good deal of descriptive information, together with some empirical research, from which we have developed certain insights into the various forms of collective behavior.

Nature of collective behavior

All sociologists talk about "collective behavior," but few attempt to define it. When they do, the definitions are not very useful. Smelser's definition, "mobilization on the basis of a belief which redefines social action" [Smelser, 1963, p. 8] will probably not be very helpful to most students. Milgram and Toch [1969, p. 507] define collective behavior as "behavior which originates spontaneously, is relatively unorganized, fairly unpredictable and planless in its course of development, and which depends upon interstimulation among participants." Collective behavior includes such topics as crowds, mobs, panics, crazes, mass hysteria, fads, fashions, propaganda, public opinion, so-cial movements, and revolutions. The last two of these topics are treated in a later chapter.

There are a number of theoretical formulations of collective behavior, none of them entirely adequate. Turner and Killian [1972, chap. 2] note that there are at least three different theoretical approaches. The earliest were the *contagion* theories [LeBon, 1896], which described crowd behavior as an irrational and uncritical response to the psychological temptations of the crowd situation. Later came the *convergence* theories, which focus upon the shared cultural and personality characteristics of the members of a collectivity and note how these similarities encourage a collective response to a situation. Finally, the *emergent norm* theories claim that in a behavior situation which invites collective behavior, a norm arises which governs the behavior. Smelser [1963, chap. 1] attempts to synthesize these approaches into an integrated theory, which, however, comes out as mainly an emergent norm theory. Smelser gives the determinants of collective behavior as:

1. *Structural conduciveness.* The structure of the society may encourage or discourage collective behavior. Simple, traditional, folk societies are less prone to collective behavior than are modern societies.
2. *Structural strain.* Deprivation and fears of deprivation lie at the base of much collective behavior. Feelings of injustice prompt many to extreme action. Impoverished classes, oppressed minorities, groups whose hard-won gains are threatened, even privileged groups who fear the loss of their privileges—all these are candidates for extreme behavior.
3. *Growth and spread of a generalized belief.* Before any collective action, there must be a belief among the actors which identifies the source of the threat, the route of escape, or the avenue to fulfillment.
4. *Precipitating factors.* Some dramatic event, or a report thereof, sets the stage for action. A cry of

"police brutality" in a racially tense neighborhood may touch off a riot. One person starting to run may precipitate a panic.

5. *Mobilization for action.* All that remains now is for action to begin.

6. *Operation of social control.* At any of the above points, the cycle can be interrupted by leadership, police power, propaganda, legislative and government policy changes, and other social controls.

Smelser's formulation has stimulated a good deal of criticism and experimentation [Oberschall, 1968; Wilkinson, 1970; Lewis, 1972]; yet it remains perhaps the most widely used theoretical approach in the study of collective behavior today.

Crowd behavior

A crowd is a *temporary collection of people reacting together to stimuli.* A busload of passengers, each buried in his or her own daydreams, is not a crowd; let the driver announce that he wishes to stop for a few drinks, and they promptly form a crowd.

Unlike most other groups, a crowd is temporary. Its members rarely know one another. Most forms of crowd behavior are unstructured with no rules, no traditions, no formal controls, no designated leaders, no established patterns for the members to follow. Crowd behavior may appear to be spontaneous and utterly unpredictable, but as we shall see, crowd behavior is not purely a matter of chance or impulse. Crowd behavior is a part of the culture. The kinds of crowds that form and the things a crowd will do and will not do differ from one culture to another. Crowd behavior can be analyzed and understood, and to some extent predicted and controlled.

Convergence theory

According to convergence theory, crowd behavior arises from the gathering together of a number of people who share the same needs, impulses, dislikes, and purposes. The people attending a Baptist revival service share a number of characteristics which differ from those of a racetrack crowd. Why are motorcycle rallies and rock festivals so much more prone to noisy disorders than are county fairs? At a rural county fair, those attending are broadly distributed by age, occupation, and social class. Most are local people, with strong ties to local groups and values, and a highly supportive attitude towards local authorities. By contrast, the motorcycle rally or rock festival attracts a quite different crowd [Shellow and Roemer, 1966]. Members are predominantly young and single. Most are outsiders, with no local ties or special concern for local feelings or property. Many in attendance are alienated from the dominant culture, and this alienation has been intensified by the customary local opposition to the holding of the rally or festival in their locality. Small wonder that "disorder" is more common than at county fairs.

Many more illustrations of convergence theory could be cited, showing how the gathering together of like-minded people is a major factor in crowd behavior.

Contagion theory

When a crowd is assembled, there are certain situational determinants of behavior which come into operation. Most of the classic studies of crowd behavior concentrated upon these.

Anonymity. At the county fair, many will meet their friends and neighbors; at the rock festival, most will be strangers. The more anonymous the crowd, the greater the potential for extreme action. The anonymity of the crowd removes the sense of individuality from the members. They do not pay attention to other members as individuals and do not feel that they themselves are being singled out as individuals. Thus the restraints on a member of a crowd are reduced, and one is free to indulge in behavior which would ordinarily be

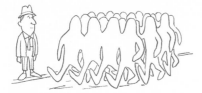

Crowds are anonymous.

controlled, because moral responsibility has been shifted from the individual to the group. At least one study [Festinger et al., 1952] claims to have confirmed these mechanisms through laboratory experimentation. Members of crowds seldom confess to any feeling of guilt after sharing in even the most outrageous atrocities, and this shift of moral responsibility to the group is part of the explanation.

Impersonality. Group behavior is typically impersonal. By this we mean that when groups interact with other groups, this interaction takes very little account of personal feelings or personal relations between members of different groups. The soldier bears no personal grudge against the enemy soldier he shoots, nor does it matter that the opposing football player is a personal friend. At the motorcycle rally, all cyclists are likely to be perceived and feared as hoodlums by the locals, while all locals become "the enemy" to the cyclists. The impersonality of crowd behavior is revealed in race riots where one member of the enemy race is as good or bad as another.

We drove around for a long time. We saw a lot of colored people, but they were in bunches. We didn't want any of that. We wanted some guy all by himself. We saw one at Mack Avenue.

Aldo drove past him and then said, "Gimme that gun." I handed it over to him and he turned around and come back. We were about 15 feet from the man when Aldo pulled up, almost stopped and shot. The man fell and we blew.

We didn't know him. He wasn't bothering us. But other people were fighting and killing and we felt like it, too. (Alfred M. Lee and Norman D. Humphrey, *Race Riot,* Holt, Rinehart and Winston, Inc., New York, 1943, p. 38.)

It should be no surprise that peaceful passersby are attacked in race riots. If the other *group* is the enemy, then *any* member of the group is automatically a victim. When FLN terrorists in Algeria tossed a grenade, killing a guest in a hotel, Europeans surged into the streets and lynched the first two Moslems they found [*Time,* Aug. 11, 1961]. But if the group setting for behavior is destroyed, then the behavior changes. For example, in the Chicago race riot of 1919, one black man outdistanced all but one of his assailants so that the two became separated from their groups and faced each other as individuals, whereupon they quit fighting [Chicago Commission, 1922, p. 22]. Removed from their groups, they realized that fighting was pointless. Group behavior is impersonal; when interaction becomes personal, it ceases to be group behavior and changes in nature.

Suggestibility. Since crowd situations are normally unstructured, there are no designated leaders and no recognized behavior patterns for the members to carry out. Furthermore their individual responsibility has been shifted to the group. Often the situation itself is confused and chaotic. In such a state of affairs, people sometimes act readily and uncritically upon suggestion, especially if the suggestion is made in a decisive, authoritative manner. The "unpredictability" of crowds is just another way of saying that crowds are suggestible [Lang and Lang, 1961, pp. 221–225]. This factor of suggestibility is, however, far from unlimited, and some sociologists feel that students of crowd behavior have overemphasized its importance [Couch, 1968].

Social contagion. At the county fair, there is no single "crowd" most of the time; instead, there are many small groups, often family groups, drifting about with no central focus. At the rock festival, a huge, closely packed crowd surrounds a single stage from whence blasts a hypnotic beat and a countercultural message. Most members lose themselves in a feeling of community and ecstasy somewhat like that of the great religious revivals of an earlier age.[1] This emotional buildup which crowd members give to one another is one of the most dramatic features of crowd behavior. This communication of feeling is most impressive in mobs and riots, but is found in orderly crowds as well. The first one or two cheers at a pep rally normally fall flat; not until we hear the deep swell of voices around us will we cheer very lustily. Every professional speaker or entertainer knows that an audience thinly scattered over a large auditorium will be unresponsive. A well-filled smaller hall is far better. Above all, the audience must be seated close together, without many empty seats separating them. Every revivalist tries to move the audience down front so that they are close to him, and solidly packed, before he starts. The phenomenon he seeks has sometimes been called by the cumbersome title *interactional amplification* although the term *social contagion* is simpler. This is the process whereby the members of a crowd stimulate and respond to one another and thereby increase their emotional intensity and responsiveness. Contagion is increased by "milling" and "rhythm." The crowd, if unseated, may push and surge back and forth, carrying individuals along with it. The crowd may break into rhythmic clapping or shouting, with successive waves of sound carrying members to higher peaks of excitement. All these processes help to explain why crowd behavior sometimes goes farther than most of the members intended. Persons who came intending to be only onlookers get caught up in the process and find themselves joining in. Many confrontations start out in a partly serious, partly festive mood, but escalate through the stages of verbal abuse, rock-throwing, tear-gassing, beating and clubbing, and sometimes shooting.

Social contagion helps to explain the great suggestibility of a crowd, once it is tuned up for

[1]See "Woodstock: Like It Was," *New York Times*, Aug. 25, 1969, pp. 1ff.

action. A person reading in solitude a hilarious scene from a popular comedy will not find it nearly so funny as when he or she sees it as a member of an audience. The "claque," a small organized group that starts and leads the applause for a star at the right moment, is a familiar fixture in the opera house. Since our own actions are reinforced by the action of others, it takes only a few to start a wave of laughter or applause.

When a crowd becomes emotionally aroused, it needs emotional release and may act upon the first suggested action which is in line with its impulses. Lynching mobs were not always concerned about which black person they lynched; if the intended victim escaped, they might lynch any black person who was handy. In Omaha in 1919, when the mayor refused to surrender a lynch victim, the mob attempted to lynch the mayor and very nearly succeeded [*Literary Digest,* Oct. 11, 1919]. In a Texas town in 1930, the victim was hidden in the vault of the courthouse; the mob burned the courthouse, then followed by wrecking the black part of town [Cantril, 1941, pp. 97–110]. The Civil War draft riots in New York City began as protests against the draft, but soon became full-fledged anti-black riots. Any suggested action, if it is in line with the established impulses and antagonisms of the members, is likely to be acted on by an emotionally aroused crowd [Lang and Lang, chap. 8].

These characteristics of crowd behavior explain why the crowd is more than a collection of individuals. Each individual member is to some degree different in the crowd from the person he or she is when alone. As Allport [in Lindzey, 1954, vol. 1, p. 28] remarks, "It used to be said in Germany that there is no such thing as a 'single Nazi.' Only with the support of a group does the peculiar subservience to the leader and his ideology take possession of the individual." We can never fully understand crowd behavior unless we understand that the crowd, like all groups, is more than merely a collection of individuals.

Emergent norm theory

Crowds are never entirely like-minded, and contagion theory does not explain why the crowd takes one action rather than another. Emergent norm theorists charge that contagion theory exaggerates the irrational and purposeless components of crowd behavior. Some early riot studies showed rioters to be predominantly young, single, unsettled, and probably unstable. But studies of the riots of the 1960s found members to be relatively representative cross sections of the categories of people involved, and apparently motivated by genuine group grievances rather than by personal instabilities [Oberschall, 1968; Moinet et al., 1972; Orum, 1974, p. 76]. The burning and looting which accompanied the ghetto riots of the 1960s was not indiscriminate. Private homes, public buildings, and agencies serving the people of the area were generally spared, while stores and offices which were perceived as exploitive were looted and burned [Oberschall, 1968; Berk and Aldrich, 1972]. Thus, these riots were not senseless outbursts of infantile or irrational rage, but were violent protests against perceived wrongs and injustices. This has led some observers to romanticize and idealize the rioters, picturing them as noble promoters of a higher morality [Fogelson, 1968; J. Skolnik, 1969; Rubenstein, 1970; Piven and Cloward, 1971], (provided, of course, the rioters were not KKK'ers, segregationists, or others with whom the observers disagreed). In opposition to this "noble crusader" image is the fact that there are some "issueless riots," which arise, not from ideology, grievance, or social protest, but from the desire for "fun and profit" [Marx, 1970].

Riots are not all alike, with the components of serious protest and "fun and profit" appearing in differing proportion on different occasions. It seems that, starting with the perceptions and grievances of the members, and fed by the contagion process, a norm eventually emerges which justifies and sets limits to the crowd behavior.

A crowd in action can be a terrifying thing. A factual account of everything said and done by an aggressive mob would be unprintable. To cite just one example, lynching victims were frequently burned alive, or slowly strangled and sometimes emasculated as well as being subjected to other inexpressible tortures [Raper, 1933, pp. 6–7, 144]. People will apparently do anything when caught up in the crowd. Is this true?

Limitations on crowd behavior

However irrational and unrestrained it may appear, crowd behavior is limited by at least four considerations: (1) the emotional needs of the members; (2) the mores of the members; (3) the leadership of the crowd; (4) the external controls over the crowd.

A crowd does only those things that most of its members would like to do.

Emotional needs of members. Crowd behavior expresses the emotional needs, resentments, and prejudices of the members. People who led boring, monotonous lives, like the medieval European peasants, appreciated an occasional witch-burning to break the monotony of their lives. People who fear deprivation, like our second-generation immigrants who have struggled from the slum to a better neighborhood and who fear that black residents will "ruin" the neighborhood, need an outlet for their fears and anxieties. In a crowd situation people may do things they ordinarily would not do, but a crowd does only those things that most of its members *would like to do.* The emotional stimulus and protection of the crowd enables its members to express the impulses, hostilities, aggressions, and rages which they are restrained from expressing in calmer moments. Many of us, for example, like to break things, but we must restrain the impulse. People in a riot can shed restraints and can tear things up without guilt feelings. If blocked from its first objective, a mob generally shifts to another. The substitute, however, still represents the hated victim, or fulfills the frustrated wish.

Homogeneous audiences are the most responsive. This observation supports the convergence theory. An audience whose members have the same interests and viewpoints will respond enthusiastically to the speaker. The political rally attracts mainly the party faithful. Its function is similar to that of a pep meeting before a football game—to arouse enthusiasm and dedication to the team. A crowd is most likely to take aggressive action when its members share a common set of prejudices and hostilities. Persons who do not share these feelings are likely to edge backward to the fringes, while the core of the crowd is made up of like-minded members.

Mores of the members. Crowd behavior is limited by the mores of its members. The crowd rarely if ever does anything which does not claim a measure of moral approval. Lynchings did not occur in areas where the mores of most people strongly condemned them. Lynchings took place only where a large proportion of the people felt that a lynching was morally justified, even necessary, under certain circumstances. The members of the lynching party normally considered themselves public bene-

factors, not guilty law breakers. Even the lynching party, then, was expressing, rather than violating, the mores of the members and probably the dominant mores of the region. We note, furthermore, that while the victim might have been killed, burned, and mutilated, he was never crucified, nor was his body ever eaten. The crowd's mores did not support these actions.

It is true that a crowd member may confess later to have shared in acts he or she realizes were morally wrong. Each person, like each group, holds a number of mutually inconsistent views, and at a given moment one or another of them is operative. It may seem very "right" to shout down a platform speaker whose ideas we see as wicked and immoral; but when the speaker for *our* side is silenced, then freedom and justice have been trampled in the dust. Our mores teach us that we should be loyal to family, friends, and fellow workers, and should do nothing that injures other people. When a strike is called in a vital industry, such as railroad transportation or telephone communication, should the worker loyally support the other strikers and thereby inconvenience and possibly injure the public, or stay on the job and injure fellow-workers? Rarely in a behavior situation does the individual have only *one* applicable moral judgment. Which of one's several sets of mores will operate in a particular situation will depend largely upon the group pressures surrounding one at that moment.

The function of crowd behavior is not to paralyze the moral judgments of its members; the function of the crowd is to isolate and neutralize some of one's moral judgments, so that certain others can find unrestrained expression. Thus a crowd is doing only those things for which the mores of the participants give considerable approval.

Crowd leadership. The leadership profoundly affects the intensity and direction of crowd behavior. Given a collection of frustrated, resentful people, a skillful leader can convert them into a vengeful mob and direct their aggression at any "enemy" who is included among their antagonisms. Likewise, a leader can sometimes calm or divert a crowd by a strategic suggestion or command.

Since most crowd behavior is unstructured, with no designated leaders, leadership is "up for grabs." Anyone may be able to assume leadership by simply calling out suggestions and commands. The most unlikely persons sometimes assume leadership. In the panic of the *Lusitania* ship disaster, it was an eighteen-year-old boy under whose direction a few lifeboats were successfully filled and launched [LaPiere, 1938, p. 459]. In many crowd situations, the members, frustrated by confusion and uncertainty, *want* to be direct- ed, and the first person who starts giving clear orders in an authoritative manner is likely to be followed. An impressive appearance is helpful, but the assured manner of one who knows what to do is essential. Let us see specifically what the crowd leader does.

1. *The leader must establish rapport.* By *rapport,* we mean a responsive trusting atten- tiveness such as any really successful speaker gets from his audience. One of your authors recalls observing a war-bond rally of workers in a large factory. A visiting dignitary first gave a speech which was a model of good speech construction and delivery, spoken in Harvard accents. It was received with polite applause. Then the plant manager began by holding out two hamlike paws and saying, "You guys see these hands? They didn't get that way pushing a pencil. They pushed a wheelbarrow for four years, and then they operated a drill press and a turret lathe and just about every damn ma- chine in this place." With these few words, he established rapport. He spoke their language. Rapport is most easily established by a leader who has the same background as the mem- bers. He or she senses their wants, recognizes their antagonisms, speaks their language, and can predict their reactions.

2. *The leader builds emotional tensions.* For some types of crowds (mobs, riots, some audiences) he or she builds up their emotional tensions by an impassioned reminder of their problems and grievances. The revivalist con- victs the sinners of their sins, the leader of the lynching mob arouses the men to defend the purity of their wives and daughters; the cheer- leader focuses all history on the outcome of tomorrow's game. In some kinds of crowds (the panic, some audiences) the leader need not arouse emotional tension, for it already exists; he or she passes directly to the next function.

3. *The leader suggests action to release the tension.* The revivalist calls for repentance; the cheerleader demands victory and lights the bonfire; the campus demonstration leader cries, "Burn the R.O.T.C. building."

4. *The leader justifies the suggested ac- tion.* Seldom does a crowd respond instantly to suggestion (except perhaps in panic behavior). Generally the leader makes some effort to justi- fy the suggestion. The revivalist pictures the new life of release from sin; the looter re- marks, "They'll never give it to us, so we'll take it." The repetition of the suggestion and its justifications permits social contagion to con- tinue to operate, so that tension continues to mount and the need for release of tension continues to grow.

Leadership can function either to stimulate or to restrain a crowd, or to direct activity from one objective to another. Leadership is, there- fore, one of the limiting factors in crowd be- havior.

External controls.   Most mob behavior occurs in the summertime when people are normally standing around and gathering in large out- door assemblies. Cold weather discourages mobs; so do hard thundershowers. Mob behav- ior is rare on army posts, where military disci- pline can be invoked to maintain order. Serv- icemen must release their tensions off the post—and do so at intervals!

The principal external controls on crowd be- havior, however, are those exerted by the po- lice. There are practically no instances of per- sons being lynched in spite of a really determined effort of law-enforcement officials to prevent the lynching. Most lynchings were preceded by either the open connivance of law-enforcement officials, or by their merely token resistance. The virtual disappearance of lynching in recent years stems in large part, not from any lack of persons who would enjoy a lynching, but from the determination of law-enforcement officials to prevent lynchings. Today, shootings and "disappearances" have replaced the classic lynchings.

Some practical knowledge about crowd control is available to police officials. Some years ago, a sociologist who was also a law enforcement official [Lohman, 1947] prepared a widely cited handbook on the handling of potential riot situations, which summarizes in simple language what social science has learned about ways of directing crowd behavior. Among the procedures used in preventing small incidents from developing into riots are: (1) preventing crowd formation by promptly arresting and carrying off noisy troublemakers and ordering the onlookers to move on; (2) meeting threatened disorder with an impressive *show of force*, bringing enough police and equipment into the area so that a *use* of force in unnecessary; (3) isolating a riot area by throwing a police cordon around it and allowing people to leave but not to enter the area; (4) diminishing a crowd by directing the persons on the fringes to "break up and go home," thus stripping the crowd down to its core and depriving the core of its mass support; (5) emphasis in police training on the officer's duty to maintain the peace, so that the officer's own prejudices do not lead him into the fatal error of ignoring attacks on those whom he does not like.

With very few exceptions, serious riots are evidence of police failure. School integration disorders in the 1960s are an example. Where local police and public officials let it be known that no disorders would be tolerated, disorders were rare. Smelser [1963, pp. 261–268] cites many cases where hesitation and indecision of police and other officials, or even their open

sympathizing with the rioters, has aided in riot development.

Some exceptions must be made to the proposition that police can control crowds if they wish. Small cities have no police reserves that can be shifted from place to place in an emergency. A local festival or celebration may bring people into a locality in numbers beyond the capacity of local police to handle. Campus demonstrations were especially difficult to control. Feeling that the campus was "theirs," campus crowds were difficult to disperse by the "peel down and send home" method. Many of the most active members of campus crowds were frequently drawn from the "nonstudent fringe," people who had neither fees, credits, nor jobs to lose. Sometimes the active leadership was provided by itinerant hardcore revolutionists who often materialize wherever demonstrations begin and who encouraged the escalation of violence. They were rarely arrested, being expert in judging just when to flee. The presence of police on campus is generally resented by students, and university administrators have become loath to summon police to the campus.

Police control of civil disturbances poses a difficult problem. Failure to use firmness early in a demonstration may encourage the crowd to grow and the disorder to become unmanageable; yet a premature police presence or the use of force is likely to "radicalize" a crowd (or a student body) and provoke an escalation of disorder. Whatever the police do is likely to be judged an error! Obviously, the capacity of police force to control crowd behavior is not unlimited [Wenger, 1973].

Some forms of crowd behavior

The audience. An audience is a crowd with interest centered on stimuli outside themselves. The stimuli are mainly one-way. With the movie, radio, or TV audience, the stimuli are entirely one-way. Every instructor, however, realizes that any performer before a "live" audience is affected by the audience reaction. Dollard tells how he was stimulated by the responsive audience in a lower-class Southern Negro church which he was invited to address:

It was all I had expected and more too. Not familiar enough with the Bible to choose an opportune text, I talked about my own state, described the country through which I had passed in coming south, spoke of the beauty of their land, and expressed my pleasure at being allowed to participate in their exercises. Helped by appreciative murmurs which began slowly and softly and became louder and fuller as I went on, I felt a great sense of elation, an increased fluency, and a vastly expanded confidence in speaking. There was no doubt that the audience was with me, was determined to aid me in every way. I went on . . .

The crowd had enabled me to talk to them much more sincerely than I thought I knew how to do; the continuous surge of affirmation was a highly elating experience. For once I did not feel that I was merely beating a sodden audience with words or striving for cold intellectual communication . . .

Mine was a miserable performance compared to the many Negro preachers I have seen striding the platform like confident panthers; but it was exactly the intensive collective participation that I had imagined it might be. No less with the speaker than with the audience there is a sense of losing the limitations of self and of unconscious powers rising to meet the unbound, unconscious forces of the group. (John Dollard, *Caste and Class in a Southern Town,* Yale University Press, New Haven, Conn., 1937, pp. 242–243.)

Within an audience, then, there may be significant two-way stimulus and response, even though the audience situation discourages the communication. The most successful performers cultivate a two-way communication which seems to make the performer a part of the group [Berger, 1971]. There is also a certain amount of communication between members, as they cheer, applaud, boo, whisper, mutter, doze, or snore. Social contagion still operates, usually at a more subdued level than in other crowds—highly subdued at a sedate church service, more freely expressive at a political

rally or a sports event. Audiences may become unruly and may even become riotous.

The riot. A riot is the action of a violently aggressive, destructive crowd. It may be a religious riot, as that between the Hindus and the Moslems in India in 1947 [Duncan, 1947; McGinty, 1947] or between Catholics and Protestants in Northern Ireland. It may be a nationality riot, like that between American servicemen and Mexicans in Los Angeles in 1943, or the so-called "zoot-suit" riot [Turner and Surace, 1956], or the many mob actions against European immigrants in the United States during the nineteenth and early twentieth centuries [Higham, 1955]. Race, religion, or nationality—no matter what the cause, the crowd behavior is much the same. A group is disliked because it is different; or it serves as a convenient scapegoat; or it is hated because it threatens competition. With suitable stimulating incidents and without effective police discouragement, persons who are individually frustrated and insecure start action; it builds and grows; the attacked group strikes back, and the riot is under way.

It may be a race riot, in which members of two races indiscriminately hunt down and beat or kill one another, as in Chicago in 1919 [Chicago Commission, 1922] or in Detroit in 1943 [Lee and Humphrey, 1943]. One study of many race riots [Lieberson and Silverman, 1965] finds that they are usually precipitated by a report of a dramatic violence by one race against the other—rape, murder, assault, police brutality—in a society where race problems have not been—and perhaps cannot be—resolved by existing social institutions, and are most likely to occur in communities that have been unresponsive to black needs and appeals [Downes, 1968].

There are other kinds of riots. The protest riot, common in colonial countries, has the object of dramatizing grievances and wringing concessions from the governing powers. The black riots in many American cities beginning in 1965 were not conventional race riots—not primarily a clash between races—but protest riots. A decade of civil rights "victories" had brought few gains to lower-class blacks who remained outside the "affluent society." While skilled and educated Negroes were gaining, lower-class blacks were falling steadily farther behind, growing more frustrated than ever. Usually precipitated by reports of police brutality (often untrue) large-scale violence, burning, and looting exploded across the country [Moynihan, 1965a; Blauner, 1966; Cohen and Murphy, 1966; Rustin, 1967; *Ebony*, special issue, August, 1967; National Advisory Commission on Civil Disorder, 1968; Boskin, 1969; Urban America, Inc., 1969]. Any riot provides the individual with the support of the crowd and a release from moral responsibility, so that he or she may express any fleeting impulse. Most riots include all these elements— flaunting of authority, attack upon disliked groups, and looting and wrecking of property, especially property belonging to the hated group.

Some campus riots, notably at Berkeley, California, in 1964 and 1965, and at Kent State in 1970, caused many Americans to wonder what our students were coming to! As riots go, most of the student demonstrations were pretty tame affairs, involving only a small fraction of the students plus some nonstudents who hung around the larger campuses. Student disorders are, of course, as old as the university. A wave of them in the 1880s hit many colleges, with Amherst's rebellion led by Calvin Coolidge and (later Chief Justice) Harlan Fiske Stone (after Stone was thrown out of another college for demonstrating) [Feuer, 1966]. These nineteenth-century rebellions were staged by students who were alienated from their college administrations but who were not alienated from the society. Recent campus disorders have typically been led by students and nonstudents deeply alienated from Establishment society and who would not be placated by anything less than major changes in contemporary social institutions [Knott, 1971].

The orgy. A revelous crowd which transgresses the normal mores is having an orgy. Like other mobs, the orgy releases tensions; but where the riot is mad with anger, the orgy is mad with joy. One cannot have an orgy by oneself; revelry must be shared or it falls flat. But a very creditable orgy may be promoted by anywhere from a handful of persons to a crowd of thousands. Exactly where "decent recreation" leaves off and the orgy begins is, perhaps, a value judgment. But to be effective in the release of tension, the orgy must involve behavior which exceeds the ordinary daily restraints and inhibitions.

In the orgy we see the factors which operate in all crowd behavior—leadership, social contagion, suggestibility, and transfer of moral responsibility to the group. Since it takes time for these forces to begin to operate, the party takes a while to get going. Before long, inhibitions are diluted, and interaction becomes less restrained. Thus many a motel party, after-the-game celebration, or convention get-together winds up as an orgy.

All societies create frustrations in their members, and all societies provide in some way for the release of tensions. In many societies the orgy is an institutionalized way for members to release their accumulated tensions. A great many primitive societies had periodic festivals or holidays in which ceremonial and orgiastic behavior were combined. Games, feasting, drinking, orgiastic dancing, and the suspension of some of the sex taboos were common features of primitive festivals. Among the Incas, for example:

Holidays might last for a day or for a week; there might be public dancing, such as when hundreds of radiantly clothed "Chosen Women" danced with Huaschar's chain; there could be games and sports; there was always drinking, of a sort one writer calls "approved license." For the Indian [Inca] was expected to get drunk, which he did, quaffing immense quantities of fermented chicha; for ritual drunkenness was as essential to a good festival as agriculture discipline to a good harvest.

Games at the festivals differed from those played by the Indian boy. . .On the day fixed for the

[December] feast, men and girls came to a predetermined place among the ripened fruit gardens, whose ripening they were to celebrate. Men and women were completely naked. At a given signal they started on a race, upon which bets were placed, toward some hill at a distance. Each man that overtook any woman in the race "enjoyed her on the spot." (Victor W. VonHagen, *Realm of the Incas,* Mentor Books, New American Library of World Literature, Inc., New York, 1957, pp. 96–97. From the series, *The Ancient Sun Kingdoms of the Americas,* The World Publishing Company, Cleveland.)

Students of revelry have assumed that the greater the accumulated tensions, the greater the temptation to find release through orgy. Casual observation would seem to support this thesis. Whenever men are isolated from female company or family life and subjected to harsh discipline, monotonous work, and unsatisfactory living conditions for long periods of time, most of them promptly go on a spree at the first opportunity. Army camps, naval stations, construction camps, lumber camps, and mining camps are classic examples. Presumably, the greater the frustrations and tensions, the more riotous the release. Ernie Pyle [1943, p. 3], the perceptive war correspondent, observed that infantry men often endured mud, rain, and dirt, and continuous chaos and uncertainty even as to where they would eat and sleep, whereas sailors ordinarily had clean clothes, good food, and a ship to call home. He then remarked that ". . . sailors didn't cuss as much or as foully as soldiers. They didn't bust loose as riotously when they hit town."

Today the automobile and the mobile home have largely destroyed the isolation of the construction camp, lumber camp, or mining camp, and the orgy has largely faded from their fringes. What no amount of moralizing could do, changing technology has accomplished. The armed services have attempted to make military life more comfortable and less frustrating, and the row of taverns, gambling places, and houses of prostitution in the nearest town is shortened, if not entirely gone.

American society has many approved forms of recreation—dancing, movie-going, participation sports, spectator sports, and many others—which doubtless serve to release tensions. Our society has not, however, institutionalized the orgy as a legitimate release. In primitive societies, the orgy is a relatively safe outlet. In a nonmechanical society, drunkenness which is limited to an occasional socially designated experience is comparatively harmless. In a society with a consanguine family system, collective property ownership, and a serene unconcern with exact biological paternity, an occasional period of sexual license creates no problems. But in our society the price of an orgy may be a painful accident, a costly fire, or a scandalous pregnancy. Our society's inability to provide safe, harmless orgies, however, also carries a price tag. In a society which produces a great many tensions within individuals, these tensions must find release in one way or another. Blocking one dangerous outlet does not guarantee that the substitute outlet will be less offensive. LaPiere comments:

That the cause of the drunken spree lies in social circumstances which demand an occasional escape, rather than, as moralists assume, in the commercial provision of opportunities for such indulgence, is illustrated by the history of an attempt to check the week-end sprees of English industrial workers. Motivated, no doubt, by the best of intentions, the stringent closing of the "pubs" in the depressing East End of London some years ago had, however, such unanticipated consequences that it was soon found advisable to remove the harsh restrictions. Withholding alcohol from workers who were accustomed to a week-end drunk reduced drunkenness and disorderly conduct, but it caused a striking increase in the frequency of wife beating, murder, and suicide. (From *Collective Behavior* by Richard LaPiere, p. 484. Copyright 1938 by McGraw-Hill Book Company. Used with permission of McGraw-Hill Book Company.)

The persistent question of how to reconcile our appetite for revelry with our need for individual safety and social order is not likely to be settled in the forseeable future.

The panic. A panic is "a collective flight based on a hysterical belief" [Smelser, 1963, p. 131]. (There are cases of individual panic, where a person is overtaken by uncontrollable fear; but our concern here is with collective panic.) A panic involves the same elements of crowd behavior, blossoming suddenly under the stress of crisis. We have done little empirical research on panic, since we dare not produce panics to order for study. There are, however, many descriptive accounts and theoretical formulations [Strauss, 1944; Foreman, 1953; Smelser, 1963]. Panic appears to be most likely to seize a group which is fatigued by prolonged stress, although many panics have spread through perfectly relaxed groups. Smelser [1963, chap. 6] sees panic as likely when people feel in great danger with a very limited escape route. Where there are ample escape routes, there is little perceived danger, little fear, and little likelihood of panic. Where there is *no* escape, the usual response is a calm acceptance of fate.

A perceived crisis produces fear, uncertainty, confusion, and a lack of decisive leadership. The role of leadership is crucial in panic prevention, for panic spreads when members lose faith in organized, cooperative effort, and each takes individual defensive action [Mintz, 1951]. In a burning building, one person shouting "Fire!" or "Let me out!" may be enough to start a panic. When a crowd is leaving in orderly manner, if there is any interruption—if someone stumbles and momentarily blocks the aisle—somebody may break out of line in a dash and touch off a panic. Often a panic is precipitated by a "front to rear communication failure." Those in front see that the escape route is blocked, and seek to turn back to find another; those in back cannot see this and push forward harder and harder as the delay lengthens. This is the usual explanation for the suffocating pileup.

In panic prevention, a leader does at least two things: He organizes the crowd so that cooperative activity can proceed, and he relieves uncertainty by specific directions and reassurances. Marshall [1947, p. 130] has pointed out that when an army unit is under heavy fire, if the unit leader says, "Let's get out of here!" panic is likely; but if he says, "Follow me to that fence," panic is unlikely. Once panic has spread, it generally continues until the crisis is past or the members are exhausted (or dead). Panic prevention depends upon a leader's assumption of authoritative direction quickly enough to organize cooperative action before some individual panics and touches off general panic.

Mass society

While *society* is as old as human social life, *mass society* is relatively new. A *mass* is not simply a lot of people, but "a relatively large number of persons, spatially dispersed and anonymous, reacting to one or more of the same stimuli but acting individually without regard for one another" [Hoult, 1969, p. 194]. As Blumer describes the mass:

It has no social organization, no body of custom and tradition, no established set of rules or rituals, no organized group of sentiments, no structure of status roles, and no established leadership. It merely consists of an aggregation of individuals who are separate, detached, anonymous, and thus, homogeneous as far as mass behavior is concerned.
(Herbert Blumer, in Alfred McClung Lee (ed.), Principles of Sociology, *Harper & Row, Publishers, Inc., Barnes and Noble Book Division, New York, 1969, pp. 86–87.)*

Mass society would be a society in which the informal, primary-group, community-based, tradition-oriented relationships of the society have been replaced by contractual, secondary-group, utilitarian relationships. It is the final stage of the shift from *gemeinschaft* to *gesellschaft* relationships. Mass society is characterized by anonymity, mobility, specialization of role and status, and by individual choices relatively independent of traditional mores or values. Since informal, primary-group, and tradi-

The elite are no longer separated from the nonelite.

tionally oriented relationships do remain important in modern societies, the "mass society" is an ideal type or model which actually exists nowhere, but whose features are increasingly predominant in most modern societies.

The traditional society was ruled by small elite groups which were well insulated from the rest of the people and ruled according to revered customs and traditions. In the mass society, tradition is an undependable basis for decision, and the elite is no longer insulated from what the nonelite are thinking and feeling. On the contrary, the elite can be influenced by the nonelite, through the ballot in democracies and through riots and noncooperation in all political systems. Because of this fact, various sections of the elite will attempt to propagandize, organize, and manipulate the nonelite in support of elite political goals [Kornhauser, 1959]. With the use of classified mailing lists and computers which can insert personal names and addresses at appropriate places in computer-written letters, it is possible for the propagandist or advertiser to create the illusion of a personal message in an impersonal mass mailing. Thus a Milwaukee nun was startled to receive a computer-written letter beginning: "Dear Mr. Mother Superior: How would you like to see a brand new Mustang parked outside P. O. Box 1043?"[2] In an in-

creasingly impersonal mass society, the illusion of the "personal touch" is greatly desired.

Much of the writing about "mass society" and "mass culture" is a mournful lament for the loss of past virtues. In contrast to our supposedly rugged, high-principled ancestors, the masses are reviled as rootless clods; of vulgar tastes, morbid or frivolous preoccupations, and having a pervasive disdain for reason and intellect [Zolla, 1968]. While this may be an accurate description of a great many people, whether this is a new development can be questioned. Philip Wylie once ventured the opinion that, after all, "Most of the people always have been slobs." Intellectual interests and "cultivated" tastes have always been shared by relatively few of the people. Mass man is *different* from his ancestors. Whether he is in any way inferior to them is uncertain.

Mass behavior

Mass society is prone to some kinds of collective behavior called *mass behavior*. This term refers to *the unorganized, unstructured, uncoordinated, individually selected behavior of masses in a mass society*. It differs from crowd behavior in that crowd behavior is brief and episodic and is acted out by people as a group, whereas mass behavior is more enduring and arises from the sum total of many individual actions. Also, crowds are collections of people, whereas masses are scattered and in no direct, continuous contact with one another. Masses cannot mill and interact as crowds do. When many people, acting individually rather than as a group, move in the same direction, this is mass behavior. A flight of refugees or the spread of beards and long hair among young people would be a good example.

The rumor

A *rumor* is a rapidly spreading report unsubstantiated by authenticated fact. While rumors may arise in any kind of society, they are most characteristic of mass societies. They may be spread by mass media or by word of mouth. Much of our casual conversation consists of rumor mongering. Every topic, from our neighbor's morals to the fate of the nation, attracts interesting and disturbing rumors. Whenever there is social strain, rumors flourish. Wherever accurate and complete facts on a matter of public concern are not available or are not believed, rumors abound. Since rumors can ruin reputations, discredit causes, and undermine morale, the manipulation of rumor is a common propaganda device.

In the definitive work on rumor, Allport and Postman [1947, p. 46] point out that a great amount of rumor mongering springs from nothing more complicated than the desire for interesting conversation and the enjoyment of a salacious or unusual tidbit. Thus a rumor of the mysterious death of one of the Beatles spread among young people in 1971 and persisted despite repeated denials [Suczek, 1972]. A person is most likely, however, to believe and spread a rumor *if it will justify his dislikes or relieve his emotional tensions.* People who dislike Republicans, hate blacks, or despise hippies will remember and repeat damaging rumors about these groups. The rumor changes continuously as it spreads, for people unconsciously distort it into the form that most perfectly supports their antagonisms. People uncritically accept and believe a rumor if it fits in with their pattern of beliefs and dislikes, or if it provides an emotionally satisfying explanation of phenomena.

Every presidential assassination has produced a flood of rumors of assassination conspiracies.[3] The conspiracy rumor is especially satisfying. It gives one the flattering feeling of having "inside" knowledge, along with a delicious sense of fearlessly denouncing evildoers.

Rumors are not very effectively dispelled by

[3]See Daniel W. Belin, Esq., *You are the Jury,* Quadrangle Books, New York 1973, for a critical appraisal of many conspiracy rumors about the death of President Kennedy.

truthful correction. The "rumor-correction center" sometimes spreads the rumor rather than the correction [Ponting, 1973]. Rumors are believed and spread because people need and like them. As Shibutani [1966, p. 139] proposes: "The process of rumor construction is terminated when the situation in which it arose is no longer problematic." This means, for example, that rumors flourish where people feel that they cannot trust government officials to tell them the truth, but rumors will subside if confidence in their officials is restored.

The fad or fashion

A *fad* is a trivial, short-lived variation in speech, decoration, or behavior. As this is written, the phrase, "Have a nice day," has been "in" long enough so that it will probably have died out by the time this book is printed.

The fad apparently originates in the desire to gain and maintain status by being different, by being a leader, and dies out when it is no longer novel. Bogardus [1950, pp. 305–309] studied 2,702 fads over many years, finding that most of them deal with superficial accessories and gewgaws. They typically grow rapidly, have a two- or three-month plateau, and then decline, although some last longer, and a few become permanent parts of the culture. One recent fad—practiced by few but enjoyed by many— was "streaking," (racing nude through a public place). It lasted for only a few months in the spring and summer of 1974, dying out as fall temperatures approached.

Fashions are similar to fads, but change less rapidly and are less trivial. The hemlines of women's dresses go up, down, up, down, while men's beards luxuriate, wither, and luxuriate again! Fashion operates only in societies with a class system. In a homogeneous, undifferentiated society, distinction through fashion does not arise, since all act and adorn themselves alike. In a rigid caste society, fashion is unnecessary, for distinction is already firmly assigned [Blumer, 1969c, p. 117]. Yet fashions do not always originate among the elite and diffuse downward, but may originate at any social level. Fashions spread as people who wish to be up-to-date make their collective selections from many competing models [Blumer, 1969b].

Fashion may involve almost any aspect of group life—manners, the arts, literature, philosophy, even the methodologies of science—but is most often seen in clothing and adornment. Fashions reflect the dominant interests and values of a society at a particular time [Harris, 1973]. In the eighteenth century, elaborate clothing reflected an ornate and decorative upper-class culture, and the confining styles of the Victorian era reflected Victorian prudishness [Flugel, 1930]. Fashion changes often reflect changes in tastes, attitudes, and values. The present trend towards reduced differentiation in sex roles [Winick, 1969] is accompanied by the trend toward unisex clothing [Stannard, 1971]. During the political conservatism and relative indifference to social problems of the placid 1950s, the popular song lyrics were trivial and romantic; as concern over social problems and competing life styles grew in the later 1960s, the popular song lyrics assumed a sharp tone of social criticism [Rosenstone, 1969]. Fashion is not entirely trivial, but often reflects the currents of change in a society.

There is much speculation, but little scientific research, on the possibility that fashion changes and choices arise from unconscious emotional needs and impulses. In one of the very few research studies, Becker [1971] concluded that those women who were first to wear miniskirts were women who had negative self-images, while the women who accepted the midiskirt craved attention so badly as to wear something ugly and sexless to attract it. Although unconscious motivation may be involved, fashion choices are not entirely irrational, for they meet genuine social needs as defined by social class, age and sex group, and other group affiliation. Fashion consciousness aids the middle-class social climber, and a distinct mode of dress or hair style fills the early teen-ager's need to "belong" in a private world not run by adults [Barber and Tobel, 1953]. Long hair and untrimmed beards for men in the early 1960's were a symbol of social protest, for a deliberate ugliness in dress and grooming was a way to shock and express contempt for the Establishment. But a decade later, beards and long hair no longer expressed social protest. Instead they had become so fashionable that experimental studies found that bearded men were rated as more handsome, masculine, and virile than their shaven compatriots [Pellegrini, 1973]. Whatever becomes fashionable is perceived as beautiful.

Fashion changes may be deliberately manipulated by the apparel industry, but only to a limited degree, for there is evidence that consumers will not passively accept everything labeled "fashionable" [Jack and Schiffer, 1948; Lang and Lang, 1961, chap. 15]. Determined efforts of the women's wear industry to promote the midiskirt in 1970 met with failure, mainly because women felt that midiskirts made them look older [Reynolds and Darden, 1972]. Here, again, fashion reflects the dominant cultural values.

The craze

Where the panic is a rush away from a perceived threat, the craze is a rush toward some satisfaction. As Smelser observes [1963, chap. 7], the craze may be superficial (miniature golf, monopoly, hula hoops, celebrity fan clubs) or serious (war crazes, nomination of a president); it may be economic (speculative boom), political (bandwagons), expressive (dance steps), religious (revivals), to mention only a few types. Flagpole sitting, dance marathons, jigsaw puzzles, canasta, and chain letters have all had their moments.

The craze differs from the ordinary fad in that it becomes an obsession for its followers. The use of LSD became a craze among a minority of college students, with an estimated 5 or 6 percent having tried LSD at least once at the peak of the craze in 1967 [Meyer, 1969, p.

201]. With Dr. Timothy Leary as its high priest, LSD was to bring the world into a new nirvana of peace, love, and creativity. But a growing fear of LSD's hazards seems to have ended its craze and reduced its users to no more than 1 percent of college students by 1969 [Meyer, 1969, p. 201].

Many crazes involve some kind of get-rich-quick scheme. The Holland tulip craze of 1634 bid up the price of tulip bulbs until their value exceeded their weight in gold. The Florida land boom of the 1920s pushed land prices to levels fantastically beyond any sound economic valuation. In the craze, the individual gets caught up in a mass hysteria and loses ordinary caution. Speculators sell to one another at climbing prices until some bad news pricks the bubble or until so many susceptible persons have joined that no new money is entering the market; then confidence falters, and the market collapses in a frenzy to unload holdings [Mackay, 1932].

Since the craze is taken over by only a small fraction of the population and is a time-consuming preoccupation, it generally wears itself out quite quickly, soon to be replaced by another for those who are susceptible.

Mass hysteria

This is some form of irrational, compulsive belief or behavior which spreads among people. It can be a brief crowd phenomenon, as when a wave of uncontrollable twitching spread through a Louisiana high school [Schuler and Parenton, 1943]. The *New York Times* [Sept. 14, 1952] reports that at a Mississippi football game, 165 teen-aged girls in a cheering section became excited and "fainted like flies." Or mass hysteria may extend beyond a single collection of people at a single moment in time. In one town, dozens of people over several weeks reported being attacked by a "phantom anesthetist" who sprayed them with an unknown drug which caused paralysis and other symptoms [Johnson, 1945]. The Salem witchcraft trials are an interesting his-

torical example of mass hysteria [Starkey, 1949]. Recurrent waves of flying-saucer reports, together with an elaborate pseudoscientific literature on flying saucers, are a more modern example of mass hysteria [Hackett, 1948; Gardner, 1957, chap. 5]. From an analysis of the reports, it can be suspected that flying-saucer reports were often the main reason for flying-saucer reports; that is, publicity about flying saucers was dependably followed by a series of new "sightings." It is, of course, a scientific possibility that some of the "unidentified flying objects" are from outer space. As stated earlier, a negative proposition (e.g., "there are no flying saucers") is impossible to prove; but the evidence for them, at present, is most unconvincing [Condon, 1969].

Why do some people succumb to mass hysteria while others seem to be immune? Our very limited research suggests that physical and psychological stress increases susceptibility. In a junior high school, there was a sudden wave of illnesses and fainting spells from a "gas" which proved to be nonexistent. A comparative study found that, in contrast to the "immunes," the "hysterics" had a record of more absences, more visits to the school nurse for trivial reasons, and more deviations of several kinds [Goldberg, 1973]. In another case of "gas" hysteria in a data-processing center where the work (key punching and sorting) was exacting but monotonous and the working conditions unsatisfactory, the women who were most dissatisfied with the work situation were the most susceptible to the phantom fumes [Stahl and Lebedun, 1974]. It thus appears that there are some personality differences between those who "keep their cool" and those who are prone to panic or hysteria, but no personality profile of the susceptible person has yet been established.

Do we, then, have satisfactory explanations for collective behavior? Not entirely. All the forms of collective behavior herein discussed seem to arise from some form of frustration or discontent. Periods of social crisis seem to foster a profusion of fads and crazes [Turner and Killian, 1972, p. 130]. Possibly recreational fads and crazes offer an escape from serious problems which appear unsolvable. All forms of collective behavior may serve to release tensions and provide some form of wish-fulfillment. We can venture some forecasts of when and where the more extreme forms of collective behavior are likely to appear and have some knowledge of how they may be controlled. With further study, we should know more.

Publics and public opinion

The term "public" is used in several senses. In popular use, "the public" is synonymous with "the people" or with practically everybody—not a very useful concept. Sociologists use the term in two senses: (1) A *public* may be defined as *a scattered number of people who share an interest in a particular topic*. There is a baseball public, an opera public, an investment public, a political-affairs public, and many others. (2) A *public* may be defined as *a number of people who are concerned over, divided upon, and in discussion about an issue*. Each important issue thus has its public, and there is no such thing as *the* public under these two definitions.

The members of a public are not gathered together like the members of a crowd. Each member of a public can communicate directly with only a handful of the other members. A public is reached mainly through the mass media. The titles of many magazines reveal the public for which each is published—*House and Garden, Field and Stream, Guns and Ammo, Western Horsemen, Cats Magazine, U.S. Camera, Stamps, Motor Trend, The Theater, Workbench, Audio, National Geographic Magazine, Holiday, Pacific Affairs,* and hundreds more. Since the members of a public can communicate effectively only through such mass media, it follows that those who control the media have considerable power to influence the opinions of that public.

Publics are created by cultural complexity.

In a simple culture there would be few if any publics. A complex culture produces many interest groups with rival axes to grind and develops many issues over which people differ. For example, one group wishes to keep our national parks in their unspoiled condition with a minimum of development; another group wants to develop them into recreation centers with resorts, airstrips, and ski lifts; still other groups wish to hunt the game, log the timber, mine the minerals, graze the grassland, or dam the streams in the parks. Such interest clashes multiply as a culture becomes more complex.

Few issues arise in a simple, stable culture; that is, few situations develop which cannot be handled by following the traditional folkways and mores of the society. But in a complex, changing culture, issues are constantly arising. In other words, situations are constantly developing which our traditional folkways and mores either will not handle at all or will handle only in a way that leaves some groups dissatisfied. For example, should "hard" pesticides which remain poisonous for a long time (such as DDT) be banned in order to protect the environment, or are they necessary for food production and disease control? Tradition gives no clear answer.

In these ways a complex changing culture creates a great many publics, each concerned with an activity, interest, or issue, As the members of a public consider the issue, and form opinions concerning it, *public opinion* is developed.

Public opinion also has two definitions: (1) *an opinion held by a substantial number of people;* (2) *the dominant opinion among a population.* According to the first usage, there can be many public opinions; according to the second, public opinion refers to a public *consensus* upon an issue. Both usages are common in the literature, and the particular meaning must be inferred from the way the term is used.

Public opinion is a creation of the mass society and the mass media. In traditional societies, *gemeinschaft* relations predominate, while an elite rules according to established traditions without very much concern for anything such as public opinion. If the ordinary people had been questioned about current "issues," their usual response would have been one of bewilderment. True enough, there were differences of interest and viewpoint in earlier societies, but these were typically thrashed out *within* the elite without involving the ordinary people (except as they suffered the consequences). Public opinion depends upon having a mass whose opinions are important to the elite, whereupon different sections of the elite seek to propagandize and manipulate this mass in support of elite interests. Democracies differ from dictatorships in that in democracies different groups among the elite compete vigorously for mass support, whereas in a dictatorship some faction among the elite gains dominance, removes or neutralizes its competitors, and enjoys a monopoly of propaganda.

Dimensions of public opinion

Public opinion has at least three dimensions. *Direction* simply states whether an opinion is for or against a proposed course of action. A count of the "yes" and "no," or the "approve" and "disapprove" opinions measures the direction of opinion. *Intensity* refers to the strength with which an opinion is held. "Yes" may mean, "Yes, absolutely, whatever the costs," or it may mean, "Yes, I guess so." *Integration* refers to the way an opinion is tied in with one's total set of beliefs and values. Is this opinion an expression of a person's general outlook or an exception to it? For example, Mr. Smith favors national health insurance (sometimes called "socialized medicine") because he favors a welfare state wherein the government provides many social services to its citizens. Ms. Jones, less enthusiastic about the welfare state, supports national health insurance because after some study she believes that it is the only practical way to organize health serv-

ices. Mr. Brown, strongly opposed to the welfare state, supports national health insurance because he dislikes physicians and wants to see their heads knocked together. Ms. Black supports it because her union tells her it is good. While identical in direction and perhaps intensity, these four opinions are basically quite different because of the way they relate to the mental context of their holders. The opinion which is well integrated with one's total value system is less easily changed by persuasion than the opinion which is divorced from or inconsistent with one's general system of beliefs and values.

Measurement of public opinion

The leaders of a group or a nation cannot lead wisely unless they know which way the people are willing to be led. The public-opinion poll is a recent invention for finding out what people are thinking. A poll is simple in concept but difficult to carry out because, as is shown above, an opinion is a rather complicated phenomenon. The pollsters prepare a set of questions on an issue, seeking to phrase the questions in such a way that the wording does not prejudice the informant's answer. Then these questions are offered to a small number of people (from a few hundred to a few thousand) so that each group or class in the total population is represented in the sample in its correct proportion. If all these preliminary arrangements are made without serious error, opinion is measured quite accurately. The Gallup Poll, for example, has predicted the vote on recent elections with an average error of less than 2 percent of the total population vote. But there are many pitfalls in public-opinion polling which a pollster must guard against in trying to attain this level of accuracy. One of the greatest is the tendency of people to state firm opinions on issues which they know nothing about, have not thought about, and really have no opinion upon. In 1959 a Los Angeles newspaperman asked a number of people the question, "Do you think the Mann Act deters or helps the cause of organized labor?" About one person in eight knew what the Mann Act is (it forbids the interstate transportation of women for immoral purposes) and realized that the question was unanswerable. But of the remainder who admitted that they knew nothing of the Mann Act, about one-half expressed decided opinions about its effects. If the "opinions" of people who know nothing about an issue are included, a poll is not very accurate. Other pitfalls surround the wording of questions, the selection of the sample, and the weighing or interpreting of responses [Parten, 1950; B. Phillips, 1966; Hennessy, 1970]. Polling is no job for amateurs!

Manipulation of public opinion

The main emphasis in public-opinion research has been upon ways of manipulating public opinion [Albig, 1957]. *Propaganda* includes all efforts to persuade people to a point of view upon an issue; everything from Sunday school lessons to billboards are propaganda; advertis-

Propaganda is not necessarily bad.

ing, sales promotion, and fund-raising drives are prime examples. The usual distinction between education and propaganda is that education seeks to cultivate one's ability to make discriminating judgments, while propaganda seeks to persuade one to the undiscriminating acceptance of a ready-made judgment. In practice, education often includes a good deal of propaganda. Teachers sometimes propagandize for their own opinions; interest groups seek to get their own propaganda, disguised as "educational materials," into the school; society virtually forces the school to propagandize for the approved moral and patriotic values. Conservatives wish the schools to propagandize for the status quo, while Marxists and other radicals insist that teachers should propagandize for the revolution. To draw a clear distinction between education and propaganda is not always possible. And it should be repeated that propaganda is not necessarily "bad"; it is merely a term applied to *all* attempts to influence other peoples' opinions and actions. Most students, beginning perhaps with a ninth-grade course in civics, have seen descriptions of the techniques of propaganda in textbook after textbook. We shall not repeat them here. Good descriptions of propaganda techniques are easily available, should the student wish to consult them [Lee and Lee, 1939; Doob, 1948, 1966; Lasswell, 1951; Qualter, 1962, ch. IV].

Does the propagandist get the greatest opinion change when his or her propaganda diverges greatly, or only slightly, from the opinions already held by the receivers? An awareness of such divergence is known as *cognitive dissonance.* Some research studies find that when the degree of divergence from the original opinion is greater, so is the opinion change; other studies reach the opposite conclusion. Whittaker [1964] reconciles these contradictory findings, saying that when the issue is one upon which the receivers hold intense opinions with a deep personal involvement, opinion change diminishes as dissonance increases. Too great a dissonance even produces a "boomerang" cognitive effect; that is, the receiver rejects the propaganda with an even stronger loyalty to his or her original opinions. Like the person who said, "I've read so much about the dangers of smoking that I've decided to give up reading," one may simply "tune out" anything which conflicts too sharply with his or her beliefs and desires. But when the issue is one on which the receiver has no intense opinions or deep personal involvement, increasing dissonance produces increased opinion change. For each receiver, there is an "optimal discrepancy" which will produce a maximum opinion change.

Limits of propaganda. If the powers of propaganda were unlimited, the side with the most money and the best public relations agency would always win. Since this does not always happen, the power of propaganda must be limited in various ways.

1. *Competing propagandas* are probably the greatest limitation. Where the state has a monopoly of propaganda, as in totalitarian states, a citizen cannot easily find any facts to use in arriving at opinions other than the officially approved ones. With a monopoly of propaganda, a propagandist can suppress and manufacture facts, and no effective rebuttal is possible. The mere *existence* of competing propagandas in a democratic state exerts a restraining influence both upon the propagandist and upon the receiver.

2. *The credibility of the propagandist* in the eyes of the receivers limits what they will accept. When his "facts" and opinions diverge from theirs, this creates tensions which the receiver can relieve either by changing opinions or by downgrading the propagandist [Aronson et al., 1963]. Credibility is reduced where the propagandist obviously has a stake in the game, so propaganda is often conducted under the name of a noble-sounding organization (Fundamental Freedoms Foundation, Tax Equality Association, Homeowners' Association) which conceals the selfish interests of the propagandists.

3. *The sophistication of the receiver* limits the effects of propaganda. In general, those who are well educated or well informed on the issue are less affected by propaganda than the poorly educated and the poorly informed.

4. *The beliefs and values of the recipient* limit the propaganda he or she will believe. Many people are fond of picturing themselves as open-minded, discriminating analysts of competing propagan-

das, but they are usually reacting mechanically to slogans and catchwords. Most people accept uncritically any propaganda which fits in with their established attitudes and values, and usually reject, equally uncritically, any which conflicts. For this reason, a propagandist rarely tries to change the basic attitudes of recipients; instead, he or she tries to get them to accept a new definition of the issue, in terms of their attitudes. For example, a propagandist for banning the use of "hard" pesticides will define the issue as one of protection versus reckless destruction of the environment; the propagandist for continuing "judicious use" of pesticides will define the issue as "food for people" versus "birdies for bird-watchers." The propagandist's task is to get the people to accept a definition of the issue that will call up those attitudes and images which support the propagandist's cause. Communist propaganda has long been ineffective in the United States because its pictures of the villainous businessman, the "oppressive" church, and a "proletariat" middle class simply struck no responsive note in the basic images, attitudes, and values of the American people.

5. *Cultural drifts and trends* limit the effectiveness of propaganda. A cultural drift is not stopped by propaganda. For this reason, all "white-supremacy" and "women's place is in the home" propagandas are doomed to futility. Propaganda may accelerate or retard a cultural trend, reinforce or weaken a value. But it is doubtful if propaganda in a democratic society can either initiate or halt a cultural trend, destroy a well-established value, or instill a new value which the culture is not already developing.

Summary

Collective behavior is a characteristic of complex cultures and is usually absent in simple societies. A *crowd* is a temporary gathering of people who are acting together. Three principal theories attempt to explain collective behavior. *Contagion theories* emphasize the psychological processes of suggestion and manipulation; *convergence theories* stress the like-mindedness of crowd members; *emergent norm theories* show how in crowd situations, a norm develops which sanctions and limits behavior. Crowd behavior is characterized by: (1) anonymity—the individual loses customary restraints and sense of personal responsibility; (2) impersonality—only the group affiliation of the person is important; (3) suggestibility—crowd members act uncritically upon suggestions; (4) social contagion—crowd members build up one another's emotional involvement. Crowd behavior is limited, however, by: (1) emotional needs and attitudes of the members; (2) the mores of the members, who rarely do anything which is not condoned by certain of their mores; (3) crowd leaders, who must establish rapport, build emotional tensions, suggest action to relieve these tensions and justify this action; and (4) external controls, mainly the police, whose ability to control crowd behavior depends partly upon their skill and partly upon the nature of the particular crowd.

Crowd behavior takes many forms. The *audience* is largely, but not entirely, a one-way crowd responding to a single stimulus. In the *riot* the members of a violently aggressive crowd release their accumulated hostilities, sometimes irrationally and sometimes purposefully. In the *orgy,* a good-natured crowd enjoys itself through uninhibited indulgence. In the *panic,* people become a crowd in sudden, disorganized flight from danger.

A *mass* is a separated number of people responding individually to the same stimuli. *Mass society* is a society in which traditional, primary-group, *gemeinschaft* relationships have been largely replaced by *gesellschaft* relationships, characterized by anonymity, mobility, specialization, and independence of traditional values. *Mass behavior* is the unor-ganized, unstructured, uncoordinated behavior of masses in a mass society. Forms of mass behavior include the *rumor,* a rapidly spreading report unsubstantiated by fact; the *fad* or *fashion,* temporarily popular variations in speech, manners, dress, or behavior; the *craze,* a short-lived mass preoccupation with a particular satisfaction; *mass hysteria,* some form of irrational compulsion which spreads among a people; and possibly others.

The term *public* is defined by sociologists both in terms of those people sharing a common interest and of those people sharing a common concern over an issue. *Public opinion* includes both the different opinions held by substantial numbers of people and the consensus opinion held by most people. Public opinion is important in mass society, where elites are influenced by masses and seek to propagandize and organize these masses in support of elite interests. Individual opinions differ in direction, in intensity, and in integration, or the way they relate to the rest of one's thinking. Consequently, it is difficult to "add up" individual opinions and measure the sum of public opinion, but professional pollsters have developed techniques which can measure opinion with considerable accuracy.

Practically every interest group today is trying to manipulate public opinion so that propaganda, often called "public relations," is one of our largest businesses. Propaganda may be less powerful than it sometimes appears to be, for its effects are limited by competing propagandas, by the credibility of the propagandists, by the sophistication of its receivers, by the established beliefs and values of the receivers, and by the existing trends within the culture.

Questions and projects

1. When we say that crowd behavior is "unstructured," what do we mean? Of what importance is its unstructured character?
2. Which has the greater potential for extreme crowd behavior—the class reunion or the family reunion? Why?
3. Why do crowd members seldom feel guilty about their mob actions?

4. Are there any situations in our culture which contain elements of the institutionalized orgy?

5. Should we fully institutionalize the orgy in American society? What benefits might accrue? What differences would arise?

6. What caused the recent student disorders in colleges and universities? Are students generally becoming more restless, or less restless? Why?

7. How does mass society differ from traditional society? Why are propaganda and public opinion more characteristic of mass society?

8. Do you think you are immune to panic? To crazes? To mass hysteria? What makes you think so?

9. Can you think of any propaganda efforts or causes which have failed in the United States because they conflicted with our cultural values? With prevailing cultural trends?

10. Write up a description of a campus pep rally as an example of crowd behavior.

11. Research studies (such as Neil Vidmar and Milton Rokeach: "Archie Bunker's Bigotry: A Study in Selective Perception and Exposure," *Journal of Communication,* 24:36–47, Winter, 1974) show that the TV show "All in the Family" is perceived by liberals as a devastating exposé of bigotry, while conservatives and bigots hear Archie "telling it like it is." What implications has this for opinion manipulators?

12. Try an experiment in rumor. Select a harmless rumor (such as that reserved faculty parking is to be abolished) and set it going by a specified number of tellings. Then record the time, frequency, and form in which it "comes back" to you as it spreads over the campus.

13. Recall and describe a crowd situation in which the behavior lagged dispiritedly for a time. Show how each of the characteristics of crowd behavior came into operation and kindled a proper enthusiasm in the members. Or, if you have the opportunity, attend and observe a crowd situation for your analysis.

14. Prepare a list of aggressive actions which you think you could engage in if placed in a suitably encouraging crowd situation. Prepare a list of actions in which you think you could not possibly share, no matter what the crowd situation. Give your reasons for each listing.

15. Run a campus public-opinion poll on a fictitious proposition such as "Do you favor or oppose the Hill-Wallerton proposal to pay college students a salary according to their point averages?" See how many will admit that they do not know of the proposal, and how many state firm opinions on it.

Suggested readings

ALLPORT, GORDON W., AND LEO POSTMAN: *The Psychology of Rumor,* Russell, New York, 1965 or "The Basic Psychology of Rumor," in WILBUR SCHRAMM (ED.): *The Process and Effects of Mass Communication,* The University of Illinois Press, Urbana, Ill., 1971, pp. 141–155. How and why rumors appear and circulate.

*BLUMER, HERBERT: "Collective Behavior," in ALFRED MCCLUNG LEE (ED.): *Principles of Sociology,* Barnes and Noble, New York, 1969, chaps. 7–12. A classic treatment of this topic in one of the College Outline Series handbooks.

BROWN, MICHAEL, AND AMY GOLDEN: *Collective Behavior,* Goodyear Publishing Co., Pacific Palisades, Calif., 1973. A textbook containing perceptive chapters (3–6) on collective behavior in disasters and (11–13) on student protest.

*KNOTT, PAUL D. (ED.): *Student Activism,* Wm. C. Brown, Publishers, Dubuque, Iowa, 1971. A brief collection of significant essays on student activism.

LANG, KURT, AND GLADYS ENGLE LANG: *Collective Dynamics,* Thomas Y. Crowell Company, New York, 1961. A textbook on collective behavior, with interesting chapters on rumor, panic, crowd behavior, fashion, public opinion, and other topics covered in this chapter.

*LEE, ALFRED MCCLUNG, AND NORMAN D. HUMPHREY: *Race Riot,* Octagon Press, New York, 1967. A classic description and analysis of the Detroit race riot of 1941.

MILGRAM, STANLEY, AND HANS TOCH: "Collective Behavior: Crowds and Social Movements," in GARDNER LINDZEY AND ELLIOT ARONSON (eds.):

Handbook of Social Psychology, Addison-Wesley Publishing Co., Reading, Mass., 1969, Vol. IV, pp. 507–610. A systematic collection of research and theory, most of which (pp. 507–584) deals with topics treated in this chapter.

MORIN, EDGAR: "Rumor in a City in Central France," *Psychology Today,* October, 1972, pp. 77ff. A sociologist's account of a vicious, titillating rumor.

*SHORT, JAMES F., JR., AND MARVIN E. WOLFGANG (eds.): *Collective Violence,* Aldine-Atherton, Chicago, 1972. A collection of essays on many kinds of violent collective behavior.

SMELSER, NEIL J.: *Theory of Collective Behavior,* The Free Press, New York, 1962. An attempt to develop and apply a theoretical system for the study of collective behavior.

TURNER, RALPH F., AND LEWIS M. KILLIAN: *Collective Behavior,* Prentice-Hall, Inc., Englewood Cliffs, N.J., 1972, chaps. 3–12. An interestingly written textbook, about half of which is devoted to the topics covered in this chapter.

*WELLS, ALAN (ED.): *Mass Media and Society,* National Press Books, Palo Alto, Calif., 1972. A collection of lively readings on mass media and popular culture.

WHITE, THEO: "Building the Big Dam," *Harper's Magazine,* June, 1935, pp. 112–121. An entertaining explanation of how and why construction camp workers used to go on payday sprees.

Five/Human ecology

Part Five describes the way people and institutions are distributed in space and the way they relate to the physical environment they occupy. Chapter 18, "Population," considers the factors in population change, migration, and composition. Chapter 19, "The Community in Mass Society," describes rural and urban communities and the emergence of a worldwide urban culture.

Chapter 18•Population

But hasn't there been a "green revolution" — miracle wheat and rice? Didn't they solve the food problem? The best answer is the story of Ireland. In the 17th century Ireland had two million people—mostly destitute. Then in the 18th century came the potato from the New World—the "green revolution" of that era. Population skyrocketed. By 1835 eight million people lived in Ireland—mostly destitute. Then came the potato blight: two million people starved, two million emigrated, four million were left—mostly destitute. *(TRB: "A Matter of Time," Reprinted by permission of* The New Republic, © 1973, *The New Republic, Inc.)*

Human ecology is the study of the interrelationships of people with their physical environments. More simply, it is the study of how people and institutions are located in space. It includes both the study of population (demography) and the study of community and regional organization.

Demographers are interested in both the size and the composition of a population. A small population with great natural resources and extensive territory will have limited economic growth and urban development. A dense population with limited natural resources will have difficulty in maintaining a high standard of living. Sometimes a population will vary from the usual sex and age distribution with certain predictable social consequences. A population with a large number of children and old people leaves a smaller proportion of people in productive labor to support them. If the sex ratio is markedly unequal, many people will be unable to marry (if marriage is monogamous) and may seek companionship outside of the normal family relationships. In many ways, population statistics are reflected in the social life of a people.

Population has been relatively stable throughout most of history. In the first 1,650 years after the birth of Christ, world population a little more than doubled. In the next 125 years it doubled again. World population is now estimated at over 3.8 billion [*UN Population and Vital Statistics,* 1973], and is expected to reach 7 billion by the year 2000 [McCormack, 1970, p. 6]. World population now grows in about six years by as many persons as it grew in the first 1,650 years following the birth of Christ. If present rates of growth were to be continued for 800 years, we should have one person per square foot of land surface of the earth [Hauser, 1960, p. 7].

Demographic concepts

In order to study population questions, one must understand the very definite meanings of

One person per square foot of land surface in less than 800 years.

demographic concepts. "Birthrate" and "death rate," for instance, are terms frequently used in demographic discussion. Usually they refer to the *crude* rate, which is the number of births or deaths per 1,000 people per year. Crude birthrates and death rates do give a picture of population trends, but they may be misleading because births and deaths are greatly affected by the age structure of the population. A population in which a large proportion of people are relatively old would show a high crude death rate even though health levels were very high. Similarly, a population with a high proportion of either the very old or the very young would have a low crude birthrate even though the women of childbearing age were busily producing children. To allow for this factor of age we frequently use *age-specific* rates, which give birthrates or death rates for specific age levels.

Standardized birthrates and death rates are rates which have been adjusted to account for differences between populations in some characteristic—age distribution, occupational distribution, rural-urban residence—which is believed to affect birthrates or death rates. For example, a birthrate standardized for age would be calculated as follows: First, some age distribution, often a life insurance "life table," is chosen as a "standard" age distribution;

then, using age-specific birthrates for a population, the birthrate for that population can be calculated as if that population had the "standard" age distribution. In this way, the true fertility rate or death probability in various populations can be compared. For example, a retirement community like St. Petersburg, Florida, has a low birthrate and a high death rate, suggesting that it is a very unhealthy place to live. But the *standardized* birthrate and death rate for St. Petersburg would give an accurate comparison of the fertility of its young people and the death probability for people of all ages between St. Petersburg and other communities. Such comparisons of standardized birthrates and death rates reveal whether any differences between crude rates for different populations are due to the factor which has been standardized or to other factors.

Sex distribution is also of interest to the demographer, for it affects the crude birthrate as well as many other social phenomena. Thus we speak of the *sex ratio,* which is the number of males per 100 females. A sex ratio of 100 indicates that the two sexes are found in equal number, one of 110 that there are 110 men to 100 women, and one of 90 that there are 90 men to 100 women.

Demographers often speak of *life expectancy.* This usually refers to the number of years of life the average infant may expect at birth, but it may also be age specific—for example, life expectancy at age sixty (average additional years of life to be expected after reaching an age of sixty).

Insurance companies use actuarial tables indicating the life expectancy at any given age. Life expectancy should be distinguished from *life span,* which refers to the length of life possible for a member of a particular species. In the last century life expectancy at birth has increased greatly, while the evidence indicates that our life span has changed little if at all.

The very elementary concepts which we have just described represent only a few of the tools used in demographic analysis, but they are probably adequate for an introductory treatment of the subject. Knowledge of the techniques of population-trend analysis is essential to those who plan business, governmental, religious, or educational programs. Some students may wish, eventually, to pursue specialized courses in this field.

Changing population composition

The composition of a population affects its social life. Washington, D.C., with its many female clerical workers, St. Petersburg with its retired people, and Columbus, Georgia, with nearby Fort Benning—these cities are different, in part, because of differences in the age, sex, and occupational composition of the population whose needs they fill.

As shown in Table 29, the age composition of the United States has been constantly changing. A high birthrate together with a relatively low death rate means that children will compose a large fraction of the total population and old people a relatively small fraction. One possible reason for the campus troubles of the sixties was that the high birthrates of the forties and fifties had given us a proportion of youth so large that they were an unusually powerful part of society [Moynihan, 1973]. This condition is changing rapidly as current low birthrates cause the proportion of youth to shrink, and the middle-aged and older to increase. From a demographic standpoint, "youth power" is still strong but by 1980 will wane, and youth will be 50 percent of the population rather than the 66 percent they constituted in 1966 [Bureau of the Census, 1967, p. 9].

We must remember that it is primarily changes in the birthrate, not in the death rate, which have changed the proportion of the aged in our population. This point is widely misunderstood by people who confuse *life span* with *life expectancy*. As stated earlier the life span measures the time which fortunate people live until carried off by "old age"; life expectancy is the mean number of years of life remaining at

TABLE 29 CHANGING AGE COMPOSITION AND DEPENDENTS IN THE UNITED STATES

Year	Dependents per 100 persons of working age (20–64)		
	Young and old	Young only (under 20)	Old only (over 64)
1820	153	146	7
1850	123	117	6
1900	94	86	8
1940	71	59	12
1966	83	66	17

Projections: Series D (1.0 to 1.1% Growth Rate)

Year	Dependents per 100 persons of working age (18–64)*		
	Young and old	Young only (under 18)	Old only (over 64)
1980	68	51	17
1990	71	53	18

*Note that definition of "working age" is changed for 1960 and later. In the "projections," Series D is the least rapid growth rate which the Census Bureau considered likely.

Source: Philip M. Hauser. Population Perspectives, Rutgers University Press, New Brunswick, N.J., 1960, p. 71; Bureau of the Census, *Population Estimates*, ser. P-25, no. 381, Dec. 18, 1967, p. 9.

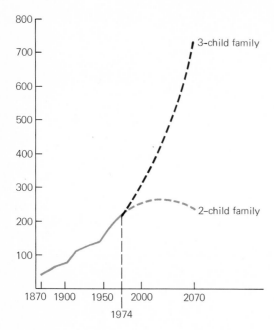

Figure 16. The population of the United States passed the 100-million mark in 1915 and reached 200 million in 1968. If families average two children in the future, growth rates will slow, and the population will reach 300 million in the year 2015. At the three-child rate, the population would reach 300 million in this century and 400 million in the year 2013. Projections assume small future reductions in mortality and assume future immigration at present levels. (Source: *Time*, Sept. 16, 1974, p. 56.)

proportion of the aged. But changes in the birthrate and in the number of children affect the proportion of the aged in a population, just as changes in the size of the freshman class affect the proportion of seniors in the student body.

Age composition has a major effect on population increase. The 1974 crude birthrate of 15.5 works out to 1.9 children per family, whereas 2.11 is generally regarded as the figure which would barely provide replacement and afford zero population growth. This would suggest that American population growth has stopped, but the facts are far different. The population is still growing at nearly record rates in gross numbers, will probably reach fifty million more by the year 2000, and will not level off until around the year 2040 [*Business Week*, Dec. 15, 1973]. Continued growth, even with a low birthrate, is part of the price we are paying for the baby boom of the fifties and sixties. We now have so many women of child-bearing age that even a birthrate below the "replacement" level still increases the population. Not until the age distribution returns to "normal," after perhaps three generations, will it be true that a two-child family brings no population growth.

Even though population growth continues, the declining U.S. birthrate is having some effect. The number of elementary school children will decrease by about four million during the 1970s. The impact is more delayed on the size of the college-age population, which will not decrease until the mid-1980s [*Metropolitan Life Statistical Bulletin*, January, 1974].

Changes in population have many social consequences. A change in the ratio of dependents to workers has great economic impact. It affects employment, living standards, and price levels. The proportion of the aged has important economic and political consequences, such as the drive for more generous pension plans, the promotion of more generous health and welfare services for old people, experimentation with retirement communities, and recreational programs. Such services for a

any given age. Life expectancy at birth has doubled in the last century and a half; life expectancy at age sixty has increased only a couple of years. In other words, infants today are far more likely to reach the age of sixty than infants a century ago, but people who have reached sixty today have only two more years of life remaining than those who reached sixty a century ago. Stated still differently, more people live to be old today, but old people today do not live much longer than old people used to live.

Life span and death rates, therefore, have played only a minor part in the increasing steadily growing segment of our population are enormously costly. With each increase in the proportion of the aged in the population, there are also proportionately fewer people working and paying taxes. In other words, an increased proportion of the aged lays a heavier tax burden upon proportionately fewer people.

The scientific study of the aged is claiming increased attention. *Geriatrics* is a branch of medicine concerned with old age and its diseases and disabilities; *gerontology* is a more inclusive field embracing the entire subject of the aged and their problems. Interest in gerontology is stimulated both by the doubling of the proportion of the aged during the twentieth century and by the shift from a rural, agricultural society, which provided a far more comfortable environment for aged people than does the urbanized and specialized, mobile society of today. The fact that women live longer than men (see Figure 17) raises the touchy question of whether "equal rights" for women demands retirement pensions that are equal with men's in total payout (and therefore less per month), or equal per month (and greater than men's in total payout).

Important as these effects have been in the United States, they are dwarfed by comparison with the impact of changing population composition in the underdeveloped countries. A sharp reduction in the death rate in these countries, mainly in infancy and early childhood, has allowed a rapid population increase,

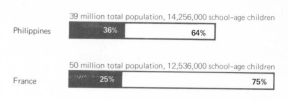

In the Philippines in 1972, 36 percent of a population of 39 million were between the ages of five and nineteen. The Philippines had slightly more school-age children than France, where 25 percent of a population of 50 million were between the ages of five and nineteen.

Figure 18. Effect of population composition on proportion of school-age children. (Source: *Demographic Yearbook*. 1972; United Nations, 1974.)

which is reflected in a very high proportion of the population under fifteen years of age. In these countries the ratio of children under fifteen to total population varies from 35 to 50 percent, while in most Western countries the ratio varies between 20 and 30 percent (see Figure 18).

This means that the poorest countries are also those with the largest proportion of children to raise and the smallest proportion of people of working age to support them. Education, for instance, is a major expense as all of the world's countries endeavor to produce a trained citizenry. The developing countries, however, often have twice as large a proportion of school-age children as the industrialized nations. Or, to put the matter another way, they could double the educational expenditures per child with no increase in the school budget if their population composition were the same as that of Western Europe.

Migration

The ancestors of the American Indians are thought to have come to the North American continent over a land bridge from Asia sometime in the remote past. All other Americans trace their ancestry to relatively recent migrants. From the time of the Pilgrim fathers, some 30 million immigrants, mostly from Europe, settled in this country and changed it

Figure 17. Life expectancy by sex at age 65 and annuity income. The annuity figures are based on the assumption of the payment of $100,000 for the purchase of an income option payable for life, with ten years guaranteed. (Source: Based on data in "Retirement Benefits for Men and Women," *Participant*, July, 1973, Teacher Insurance and Retirement Association, July, 1973.

from a wilderness of food gatherers and hunters to the nation we know today. International immigration is now less important than in previous years, but a tremendous movement within the country leads to a constant redistribution of population.

Push, pull, and channels

The forces affecting migration may be grouped under three headings: (1) push, (2) pull, and (3) channels. *Push* relates to unfavorable conditions in the homeland which make people want to leave. The shifts of national boundary lines after World War II and the rise of intolerant political states, especially Communist, have made life in their native lands intolerable for many people. In 1973 it was estimated that 14 million people who had been forced to leave their ancestral homes had not yet found a permanent place of residence [*World Refugee Report,* U.S. Committee For Refugees, 1974, p. 6].

. . . except for the American Indians, they are all the descendants of immigrants.

Pull refers to the attractive features in the receiving country. Immigration proceeds toward the area of greater opportunities, as these are perceived by the individual. This perception is a cultural definition and not necessarily an objectively valid judgment. It is not the overall opportunity for economic development which is decisive, but the ease with which the individual can move into a situation with relatively little cultural readjustment. Alaska, for instance, is much more sparsely settled than California or New York and may have greater potential economic opportunities. Yet dozens of immigrants move to these states for every one who enters Alaska, simply because they seek an opportunity to make a living in an area where they believe they will be comfortable.

Channels refer to the means of movement from one area to another. They include the availability of transportation, of information, of help in overcoming financial obstacles, and the presence or absence of barriers in both the homeland and the receiving country. The twentieth century has seen the development of marvelous means of transport accompanied by severe restrictions of immigration. Physically it was never easier to move from one country to another. Socially or politically, it has seldom been more difficult. In previous centuries, people could often migrate without restrictions of any kind. Even passports were seldom required. Today we take it for granted that countries will select the type and number of immigrants they wish to receive and that individuals will be unable to move unless some governmental bureau has given permission. Among the early immigrants to America were prostitutes, prisoners from penal colonies, illiterates, adherents of radical political movements, the diseased and the physically deformed, none of whom would be admitted today. Indeed, it is certain that many of the early migrants whose memory is now enshrined by the Daughters of the American Revolution and similar organizations would not be able to qualify for entry under our present laws.

International migration

Increasing population and a developing nationalism have combined to make governments wish to restrict immigration to the type of immigrants they feel can most easily be assimilated and to the number the nation can easily absorb into its economy.

Immigration patterns in the United States changed when new immigration laws became effective in 1968. The rigid national quota system (which allowed only 100 immigrants a year from most Asian and African countries) was replaced by a new system giving priority to relatives and to those with occupational skills useful to the United States. Meanwhile, prosperity in Northwestern Europe made migration to the United States less attractive than in the past. The result is that the proportion of immigration from the United Kingdom and Northern Europe has sharply decreased and that from Southern Europe and Asia has increased. For instance, immigration from the Philippines has increased tenfold and that from Portugal more than sixfold, while the proportion from Germany and the United Kingdom dropped by more than one-half between 1965 and 1970. Total immigration has increased slightly, moving from 296,697 in 1965 to 373,326 in 1970 [*Metropolitan Life Statistical Bulletin,* November, 1970, p. 9].

Most of the rest of the world, like the United States, has also followed selective or restrictive immigration policies. The countries which encourage immigration are those like Brazil, Canada, and Australia, which are considered underpopulated and welcome immigrants as a means of developing their resources. Since Australia and Canada restrict Oriental and African immigration, however, even those countries cannot be described as having a completely open immigration policy.

Doubts about the United States policy center on the extent of illegal immigration and the effect of immigration on population increase. Illegal immigration is hard to measure, but more than 400,000 were arrested in 1971 [*Commission on Population and the American Future,* 1972, p. 202]. The majority of illegal immigrants are Mexicans who crossed the border illegally, but there are many other nationalities, most of whom enter the country as legal visitors and then overstay their visas.

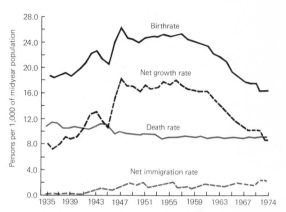

Figure 19. Annual rates of net growth, births, deaths, and net immigration in the United States, 1935 to 1974. (Source: Bureau of the Census, *Current Population Reports,* series P-25, no. 442, Mar. 20, 1970; Abrams and Abrams, "Immigration Policy," *The Public Interest, Winter, 1975, pp. 15–17.)

Legal immigration accounts for almost a quarter of our population growth [Ibid., p. 202], and it may be that the total impact, including illegal immigrants, is responsible for half the American population growth now taking place. Taken by itself, the proportionate contribution of immigration to population growth may not be too significant [Keely, 1974]. But as natural increase declines, any immigration would play a greater proportionate role.

The 1,600-mile border with Mexico is obviously difficult to police, and the Immigration Service feels that its funds are inadequate. In addition, there is much business pressure to "go easy" on the illegal immigrants. Fruit growers and many other businesses feel that it is difficult to get native Americans to take lower-level jobs and that only through employing aliens, many of whom are illegal entrants, can they keep operating. Congressman Emmanuel Celler expressed this idea as follows: "You couldn't conduct a hotel in New York, you couldn't conduct a restaurant in New York if you didn't have rough laborers. We haven't got the rough laborers any more . . . Where are we going to get people to do that rough work?" [Abrams and Abrams, 1975, p. 26].

Despite current restrictions, the United States is still one of the few countries taking large numbers of immigrants. At present levels of legal and illegal immigration, it would be necessary for American citizens to cut their family size below two children if zero population growth is to be achieved [*The Commission on Population Growth and America's Future*, 1972, p. 201]. As birthrates fall, immigration becomes a more significant factor in population increase; yet it is difficult to control, and both humanitarian and economic defenses can be made for allowing immigration to continue.

Internal migration

In a normal year, one American family in five will move. The past fifty years have seen millions of people moving to the cities of the North and the West from the agricultural areas of the South and the Middle West, plus a considerable movement of Puerto Ricans to the mainland. At present, internal migration patterns are shifting, with more people moving South, West, and to the small towns, but *migration* continues unabated.

While this internal migration is different in form from international migration, the consequences of the two shifts are much the same. The movement into a new region changes the population composition, provides new labor, and introduces a group of people ignorant of the local folkways, who have to make their adjustment to a strange cultural setting. Southern whites and blacks, along with Puerto Ricans and others, thus make many of the same contributions and experience many of the same problems as did the European immigrants of an earlier day.

Social and cultural aspects of population change

What causes a change in the rate of population growth? There is no evidence that groups differ in their biological capacity to reproduce and to survive, or that this capacity changes from time to time. Research on birthrates concerns both *fecundity*, the biological capacity to reproduce, and *fertility*, the actual rate of reproduction. Fecundity varies greatly between individuals, but we have no evidence of major differences between large population groups. Since our biological capacity to reproduce appears to be constant, social and cultural factors must explain most variations in birthrates and death rates.

Changes in death rates

Throughout most of history, both birthrates and death rates have been high, with only a small rate of natural increase. In the Bronze Age of ancient Greece, expectation of life at birth was an estimated 18 years. By the opening of the nineteenth century it had doubled to about 36 years. A century and a half later it has doubled again, standing at 71.2 years in the United States (specifically, 68.3 for white males, 76 for white females, 61.2 for nonwhite males, and 69.9 for nonwhite females). Between 1900 and 1973 our crude death rate fell by almost one-half, from 17.2 to 9.8 deaths per 1,000 people. What has caused such a sharp decline?

A great many factors, stretching backward for hundreds of years, have contributed to the drop in the death rate. Improved transportation made it possible to transport a food surplus and to alleviate a local famine. Improvements in food preservation made it possible to preserve a food surplus. The growth of nationalism brought political institutions which were better able to cope with local crop failures and threatened famines. But medicine, sanitary engineering, and public-health measures were mainly responsible for the dramatic drops of the past century. After Pasteur and the germ theory of disease, many epidemic diseases quickly yielded to preventive measures. Pure food and water supply routed others. In the

Western countries today, the great killers of the past—smallpox, cholera, diphtheria, typhoid, and scarlet fever—have become so rare that it is hard to find cases for medical students to observe.

The decline in the death rate in Europe began about 1750 in England and France and generally preceded any decline in the birthrate. A country with a falling death rate and a stationary birthrate will show an explosive rate of population increase. This is what explains the rapid population growth of recent centuries.

Age at marriage and marriage rate

One factor in the birthrate is the proportion of people who get married and the ages at which they marry (see Table 31). A study of marriages in Korea found that women married under nineteen had an average of 4.02 children during their childbearing years compared to 2.5 children for those married after the age of twenty-five [Kim et al., 1974, p. 647]. Early marriage not only increases the number of years of childbearing; early marriage is also associated with lower social-class background, together with attitudes and practices which favor large families.

For many years, Ireland was known as a place where the birthrate was kept down because about a fourth of the population never married and the rest married late—around thirty-five years for men and thirty for women [Blanshard, 1953]. Today, the marriage rate has risen, and the median age of marriage has fallen to twenty-four for women and twenty-six for men. The Irish birthrate remains low, which is now attributed to the use of the pill, which is widely used despite official disapproval [Walsh, 1972]. The Chinese discourage marriage until the woman is about twenty-five and the man about twenty-eight ["China's Birth Rate," AP dispatch in the *New York Times,* May 6, 1973, p. 5]. By comparison, the median age of marriage in the United States in 1973 was 21 for women and 23.2 for men.

The marriage rate is also related to the sex composition of the population. One would assume that usually the number of both sexes is approximately equal and that the age distribution is "normal"; but actually this is seldom true. In the United States female workers are attracted to well-established urban areas; Washington, D.C., in 1970 had a sex ratio of 86.7 (that is, 100 females for every 86.7 males). Areas of recent settlement attract more men; Alaska had a sex ratio of 119.1.

TABLE 30 INTERNATIONAL CATHOLIC-PROTESTANT BIRTHRATE COMPARISONS

Country	Crude birth-rate	Birth-rate order	Catholic rank order	Per-cent Catholic
Iceland	22.4	1	6	2
Italy	16.3	2	1	99
Norway	16.3	2	7	1
Netherlands	16.1	4	4	49
United Kingdom	14.9	5	5	9
Austria	13.9	6	3	89
Belgium	13.8	7	1	99
Finland	12.7	8	7	1

Source: Birthrate data from *United Nations Statistical Yearbook*, 1973; Catholic percentages derived from data in Statesman's Yearbook, 1970–1971.

TABLE 31 PROPORTION OF PERSONS MARRIED AND MEDIAN AGE AT FIRST MARRIAGE IN THE UNITED STATES, 1890 to 1973

Year	Proportion married, 14 years old or older standardized for age		Median age at first marriage	
	Male, percent	Female, percent	Male	Female
1890	61.2	59.4	26.1	22.0
1900	59.9	58.7	25.9	21.9
1910	60.4	60.1	25.1	21.6
1920	61.3	60.4	24.6	21.1
1930	62.1	61.2	24.3	21.3
1940	62.8	61.0	24.3	21.6
1950	68.0	66.1	22.8	20.3
1955	69.3	67.4	22.6	20.2
1960	70.0	67.8	22.8	20.3
1965	67.9	63.9	22.8	20.6
1973	74.5	68.1	23.2	21.0

Source: Department of Commerce, Bureau of the Census, *U.S. Census of Population*, vol. 2, part 1, *Current Population Reports*, ser. P-20, nos. 96 (1960) and 105 (1965). 1969 data from *Metropolitan Life Statistical Bulletin*, November, 1970, p. 5; *Statistical Abstract of the United States*, 1974.

Such unbalanced sex ratios reduce the marriage rate.

From 1900 to 1955, the U.S. population married at steadily younger ages. Since 1955, this trend has been reversed, although only to a slight degree. The median age at marriage for men had risen from 22.26 years in 1955 to 23.2 in 1973, and the median age for women had risen from 20.2 years to 21 [*Metropolitan Life Statistical Bulletin*, November, 1970, p. 5, and *Statistical Abstract of the United States*, 1974, p. 150]. It remains to be seen whether this is a minor statistical fluctuation or whether women's liberation and a general disparagement of marriage have made early marriage (and in some cases, any marriage) less attractive. If early marriage is losing its appeal, this will be another factor reducing the birthrate.

Social status and the birthrate

The folk proverb that the "rich get richer and the poor get babies" describes fairly correctly the relationship between social status and the birthrate. In general, a low birthrate is more characteristic of white urbanized, well-educated, and high-income groups, and a high birthrate is more apt to be found among nonwhite, rural, poorly educated, and low-income groups. Groups in which these characteristics are mixed usually have intermediate fertility rates.

Recent studies show wide variation among lower-class people in their readiness to make use of contraceptive techniques. Apparently there are many who greatly prefer small families and will make use of contraceptive techniques when materials and information are made available by Planned Parenthood clinics or similar agencies [Jaffe and Polgar, 1968].

TABLE 32 NUMBER OF CHILDREN EVER BORN, PER WOMAN 35 TO 44 YEARS OLD, BY SELECTED CHARACTERISTICS, 1970

Subject		Negro	White
All women		3.5	2.9
Type of residence:			
Urbanized area		3.2	2.7
Other urban		3.8	2.9
Rural nonfarm		4.7	3.1
Rural farm		5.4	3.5
Years of school completed:			
Elementary:	Less than 8 years	4.1	3.4
	8 years	4.0	3.2
High school:	1 to 3 years	3.8	3.1
	4 years	3.0	2.8
College:	1 to 3 years	2.7	2.8
	4 years or more	1.9	2.3
Labor force status:			
In labor force		3.1	2.5
Not in labor force		4.1	3.2

Source: U.S. Department of Commerce, Social and Economic Statistics Administration, Bureau of the Census, "The Social and Economic Status of the Black Population in the United States," 1972, Series P-23, no. 46, July, 1973, p. 74.

This is revealed in Figure 20, which compares the changes in the birthrates of less affluent and more affluent families, with the less affluent families showing the greater decline. Likewise, the nonwhite birthrates, although still higher than the white birthrates, had shown a proportionately greater decline. This would seem to indicate that the greatly increased provision of family planning clinics in recent years had been effective in lowering the birthrate of once highly fertile groups. If this trend continues, we may see racial, regional, and economic birthrate differences disappear.

The planning attitude and family limitation. In rural areas a large family has labor value. In the modern city child labor is prohibited, and each additional child adds to the family expenses without increasing its income. Supposedly, in the city only the wealthier couples could afford large families, whereas the poor would find a large family a difficult burden. Such reasoning assumes that both the poor and the more well-to-do have the same tendency to plan their lives. In the discussion of the deferred-gratification pattern in the chapter on social mobility, we found that planning was not a typical lower-class pattern. Instead of trying to control their environment, lower-class people are likely to consider themselves creatures of fate, subject to forces beyond their control. Most of them do not *desire* larger families than middle-class people [Chilman, 1968] but they *get* larger families because they have neither strong motivation to limit family size nor easy access to birth-control techniques.

Table 32 indicates the effect of social status factors. Notice that the birthrate is higher in rural than in urban districts and it rises as education decreases. The black birthrate is higher than the white in most categories, but it shows the same relationship to social status categories; among the college educated, the black birthrate is actually lower than the white. Note, too, that women in the labor force have smaller families than those not employed. This supports a current theory that feminine liberation is a vital aspect of population control.

Malthus on population

The argument about population pressure still swirls around the ideas of the Rev. Thomas R. Malthus, an English clergyman whose *Essay on Population* in 1798 called the world's attention to this topic. Malthus believed that the essential reason for poverty was the pressure of population growth on the world's resources. He reasoned that the effects of natural fertility were held in check only by such negative forces as famine, war, and pestilence. Whenever an improvement in productive technology yielded an economic surplus, these products would soon be consumed by an expanding population.

Malthus did not deny the possibility of increasing industrial and agricultural production, but he believed that the increase would be unable to keep up with population growth, and expressed his belief that population tends to multiply in geometric ratio (2, 4, 8, 16, etc.) while production can only increase in an arithmetic ratio (1, 2, 3, 4, etc.). Each increase in population becomes a basis for a further increase in the next generation, but each increase in the yield from an acre of land is not a basis for a still further increase the following season. Instead, having boosted the yield this year, producers will find it harder, not easier, to boost the yield still higher next year.

People increase through multiplication whereas the food supply increases only by addition and is constantly being outrun by the growth of population. Malthus urged later marriages as a means of keeping down the birthrate, but he was pessimistic about the chance that this policy would be followed. He saw no practical possibility of averting hunger, famine and pestilence. Organized charity and relief would only enable a few more to survive

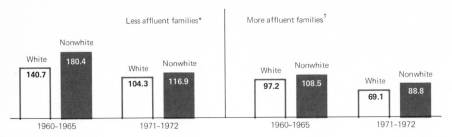

*Incomes no more than 25 percent above poverty level.

†Incomes more than 25 percent above poverty level.

Figure 20. Number of live births per 1,000 women aged 15–44.
Incomes under 125 percent of the poverty figure in 1972 were under $5,343. (Source: Based on
table in Frederick S. Jaffe, "Low Income Families: Fertility in 1971–1972," *Family Planning
Perspectives*, 6:109, Spring, 1974.)

today so that they might starve tomorrow. Because of these gloomy predictions of Malthus, economics became known as the "dismal science."

In the 1920s it was popular to believe that the events of the preceding century had disproved the Malthusian hypotheses. The world had seen the greatest population growth in its history, and at the same time the standard of living had improved rather than declined. Why did Malthus's gloomy predictions fail to materialize? One reason is that Malthus failed to foresee the widespread use of improved methods of contraception. The contraceptive devices of his day were so crude and inefficient that he and other writers paid little or no attention to them. Another reason was that Malthus could not be expected to foresee the magnitude of the industrial and agricultural revolution of the nineteenth and twentieth centuries. Great new land areas in North and South America and Australia were brought under cultivation. Improvements in agriculture rapidly boosted output per acre. For a time, birthrates in the Western world were falling so rapidly and production was rising so rapidly that Malthus began to sound like a gloomy scold instead of a gifted thinker. Recently, however, Malthus has been restored to fashion by scholars known as the "neo-Malthusian school."

These neo-Malthusians note that the population of the world in the time of Malthus was less than 1 billion people; today, it is over 3.8 billion. Further, the population growth of about one-half of 1 percent a year, which alarmed Malthus, has grown to a rate of around 2 percent a year, or four times as great. Similarly, North and South America were sparsely populated at the time of Malthus, but practically all of their productive land is now in full use.* In other words, what might have been considered the "slack" has now been taken up so that, while the alarm of Malthus may have been premature in his day, it is quite justifiable in the current situation. Even the North American continent faces severe problems, although it is lightly populated as compared with Europe or Asia. Many areas in the United States are already short of water, and this condition is bound to worsen as population soars. Further, Americans now pay high prices for the importation of oil and other minerals, which, until recently, were adequately provided from domestic sources. In spite of these problems, it may be that the United States can maintain its present population at a high level. But can it do so for a population 50 percent larger, or twice as large, or four times as large?

*Some optimists view the "untapped tropical jungle lands" hopefully, but most jungle lands are deficient in minerals. When stripped of their forest cover, they soon form a hard, concretelike crust which absorbs little water. They are unsuitable for intensive cultivation by any presently known technology. See David W. Ehrenfeld, *Conserving Life on Earth* (New York, Oxford University Press, 1972), pp. 44–46; also, F. R. Fosberg, *Tropical Africa and South America: A Comparative Study* (Washington, D. C. Smithsonian Press, 1973).

Some other parts of the world are in a better position than the United States in terms of population density, but most are worse. In the view of the neo-Malthusians, the appearance of crisis is only a matter of time. Many countries face a real crisis now [Hardin, 1974]. Others will find that population doomsday is perhaps twenty to thirty years away. Only a few may have a century if they can protect themselves from the onslaughts of desperate people in the overpopulated countries. But for all countries, the ghost of Malthus hovers over their destiny.

Famine and the triage reaction

In 1967, when the granaries of the United States were still bulging with "surplus" food, a book appeared entitled, *Famine, 1975* [Paddock and Paddock, 1967]. As indicated by the title, the book predicted that by 1975, the world would face famine conditions which it would be impossible completely to alleviate. The authors suggested that the United States and other food-exporting nations might have to use the *triage* procedure, a practice developed to cope with the heavy casualties of trench warfare in World War I. Triage comes from the French verb *tier*—"to sort." Since medical facilities were limited, it was necessary to sort out three categories of wounded and assign medical care accordingly. One category, the "walking wounded," might be suffering, but it could survive without immediate medical attention. Another category, "the can't be saved," would probably die regardless of what was done and hence were not provided immediate treatment. Medical care was reserved for the third category, who, it was thought, could be saved with immediate medical care.

Paddock and Paddock argued that the world was rapidly approaching a situation in which the shortage of food would be as desperate as the shortage of physicians in war time. Hence they suggested that by 1975, the food-exporting nations would have to sort out the food-deficit nations and decide which could survive without aid, which were in so desperate a condition that starvation could not long be averted regardless of the efforts of other nations, and which could be saved by the limited amount of aid available.

At the time the book was written, the *triage* formula seemed both immoral and unnecessary. Not only did the United States and some other nations have large stocks of food, but the "green revolution" had greatly expanded food production throughout the world. But when 1975 arrived, the book's predictions seem altogether too sound. The surplus food stocks had largely disappeared, the green revolution had foundered on inclement weather and difficulties with fertilizers and pesticides, and the spectre of famine was real in many countries. Delegates to the World Food Conference in Rome in late 1974 requested an American commitment of food shipments which President Ford felt could not be met by the supplies available. A *New York Times* report [Feb. 2, 1975, p. 1] that the gap between world demand and world supply of food was "only" 3.5 million tons was hailed as a "hopeful" situation.

Some critics claim that the moment for *triage* is here [Greene, 1975]. They argue that indiscriminate food shipments will only mag-

TABLE 33 IS TIME RUNNING OUT FOR ZERO POPULATION GROWTH?

Country	Population circa 1970 (in millions)	Population size (in millions) in 2050 if replacement fertility is reached:		
		In 1980	In 2000	In 2040
Developed	1,122	1,482	1,610	1,853
Developing	2,530	4,763	6,525	11,591
World	3,652	6,245	8,135	13,444

Source: Tomas Frejka, *Reference Tables to "The Future of Population Growth,"* New York, The Population Council, 1973.

nify human misery by encouraging hungry populations to go on increasing while postponing the programs needed to bring their population growth under control [Hardin, 1974]. They take the position that it is better to allow 10 million people to starve today than 100 million starve later, after our capacity to feed them is exhausted.

Is such a brutal choice inescapable? Is control over population growth a practical possibility? What are the possible means through which population growth might be controlled?

Controlling population growth

Population grows because of an excess of births over deaths. The dramatic increase in population in the last century has come because the death rate, which in 1800 was around 40 per 1,000, has dropped to about 10 per 1,000. What, in a limited sense, might be called "death control" came first in the industrialized countries and was soon followed by a slower decline in the birthrate. The net result was a natural increase allowing the population to double in about a century. In the developing areas, the death rate did not decline greatly until after World War II, but now it has dropped nearly to the levels of the industrial countries, while the birthrate has shown little change (see Figure 21). The result is that a section of the world which is already densely populated faces the prospect of doubling the population every twenty-eight years unless birthrates can be reduced drastically and quickly.

In the Western nations, industrialization and urbanization brought higher levels of education, the development of mass markets for consumer goods, and an eventual desire to have smaller families. Thus, according to this "theory of demographic transition," industrialization and modernization unleash forces which eventually bring down birthrates. There are two difficulties in applying this theory to the developing nations. First, it may not hold true for non-Western nations; second, even if it does, it may not operate quickly enough to avoid unmanageable population explosions.

Something about the dynamics of population control may be learned from the Japanese experience. Although highly industrialized, Japan still has many aspects of its ancient culture, and the attitudes of its people are a blend of the modern and the traditional. The Japanese population grew from 56 million in 1920 to 73 million in 1940. *This increase alone* would have populated Japan with 114 persons per square mile, a density exceeded by only twelve of the American states. Defeat in war and the loss of expanding empire made population pressure even more unmanageable. Following World War II, the government encouraged population restriction through legalized abortion and contraception. By 1953, it was estimated that about one-half of all conceptions were ended by abortion [Muramatsu, 1960]. The Japanese birthrate fell from 34.3 in 1947 to 17.2 in 1957, almost exactly one-half. This is the most precipitous intentional decline in a nation's birthrate known to history [Hunt, 1962].

Japan may be the first country in the world to end population growth. A 1969 report of the Japanese Population Council indicated that the birthrate had fallen to two children per Japanese woman and that, if the trend continued, population growth would end by 1983 [*Otago Daily Times,* Aug. 8, 1969, reprinted in *Population Bomb Press Clippings,* November, 1969]. Some Japanese fear a labor shortage which will slow Japanese industrial expansion, and advocate a change in population policy. Others think that a stabilized population is desirable and that Japan has reached its optimum population [Boffey, 1970; *Japan Report,* 1974].

A major reason for the Japanese success in population control as contrasted with its relative failure in most other countries is that the Japanese adopted a technique which most other countries have been reluctant to sanction. Abortion is morally repugnant to many people, but it is a technique which always

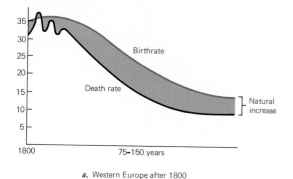

a. Western Europe after 1800

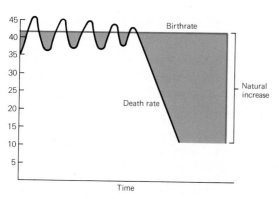

b. Less developed countries, mid–20th century
(The sharp drop in the death rate began between
1940 and 1960, depending upon the specific country)

Figure 21. Approximation of the birth and death rates for two different groups of nations over time. (Source: Shirley Foster Hartley, "Our Growing Problem: Population," *Social Problems*, 21:194, Fall, 1973.)

also important. The government encountered little resistance to its population control program because the traditional values of Japanese society were not an obstacle. The Japanese traditional family system was more concerned with the well-being of the heir than with large numbers of offspring. Abortion and infanticide had long been occasional practices. Neither of the dominant religions, Buddhism and Shintoism, objects to family planning. Japan is an urban industrial country with an efficient governmental bureaucracy and a literate population. All these circumstances made the task far simpler than in a country like India with widespread illiteracy, primitive village life, some religious hostility to family planning, and a different emphasis in the familistic system. In such a setting the average village Indian lacks either the means or the motivation for family planning. Just one anecdote will tell something of the problem facing family planners in many underdeveloped areas. In one district the literacy barrier was surmounted by a large poster showing a three-child native family in comfortable surroundings, contrasted with another larger family amid squalor. But the reaction was unexpected. Instead of admiring the greater comfort of the small family, the observers murmured, "That poor family—only three children!"

works, is relatively simple and cheap, and does not require any change in sexual habits. The Japanese accepted abortion, and only gradually has a part of the population learned to practice contraception. Other countries have also found their people slow to accept contraception but have been reluctant to make either abortion or sterilization readily available. The result is that the Japanese are approaching a stable population while most other countries still have a rapidly growing population.

While the Japanese acceptance of abortion may be the chief reason for the success of their population control programs, other factors are

Family planning in less developed areas

Some countries whose people are not greatly concerned about family size are still making serious efforts toward family planning. The most obvious example is the development of public birth control clinics which make contraceptive practices available either free or at little cost, and which propagandize for their use. To date, most countries still have limited programs. Berelson [1974, p. 8] classifies only four as "strong"—Taiwan, South Korea, Hong Kong, and Singapore. In 1971, only about 12 percent of the women "at risk" in the less developed countries (outside of China) were practicing contraception [Robbins, 1973, p. 3]. The family clinics are often given feeble support and frequently seek to serve a population which has little desire for their services, but they are beginning to have an impact.

How can motivations be changed so that people in a peasant society, who have traditionally welcomed large families, will utilize family planning? The obvious answer is that as the nature of the society changes, so will the attitude toward size of family. When standards of living rise, when children are seen as students rather than little laborers, when many women are employed outside the home and when lower infant mortality removes the fear of being without an heir, then small families will come into favor. In other words, economic development promotes family limitation, as outlined by the "theory of demographic transition."

The trouble with this view is that, in many countries, the problems caused by overpopulation are so massive that economic development may never take place. Whereas in the Western nations, "death control" *accompanied* industrialization, "death control" *preceded* the modernization and industrialization of most of the developing nations by several decades. This gave them explosive population growth before the conditions for birth control had developed. What is needed now is an approach that will reduce population growth so that economic development has a better chance. As Shirley Hartley expresses the idea: "The gap between the rich and the poor nations continues to increase, not because there are no improvements in the less developed nations, but because they are watered down by population increase. Had population remained stable during the 1960s the 'Development Decade' would have been a great success" [Hartley, 1973, p. 202].

Most countries have continued a pronatalist policy favoring large families. Through tax deductions, family allowances or free services, they have actually rewarded people for having large families. Today, many believe that perhaps this policy should be reversed and people should be rewarded for restricting the number of births. It usually takes the form of direct payments for successful contraceptive usage. Such payments cost less than the country would save by reducing births. Some examples of incentives include the payment of forty-five rupees plus some goods and a free lottery ticket to men who accept vasectomy in some provinces in India; reduced school fees for a two-child family, with reduction cut in half with a third child and forfeited with a fourth in Taiwan; paid maternity leave limited to three children and public housing assigned without regard to size of family (formerly preference given to largest families) in Singapore. All these measures are of recent origin, but information available indicates that they do have some success in stimulating acceptance of family planning [Berelson, 1974, pp. 5–6].

The Chinese example. China is a classic example of all the elements which usually contribute to a high birthrate: the large family ideal, high illiteracy, low per capita income, and mostly agricultural employment. Although national statistics are dubious, reports from some individual districts where reliable data are available indicate that a great deal of progress has been made. Shanghai, for instance, in 1972 reported a birthrate of 10.75, and a rural commune claimed an even lower rate of 10.4, as contrasted with a rate of 45 in 1963 [Djerassi, 1974, p. 48].

The Chinese are a tightly organized society in which the individual is under enormous pressure to follow national policies. This may be a major aspect of its success in changing birthrates and is a feature which most other countries would not care to emulate. However, other aspects of the Chinese experience are worth noting. First, the Chinese have used every type of measure for birth control, including all types of contraceptives, abortion and sterilization, and have sought to adapt the pill to the Chinese women in a way that reduces side effects [Djerassi, 1974, p. 26]. Second, the Chinese have promoted later marriage to reduce "exposure" to impregnation. This is done by rules banning marriage for those receiving state scholarships, extra clothing allowances for those married after age thirty, and a policy of frequent separation of couples in early years of marriage [Morrison and Salmon, 1973, p. 875]. Since the current estimate for the world is that at least one person in five is Chinese, their success in family limitation is of major significance.

Abortion and sterilization. Family planning clinics outside of Eastern Europe and Japan seldom offer sterilization and even less often abortion. Most contraceptive practices require some degree of planning and continuous application, and there is some risk of unpleasant or harmful side effects. In either abortion or sterilization, the risk is minimal, planning is not needed and, in the case of sterilization, one operation eliminates childbearing.

A sterilization program is given credit for the 1960–1965 reduction of the Puerto Rican birthrate from 5.2 to 4 births per woman [Presser, 1969]. Similarly, research in India has found that sterilization will reduce four times as many births as persuading women to try a contraceptive device [Simmons, 1971, p. 56]. In the Soviet Union, abortions have run as high as three times the number of live births [Tietze and Dawson, 1974, p. 14]. In the United States, there was one abortion for every five births in 1974, running much higher in some states [Lowe, 1974]. The abortion effect is seen in Rumania, whose birthrate was 14.3 per 1,000 in 1966 when abortion was legal; in 1967, abortion was made illegal and the birthrate jumped to almost 40 per 1,000 [Tietze and Dawson, 1974, p. 49]. Abortion is more prevalent in Eastern Europe than elsewhere, but it seems to be an important aspect of population control in most countries. As Berelson points out, "making abortions legal or illegal may be

one of the most effective single ways the modern state has of changing birthrates up or down" [1974, p. 6].

Probably the ideal approach is one where people voluntarily follow contraceptive practices. However, some people in the most industrialized countries, and a large proportion of people in the less developed areas, find this kind of planning mentality difficult to accept. If objections to abortion or sterilization cause these operations to be eliminated from family planning clinics, there is little likelihood of a rapid reduction in the birthrate.

Ideological viewpoints

It is often assumed that Roman Catholic teachings are a major obstacle to securing a lowered birthrate. This assumption is valid if one looks at the effect of Catholic influence on government policies. However, if one looks at the birthrates of adherents of different religious bodies, the situation is more ambiguous. Comparisons of Protestant and Catholic areas show no consistent pattern. Sometimes the Catholic and sometimes the Protestant area has the higher rate [Hunt, 1967]. In Europe, the highest birthrate is often found in Iceland, which is only 2 percent Catholic, and the lowest in Austria or Belgium, which are 99 percent Catholic. In the United States, recent surveys found that five out of six American Catholics approve of "artificial contraception," while 70 percent believe that legal abortion should be available to those who desire it [*Time*, Jan. 13, 1975, p. 55].

The question of government policy is another matter. Until recently, governments of many Catholic countries refused to participate in birth control programs, and Catholic influence is constantly seeking to limit the extent and effectiveness of the programs which have been adopted. Dissent from Vatican policy by many priests and bishops, as well as laymen, has not succeeded in changing the official position of opposition to any artificial means of birth control. The official Catholic position has been especially hostile to the legalization of abortion. Catholic teachings appear to have had little influence on the practices of individuals, but Catholic political pressure has sought to inhibit governments from adopting effective programs to popularize birth control.

Another objection has come from some American blacks, who charge that the promotion of birth-control clinics is a genocidal plot to prevent blacks from having the power which might come from a growing population [Darity et al., 1971; Innis, 1974]. There is, however, little evidence that either Catholic or black militant views have much influence on family behavior. Black fertility has exceeded that of whites, but it is rapidly declining and can best be understood in terms of more general social status factors, such as income, education, urban or rural residence, and female participation in the labor force.

The position of the pronatalist black militants is similar to the stand taken by some spokesmen in developing countries, who see family limitation as an effort to weaken their country's power. Hernandez [1974] expresses the Third World view that their real problem is poverty and powerlessness, not population, that only after a social revolution has brought prosperity and power to Third World peoples can population programs be successful. Both positions are supported by the Marxian theory that population pressure is irrelevant, since capitalism is the cause of most human problems.

Both the Catholic and the Marxist viewpoints were expressed at the first World Conference on Population, held in Bucharest in August, 1974. The Vatican sent a delegation to the Bucharest conference but opposed all proposals for the spread of contraception. Its viewpoint was seconded by Argentina, which regards itself as underpopulated and is pursuing pronatalist policies designed to raise the birthrate [Mauldin et al., 1974, p. 371: Hemmer, 1975, p. 9].

Since Marxists believe that most evils result from the capitalist system, they are loath to admit that there is such a thing as overpopulation [Vermisher, 1973; Conner, 1974; Pishunov and Steshenko, 1975]. China has taken energetic steps toward the stabilization of its own population, but the opportunity to embarrass the Western countries was too great a temptation, and the Chinese took a leading role in attacking population control.

At the same time that the Chinese were denouncing population control, they demanded that the secretariat suppress all reference to the birth control measures in China in official documents [Hemmer, 1975, p. 9]. They portrayed the concern for population as a plot to divert the underdeveloped world from its real concerns. Typical of the statements was one from Huang Shutse, Vice-minister of Health: "Is it owing to overpopulation that unemployment and poverty exist today? No, absolutely not. It is due to the exploitation, aggression and plunder of the super powers" [*Chicago Sun-Times,* Aug. 22, 1974, p. 32]. Huang went on to laud population growth in the developing areas as "an important condition for the fight against imperialism" [*Time,* Sept. 9, 1974, p. 37]. The Soviet effort to join in the attack was not altogether successful, since the Chinese blamed both the Soviets and the United States for the Third World problems.

The Chinese attack struck a responsive chord with the developing countries, with the result that the conference became a field day

Both Catholic and Marxist leaders oppose contraceptive programs.

for the denunciation of the "superpowers," with a consequent lessening of attention to the population issues which had produced such a conference. After oratory subsided, some rather mild resolutions were passed in support of population planning, which did not fully reflect the substantial commitment to population control in much of the world.

Population prospects

The industrialized countries

A glance at Figure 21 would seem to indicate that the industrialized countries have things pretty well under control. The industrialized countries are growing at the rate of about 1 percent a year and the less developed areas at 2.5 percent. This means that industrialized countries will double their population in seventy years, and the less developed in twenty-eight [Berelson, 1974, p. 5]. Like the United States, many of the industrialized countries have a dwindling birthrate and may expect their populations to stabilize in fifty to seventy-five years if present trends continue.

This pleasant prospect is marred by the possibility that the declining birthrate may be a temporary fluctuation rather than a long-term trend. Judith Blake [1974] notes, for example, that opinion surveys show a tolerance for families with three or four children, which, if it again became a common norm, would cause the American birthrate to skyrocket as it did in the first twenty years after World War II. She also notes the aversion to either childlessness or the one-child family, and finally the tendency to begin procreation in the first years of marriage. In the early 1970s, the decline in births in the United States has been greater than predicted. But notions of desired family size have been as changeable as the length of women's hemlines, and a swing back to a larger-size family is entirely possible.

At the Bucharest Conference on Population

. . . the "exaggerated consumerism" of the industrialized nations.

there were bitter comments from the less developed countries that the real problem was not their own population increase but the "exaggerated consumerism" of the industrialized nations. As a rationale for the population crisis in less developed countries, this is not very convincing, since there is no level of living low enough to allow population to double every twenty-eight years without creating human misery. However, as a reminder to the industrialized countries that they too have a problem, the complaint has some point. Its substance is summarized by Paul R. Ehrlich:

A preliminary census report was recently released which indicates that the population of the United States may grow by "only" 75 million people by the end of the century.

Assume for a moment that the demographic projections, which have often been too low in the past, are accurate, and that in the year 2000 the population of the United States is "only" some 280 million people. What might that mean to us and to the world?

Each American has roughly 50 times the negative impact on the Earth's life-support systems as the average citizen of India. Therefore, in terms of eco-system destruction, adding 75 million more Americans will be the equivalent of adding 3.7 bil-

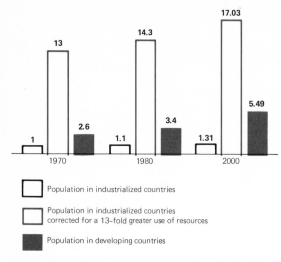

Population in industrialized countries

Population in industrialized countries corrected for a 13-fold greater use of resources

Population in developing countries

Figure 22. The population explosion measured in terms of comparative resource use (billions). The assumption that resource utilization is thirteen times higher in the industrialized countries is based on Bernard Berelson et al., "World Population: Status Report 1974," *Reports on Population Planning,* January, 1974, p. 9. The less developed countries' growth is projected at the current annual rate of 2.5 percent and industrialized countries at 0.9 percent. (Source: Population estimates from *War On Hunger,* 8:8, December, 1974.)

lion Indians to the world population. (Paul R. Ehrlich, *New York Times,* Nov. 4, 1970, p. 47. Copyright © 1970 by The New York Times Company. Reprinted by permission).

Ehrlich's statement is based on his estimate of the total proportion of essential resources consumed by industrialized nations and may be considered extreme by some authorities. The Population Council makes the more conservative estimate that the per capita domestic product of developing countries is one-thirteenth that of the industrialized nations [Berelson, 1974, p. 9]. Figure 22 shows the enormous increase in the population of developing countries but also shows that, in terms of total consumption, population increase in the industrialized countries will place an even greater demand on world resources.

Unless the birthrate of the industrialized countries drops considerably below the replacement level of 2.11 children per family, the industrialized countries will have a substantial increase—perhaps another 300 million—before zero population growth is reached. One scholar [Miller, 1960] claims that rapid population growth requires an increase in government controls of many kinds, promotes the bureaucratization of society, and reduces the range of individual liberties. Already in England, that historic citadel of individual liberty, the state will take away a farmer's land (with compensation) if he does not farm it efficiently; the national interest cannot allow a landowner the luxury of inefficient land use. In the Netherlands one is not permitted to build a one-story house; the land cannot be spared. Individual liberty in modern societies is a luxury which is gradually sacrificed as population pressure grows intense. How much of it should be sacrificed in order to feed more and more people? Some years ago Landis framed the issue in this manner:

Certainly individualized Western man has reached the point where he is unwilling to devote his full energies to food supply. The dream of luxuries, of leisure which comes from having plenty, has motivated him to cross oceans in quest of spices, and has led him to penetrate nature's deep secrets with microscope and telescope. He will not willingly settle for a life motivated primarily by a struggle for appeasement of hunger. He can hardly conceive of the fact that millions live on that level already.

The world now supports around 2.4 billion people [in 1950; increased to 3.5 billion by 1970]. It perhaps could sustain a maximum of somewhere between 5 and 10 billion, but to do so would require a maximum of free migration between continents and nations and the exertion of all human effort toward producing the maximum of food. Is man willing to devote all his energies to feeding the world, as will be required in a hundred to a hundred fifty years, assuming present rates of population growth? (Paul H. Landis, "Is There Room for the Next 1,000,000,000 People?" *The Clearing House,* 28:140–141, November, 1953.)

The less developed countries. The non-Western world is now in the earlier stages of demographic transition. Death rates have been plunging precipitously as non-Western lands gained epidemic control in the post-World War II years. For example, the death rate in Ceylon fell by one-half in a single decade [Morgan, 1956]. In such countries a rapidly falling death rate and an approximately stationary birthrate give a rate of population growth which soon becomes unmanageable (see Figure 21).

Until recently, efforts to reduce the birthrate in the less developed areas were making little headway. During the 1960s, though, there was a slight evidence of a slowdown in the growth rate in at least a dozen countries of small to medium size [Berelson, 1974, p. 7], as well as reports of a drastic reduction in China. In other countries, the picture is less clear, and perhaps the best that can be said is the statement by Berelson: "It is likely that the 1960s marked the beginning of a worldwide fall in the fertility of developing countries—likely, but not yet certain" [Berelson, 1974, p. 7].

The decline in these few "successful" countries was around ten points for the decade, meaning that birthrates over 40 per 1,000 came down to around 30—which is still twice the rate in most developed countries. Even if we assume an immediate drop to the two-child-per-family (2.11) replacement level, the developing areas would add over 1.5 billion people before reaching a stable level. There is no possibility of this happening. If world birthrates could be reduced to replacement levels by the year 2000, then world population would stabilize at around 8.5 billion by the end of the twenty-first century [Nortman, 1972]. But if present growth rates were to continue, world population would reach 20 billion by the year 2050. This will not happen either, for long before this figure is reached, it is likely that famine, pestilence, war, or possibly environmental disaster will have "controlled" world population [Meadows et al., 1972; Laqueur, 1974]. The choice is clearly between family planning and famine, and it may already be too late.

To add a final cheerful note: there is considerable evidence that an unfavorable climatic change about 1500 reduced the food supply and was partly responsible for the decimations of the sixteenth century; then a favorable climatic shift two centuries later contributed to world population growth after 1700 [Braudel, 1974]. There is some evidence that another unfavorable cooling cycle may be starting [Douglas, 1975]. If true, then the forecasts in this chapter will prove to be far too optimistic.

The sociology of death

To most people, the role of the death rate in population growth is of less interest than the meaning of death for themselves and their associates. This is especially true in a time when medical science has altered the manner in which death comes and thereby raised questions about its cultural interpretation. Death is inevitable in all societies, but is defined and treated differently in various cultures. The attitudes toward death, the tests which determine when death has arrived, the ceremonies which follow, whether the dead are viewed as "gone" or still "here"—all these are culturally determined.

Consider the deceptively simple question of when life begins, which lies at the heart of the abortion controversy. Is there a human being at the moment of the union of the sperm and ovum? Does life begin at some specified stage of fetal development or does it begin at birth, when the fetus has been separated from the body of the mother? There is no complete agreement on this issue, and different definitions may classify the act of abortion either as murder or as simple surgery [Green, 1972, p. 295].

Nor is there a simple biological test for the end of life. Improvements in medical care which prolong life have also brought confusion in determining when death has arrived. When the heart can be kept beating and the lungs breathing indefinitely, the older signs of the end of life are no longer sufficient. Is one alive when all power of thought and all control of bodily movements are lost? Is it murder to withdraw the special ministrations which have kept the vital functions operating when there is no hope of recovery? These questions draw us into a type of decision making seldom necessary in the past.

As far back as we have any record, societies have developed special ceremonies to mark the passing of the loved one, to comfort the bereaved, and to reintegrate friends and relatives into viable social relationships. Funerals are the last of the "rites of passage" [van Gennep, 1960] and are regarded as especially important. The Irish wake, a time when people gathered in the house of the deceased to drink and socialize as they mourned the dead, was an effective form of social therapy. Preparations for the wake kept the family busy; lamentation and weeping provided emotional release, as did the drinking; and the visits by friends and neighbors reaffirmed their place in a social network [Kane, 1968]. By contrast, the conventional middle-class American funeral gives friends and relatives little chance to socialize or to find emotional catharsis through an unrestrained expression of grief.

Funeral ceremonies offer the last chance for a display of wealth which will indicate the importance of the deceased and his or her family. For prominent government figures (as well as notorious gangsters) this is marked by an assemblage of dignitaries, a crowd of people, elaborate ceremonies, and burial in an impressive mausoleum. The passing of lesser mortals is marked by similar ceremonies on a smaller scale, in which burial in a pauper's grave is the final disgrace, while an elaborate casket and tomb indicate both the affection and the status of the survivors. To some extent, it seems true that the less prosperity the individual has had in life, the more important it is to make an impressive exit. The possession of assets, through insurance and sometimes the contribution of friends, makes it possible for the poor to have a funeral as fine as that of the more affluent. One survey found, in fact, that funeral expenses were surprisingly unaffected by socioeconomic status, averaging $1,222 for those of high status compared with $1,184 for those of low status [Salomone, 1968, p. 56].

Whether funeral rites are a meaningless ceremony or a helpful therapeutic process probably depends as much on the attitudes with which death is approached as it does on the nature of the final rites. Some observers classify American society as a youth-oriented culture which has difficulty accepting the onset of age and is not emotionally prepared for the end of life. For some people, emotional acceptance is based on a religious conviction that, in some form, life goes on and the grave is a new beginning rather than an end. Others are not able to accept the idea of personal immortality, but are sustained by the concept that their personal lives are a significant part of a greater society. Too many, however, have not found any rationale which prepares them for acceptance of this final stage, either for themselves or their friends and relatives, so that the last act of life is seen as empty and meaningless [Strauss, Glasser and Quint, 1968].

After a long period of neglect, it is again permissible to discuss the fact of death and its meaning. The media are using feature programs and popular articles, and courses of study are beginning to appear in the sociology and psychology departments of universities. There are no easy answers, but at least we are beginning to look with candor at the meaning of both life and death, and the ceremonies and attitudes which define their meaning.

Summary

Human ecology is the study of the interrelationships of people with their physical environment. *Demography* is concerned with the age and sex composition of the population, its movement, both within and across national frontiers, and its rate of growth.

The *age* and *sex composition* of a population affects its social life in many ways. Changes in age composition are due mainly to changes in birthrates and death rates and are presently increasing the proportions of both aged and children in many populations. The increased proportion of youth is a major handicap to underdeveloped countries, since it increases educational costs while reducing the proportion of the population in productive labor. The permanent rise of a rather large group of old people has prompted the rise of *geriatrics* and *gerontology,* disciplines devoted to the problems of the aged.

Migration is affected by the *push* given to people by unsatisfactory conditions at home, by the *pull* of attractive opportunities elsewhere, and by the *channels* or means through which they are able to migrate. The United States received a constant stream of immigrants until the enactment of restrictive legislation in 1921. Since then immigration has been restricted not only by the United States but also by many other countries. Most migration today is internal, especially from farm to city within a country. Political dislocations have produced record numbers of refugees, but although transportation is easy, social restrictions made refugee resettlement more difficult than ever before. In the United States, immigration is again a significant source of population increase. The sources of immigrants have shifted, and currently, more immigrants are coming from Asia than from Europe. Illegal immigration is increasing and may exceed the legal admissions.

Birthrates tend to vary inversely with social status, but in recent years in the United States, the birthrates of the poor and of blacks at all income levels have been dropping sharply.

Malthus noted that population growth tends to outrun its food supply. He dismissed the idea of the effectiveness of contraception and predicted inevitable overpopulation and misery unless people controlled population growth by postponing marriage. The rapid colonial expansion and industrial and agricultural development of the nineteenth century delayed the fulfillment of Malthus's predictions, but they now appear likely to be fulfilled in at least some parts of the world. Family planning is being used in some areas, but many cultural barriers impede its acceptance in the areas where the most unmanageable population explosions are likely to occur.

In the past three centuries a nearly stable world population has exploded into fantastic growth. Effective death control has cut the death rate in nearly all areas of the world, while only in some areas has the birthrate fallen appreciably, and in none has it fallen enough to restore a historic stability of population.

A society's birthrate is largely a result of the average age at marriage, the proportion of people who marry, and their use or nonuse of birth control. Family planning meets ideological objections from Marxists and Catholics. It is regarded as genocide by some black militants and some leaders in the developing countries. Developing countries are rapidly increasing in population. In the industrial countries, population growth is slower but takes a major proportion of natural resources. Family planning programs have made only a minor impact in most developing countries. For more effective control, it will be necessary to offer monetary and social incentives for small families and to use such methods as abortion and sterilization. The momentum from earlier years of high birthrates, which increased the proportion of women of childbearing age, is so great that even a drop to a replacement birthrate would not end population growth for another seventy years. Each society defines the meaning of death and supplies appropriate ceremonies. Modern medical procedures have complicated the definition of death and created new questions about the proper treatment of the dying.

Questions and projects

1. What has been the rate of population growth throughout most of history? Why have world rates of population growth changed recently? How long will present rates of growth continue?
2. What factors other than birth control affect the rate of reproduction?
3. Should the United States eliminate or greatly reduce immigration? Why is it difficult to control illegal immigration?
4. What were the ideas of Malthus? Do you feel that the passage of time has outdated or confirmed these ideas? Why or why not?
5. Is it true that the countries of Asia, Africa, and Latin America are now undergoing a population cycle similar to that experienced by the United States and Western Europe at an earlier date?
6. How would you explain the tendency of inhabitants of underdeveloped areas to react more favorably to the use of sterilization and abortion than to contraception?
7. Will it be necessary to use compulsory methods of birth control to control population increase? What reason is there for thinking voluntary methods will or will not be successful?
8. How would you explain the tendency toward an excess of females in American cities and an excess of males in the rural districts?
9. The United States seems to be moving toward lower birthrates, which will result in a smaller proportion of children and a larger proportion of the aged. What effect will this have on economic and political trends?
10. Why do Communist spokesmen, the Papacy, and some militant blacks object to birth-control programs? Are their objections well founded?
11. Do you believe that a couple has a right to bear as many children as they want and can provide for?
12. Using the most recent *Statistical Abstract* of the United States, compare the population growth of your state with others. What factors would appear to affect the relative position of your state? What adjustments do you feel your state will be required to make to meet the needs indicated by population changes?
13. Using the *United Nations Demographic Yearbook,* compare birth and death rates in the Philippines, India, and Mexico with those in Great Britain, France, and the United States. What conclusions would you draw about the probable future of population growth in these countries?

Suggested readings

ABRAMS, ELLIOTT, AND FRANKLIN S. ABRAMS: "Immigration Policy—Who Gets in and Why?", *The Public Interest,* 9:2–29, Winter, 1975. An incisive article which raises the principal issues concerning both legal and illegal immigration. Should be read in conjunction with KEELEY, CHARLES B.: "Immigration Composition and Population Policy," *Science,* 185:587–593, Aug. 16, 1974. Keeley's article supplies necessary comparative material.

BERELSON, BERNARD: "World Population: Status Report, 1974," *Reports on Population/Family Planning,* No. 15, 1–47, January, 1974. A current report on world population trends and family planning programs. It is readable, concise, and complete.

BLAKE, JUDITH: "Can We Believe Recent Data on Birth Expectations in the United States?", *Demography,* 11:44, February, 1974. This article tells why demographers suspect that the fall of the American birthrate may not be permanent.

CHANDRASEKHAR, S.: *Abortion in a Crowded World,* University of Washington Press, Seattle, 1974. An eminent Indian demographer discusses the role of abortion in population control programs in India.

EHRLICH, PAUL, AND ANNE H. EHRLICH: *Population, Resources, Environment: Issues in Human Ecology,* 2d ed. W. H. Freeman and Company, San Francisco, 1972. An impassioned and scholarly plea for effective action to deal with the crisis in ecology.

FORD, THOMAS F., AND GORDON F. DE JONG (EDS.): *Social Demography,* Prentice-Hall, Inc., Englewood Cliffs, N.J., 1970. A series of readings indicating the manner in which population composition interacts with social structure.

*HANDLIN, OSCAR: *The Newcomers,* Harvard University Press, Cambridge, Mass., 1959. A comparison of Puerto Rican adjustment in New York City with that of previous immigrants.

HARDIN, GARRETT: "Lifeboat Ethics: The Case Against Helping the Poor," *Psychology Today,* 38:43, September, 1974. Taking the analogies of the commons, which was ruined for all because no one controlled the number of cows grazing, and the overcrowded lifeboat which sank, Hardin argues that it is futile for the United States to help nations which refuse to limit population.

MORRIS, JUDY K.: "Professor Malthus and His Essay," *Population Bulletin,* 22:7–27, February, 1966. Background and current relevance of the Malthusian theory.

PADDOCK, WILLIAM, AND PAUL PADDOCK: *Famine 1975!,* Little, Brown and Company, New York, 1967. The book in which the authors predicted that *triage* would become a live issue in 1975. A readable, provocative and still timely book.

Sociological Symposium, 1:1–95, Fall, 1968. This issue is devoted entirely to the sociology of death. It includes the following articles: "The Rabbi and the Funeral Director," "The Bier Baron," "The Non-Accountability of Terminal Care," and "The Inevitable Death Orientation."

SPENGLER, JOSEPH J.: *America's Population Prospects,* W. H. Freeman and Company, San Francisco, 1975. Relates domestic population trends to worldwide resource shortages, and the effect of current population changes on our policy decisions.

VERNON, GLENN: *The Sociology of Death: An Analysis of Death Related Behavior,* Ronald Press, Inc., New York, 1970. A thorough analysis of all the major issues related to this topic.

Zero Population Growth, National Reporter, Los Altos, California, 94022. A journal, published by the organization with the same name, presenting articles and news items supporting the idea that no couple should bear more than two children.

Chapter 19 • The community in mass society

. . . if the anonymity New York grants us is a problem, it is also a blessing. In small towns it is natural and easy to be passing friendly with everyone nearby, and in small towns it works. But in New York there are too many people nearby. Just try to imagine walking down Madison Avenue and being friendly to everyone you meet there! Not only would you never get where you were going, but you would be making a nuisance of yourself to thousands of people with their own errands to run. The very multitude of people makes it necessary for us to stare through and beyond one another.

. . . were I living in an apartment house, I would not care to know who lives above me, below me, or in the next apartment on either side. I want to choose my friends: I do not care to have them thrust upon me by the rental agent. And I do not want people dropping in to borrow whatever people borrow, nor to chitchat whatever neighbors chitchat . . .

It *can* be lonely at times inside that anonymity, but let a small-town friendliness echo through those canyons and the future would be chaos forever, bumper to bumper and nose to nose from here to infinity. *(John Ciardi,"Manner of Speaking,"* Saturday Review, *Feb. 12, 1966, pp. 16-17.)*

The social life people lead is affected by the kind of community in which they live. The community is as old as humanity—or even older, for our subhuman ancestors probably shared a community life. *A community is a local grouping within which people carry out a full round of life activities.* Defined in greater detail [Hillery, 1955; Jonassen, 1959, p. 20], a community includes (1) a grouping of people, (2) within a geographic area, (3) with a division of labor into specialized and interdependent functions, (4) with a common culture and a social system which organizes their activities, (5) whose members are conscious of their unity and of belonging to the community, and (6) who can act collectively in an organized manner. For it to qualify as a true community, its members must be able to experience all or nearly all aspects of the culture within its boundaries. The handful of houses in a hamlet do not form a community, for their occupants must travel elsewhere for many of their needs and relationships. While in strict correctness the term "community" refers to a grouping of people, and not to the territory they occupy, both usages are fairly common in sociological literature. The term is also loosely used to describe almost any subculture or category of people, whether geographical (Hickory Corners, New York City, the "world community") or social (the "community of scholars," the "black community," the "artistic community"), but these are not the usual sociological uses of the term.

It has been traditional to classify communities as rural or urban, depending upon whether their populations were small and agricultural, or larger and industrial or commercial. The classification was never entirely satisfactory, for it made no provision for the fishing village, the mining camp, the trading post, or many other special types of communities. Modern transportation has so eroded the boundaries between city and country that we actually have a gradual shading of one community into the other and not two distinct types of community. One analysis locates four types of community along the rural-urban continuum: the rural community, the "fringe" community, the town, and the metropolis [Arensberg and Kimball, 1965]. While these are ideal types and thus in a sense artificial, they are useful tools for analysis.

Community and mass society. The concepts of community and mass society are, in a sense, contradictory. The concept of community emphasizes the unity of a settlement of people, their identification with one another, their ability to act together, and their common sharing of traditions, interests, and values. The concept of mass society poses an aggregation of separate, detached, anonymous individuals with a social organization based on contract instead of kinship, where ties between persons are utilitarian instead of personal or sentimental, where there are no generally revered traditions and no established leadership elite (see p. 376). Thus defined, there could be no true community in a true mass society. But both concepts describe ideal types, and an ideal type is always an exaggeration of reality. The concept of mass society highlights certain features and trends which are, to a considerable degree, characteristic of modern societies. The concept of community describes some features of social organization which are true, to a considerable degree, of most local settlements of peo-

. . . where ties between persons are utilitarian instead of personal.

ple. While perfect examples are difficult to find, the concepts are useful as starting points for study.

The rural community

The physical and social conditions of urban and rural life are different. Consequently there are differences in the personality and behavior of urban and rural people. These differences have provided endless source material for the novelist and the playwright, and continue to interest the sociologist.

The folk society

Some sociologists have seen the concept of the folk society as a close parallel to traditional rural life. This concept is somewhat reminiscent of the gemeinschaft described in Chapter 8. Redfield describes the folk society:

Such a society is small, isolated, nonliterate and homogeneous with a strong sense of group solidarity. The ways of living are conventionalized into that coherent system which we call a "culture." Behavior is traditional, spontaneous, uncritical and personal; there is no legislation or habit of experiment and reflection for intellectual ends. Kinship, its relationships and institutions, are the type categories of experience and the familial group is the unit of action. The sacred prevails over the secular;

the economy is one of status rather than of the market. (Robert Redfield, "The Folk Society," *American Journal of Sociology,* 52:293–308, January, 1947. Copyright, 1947 by The University of Chicago and used with the permission of the author and the *American Sociological Review.*) For criticism and discussion of the folk-society concept, see Oscar Lewis, *Life in a Mexican Village,* The University of Illinois Press, Urbana, 1951; Horace Miner, "The Folk-Urban Continuum," *American Sociological Review,* 17:529–537, October, 1952.)

The folk society is most perfectly illustrated by the primitive agricultural society—tradition-bound, informal, homogeneous, and unchanging. Its opposite is the mass society—large, impersonal, changing, and dominated by secondary contacts and mass communication processes—reminiscent of the gesellschaft. Much of the discussion of rural-urban differences is in terms of folk society—mass society contrasts.

Today, however, the rural life is losing its folk-society flavor. What are the traditional features of rural life and how are they changing?

Traditional characteristics of rural life

Rural communities are not all alike. Edwards [1959] distinguishes at least five types of rural communities: the town-country community with farms scattered about a village center; the open-country community without any village center; the village community, whose subtypes include the fishing village, the mining village, and the mill village; the line village, with farm homes strung along the road at the ends of long, narrow farms; and the plantation. Yet certain characteristics are common to nearly all kinds of rural communities.

Isolation. Perhaps the most conspicuous feature of American rural life in times past was its isolation. Throughout much of the world, rural people are clustered into small villages, within walking distance of the surrounding farmland. In the United States, the isolated homestead became the usual pattern of rural settlement, a pattern that was productively more efficient but socially isolating. Not only was the local group isolated from other groups but each family was isolated from other families. With a thinly scattered population, personal contacts were few. Each contact involved the perception of an individual as a complete person, not simply as a functionary. There were few impersonal contacts in folk or rural societies—no anonymous bus drivers, ticket sellers, grocery clerks, or policemen. Nearly every contact was with an acquaintance who was treated, not only in terms of economic function, but also in terms of one's total personality and all the many facets of one's status in the community.

The hospitality pattern of the American frontier, wherein the traveler was welcome to spend the night at almost any farmhouse, was a practical response both to frontier needs—where else would the traveler stay?—and to frontier loneliness. The traveler brought news, contact with the outside world, and a break in monotony. Even today the hospitality pattern survives under conditions of extreme isolation. On the Alaska Highway the mores of the region require one to offer assistance to any stranded motorist, who may actually die if assistance is not given. The hospitality pattern is a perfect illustration of how customs and mores arise in response to social needs and change as these needs change.

Homogeneity. Taken as a whole, American settlers were a quite heterogeneous lot. But within a given locality, the settlers were likely to be quite homogeneous in ethnic and cultural background. They showed a strong tendency to follow earlier migrants from their home communities, so that the settlers from a particular country and district tended to be clustered into rather homogeneous settlements. This homogeneity, together with the comparative isolation of settlements from one another, helped to encourage the conservatism, traditionalism, and ethnocentrism of American rural communities.

Agricultural employment. Nearly all were farmers or hired hands, while even the minister, doctor, teacher, storekeeper, and blacksmith were deeply involved in an agricultural way of life. All faced common problems, performed common tasks, and shared a common helplessness before the awesome natural forces which man could not control.

Subsistence economy. The traditional American homestead tried to produce nearly everything it consumed. The bulging smokehouse, the well-stocked fruit cellar, and the shelves sagging with home-canned goods were a source of pride to the farm family. In a rapidly expanding economy with a chronic shortage of money and credit, a subsistence-and-barter economy was a socially useful adaptation. Thrift was an honored value, and conspicuous consumption was seen as an urban vice. A farmer's status was measured by his lands, his herds, his barns, his crops, and the inheritance he could pass on to his children—all highly visible, thus making conspicuous consumption unnecessary as symbols of success.

Living within a subsistence rather than a market economy, rural people were inclined to be suspicious of intellectuality and "book learning." The farmer was most likely to see a piece of paper when some "city slicker" was trying to do him out of something. Distrust of city people and disapproval of urban life were predictable rural attitudes.

These are some of the influences which shaped American rural personality. Hospitable and cooperative, conservative and religious, hard-working and thrifty, ethnocentric and intolerant—these characteristics were products of the physical and social conditions of rural life in America. Today these conditions have vastly changed. And so has the social behavior of rural people.

The rural revolution

Reduced isolation. Two generations ago the isolation of rural life could be measured by the contrast between the styles shown in the Sears, Roebuck catalog and those on the pages of a metropolitan newspaper. Today the styles are similar. The automobile and good roads have wrought a transformation of rural and village life which is difficult for the present generation of students to appreciate. Thousands of small villages have ceased to be true communities, as good roads have carried their trade, their storekeepers, their professionals, and their recreation to a nearby city. If close enough to the city, they have become suburbs; if too distant, they have often become the half-empty shells of decaying houses and aging people, as are so many of the villages of America today. Transportation, plus the press, movies, radio, and television, have ended the social isolation of rural America. The true provincial today may be the urban slum dweller, who may spend years without venturing beyond one set of canyons, or possibly the suburbanite living within the walls of a one-class, one-age-group, lily-white neighborhood.

Commercialization and rationalization of agriculture. Without a revolution in agricultural productivity, there could have been little urban growth. In 1790 it required the surplus of nine farm families to support one urban family; today twenty-four nonfarm families are supported by each farm family. Farming used to be a way of life which called for no special knowledge beyond that which farm youth absorbed unavoidably as they grew up. Today farming is a highly complex operation demanding substantial capital, specialized knowledge, rapid changes in productive technology, and continuous market analysis. The "average" American farm represents an investment of at least $130,000 in land and buildings, and this "average" includes many which are too small or ill-equipped to be efficient. This investment is rising rapidly. Most of the new harvesting machines for harvesting cherries, oranges, celery, and other crops cost from $20,000 to $40,000 each. Today's successful farm has become a roofless factory, using a variety of managerial skills comparable to those needed for many another business, and more often described as "agribusiness."

As farming has grown more demanding, the number of farm families has fallen precipitously—from 6.7 million and 22 percent of all American families in 1935 to 2.1 million and 4.0 percent of all families in 1971. Meanwhile the average size of farms has steadily increased from 143 acres in 1925 to 385 acres in 1973.

Farms are growing larger because of changes in farm technology. Mechanization allows one farm family to handle more acreage, and more acreage permits a more efficient use of farm machinery. Consequently, larger farms are more efficient. Production costs per unit of production on small farms are more than twice as high as on larger farms [Tweeten and Schreiner, 1970, p. 43]. These trends towards fewer and larger farms seem to be slowing down in recent years and may "bottom out" before long. The family farm remains the typical farm operation, and there is no indication that huge corporate "factories in the field" will displace the family farm.

Because of these changes in agricultural technology, the farm population is rapidly shrinking. In 1790 the rural (farm and nonfarm) residents comprised 94.8 percent of the population. By 1920, when "farm" and "rural nonfarm" people were first separated in the census, farm people constituted 30.1 percent of the population; in 1972 only 4.6 percent, and they are still diminishing in proportion. We were once a nation of farmers. Today farmers are becoming one of the smallest of our major occupational groups. At present more than 1 million of our farm families are unnecessary for agricultural production and could leave the farm tomorrow without ever being missed. These are "marginal" farmers, who have too little land, equipment, and capital, or too little energy or managerial skill to farm very profitably. One-third of our farms are part-time or postretirement operations. But of our full-time farm operations, one-fourth produce less than $5,000 of farm produce per year (and this is gross produce, not net income after expenses). These farms contribute little to our national

Figure 23. Farm population, farms, and farm size, 1950–1972. (Source: Data from U.S. Dept. of Agriculture, Economic Research Service, and *Statistical Abstract of the United States*, 1973, p. 583.)

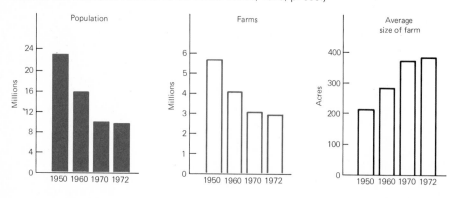

farm product and do not provide a decent living to their operators. Yet an estimated three-fifths of the farm poor are too old, too handicapped, or too uneducated to transfer to other occupations even if offered job training [Burchinal and Siff, 1964]. They steadily disappear from farming through retirement and rarely through transfer to other employment. As they retire, their lands are added to other farms. Thus the number of farmers and the farm population shrinks, while the average size of farms increases. As the farm became part of the market economy, the attitudes appropriate to a subsistence economy have languished. Thrift, as an absolute value, seen as *good* in and of itself, is also a useful practice in a subsistence economy. In a market economy it becomes an anachronism. Farm people today appear to have as avid an appetite for new cars and color television sets as urbanites. After all, values grow out of the experience of the group. In a subsistence economy of limited productivity, where there is rarely enough of anything, especially money, the elevation of thrift to an absolute value is practical and sensible. With the development of a highly productive market economy, thrift becomes pointless as an end in itself. Instead, reasonable thrift becomes a means to an end, such as saving money on inessentials in order to afford the major purchase of a home or a new car. This and many other value changes have accompanied the technological revolution in American agriculture.

These processes are in operation throughout the Western world. In the six European Common Market countries, employment in agriculture fell by over one-third since 1955 [*New York Times,* Mar. 28, 1971, p. 6]. Germany, Holland, and Belgium have less than 10 percent of their labor force in agriculture, France about 15 percent, and Italy about 22 percent. Their rural areas face the same problems of farm unemployment and lack of training for other employment, while their cities have the same problems of congestion, housing, pollution, and taxation.

Urbanization of rural life. It is no longer possible to identify rural rustics by outmoded dress or bucolic manner. Although there are still some differences between the modal personalities, life-styles, and value systems of rural and urban dwellers, all the historic rural-urban differences are shrinking. Every rural activity from agriculture [Winfield, 1973] to mate selection [Wakil, 1973] has been "urbanized in that the values and norms governing the activity do not differ significantly between urban and rural people." To a high degree, rural life is becoming urbanized, as historically urban patterns have spread into rural areas. Taylor and Jones [1964] speak of the "urbanized social organization" of America, and every rural sociology textbook reflects this urbanization of rural life [Copp, 1964; Rogers and Burdge, 1972]. This process is widespread but uneven. Rural areas closer to large cities, and those where agriculture is most highly rationalized and commercialized show the highest degree of urbanization; more isolated areas and areas where farming practices are more traditional show fewer urban influences. But everywhere, the steady urbanization of rural society is evident.

There are many examples of urbanization. The electric pump and the septic tank have brought urban plumbing to the rural home.

It is no longer possible to identify rural rustics by their outmoded dress or bucolic manner.

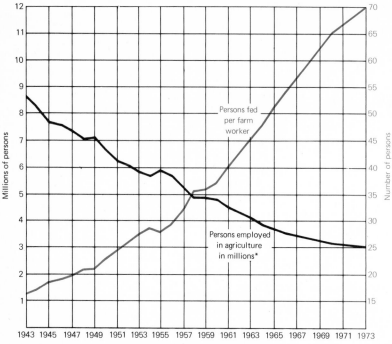

*Full-time agricultural workers, plus part-time workers equated to full-time basis.

Figure 24. The agricultural revolution in the United States.
(Source: *Statistical Abstracts of the United States*, various dates.)

The rural birthrate has been dropping closer to the urban birthrate—77 percent higher in 1940, 40 percent higher in 1950, 34 percent higher in 1960, and 18 percent higher in 1972. Our population today is predominantly urban. In 1972 only 4.6 percent of our people lived on farms, with 69 percent in metropolitan areas and 25 percent living in smaller cities, towns, villages, and "rural nonfarm" areas. Most of these rural nonfarm people (unless retired) are urban commuters, who become a powerful urbanizing influence upon rural life. In many urban fringe areas, people are divided between farm and nonfarm employment, and any classification of such areas as either rural or urban is arbitrary. Although "rural" and "urban" survive as words and as statistical categories, the rural-urban distinction is no longer very important.

Rural neglect

Political power has migrated to the city along with the people. Rural social problems are as great as or greater than urban problems. For example, half the nation's poor are in rural America, where poverty is twice as common as in urban America, yet the metropolitan areas get nearly three-fourths of all federal health and welfare funds [Tamblyn, 1973, p. 15]. Rural areas have proportionately more dilapidated housing, in which room crowding (persons per room) is greater than in urban areas [Carnahan et al., 1974]. Yet the urban ghetto and the "urban crisis" get attention and funds. Metropolitan cities have well-organized minorities who must be pacified, and have professional staffs of money-sniffers who are skilled in the arts of grantsmanship, while ". . . the poorer a [rural] county happened to be, the less chance it had to obtain the funds necessary for local development" [Hanson, 1973, p. 240]. A raft of research organizations, such as The Urban Institute and the Center for Urban Policy Research, are devoted to the study of urban problems, but there is no rural equivalent. The only one of the

The rural-urban distinction is no longer very important.

New Deal farm programs intended to aid the marginal farmers—the Farm Security Administration—was liquidated in 1946, while most of the other farm programs survive [Ford, 1973, Chap. 3]. The land grant colleges and the Agricultural Extension Service concentrate upon promoting the mechanization and commercialization of agriculture, and have little interest in marginal farmers, the farm poor, or rural social problems [Hightower, 1973]. Consequently, not much is done about them.

The urban community

The development of cities

In order for the primitive Stone Age village to overshoot its few dozen households and expand to a size of several hundred thousand, it had to have a food surplus, a water supply, and a transportation system. Since a river valley provided all three, the first large cities arose six or seven thousand years ago in the valleys of the Nile, the Tigris, and the Euphrates. Surplus food to support an urban population was abundant in the fertile valley, and the slow-flowing rivers provided simple transportation. Although most ancient cities remained tiny by modern standards, a few reached a size of several hundred thousand, complete with problems of water supply, sewage disposal, and traffic congestion.

The growth of cities unleashed revolutionary changes. The primitive village was a folk society, organized on a kinship basis and guided by customary procedures. A number of conditions are necessary for a large city: (1) a division of labor into many specialized occupations; (2) social organization based upon occupation and social class rather than kinship; (3) formal government institutions based on territory rather than family; (4) a system of trade and commerce: (5) means of communication and record keeping; and (6) rational technology. These developments proceed steadily as small towns grow into large cities. Obviously the large city could not arise until the culture had made a number of necessary inventions; at the same time, the development of the city proved a great stimulus to the making and improving of such inventions as carts and barges, ditches and aqueducts, writing, number systems, governmental bureaucracies, and many others.

Towns and cities are of many kinds—temple towns, garrison towns, mining towns, political capitals, resort centers, industrial cities, trading centers, and others. The "company town" is a unique kind of community which has now nearly disappeared [Allen, 1966]. Most large cities are diversified, carrying on a number of kinds of activity. An early sociologist, Cooley [1894], noted that cities tend to grow wherever there is a "break" in transportation so that goods must be unloaded and reloaded for transshipment. Port cities like London, Montreal, and New Orleans are located up a navigable river at the point where large ocean vessels can go no further. Denver lies at the foot of a mountain range, Pittsburgh at the confluence of two rivers. The break-in-transportation theory does not necessarily apply to resort centers like Las Vegas, Aspen, or Monte Carlo, to political capitals like Washington or Brazilia, or to other specialized cities for which transportation was relatively unimportant, but the break-in-transportation theory still serves to explain the location of most cities.

In the Western world, urbanization has accompanied industrialization. Commercial and industrial development provided an urban "pull" changing agricultural technology and high rural birthrates combined to provide a rural surplus of people. In many undeveloped countries today, however, urbanization is rushing along without a proportionate industrial development. Death rates in the developing countries have been falling rapidly in recent decades. Agriculture cannot absorb the population increase, so people flock to the cities, even though they have little prospect of finding jobs or housing [Ham, 1973]. In Indonesia, for example, the population of the cities has doubled every ten to fifteen years without proportionate increase in either urban industrial output or agricultural productivity. The results seem to be an intensification of every type of problem:

Since the war the supplies of food to the cities of Java have diminished at the same time as the number of city people to be fed has increased. . . . The result is that much of the food consumed in the cities is now brought from abroad. . . . A city whose physical structure was designed for half a million is now the home of about six times that number. . . . There is a free movement of population and so the erection of housing facilities in the cities, improvement of roads, introduction of subsidized bus service—in short any alleviation of the discomforts of city life—will operate, along with subsidized rice, to draw people from the crowded countryside. . . . Efforts of town planning and house construction are frustrated; people are drawn to the cities faster than decent places for them to live can be found. (Nathan Keyfitz, "The

Ecology of Indonesian Cities," *American Journal of Sociology,* 66:348–354, January, 1961. Copyright, 1961, by The University of Chicago.)

The result of such urban growth is a type of slum practically unknown in the United States, the *suburban squatter slum.* Nearly every major city in Asia, Africa, and South America has on its outskirts a large area occupied by people living on land they do not own or rent, in flimsy shanties which they have built of scrap materials—shipping crates, scrap lumber, old signboards, flattened tin cans, old bricks, or anything else that can be scrounged. Generally there are no urban services—power, water, or sewers—and people live in a squalor which makes American slums look like castles by comparison. From one-fourth to one-half of the "urban" residents of much of the world— 50 percent in Ankara, Turkey; 40 percent in Caracas, Venezuela—live in such wretchedness [Howton, 1967; Juppenlatz, 1970, p. 15].

Here the brutal consequences of the population explosion are evident. A falling death rate and a birthrate that remains high give a rate of population growth which exceeds the rate of expansion of the economies of the underdeveloped countries. Add to this, in most cases, a political system that is at best inefficient, and very often is both corrupt and inefficient, and human misery is the inevitable result. Yet the squatter slum is not entirely dysfunctional, for it does provide—however painfully—a transitional bridge between peasant village life and the urban economy [Berry, 1973, pp. 83–91].

The ecological pattern of cities

Most cities look as though they just happened—grew without plan or design—and they did. While a few major cities such as Washington, D.C., once had a plan, they have long since outgrown it. But while most city growth is not planned, neither is it entirely haphazard. Cities have structure, and there is some reason for the arrangement of their parts. Several sociolo-

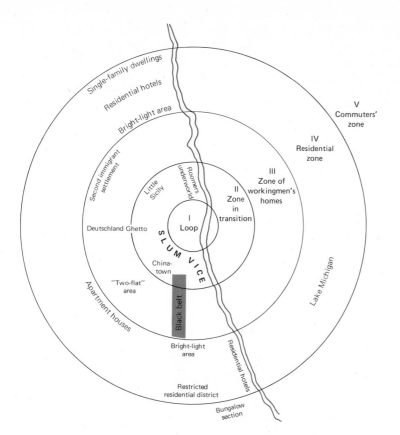

gists have sought to discover the underlying pattern according to which a modern city develops.

Patterns of urban design. Burgess's *concentric zone pattern,* shown in Figure 25, is one such attempt. Based upon his studies of Chicago in the early 1920s, it shows a central business district at the center, surrounded by a slum consisting of old buildings which are gradually being replaced by the expansion of the business district. This in turn is surrounded by zones of successively better-class residences.

Do real cities resemble the Burgess pattern? Each American city (with the possible exception of Los Angeles) has a central business district, partly or entirely surrounded by a slum. This surrounding zone contains the oldest buildings in the city, undesirable because of decay, dirt, and congestion. Housing quality tends to improve as one moves outward from this slum, and much of the choice residential area is located in the suburbs. But this pattern does not fit preindustrial cities, whose sequence of zones was reversed, with the rich living close to the center and the poor on the fringes [Sjoberg, 1960; Abbott, 1974]. Nor does the concentric zone pattern describe city growth since automobile transport became dominant. Thus it fits cities at a particular time and place. And even then, these zones are not unbroken bands surrounding the city, nor are they circular in shape. Instead, the various grades of residence are rather irregularly dis-

Figure 26. Changes in the location of fashionable residences. This graph represents Hoyt's sector theory. The solid colored spaces show how the fashionable residential areas shifted outward from the city center between 1900 and 1936. (Source: Homer Hoyt: *The Structure and Growth of Residential Neighborhoods in American Cities*, Federal Housing Administration, Washington, D.C., 1939, p. 115.)

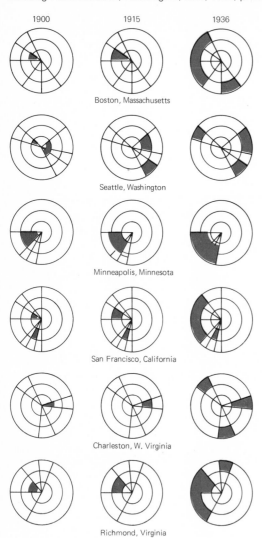

1900   1915   1936

Boston, Massachusetts

Seattle, Washington

Minneapolis, Minnesota

San Francisco, California

Charleston, W. Virginia

Richmond, Virginia

tributed and often concentrated on one side of the city.

This observation led Hoyt [1933] to frame his *sector theory of city growth,* holding that a particular kind of land use tends to locate and remain in a particular sector of the city. Figure 26 shows how this theory is borne out in several American cities over several decades. Thus industry tends to locate in one sector, upper-class housing in an opposite sector, and working-class housing in intermediate sectors; then as time passes, each of these sectors simply expands outward until some change in topography breaks up the pattern.

The *multinuclear theory* [Harris and Ullman, 1945] holds that a number of centers—business, shopping, manufacturing—and residential areas become located early in a city's history. Topography, cost, and historical accident all enter into these early choices. These concentrations tend to survive and fix the pattern of later city growth. Larger cities, which usually represent the growing together of once separate villages or communities, provide multiple nuclei. These three patterns are shown in comparison in Figure 27.

Still another pattern can be recognized—one so simple that it has not been dignified by being called a theory. It relates land use to topography. Railroads tend to follow the river valley; heavy industry locates along the railroad; upper-class residence seeks the highlands; and the intermediate levels of housing are scattered in between.

The existence of alternative theories shows that none of them is entirely satisfactory. None of them is perfectly illustrated by any American city, and many cities outside the United States will show very little resemblance to any of these patterns; for example, Calcutta stretches for some 35 miles along the Ganges River [A. J. Rose, 1967, chap. 11]. Each pattern is an idea which real cities more or less perfectly resemble. Since most American cities do show some resemblance to one of these patterns, the theories are helpful in revealing their prevailing structure.

City structure today is being revolutionized by transportation. In most cities the central business district has ceased to expand, and the commercial growth leapfrogs to the suburban shopping centers. A growing ring of decay is left surrounding the business district, as it no longer razes its fringe as it expands. An aging and decaying central city is soon trapped by declining tax sources and mounting tax expenditures. This is the basic reason why nearly every city in the country is caught in a financial crisis and has made some efforts at urban renewal.

Slums. A slum is a deteriorated area of the city inhabited by poor people. As mentioned earlier, most Asian, African, and South American cities have large "shanty" slums on their outskirts. Slums in the United States are generally in the inner-city areas, the "area in transition" in Burgess' concentric zone pattern. The oldest housing in the city is generally found in this area separating the central business district from the newer residential districts. Old buildings, however, do not cause slums. Old buildings, when structurally sound, are sometimes remodeled into highly fashionable residential districts. *It is the low income of the residents which creates a slum* [Muth, 1969]. There are several steps in the conversion of old housing into slum housing: (1) older housing units are subdivided, often through illegal makeshift conversions, so that some units lack even the facilities for cleanliness (when three families share a bathroom, nobody cleans it); (2) with subdivision, there is an enormous increase in overcrowding and congestion, with buildings deteriorating through heavy use and lawns worn bare or turned into parking space; (3) building owners neglect maintenance or improvement, which are discouraged by taxing policies which penalize improvements; (4) people who have always been poor (perhaps for generations) and have always lived in old houses generally take poor care of property. Thus a vicious circle of cause and effect is maintained: slum landlords justify their neglect of property maintenance because slum tenants do not "take care" of property, while slum tenants typically have not developed habits of property care because they have never had any property worth taking care of.

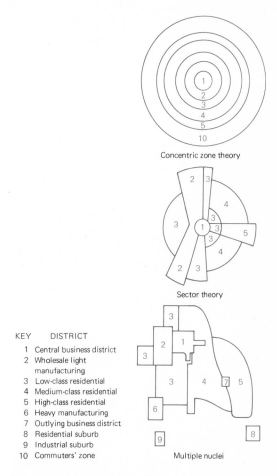

KEY   DISTRICT
1 Central business district
2 Wholesale light manufacturing
3 Low-class residential
4 Medium-class residential
5 High-class residential
6 Heavy manufacturing
7 Outlying business district
8 Residential suburb
9 Industrial suburb
10 Commuters' zone

Concentric zone theory

Sector theory

Multiple nuclei

Figure 27. Three patterns of city structure. Generalizations of internal structure of cities. The concentric-zone pattern is a generalization which Burgess proposed as an ideal type to apply more or less perfectly to all cities. The arrangement of the sectors in the sector theory varies from city to city. The diagram for multiple nuclei represents one possible pattern among innumerable variations. (Source: C. D. Harris and E. L. Ullman, "The Nature of Cities," *The Annals*, 242:13, November, 1945.)

Slumlords are often blamed for the wretchedness of the slums. The stereotype slumlord lives handsomely in a manicured suburb or a posh Florida condominium, insulated from his grubby tenants by layers of realty corporations whose collectors have ingenious ways of collecting rents. Such slumlords, if they were ever common, are uncommon today. The typical slumlord is very often a minority person who owns one or two properties, either lives in one of them or in the immediate area, and gets a minor part of his income from rentals [Sternlieb and Burchell, 1973, Chaps. 2, 3]. He most often became a landlord because he couldn't afford a single-family dwelling and depends upon rentals to help meet the mortgage payments. Often they do not, and "residential abandonment" has become a major urban problem. Complete blocks and even entire districts are today being abandoned to the rats, vandals, and squatters [Rogin, 1971; Sternlieb and Burchell, 1973]. The reason for abandonment is simple; rental income is insufficient to cover costs.

Tax policies are a prime factor in property deterioration, for improvements bring increased tax assessments. Building code enforcement is seldom very effective in preventing deterioration. Owner-occupants are not the problem; theirs are the best-maintained slum properties. Absentee owners and realty corporations, however, may be difficult to track down, and are experts at avoiding compliance. Finally, if fines are imposed, they are generally so small that it is cheaper to pay them than to make the repairs.

Slum clearance and low-cost housing projects had some success during the 1930s and 1940s when the program was new. Early studies showed greatly lower rates for crime and other antisocial behaviors in housing projects than in surrounding slum areas [Barer, 1946; Dee, 1956]. But as years passed, and both the levels of prosperity and the housing supply improved, the projects tended to fill up with the black welfare poor. No other residential area will accept low-income housing, for nobody wants the poor, especially when they are non-white. Small "scatter" public housing was also rejected, and projects became high-rise monsters located in the black ghetto (where black politicians welcomed a solid black constituency). Thus the project poor became isolated from the rest of society. In many projects, children lived in a world where stable families with working fathers were too few and illegitimate births and irregular families so common that there was little chance to learn the conventional norms of study, work, marriage, and social life. Some projects became so afflicted with crime, vandalism, filth, and disorder that "normal" families fled them, rents failed to cover costs, and a cycle of abandonment and demolition began [Griffin, 1974, pp. 159–160].

The early hope that better housing would bring a change toward stable (middle-class) work and family life norms has not been fulfilled. Housing alone does not "elevate" people's behavior patterns [Morris and Mogey, 1965, pp. 162–163; Weller and Luchterhand, 1973]. Public housing cannot provide a decent life environment unless stable families and middle-income people are included to give a more normal population [Fuerst, 1974], and this is politically impossible. There is little realistic prospect for public housing in the United States for the foreseeable future. It now appears that rental supplements, providing low-income people with income with which to rent private housing, is a more practical alternative [Sternlieb, 1969, p. 234; *Business Week,* Mar. 31, 1975, p. 78].

The slum is sometimes pictured as an area totally lacking in social organization. This is incorrect, for there is a pattern of social organization in the slum [Whyte, 1955; Suttles, 1968]. The slum is highly provincial, with people rarely venturing beyond the "turf" of their ethnic group. The overall pattern is one which Suttles calls "ordered segmentation" [pp. 225–227]. Each ethnic group has its boundaries, within which most social relationships are confined and socially controlled. Programs which disrupt these established boundaries therefore weaken the social controls of the area.

There are rural areas which are true slums in

all but location. As described in Fetterman's *Stinking Creek* [1970], rural slum housing is more dilapidated, has even fewer utility services, and room crowding is even greater. Poverty and hopelessness are equally widespread, social services are even less adequate than in the urban slum, and "welfare" is the principal source of income. The rural slum is equally grim but receives even less attention than the urban slum.

Metropolitan areas and suburbs. Modern transportation is responsible for the suburb and the metropolitan area. A "standard metropolitan statistical area" is defined by the census as a county or group of counties containing at least one city (or a pair of adjoining cities) with over 50,000 people. Adjacent counties are included if they are metropolitan in character, as measured by certain criteria. In 1970, some 69 percent of the nation's population lived in our 212 metropolitan areas.

The suburb is the fastest growing part of America. Between 1960 and 1970 the suburbs of our metropolitan areas grew by 26 percent, while our rural population remained unchanged and the central cities were growing by only 6.4 percent. The suburbs accounted for nearly two-thirds of the nation's population growth during the 1950s, but for more than three-fourths of the nation's population growth during the 1960s.

This explosion of the suburbs is a part of what has recently come to be known as *urban sprawl.* Vast strip cities are developing from Boston to Baltimore, another from Buffalo to Detroit, across Michigan and on through Chicago around to Milwaukee and many others. These strip cities fit no traditional pattern of city structure. In time, new theoretical constructs will be developed to describe them. Urban sprawl and strip cities bring a host of problems with them [Whyte, 1958]. Land resources are used wastefully, and the region is locked into a permanent pattern of dependence upon the automobile [McKee and Smith, 1972]. The existing structures of township, city, and county government are quite inadequate to

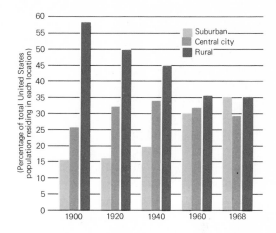

Figure 28. Shift of the United States population to the suburbs, 1900–1970. (Source: U.S. Department of Commerce, Bureau of the Census, U.S. Census of Population, 1960; Selected Area Reports, Standard Metropolitan Statistical Areas, Final Report DC (3)-ID: Current Population Reports, Trends in Social and Economic Conditions in Metropolitan Areas, series P-23, no. 27, February, 1969; and Current Population Reports, Provisional Estimates of the Population of 100 Large Metropolitan Areas: July, 1967, series P-25, no. 441, December 1968, *Statistical Abstracts of the United States.*)

organize this developing urban monstrosity. With over 1,400 separate political units in the New York metropolitan area, each with its vested interests to defend, any coherent overall planning becomes almost an impossibility. Some observers believe that the problems of these metropolitan areas are so difficult that they will not be solved, and that the largest metropolitan areas will go into a relative decline [Vernon, 1960]. Some other observers believe that bold planning *can* solve the problems of urban sprawl and urban blight [Jacobs, 1961; Gruen, 1964; Abrams, 1965: Erber, 1970; Griffin, 1974]. Urban sprawl is not exclusively an American problem; it is taking place all over the world, even in the Soviet Union, despite official efforts to stem the growth of the larger cities [Anderson, 1966]. Urban growth proceeds for much the same reasons and has much the same consequences everywhere in the world.

Any coherent planning becomes an impossibility.

Changing racial structure. Since 1940, the black population of our central cities has been growing rapidly while the white population has been fleeing to the suburbs. Between 1940 and 1950, while the white population of all central cities was growing by 3.7 percent, the black population grew by 68 percent; between 1950 and 1960, the figures were 4.9 percent for whites and 49.8 percent for blacks. Between 1960 and 1970, the white population of the central cities declined by 5.4 percent while their black population grew by 32.8 percent. Between 1950 and 1970, blacks increased from 12.2 to 20.5 percent of the population of the central cities, while declining from 6.6. to 5.3 percent of the population of the suburbs. Most of the black suburbanites live within predominantly black suburbs [Farley, 1970]. The growth of the black population of central cities is slowing down, partly because the rural pool of possible black urban migrants is running low, and racial segregation in the cities, while still high, is definitely declining [Glazer, 1974]. Eighty-one percent of American blacks are now urban, making them the most highly urbanized segment of our population. Four major central cities now have black majorities—Atlanta, Gary, Newark, and Washington, D.C.—and several more will soon join them.

Urban ecological processes

Change is continuous in the American city. The means through which the distribution of people and institutions change are known as *ecological processes.* To understand them we must begin with the *natural area,* a collection of people and activities which are drawn together in mutual interdependence within a limited area. The single-men's district of flophouses and cheap hotels, cheap restaurants, pawn shops, burlesque shows, taverns, and missions, all catering to the needs of low-income homeless men, is an example of a natural area. Other natural areas include the department-store section, the entertainment area, the communities of recent immigrants, the rooming-house district, the college students' residential area, the warehouse district, and many others. Natural areas are unplanned. They arise from the free choices of individuals. Persons having similar needs and preferences are drawn together into an area where these are most easily fulfilled, and their association creates a natural area.

The *neighborhood,* unlike the natural area, may be either planned or unplanned. A neighborhood is an area where people neighbor, and not all areas are neighborhoods. There is very little neighboring in some areas, such as the rooming-house district, and more neighboring in the ethnic communities and family-residence areas. Some urban neighborhoods are consciously planned, with housing, communication, shopping, and recreation facilities deliberately arranged to encourage neighboring. More often the neighborhood is an unplanned product of people's need for social relations. Neighboring is greatest in family-residence areas where people face common problems of child rearing and crabgrass fighting. Neighborhoods and natural areas are constantly being formed, dissolved, and relocated through the urban ecological processes of *concentration, centralization, decentralization, segregation,* and *invasion.*

Concentration is the tendency for people and institutions to gather where conditions are favorable. It produces the growth of cities. *Centralization* is the clustering together of the economic and service functions within the city. People come together to work, to play, to shop, then return to other areas to live. The shopping district, the factory district, and the entertainment district are empty of people for a part of each day or night. The central business district is a prime example of centralization. *Decentralization* describes the tendency of people and organizations to desert the center of the city for outlying areas where congestion is less and land values are lower. The automobile and motor truck and electric power have greatly encouraged residential, commercial, and industrial decentralization—a tendency which greatly complicates the task of anyone who seeks to diagram the pattern of the city.

Segregation refers to the concentration of certain types of people or organizations within a particular area. The "Gold Coast," the ghetto and the produce market areas are examples, along with the hotel and banking districts, the theater district, and "used-car row." Segregation may be either voluntary or involuntary. Most immigrant groups voluntarily segregated themselves, for life was more comfortable this way. The ethnic neighborhood in the large American cities was partly voluntary and partly involuntary [Wirth, 1928]. The ghetto is an example of involuntary segregation, as low income, realtor practices, the threat of violence, and "neighborhood improvement associations" combined to limit black residence to restricted black areas [Abrams, 1955; Grier and Grier, 1960].

Invasion takes place when a new kind of people, organization, or activity enters an area. Residential areas may be invaded by business; a business area may be invaded by a new kind of business; residents of a different class level or ethnic group may move into a residential area. Generally the invasion is of a higher-status area by a lower-status group or activity. This direction of invasion is a normal outcome of the process of city growth and of aging. A once-exclusive residential area of homes which are no longer fashionable is invaded by people a class level below the present occupants. A generation later the same area may be invaded by persons still another class level lower, or by blacks or other ethnics, or by secondhand stores and other business houses. Occasionally the direction is reversed. Many large cities today contain some areas where dilapidated housing is being renovated or rebuilt into an upper-class residential area. Many upper-income people have fled to the suburbs because attractive new housing is located there. Many would like to remain close to the city's center if satisfactory housing is available. Some areas have therefore traveled the complete cycle of upper-class residence to slum to upper-class residence. In all likelihood, the cycle will now be repeated.

Stages in the invasion cycle. Several sociologists have sought to define the several stages of an invasion cycle [McKenzie, 1925, p. 25; Gibbard, 1938, pp. 206–207; Lee, 1955, pp. 257–260]. The *initial* stage brings a small number of people into the area and may not even be noticed for a time. When the old occupants become aware of an invasion, a *reaction* stage begins, whose intensity depends upon the cultural and racial characteristics of the invaders, the attitudes of the old residents, and the neighborhood solidarity. Opposition is most likely when the invaders are black. A common device is the "civic," "protective," or "neighborhood-improvement" association. This organization seeks to prevent residents from selling or renting to the invaders, and to discourage the invaders from seeking to buy or rent in the area. Such associations are most effective when most of the homes are owned by their occupants. If the reaction fails to stop the invaders, then the *general influx* stage soon follows. When there are enough of the newcomers to make the old residents unwilling to remain, the "tip point" has been reached, and the old residents rapidly abandon the area to the newcomers. The *climax* is the complete replacement of the old residents with newcomers or with commercial or institutional land use. The final stage is *succession,* in which the area may remain in a disorganized and chaotic state, or may become well-organized around its new residents or land use.

This invasion cycle is continuously in operation in every American city. The processes of growth and aging make it inevitable. It is a costly process—costly in terms of human frustration and economic waste—but no one has suggested a practical alternative. Zoning is not an alternative—it is simply a technique for making invasion and succession more deliberate and orderly, and for protecting vested interests in the process [Babcock, 1966].

It is through these ecological processes that the city continues to change. City planners today are trying to control and direct the processes in order to make them less wasteful and painful.

Urban life and personality

The city is a place of contrasts. Cities are centers of learning, of the arts, of science and medicine, of excitement, glamor, and "progress," while rural areas have been charged with provincialism, superstition, ignorance, and bigotry. Cities are also centers of vice and crime, of frivolous extravagance, of unbridled self-indulgence, and of insincere pretension. In short, the city reveals in vivid contrast most of the dominant characteristics of the culture, and has been a source of endless inspiration to artists and writers, as in this example:

For Manila is a city like all cities—changeless and changing. Giving and taking back. Harsh and yet tender as a child's caress. And unlike other cities,

it is the east and the west meeting at last. It is the Malay and the Latin. The American and the Chinese. . . . The city of the strident voice and the brick and cement jungles, and the city with the hidden lullabies and the warm hand. Cankered by ugliness and evil, spiked with violence and sudden death, it has its moments of breathless beauty and primal innocence. And if a man could see his way clear through to the very core of the city, he might yet apprehend the final meaning which could be the germ of his fulfillment. (Vincente Rivera, Jr., "This is Manila," *Sunday Times Magazine* (Manila), Nov. 20, 1953, pp. 9–10.)

A vacation is merely a change of scene for tightly scheduled activities.

Even though poetic rather than sociological, this description still carries a sense of the heterogeneity and contrast of the city. What are the dominant characteristics of the city, and how do they shape urban life and personality?

Speed and tension. The city is always in a hurry. Work and play are timed by the clock as we proceed from deadline to deadline. Lunches become business appointments, or possibly the busy executive eats lunch at his desk, barking commands between bites, while even the most humble worker must catch the bus and punch the time clock. Genuine relaxation is impossible for many urbanites, and a vacation is merely a change of scene for tightly scheduled activities.

Anonymity. The sheer pressure of numbers makes for anonymity. Of course there are groups within which the urbanite is known as a person, but much of his routine life is spent in the anonymous crowd—the *Lonely Crowd* of David Riesman [1950]. The heterogeneity of city life, with its mixture of people of all races, creeds, classes, occupations, and ethnic origins heightens this sense of anonymity. Differing interests separate people from any intimate acquaintance with others whom they meet in passing.

In the "skid rows" are the extremes of urban anonymity—the forgotten men and women of obscure past and uncertain future. They exist outside the pale of organized conventional living, their lives centered in the rooming- or flophouse, the cheap tavern, and perhaps the rescue mission. Here deviants may cluster and pursue their deviation with a minimum of interference. They are the defeated refuse of our social system, resigned, and often contented with a social role which demands little and offers little [Bogue, 1963; Wallace, 1965, 1968]. In recent years, the skid rows have been shrinking and may soon disappear [VanderKooi, 1973].

Social distance. City people are physically crowded but socially distant. Social distance is a product of anonymity, impersonality, and heterogeneity. Ethnic differences are one form of heterogeneity, dividing people into groups which often dislike or disdain one another. But occupational differences may be even more important sources of social distance. Unlike the agricultural community, the city has no common occupational focus which serves as a common interest for urbanites. Workers may follow any one of thousands of different occupations and have little understanding of, or interest in, other lines of work. The varieties of work attract people with a great range of education, skills, training, and temperament. This diversity of interests, backgrounds, and economic levels means that the individual learns to reveal only the side of the personality which the other person can be expected to understand. This constant masking of one's true

feelings adds up to a great lack of understanding. The great city which multiplies contacts also produces loneliness. From this loneliness a person often flees into a frantic effort to adapt to changing popular tastes in order to prove to blasé neighbors that one really "belongs" and thus merits at least a segment of their attention. The city is a place of outward conformity and inner reservations, of "front" and conspicuous consumption, of "keeping up with the Joneses." When people cannot know us for what we are, they must judge us by what they see. Hence the great importance of the well-tailored appearance, the impressive car, the occupational title, and the "good" address.

City people may have as many primary-group associates as rural people, and may see them more often. But whereas *most* of the rural person's daily contacts are primary, *most* routine social contacts in the city are impersonal, segmented, and correct. Formal politeness takes the place of genuine friendliness. The telephone and the printed checklist make it possible to contact people impersonally when necessary while keeping them at a distance. Urbanites become nigh-dwellers, not neighbors. Apartment dwellers may live for years with little or no acquaintance with many of the other occupants. Geography is a basis for grouping among rural farm people, both because of scarcity of neighbors and because of the community of interests which develops from their common problems and life-styles. Urban dwellers have no such scarcity of neighbors, and one's immediate neighbors rarely share much community of interest with one. Instead, those persons with whom one shares a community of interest are likely to be scattered throughout the area. Thus common interest replaces geographic proximity as a basis for grouping in the city. Toward that great mass of people with whom one rubs elbows daily, but with whom one shares neither kinship nor common interest, one is formal and correct. The ability of urbanites to look past or through people without seeing them is quite disconcerting to many rural visitors.

Regimentation. The pressure of numbers requires that urban life be highly regimented. Traffic lights control the flow of traffic; elevators and escalators move on schedule. The city dweller learns to work by the clock, under close supervision, often following instructions to the letter without any effort to understand what one is doing or why. Changes in routine are decreed from above and must be coordinated by the electronic computer, which places each human robot in the right spot at the right time performing the right function. Even recreation for children is organized, and the harried housewife races to get Junior to his club at 4:15 so that he will be on time for the period of "freeplay." Such control is sometimes irksome, but the true city dweller has learned to accept the idea that most of life is according to plan, and to justify subservience to regulation on the ground of efficiency.

What results do these conditions of urban life have on personality? Very little actual research has been done on this question, although it has attracted a great deal of sociological speculation. Some sociologists suspect that urban life produces greater emotional tension and insecurity than does rural life, and some empirical evidence supports this conclusion. The rates of mental illness are higher in the city than in rural areas. It is, however, not clear whether the city causes more mental disorder, attracts the maladjusted person to the city, or merely locates and diagnoses more accurately the extent of mental illness in the population. One well-controlled study some years ago found that farm and small-town children show a higher level of personal adjustment than urban children, with greater self-reliance, a greater sense of personal worth, and fewer feelings of nonbelonging [Mangus, 1948]. Although insecurity and rejection are entirely possible in a rural setting, the heterogeneous and anonymous nature of the city probably increases insecurity and the sense of nonbelonging.

Segmentation of personality is a necessary technique for coping with the multiple human contacts of an urban area. Most routine urban contacts are of secondary-group rather than primary-group in nature. Most contacts are instrumental; that is, we use another person as a necessary functionary to fulfill our purposes. We do not ordinarily interact with entire persons, but with people in terms of their formal roles as mailmen, bus drivers, elevator operators, salespersons, and other functionaries. We thus interact with only a segment of the person, not with the whole person. Such casual, superficial, short-lived relations with segments of people constitute a large part of the urbanite's social contacts, in contrast to the rural dweller, who has relatively fewer contacts with anyone whom he does not know well or with whom he fails to interact as a complete person [Sorokin and Zimmerman, 1929, pp. 48–58]. Even the superficial camaraderie with the taxicab driver is not genuine informal social interaction, but is a standardized part of the service [Davis, 1959].

All this does not, however, mean that the urbanite feels any less sense of local identity than country people. A recent study finds that feelings of attachment to the community are highly affected by length of residence in the community, but are not affected by the size of the community [Kasarda and Janowitz, 1974]. Nor are urbanites less happy, for research shows that happiness, also, is unrelated to community size [Fischer, 1973b]. Urban life and personality are in some degree different from, but not necessarily less desirable than, rural life and personality.

The worldwide urban culture

Is there an urban culture which is shared by cities everywhere, or are these conditions of urban life and personality unique to the Western world? The descriptions of cities, city life, and urban problems show a good deal of similarity, wherever the cities are located [Motwani, 1951; Miner, 1952, 1967; Abu-Lughod, 1961; Rose, 1967]. An urban society operates in roughly similar fashion wherever urbanization has taken place. Regardless of the cultural setting, urbanization brings certain inescapable consequences—population density, anonymity, impersonality, regimentation, and segmentation of personality. Urban people reveal certain differences from country people everywhere. All over the world, the rural village communities are changing, old traditions are crumbling, and new technologies and new patterns of work and social life are emerging [Halpern, 1967].

The antiurban bias

Ever since their earliest appearance, cities have been viewed with suspicion by rural peoples. The Old Testament prophets were rural men, denouncing the sins and vices of the wicked cities. Jefferson despised cities and felt that only a nation of freeholding farmers could possibly remain a democracy. Even many city people share the antiurban bias, which sees the city as a center of sin and crime, of trickery and hypocrisy, of political corruption, of frivolity and superficiality, and of vexing problems of all sorts. Meanwhile the country is assumed to be a haven of simple honesty and rugged integrity, where good things grow and God's own people dwell. The antiurban bias is revealed in the widespread assumption that the country or small town is a better place to raise children, that farming and raising food is more noble than other work, that "grass roots democracy" is more genuine and rural voters more trustworthy, and that rural life and rural people are simply "better" in nearly every way. Even social research follows the antiurban bias. Most urban research shows what a mess the city is in, while funded research on rural life is generally screened to avoid any data which would challenge the assumption that "the rural community is a good place to live" [Olson, 1964].

All of these assumptions are dubious, and many of them are demonstrably false. Urban and rural life are *different,* but whether one is better than the other is a question of values. The "goodness of life" in a community cannot be measured until we agree on what measures to use. If high health levels, high average incomes, higher educational levels, and many social amenities are the values chosen, then city life is better. If a quiet, less complicated life is preferred, then the country has the edge. Obviously, this is a philosophical question, not a scientific question, and it should be remembered that the assumption of rural (or urban) superiority represents a bias, not a fact.

Rural and urban convergence

Although "rural" and "urban" are useful concepts, there has never been a sharp dividing line between them. Even before the suburban movement and the urbanization of rural life, the two life-styles converged in the *town.*

The town

The town is intermediate between rural and urban communities. It is too large for all inhabitants to be acquainted with one another, yet small enough for informal relationships to predominate. Social behavior more closely resembles the rural than the metropolitan city pattern. There is no census definition for the town; the census classifies any settlement of over 2,500 persons as "urban" and all else as "rural." Sociological studies of the town have seldom bothered to define it, but the towns studied have never exceeded a few thousand people.

Most towns are either county seats or rural trading centers. The county seat towns are usually stagnant, and the rural trading towns are usually declining as the rural farm population falls. A great many of the youth must migrate elsewhere for employment, giving the town an abnormal population distribution and a "dead" atmosphere. About the only towns showing growth are those close enough to cities to become commuter suburbs, or so located as to attract industry (having water supply, labor supply, transportation, and proximity to markets), or those where tourism and recreation are thriving.

The local autonomy of the small town has eroded under the impact of the mass society. Martindale and Hanson [1969, p. 6] find the townspeople divided between "locals" who would like to preserve local self-sufficiency and "cosmopolitans" who would orient local life to the national economy and the mass society.

The rural nonfarmers

The "rural nonfarm" category has been our most rapidly growing population segment, increasing by 32 percent between 1950 and 1960, and by 48 percent between 1960 and 1970, by which time one-fifth of the population fell into this category. While often called "suburbanites," either their villages are too small (under 2,500) or their settlement is too thinly scattered to be defined as "urbanized areas." These people are not engaged in farming, and many commute to urban areas for jobs, shopping, and entertainment. They are "rural" only by census definition; their lifestyle is a rural-urban blend.

The fading rural-urban distinction

Urban-rural differences of all sorts are rapidly shrinking in the Western world, and soon this will probably be true everywhere. Suburbanites who sought to flee the racial tensions, congestion, pollution, and tax crises of the city are now finding these problems catching up with them. Even this difference is fading.

The rural-urban distinction has already become secondary to the occupational distinction in importance [Stewart, 1958; Dewey, 1960]. The distinctive rural pattern of life is more closely linked to an agricultural occupation than to mere residence in a rural area. A study of rural-urban differences in interpersonal relations found that farm people differed considerably from urban residents, while there was comparatively little difference between urban and rural nonfarm people [Reiss, 1959]. Clearly, occupation has become more important than rural or urban residence as a clue to one's personality and way of life. Many sociologists today are concluding that the urban-rural distinction is no longer an important one for social analysis [Abrahamson, 1974]. We now have an *urban* culture, in which place of residence is one of the least important of all social indicators in the United States. In less developed and urbanized societies, however, the rural-urban distinction remains significant [Rosen, 1973].

Nor should it be assumed that urbanization *necessarily* brings anomie, disorganization, and a lack of informal primary-group relationships. Earlier observers of urbanism were impressed by these features of urban life [Park et al., 1925; Sorokin and Zimmerman, 1929; Wirth, 1938]. But either the observers exaggerated these characteristics, or urbanites have changed. Some modern studies have found that alienation and anomie are no more widespread in highly urbanized than in less highly urbanized areas [Greer and Kube, 1959; Fischer, 1973a]. As urbanism increases, neighboring and participation in formal organizations decline, but primary-group relationships within kinship and friendship groups increase. When rural people migrate to the city, they do not enter a social vacuum but rely heavily upon relatives for social interaction [Blumberg and Bell, 1959]. Instead of the extended family declining in importance with urbanization, research finds that the extended family is an even more important unit in large cities than in rural areas [Key, 1961]. Apparently as urbanism increases and people tend to become anonymous members of the community, they rely more heavily upon close friends and relatives for intimate response, identity, and a sense of belonging. The rise of the proportion of secondary contacts with urbanism implies no absolute weakening of primary-group life.

The future of cities

Much of the popular literature on the "crisis of the cities" implies that the city is doomed. This is nonsense! Unless modern civilization disappears, the city will survive, because the large city is essential to modern civilization. True, the problems of the modern city are grave, but ways to solve or endure them will be found.

The new town movement

It is well over a century since the first "new towns" were founded in England and the United States. The idea was to avoid the dreary squalor of endless big-city growth by founding many self-contained, self-supporting new towns, pleasantly planned for efficiency and beauty. A few striking successes, such as Tapiola, Finland, show how a city can be both efficient and lovely [Clapp, 1971; Evans, 1972; Thomas and Cresswell, 1973].

While holding promise of a far more pleasant life for those fortunate enough to inhabit them, new towns are no cure for the problems of existing cities. They require a huge initial investment, and most of the new town developments in the United States are in financial difficulty. In the United States, they generally have a "country club" atmosphere, excluding all who are not moderately prosperous. By design, the new towns are kept to a modest size, and cannot be the magnet for artists, intellectuals, power-seekers, and "happenings" which make the great city a less secure but more exciting place to live. Some residents of the new towns complain that life there is safe, efficient, and comfortable, but just a bit dull. Thus the new towns escape some urban problems while creating others; yet on balance, the new towns offer to some people a more civilized pattern of urban living

than they now experience [Business Week, Nov. 22, 1969, pp. 130ff.: Canty, 1969; Schaffer, 1970; Knittel, 1973; Brooks, 1974]. But a new town would need to be completed every week if even a third of America's urban growth were to be accommodated, and, as this is written, most of the new towns in the United States are in serious financial difficulty [Business Week, Mar. 24, 1975, pp. 70–71]. Consequently, most of our urban growth may be expected to follow conventional patterns.

City planning and urban renewal

One commonly recommended antidote for urban problems today is city planning. Practically every city has a city-planning board, although often it does little but decide upon the location of highways, public buildings, and upon zoning changes. Any comprehensive planning is certain to meet opposition from many vested interests. Yet without comprehensive planning and execution of these plans, the American city faces accelerating decay. Slums are spreading faster than they are being cleared. Uncoordinated, piecemeal development of the urban fringe and of the "strip" cities is certain to mean great waste and agonizing future problems. Sewers, water mains, and expressways, built *after* many homes and buildings are constructed, will require expensive demolition. One suburb will wind up with lots of children to educate, while another suburb will have the industrial properties which make up the tax base needed to finance good schools. Certain areas will begin to have costly floods when the development of adjacent areas alters the watershed. Quiet residential areas will become noisy thoroughfares because of developments in adjacent areas. Problems like these are the fruit of uncoordinated, unplanned regional development. There are, as yet, few planning authorities with power to make, let alone enforce, the execution of plans for an entire metropolitan area. Eventually, after the problems have become intolerable and most of the mistakes have already been made, we shall probably create the plans. They will need to include the provision of adequate public facilities such as recreation centers, public-health units, and schools; the necessary supplies of clean air, light, and water, along with provisions for sewage disposal; the guidance and control of the restless youth of our cities; and finally the overwhelming problem of urban traffic. In some cases the unit of planning is an urban neighborhood, whereas other problems may demand state, regional, or even national attention.

Urban renewal programs are now a fixture of nearly every large American city. Congress in 1966 authorized a "model cities" program, administered by the Model Cities Administration of the Department of Housing and Urban Development. This was intended to show, in a few cities, what a coordinated attack on a city's multiple problems could accomplish. The success to date has not been impressive. Many new civic and office buildings, and some middle-income housing have been built. Slums have been shifted around. New Haven, Connecticut, had a most impressive series of urban renewal projects, designed to rescue the decaying areas of the city with reconstruction, to rescue disadvantaged groups with job training and other services, and, hopefully, to prevent the outbreak of riots and civil disorders. Yet all this did not prevent New Haven from having a riot in 1967. According to some critics, a failure to consult the poor, whom many of the "improvements" displaced rather than helped, was primarily responsible [Powledge, 1970]. Following the wave of urban riots of 1967, many cities launched new programs designed to ease urban tensions, but they have been more palliative than corrective, and have been, at best, no more than a modest success [Bayton, 1969; Marshall Kaplan, 1970; Pressman and Wildausky, 1974]. In some cases, renewal and model cities plans ran into furious local opposition from citizen groups, which charged that the plans favored developers and

business interests at the expense of the people [Frazier, 1972; Stein, 1972].

The enormously difficult questions of how to arrest urban blight and reconstruct the social life of our cities are too complicated to be treated here. These problems fill other textbooks for other courses. Meanwhile, debate on the means and ends of urban planning and reconstruction continues [Bellush and Hausknecht, 1967; Erber, 1970; Chartrand, 1971; Carey and Mapes, 1972; Warren, 1973]. Cities are as old as recorded history, but only within the lifetime of living people have we begun to live in an urban society. And only within the memory of today's college undergraduates have we begun seriously to consider how we can organize an urban society for our comfort and contentment.

Summary

A *community* is usually defined as the residents of an area within which all a group's life activities can be carried on. Rural and urban people have been different because the physical and social conditions of life were different in urban and rural communities. The traditional rural community tended to be a folk society. Its isolation, homogeneity, agricultural occupation, and subsistence economy all tended to develop people who were thrifty, hardworking, conservative, and ethnocentric. Changing technology has brought a rural revolution, with reduced isolation, commercialized large-scale farming, and a way of life very similar in many respects to urban patterns.

Cities become possible when an agricultural surplus develops, together with improved means of transportation, and tend to be located at "breaks in transportation." Attempts to explain the ecological pattern of American cities have produced the concentric zone, sector, and multiple-nuclei theories, none of which any city perfectly fits but which many cities somewhat resemble. The most significant current developments in city structure are the *metropolitan area,* including the *suburb,* which now accounts for most of our current population growth. The rapid growth of the black population of the central cities is now slowing down, since most blacks are now urban. As yet, there has been little black migration to the suburbs.

Slums are a product of the low income of slum residents, setting in motion a cause-and-effect circle of property neglect by landlords and property abuse by tenants. Public housing has had only limited success in arresting urban blight, in part because it intensifies the isolation of the poor from the rest of the society.

The city is a conglomeration of *natural areas,* constantly forming and shifting through the *ecological processes* of concentration, centralization, decentralization, segregation, and invasion. The *invasion cycle* has several stages: the initial influx, reaction, general influx, climax, and succession.

Urban life and personality are affected by the physical and social conditions of urban living—speed and tension, anonymity, social distance, and regimentation. These conditions produce impersonality, insecurity, and segmentation of personality, which appear to be universal characteristics of urbanization all over the world. The widespread assumption that these differences make rural life and rural people "better" is known as the *antiurban bias.* Today, urban and rural differences are rapidly shrinking in the Western world and will eventually do so elsewhere. The rural-urban distinction is already less important than occupational classification as a clue to one's personality and way of life. The *town* is an example of rural-urban convergence, with townspeople divided upon whether to seek to retain small-town self-sufficiency or to seek integration into the national economy. The rapidly growing rural non-farm category holds a blend of rural and urban life.

The *new town movement* is an attempt to siphon people and industry into new planned communities. *Urban renewal* and *city planning* are an attempt—not yet highly successful—to grapple with the increasingly grave problems of the city.

Questions and projects

1. Why did prehistoric people build no cities?
2. To what extent does folk society survive in rural America today? Where and why has it most completely disappeared from rural America?
3. How are the personality characteristics of rural and urban people a product of their physical and social conditions of life? What sort of problems are faced by rural migrants to the city?
4. What has produced the rural revolution? What has this done to rural-urban differences?
5. Why has "conspicuous consumption" been more of an urban than a rural pattern? Is this relation changing today? How or why?
6. Are the "rural nonfarm" people closer to the rural or to the urban pattern in personality and life style?
7. Are rural social problems as grave as urban social problems? Why do they attract less concern?
8. What causes city slums? What causes rural slums? How do rural slums resemble and differ from city slums?
9. Who is to blame for inner-city property decay and abandonment?
10. Why should urban planning be so difficult? Why can't planners devise a workable plan and carry it through?
11. Take the city you know best and apply each of the three theories of city structure. Which fits it best? How well does the theory describe the actual arrangement of this city?
12. Trace the stages of the invasion cycle for an area of the city you know best. Try to date each stage. How long did each stage last and how long did

the entire cycle require? Was it a happy or painful period?

13. What factual data can you find to measure the "goodness" of life in rural and urban society? What values are used in this evaluation?

14. Read Edward T. Chase, "Jam on the Côte d'Azur," *Reporter,* Sept. 28, 1961, pp. 44–46, or Wilfred Owen, *Cities in the Motor Age,* The Viking Press, Inc., New York, 1959. Then prepare your answer to the question. Are automobiles an asset or a blight upon the modern city?

Suggested readings

*BANFIELD, EDWARD D.: *The Unheavenly City: The Nature and Future of Our Urban Crisis,* Little, Brown and Co., Boston, 1970; *The Unheavenly City Revisited,* Little, Brown and Co., Boston, 1974. A diagnosis of urban ills which is highly critical of all "liberal" remedies.

BELL, WENDALL, AND MARION D. BOAT: "Urban Neighborhoods and Informal Social Relations, " *American Journal of Sociology,* 62:391–398, January, 1957; Bobbs-Merrill reprint S-14. Research data on the extent and intimacy of neighborhood contacts in the city.

FUERST, J. S.: "Class, Family, and Housing," *Society,* Nov./Dec., 1974, pp. 48–53. Tells why public housing filled with the welfare poor, with no stable middle-income families, is doomed to failure.

GRIFFIN, CHARLES W., JR.: *Taming the Last Frontier: A Prescription for the Urban Crisis,* Pitman Publishing Co., New York, 1974. A semipopular discussion of needs and plans for city survival.

*HALPERN, JOEL M.: *The Changing Village Community,* Prentice-Hall, Inc., Englewood Cliffs, N.J., 1967. A brief description of the revolutionary changes in village life throughout the world.

*HARRISON, BENNETT: *Urban Economic Development,* The Urban Institute, Washington, D.C., 1974. Discusses the problem of economic rehabilitation of the ghetto.

*JACOBS, JANE: *The Death and Life of Great American Cities,* Random House, Inc., New York, 1961. An attack on conventional city planning and a call for a different approach.

MARTINDALE, DON: "Prefatory Remarks: The Theory of the City," introduction to MAX WEBER, *The City,* The Free Press of Glencoe, Inc., New York, 1958. A penetrating review of sociological theory on the city.

*MICHELSON, WILLIAM H.: *Man and His Urban Environment,* Addison-Wesley Publishing Company, Inc., Reading, Mass., 1970. An attempt to integrate significant theory and research on the relation between urban environments and man's social life. Advanced content written in simple language.

ROGERS, EVERETT M., AND RABEL J. BURDGE, *Social Change in Rural Societies,* Appleton-Century-Crofts, Inc., New York, 1972. A textbook in rural sociology.

STERNLIEB, GEORGE, AND ROBERT W. BURCHELL: *Residential Abandonment: The Tenement Landlord Revisited,* Center for Urban Policy Research, Rutgers University, New Brunswick, N.J., 1973. Why and how slum property decays and becomes abandoned.

*WALLACE, SAMUEL E., *Skid Row as a Way of Life,* Harper & Row, Publishers, Inc., New York, 1965. A readable but sociologically sophisticated analysis of vagrancy and the skid row subculture.

WIRTH, LOUIS W.: "Urbanism as a Way of Life," *American Journal of Sociology,* 44:1–25, July, 1938; Bobbs-Merrill reprint S-320. A classic essay describing urban life and personality.

Six/Social change and social policy

Part Six deals with change and the effort to effect change. Chapter 20, "Social and Cultural Change," discusses the forces which encourage and resist change and the social consequences of change when it is accomplished. Chapter 21, "Social Movements," describes some more or less organized efforts of people to promote changes they desire or to resist changes they deplore.

Chapter 20 ● Social and cultural change

Homouda Awadan's nights have been restless recently, mainly because his cow no longer sleeps in the same room with him.

Awadan is one of 2,000 peasants moved last summer from overpopulated mud-hut villages to Ibis, a modern village with brick houses, electric lighting, running water and special pens for cattle.

The operation is sponsored by the U.S. Point Four program and the Egyptian Agriculture Department.

Life in the modern village has posed many problems to the fellaheen [peasants], many of whom came from villages that have seen little change since the days of the pharaohs.

All his life Awadan has slept with his cow, his chief work animal and provider of milk, yogurt and white cheese. Keeping the animal inside the house kept his floor littered with animal refuse, but Awadan could not take a chance on the beast being stolen.

"For the past three nights I have been waking in the middle of the night to check on my cow down in the village," said Awadan, still not used to the separation from his most treasured possession.

Awadan often yearns for the uncomplicated life of the mud village, but he remembers the five acres of land the government gave him and decides to stay. He never owned land be-

fore. He had to rent it from a big landowner.

Sheikh Rashad, director of the co-operative union at Ibis village, said it took much convincing to move the fellaheen into the model village. They are not inclined to move, no matter how crowded, he said.

In spite of all preparations, unexpected situations arose, Rashad said. Stacks of dry wood soon began appearing on top of the houses, similar to the mud villages, he added. At Ibis they had special storage rooms for wood, but the fellaheen would not use them. *(Associated Press, Nov. 9, 1959.)*

All cultures are constantly changing—some rapidly and some very slowly. Even when it tries to do so, no society succeeds in exactly copying and transmitting the culture of its ancestors. This fluidity is most easily illustrated by language changes. English has changed so greatly that most students have their troubles with Shakespeare and are hopelessly lost in Chaucer. In 1755 Samuel Johnson published his dictionary in the hope that it would stabilize word meanings and stop language changes, but soon he confessed that he had failed. None of the historic efforts to preserve a culture without change has been more than temporarily and partially successful. Social change is continuous and irresistible. Only its speed and direction vary.

There is a distinction between _social change_—changes in the social structure and social relationships of the society—and _cultural change_—changes in the culture of a society. Some social changes might include changes in the age distribution, average educational level, or birthrate of a population; or the decline of informality and personal neighborliness as people shift from village to city; or the change in the relationship between workers and employers when unions become organized; or the change of the husband from the boss to a partner in today's democratic family. Cultural changes might include such things as the invention and popularization of the automobile, the addition of new words to our language, changing concepts of propriety and morality, new forms of music, art, or dance, or the general trend toward sex equality. Yet the concepts overlap. The trend toward sex equality involves both a changing set of cultural norms concerning male-female roles, and some changing social relationships as well. Nearly all important changes involve both social and cultural aspects. In practice, therefore, the distinction is seldom a very important one, and the two terms are often used interchangeably. Sometimes the term _sociocultural change_ is used to include changes of both kinds.

There is an important distinction between social change and _progress_. The term "progress" carries a value judgment. Progress means change in a desirable direction. Desirable as measured by whose values? Are faster automobiles, taller buildings, higher incomes, and greater acceptance of divorce and abortion desirable? Not all Americans are agreed. Since progress is an evaluative term, social scientists prefer the neutrally descriptive term "change."

There are a number of different theories of social and cultural change [Ryan, 1969, chap. 2; Applebaum, 1970; Allen, 1971]. The equilibrium and conflict theories of change were discussed in Chapter 4. Cyclical theories of change are as old as Aristotle, and among many modern proponents of cyclical theories of change, those of a philosopher, Spengler [1918], an historian, Toynbee [1935–1961], and a sociologist, Sorokin [1941] are notable. But a study of the conflicting grand theories of change may be of less use to the introductory student than a study of the conditions and processes of change.

Process of social change

Discovery

A _discovery_ is _a shared human perception of an aspect of reality which already exists._ Humans discovered the principle of the lever, the circulation of the blood, and the conditioned reflex. A discovery is an addition to the world's store of verified knowledge. A discovery adds something new to the culture because, although this aspect of reality may always have existed, it became part of the culture only after its discovery.

A discovery becomes a factor in social change only when it is put to use. A discovery may become part of the background of knowledge which people use in evaluating their present practices. Thus the recent discoveries of physiology and psychology that males and females are alike in their intellectual capacities did not _compel_ men to alter their attitudes toward the status of women; but the discoveries made the nineteenth-century patriarch look ridiculous and diluted men's determination to preserve traditional male dominance.

When new knowledge is used to develop new technology, vast changes generally follow. The ancient Greeks knew about the power of steam, and before A.D. 100 Hero of Alexandria had built a small steam engine as a toy, but steam power produced no social changes until it was put to serious use nearly 2,000 years later. Discoveries become a factor in social change when new knowledge is put to new uses.

Invention

An _invention_ is often defined as _a new combination or a new use of existing know-_

ledge. Thus George Selden in 1895 combined a liquid-gas engine, a liquid-gas tank, a running-gear mechanism, an intermediate clutch, a driving shaft, and a carriage body, and patented this contraption as an automobile. None of these ideas were new; the only novelty was the combined use of them. The Selden patent was attacked and eventually revoked by the courts on the ground that he did not originate the idea of combining these items.

While existing elements are used in a new invention, it is the *idea* of combining them in a useful way that produces something which never before existed. Thus iron, with the addition of small amounts of other metals, became steel, a new metal with properties which no metal known at that time could equal. Likewise a round slice of tree log and a length of tree limb were not new, but the wheel and axle were new. The wheel did not exist until someone had, and carried to successful use, the idea of using a limb and a slice of a tree log in this manner.

Inventions may be classified as *material inventions,* such as the bow and arrow, telephone, or airplane, and *social inventions,* such as the alphabet, constitutional government, or the corporation. In each case, old elements are used, combined, and improved for a new application. Invention is thus a continuing process, with each new invention the last in a long series of preceding inventions and discoveries. In a popularly written book, Burlingame [1947] has analyzed a number of familiar inventions, showing how each began hundreds or thousands of years ago and passed through dozens of preliminary inventions and intermediate stages. Invention is not strictly an individual matter; it is a social process involving an endless series of modifications, improvements, and recombinations. As Gillin [1948, pp. 158–163] pointed out, each invention may be new in *form, function,* and *meaning.* "Form" refers to the shape of the new object or the actions of the new behavior trait; "function" refers to what the invention does; "meaning" refers to the long-range conse-

quences of its use. To these three, we might also add that an invention may be new in *principle,* that is, in the basic scientific law upon which it is based.

The jet engine and the piston engine use the same principle (expansion of burning gases) but differ in form (one uses expanding gases directly for thrust, the other to push a piston in a cylinder). The steam engine and the piston gasoline engine are similar in form but differ in principle (one creates expanding gases by boiling water, the other by burning gasoline). The bow and arrow differs in both principle and form from the primitive spear but has the same function and meaning. The wheeled cart was new in all respects (in principle, since the load was carried by wheel and axle instead of being dragged or packed; in form, since it was new in design; in function, since it carried both people and possessions; in meaning, since it made large-scale, long-distance overland transport possible). Very few inventions are new in all four respects.

The term *innovation* has sometimes been used to include both discoveries and inventions [Barnett, 1953, pp. 7–8]. In either case, something new has been added to the culture.

Diffusion

Even the most inventive society invents only a modest proportion of its innovations. Most of the social changes in all known societies have developed through *diffusion, the spread of culture traits from group to group.* Diffusion operates both within societies and between societies. Jazz originated among black musicians of New Orleans and became diffused to other groups within the society. Later it spread to other societies and has now been diffused throughout the civilized world.

Diffusion takes place whenever societies come into contact. Societies may seek to prevent diffusion by forbidding contact, as did the Old Testament Hebrews:

When the Lord thy God shall bring thee into the

Most of the content of any complex culture has been diffused from other societies.

land whither thou goest to possess it, and hath cast out many nations before thee . . . thou shalt smite them and utterly destroy them; thou shalt make no covenant with them, nor shew mercy unto them; neither shalt thou make marriages with them. . . . For they will turn away thy son from following me, that they may serve other gods. . . . But . . . ye shall destroy their altars, and break down their images, and cut down their groves, and burn their graven images with fire. (Deuteronomy 7:1–5.)

Like most efforts to prevent intercultural contacts, this prohibition failed. The Old Testament tells how the Hebrews persisted in mingling and intermarrying with the surrounding tribes, adopting bits of their cultures in the process. Whenever cultures come into contact, some exchange of culture traits always takes place.

Most of the content of any complex culture has been diffused from other societies. Ralph Linton has written a famous passage which tells how 100 percent Americans have actually borrowed most of their culture from other societies.

Our solid American Citizen awakens in a bed built on a pattern which originated in the Near East but which was modified in Northern Europe before it was transmitted to America. He throws back covers made from cotton, domesticated in India, or linen, domesticated in the Near East, or silk, the use of which was discovered in China. All of these materials have been spun and woven by processes invented in the Near East. He slips into his moccasins, invented by the Indians of the Eastern wood-

lands, and goes to the bathroom, whose fixtures are a mixture of European and American inventions, both of recent date. He takes off his pajamas, a garment invented in India, and washes with soap invented by the ancient Gauls. He then shaves, a masochistic rite which seems to have been derived from either Sumer or Ancient Egypt.

Returning to the bedroom, he removes his clothes from a chair of Southern European type and proceeds to dress. He puts on garments whose form originally derived from the skin clothing of the nomads of the Asiatic steppes, puts on shoes made from skins tanned by a process invented in ancient Egypt and cut to a pattern derived from the classical civilizations of the Mediterranean, and ties around his neck a strip of bright-colored cloth which is a vestigial survival of the shoulder shawls worn by seventeenth century Croatians. Before going out for breakfast he glances through the window, made of glass invented in Egypt, and if it is raining puts on overshoes made of rubber discovered by the Central American Indians and takes an umbrella, invented in southeastern Asia. Upon his head he puts a hat made of felt, a material invented in the Asiatic steppes.

On his way to breakfast he stops to buy a paper, paying for it with coins, an ancient Lydian invention. At the restaurant a whole new series of borrowed elements confronts him. His plate is made of a form of pottery invented in China. His knife is of steel, an alloy first made in southern India, his fork a medieval Italian invention, and his spoon a derivative of a Roman original. He begins breakfast with an orange, from the eastern Mediterranean, a cantaloupe from Persia, or perhaps a piece of African watermelon. With this he has coffee, an Abyssinian plant, with cream and sugar. Both the domestication of cows and the idea of milking them originated in the Near East, while sugar was first made in India. After his fruit and first coffee he goes to waffles, cakes made by a Scandinavian technique from wheat domesticated in Asia Minor. Over these he pours maple syrup, invented by the Indians of the Eastern woodlands. As a side dish he may have the egg of a species of bird domesticated in Indo-China, or thin strips of the flesh of an animal domesticated in Eastern Asia which have been salted and smoked by a process developed in northern Europe.

When our friend has finished eating he settles back to smoke, an American Indian habit, consuming a plant domesticated in Brazil in either a pipe, derived from the Indians of Virginia, or a cigarette, derived from Mexico. If he is hardy enough he may even attempt a cigar, transmitted to us from the Antilles by way of Spain. While smoking he reads the news of the day, imprinted in characters invented by the ancient Semites upon a material invented in China, by a process invented in Germany. As he absorbs the accounts of foreign troubles he will, if he is a good conservative citizen, thank a Hebrew deity in an Indo-European language that he is a 100 percent American. (Ralph Linton, *The Study of Man,* © 1936, renewed 1964. Pp. 326–327. Reprinted by permission of Prentice-Hall, Englewood Cliffs, N.J.)

Diffusion is always a two-way process. Traits cannot diffuse unless there is some kind of contact between peoples, and these contacts always entail some diffusion in both directions. Europeans gave horses, firearms, Christianity, and whisky to the Indians in exchange for corn, potatoes, tobacco, and the canoe. Yet the exchange is often lopsided. When two cultures come into contact, the society with the simpler technology generally does the more borrowing. Within societies, low-status groups generally borrow more than high-status groups. Slave groups generally absorb the culture of their masters, while their own is forgotten or deliberately extinguished.

Diffusion is a selective process. A group accepts some culture traits from a neighbor, at the same time rejecting others. We accepted much of the Indian's food but rejected his religion. Indians quickly accepted the white man's horse but long rejected the white man's cow.

Diffusion generally involves some modification of the borrowed element. As noted earlier, each cultural trait has *principle, form, function,* and *meaning.* Any or all of these may change when a trait is diffused. When Europeans adopted Indian tobacco, they smoked it in a pipe somewhat like the Indian pipe, thus preserving the form, although they also added other forms—cigars, cigarettes, chewing tobacco, and snuff. But they entirely changed function and meaning. Indians smoked tobacco as a ceremonial ritual; Europeans used it

first as a medicine, and later for personal gratification and sociability. The outward forms of Christianity have been diffused more readily than the functions and meanings. In missionary areas many converts have accepted the forms of Christian worship while retaining many of their traditional supernatural beliefs and practices. Non-Western peoples have put tin cans and other Western artifacts to a variety of uses, both utilitarian and aesthetic. American colonists accepted maize (corn) from the Indians unchanged; it traveled to Europe, where it was used as food for animals but not for people; it was then diffused to West Africa, where it became a favorite food and even an offering to the gods. Endless examples could be cited to show how traits are nearly always modified as they are diffused.

Sociologists and anthropologists have made many research studies of the diffusion process [Allen, 1971, chap. 12]. Most of our aid programs in underdeveloped countries, as well as those for "underprivileged" groups in our own country, are primarily efforts to promote diffusion. Consequently, it is one of the most important topics in sociology.

Factors in the rate of change

Discovery, invention, and diffusion are processes of change. But what causes them to happen? We cannot answer this question without first examining the meaning of the term *cause.* A cause is sometimes defined as a phenomenon which *is both necessary and sufficient* to produce a predictable effect. It is necessary in that we never have this effect without this cause, and sufficient in that this cause, alone, always produces this effect. Thus defined, very few causes have been established in social science. Does drunkenness cause divorce? Many long-suffering souls put up with a drunken mate, while others divorce mates who are bone dry. Obviously, drunkenness is neither a necessary nor a sufficient condition to produce a divorce. Most causation in social science is multiple—that is, a number of factors interact in producing a result. What factors interact in producing a social change?

First of all, we note that the factors in social change are predominantly social and cultural, not biological or geographic. Not everyone accepts this view. Some people would attribute the rise and fall of great civilizations to changes in the biological characteristics of nations. Often these theories have a racial twist; a great civilization is said to arise from a vigorous, creative race, and falls when the race mixes with lesser breeds and dilutes its genius. According to an opposite version, a great burst of creativity follows a fortunate intermixture of races and dies out as the hybrid strain runs out. Most scientists reject all such theories. There is no convincing scientific evidence that any race differs from any other race in its biological basis for human learning, or that human biology has changed significantly during the last twenty-five thousand years or so. During the period of recorded history, our biological attributes appear to have been a constant, not a variable, in our behavior.

Physical environment

Major changes in the physical environment are quite rare, but very compelling when they happen. The desert wastes of North Africa were once green and well populated. Climates change, soil erodes, and lakes gradually turn into swamps and finally plains. A culture is greatly affected by such changes, although sometimes they come about so slowly that they are largely unnoticed. Human misuse can bring very rapid changes in physical environment which, in turn, change the social and cultural life of a people. Deforestation brings land erosion and reduces rainfall; overgrazing destroys the vegetation cover and promotes erosion. Much of the wasteland and desert land of the world is a testament to human ignorance and misuse [Mikesell, 1969; Horton and Leslie, 1974, chap. 20]. Human environmental de-

struction has been at least a contributing factor in the fall of most great civilizations.

Many human groups throughout history have changed their physical environments through migration. Especially in primitive societies, whose members are very directly dependent upon their physical environment, migration to a different environment brings major changes in culture. Civilization makes it easy to transport a culture and practice it in a new and different environment. The British colonial in the jungle outpost often persisted in taking afternoon tea and dressing for dinner. Yet no one would suggest that he was unaffected by the jungle environment; even civilized cultures are affected by a change of physical environment [Hoffman, 1973].

Population changes

A population change is itself a social change, but also becomes a causal factor in further social and cultural changes. When a thinly settled frontier fills up with people, the hospitality pattern fades away, secondary-group relations multiply, institutional structures grow more elaborate, and many other changes occur. A rapidly growing population must either migrate or improve its productive techniques. Great historic migrations and conquests—of the Huns, the Vikings, and many others—have arisen from the pressure of a growing population upon limited resources. Migration encourages further change, for it brings a group into a new environment, subjects it to new social contacts, and confronts it with new problems. No major population change leaves the culture unchanged. As this is written, many scholars are gravely wondering whether the population explosion threatens the total destruction of modern civilization.

Isolation and contact

Societies located at world crossroads have always been centers of change. Since most new traits come through diffusion, those societies in closest contact with other societies are likely to change most rapidly. In ancient times of overland transport, the land bridge connecting Asia, Africa, and Europe was the center of civilizing change. Later, sailing vessels shifted the center to the fringes of the Mediterranean Sea, and still later to the northwest coast of Europe. Areas of greatest intercultural contact are the centers of change. War and trade have always brought intercultural contact, and today tourism is adding to the contacts between cultures [Greenwood, 1972].

Conversely, isolated areas are centers of stability, conservatism, and resistance to change. Almost without exception, the most primitive tribes have been those who were the most isolated, like the polar Eskimos or the Aranda of Central Australia. Even among civilized peoples, isolation brings cultural stability. The most "backward" American groups have been found in the inaccessible hills and valleys of the Appalachians [Sherman and Henry, 1933; Surface, 1970].

Leyburn [1935] has shown how European groups who migrated to remote, isolated frontiers often retained many elements of their native culture long after they had been discarded by their parent society. Thus by the nineteenth century, the social life of the Boers in the Transvaal resembled the life of the late seventeenth-century Dutch more than that of their contemporaries in the Netherlands.

Ethnic enclaves, whose isolation is social and voluntary rather than geographic, show a similar conservatism, whether it be Americans in Spain [D. Nash, 1967], Amish in America [Hostettler, 1964], or Tristan Islanders in England [Munch, 1964, 1970]. Isolation invariably retards social change.

Structure of society and culture

The structure of a society affects its rate of change in subtle and not immediately apparent ways. Inkles and Smith [1974] conducted depth interviews in six developing countries, seeking to find out what made persons receptive to change. They found that persons who worked in a factory, had several years of education, and read newspapers were more receptive. A society which vests great authority in the very old people, as classical China did for centuries, is likely to be conservative and stable. A society which stresses conformity and trains the individual to be highly responsive to the group, such as the Zuñi, is less receptive to change than a society like the Ileo, who are highly individualistic and tolerate considerable cultural variability [Ottenberg, 1959].

A highly centralized bureaucracy is highly favorable to the promotion and diffusion of change [Dowdy, 1970], although bureaucracies have sometimes been used in an attempt to suppress change, usually with no more than temporary success.

When a culture is very highly integrated, so that each element is tightly interwoven with all the others in a mutually interdependent system, change is difficult and costly. Among a number of Nilotic African peoples, such as the Pakot, Masai, and Kipsizis, the culture is integrated around the cattle complex. Cattle are not only a means of subsistence; they are also a necessity for bride purchase, a measure of status, and an object of intense affection [Schneider, 1959]. Such a system is strongly resistant to social change. But when the culture is less highly integrated, so that work, play, family, religion, and other activities are less dependent upon one another, change is easier and more frequent. A tightly structured society, wherein every person's roles, duties, privileges, and obligations are precisely and rigidly defined, is less given to changes than a more loosely structured society wherein roles, lines of authority, privileges, and obligations are more open to individual rearrangement.

The structure of American society is highly conducive to social change. Our individualism, our lack of rigid social stratification, our relatively high proportion of achieved statuses, and our institutionalization of research all encourage rapid social change. Today tens of thousands of workers are systematically employed in finding new discoveries and inventions. This exploration is something new in the world's history. Our dazzling and sometimes upsetting rate of change is one consequence.

Attitudes and values

To us change seems normal, and most Westerners pride themselves upon being progressive and up to date. By contrast, the Trobriand Islanders off the coast of New Guinea had no concept of change, and did not even have any words in their language to express or describe change [Lee, 1959a, pp. 89–104]. When Westerners tried to explain the concept of change, the islanders could not understand what they were talking about. Societies obviously differ greatly in their general attitude toward change. A people who revere the past, worship their ancestors, honor and obey their elders, and are preoccupied with traditions and rituals will change slowly and unwillingly. When a culture has been relatively static for a long time, the people are likely to assume that it should remain so indefinitely. They are intensely and unconsciously ethnocentric; they assume that their customs and techniques are correct and everlasting. A possible change is unlikely even to be seriously considered. Change in such a society occurs mainly when it is too gradual to be noticed.

A rapidly changing society has a different attitude toward change, and this attitude is both cause and effect of the changes already taking place. Rapidly changing societies are aware of social change. They are somewhat skeptical and critical of some parts of their traditional culture and will consider and experiment with innovations. Such attitudes powerfully stimulate the proposal and acceptance of changes by individuals within the society. There may be variations between localities in attitude toward change. One study finds that farmers' acceptance of agricultural innova-

tions is affected by their impression of their local community's receptivity to the idea of change [Flinn, 1970].

Different groups within a locality or a society may show differing receptivity to change. Every changing society has its liberals and its conservatives. Literate and educated people tend to accept changes more readily than the illiterate and uneducated [Nwosu, 1971; Waisanen and Kumata, 1972]. The Amish in the United States have been notably resistant to change of every kind except, sometimes, in farming techniques. And a group may be highly receptive to change of one kind but highly resistant to changes of other kinds. Thus we can enter many churches of strikingly modern architecture and hear a sermon basically unchanged since the days of Luther.

Attitudes and values affect both the amount and the direction of social change. The ancient Greeks made great contributions to art and learning but little to technology. Work was done by slaves; to concern oneself with a slave's work was no proper task for a Greek scholar. No society has been equally dynamic in all aspects, and its values determine in which area—art, music, warfare, technology, philosophy, or religion—it will be inventive.

Perceived needs

A society's rate and direction of change are greatly affected by the needs its members perceive. "Needs" are subjective; they are real if people feel that they are real. In many underdeveloped and malnourished parts of the world, people not only need *more* food, they also need *different* foods, especially vegetables and legumes. Agricultural changes which bring *more* food are more readily accepted than those bringing *different* foods, for which they feel no need [Arensberg and Niehoff, 1971, p. 155]. Until people feel a need, nothing changes; only the perceived needs of a society count.

Some practical inventions languish until the

society discovers or develops a need for them. The zipper fastener was invented in 1891 but ignored for a quarter century. The pneumatic tire was invented and patented by Thompson in 1845 but was ignored until the popularity of the bicycle created an awareness of need for it; then it was reinvented by Dunlop in 1888.

It is often stated that changing conditions create new needs—genuine, objective needs, not just subjectively "felt" needs. Thus, urbanization created a need for sanitary engineering; the modern factory system created a need for labor unions; and the high-speed automobile created a need for superhighways. A culture is integrated, and therefore any changes in one part of the culture create a need for adaptive changes in related parts of the culture.

It is doubtless true that failure to recognize an objective need may have unpleasant consequences. For centuries, sickness and death were the price of our failure to recognize that urban growth made sanitary engineering a necessity. A more recent failure to recognize that death control creates a need for birth control has brought half the world to the brink of starvation. All this does not alter the fact that it is only those "needs" which are perceived as necessary which stimulate innovation and social change.

Necessity, however, is no guarantee that the needed invention or discovery will be made. At present, we perceive that we need cures for cancer and for the common cold, a pollution-free power source, and an effective protection against radioactivity. There is no certainty that we shall develop any of these. Necessity may be the mother of invention, but invention also needs a father—a cultural base to provide the necessary supporting knowledge and technique.

The cultural base

The cave man could make exceedingly few material inventions, for he had very little to work with. Even the bow and arrow combines a number of inventions and techniques—notching the bow ends, tying the bowstring, hafting and pointing the arrow, plus the idea and technique of shooting it. Not until these components were invented was it possible to invent the bow and arrow. By the *cultural base,* we mean *the accumulation of knowledge and technique* available to the inventor. As the cultural base grows, an increasing number of inventions and discoveries become possible. The invention of the geared wheel provided a component which has been used in countless inventions. The discovery of electromagnetism and the invention of the vacuum tube provided necessary components for hundreds of more recent inventions.

Unless the cultural base provides the necessary preceding inventions and discoveries, an invention cannot be completed. Leonardo da Vinci in the late fifteenth century sketched many machines which were entirely workable in principle and detail, but the technology of his day was incapable of building them. His drawings for the aerial bomb, hydraulic pump, air-conditioning unit, helicopter, machine gun, military tank, and many others were clear and workable, but the fifteenth century lacked the advanced metals, the fuels, the lubricants, and the technical skills necessary to carry his brilliant ideas into practical reality. Many inventive ideas have had to wait until the supporting gaps in knowledge and technique were filled in.

When all the supporting knowledge has been developed, the appearance of an invention or discovery becomes almost a certainty. In fact, it is quite common for an invention or discovery to be made independently by several persons at about the same time. Ogburn [1950, pp. 90–102], a sociologist who specialized in the study of social change, listed 148 such inventions and discoveries, ranging from the discovery of sun spots, independently discovered by Galileo, Fabricius, Scheiner, and Harriott, all in 1611, to the invention of the airplane by Langley (1893–1897), Wright (1895–1901), and perhaps others. In fact, disputes over who was first with an invention or a scientific discovery are common and sometimes acrimonious [Merton, 1957c]. When the cultural base provides all the supporting items of knowledge, it is very probable that one or more imaginative persons will put these items together for a new invention or discovery.

Cross-fertilization. The great importance of the cultural base is revealed by the principle of *cross-fertilization,* which states that discoveries and inventions in one field became useful in an entirely different field. Pasteur's germ theory of disease grew out of his efforts to tell France's vintners why their wine turned sour. The vacuum tube, developed for radio, made possible the electronic computer, which now aids research in nearly everything from astronomy to zoology. Certain radioactive materials, byproducts of the search for more deadly weapons, are now invaluable in medical diagnosis, therapy, and research. Stouffer's studies [1949], designed to show the armed services how to get more effective fighting men, also provided knowledge that was useful to students of group dynamics, race relations, and several other fields of sociology.

The exponential principle. This principle states that, as the cultural base grows, its possible uses tend to grow in a geometric ratio. To illustrate: If we have only two chemicals in a laboratory, only one combination (A-B) is possible; with three chemicals, four combinations are possible (A-B-C, A-B, A-C, and B-C); with four chemicals, ten combinations; with five chemicals, twenty-five, and so on. As the size of the cultural base grows by addition, the possible combinations of these elements grow by multiplication. This helps to explain today's high rate of discovery and invention [Hamblin et al., 1973]. A vast accumulation of scientific technical knowledge is shared by all the civilized societies, and from this base new inventions and discoveries flow in a rising tide.

Resistance to and acceptance of social change

Not all proposed innovations are accepted by the society. A process of *selective acceptance* operates as some innovations are accepted instantly and some only after long delay; some are rejected entirely; and others are accepted in part. Thus we accepted completely the Indians' corn, accepted and modified their tobacco, accepted in a very small, highly modified way their totemic clans (Boy Scout "beaver" and "wolverine" patrols), and totally rejected their religion. Acceptance of innovations is never automatic and is always selective according to a number of considerations.

Specific attitudes and values

Aside from its general attitude toward change, each society has many specific attitudes and values which cling to its objects and activities. When government agents introduced hybrid corn to the Spanish-American farmers of the Rio Grande Valley a few years ago, they readily adopted it because of its superior yield; but within three years, they had all returned to the old corn. They didn't like the hybrid corn because it didn't make good tortillas [Apodaca, 1952]. People's established likes and dislikes are important factors in social change.

If an object has a purely utilitarian value—that is, if it is valued because of what it will do—change may be accepted quite readily. Thus a study [Fliegel and Kivlin, 1966] of the acceptance of new farm practices by American farmers finds that those which are perceived as most profitable and least risky are most readily accepted. If some feature of the traditional culture is valued intrinsically—valued for itself, aside from what it will do—change is less readily accepted. To the American farmer, cattle are a source of income, to be bred, culled, and butchered whenever most profitable. But to many of the Nilotic peoples of Africa, cattle represent intrinsic values. The owner recognizes and loves each cow. To slaughter one would be like killing one of the family. A Pakot with a hundred cattle is rich and respected; one with only a dozen is poor; the man with no cattle is ignored as though he were dead. Efforts of colonial officials to get such peoples to manage their herds "rationally"—to cull their herds, breed only the best, and stop overgrazing their lands—have generally failed.

The average American, who usually takes a coldly rational, relatively unsentimental view of economic activities, finds it hard to appreciate the sentiments and values of non-Western peoples. He is irritated by the Biaga of Central India, who refused to give up their primitive digging sticks for the far superior moldboard plow. Why? The Biaga loved the earth as a kindly and generous mother; they would gently help her with the digging stick to bring forth her yield, but could not bring themselves to cut her "with knives" [Elwin, 1939, pp. 106–107]. The American is annoyed by the Ettwah Indians' unwillingness to adopt green manuring (plowing under a crop of green sanhemp as fertilizer). But to this Indian, "green manuring involves a very cruel act of plowing under the sanhemp leaf and stalk before they are ripe. This act involves violence" [Mayer, 1958, p. 209]. Yet is there any basic difference between these illustrations and an American's refusal to eat horse meat because it conflicts with his or her values? How about those American groups who reject abortion, divorce, or alcoholic beverages, or movies, or card playing because these would conflict with their values? To each of us, it seems entirely logical and right to reject any innovation that conflicts with our mores or values; when another group does likewise, their refusal often impresses us as stubborn ignorance. Such is ethnocentrism!

Demonstrability of innovations

An innovation is most quickly accepted when its usefulness can be easily demonstrated. The American Indians eagerly accepted the white man's gun, but have not accepted the white man's medicine, whose superiority is less easily demonstrated. Many inventions are so inefficient in their earlier stages that general acceptance is delayed until they are perfected. During the automobile's first three decades of development, public scorn was expressed by the derisive advice to "get a horse!" Early imperfections delay, but rarely prevent, the eventual acceptance of workable inventions.

An innovation is most quickly accepted when its usefulness can be easily demonstrated.

Some innovations can be demonstrated quite easily, on a small scale; others cannot be demonstrated without costly, large-scale trials. Most mechanical inventions can usually be tested in a few hours or days, and at modest cost. Most social inventions such as the corporation, social organization based on role rather than on kinship, or world government, are not easily tried out in the laboratory or testing bureau. Many social inventions can be tested only through a long-term trial, involving at least an entire society. We hesitate to adopt an innovation until we have been shown how it works; yet we can determine the practical value of most social inventions only by adopting them. This dilemma slows their acceptance.

Compatibility with existing culture

Innovations are most readily accepted when they fit in nicely with the existing culture. The horse fitted easily into the hunting culture of the Apache, as it enabled them to do better what they were already doing. Not all innovations mesh so well. Innovations may be incompatible with the existing culture in at least three ways.

First, *the innovation may conflict with existing patterns.* In many developing countries, the idea of appointment and promotion on a merit basis is incompatible with the traditional family obligation to take care of one's relatives. Many current conservationist proposals in the United States conflict with our traditional concepts of land use, property rights, and personal liberties.

When an innovation conflicts with existing culture patterns, there are at least three possible outcomes: (1) It may be rejected, just as most Americans have rejected communism; (2) it may be accepted, and the conflicting cultural traits may be adjusted to it, as we have altered our child-labor practices to permit compulsory public education; (3) it may be accepted and its conflict with the existing culture may be concealed and evaded by rationalization, as in those areas (including France and, until recently, five of the United States) where contraceptives are freely sold "for prevention of disease," although the sale of contraceptives is forbidden by law. While not always decisive, conflict with the existing culture discourages acceptance of an innovation.

Sometimes an apparent conflict can be avoided by role compartmentalization. As an example, the Kwaio of the Solomon Islands have chiefs every Tuesday! Their social organization included no chiefs, but it became necessary to invent some to handle dealings with white officials after World War II. To avoid conflict between these new "chiefs" and the traditional holders of authority and influence, they simply agreed that the chiefs would "reign" only on Tuesdays when the white officials called [Keesing, 1968]. In this way, a potentially disruptive innovation was insulated from the rest of the culture.

Second, *the innovation may call for new patterns not present in the culture.* The American Indians had no patterns of animal husbandry into which the cow could be fitted. When they were first given cows by government agents, they hunted them as game animals. A society generally tries to use an innovation in old, familiar ways. When this fails, the society may develop new ways of making effective use of the new element. Thus we have disguised each new building material to make it look like an old, familiar material. Early concrete blocks were faced like rough-finished stone; asphalt and asbestos shingles were finished to look like brick or wood; aluminum siding is still made to look like wood. Then, after some years, each of these materials begins to be used in designs and ways which make full use of its own properties and possibilities. Most innovations call for some new patterns in the culture, and it takes time to develop them.

Third, *some innovations are substitutive, not additive,* and these are less readily accepted. It is easier to accept innovations which can be added to the culture without requiring the immediate discard of some familiar trait complex. American baseball, jazz, and the "western" movie have been diffused throughout most of the world. Each could be added to almost any kind of culture without requiring surrender of any native traits. But the approximate equality of the sexes, democracy, or rational business enterprise have diffused more slowly; each requires the surrender of traditional values and practices. Many non-Western peoples have readily accepted the procedures and materials of scientific medicine—inoculations, antibiotics, analgesics, and even surgery—for these could coexist with their traditional folk medicine. The ill Navaho could swallow the government doctor's pill while the Navaho healing dance continued. But often these peoples neither understand nor accept the scientific foundations of medicine, such as the germ, virus, and stress theories of disease, or the rest of the medical subculture, for these conflict with their traditional belief system [Gould, 1965; Wolff, 1965; J. Nash, 1967]. Whenever the nature of the choice is such that one cannot have *both* the new and the old, the acceptance of the new is usually delayed.

Costs of change

The very poor resist all change because they cannot afford to take *any* risk [Arensberg and Niehoff, 1971, pp. 149–150]. Change is nearly always costly. Not only does change disrupt the existing culture and destroy cherished sentiments and values, but it also involves some specific costs.

Technical difficulties of change. Very few innovations can simply be added to the existing culture; most innovations require some modification of the existing culture. Only recently did England replace an awkward and clumsy monetary system with a decimal currency, while the United States has been debating and postponing a switch to the metric system of measures for over a century. Why have such clumsy systems been retained for so long? Because the changeover is so difficult. England's switch to a decimal currency in 1967 proved to be far more complicated than simply learning a new system. Changes in cash registers, coin machines, bookkeeping records, standardized merchandise sizes, and arguments over pound fractions were all involved. Learning the metric system would be very simple, but the task of making and stocking everything from window frames to nuts and bolts in both size ranges for

a half century or so is overwhelming. Railroads would be more efficient if the tracks were a foot or two farther apart to permit wider cars; but the cost of rebuilding the tracks and replacing the rolling stock is prohibitive. New inventions and improved machines often make present machinery obsolete and destroy the market for technical skills which workers have spent years in developing.

Vested interests and social change. The costs of social change are never evenly distributed. The industry which is made obsolete and the workers whose skill is made unmarketable are forced to bear the costs of technical progress, while others enjoy the improved products. Those to whom the status quo is profitable are said to have a *vested interest.* Communities with an army post or navy yard nearby find that all this government money is good for business, so these communities have a vested interest in retaining these military establishments. Students attending state universities have a vested interest in tax-supported higher education. Nearly everyone has some vested interests—from the rich with their tax-exempt bonds to the poor with their welfare checks.

Most social changes carry a threat, real or imaginary, to some vested interests who then oppose these changes. Examples are almost endless. In 1579 the Council of Danzig, acting in response to pressure from weavers, ordered the strangulation of the inventor of an improved weaving machine; and the spinsters of Blackburn, England, invaded Hargreave's home to destroy his spinning jennies [Stern, 1937]. The early railroads were opposed by landowners who didn't want their lands cut up, and by canal owners and toll-road companies; and then in turn the railroads became vigorous opponents of the automobile and helped to block construction of the St. Lawrence Seaway. Employer opposition to the organization of labor unions was long and bitter, and still continues in some places, while unions resort to "featherbedding" in the effort to retain jobs made unnecessary by technical change. Each group is an ardent advocate of progress in general, but seldom at the expense of its own vested interests.

Vested interests, however, appear as promoters of change whenever they believe the proposed change will be profitable to them. American corporations spend billions of dollars each year to develop new products which they can sell profitably. Many business groups in the Great Lakes area energetically supported the St. Lawrence Seaway proposal. Such government enterprises are normally denounced as socialism by vested interests which are not enriched thereby, while those vested interests whom the proposal benefits will find other terms to describe it. (Apparently, *socialism* operates when the government spends money to benefit *you,* not me!) Business interests have sought and obtained many kinds of government regulation and "interference" when it seemed in their interest to do so. Labor unions have been most eloquent supporters of laws to limit child labor. The great Chicago fire of 1871 showed the weakness of competing private fire-fighting companies, and, more important, imposed such heavy losses upon fire insurance companies that they threw their support behind the proposal for tax-supported municipal fire departments. Many social reforms have finally been secured, after long agitation, because powerful vested interests came to redefine their interests and decided that the reform would benefit them.

Role of the change agent

Who proposes a change and how does this person go about it? The identity of the originator greatly affects acceptance or rejection. Any proposal of the Communist party in the United States is doomed to certain defeat. Opponents of all sorts of proposals often label them Communist in order to defeat them. Innovations which are first adopted by persons at the top of the prestige scale and power system are likely to filter downward quite rapidly; those first adopted by low-status persons are likely to percolate upward more slowly, if at all.

Successful change agents often seek to make the change appear innocuous by identifying it with familiar cultural elements. King Ibn Saud introduced radio and telephone to Saudi Arabia by quoting the Koran over them. Franklin D. Roosevelt's leadership rested partly upon his ability to describe significant reforms in terms of homespun American sentiments and values.

Change agents must know the culture in which they work. This point is stressed in the many guidebooks for aid officials working in development programs in underdeveloped countries [Arensberg and Niehoff, 1971; Leagins and Loomis, 1972; Loomis and Beagle, 1975]. The thoughtless ethnocentrism of Western social scientists and technicians has often doomed their efforts to failure [Alatas, 1972; Selwyn, 1973]. Government attempts to settle Navajo Indians as individual families on irrigated land were unsuccessful, for the Navajo were accustomed to work land cooperatively along extended kinship lines. An amusing illustration of how ignorance and ethnocentrism handicapped a change agent is found in Micronesia, where an American labor relations expert sought to recruit Palauan workers for a mining operation. He first demanded to see the "chief"—a request which posed a problem since they had no chief in their social structure. Finally they produced a person with whom the American expert sought to establish rapport by throwing an arm around his shoulders and laughingly tousling his hair. In Palauan culture this was an indignity roughly equivalent, in our culture, to opening a man's fly in public [Useem, 1952]. Needless to add, this expert was not very successful.

Sometimes a change agent succeeds in promoting a change, only to find that the results are an unhappy surprise. In one South African area the Western workers noticed that the native mothers were exhausted by nursing their babies for two years; they successfully introduced bottle feeding. The innovation had the effect of evading the native taboo upon sexual relations during lactation, so that instead of bearing a child every three or four years, the women now bore a child every year or so, and were more exhausted than ever [Lee, 1959*b*]. Change agents must thoroughly understand the interrelations of the culture if they are to be able to predict the consequences of a particular change. At this moment, when thousands of American representatives are functioning as change agents in nearly every underdeveloped country of the world, we might remind ourselves of the necessity for change agents to be observant students of the society they wish to help, if they are to avoid unhappy consequences.

The efforts of the change agent are not always appreciated. The inventor is often ridiculed; the missionary may be eaten; and the agitator or reformer is usually persecuted. Radicals are likely to be popular only after they are dead, and organizations (like the Daughters of the American Revolution) dedicated to the memory of dead revolutionists have no fondness for live ones. Those who sought to change the segregated racial patterns of American society may become heroes in the history books, but they faced jail and physical violence during their lifetime. Change agents do not always observe all laws, but even meticulous law observance is no protection. It was impossible to be a labor organizer in the 1930s or a civil rights worker in the 1950s without being beaten, jailed, or even worse.

Persecution of change agents and social reformers has a long history. Huss and Servetus were burned at the stake, while Luther and Wycliffe narrowly escaped. Florence Nightingale fought against family opposition, public ridicule and scorn, and official jealousy, intrigue, and slander in her efforts to change the image of nurse from slattern to professional. Jane Addams was showered with honors in her old age in recognition of the acts for which she was reviled when conducting them. Change agents are likely to be honored only when they are very old or very dead.

The deviant as change agent. Many change agents are deviants of some sort. The nonconformist may unwittingly launch a new fashion, speech form, or dance step. Inventors are people who love to tinker; they are more excited by the challenge of a new idea than by the possibility of riches [Barnett, 1953, pp. 150–156]. Social reformers are necessarily people who are disenchanted with some aspect of the status quo. Without deviants, there would be many fewer social changes.

Persuasive and abrasive techniques of promoting change

Most of the conventional wisdom on social change has recommended that change agents should operate as "tactfully" as possible. Standard recommendations have been to make no extreme demands that would alarm people or arouse strong opposition, but to be gradualist and settle for piecemeal change; make demands sound as innocuous and inoffensive as possible; present them as small continuations of present trends and traditions, not as radical departures; avoid insulting or antagonizing anyone if possible; assume the good faith and decent intentions of opponents as long as possible; seek persuasion and consensus, not confrontation and acrimony.

During the 1960s, a number of groups, including campus activists, black militants, war protestors, and welfare rights activists, inverted this conventional wisdom by following deliberately abrasive procedures. The apparent objective is to startle, shock, confuse, alarm, intimidate, and paralyze the authority figures and "soften them up" until they are ready to make major concessions. Tactics include the use of abusive, insulting, and sometimes obscene language; extreme and often outrageous demands which are promotional, consciousness-raising tactics rather than serious goals; impugning and denying the good faith and motives of authority figures and opponents; obstructing routine activities by mass sit-ins, disruption of lectures and meetings, and other forms of demonstration and confrontation [Searle, 1968; W. Anderson, 1969; Massimo, 1969; Etzioni, 1970; Kelman, 1970; Franklin, 1971; Green, 1971; Knott, 1971].

Which set of techniques is more effective? Many policy changes accompanied the disorders of the 1960s. It can be argued that students, women, and minorities would not have so greatly enlarged their rights through reliance upon genteel persuasion. There is some research evidence, for example, showing that government grants and welfare payments increased (temporarily) in cities that had riots in the 1960s [Betz, 1974]. It is possible that there are some situations where only persuasive techniques are effective, such as in promoting agricultural practices among peasant peoples, and other situations where abrasive techniques are more effective. For example, when attempting to get somebody to *stop* doing something (e.g., stop enforcing dormitory regulations), abrasive techniques may have greater impact. Much more research is needed before any firm answers can be given.

Adversary techniques. Somewhat intermediate between the above alternatives are a series of *adversary* techniques which are becoming increasingly popular. Collective bargaining, strikes and boycotts, affirmative action, and class action lawsuits are examples. No longer can the rejected job applicant, the disappointed Ph.D. candidate, or the disgruntled customer be trusted to roll over and play dead. Today he or she may initiate an adversary proceeding. Both persuasion and pressure tactics are used in adversary proceedings. They do not include deliberate insult or needless provocation of adversaries, but neither do they include any tender concern for the adversaries' feelings.

Adversary negotiations often become acrimonious, since a conflict process is in operation. Although the goal is accommodation, all adversary interaction carries an inherent temptation to anger, to a hardening of in-group solidarities, and to a sharpening of conflict

alignments. Yet in a democratic society with many opposing interests and viewpoints, adversary relationships increase along with the increasing power equality of these different groups and categories of people.

Social and personal disorganization

Social effects of discovery and invention

No social change leaves the rest of the culture entirely unaffected. Even an "additive" innovation draws time and interest away from other elements of the culture. Some innovations are shattering in their impact. When the missionaries passed out steel axes to the Yir Yoront of Australia, the gift appeared to be an innocuous gesture, but the stone ax was so tightly integrated into the culture that a chain reaction of disruption spread through the social structure [Sharp, 1952]. The stone ax was a symbol of adult masculinity. It might be lent to women and to youths, and the lines of ax borrowing were very important features of the social organization. When superior steel axes were passed out indiscriminately, and owned by women and youths, the symbol of authority was so undermined that authority itself became clouded, relations were confused, and reciprocal obligations became uncertain. The stone for the axes was quarried far to the south, and traded northward along trade routes through an established system of trading partners, who also shared in important ceremonials. With the substitution of the steel ax, trading relationships languished, and this rich ceremonial sharing was lost. Deep and serious disturbance of Yir Yoront culture is traced to the single innovation of the steel ax. The illustration is dramatic; but have the effects of the automobile or the radio upon American culture been less far-reaching? Ogburn [1933, pp. 153–156] has compiled a list of 150 social changes which he attributes to the radio; and television has brought still more.

Ogburn distinguishes three forms of the social effects of invention. (1) *Dispersion, or the multiple effects of a single mechanical invention,* is illustrated by the many effects of the radio, or by the automobile, which shortens travel time, supports a huge manufacturing and servicing industry, provides a market for vast quantities of gasoline and oil, steel, glass, leather, and other materials, requires a massive road-building program, alters courtship and recreational behavior, promotes suburbs and shopping centers, and has many other consequences. (2) *Succession, or the derivative social effects of a single invention,* means that an invention produces changes, which in turn produce further changes, and so on. The invention of the cotton gin (a) simplified cotton processing and made cotton more profitable; this result (b) encouraged the planting of more cotton; and the planting (c) required more slaves; the increase in slavery and growing Southern dependence upon cotton export (d) helped to provoke the Civil War, which (e) greatly stimulated the growth of large-scale industry and business monopoly; these in turn (f) encouraged antitrust laws and labor unions; and the chain still continues. While these developments were not entirely due to the cotton gin, it helped to produce them all. (3) *Convergence, or the coming together of several influences of different inventions,* may be variously illustrated. The six-shooter, barbedwire fencing, and the windmill facilitated the settlement of the great American plains. The automobile, the electric pump, and the septic tank made the modern suburb possible. Nuclear warheads, intercontinental missiles, and radar detection systems have, in the opinion of many military theorists, made total war obsolete.

Much has been written about the social effects of invention. It does not matter whether the new trait has been invented within the society or diffused into it; the social effects are equally great from either method. Guns "made all men the same size" and ended the power advantage of the horsed knight in armor; cannons ended the relative impregnability of the medieval castle and strengthened the king at the expense of the provincial nobility. A diffused trait often finds a society quite unable to cope with it successfully. For example, primitive societies which brew their own alcoholic beverages generally have cultural controls over their use, but primitive societies which have received alcohol from white men have had no such controls, and the effects have been generally devastating [Horton, 1943]. To cite one instance, the Eskimo of St. Lawrence Island, when first introduced to alcohol, promptly went on a month-long drunk and missed the annual walrus migration; the following winter most of them died of starvation [Nelson, 1899]. Innovations, whether discovered, invented, or diffused, can be equally disruptive.

Unequal rates of change

Since a culture is interrelated, changes in one aspect of the culture invariably affect other aspects of the culture. The affected traits will usually be adapted to this change, but only after some time has passed. This time interval between the arrival of a change and the completion of the adaptations it prompts is called *cultural lag,* a concept developed by Ogburn [1922, pp. 200–213]. As an illustration, he pointed out that about 1870, workers in large numbers began entering factories where they were often injured in unavoidable accidents. But not until another half century had passed did most states get around to enacting Workmen's Compensation laws. In this instance, the cultural lag was about fifty years.

A cultural lag exists wherever any aspect of the culture lags behind another aspect to which it is related. Probably the most pervasive form of cultural lag in present Western societies is the lag of institutions behind changing technology. For example, in most states the size of a county was based upon the distance one could travel to the county seat and return in the same day; despite improved transportation, the county unit still remains at

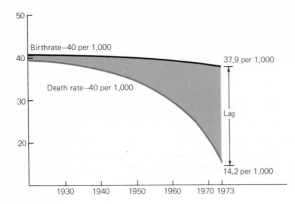

Figure 29. Cultural lag: death control and birth control in developing countries. (Source: Based on data in Dorothy Nortman and Elizabeth Hofstatter, "Population and Family Planning Programs: A Factbook," Reports on Population Planning, 6:2, December, 1974.)

its old size, inefficient for many of its functions. The metropolitan area sprawls over a hodgepodge of many different state, county, city, and township units, so that efficient area planning, government, and law enforcement become an impossibility. For a full century, urbanization and industrialization were destroying the possibility for the individual worker to ensure the security of his family by depending upon himself, his relatives, and his neighbors; yet only after the Great Depression of the 1930s dramatized this fact did we establish social security, unemployment insurance, and other welfare measures.

Some cultural lags involve the lag of one part of the material culture behind a related part of the material culture. For a quarter century after we replaced the horse with the automobile, we continued to build the garage out behind the house, back where the smelly stables used to go. Sometimes the material culture lags behind changes in the nonmaterial culture. For example, educational research has long since discovered that movable classroom furniture aids in organizing learning activities; yet thousands of classrooms still have inflexible rows of desks screwed to the floor. Finally, one aspect of the nonmaterial culture

may lag behind other related aspects of nonmaterial culture. As shown in Figure 29, the world's lag in the use of birth control following our brilliant success in death control has produced the population explosion, probably the world's most catastrophic cultural lag.

The concept of cultural lag applies to differing rates of change *within* a society, not to rates of change between societies. It describes the disharmony between related parts of a single culture, produced through unequal rates of change. Cultural lags are most numerous in a rapidly changing culture. They are symptoms, not of a backward society, but of a highly dynamic and increasingly complex society. But even if all people were wise, objective, and adaptable, they would still need some time to discover what adaptations a new change would require, and more time to work out and complete those adaptations. Most of us, however, are pretty ignorant about matters outside our specialty, are prejudiced and swayed by vested interests, and are not nearly so adaptable as we like to imagine. Cultural lags are numerous and persistent.

Social change and social problems

A social problem may be defined as a condition which many people consider undesirable and want to correct [Horton and Leslie, 1974, pp. 4–7]. A perfectly integrated society would have no social problems, for all institutions and behavior would be neatly harmonized and defined as acceptable by the values of the society. A changing society inevitably develops problems. Either the conditions themselves change and become unacceptable (population growth, soil erosion, and deforestation create a conservation problem), or the society's changing values define an old condition as no longer tolerable (child labor, poverty, racism, or lack of education). Social problems are part of the price of social change. The detailed analysis of social problems, however, belongs in another textbook and another course.

Disorganization and demoralization

As has been repeatedly suggested in this chapter, all new elements disrupt the existing culture to some extent. If a culture is well organized, with all its traits and institutions fitting closely together, change in any one of them will disorganize this arrangement. In today's world, change is most rapid in the developing countries; as a country approaches full "modernization," the rate of change slows down [Fierabend and Fierabend, 1972]. Thus it is the developing countries that are suffering the greatest disorganization, both because of their high rate of change and because of their relative unfamiliarity with the change process. Modernization and "progress" bring new hardship to many of the poor, who endure the resultant price inflation without sharing in the benefits [Scott and Kerkvliet, 1973]. Modernization promotes new systems of social stratification and encourages increased ethnic competition within developing countries [Bates, 1974]. "Progress" is a mixed blessing.

When a culture becomes highly disorganized, the people's sense of security, morale, and purpose in life is damaged. When people are confused and uncertain, so that their behavior is also inconsistent, hesitant, and contradictory, they are described as *personally disorganized*. If their disorganization proceeds until they lose their sense of purpose in life and become resigned and apathetic, we describe them as *demoralized*. They have lost their morale, and often their behavior controls are lost as well. A demoralized people is likely to suffer population decline, through a lowered birthrate, a higher death rate, or both. The capacity of a thoroughly demoralized people simply to die out has attracted the attention of a number of anthropologists [Rivers, 1922; Maher, 1961].

The extermination of the buffalo demoralized the American Indians of the Great Plains [Lesser, 1933; Wissler, 1938; Sandoz, 1954; Deloria, 1970]. The buffalo provided food, clothing, and shelter; in all, over fifty separate parts of the buffalo carcass were used by the Indians. The buffalo hunt provided the principal object of the Indian's religious ceremonials, the goal of his maturing, and a road to status and recognition. His other avenue to status—warfare—was also dependent upon an ample supply of dried buffalo meat. When the government exterminated the buffalo in order to pacify the Indians, it demoralized them as well. The integrating and status-giving functions of the war party and the buffalo hunt were lost. Religious ceremonials were now empty and meaningless. The hunting economy was totally destroyed, and the Indians lived, and sometimes starved, on government handouts. The traditional goals and values which gave zest and meaning to life were now unavailable, and to substitute the white man's goals and values was an almost impossible task of learning. In the few instances where Indians did successfully adopt the white man's economy, this, too, was soon destroyed by the white man's hunger for the Indians' land [Foreman, 1932; Collier, 1947, pp. 199–219; Deloria, 1970]. Suffering from the destruction of their own culture, denied access to the white man's culture, ravaged by the white man's diseases, and corrupted by his alcohol, many Indian tribes became deeply demoralized. Depopulation was almost universal, and only in recent decades has Indian population begun to rebuild. This story of devastatingly disruptive social change, disorganization of the culture, and personal disorganization and demoralization of the people has been repeated hundreds of times in the world's history.

Not all native peoples, however, have been demoralized by their contacts with Western societies. The Palauans of Micronesia worked out an interdependent blend of traditional culture and Western commercialism. They happily drove trucks and pounded typewriters to earn money to buy the traditional clan gifts, and used motor launches to carry their sweet potatoes to traditional festivals [Mead, 1955, p. 128]. Whether change disrupts a society to the point of demoralization depends upon the nature of the changes, the way they are introduced, and the structure of the society upon which they impinge.

Is change least painful when it comes slowly? Not necessarily. Since culture involves interrelations, it is generally easier to accept a cluster of related changes than to accept them one at a time. For example, if a primitive people acquires clothing without soap, then filth and disease are predictable; if given clothes without sewing machines, then they will be clothed in tatters. With mud floors to sit upon, and no place to store clothing and these other artifacts, filth and clutter are a certainty. But if all these elements—clothes, soap, sewing machines, and floored houses with shelves and closets—are adopted together within a single generation, these changes can be made far more easily than if they are spaced over several generations.

Western cultural diffusion generally converts the native village into a depressing slum, not because the people adopt too many new traits but because they adopt too few. It may even be psychologically easier to make a lot of changes than a few. As Margaret Mead [1956, pp. 445–446] has observed, "A people who choose to practice a new technology or enter into drastically new kinds of economic relationships will do this more easily if they live in different houses, wear different clothes and eat different, or differently cooked, food." Much of the social disorganization which accompanies social change stems from the fact that a people who are willing to adopt new trait complexes are blocked from doing so. Sometimes they are blocked by their own limited resources and sometimes by the unwillingness of the dominant whites to admit them into full participation in Western civilization. The Mau Mau terrorism in Kenya in the 1950s was largely attributable to the frustration of the Kikuyu's intense desire to share in Western civilization [Bascom and Herskovitz (eds.), 1959, p. 4].

We need, therefore, to revise the notion that slow change is necessarily more comfortable than rapid change. In some situations, the rapid wholesale change of a way of life may be infinitely less disturbing than piecemeal changes, as Mead [1956, chap. 18] has shown in her study of the Manus, who moved from the Stone Age into Western civilization in a single generation. The reason may be that slow change allows cultural lags to accumulate, not to be corrected until they become painful. Rapid change may actually produce fewer lags, because many of the related items of the culture may be changed at the same time.

Change has come with dazzling speed upon contemporary Western societies. Within a few short generations, the Western peoples have shifted from life in rural, agricultural folk societies to life in an immensely complex urban, industrial, impersonal mass society. Are contemporary Western societies disorganized? Certainly! Cultural lags are numerous at every point. The school is constantly straining to prepare children for a society which changes even before they become adult. A century ago husband and wife could each assume a quite clearly defined role; today neither can be at all sure what she or he will be expected to be and do in their marriage. Every level of government is struggling with tasks which few of our grandfathers would have guessed it would ever assume. Although the traditional informal controls of the folk society are failing to regulate the behavior of individuals in this impersonal urban world of ours, we are still hunting for effective substitutes.

There is national consensus upon neither goals nor means in American society. Popular faith in all American institutions and professions has been eroding in recent years [Harris Poll, Sept. 30, 1974].

These are symptoms of social disorganization—of failure of traditional controls, role confusion and uncertainty, conflicting moral codes, and declining confidence in established institutions. In such a society, people become disorganized. Many fail to internalize a coherent system of values and behavior controls. A smaller number become seriously disorganized and grow so erratic and contradictory in behavior that they are diagnosed as mentally ill and in need of psychotherapy. Whether those who embrace countercultural life-styles are simply personally disorganized or are well organized around a deviant life organization is a question which is bitterly debated.

If our society is so badly disorganized, why are we not all mentally ill? Despite our accelerating rate of social change during the past century, the available evidence indicates that the frequency of mental illness has not significantly increased [Goldhamer and Marshall, 1953; Dunham, 1969; Wagenfeld, 1972]. More persons are diagnosed and treated than formerly, but this proves only that more cases of mental illness are being located and treated. Measuring the frequency of mental illness, either present or past, is a difficult research problem [Manis et al., 1964; Phillips and Clancy, 1970]. It is possible that there is no more mental illness today because we have become able to develop personalities that are adaptable to social change [Mead, 1947]. Children in our society are socialized to anticipate and appreciate change. The strain of change may be considerably reduced by a socialization which seeks to prepare persons to adapt themselves. Since adult roles are uncertain, we seek to socialize and educate children to function successfully in several roles, not just in one. Finally, we have developed social case work and psychiatry for persons who cannot work out an effective life pattern by themselves. Over much of the world today, the rate of social change is accelerating. Whether the human race can adapt itself as rapidly as its social life is changing is still a moot question.

A popular writer [Toffler, 1970] has given the term "future shock" to the stresses and anxieties provoked by rapid change. Recent research provides some support for the thesis that stress and anxiety is linked with the perceived rate of change [Lauer, 1974]. Some social scientists are doubtful that we shall make the changes necessary to grapple with such problems as the population explosion, pollution, and resource exhaustion. They fear that civilization may

Children in our society are socialized to anticipate and appreciate change.

collapse in depression, famine, pestilence, warfare, and chaos [Heilbroner, 1974; Laqueur, 1974]. Such pessimism is far from new. The fifteenth century, for example, was an epoch of profound pessimism [Huizinga, 1924, p. 22]. Time will tell whether today's "men of good fear" are any more correct.

Social planning: Can change be directed?

Is it possible to control and direct social changes so that they will be less painful and costly? Social scientists disagree. Some feel that social change is caused by social forces beyond our effective control [Sorokin, 1941, 1948; La-Piere, 1965]. For example, when the necessary supporting knowledge is developed, an invention will be made by someone, even if this invention is most troublesome to human existence. The hydrogen bomb is an example. Although we fear it may destroy us, we go on advancing it because others will do so anyway. Could the Indian wars possibly have been avoided? The Indians had land we wanted for our growing population, and our advance was certain to destroy the Indian's way of life. The many unnecessary brutal episodes were merely the symptoms, not the cause, of a conflict which was unavoidable, given these groups with their respective needs and cultural backgrounds. Practically any great social change can be thus described in terms of blind social forces, so that we conclude that what *did* happen was about the only thing that *could* happen in that situation.

Some social scientists, however, believe that we *can* exert *some* influence over the course of social change [Mannheim, 1949; Bottomore, 1962, pp. 283–284; Horowitz, 1966]. They believe that some degree of social planning is possible. *Social planning* is defined [Himes, 1954, p. 18] as "a conscious interactional process combining investigation, discussion, agreement, and action in order to achieve those conditions, relationships, and values that are regarded as desirable." More simply, social planning is an attempt at the intelligent direction of social change [Riemer, 1947; Adams, 1950; Gross, 1967; Bennis, et al., 1969, chap. 1; Kahn, 1969; Havelock, 1973; Friedmann, 1973; Gil, 1973; Kramer and Specht, 1975]. In his *The Active Society* [1968], Etzioni argues that, rather than drifting aimlessly, a society can guide social change to achieve humane social goals. He sees this social guidance, not as a pattern imposed by a ruling elite, but as a result of the efforts of active-minded publics who mobilize to demand changes in accord with their needs and interests. But just how the conflicting wishes of different publics are to be reconciled would remain a perplexing problem.

Elite direction of social planning is characteristic of the Communist societies. Decision making has been highly centralized, and plans have been exceedingly intricate and detailed. Recently there has been some decentralization of decision making in the USSR, with less attempt to specify all details [Shaffer, 1968; Smolinski, 1968]. Planning which attempts to program practically all the activities of a society is less successful than planning that is limited to only one, or a small number, of activities or goals. This kind of social planning

is an old American tradition. When the framers of our Constitution rejected primogeniture (the European provision that the lands pass intact to the eldest son) and entail (the provision that prevents him from selling them), these American planners were seeking to construct a society of small, landowning farmers instead of a society of landed estates. This purpose was reinforced by the Homestead Act of 1862, which gave public lands in small parcels to individual farmers instead of selling it in large blocks to the highest bidders. Zoning ordinances, building codes, public education, and compulsory school attendance laws are examples of social planning. Some problems which call for planning at the national or international level include the use of the world's water resources and fishing rights, use of mineral resources under international waters, and many others.

A critic of planning would contend that such planning efforts do not really change anything, but are merely a slightly more orderly way of carrying out changes that are inevitable anyway. The comment perhaps sums up the matter. Certainly, no social planning will prevent or reverse a change which present knowledge and longtime trends are creating. There is, for example, no way of returning to the "simple life," nor is it possible by planning to steer social change in a direction contrary to most people's wishes and values. The major social changes are probably uncontrollable, but social planning may be able to reduce the delays and costs of integrating them into the culture.

Summary

All societies change continuously. New traits appear through *discovery* and *invention,* or through *diffusion* from other societies.

The rate of social change varies enormously from society to society and from time to time. In rare instances, certain *geographic changes* produce great social change. More often, *migration* to a new environment brings changes in social life. *Changes in population size or composition* always produce social changes. Since *isolation* retards change and cross-cultural contacts promote change, physically or socially isolated groups show fewer changes. The *structure of the society and culture* affect change: A highly conformist, traditional society or a highly integrated culture is less prone to change than the individualistic, permissive society with a less highly integrated culture. A society's *attitudes and values* greatly encourage or retard change. The *perceived needs* of a people affect the speed and direction of change. Perhaps most important of all, the *cultural base* provides the foundation of knowledge and skill necessary to develop new elements; as the cultural base expands, the possibilities of new combinations multiply in an *exponential* manner, while knowledge in one area often *cross-fertilizes* other areas of development.

Not all innovations are accepted. The attitudes and values of a group determine what kind of innovations a group is likely to accept. If an innovation's usefulness can be demonstrated easily and cheaply, the proof is helpful; but many social inventions cannot be tested except through a complete acceptance. Compatible innovations are more readily accepted than those which clash with important features of the existing culture. Technical difficulties of fitting a change into the existing culture often cause great economic cost and personal inconvenience. Vested interests normally oppose change, but they occasionally discover that a proposed change is to their advantage. The change agent's ingenuity and

social position affect his success in introducing changes. Unless the change agent knows the culture very well, he may fail in his efforts, because he generally miscalculates the consequences of his changes and the techniques needed to promote them. Whether promoting change through "tactful" persuasion, abrasive insistence, or some combination of the two in an adversary proceeding is debatable, and may vary with the change situation.

Social and personal disorganization are costs of social change. Discoveries and inventions, as well as diffused new traits and complexes, often set off a chain reaction of change which disrupts many aspects of the culture. The different parts of the culture, interrelated, and interdependent though they are, do not change at the same rate of speed. The time interval between the appearance of a new trait and the completion of the adaptations it forces is called *cultural lag.* All rapidly changing societies have many cultural lags and are somewhat *disorganized.* In a disorganized society, persons who may have greater difficulty in finding a comfortable behavior system become themselves disorganized. When they lose hope of finding a rewarding way of conducting their lives and cease trying, they have become *demoralized* and may actually die out as a group. In an effort to speed and simplify this process and reduce the costs and wastes of social change, *social planning* is increasingly being attempted. Social scientists are not agreed upon the degree of success to be expected from the direction of social change by social planning.

Questions and projects

1. Why are social scientists hesitant to use the term "progress"?
2. Is knowledge of the diffusion process likely to reduce ethnocentrism?
3. What are some of the change-promoting features

of American society? What are some of its change-resisting features?
4. Is the rate of invention likely to continue rising, or to fall off? Why?
5. Why will a person who insists upon the latest

cars, fashions, and gadgets often be entirely satisfied with ancient social philosophies?

6. How many of those persons whom we now consider "great" were noncontroversial during their lives? How many achieved greatness by promoting changes and how many by preventing changes?

7. Is it possible for a change agent to promote a major change without arousing violent hostilities?

8. What are some recent social changes in our society which you consider undesirable? Some which you consider desirable? What values are you using in making these judgments?

9. Why should social change be so difficult? Why can't people simply get together, decide what changes are desirable, and then promote them?

10. Evaluate this statement: "The more successfully we progress, the fewer cultural lags and social problems we shall have."

11. For each of the three alternative change techniques—persuasion, abrasion, and adversary action—outline a change situation for which this technique would be most likely to succeed.

12. Substantial racial integration in the United States has been accomplished in recent years through piecemeal action, one issue at a time. Would it have been easier or more difficult to have rapidly integrated all activities and services at the same time?

13. Can social planning ever change "human nature"? Must it, in order to succeed?

14. Read one of the following novels, which describe Americans operating as change agents in other societies, and explain the agents' successes or failures in that capacity: Ronald Hardy, *The Place of the Jackals;* Graham Greene, *The Quiet American;* James Ullman, *Windom's Way;* Kathryn Grondahl, *The Mango Season;* Margaret Landon, *Never Dies the Dream;* Thomas Streissguth, *Tigers in the House.*

Suggested readings

ADAMS, E. M.: "The Logic of Planning," *Social Forces,* 28:419–423, May, 1950. A brief outline of the principles of social planning in a democracy.

ALLEN, FRANCIS R.: *Socio-cultural Dynamics: An Introduction to Social Change,* The Macmillan Company, New York, 1971. A textbook on theories of social and cultural change.

*APPELBAUM, RICHARD P.: *Theories of Social Change,* Markham Publishing Co., Chicago, 1970. A concise summary of current sociological thought on social change.

*BARNETT, H. G.: *Innovation: The Basis of Cultural Change,* McGraw-Hill Book Company, New York, 1953. An anthropologist's analysis of the development and acceptance of innovations.

*BASCOM, WILLIAM R., AND MELVILLE J. HERSKOVITS (EDS.): *Continuity and Change in African Cultures,* The University of Chicago Press, Chicago, 1959. Two essays—Simon Ottenberg, "Ibo Receptivity to Change" (pp. 130–143), and Harold K. Schneider, "Pakot Resistance to Change" (pp. 144–167)—seek to explain the opposite reactions of two societies to social change.

BENNIS, WARREN G., KENNETH D. BENNE, AND ROBERT CHIN: *The Planning of Change,* Holt, Rinehart and Winston, Inc., New York, 1969. A comprehensive textbook on social planning and change.

BREED, WARREN: *The Self-Guiding Society,* Free Press, New York, 1971. A popularization of Amitai Etzioni's *The Active Society* (Free Press, 1969), arguing that social change can be intelligently directed by mobilized groups of people.

HANSON, MARK: "The Improbable Change Agent and the PhB," *Rural Sociology,* 38:237–242, Summer, 1973. An entertaining account of how a patient change agent works to promote change in a poor rural American county.

LEE, DOROTHY: "The Cultural Curtain," *Annals of the American Academy of Political and Social Science,* 323:120–128, May, 1959. An interesting article showing, with many illustrations, the need for change agents to understand the culture in which they promote change.

*OGBURN, WILLIAM F.: *Social Change,* The Viking Press, Inc., New York, 1922. The classic study of social change.

*ROCHLIN, GENE I. (ED.): *Scientific Technology and Social Change: Readings from Scientific American,* W. H. Freeman and Company, San Francisco, 1974. A collection of articles on technology, resources, and energy as factors in social change.

RYAN, BRUCE F.: *Social and Cultural Change,* Ronald Press Co., New York, 1969. A basic textbook on social and cultural change.

*SPICER, EDWARD H. (ED.): *Human Problems in Technological Change,* Russell Sage Foundation, New York, 1952. A casebook describing a number of societies where important changes were introduced, showing the process of adoption and the social consequences of these changes.

*SWANSON, GUY: *Social Change,* Scott, Foresman and Co., Glencoe, Ill., 1971. A concise treatment of social change.

Chapter 21 • Social movements

Last night I told Jim: "I been working in the same factory as you 10 years now. We go in at the same time, come out at the same time. But I do all the shopping, get the dinner, wash the dishes and on Sunday break my back down on the kitchen floor. I'm real tired of doin' all that. I want some help from you." Well, he just laughed at me, see? Like he done every time I mentioned this before. But last night I wouldn't let up. I mean, I really *meant* it this time. And you know? I thought he was gonna let me have it. Looked mighty like he was gettin' ready to belt me one. But you know? I just didn't care! I wasn't gonna back down, come hell or high water. You'll just never believe it, he'd kill me if he knew I was tellin' you, he washed the dishes. First time in his entire life." *(Quoted from Vivian Gornick, "Consciousness," New York Times Magazine, Jan. 10, 1971, p. 22. Copyright © 1971 by The New York Times Company. Reprinted by permission.)*

These few phrases introduce one of the most recent, and yet one of the oldest, of our social movements. What are social movements? Why do they appear? What are the conditions under which they succeed or fail?

Nature and definition of social movements

Early sociologists saw social movements as efforts to promote change. More recent sociologists view social movements as efforts either to promote or to resist change. For example, Turner and Killian [1957, p. 308] define a social movement as *"a collectivity acting with some continuity to promote or resist a change in the society or group of which it is a part."*

This definition covers a wide range of movements: religious movements such as Hare Krishna or the Jesus Movement, or the growing popular interest in psychedelic and occult experience [Marty, 1970; McFerran, 1972; Zaretsky and Leone, 1974]; reform movements such as women's liberation or gay liberation; revolutionary movements such as communism or the New Left; and many others.

Social movements are not institutions. Social institutions are relatively permanent and stable elements of a culture, whereas social movements are highly dynamic and have an uncertain lifespan. Institutions hold institutional status; that is, nearly everyone regards them as necessary and valuable aspects of the culture. A social movement lacks institutional status, for vast numbers of people view it with indifference or hostility. If a movement gains general or nearly universal support, its work is done and its active life, as a movement, is over.

Social movements are also distinguished from associations. An association is generally a formal organization, with members, officers, and a written constitution. A social movement often comes to include several movement organizations, but movements contain many participants who are not members of these supporting associations. Some movements are almost totally unorganized.

Social movements sometimes act as pressure groups, but most pressure groups are not social movements. Most pressure groups merely want the existing norms and values of the society to be interpreted to their benefit. But social movements are primarily and consciously concerned with promoting or resisting actual changes in these social norms and values. Occasionally, but only occasionally, do social movements function as pressure groups.

Social trends, such as the suburban migration or the increasing divorce rate, are not social movements; neither are changes in attitude or behavior, such as the growing acceptance of marijuana, for the element of collective action is missing.

Sociologists and other social scientists are much interested in the scientific analysis of social movements. They study them in several ways, including: (1) participant-observer studies, in which the sociologist joins the movement to observe it from the inside [Festinger et al., 1956; Lincoln, 1961; Ilfeld and Lauer, 1964]; (2) historical or longitudinal studies, combing published accounts, historical documents, newspaper files, and other sources [Edwards, 1927; Gusfield, 1955; O'Neill, 1969; Unger, 1974]; (3) comparative-membership studies, analyzing a sample of members or leaders (a) statistically, according to age, sex, class, occupation, education, and other characteristics in an effort to find out who joins and why [Lipset, 1950; Almond et al., 1954; Flacks, 1967; Lee, 1968; Aron, 1974], or (b) by interviews and biographical accounts, in an effort to discover their common feelings and motives [Crossman, 1949; Ernst and Loth,

1952; Kerpelman, 1969; Wilkes, 1970]; (4) content analyses of a movement's statements and propaganda [Lasswell and Blumenstock, 1939].

Social situations favoring social movements

Social movements do not "just happen." They arise wherever social conditions are favorable, and these conditions will have produced many people who are ready and willing to promote them. What kinds of social conditions are favorable to the appearance and spread of social movements?

Cultural drifts

Gradual, broad, sweeping changes in values or behavior are constantly going on in all civilized societies today (and in most primitive societies as well). Such changes are called *cultural drifts*. The concept originated with Herskovits [1949, p. 581], who describes it as a process "where minor alterations slowly change the character and form of a way of life, but where the continuity of the event is apparent." In the course of a cultural drift most of the people develop new ideas of what society should be like and how society should treat them. The long development of democratic society is an example of cultural drift. Some other examples include the emancipation of women, the changed attitude toward leisure and recreation, and the trend toward increasing equality in status and income.

Each cultural drift arises through the interaction of many causative factors. Each is far too extensive to be produced by any one social movement, although one or more movements may be involved in the change process. Cultural drifts thus often provide an opportunity for social movements to prod and hasten developments already under way. For the past century, a cultural drift has been running toward more nearly equal rights for all kinds of groups—age, sex, religious, political, racial, or ethnic. This cultural drift makes it almost a certainty that present social movements seeking social equality for racial and ethnic minorities with whites will eventually succeed, while present movements to resist such changes will eventually fail. Thus do cultural drifts aid or doom a social movement.

Social disorganization and social movements

"I took away their despair," said Nasser to explain his devoted following in the Arab world. Before a person can be a leader, there must be people ready to be led somewhere. Not many such people are found in stable, well-integrated societies, whose members are generally complacent and secure, feel no discontent, and have no interest in change. They rarely join social movements. It is the changing society—simple or complex—in which social movements flourish.

A changing society is always to some extent disorganized. As we outlined in the last chapter, societies differ greatly in the speed with which they change and in the degree to which a particular change disorganizes the culture. Social disorganization brings confusion and uncertainty to a society's members, since their traditions no longer form a dependable guide to behavior. In a disorganized society, individuals tend to become rootless and anomic. Leo Srole has drawn up an anomie scale which reveals some of the characteristics of the anomic frame of mind. In ascending order of intensity, these characteristics are: (1) a feeling that the community leaders are indifferent to human needs; (2) a feeling that little can be accomplished in a society which one sees as basically unpredictable and disorderly; (3) a feeling that one's life goals are slipping out of reach; (4) a general sense of futility; and (5) a conviction that one cannot count on personal associates

for social and psychological support [Merton, 1957a, pp. 164–169]. Anomie is often accompanied by alienation, which adds feelings of powerlessness and social isolation (see pp. 135–136).

Alienation and anomie become widespread states of mind in a disorganized society. Their symptoms are insecurity, confusion, restlessness, and suggestibility. Once-honored rules no longer seem binding and once-cherished goals no longer attainable, while no other rules or goals seem worth the effort. Such a confused and frustrated setting is ideal for the appearance and growth of social movements.

The spread of the Ghost Dance among the American Indians illustrates the relationship between social disorganization and social movements [McKern and McKern, 1970]. This was a dance which, if performed properly, was supposed to bring the end of the white man and the return of the buffalo. It originated among the North Paiutes of Nevada and spread in two waves in 1870 and 1890. However, it spread only among those peoples whose tribal life was seriously disrupted, mainly by the destruction of the buffalo [Lesser, 1933]. Each tribe participated in Ghost Dance ceremonials with an intensity roughly proportional to the amount of deprivation they suffered through the disruption of their tribal life [Nash, 1937]. The Sioux, flushed with recent victories and favorable treaties under Red Cloud, ignored the Ghost Dance in the 1870s; but by 1890, wretched and dispirited on a reservation, they eagerly adopted it. The Navaho, who remained prosperous and comfortable throughout this period, greeted the Ghost Dance with an amused and tolerant indifference; but when the Great Depression of the 1930s brought acute distress to the Navaho, aboriginal ceremonials had a remarkable revival [Kluckhohn, 1938].

Frustration and confusion, rather than extreme poverty and misery, spawn social movements. People can be emotionally secure and contented at a miserable level of bare subsistence, if their value system defines this deprivation as a necessary and proper condition of life. Corruption, social inequality, and social injustice do not necessarily doom a social system. Many social systems have remained stable and unshakable for centuries, despite grinding poverty, rampant corruption, and gross exploitation. Such a social order can survive as long as most members can attain the goals they have been encouraged to pursue. Human beings are so pliable and educable that almost any kind of social system will appear good to them if it has a fair degree of internal consistency and if they have been properly socialized to live within it. Therefore, traditional societies are often highly stable until they once begin to change; once the traditional customs and values are questioned, the people may experience a tremendous inflation of wishes, sometimes called a "revolution of rising expectations." Revolutions are most likely to occur, not when a people are most miserable, but after things have begun to improve [Brinton, 1938, pp. 40–44; Street and Street, 1961]. What apparently happens is that, although people have begun to live better, their scale of wants expands so much more rapidly that they are more frustrated than ever. Revolutions and other uprisings are especially likely to break out after a downturn has interrupted a period of improvement, creating an intolerable gap between rising expectations and falling realizations [Davies, 1962; Geschwender, 1968].

Social discontent

Social discontent is a widespread general dissatisfaction with the existing society. It has at least three roots: relative deprivation, perception of injustice, and status inconsistency.

Relative deprivation. The concept of *relative deprivation,* proposed by Stouffer [1949], means that one *feels* deprived according to the gap between what one has and what one feels one should have [Morrison, 1971]. Farmers in the National Farm Organization felt deprived

The concept of relative deprivation.

when they compared their income and working hours with those of factory workers [Morrison and Steeves, 1967]. The greatest discontent and protest among college students in the 1960s arose, not at the inferior colleges with a conformist atmosphere and little student freedom, but at the finest and most liberal schools, where student expectations were high. Consequently, schools where the students had the least objective cause for complaint were nonetheless the schools with the greatest gap between student expectations and institutional realities [Keniston, 1969, p. 238]. Wherever hopes and expectations rise faster than realizations, feelings of relative deprivation increase.

Relative deprivation is increasing throughout most of the underdeveloped world. The traditional folk societies are being disorganized at a rapid rate. All over the world, the impoverished peoples are getting the notion that poverty, hunger, and illness are not necessary after all. They are beginning to long for bicycles, radios, refrigerators, and all the other things that glitter along the slope of endlessly ascending desires. They hunger for these treasures but have little real understanding of what it takes to produce them. Therefore, even where people are beginning to get some of the things they covet, the satisfactions come with a tantalizing and unbearably frustrating slowness. A weakening of traditional and tribal controls generally accompanies this enormous inflation of desires. It will be a remarkable achievement if the underdeveloped areas are able to carry through an orderly program of economic and social development. Meanwhile, the population explosion in the underdeveloped countries, combined with limited rural opportunity, is sending hordes of peasant peoples to the cities, where they huddle in squalid suburban slums, as described on page 424. Uneducated and untrained, many are unemployed and often come to share the "culture of poverty" which Oscar Lewis has so eloquently described [1959, 1963a, 1963b, 1965, 1966a, 1966b]. Cut off from the extended family and village life which formerly made their poverty bearable, and unable to enter successfully into the urban culture, these rootless, alienated unfortunates are the potential shock troops for tomorrow's revolutionary movements.

Perception of injustice. Social injustice is not an objective social fact; it is a subjective value judgment. Is it just or unjust that one person should have ten times, or ten thousand times, as much wealth as another? This depends upon one's beliefs and values. In a number of countries the masses live in abject poverty while the rich live in sybaritic splendor, pay virtually no taxes, and block all attempts at social reform. Is such a social system unjust? Most readers will probably think so; but whether a social system is unjust is not the crucial question. It is when a social system is *perceived* as unjust by its members that they become frustrated and alienated. Perceived social injustice thus provides both a desire for change and a moral justification for breaking heads, if necessary, to get it [Turner, 1968].

A sense of injustice is not limited to the miserable poor. Any group, at any status level, may come to feel itself the victim of social injustice. A wealthy class, firmly believing that its wealth and privileges are just and proper, may suffer an intense and righteous sense of injustice when faced with "confiscatory" taxes or land-reform policies intended to benefit others. Whether such policies are "objectively" just is impossible to establish, since "justice"

is a matter of values. But a *feeling* of social injustice provides fertile soil for social movements, equally among the rich, the poor, and the in-betweens.

Status inconsistency. *Status inconsistency*, described on pages 105–106, develops when one's several statuses are not equally ranked [Lenski, 1954; Goffman, 1957; Malewski, 1966]. People who have a strong feeling of status inconsistency are likely to feel deprived and improperly recognized and rewarded.

These three factors—relative deprivation, perception of injustice, and status inconsistency—when all are present in the same person, make for a discontent and readiness to join social movements.

Structural preconditions for social movements

In a provocative synthesis, Stockdale [1970] suggests five preconditions for the appearance of collective action: (1) *social discontent;* (2) *structural blockage* (barriers in the social structure which prevent people from removing the sources of their discontent); (3) *contact* (interaction between the discontented); (4) *efficacy* (a feeling of expectation that proposed action will relieve discontent); and (5) *ideology* (a body of beliefs which justify and support the proposed action). When all these are present, collective action is almost inevitable. Table 34 shows Stockdale's application of this synthesis to several recent social movements. A synthesis of this sort, if sound, should enable us to predict the rise of social movements in the near future. A longitudinal study would be needed to test Stockdale's propositions.

Personal susceptibility to social movements

In a stable, well-integrated society with very few social tensions or alienated groups, there are few social movements and few people who are interested. Contented people rarely join social movements. Those who are at peace within themselves and with their society are likely to be fully absorbed in their own activities. They generally view social movements with either amusement, indifference, or hostility. But in a changing, continuously disorganized society, the fully contented person is a rarity. More people in such a society believe they perceive social injustice and become dissatisfied or alienated. It is the dissatisfied who build social movements. The frustrated and misplaced, the restless and rootless, those who putter in boredom, those who seethe with hostility, those who are oppressed by the futility of their present lives, those who rage against what they perceive as social injustice—these are the material of which most social movements are built. Let us note some of the circumstances apparently associated with such states of mind.

Mobility

People on the move have little chance to put down roots and become integrated into the life of the community. Their mobility not only weakens the community's control over them, it also deprives them of the emotional satisfactions of really belonging to the local group. California, whose population doubled in less than a generation, seems to be the birthplace of more movements, cults, and sects than any other several states combined, while in low-mobility states like Vermont, an agitator can address the largest crowds in a whisper.

When mobility is forced upon people by changing circumstances, they are even more in need of a social movement as an emotional refuge. Cohn's [1957] study of European millenarian movements in the Middle Ages found that millenarian fantasies were strongest among the uprooted peasants who were forced off the land to become urban workers or beggars and unemployed. They suffered the effects of geographic mobility and downward social mobility combined. But mobility of ei-

ther sort almost always produces social movements.

We should remember, of course, that this is a joint cause-and-effect relationship. That is, many people are mobile because they are rootless, and many people are rootless because they are mobile. No matter what the circumstances, high-mobility groups generally provide more than their share of a movement's converts.

Marginality

Persons who are not fully accepted and integrated into a group are termed *marginal*. The concept of marginality is more fully explained on page 307. Marginal persons are likely to feel uneasy and insecure, anxious for acceptance and resentful that it has been withheld. Stated differently, they are aware of a discrepancy between their self-image and the public image of them, and the inconsistency is frustrating.

Contented people rarely join social movements.

Marginality often seems to produce overconformity, as is shown by the fierce patriotism of the newly naturalized citizen, the tireless zeal of the new religious convert, or the meticulous etiquette of the new-rich. But sometimes marginal people give up this search for acceptance and join an unpopular social movement, as though to say, "Here, at least, *someone* appreciates me!" In fact, much of the membership and leadership of many social movements seems to have come from marginal groups in society [Lasswell and Blumenstock, 1939, pp. 277–300; Hoffer, 1951]. This does not mean that only marginal people join movements. In the case of the Cooperative Commonwealth Federation, a socialist political movement in Saskatchewan, the established leaders among the farm people became active CCF members; yet among the town businessmen, mainly the marginal persons joined [Lipset, 1950]. Since the CCF reflected basic changes in the value system of rural Saskatchewan, the opinion leaders among the farmers were among the first to join. But since the movement did not reflect the dominant values of the business community, it attracted those businessmen whose marginal acceptance had prevented them from fully internalizing the values of the business group.

Most movements draw many of their early members and leaders from the marginal persons and groups in the society. Marginal people are more susceptible because they are anxious for acceptance somewhere and are less firmly wedded to the norms and values of the groups which have only partly accepted them. But until a movement succeeds in also attracting the leaders and decision makers of the group it aims at, it generally remains weak and ineffectual.

Social isolation

Considerable research shows that persons and groups who are isolated from the community are more alienated and are more receptive to mass movements than groups whose status and work integrates them into the community. Kornhauser [1959, p. 159] says that ". . . free-lance intellectuals appear to be more disposed toward mass movements than intellectuals in corporate bodies, especially universities." The worker groups who are most receptive to social movements, especially to violent movements, are those whose work cuts them

off from the larger society, such as miners, maritime workers, and longshoremen [Kornhauser, 1959, chap. 12]. Because of either geographical location or social structure, these workers have few social contacts with other groups in the society. They rarely belong to the mixed-membership voluntary associations which thrive among other groups. They have few opportunities to participate in the formal and informal life of the community; their ties to the established order are weak, and they are more easily mobilized to overthrow it.

Changing social status

No evidence shows that activity in social movements is more intense at one class level than another, but evidence does show that a *change* of status increases susceptibility. Upward mobility brings a person into new class groupings in which his or her position is marginal and where he or she is somewhat insecure. But a loss of social status, or threatened loss, is still more unsettling. A few years ago, when this topic was of interest to scholars, they produced a good deal of evidence that those who feel they are suffering downward mobility are abnormally hostile toward other groups and are more often violent and authoritarian in their social attitudes [Bettelheim and Janowitz, 1950, pp. 55ff; Srole, 1956; Kaufman, 1957], and are good candidates for social movements [Geschwender, 1968]. In Germany the farmers who voted most heavily for Hitler between 1932 and 1934 were neither the rich nor the poor, but were the commercial-type farmers who were most vulnerable to market changes [Loomis and Beagle, 1946; Heberle, 1951, pp. 222–236]. In other words, the farmers who feared that they might become poor turned Nazi more regularly than did those who were already poor. But all the observers of Nazism agree that the strongest support before the Nazis gained power came from the lower-middle-class shopkeepers, tradesmen, and artisans who, having lost their savings in the

TABLE 34 STRUCTURAL PRECONDITIONS FOR THE EMERGENCE OF COLLECTIVE ACTION: FOUR EXAMPLES

Example	VARIABLES				
	Discontent (Inequity)	Structural blockage	Contact	Efficacy	Ideology
Ghetto riots	High level of discontent. Inputs of education, skills and energy tend to be inequitably rewarded—low levels of income, cultural deprivation.	Individual efforts to improve situation blocked by discrimination in jobs, housing, etc.	High level of contact among alienated ghetto dwellers. Critical mass of potential partisans.	Costs of collective action high, although individuals may perceive low potential personal costs. Chances of removing original source of discontent low.* Probable satisfaction in acting against the system.	Legitimacy of the present system questioned on both local and societal levels. Whites and "black bourgeoisie" depicted as colonial exploiters.
Delano grape strike	High level of discontent. Inputs of physical effort and skills receive lower returns than could be obtained in off-farm employment.	Individual unable to improve situation by increased effort, skills or negotiation. Discrimination.	Migrants in Delano area less geographically mobile than migrants in other sections of the country. Greater contact for longer time periods.	Costs of participation low relative to potential outcomes.† Collective bargaining has been successful in industry.	Growers are depicted as greedy affluent capitalists who exploit migrants. Acceptance of collective bargaining.
Student protest (active)	High levels of discontent. Students object to being "processed" through an impersonal bureaucratic system and "channeled into an unjust society." Many altruistically concerned with inequity situations of minorities.	Individual efforts to "work through channels" usually ineffective.	Protests occur only when "critical mass" of dissatisfied students are in frequent contact.	Sanctions not generally severe in early cases of student protest.*	University depicted as an impersonal bureaucratic system which processes students and channels them into an unjust society.
National Farmers Organization (NFO)	High level of discontent. Inputs of education, skills, capital and energy receive lower returns than could be earned in off-farm work.	Individual has almost no influence on prices received and only limited control of production costs.	Potential partisans are contacted by recruiters. Meetings are "rites of intensification."	Costs to participants low relative to potential outcomes.† Collective bargaining has been successful in industry.	Processors and distributors of agricultural products depicted as exploiters of farmers. Acceptance of collective bargaining.

*For any given level of discontent, the emergence of collective action is generally positively related to the efficacy of collective action (inversely related to severity of sanctions). Where the level of discontent is very great, collective action may occur even with the threat of extreme sanctions.

†Costs and potential payoffs to grape strikers and NFO members are principally economic. Leaders attempt to convince potential partisans that the probability of success is high and potential payoffs are great. The costs for specific individuals, however, may be high.
Source: Quoted by permission from Jerry D. Stockdale, "Structural Preconditions for Collective Action," paper presented at the 1970 annual meeting of the Society for the Study of Social Problems.

postwar inflation, were now being squeezed between the gains of organized labor and the rationalization of production and distribution by the big corporations and department stores [Gerth, 1940; Mannheim, 1940, pp. 102ff.; Fromm, 1941, pp. 211–216]. The same groups formed the core of the French Poujadist movement in the 1950s, a tax-revolt movement centered among the small shopkeepers who were threatened by big-business retailing [Heberle, 1956; Lipsedge, 1956]. The most violent reaction to Martin Luther King's demonstration marches came in Northern upper-working-class neighborhoods whose residents, often first- or second-generation immigrants, had clawed their way out of the slum and feared that black neighbors would recreate the slum they had escaped [Giles, 1967]. A study [Rother, 1967] of John Birch Society members found that, as compared with a control group of nonmembers, the John Birch Society members had experienced far more mobility, mostly downward, and the study concluded by attributing their political extremism to their status frustrations. Probably no development is more likely to inspire a social movement than a perceived threat to the economic security and social status of some segment of the society.

Lack of family ties

The advice, "Marry and settle down," is not just a piece of rhetoric; it actually happens. When men and women get a little home with a big mortgage and the responsibility of new mouths to fill and feet to cover, they may lose their urge to man the barricades! The more extremist and unpopular the movement, the more strongly do family ties discourage one's participation. Activity in a social movement is time-consuming and competes with family responsibilities.

A person with a warm, richly satisfying family life has no emotional need to find a cause to fill the emotional void in his or her life, which some scholars see as the main reason people join social movements [Hoffer, 1951]. Membership studies of social movements have generally found a disproportionate share of members who either have no families or are estranged from their families. This is especially true with the more radical movements. Thus Ernst and Loth's [1952, pp. 1–15] study of former American Communist party members found that most of them joined the party during their late teens or early twenties, while still unmarried, and while engaged in bitter emancipation conflicts with their parents. During the 1930s, youths with a strong emotional need to tell their devout-Baptist-Republican-businessman fathers, "You can't run *my* life!" often joined the Communist party. A decade ago they might have joined the New Left or the hippie dropouts; today they are joining Hare Krishna or the Jesus movement. One psychiatrist, after psychoanalytic interviews with a sample of campus revolutionists, concludes that most of them came from homes which superficially appeared to be permissive, but in which parents withdrew from and emotionally abandoned their children. He asserts that their parents' failure to provide reassurance and guidance left these children immature and lacking in the confidence and ability to pursue conventional life goals [Hendin, 1971]. Another study, supporting the immaturity thesis, found that the reality perceptions of a sample of high school activists resembled those of elementary school children more closely than they resembled those of nonactivist high school students [Crain and Crain, 1974]. But some studies disagree with this analysis and find such background factors not very important [Aron, 1974]. However, there is not enough definitive research to permit psychiatric generalizations about campus revolutionaries or other movement activists. Are they immature or unstable persons who are displacing their own emotional conflicts upon the society? Or are they fearlessly unmasking the hypocrisy and exploitation of an unjust society? It is possible that both propositions are in some measure correct.

Since a stable, tightly knit family life discourages activity in social movements, most revolutionary movements, from early Christianity to the New Left, have attacked the family. The Apostle Paul counseled Christians to remain single and undistracted if they were able to. One of the first moves of the new Communist government of China was to launch a vigorous, calculated attack upon the extended family, aiming to undermine family authority, sever the lines of family obligation, and transfer personal loyalties and emotional moorings from the family to the Communist party [Chandrasekhar, 1959; Yang, 1959]. But a new regime, after it is firmly established, supports and uses the family as a conservative and stabilizing force. Thus the early Communist regime in Russia attacked the family, endorsed free love, ridiculed parental authority, and encouraged postcard divorce; in Russia today, parental authority is supported, divorce is exceedingly difficult, public morals are puritanical, and affectionate family life is officially encouraged [Alt and Alt, 1959; Kharchev, 1961; Leslie, 1973, pp. 136–138]. There is no inconsistency in this about-face. It merely reveals a revolutionary movement at different stages in its career.

Personal maladjustment

In the preceding pages we have repeatedly hinted that the maladjusted are especially susceptible to social movements. Those who have failed to find a satisfying life role and a comfortable, secure status are very likely, consciously or unconsciously, to be shopping for something to bring purpose and meaning to their lives. In a perceptive discussion, Hoffer [1951, pp. 45–46] has distinguished the temporary from the permanent misfits. The temporary misfits are "people who have not found their place in life but still hope to find it." Adolescent youth, unemployed college graduates, demobilized veterans, and new immigrants are examples. Restless, frustrated, and

fearful that opportunity may elude them, they are good fodder for movements but are not very dependable. As rapidly as the society can offer rewarding jobs and statuses to them, they are likely to lose interest in social movements. The permanent misfits are those who, because of limited talent or some impassable social barrier, are forever blocked from the role and status they crave. The unsuccessful artist or writer, the middle-aged craftsman whose trade is destroyed by automation and who must compete as an unskilled laborer, the single person who desperately wants a home and children but has no hope of finding them—all are permanent misfits, since there is little prospect of their ever finding a life role and status rewarding enough to absorb their interests. They remain frustrated and in emotional need of something to fill the aching void in their lives.

Are social movements, then, only a refuge for the homeless failures and misfits of society? Do such people join a movement in a sort of emotional reflex, and not as an act of intellectual judgment? Yes, to some extent. Heberle [1951, p. 113] remarks, "The neurotic, maladjusted, unbalanced or psychopathic seem to be attracted not so much by the ideas [of a movement] as by the sense of oneness, of belonging, which appeases their feelings of insecurity, of helplessness, of isolation." Certainly there are both rational and nonrational factors in movement participation. In at least some cases, rational self-interest lies at the base of one's behavior in social movements [Olson, 1965; Oberschall, 1973]. In other instances, the nonrational factors may be more important. One young activist who died in a bomb-making accident was described by an associate in these words: "Angel didn't necessarily want to believe in revolution. She just wanted to *believe.* I believe she would have taken anything, fascist or revolutionary, just as long as it didn't have a complicated, ambiguous line" [Wolff, 1974, p. 18].

Members of the more extreme movements often shift from one movement professing one set of beliefs to another movement professing an opposite set of beliefs with very little intellectual difficulty. Thus, "Hitler looked on the German Communists as potential National Socialists . . . [Nazi] Captain Roehm boasted that he could turn the reddest Communist into a nationalist in four weeks. On the other hand, [Communist] Karl Radek looked on the Nazi Brown Shirts (S.A.) as a reserve for future Communist recruits" [Hoffer, 1951, p. 17]. Later history showed all these men to be correct. While it is dangerous to generalize about motives, such evidence lends support to the belief that many people join extremist movements to satisfy their emotional compulsions, while the rational programs of these movements are unimportant so long as the members' emotional yearnings are fulfilled.

Are the less extreme movements equally nonrational? Probably not. When a movement expresses a developing consensus of opinion among the more influential members of the society, as the temperance movement did in the nineteenth century [Gusfield, 1955], as the Cooperative Commonwealth Federation did in Saskatchewan [Lipset, 1950], or as the civil rights movement did in the 1950s, such a movement attracts the responsible leaders of the community, not the misfits. Probably most of the members of a movement find some element of emotional compensation in their activity, as nearly all of us find it in our own behavior. But the evidence would not justify a conclusion that movements arise solely from the people's need to scratch their emotional itch.

All the above conditions help to prepare people who are receptive to the appeal of a social movement. This receptivity does not "cause" important mass movements. Unless there is deep and widespread social discontent, any movement growing purely from the misfits' hunger for a crusade will have no future. But when social unrest is intense and alienation and anomie become normal, then the homeless, the status cliff-hangers, and the misfits become the shock troops of mass movements which can set an entire nation on fire. The ultimate consequences depend upon the actions of the responsible leaders of the society. If they perceive social injustices in need of correction and social tensions in need of resolution, assume leadership, and channel this mass protest into constructive social reforms, the main features of the social system may be conserved. But if they seek to block social reforms which are passionately sought and long overdue, as did the eighteenth-century French or the early twentieth-century Russian aristocrats, they guarantee the eventual destruction of the social system.

Types of social movements

To classify social movements is not always easy, for sometimes a movement is intermediate or mixed in nature, or is different at different stages of its career. As always, the categories below are "ideal types," into which actual movements more or less perfectly fall.

Migratory movements

After the American Revolution, an estimated 100,000 British sympathizers either fled or were exiled, mostly to Canada [Brown, 1969]. Following the Civil War, about 10,000 Southerners left the country rather than endure the Yankee Reconstruction and established colonies in Mexico and Brazil [Nunn, 1956; Ross and Kerner, 1958]. Sometimes discontent with present circumstances, together with the lure of a greener distant pasture, leads large numbers of people to migrate. The mere fact that a lot of people migrate does not create a migratory social movement, nor is one created purely by the number of people who move, each for private and widely varied reasons. We have a migratory social movement when there is a common focus of discontent, a shared purpose or hope for the future, and a widely discussed and shared decision to move to a new location, regardless of whether they migrate as an organized group or as individuals and families. The northward migration of Southern blacks began to assume the proportions of a social movement about the time of World War I and only recently has begun to subside. A more spectacular example is the Irish migration in which over 750,000 of the Irish people, already economically distressed and politically discontented, left their country in the five years following the great potato-crop failures beginning in 1845 [Morehouse, 1928]. In the seventeen years before the Berlin Wall was built in 1961, over 4 million East Germans fled the dull grey monotony of the German Democratic Republic. This was over one-fourth of that country's population, making this one of the greatest mass migrations in history [Gilroy, 1961; Bailey, 1961].

Migration is often difficult today. Every Communist country in the world has fences, armed guards, and police dogs to keep its people in, while the capitalist democracies, despite all their imperfections, have guards and fences to keep people out. Migration is not always available to a distressed people.

Zionism: a contemporary migratory social movement. For over 2,000 years, Jews have dreamed of a return to the "Promised Land." A succession of self-styled messiahs following the end of the Middle Ages stimulated much excitement, but no solid accomplishments. Yet interest remained, and Theodore Herzl fanned this impulse into a political movement at the first Zionist congress in 1897. But the attractions of the Zionist movement paralleled the degree of Jewish persecution throughout the world. Migration to Palestine (now Israel) during the 1920s was limited by the British government which ruled Palestine under a League of Nations mandate, and allowed only a trickle of immigrants. During the 1930s, migration multiplied greatly as Jewish persecution in Europe mounted, much of this migration in violation of British regulations. By 1948, when the United Nations attempted to resolve the

Arab-Jewish question by partitioning Palestine into separate states, the Jewish population of Palestine was only 35 percent native-born. Jewish immigration continued at a high rate, with the native-born fraction of the Jewish population of Israel falling as low as 25 percent in 1951, then rising to 37 percent in 1960.

Arab opposition to Jewish migration and to the establishment of the state of Israel led to wars in 1947, 1956, 1967, and 1973, and this conflict remains unresolved. Many accounts sympathetic to the Israeli cause are available [Hurewitz, 1968; Eckhardt and Eckhardt, 1970; Segre, 1971], an occasional critical account is found [Lilienthal, 1965], and, rarely, an Arab point of view appears in English [Abu-Lughod, 1970]. Meanwhile Jewish migration to Israel continues, and the future rate of migration will be as greatly determined by what happens to Jews elsewhere as by what happens in Israel.

Expressive movements

When people are bottled up within a confining social system from which they cannot flee and which they feel powerless to change, the result generally is an expressive social movement. In the expressive social movement individuals come to terms with an unpleasant external reality *by modifying their reactions to that reality,* not by modifying the external reality itself. Through some kind of activity—dreams, visions, rituals, dances, games, consciousness-altering drugs, or other forms of emotional expression—one finds enough emotional release to make life bearable. Often the expressive movement is millenarian. Dozens of movements have helped people to ignore a miserable present by fixing their gaze upon a glorious millennium that is about to dawn [Cohn, 1957; Watson, 1973].

Most millenarian movements are purely escapist in that they occupy people with happy dreams while the existing realities remain unchanged. Yet the millenarian movement may pave the way for eventual reform or revolt because it cuts ties to the past, and may function as a unifying and arousing force in a passive population. Thus it may serve as a connecting link between prepolitical and actively political movements [Talmon, 1962].

Expressive movements are many and varied. The medieval flagellants sought a release from their sense of sin and personal unworthiness (and possibly gratified other compulsions) by masochistic orgies [Cohn, 1957, chap. 6]. Expressive movements would include the great surge of interest and collective activity surrounding pseudoscientific, mystic, and occultist preoccupations, ranging from UFOs to satanism [Evans, 1973; Sladek, 1973; symposium, *The Humanist,* September, 1974, pp. 4–33]. Some scholars would include crazes, fads, and fashions as expressive movements [Blumer, 1969a, pp. 114–119], but the present writers consider them too trivial to be social movements and have discussed them in Chapter 17, "Collective Behavior."

The Jesus Movement: a contemporary expressive movement. The 1960s brought the counterculture along with a great surge of youthful idealism and reformism in all the industrialized democracies. The 1970s brought disillusionment. Social problems proved to be resistant to easy solutions; confrontations were found to be dangerous and often unproductive. The collapse of the New Left (see pages 484–485) has been followed by a turning of thoughts and concerns inward, away from the society and toward the self.

Aside from the mainline orthodox churches, practically every kind of religious experience has attracted new interest and support. The Jesus Movement proclaims a simple, fundamentalist, evangelistic Christianity along with a rejection of materialism, violence, drugs, and nonmarital sex. There are many movement organizations, ranging from the relatively orderly and formal Campus Crusade for Christ to the commune-based Children of God. In 1971, this organization claimed around

3,000 members in about 30 communes. Personal life-styles range from "straight" to "hip"; long hair and bare feet are common, but personal cleanliness is the rule. Members are almost exclusively white, middle- or upper-class in origin. Most members have experienced and wearied of the drugs, sex, and intellectual chaos of the counterculture.

The Jesus Movement is heavily pentacostal (speaking in tongues), apocalyptic (anticipating an early Armageddon, with destruction of the world and a second coming of Christ), and bears heavy overtones of occultism [Ward, 1972, chap. 8]. The Children of God communes "provide an alternative community for a class which had already experienced alienation" [Ellwood, 1973, p. 12]. In place of the drug "high," the Jesus Movement provides a way of getting "high" on Jesus, with the emotional ecstasy of fundamentalist Christianity and "Jesus rock" music, of coming forward to be "saved," and anticipating the apocalypse [Howard, 1974, p. 208]. The movement offers the sustaining warmth and companionship of the counterculture and the high sense of purpose of radical activism without its violence, dangers, and "sinful" indulgences. Yet the Jesus Movement is not purely escapist. As Howard notes, "The Jesus Movement provides a way for dissident youth to be reintegrated into society" [p. 207]. Critics object to the movement's anti-intellectualism, its primitive theology, and its withdrawal from responsible political action [Ellwood, 1973, p. 132]. Defenders contrast the serene, orderly lives of the "Jesus people" with the vacuous destructiveness of the less lovely segments of the counterculture, and pronounce it an improvement.

Utopian movements

Ever since Sir Thomas More wrote his *Utopia,* the term has meant a society of such perfection that it can be found only in the imagination. Many other writers had a try at describing a perfect society, from Plato in his *Republic* to

B. F. Skinner in *Walden II*. Many attempts to create such a perfect society were made in the eighteenth and nineteenth centuries when utopian movements were popular [Nordhoff, 1875; Davis, 1930, chap. 2; Roberts, 1971, chaps. 2–4; Leslie, 1973, chap. 5; Kinkade, 1974]. Since these idealists are never able to experiment with an entire society, the utopian movement is *an attempt to create an ideal social system within a small community of dedicated followers;* later this system might expand to include the entire society. Many of the utopian communities of the past which were strongly religious survived longer because they did not have to "pay off" in personal happiness or material well-being. The payoff was in following the will of God. But other utopian communities, like Brook Farm and the Oneida Community, were secular in ideology. They were based on a conception of humanity as basically good, cooperative, and altruistic, needing only a favorable setting to unlock these virtues. Most of the religious and all of the secular utopian movements failed, either because of inner contradictions and impracticabilities or because of conflict with the external society [Burton, 1939; Halloway, 1951; Bestor, 1950, 1970; Kanter, 1972; Veysey, 1974].

The utopian ideal, however, remains very much alive. Skinner's *Walden II* [1948] is possibly the best-known example of contemporary utopian literature, but there are many other modern utopians [Kateb, 1971]. It is likely that people will never cease trying to imagine a more perfect society.

The commune: a contemporary utopian social movement. The commune, described on page 207, is popular among those who are variously called hippies, dropouts, freaks, or members of the "alternative society." While some of the communes are filled with obvious misfits who could not "make it" under any social system, some other communes are composed of highly talented, well educated people who appear to be emotionally stable. All share a conviction that conventional society is hypocritical, exploitative, destructive of human values, decadent, and hopelessly doomed by its own contradictions. They see their alternative society as an answer to loneliness, alienation, exploitation, and social injustice.

In some communes the members hold regular jobs; but in many, the main source of funds is welfare, plus some income from odd jobs, occasional work, sale of handicraft objects, and contributions from parents. The nonworking commune is thus parasitic upon the society, and therefore cannot serve as the utopian model for the entire society to copy. If the alternative society of the commune is to be generally accepted, the commune in which most people work will need to be the model.

The alternative-society movement, like all utopian movements, faces the scorn and opposition of conventional people. Reports of police harassment are common, and some rural communes have been literally "run off" by local residents who, among other objections, may have feared the commune's attraction for their own youth. Since communards are typically rather gentle people without weapons or much inclination to fight, they have been prey to thievery and to the bullying of motorcycle toughs, for whom terrorizing a commune is a favorite sport.

To date, communards have been drawn mainly from white, middle- or upper-class youth. Will the commune spread among the black and the poor, many of whom have long practiced a semi-communal sharing of their meager resources [Davis, 1946]? Possibly, but it is also possible that the commune appeals only to those who have experienced the comfortable, conventional life-style of the middle and upper classes and found it unsatisfying.

Reform movements

The reform movement is *an attempt to improve the society without greatly changing its basic social structure.* Reform movements are difficult in an authoritarian society, whose rulers tolerate no active opposition. Reform movements can operate easily only in a democratic atmosphere where people have considerable freedom to criticize existing institutions and may secure changes in them when the majority wishes.

American history is crowded with reform movements—abolition, feminism, prohibition, and many others. At any moment, dozens of "mimeograph organizations" (consisting of a post office box number, a mimeograph machine, a mailing list, and a set of optimistic hopes) are seeking to arouse enough public interest to spark a reform movement. A number of conservation groups and organizations labored for years before enough public interest developed to fuel the current environmentalist movement. One of the most recent reform movements is the Gay Liberation Movement, in which many homosexuals have "come out of the closet" and organized to demand acceptance of homosexuality as a legitimate alternative life-style [Miller, 1971; Humphreys, 1972; Alvarez and March, 1974; Jay and Young, 1974]. Our democratic atmosphere, our Judeo-Christian values, and our tradition of voluntarism have combined to make reform movements a conspicuous feature of past and present American history.

Women's Liberation: a contemporary reform movement. The feminist movement of the nineteenth and early twentieth centuries, after considerable dispute over goals and tactics, finally united upon the goal of woman suffrage, and soon dissolved after this goal was won [O'Neill, 1969]. Today's Women's Liberation Movement found its ideology in books such as Simone de Beauvoir's *The Second Sex* [1953], Betty Friedan's *The Feminine Mystique* [1963], and Kate Millet's *Sexual Politics* [1970]. One of the sparks which ignited the movement was the condescending treatment of women in the New Left [Piercy, 1970]. As one woman reports, "Suddenly women found themselves *serving,* as secretary, mother and

concubine, while men did all the speaking, writing and negotiating—and these were men who professed to reject the 'oppressive' ritual machinery of their society" [Gottlieb, 1971, p. 27].

While pique may have thrown the spark, it fell upon the tinder of undeniable sex discrimination and the recent decline in the status of women in American society (see pages 208–210 for documentation and a description of the philosophy and goals of Women's Lib). The movement consists of hundreds of local groups, many of which are affiliated with a national organization. The National Organization of Women (NOW) is the largest and probably the most conservative, whose goal is to "bring women into full participation in the mainstream of American society now, exercising all the privileges and responsibilities thereof in truly equal partnership with men" [Wilkes, 1970, p. 143]. Some other groups are more radical, such as Women's International Terrorist Conspiracy From Hell (WITCH) or Women's Radical Action Project (WRAP), and a continuous reshuffling of organizational structures can be expected. The more radical members of Women's Lib are generally ardent New Leftists, who see the liberation of women as merely one aspect of a total revolution in the society.

Membership studies show that the members are predominantly white, educated, middle-class, relatively young, atheist or agnostic in religion, and independent and "modern" in outlook [Tavris, 1973; Dempewolff, 1974]. One sociologist-member claims that conversion to Women's Liberation requires that a woman have: (1) means and resources to pursue some alternative to the traditional female sex role; (2) a political sophistication about the uses of power; (3) a sense of achievement discrepancy between her potentials and her accomplishments; and (4) a long-term pattern of defiance of traditional values, with practically all members being religious unbelievers, sexually "emancipated," and illegal drug users or experimenters [Micossi, 1970]. The main conversion technique is the "consciousness-raising" session, in which a group of ten or fifteen women, under a leader, are encouraged to examine and discuss their personal experiences in the light of "sexism" (the ascribing of subordinate roles to women) and "male chauvinism" (patronizing condescension to women) [Gornick, 1971]. Consciousness-raising sessions are devoted to arousing an awareness of the many subtle ways in which women's subordinate role is maintained. The movement has its critics [Mailer, 1971; Decter, 1972; Staines et al., 1974], and many men who give verbal assent continue to behave traditionally [Tavris, 1973].

Is Women's Liberation a rational response to the culture lag between our democratic egalitarian ethos and our patterns of sex discrimination? Or is it a displacement of the emotional problems of unhappy and neurotic women? Are they unhappy and neurotic because of cultural lags in the status and treatment of women, or because of emotional difficulties which would make them unhappy and neurotic in any cultural setting? While reliable evidence is lacking, it is likely that all these propositions are in some part true. At the least, the relatively moderate goals of NOW are no more than are required by the democratic ethos and the Civil Rights Act of 1964. It is also likely that, as with most social movements, the more active members—the "true believers" Hoffer describes [1951]—derive their commitment from their own emotional discontents. Journalistic biographical sketches of a few leaders and members show a high proportion who have a history of marital failure, and of frustration and dissatisfaction with female sex roles [Wilkes, 1970; Gornick, 1971]. Some members reveal an aggressive hostility toward men and would much prefer a karate black belt to a wedding ring. However, while it is likely that Women's Liberation attracts a high proportion of frustrated, hostile people, this is true of many movements, and does not necessarily invalidate a movement's claims. While the more radical goals of Women's Liberation may

never be attained, the movement appears to have revived a cultural drift towards sex equality which had been stalled for decades. The status of women in society will probably be different in many ways in the year 2000 [Tripp, 1974].

It is possible, however, that the Women's Liberation Movement may have "peaked" in the early 1970s. As this is written, it appears that support for the passage of the Equal Rights Amendment is wavering. It may be significant that the best-selling book in 1974 [Morgan, 1973] concentrated upon telling women how to be sexy, beautiful, submissive housewives, and that two sets of study courses, teaching women how to be nonliberated, are proving to be tremendously popular [*Time,* Mar. 10, 1975, p. 77]. It may be that the second American feminist movement is drawing to a close.

Revolutionary movements

A *revolution* is *a sudden, usually violent, and relatively complete change in a social system.* It is distinguished from the coup d'etat, or palace revolt, which replaces the individuals who rule, but leaves the institutions and the power system of the society unchanged. The term is sometimes applied to gradual, sweeping, peaceful changes such as the industrial revolution or the "sexual revolution," but this is a different usage of the term. The revolutionary movement seeks to overthrow the existing social system and replace it with a greatly different one. Unlike the reformer who wants to correct some imperfections in the present social order, the revolutionist considers the system not worth saving. The reformer is, therefore, the revolutionist's worst enemy, for social reforms may drain off the discontent upon which the revolutionist wishes to build a revolution.

A democracy is poor soil for revolution. A revolutionary movement must be rooted in a tremendous social discontent; but in a democracy, social unrest generally leads to social reform, and reform indefinitely postpones the revolution. But where authoritarian government blocks the popular wish for reform, the reformer must then attack the government, and thus becomes a revolutionist. Revolutionary movements flourish where reform is blocked so that the revolutionary movement is the people's only alternative to their present misery. It is no accident that the Communist party has been weakest in democratic countries such as the United States, England, and the Scandinavian countries, and is far stronger in countries with a tradition of repressive government, or where government is nominally democratic, yet is so structured as to be an ineffective instrument of the popular wish for reform. In France and Italy, many people despair of reform and turn to revolutionary parties [Cantril, 1958].

Edwards [1927] and Brinton [1938] have independently arrived at a practically identical sequence of stages which they believe to be typical of most successful revolutions: (1) an accumulation of deep unrest, stretching over many years; (2) the defection of the intellectuals, who grow increasingly critical of the status quo; (3) the emergence of an economic incentive for revolt and a social myth or set of beliefs to justify it; (4) the revolutionary outbreak, aided by the hesitation and weakness of the ruling group; (5) the rule of the moderates, who soon fail to control the various groups among the revolutionists or to satisfy the aroused passions of the populace; (6) the rise of the radicals or extremists, who gain power and begin to exterminate all opposition; (7) the reign of terror; (8) the return to normality, as moderates regain power, consolidate the achievements of the revolution, and restore some aspects of the prerevolutionary society. More recent theorists have, with some embellishments, generally supported the Edwards-Brinton sequence [Schwartz, 1971; Methvin, 1973]. The Edwards-Brinton outline is based largely on the French and Russian revolutions. The more recent Mexican revolution followed it fairly closely, while the Chinese and Cuban revolutions appear to be following it somewhat less closely.

Sometimes it is difficult to classify a movement as clearly reform or clearly revolutionary, since the supporters cover a broad spectrum ranging from moderate reformers to violent revolutionists. Women's Lib is an example. The Black Panther party is revolutionary in goals and tactics, at least as it affects black people, although it would leave white society relatively unchanged [Foner, 1970; Howard, 1974, chap. 2].

The New Left: a recent revolutionary movement. The spirit of protest among mainly the younger people also ranged from reformist to revolutionary. The young reformers and the young revolutionists were in considerable agreement in their indictment of the present society as unjust, exploitative, and destructive of humanity, but they differed in their prescription. The reformers worked "within the system" to effect change, using nonviolent demonstration and political activity as means. Reformers admired "Nader's Raiders," the team working with Ralph Nader, and supported the environmentalist movement, while revolutionists considered such efforts irrelevant or even counterproductive. The New Left was especially contemptuous of the liberal. One observer reported that "All New Leftists agree on *liberal*. He is universally defined as a hypocritical, selling-out vacillator, a guilt-ridden moralist unable to act decisively because he sees all sides of an issue; a picker at tiny parts of a problem who thereby fails to solve any of it; an immoral man" [Romm, 1970, p. 247].

There are numerous published descriptions of the revolutionary New Left. Some are critical [Feuer, 1968; Gerberding and Smith, 1970; Kelman, 1970], some are neutrally descriptive and analytical [Cohen and Hale, 1966], and some are sympathetic [Hoffman, 1968; Lynd, 1969; Oglesby, 1969; Bone, 1975]. Some are compilations of New Left statements, handbills, posters, and other material [Berke, 1969; Romm, 1970].

Like most revolutionists, many New Leftists were at times undemocratic in seeking to impose their views, even when they were minority views, upon the majority by any means considered effective. Sometimes they were ruthlessly intolerant of dissent [Kelman, 1970], shouting down public speakers whom they wished to silence and disrupting meetings they wished to paralyze.[1]

The Students for a Democratic Society (SDS) were the leading movement organization. With a peak membership of 100,000, the SDS provided a focus for youth discontent, antiwar protest, and promotion of the hippie youth culture. While committed to the ideal of participatory democracy, the SDS nonetheless drifted into control by an elitist hierarchy, again illustrating Michels' "iron law of oligarchy" (see p. 221) [Stone, 1972]. The SDS was weakened by its male chauvinism, its narrowly middle-class base, its lack of a coherent, long-range program, and its naïve activism, which quickly reverted to a defeatist cynicism when it was not immediately successful [O'Brien, 1972].

The New Left Movement disintegrated rapidly after 1969, when the SDS dissolved into warring factions [Unger, 1974, chap. 6]. In the mid-1970s the counterculture has lost much of its following, the campus is relatively quiet, and graduating seniors are once again welcoming recruiters from ITT and Dow Chemical, those demons of the New Left. Yet radicalism is not dead. To a degree, it has moved from the dorms and the quadrangles into the faculty offices. In the major universities, avowed Marxist professors teach, use Marxian textbooks, and introduce courses in "Marxian Methodology." Most of the former radical activists are now working in schools, social agencies, and corporate executive suites, but most of them remain liberal-to-radical in their attitudes, and remain potential recruits for another round of radical activism when conditions are favorable [Fendrich and Tarleau, 1973].

Resistance movements

The revolutionary movement arises among people who are dissatisfied because social change is too slow. The resistance movement arises among those dissatisfied because change is too fast. The resistance movement is an effort to block a proposed change or to uproot a change already achieved. The Ku Klux Klan is perhaps our best-known resistance movement, organized in the South after the Civil War to keep blacks "in their place" by terror and intimidation [Brown, 1902, part 4; Mecklin, 1924], and reborn in the North after World War I as a nativistic movement [VanderZanden, 1960; Alexander, 1965]. The nativistic movement is an attempt to protect the purity of the group and its culture from new or foreign intrusions [Higham, 1955; Friedman, 1967]. The Native American party and the Know-Nothing movements of the 1830s and 1840s were anti-immigrant and anti-Catholic, and coincided with an increase of Irish and German immigration to the United States. As in most resistance movements, there was a large element of scapegoating in the focusing of frustrations arising from many sources upon the immigrant, who was blamed for practically all troubles.

In a democratic society, all periods of rapid change will stimulate resistance movements. The New Deal era of reform produced a large number of resistance-movement organizations [Schlesinger, 1960, vol. 3, chap. 1]. Some, like the Committee for Constitutional Government and the American Liberty League, were largely fund-collecting offices for the distribution of anti-New Deal propaganda. Others, like the Silver Shirts, the Black Legion, and the Christian Americans, were would-be mass movements which united opposition to New Deal reforms with anti-Semitism, isolationism, and antiforeign sentiments in a fascist-type organi-

---

[1]We sought to include some Liberation News Service releases illustrating the use of these tactics, but were denied reprint permission by Liberation News Service.

zation [Lowenthal and Guterman, 1949; Carlson, 1943, 1946]. More recently the movement of extreme resistance to liberalism, internationalism, and welfare statism has come to be known as the "radical right" [Bell, 1963; Howard, 1974, chap. 11]. Still more recently the "New Right" (sometimes called the "Libertarians") has appeared, differing slightly from the radical right in being less preoccupied with anticommunism, and favoring a thorough and consistent return to laissez faire economics and minimum government activity [Lipset, 1968; Lehr and Rossetto, 1971].

The White Citizens' Councils appeared in the wake of the Supreme Court's 1954 school desegregation decision. Unlike many movement organizations, this one drew many of the "community influentials" and political leaders of the South. For a time, the Southern "establishment" was solidly united in opposition to school desegregation and in support of the White Citizens' Councils [Cater, 1956; Routh and Anthony, 1956; VanderZanden, 1959]. As is usually the case with resistance movements, it failed and dissolved. For some years the John Birch Society was a prominent resistance organization, opposing "communism," which they defined to include all faintly liberal causes and programs [Grove, 1961; Mosk and Jewel, 1961; Epstein and Forster, 1967; Schamp, 1970]. Though still active, it has attracted relatively little recent attention.

Right to Life: A contemporary resistance movement. Abortion is older than written history. Legal prohibition of abortion in the United States dates from the 1830s, and was based on the medical dangers of abortion at a time when 30 percent of all abortions were fatal to the woman [Greenhouse, 1970]. As these declined until abortion became medically far less hazardous than childbirth, the opposition shifted to the argument that abortion is murder. This rests upon the assumption that a human being is created at the moment of conception—a theological proposition which cannot be scientifically evaluated.

By 1972, nearly two-thirds of all Americans agreed that "The decision to have an abortion should be made solely by a woman and her doctor" [Pomeroy and Landman, 1973]. By 1974, some 70 percent of all American Catholics agreed that legal abortions should be available to those who desired them [*Time*, Jan. 13, 1975, p. 55]. But the Supreme Court's 1973 decision legalizing early abortion stimulated a classic resistance movement aimed at reversing this decision.

A number of antiabortionist groups and organizations (which prefer to be called "Pro-Life") appeared, including Alternatives to Abortion, Birthright USA, American United for Life, National Right to Life Committee, and others. Sponsorship is heavily, but by no means exclusively, Catholic. The movement is too new for the customary membership studies to be available, but membership seems to be heavily concentrated among those who are religiously and politically conservative. Tactics include support of a "pro-Life" constitutional amendment empowering states to forbid abortion, an energetic publicity campaign featuring gory color pictures of aborted fetuses, and the pressing of any litigation which might reduce abortion availability or intimidate medical personnel [*Time*, Feb. 24, 1975, p. 67]. Local informational meetings and letters to the editor are extensively used.

The Right to Life Movement, in trying to reverse the majority public opinion on legalized abortion, would appear to be resisting a number of powerful cultural drifts and social trends. Whether it will succeed is doubtful.

Life cycle of social movements

No two movements are exactly alike; yet different movements have much in common. Most completed movements pass through much the same set of four stages—of unrest,

Agitators seem to pop up everywhere.

excitement, formalization, and institutionalization, first suggested by W. E. Gettys [Dawson and Gettys, 1934, pp. 708–709], who applied them to his study of the Methodist movement in England. A few accomplish their purpose without needing to enter the later stages. Other life cycles suggested by Zald and Ash [1969] and by Blumer [1969a, pp. 103–114] are quite similar, differing only in details.

The unrest stage

All movements are rooted in social unrest. When people grow bored and restless, or develop a sense of social injustice, or when some change has disrupted an established way of life, they develop an unstable volatility which we call social unrest. When they confront situations that their traditional ideology cannot explain, they are frustrated. For example, the Great Depression of the thirties brought actual destitution to millions of workers who had been socialized to believe that there must be something wrong with a man who cannot support his family. The emotional experience was shattering for unemployed men, many of whom agonized painfully about accepting relief when it was offered. Social change, social

disorganization, and social unrest are inseparable. This stage may be very prolonged, lasting as many as several generations.

The excitement stage

Unrest is vague, generalized, and unfocused. When it becomes focused on certain conditions, and when certain "causes" of misery are identified so that proposals for action fill the air, the excitement stage has come. During this stage it is easy to gather an audience, and agitators seem to pop up everywhere. Many fledgling movements are launched, mostly to founder on the rocks of clumsy leadership or ineffective appeals. Sometimes a magnetic agitator, working on people whose needs have made them receptive, can rouse a huge following almost overnight. To convert such a mass into an effective movement requires a skillful organizer. The excitement stage is typically brief, leading quickly either to action or to a loss of interest.

The formalization stage

Some of the migratory and expressive movements may be able to operate without formal organization, but those which seek to modify the society must become organized. An excited mass of followers will drift away unless their enthusiasms are ordered and directed. In the formalization stage, one or more movement organizations are formed, chains of officers are appointed, fund raising is systematized, and the ideology of the movement is clarified. The ideology reminds people of their discontents, identifies the villains, states the movement's objectives, outlines the strategy and tactics for attaining the stated porposes, and provides the moral justification for all these actions. Formalization converts an excited mass into a disciplined membership and a vague cause into a practical enterprise. This, too, is a brief phase leading quickly into institutionalization. Often rivalry and ideological disagreements among movement organizations splinter and destroy the movement. In the effort to prevent such "factionalism," many movement organizations become authoritarian, intolerant, and elitist [Geschwender, 1974].

The institutionalization stage

Institutionalization eventually overtakes most movements if they last long enough. The movement crystallizes into a definite pattern, including traditions to uphold and possibly vested interests to defend. Efficient bureaucrats replace zealous agitators as leaders, and members feel themselves supporters of a worthy organization rather than campaigners in a sacrificial crusade. The acquisition of elaborate office suites or buildings (as by labor organizations in recent years) is evidence that the institutionalization of the movement is complete and its active phase as a movement is over. This institutionalization stage may last almost indefinitely.

The dissolution stage

Most scholars end the movement's cycle with the institutionalization stage. But this is not really the end, for different movements come to different conclusions. A movement may die at any stage in its career. Some movements achieve their objectives and then disappear, like the movement for women's suffrage. The officers of a movement which is killed through success may attempt to switch the movement to a new objective, as the National Foundation did after polio was conquered. Such a change of direction is rarely successful. Some movements, however, do undergo a transition in which the movement comes to pursue objectives quite different from the original ones. As an example, the Townsend movement for liberal old-age pensions in the 1930s lost most of its members when returning prosperity and the growth of other pension plans undercut its program, but the Townsend clubs survived for quite a number of years as recreational groups of older people who were only mildly interested in the pension plan [Messinger, 1955]. A movement may shrink into a sectlike band of followers, doggedly pursuing an objective which is probably forever unattainable, such as the prohibitionist movement embodied in the Women's Christian Temperance Union [Gusfield, 1955]. Some movements achieve full institutional status and make a contribution to the institutions of the society. This progress is illustrated by the many religious sects which have completed the transition into denominations.

Appraisal

Do social movements do more good than harm? That is like asking if wind does more good than harm. Social movements are one of the ways a society changes itself. The changes, though often painful, would not occur unless some social force produced them.

Are the members emotionally sick people finding outlet for their compulsions, or are they generous humanitarians seeking to alleviate human suffering? Some of each. Some movements have more of one than of the other characteristic, but most movements have both, just as each person may have some of both within his or her own personality.

Will there be more new movements in the future? Yes, for social movements inevitably accompany rapid social change. What kinds? This we cannot predict. Authoritarian society encourages migratory, expressive, and perhaps revolutionary movements. An optimistic era like the eighteenth century abounds in utopian and reform movements, while, as Stephan Runciman [1956, p. 14] notes, "a disillusioned age turns to religion, as an escape from the uncertainties of the world." We can be certain only that social movements will continue to express people's dissatisfaction with the society in which they find themselves.

Summary

Social movements are collective attempts to promote or resist change, either in the society or in its members. Broad cultural drifts provide a favorable setting for social movements pushing in the same direction as the cultural drift. Social change and social disorganization produce the frustration, alienation, anomie, and confusion which make people more receptive to social movements. Perceived social injustice provides both the desire for change and the moral justification for a movement's actions. Mobility, marginality, social isolation, changing social status, lack of family ties, and personal maladjustments all tend to make persons more receptive.

Movements are of several types: *migratory,* wherein people physically flee a frustrating society; *expressive,* wherein they modify themselves rather than the society and find emotional outlet through expressive behavior; *utopian,* wherein a small band seeks to create a perfect society in miniature; *reform,* wherein a group seeks to persuade a democratic society to correct its imperfections; *revolutionary,* wherein people seek to replace the existing social system with a new one; and *resistance,* wherein conservatives seek to block or uproot social changes they dislike.

Sociologists and historians seek to describe a "typical" life cycle which movements may approximate: an *unrest* stage of widespread but unfocused discontent; an *excitement* stage, during which discontent is increased and focused; a *formalization* stage, when mass excitement is organized into effective action; an *institutionalization* stage, when the movement crystallizes into a bureaucracy, and a *dissolution* stage, when an active movement receives one of several kinds of funerals. While not always rational and sometimes annoying, social movements help a democratic society to take up cultural lags and remain passably integrated.

Questions and projects

1. How is a social movement distinguished from institutions, associations, pressure groups, cultural drifts, or social trends?
2. How do cultural drifts affect social movements? Considering present cultural drifts, what do you think will be the eventual success of the prohibitionist movement? Of the Women's Liberation Movement? Of the movement to outlaw legal abortion?
3. Why are social movements most likely to arise after a society begins to improve its material conditions rather than when it is in abject poverty?
4. Compared with other Western countries, has the United States had few or many social movements? Why?
5. What factors affect a person's receptivity to social movements?
6. Among the several types of social movements, which are the most numerous in present American society? Why?
7. Can you think of any social movements in the United States not mentioned in this chapter? In which classification would you place each?
8. What determines a person's decision to support one of several movements? Is it pure chance? The ideas and goals of the particular movement? The emotional needs it fills? Or what?
9. Is a movement likely to appeal to different kinds of people at different stages in its career? Why?
10. Some movements seem to attract mainly misfits and neurotics, while others attract the solid "respectables" of the community. Why? Sometimes a movement attracts the opinion leaders of one group and the misfits of another group. How do you explain this phenomenon?
11. Applying Stockdale's synthesis in Table 34, what predictions would you make about the

prospects that the Women's Liberation Movement will succeed in inspiring "collective action" on a mass scale?

12. How do you explain the failure of the Communist party to build a mass movement in the United States?

13. Americans in the Vietnam war attempted to protect native villagers by "relocating" them in "safe" areas. How effectively did this protect them from revolutionary ideas?

14. The New Left Movement was the subject of numerous books and articles between 1969 and 1971, and of practically none since then. What does this suggest?

15. If it were shown that most of the leaders of a particular movement are psychologically maladjusted persons, how would this affect your evaluation of the movement? Apply your answer to Women's Liberation, the Jesus Movement, the Right to Life Movement, and the environmentalist movement.

16. Suppose you were a promoter, seeking a favorable area in which to launch a social movement. What statistics would you use in finding a receptive location?

17. Do you know anyone who has a long history of involvement in "far-out" causes or movements? What is this person like? Do you know another person with a long activity in more moderate movements and organizations? How does the second person compare with the first?

18. Take three or four students whom you know very well and estimate, according to the information in this chapter, the receptivity of each one to social movements. How about yourself? Are you a good or poor prospect for membership? In what kind of movement? Would your judgments be scientific conclusions or subjective impressions?

Suggested readings

Annals of the American Academy of Political and Social Science, "Protest in the Sixties," vol. 382, March, 1969. A collection of theory and research on social movements.

BARBER, BERNARD: "Acculturation and Messianic Movements," *American Sociological Review,* 6:663–669, October, 1941; Bobbs-Merrill reprint S-332. Shows how messianic movements arose among American Indian peoples as a reaction to the disorganization of their tribal life.

BLUMER, HERBERT: "Social Movements," in ALFRED M. LEE (ED.), *Principles of Sociology,* College Outline Series, Barnes & Noble, Inc., New York, 1969, pp. 99–120. A concise outline of the field of social movements.

CARDEN, MAREN LOCKWOOD: *The New Feminist Movement,* Russell Sage Foundation, New York, 1974. A current report on Women's Liberation.

ELLWOOD, ROBERT S., JR.: *One Way: The Jesus Movement and Its Meaning,* Prentice-Hall, Inc., Englewood Cliffs, N.J., 1973. A brief analysis of the Jesus Movement.

*FONER, PHILIP S. (ED.): *The Black Panthers Speak,* J. B. Lippincott Company, Philadelphia, 1970. A collection of statements by Black Panther party leaders, plus some other commentary.

GERBERDING, WILLIAM P., AND DUANE E. SMITH: *The Radical Left: The Abuse of Discontent,* Houghton Mifflin Company, Boston, 1970. A collection of commentary on the New Left Movement.

*HOWARD, JOHN R.: *The Cutting Edge: Social Movements and Social Change in America,* J. B. Lippincott Co., Philadelphia, 1974. A descriptive analysis of many current social movements.

*KELMAN, STEPHEN: *Push Comes to Shove: The Escalation of Student Protest,* Houghton Mifflin Company, Boston, 1970. A Harvard student's account of the student strike at Harvard.

*KNOTT, PAUL D.: *Student Activism,* Wm. C. Brown Company, Publishers, Dubuque, Iowa, 1971. A brief, readable collection of commentary on the student protest movement.

LANG, KURT, AND GLADYS ENGEL LANG: *Collective Dynamics,* Thomas Y. Crowell Company, New York, 1961, chaps. 16, 17. Two detailed and perceptive chapters on social movements, in a textbook on collective behavior.

*MORGAN, ROBIN (ED.): *Sisterhood Is Powerful: An Anthology of Writings from the Women's Liberation Movement,* Random House, Inc., New York, 1970. A series of trenchant statements of the Women's Lib ideology.

MCLAUGHLIN, BARRY (ED.): *Studies in Social Movements: A Psychological Perspective,* The Free Press, New York, 1969. A collection with emphasis upon motivation and interaction in social movements.

OGLESBY, CARL: *The New Left Reader,* Grove Press, Inc., New York, 1969. A collection of statements by various New Left leaders.

*ROBERTS, RON E., AND ROBERT MARCH KLOSS: *Social Movements: Between the Balcony and the Barricade,* C. V. Mosby Co., St. Louis, 1974. A brief, readable textbook on social movements.

UNGER, IRWIN: *The Movement: A History of the American New Left, 1959–1972,* Dodd, Mead and Co., New York, 1974. A readable history of the rise and fall of the New Left.

VANDERZANDEN, JAMES W.: "The Klan Revival," *American Journal of Sociology,* 65:456–462, March, 1960; Bobbs-Merrill reprint S-299. A membership study of the revived Ku Klux Klan, showing social backgrounds and possible motivations of current members.

WILSON, JOHN: *Introduction to Social Movements,* John Wiley and Sons, Inc., New York, 1973. An analytical textbook on social movements.

Bibliography

ABBOTT, WALTER F.: "Moscow in 1897 as a Preindustrial City: A Test of The Inverse Burgess Zonal Hypothesis," *American Sociological Review,* 39:542–550, August 1974.

ABRAHAMSON, MARK: "The Social Dimensions of Urbanism," *Social Forces,* 52:376–383, March 1974.

ABRAMS, CHARLES: *Forbidden Neighbors: A Study of Prejudice in Housing,* Harper & Row, Publishers, Inc., New York, 1955.

———: *The City is the Frontier,* Harper & Row, Publishers, Inc., New York, 1965.

ABRAMS, ELLIOTT, and FRANKLIN S. ABRAMS: "Immigration Policy—Who Gets In and Why?", *The Public Interest,* 38:3–29, Winter 1975.

ABU-LUGHOD, IBRAHIM (ed.): *The Arab-Israeli Confrontation of June 1967: An Arab Perspective,* Northwestern University Press, Evanston, Ill., 1970.

ABU-LUGHOD, JANET: "Migrant Adjustment to City Life: The Egyptian Case," *American Journal of Sociology,* 65:22–32, 1961.

ADAMS, E. M.: "The Logic of Planning," *Social Forces* 28:419–423, 1950.

ADAMS, PAUL, et al.:*Children's Rights: Toward the Liberation of the Child,* Praeger Publishers, New York, 1972.

ADORNO, T. W., ELSE FRENKEL-BRUNSWICK, D. J. LEVINSON, and R. N. SANFORD: *The Authoritarian Personality,* Harper & Row, Publishers, Inc., New York, 1950.

ALATUS, SEYD HUEESIN: "The Captive Mind in Developmental Studies: Some Neglected Problems and the Need for an Autonomous Social Science Tradition in Asia," *International Social Science Journal,* 24:9–25, 1972.

ALBIG, WILLIAM: "Two Decades of Opinion Study: 1936–1956," *Public Opinion Quarterly,* 21:14–22, 1957.

ALCOCK, JAMES E.: "Cooperation, Competition and the Effects of Time Pressure in Canada and India," *Journal of Conflict Resolution,* 18:171–178, June 1974.

ALDOUS, JOAN: "Wives' Employment Status and Lower-class Men as Husband-Fathers: Support for the Moynihan Thesis," *Journal of Marriage and the Family,* 31:469–476, August 1969.

ALEXANDER, CHARLES C.: *The Ku Klux Klan in the Southwest,* University of Kentucky Press, Lexington, 1965.

ALINSKY, SAUL D.: "The War on Poverty—Political Pornography," *Journal of Social Issues,* 21:41–47, January 1965.

ALLAND, ALEXANDER: *The Human Imperative,* Columbia University Press, New York, 1972.

ALLEN, FRANCIS R.: *Socio-Cultural Dynamics: An Introduction to Social Change,* The Macmillan Company, New York, 1971.

ALLEN, JAMES B.: *The Company Town in the American West,* University of Oklahoma Press, Norman, 1966.

ALLPORT, GORDON W., and LEO POSTMAN: *The Psychology of Rumor,* Holt, Rinehart and Winston, Inc., New York, 1947.

ALMOND, GABRIEL A., et al.: *The Appeals of Communism,* Princeton University Press, Princeton, N.J. 1954.

——— and SIDNEY VERBA: *The Civic Culture: Political Attitudes and Democracy in Five Nations,* Princeton University Press, Princeton, N.J., 1963.

ALSOP, STEWART: "America's Big New Rich," *Saturday Evening Post,* July 17, 1965, pp. 23–28.

ALT, HERSCHEL, and EDITH ALT: *Russia's Children,* Bookman Associates, Inc., New York, 1959.

ALVAREZ, WALTER C., and SUE MARCH: *Homosexuality vs. Gay Liberation: A Confrontation Doublebook,* Pyramid Publications, New York, 1974.

America, "Rome and New York," Aug. 24, 1957, p. 518.

ANDENAES, JOHANNES: "Moral or Educative Influence of Criminal Law," *Journal of Social Issues,* 27:17–32, No. 2, 1971.

ANDERSON, CHARLES H.:*Toward a New Sociology,* Dorsey Press, Homewood, Ill., 1971.

———: *The Political Economy of Social Class,* Prentice-Hall, Inc., Englewood Cliffs, N.J., 1974.

ANDERSON, RAYMOND H.: "Soviet Urban Sprawl Defies Official Efforts to Curb the Growth of Cities," *New York Times,* Nov. 13, 1966, p. 122.

ANDERSON, SCARVIA B., et al.: *Social Studies in Secondary Schools: A Survey of Courses and Practices,* Princeton University Press, Princeton, N.J., 1964.

ANDERSON, WALT (ed.): *The Age of Protest,* Goodyear Publishing Co., Palisades Park, Calif., 1969.

ANDREWS, LEWIS M.: "Communes and the Work Crisis," *Nation,* 211:460–463, Nov. 9, 1970.

APODACA, ANADETO: "Corn and Custom: The Introduction of Hybrid Corn to Spanish American Farmers in New Mexico," in EDWARD H. SPICER (ed.), *Human Problems in Technological Change,* Russell Sage Foundation, New York, 1952, pp. 35–39.

APPELBAUM, RICHARD P.: *Theories of Social Change,* Markham Publishing Company, Chicago, 1970.

ARDREY, ROBERT: *The Territorial Imperative,* Atheneum Publishers, New York, 1966.

ARENSBERG, CONRAD M., and SOLON T. KIMBALL: *Culture and Community,* Harcourt, Brace and World, Inc., New York, 1965.

ARENSBERG, CONRAD M., and ARTHUR M. NIEHOFF: *Introducing Change: A Manual for Community Development,* Aldine-Atherton, Chicago, 1971.

ARGYRIS, CHRIS: "We Must Make Work Worthwhile," *Life,* May 5, 1967, pp. 56ff.

ARMOR, DAVID J.: "The Evidence on Busing," *The Public Interest,* 28:90–126, Summer 1972.

ARNOLD, DAVID O. (ed.): *The Sociology of Subcultures,* The Glendessary Press, Berkeley, 1970.

ARNOLD, THURMAN: *The Folklore of Capitalism,* Yale University Press, New Haven, Conn., 1937.

ARNOTT, CATHERINE C.: "Husbands' Attitude and Wives' Commitment to Employment," *Journal of Marriage & the Family,* 34:673–684, November 1972.

ARON, RAYMOND, in International Sociological Association in Collaboration with JESSIE BERNARD, T. H. PEAR, RAYMOND ARON, and ROBERT C. ANGELL: *The Nature of Conflict,* UNESCO, Paris, 1957.

ARON, WILLIAM S.: "Student Activism of the 1960s Revisited: A Multivariate Analysis Research Note," *Social Forces,* 52:408–414, March 1974.

ARONSON, ELLIOT, et al.: "Communicator Credibility and Communication Discrepancy as Determinants of Opinion Change," *Journal of Abnormal and Social Psychology,* 67:31–36, 1963.

ASCH, S. E.: "Effects of Group Pressure upon the Modification and Distortion of Judgments," in HEINZ GUETZKOW (ed.), *Groups, Leadership, and Men,* U.S. Office of Naval Research, Carnegie Press, Carnegie Institute of Technology, Pittsburgh, 1951.

ASHTON, ROBERT JR.: "Progress Comes to Black Mesa," *National Parks and Conservation Magazine: The Environmental Journal,* September 1971, pp. 4–9.

AUGUSTUS, AMELIA: "Malevolent Neglect," *The Interdependent,* 1:1, December 1974.

BABCHUCK, NICHOLAS, and JOHN A. BALLWEG: "Black Family Structure and Primary Relations," *Phylon,* 33:334–347, Winter 1972.

BABCOCK, RICHARD F.: *The Zoning Game: Municipal Practices and Policies,* University of Wisconsin Press, Madison, 1966.

BACH, GEORGE R.: "The Marathon Group: Intensive Practice of Intimate Interaction," *Psychological Reports,* 118:995–1002, 1966.

BACHMAN, JERALD B., et al.: *Dropping Out—Problem or Symptom,* Institute for Social Research, Ann Arbor, Mich., 1972.

BAILEY, GEORGE: "The Disappearing Satellite," *Reporter,* Mar. 16, 1961, pp. 20–23.

BAILEY, ROBERT JR.: "Urban Radicals: Activists in an Alinsky Community Organization," *Growth and Change,* 4:3–9, July 1973.

BAIN, READ: "Our Schizoid Culture," *Sociology and Social Research,* 19:226–276, 1935.

———: "The Self- and Other-words of a Child," *American Journal of Sociology,* 41:767–776, May 1936.

BAKER, CHARLES R.: "White Citizens' Councils Fight for Segregation Now," *Homefront* (newsletter of the Institute for American Democracy, Washington, D.C.), January 1970.

BALES, ROBERT F.: "Small-group Theory and Research," in ROBERT K. MERTON, LEONARD BROOM, and LEONARD S. COTTRELL, JR. (eds.), *Sociology Today: Problems and Prospects,* Basic Books, Inc., New York, 1959, pp. 293–308.

BANFIELD, EDWARD C.: *The Unheavenly City,* Little, Brown and Company, Inc., Boston, 1970.

———: *The Unheavenly City Revisited,* Little, Brown and Company, Inc., Boston, 1974.

BANTON, MICHAEL: *Race Relations,* Basic Books, Inc., New York, 1967.

BARBER, BERNARD, and LYLE S. TOBEL: "Fashion in Women's Clothes and the American Social System," *Social Forces,* 31:124–131, 1953.

———: "Social Mobility in Hindu India," in JAMES

SILVERBERG (ed.), *Social Mobility in the Caste System in India,* Mouton and Company, The Hague, 1968, pp. 18–35.

BARBER, THEODORE X., and WILLIAM B. MEEKER: "Out of Sight, Out of Mind," *Human Behavior,* Aug. 1974, pp. 56–60.

BARER, NAOMI: "Delinquency Before, After Admission to New Haven Housing Development," *Journal of Housing,* 3:27, January 1946.

BARNES, C. A.: "A Statistical Study of the Freudian Theory of Levels of Psychosexual Development," *Genetic Psychology Monographs,* 45:105–174, 1952.

BARNETT, H. G.: *Innovation: The Basis of Social Change,* McGraw-Hill Book Company, New York, 1953.

BARON, HAROLD M., with HARRIET STULMAN, RICHARD ROTHENSTEIN, and RENNARD DAVIS: "Black Powerlessness in Chicago," *Trans-action,* 6:27–33, November 1968.

BASCOM, WILLIAM R., and MELVILLE J. HERSKOVITZ (eds.): *Continuity and Change in African Cultures,* University of Chicago Press, Chicago, 1959.

BATES, ROBERT H.: "Ethnic Competition and Modernization in Contemporary Africa," *Comparative Political Studies,* 6:457–484, January 1974.

BAVELAS, ALEX: "Communication Patterns in Task-oriented Groups," in DORWIN CARTWRIGHT and ALVIN F. ZANDER (eds.), *Group Dynamics,* Harper & Row, Publishers, Inc., New York, 1953, pp. 493–494

BAYTON, JAMES A.: *Tension in the Cities: Three Programs for Survival,* Chilton Book Company, Philadelphia, 1969.

BECKER, HOWARD S.: *Outsiders,* The Free Press, New York, 1963.

———: "Whose Side Are We On?", *Social Problems,* 14:239–247, Winter 1967.

BECKER, JOHN: Research note in *Behavior Today,* Feb. 22, 1971, p. 2.

BECKMAN, LEONARD: "Clothes Make the Person: Social Roles and Uniforms," *Psychology Today,* April 1974, pp. 49–51.

BELL, DANIEL: *The Coming of Post-Industrial Society: A Venture in Social Forecasting,* Basic Books, Inc., New York, 1973.

———: "The Power Elite—Reconsidered," *American Journal of Sociology,* 64:238–250, 1958.

——— (ed.): *The Radical Right: The New American Right, Expanded and Updated,* Doubleday & Company, Inc., Garden City, N.Y., 1963,

BELL, INGE POWELL: "The Double Standard," *Transaction,* November–December 1970, pp. 75–80.

BELLUSH, JEWEL, and MURRAY HAUSKNECHT (eds.): *Urban Renewal: People, Policies, and Planning,* Doubleday & Company, Inc., Garden City, New York, 1967.

BEN-DAVID, JOSEPH: "Scientific Productivity and Academic Organization," *American Sociological Review,* 25:828–843, 1960.

BENDER, EUGENE L., and GEORGE KAGIWADA: "Hansen's Law of 'Third Generation Return' and the Study of American Religico-Ethnic Groups," *Phylon,* 2:360–370, Winter 1968.

BENEDICT, RUTH: *Patterns of Culture,* Houghton Mifflin Company, Boston, 1934.

———: "Continuities and Discontinuities in Cultural Conditioning," *Psychiatry,* 1:161–167, 1938.

BENGTSON, VERN L., and JOSEPH A KUYPERS: "Generative Differences and the Developmental Stake," *Aging and Human Development,* 2:249–260, November 1971.

BENNIS, WARREN G., KENNETH D. BENNE, and ROBERT CHIN: *The Planning of Change,* Holt, Rinehart and Winston, Inc., New York, 1969.

BERELSON, BERNARD (ed.): *Family Planning and Population Programs,* Basic Books, Inc., New York, 1969.

———et al.: "Family Planning and Population Programs: A Review of World Development," University of Chicago Press, Chicago, 1966.

———: "World Population: Status Report 1974," *Reports on Population Family Planning,* January 1975, pp. 1–47.

BERG, IVAR: "Rich Man's Qualifications for Poor Man's Jobs," *Trans-action,* March 1969, pp. 45–50.

BERGER, BENNETT, et al.: "Child-rearing Practices of the Communal Family," in ARLENE S. SKOLNICK and JEROME H. SKOLNICK (eds.), *Family in Transition,* Little, Brown and Company, Boston, 1971, pp. 509–523.

BERGER, BENNETT M.: "Audiences, Art and Power," *Trans-action,* May 1971, pp. 26–30.

BERGER, PETER L., and BRIGETTE BERGER: "The Blueing of America," *The New Republic,* Apr. 3, 1971, pp. 20–23.

BERK, RICHARD A., and HOWARD E. ALDRICH: "Patterns of Vandalism During Civil Disorders as an Indicator of Selection of Targets," *American Sociological Review,* 37:533–547, October 1972.

BERKE, JOSEPH (ed.): *Counter-Culture,* Peter Owen, Ltd., London, 1969.

BERNARD, JESSIE: "Autonomic and Decisive Competition," *The Sociological Quarterly,* 1:25–38, January 1960.

BERNSTEIN, BASIL: "Elaborated and Restricted Codes: An Outline," *Sociological Inquiry,* 36:254–261, Spring 1966.

BERRY, BREWTON: *Race and Ethnic Relations,* Houghton Mifflin Company, Boston, 1965.

BERRY, BRIAN J. L.: *The Human Consequences of Urbanization,* The Macmillan Company, London, 1973.

BESTOR, ARTHUR E., JR.: *Backwoods Utopias: The Sectarian and Owenite Phases of Communitarian Socialism in America: 1663–1829,* University of Pennsylvania Press, Philadelphia, 1950, 1970.

BETTELHEIM, BRUNO, and MORRIS JANOWITZ: *The Dynamics of Prejudice,* Harper & Row, Publishers, Inc., New York, 1950.

—— and ——: "Does Communal Education Work? The Case of the Kibbutz," *Commentary,* 33:117–125, February 1962. Reprinted in EDWIN M. SCHUR (ed.), *The Family and the Sexual Revolution,* Indiana University Press, Bloomington, 1964, pp. 293–307.

—— AND ——: *The Children of the Dream,* The Macmillan Company, New York, 1969.

BETZ, MICHAEL: "Riots and Welfare: Are They Related?", *Social Problems,* 21:345–355, 1974.

BICKMAN, LEONARD: "Clothes Make the Person: Social Roles and Uniforms," *Psychology Today,* April 1974, pp. 49–51.

BIDDLE, BRUCE J., and EDWIN J. THOMAS (eds.): *Role Theory: Concepts and Research,* John Wiley & Sons, Inc., New York, 1956.

BIDERMAN, ALBERT D.: "Social-Psychological Needs and 'Involuntary' Behavior as Illustrated by Compliance in Interrogation," *Sociometry,* 23:120–147, 1960.

BIERSTEDT, ROBERT A.: "An Analysis of Social Power," *American Sociological Review,* 15:730–738, December 1950.

——: *The Social Order,* McGraw-Hill Book Company, New York, 1963.

BILLER, HENRY B.: "Father Absence and the Personality Development of the Male Child," *Developmental Psychology,* 2:181–201, April 1970.

BINFORD, SALLY: "Apes and Original Sin," *Human Behavior,* November–December 1972, pp. 65–71.

BIRCH, HERBERT G., and JOAN DYE GUSSOW: *Disadvantaged Children: Health, Nutrition, and School Failure,* Harcourt, Brace & World, Inc., New York, 1970.

BISHOP, JOSEPH W., JR.: "Lawyers at the Bar," *Commentary,* August 1974, pp. 48–53.

BLACK, JEANNE HUMPHREY: "Conceptions of Sex-role; Some Cross-cultural and Longitudinal Perspectives," paper presented to 127th annual meeting of American Psychiatric Association, Detroit, May 1974.

BLAKE, JUDITH: "Can We Believe Recent Data on Birth Expectations in the United States?" *Demography,* 11:25–44, February 1974.

BLANSHARD, PAUL: "The Irish and Catholic Power," Beacon Press, Boston, 1953.

BLAU, PETER MICHAEL, and W. RICHARD SCOTT: *Formal Organizations: A Comparative Approach,* Chandler Publishing Company, San Francisco, 1962.

——and O. DUDLEY DUNCAN: *The American Occupational Structure,* John Wiley & Sons, Inc., New York, 1967.

BLAUNER, ROBERT: *Alienation and Freedom: The Factory Worker and His Industry,* University of Chicago Press, Chicago, 1964.

——: "Whitewash over Watts," *Trans-action,* 3:3–9, March–April 1966.

BLOOD, ROBERT A., and DONALD M. WOLFE: *Husbands and Wives,* The Free Press, New York, 1960.

BLOOD, ROBERT O., JR., and DONALD M. WOLFE: "Negro–White Differences in Blue-Collar Marriages in a Northern Metropolis," *Social Forces,* 48:59–64, September 1969.

BLOODWORTH, DENNIS: "How Mao Rides the Dragon," *The Observer* (London), Sept. 11, 1966; reprinted in *Current,* October, 1966, pp. 48–50.

BLOOM, B. S.: "The Thought Process of Students in Discussion," in SIDNEY J. FRENCH (ed.), *Accent on Teaching,* Harper & Row, Publishers, Inc., New York, 1954.

BLOOM, LEONARD: *The Social Psychology of Race Relations,* Schenkman Publishing Company, Cambridge, Mass., 1972.

BLUMBERG, LEONARD, and ROBERT R. BELL: "Urban Migration and Kinship Ties," *Social Problems,* 6:328–333, Spring 1959.

BLUMBERG, PAUL: "The Decline and Fall of the Status Symbol: Some Thoughts on Status in a Post-Industrial Society," *Social Problems,* 21:480–498, April 1974.

BLUMER, HERBERT: "Collective Behavior," in ALFRED MCCLUNG LEE (ed.), *Principles of Sociology,* Barnes & Noble, Inc., New York, 1969 (a), pp. 65–122.

———: "Social Movements," in ALFRED M. LEE (ed.), College Outline Series: *Principles of Sociology,* Barnes & Noble, Inc., New York, 1969 (b), pp. 99–120.

———: "Fashion: From Class Differentiation to Collective Selection," *Sociological Quarterly,* 10:275–291, Summer 1969 (c).

BODE, JERRY G.: "Status Mobility of Catholics vis-a-vis Several Protestant Denominations: More Evidence," *Sociological Quarterly,* 11:103–110, Winter 1970.

BOFFEY, P. M.: "Japan: A Crowded Nation Wants to Boost Its Birthrate," *Science,* 167:960–962, Feb. 13, 1970.

BOGARDUS, EMORY S.: "A Race Relations Cycle," *American Journal of Sociology,* 35:612–617, 1930.

———: *Fundamentals of Social Psychology,* Appleton-Century-Crofts, New York, 1950.

———: "Racial Distance Changes in the United States During the Past Thirty Years," *Sociology and Social Research,* 43:127–135, 1958.

———: "Racial Reactions by Regions," *Sociology and Social Research,* 43:286–290, 1959.

BOGUE, DONALD J.: *Skid Row,* The Community and Family Study Center, Chicago, 1963.

BOISNERT, M. J.: "Behavior Modification as an Alternative to Psychotherapy," *Social Casework,* 55:43–47, January 1974.

BONE, CHRISTOPHER: *The Disinherited Children: A Study of the New Left and the Generation Gap.,* Halsted Press, New York, 1975.

BOSKIN, JOSEPH: "The Revolt of the Urban Ghettos," *Annals of the American Academy of Political and Social Science,* 382:1–14, March 1969.

BOTTOMORE, T. B.: *Sociology: A Guide to Problems and Literature,* George Allen and Unwin, Ltd., London, 1962, pp. 283–284.

BOUMA, DONALD H.: "The Analysis of the Social Power Position of a Real Estate Board," *Social Problems,* 10:116–128, Fall 1962 (a).

———: "The Legitimation of the Social Power Position of a Real Estate Board," *American Journal of Economics and Sociology,* 21:383–392, October 1962 (b).

———: *Why Kalamazoo Voted No,* W. E. Upjohn Institute for Employment Research, Kalamazoo, Mich., 1962 (c).

———: *Kids and Cops,* William B. Eerdmanns Publishing Co., Grand Rapids, Mich., 1969.

———: "Issue-analysis Approach to Community Power: A Case Study of Realtors in Kalamazoo," *The American Journal of Economics and Sociology,* 29:241–252, July 1970.

———and DONALD G. WILLIAMS: "Police-school Liaison: An Evaluation of Programs," *Intellect,* November 1972, pp. 119–122.

BOUMA, GARY D.: "Assessing the Impact of Religion: A Critical Review," *Sociological Analysis,* 31:172–179, Winter 1970.

BOVARD, EVERETT W., JR.: "Group Structure and Perception," *Journal of Abnormal and Social Psychology,* 46:398–405, 1951.

BRACEY, JOHN H., JR., AUGUST MEIER, and ELLIOTT M. RUDWICK: *Black Matriarchy: Myth or Reality,* Wadsworth Publishing Co., Belmont, Calif., 1971.

BRADY, THOMAS F.: "French Worker-Priests Must Abandon Politics," *New York Times,* Jan. 31, 1954, sect. 4, p. 7.

BRAUDEL, FERNAND: *Capitalism and Material Life,* Harper & Row, Publishers, Inc., New York, 1974.

BRAUNGART, ROBERT: Research note in *Behavior Today,* Nov. 9, 1970, p. 3.

BRILL, HARRY: *Why Organizers Fail,* University of California Press, Berkeley, 1971.

BRIM, ORVILLE G., JR.: "The Acceptance of New Behavior in Child-rearing," *Human Relations,* 7:473–491, 1954.

BRINTON, CRANE: *The Anatomy of Revolution,* W. W. Norton & Company, Inc., New York, 1938.

BRONFENBRENNER, URIE, with the assistance of JOHN C. CONDRY, JR.: *Two Worlds of Childhood: U.S. and U.S.S.R.,* Basic Books, Inc., New York, 1970.

BROOKS, RICHARD OLIVER: *New Towns and Communal Values: A Case Study of Columbia, Maryland,* Frederick A. Praeger, Publishers, New York, 1974.

BROOM, LEONARD, and F. LANCASTER JONES: "Status Consistency and Political Preference: The Australian Case," *American Sociological Review,* 35:989–1001, December 1970.

———and PHILIP SELZNICK: *Sociology,* Harper & Row, Publishers, Inc., New York, 1972.

BROVERMAN, INGE K., et al.: "Sex-role Stereotypes: A Current Appraisal," *Journal of Social Issues,* 28:2, 59–78, 1972.

BROWN, JUDITH K.: "A Note on the Division of Labor by Sex," *American Anthropologist,* 72:1073–1078, October 1970.

BROWN, ROBERT L.: "Social Distance as a Function of Mexican-American and Other Ethnic Identity,"

Sociology and Social Research, 57:273–287, April 1973.

BROWN, WALLACE: *The Good Americans: The Loyalists in the American Revolution,* William Morrow and Co., Inc., New York, 1969.

BROWN, WILLIAM G.: *The Lower South in American History,* The Macmillan Company, New York, 1902.

BROWN, WILLIAM O.: "Culture Contact and Race Conflict," in E. B. REUTER (ed.), *Race and Culture Contacts,* McGraw-Hill Book Company, New York, 1934.

BRUNSWICK, ANN F.: "A Generation Gap? A Comparison of Some Generational Differences Between Blacks and Whites," *Social Problems,* 17:358–371, Winter 1970.

BRUYN, SEVERYN T.: *The Human Perspective in Sociology: The Methodology of Participant Observation,* Prentice-Hall, Inc., Englewood Cliffs, N.J., 1966.

BRYAN, CLIFFORD E., and ROBERT L. HORTON: *Basic Facts on the Generation Gap,* Learning Systems Co., Homewood, Ill., 1974.

BUCHANAN, PATRICK: "Reflections on '74: Power of the Press and a Departing Star," *TV Guide,* Jan. 11, 1975, pp. 5–6.

BURCHARD, WALDO: *The Role of the Military Chaplain,* University of California Press, Berkeley, 1963.

BURCHINALL, LEE G., and HILDA SIFF: "Rural Poverty," *Journal of Marriage and the Family,* 26:399–405, November 1964.

BUREAU OF THE CENSUS, SOCIAL AND ECONOMIC STATISTICS ADMINISTRATION, U.S. DEPARTMENT OF COMMERCE: *The Social and Economic Status of the Black Population of the United States, 1972,* Current Population Reports Series P-23, No. 46, 1973.

BURGESS, ERNEST W., and HARVEY J. LOCKE: *The Family: From Institution to Companionate,* American Book Company, New York, 1953.

BURLINGAME, ROGER: *Inventors Behind the Inventor,* Harcourt, Brace & World, Inc., New York, 1947.

BURMA, JOHN H.: "The Measurement of Negro Passing," *American Journal of Sociology,* 52:18–22, 1946.

BURNHAM, JAMES F.: *The Managerial Revolution,* The John Day Company, Inc., New York, 1941.

BURNS, HAYWOOD: "Can a Black Man Get a Fair Trial in This Country?" *New York Times Magazine,* July 12, 1970; reprinted in ROBERT K. YIN, *Race,*

Creed or National Origin, F. E. Peacock, Itaska, Ill., 1973.

BURTON, ARTHUR (ed.): *Encounter: The Theory and Practice of Encounter Groups,* Jossey-Bass, Inc., San Francisco, 1969.

BURTON, KATHERINA: *Paradise Planters: The Story of Brook Farm,* David McKay Company, Inc., New York, 1939.

BUSINESS WEEK: "Sociologists Invade the Plant," Mar. 21, 1959, pp. 95ff.

———: "How Welfare Keeps Women from Working," Apr. 7, 1973, p. 51.

———: "The Burgeoning Benefits of a Lower Birth Rate," Dec. 15, 1973, p. 41.

CADWALLADER, MERVYN: "Marriage as a Wretched Institution," *Atlantic,* November 1966, pp. 62–66.

CALVIN, A. D., and WAYNE H. HOLTZMAN: "Adjustment to the Discrepancy between Self-Concept and the Inferred Self," *Journal of Consulting Psychiatry,* 17:39–44, 1953.

CAMERON, PAUL: "Social Stereotypes: Three Faces of Happiness," *Psychology Today,* August 1974, pp. 63–64.

CANTRIL, HADLEY: *The Psychology of Social Movements,* John Wiley & Sons, Inc., New York, 1941.

———: *The Politics of Despair,* Basic Books, Inc., New York, 1958.

CANTY, DONALD (ed.): *The New City,* Frederick A. Praeger Publishers, Inc., New York, 1969.

CAPLOW, THEODORE: *The Academic Marketplace,* Basic Books, Inc., New York, 1958.

CARDEN, MAREN LOCKWOOD: *The New Feminist Movement,* Russell Sage Foundation, New York, 1973.

CAREY, LYNETTE, and ROY MAPES: *The Sociology of Planning,* B. T. Balsford, Ltd., London, 1972.

CARLSON, J. R.: *Under Cover,* E. P. Dutton & Co., Inc., New York, 1943.

———: *The Plotters,* E. P. Dutton & Co., Inc., New York, 1946.

CARNAHAN, DOUGLAS, WALTER GOVE, and OMER R. GALLE: "Urbanization, Population Density, and Overcrowding: Trends in the Quality of Life in Urban America," *Social Forces,* 53:62–72, September 1974.

CARTWRIGHT, DORWIN, and ALVIN F. ZANDER (eds.): *Group Dynamics: Theory and Research,* Harper & Row, Publishers, Inc., New York, 1960.

CASLER, LAWRENCE: *Is Marriage Necessary?* Behavioral Sciences Publications, New York, 1974.

CATER, DOUGLAS: "Civil War in Alabama's Citizens' Councils," *Reporter,* May 17, 1956, pp. 19–21.

CAVAN, RUTH SHONLE: "Jewish Student Attitudes Toward Interreligious and Intra-Jewish Marriage," *American Journal of Sociology,* 76:1064–1071, May, 1971.

CENTERS, RICHARD: *The Psychology of Social Classes,* Princeton University Press, Princeton, N.J., 1949.

CHAMBERS, ROSALIND C.: "A Study of Three Voluntary Organizations," in D. V. GLASS (ed.), *Social Mobility in Britain,* The Free Press, New York, 1954, pp. 384–406.

CHANDLER, MICHAEL: Research note in *Behavior Today,* Dec. 14, 1970, p. 2.

CHANDRASEKHAR, S.: "Mao's War with the Chinese Family," *New York Times Magazine,* May 17, 1959, pp. 21ff.

CHARTRAND, ROBERT LEE (ed.): *Hope for the Cities,* Spartan Books, New York, 1971.

CHICAGO COMMISSION ON RACE RELATIONS: *The Negro in Chicago,* University of Chicago Press, Chicago, 1922.

CHILMAN, CATHERINE S.: "Fertility and Poverty in the United States: Some Implications for Family-Planning Programs, Evaluation and Research," *Journal of Marriage and the Family,* 30:207–227, May 1968.

CHINOY, ELY: "The Tradition of Opportunity and the Aspirations of Automobile Workers," *American Journal of Sociology,* 57:453–459, 1952.

CHRISTENSEN, HAROLD T., and CHRISTINA F. GREGG: "Changing Sex Norms in America and Scandinavia," *Journal of Marriage and the Family,* 32:616–627, November 1970.

CLAPP, JAMES A.: *New Towns and Urban Policy,* Dunellen Publishing Company, New York, 1971.

CLARK, TERRY N.: "Community Structure, Decision-Making, Budget Expenditures, and Urban Renewal in 51 American Communities," *American Sociological Review,* 33:576–593, August 1968.

CLAUSEN, CONNIE: *I Love You, Honey, but the Season's Over,* Holt, Rinehart and Winston, Inc., New York, 1961.

CLEAVER, ELDRIDGE: *Soul on Ice,* Dell Publishing Company, New York, 1968.

CLINARD, MARSHALL B.: *Sociology of Deviant Behavior,* Holt, Rinehart and Winston, Inc., New York, 1968, 1972.

CLINE, HOWARD F.: *Mexico,* Oxford University Press, New York, 1963.

CLOWARD, RICHARD A., and FRANCES SCOTT PIVEN: *The Politics of Turmoil: Essays on Poverty, Race, and the Urban Crisis,* Pantheon Books, New York, 1974.

COHEN, ALBERT K.: *Delinquent Boys: The Culture of the Gang,* The Free Press, New York, 1955.

COHEN, HARRY: *The Demonics of Bureaucracy: Problems of Change in a Government Agency,* Iowa State University Press, Ames, Iowa, 1965.

COHEN, JERRY, and WILLIAM S. MURPHY: *Burn, Baby, Burn,* E. P. Dutton & Co., Inc., New York, 1966.

COHEN, LELAND B.: *Jewish Intermarriage: Analysis of the National Jewish Population Study,* (mimeo), August 1974.

COHEN, MARSHALL: "Civil Disobedience in a Constitutional Democracy," *Massachusetts Review,* 10:211–216, Spring 1969.

COHEN, MITCHELL, and DENNIS HALE (eds.): *The New Student Left,* Beacon Press, Boston, 1967.

COHEN, NATHAN E.: *The Citizen Volunteer: His Responsibility, Role and Opportunity in Modern Society,* Harper & Row, Publishers, Inc., New York, 1960.

COHN, NORMAN: *The Pursuit of the Millennium,* Essential Books, Fair Lawn, N.J., 1957.

COLEMAN, JAMES S., et al.: *Equality of Educational Opportunity,* U.S. Department of Health, Education and Welfare, Washington, D.C., 1966.

—— et al.: *How Do the Young Become Adults?* Report No. 130, Center for Social Organization of Schools, Washington, D.C., 1972.

—— et al.: *Youth: Transition to Adulthood: Report of the Panel on Youth of the President's Science Advisory Committee,* University of Chicago Press, Chicago, 1974.

COLEMAN, RICHARD P., and BERNICE L. NEUGARTEN: *Social Status in the City,* Jossey-Bass, San Francisco, 1971.

COLFAX, J. DAVID, and JACK L. ROACH (eds.): *Radical Sociology,* Basic Books, Inc., New York, 1971.

COLLIER, JOHN: *Indians of the Americas,* W. W. Norton & Company, Inc., New York, 1947.

COMMISSION ON POPULATION GROWTH AND THE AMERICAN FUTURE: *Population and the American Future,* New American Library, New York, 1972.

COMPTE, AUGUSTE: *Positive Philosophy,* translated by Harriet Martineau, C. Blanchard Company, New York, 1855.

CONDON, EDWARD U.: "UFO's I Have Found and Lost," *Bulletin of the Atomic Scientists,* 35:6–8, December 1969.

CONNELL, R. W.: "Political Socialization of the American Family: The Evidence Reexamined," *Public Opinion Quarterly,* 36:323–333, Fall 1972.

CONNER, CLIFF: "Hunger: U.S. Agribusiness and World Famine," *International Socialist Review,* September 1974, pp. 20–31.

CONVERSE, PHILIP E.: "Country Differences in Use of Time," in ALEXANDER SZALAS (ed.), *Use of Time: Daily Activities of Urban and Suburban Populations in 12 Countries,* Mouton and Company, The Hague, 1972.

COOLEY, CHARLES HORTON: "The Theory of Transportation," *Publications of the American Economic Association,* Vol. 9, No. 3, 1894.

———: *The Nature of Human Nature,* Charles Scribner's Sons, New York, 1902.

———: "A Study of the Early Use of Self Words by a Child," *Psychological Review,* 15:339–357, 1908.

COOPER, DAVID: *The Death of the Family,* Pantheon Books, A Division of Random House, Inc., New York, 1970.

COPP, JAMES H. (ed.): *Our Changing Rural Society: Perspectives and Trends,* Department of Publications, State University of Iowa, Iowa City, 1964.

CORTEZ, JUAN B., and FLORENCE M. GATTI: "Physique and Propensity," *Psychology Today,* October 1970, pp. 42ff.

COSER, LEWIS: *The Functions of Social Conflict,* The Free Press, New York, 1956,

——— and BERNARD ROSENBERG: *Sociological Theory,* The Macmillan Company, New York, 1969.

COSER, LEWIS A.: "Some Functions of Deviant Behavior and Normative Flexibility," *American Journal of Sociology,* 69:172–181, September 1962.

———: *Continuities in the Study of Social Conflict,* The Free Press, New York, 1967.

COTE, WILLIAM E.: "Rift Runs Deep in Staff Strike Against MEA," *Kalamazoo Gazette,* Sept. 28, 1974, p. 5.

COUCH, CARL J.: "Collective Behavior: An Examination of Some Stereotypes," *Social Problems,* 15:310–322, Winter 1968.

COURSEY, ROBERT D.: "Clothing Doth Make the Man, in the Eye of the Beholder," *Perceptual and Motor Skills,* 36:1259–1264, June 1973.

CRAIN, WILLIAM C., and ELLEN F. CRAIN: "The Growth of Political Ideas and Their Expression Among Young Activists," *Journal of Youth and Adolescence,* 3:105–132, No. 2, 1974.

CREED, E. R.: "Genetic Adaptation," in J. ROSE (ed.), *Technological Injury: The Effects of Technological Advances on Environment, Life and Society,* Gordon and Breach Science Publishers, London, 1969, pp. 119–134.

CRESSEY, DONALD R.: *Theft of a Nation: The Structure and Operations of Organized Crime in America,* Harper & Row, Publishers, Inc., New York, 1969.

CROSSMAN, RICHARD (ed.): *The God That Failed,* Harper & Row, Publishers, Inc., New York, 1949.

CROW, JAMES F.: "Genetic Theories and Influences: Comments on the Value of Diversity," *Harvard Educational Review,* 39:301–309, Spring 1969.

CROWLEY, JAMES W.: "Religious Preference and Worldly Success: An Empirical Test in a Midwestern City," *Sociological Analysis,* 32:71–80, Summer, 1971.

CUBER, JOHN F.: "Marginal Church Participants," *Sociology and Social Research,* 25:57–62, September 1940.

CURTIS, JAMES: "Voluntary Association Joining: A Cross-National Comparative Note," *American Sociological Review,* 36:872–880, October 1971.

CURTIS, RUSSELL L., JR., and LOUIS A. ZURCHER, JR.: "Voluntary Associations and the Social Integration of the Poor," *Social Problems,* 18:339–357, Winter 1971.

DAHL, ROBERT A.: "A Critique of the Ruling Elite Model," *American Political Science Review,* 52:463–469, 1958.

———: *Who Governs?* Yale University Press, New Haven, Conn., 1961.

DAHRENDORF, RALF: "Conflict Groups, Group Conflicts and Social Change," in *Class and Industrial Society,* Stanford University Press, Stanford, Calif., 1959, pp. 202–223.

———: "Towards a Theory of Social Conflict," in AMITAI ETZIONI and EVA ETZIONI (eds.), *Social Change,* Basic Books, Inc., New York, 1964, pp. 100–123.

DAI, BINGHAM: "Obsessive-Compulsive Disorders in Chinese Culture," *Social Problems,* 4:313–321, 1957.

DALE, EDWARD EVERETT: *The Range Cattle Industry,* Univ. of Oklahoma Press, Norman, 1930.

DANIELS, ROBERT V.: *A Documentary History of Communism, Volume II,* Random House, Inc., New York, 1960.

DARITY, WILLIAM A., CASTELLANO B. TURNER, and H. JEAN THIEBAUX: "Race Consciousness and Fears of Black Genocide as Barriers to Family Planning," paper presented at Ninth Annual Meeting of the National Association of Planned Parenthood Physicians, Kansas City, Mo., 1971; reprinted in *Population Reference Bureau,* Selection No. 37, June, 1971, pp. 5–12.

DARWIN, CHARLES: *On the Origin of the Species,* Introduction by Ernst Mayer, Harvard University Press, Cambridge, Mass., 1964.

DAVIDSON, BASIL: *The Lost Cities of Africa,* Little, Brown and Company, Boston, 1959.

———: *The African Past,* Little, Brown and Company, Boston, 1964.

———: *African Kingdoms,* Time, Inc., New York, 1966.

DAVIDSON, SARA: "Open Land: Getting Back to the Communal Garden," *Harper's,* June 1970, pp. 91–102.

DAVIES, JAMES C.: "Toward a Theory of Revolution," *American Sociological Review,* 17:5–19, 1962.

DAVIS, ALLISON: "The Motivation of the Underprivileged Worker," in WILLIAM F. WHYTE (ed.), *Industry and Society,* McGraw-Hill Book Company, New York, 1946, pp. 84–106.

DAVIS, FRED: "The Cabdriver and His Fare: Facets of a Fleeting Relationship," *American Journal of Sociology,* 65:158–165, 1959.

DAVIS, JEROME: *Contemporary Social Movements,* Appleton-Century-Crofts, Inc., New York, 1930.

DAVIS, KEITH: *Human Relations at Work,* McGraw-Hill Book Company, New York, 1972.

DAVIS, KINGSLEY: *Human Society,* The Macmillan Company, New York, 1949.

DAWSON, CARL, and W. E. GETTYS: *Introduction to Sociology,* The Ronald Press Company, New York, 1934, 1948.

DEAN, DWIGHT G.: "Alienation: Its Meaning and Measurement," *American Sociological Review,* 26:753–758, 1961.

DEASY, LEILA CALHOUN: "Socio-Economic Status and Participation in the Poliomyelitis Vaccine Trial," *American Sociological Review,* 21:185–191, 1956.

DE BEAUVOIR, SIMONE: *The Second Sex,* Alfred A. Knopf, Inc., New York, 1953.

DE BELL, GARRETT: *The Environmental Handbook: Prepared for the First National Environmental Teach-in, April 22, 1970,* Ballantine Books, New York, 1970.

DEBO, ANGIE: *A History of the Indians of the United States,* University of Oklahoma Press, Norman, 1970.

DECTER, MIDGE: *The New Chastity and Other Arguments against Women's Liberation,* Coward, McCann and Geohegan, Inc., New York, 1972.

DEE, WILLIAM L. J.: "The Social Effect of a Public Housing Project on the Immediate Community," in MEYER WEINBERG and OSCAR E. SHABAT, *Society and Man,* Prentice-Hall, Inc., Englewood Cliffs, N.J., 1956, pp. 329–339.

DEEDY, JOHN: "There are Many Forms of Minority," *New York Times,* Feb. 9, 1975, sect. 4, p. 3.

DEFRONZO, JAMES: "Embourgoisement in Indianapolis," *Social Problems,* 21:260–283, Fall 1973.

DELORA, JOANN S., and JACK R. DELORA (eds.): *Intimate Life Styles: Marriage and Its Alternatives,* Goodyear Publishing Company, Inc., Pacific Palisades, Calif., 1975.

DELORIA, VINE, JR.: *Custer Died for Your Sins: An Indian Manifesto,* The Macmillan Company, New York, 1970.

DEMPEWOLFF, J. A.: "Some Correlates of Feminism," *Psychological Reports,* 34:671–676, April 1974.

DENZIN, NORMAN K.: *The Research Act in Sociology: A Theoretical Introduction to Research Methods,* Butterworth and Co., London, 1970.

DEUTSCH, MORTON: "An Experimental Study of the Effects of Cooperation and Competition upon Group Process," *Human Relations,* 2:199–231, 1949.

DEWEY, RICHARD: "The Rural-Urban Continuum: Real but Relatively Unimportant," *American Journal of Sociology,* 66:60–66, 1960.

DICHTER, ERNEST: *Motivating Human Behavior,* McGraw-Hill Book Company, New York, 1971.

DIEBOLD, JOHN: "Management Can Learn from Japan," *Business Week,* Sept. 29, 1973, p. 14.

DITTES, JAMES E., and HAROLD H. KELLEY: "Effects of Different Conditions of Acceptance upon Conformity to Group Norms," *Journal of Abnormal and Social Psychology,* 53:100–107, 1956.

DJERASSI, CARL: "Fertility Limitation Through Contraceptive Steroids in the People's Republic of China," *Studies in Family Planning,* 5:13–29, January 1974.

DJILAS, MILOVAN: *The New Class,* Frederick A. Praeger Publishers, New York, 1957.

DOBZHANSKY, THEODOSIUS: *Mankind Evolving: The*

Evolution of the Human Species, Yale University Press, New Haven, Conn., 1962.

DODSON, DAN W.: "The Creative Role of Conflict Re-examined," *Journal of Intergroup Relations,* 1:5–12, 1959.

DOLLARD, JOHN, et al.: *Frustration and Aggression,* Yale University Press, New Haven, Conn., 1939.

DOMHOFF, G. WILLIAM: *Who Rules America?* Prentice-Hall, Inc., Englewood Cliffs, N.J., 1967.

————: *The Higher Circles,* Random House, Inc., New York, 1970.

DOOB, LEONARD: *Propaganda,* Holt, Rinehart and Winston, Inc., New York, 1948.

————: *Public Opinion and Propaganda,* Archon Books, The Shoe String Press, Inc., Hamden, Conn., 1966.

DORN, H. F. M.: "Tobacco Consumption and Mortality from Cancer and Other Diseases," *Public Health Reports,* 74:581–593 (1959).

DOUGLAS, JACK D. (ed.): *The Relevance of Sociology,* Appleton-Century-Crofts, New York, 1970.

DOUGLAS, JOHN H.: "Climate Changes: Chilling Possibilities," *Science News,* 107:138–140, Mar. 1, 1975.

DOUVAN, ELIZABETH: "Employment and the Adolescent," in F. IVAN NYE, *The Employed Mother in America,* Rand McNally & Company, Chicago, 1963, pp. 142–164.

DOWDY, EDWIN: "Aspects of Tokugawa Bureaucracy and Modernization," *Australian Journal of Politics and History,* 16:375–389, December 1970.

DOWNES, BRYAN T.: "The Social Characteristics of Riot Cities: A Comparative Study," *Social Science Quarterly,* 49:504–520, December 1968.

DOWNS, ANTHONY: *Who Are the Urban Poor?* Committee for Economic Development, New York, 1970.

DRAPER, THEODORE: "The Psychology of Surrender," *Atlantic Monthly,* 176:62–65, 1945.

DUBOIS, CORA: *The Peoples of Alor,* University of Minnesota Press, Minneapolis, 1944.

DUNCAN, DAVID DOUGLAS: "In the Middle of an Indian Massacre," *Life,* Oct. 6, 1947, pp. 6ff.

DUNHAM, H. WARREN, and S. KIRSON WEINBERG: *The Culture of the State Mental Hospital,* Wayne State University Press, Detroit, Mich., 1960.

———— and ————: "City Core and Suburban Fringe: Distribution Patterns of Mental Illness," in

STANLEY PLOG and ROBERT EDGERTON (eds.), *Changing Perspectives in Mental Illness,* Holt, Rinehart and Winston, Inc., New York, 1960, pp. 337–363.

DURKHEIM, EMILE: *Le Suicide: Etude de Sociologie,* translated by J. A. Spaulding and G. Simpson, The Free Press, New York, 1951.

DUSEK, JEROME B., and EDWARD J. O'CONNELL: "Teacher Expectancy Effects on the Achievement Test Performance of Elementary School Children," *Journal of Educational Psychology,* 65:371–377, No. 3, 1973.

DYE, THOMAS R., EUGENE R. DECLERCQ, and JOHN W. PICKERING: "Institutional Elites," *Social Science Quarterly,* 54:8–28, August 1973.

EASTERLIN, RICHARD J.: "Does Money Buy Happiness?" *The Public Interest,* 30:3–11, Winter 1973.

EBENSTEIN, WILLIAM: *Today's Isms: Communism, Fascism, Capitalism, Socialism,* Prentice-Hall, Inc., Englewood Cliffs, N.J., 1973.

ECKHARDT, ALICE, and ROY ECKHARDT: *Encounter with Israel: A Challenge to Conscience,* Association Press, New York, 1970.

EDWARDS, ALLEN A.: "Types of Rural Communities," in MARVIN B. SUSSMAN (ed.), *Community Structure and Analysis,* Thomas Y. Crowell Company, New York, 1959.

EDWARDS, LYFORD P.: *The Natural History of Revolution,* University of Chicago Press, Chicago, 1927.

EFRON, EDITH: *The News Twisters,* Nash Publishing Company, Los Angeles, 1971.

————: "So This is Adversary Journalism," *TV Guide,* Jan. 18, 1975, pp. 5–6.

————: "Some Admissions: Yes, There Was Hate and Bias," *TV Guide,* Dec. 28, 1974, pp. 3–4.

EGAN, GERARD: *Encounter Group Processes for Interpersonal Growth,* Wadsworth Publishing Company, Inc., Belmont, Calif., 1970.

EGGAN, DOROTHY: "The General Problem of Hopi Adjustment," *American Anthropologist,* 45:357–373, July 1943.

EHRLICH, PAUL, and ANNE H. EHRLICH: *Population, Resources, Environment: Issues in Human Ecology,* Prentice-Hall, Inc., Englewood Cliffs, N.J., 1970.

EKMAN, PAUL, and WALLACE V. FRIESEN: "Detecting Deception from the Body or Face," *Journal of*

Personality and Social Psychology, 19:288–297, March 1974.

ELLIS, EVELYN: "Social Psychological Correlates of Upward Social Mobility among Unmarried Career Women," *American Sociological Review,* 17:558–563, 1952.

ELLWOOD, ROBERT S., JR.: *One Way: The Jesus Movement and Its Meaning,* Prentice-Hall, Inc., Englewood Cliffs, N.J., 1973.

ELMEN, P.: "Focus on Ireland: A Land Where Faith Matters," *Christian Century,* Feb. 3, 1971, pp. 88–170ff.

ELWIN, VARRIER: *The Biaga,* John Murray (Publishers), Ltd., London, 1939.

EPSTEIN, BENJAMIN R., and ARNOLD FORSTER: *The Radical Right: A Report on the John Birch Society and Its Allies,* Vintage Books, New York, 1967.

ERBER, ERNEST (ed.): *Urban Planning in Transition,* Grossman Publishers, New York, 1970.

ERNST, MORRIS, and DAVID LOTH: *Report on the American Communist,* Holt, Rinehart and Winston, Inc., New York, 1952.

ERSKINE, HAZEL: "The Polls: Pacifism and the Generation Gap," *Public Opinion Quarterly,* 36:616–627, Winter 1972–1973.

ETZIONI, AMITAI: *The Active Society: A Theory of Societal and Political Processes,* The Free Press, New York, 1968.

——: *Demonstration Democracy,* Gordon and Breach, Science Publishers, Inc., New York, 1971.

——: "Life, Dying, Death: Ethics and Open Decision," *Science News,* 106:109, August 1974.

EULAU, HANS: "Identification with Class and Political Role Behavior," *Public Opinion Quarterly,* 20:515–529, 1956.

EVANS, CHRISTOPHER: *Cults of Unreason,* George W. Harrap and Co., Ltd., London, 1973.

EVANS, FREDERICK J.: "The Power of a Sugar Pill," *Psychology Today,* April 1974, pp. 55–59.

EVANS, HAZEL (ed.): *New Towns: The British Experience,* John Wiley and Sons, Inc., New York, 1972.

EVANS, SUE L., JOHN B. RINEHART, and RUTH A. SUCCOP: "Failure to Thrive: A Study of 45 Children and Their Families," *Journal of Child Psychiatry,* 11:440–457, July 1972.

EYSENCK, HANS J.: *The I.Q. Argument: Race, Intelligence, and Education,* The Library Press, New York, 1971.

FAIRCHILD, HENRY PRATT (ed.): *Dictionary of Sociology,* Philosophical Library, Inc., New York, 1957.

FAIRFIELD, RICHARD: *Communes, USA: A Personal Tour,* Penguin Books, Baltimore, 1972.

FANFANI, AMINTORE: *Catholicism, Protestantism and Capitalism,* Sheed & Ward, Inc., New York, 1955.

FARIS, R. E. L.: "The Alleged Class System in the United States," *Research Studies of the State College of Washington,* vol. 22, June 1954.

FARLEY, JENNIE: "Maternal Employment and Child Behavior," *Cornell Journal of Social Relations,* 3:58–71, Fall 1968.

FARLEY, REYNOLDS: "The Changing Distribution of Negroes within Metropolitan Areas: The Emergence of Black Suburbs," *American Journal of Sociology,* 75:512–529, January 1970.

—— and ALMA F. TAUBER: "Racial Segregation in the Public Schools," *American Journal of Sociology,* 79:888–905, January 1974.

FARSON, RICHARD: *Birthrights,* The Macmillan Company, New York, 1974.

FAST, JULIUS: *Body Language,* M. Evans, distributed in Association with J. B. Lippincott Co., New York, 1970.

FAVE, L. RICHARD: "The Culture of Poverty Revisited: A Strategy for Research," *Social Problems* 21:609–621, June 1974.

FELDMESSER, ROBERT A.: "The Persistence of Status Advantages in Soviet Russia," *American Journal of Sociology,* 59:19–27, 1953.

FELSON, MARCUS, and DAVID KNOKE: "Social Status of the Married Woman," *Journal of Marriage & the Family,* 36:516–521, August 1974.

FENDRICH, JAMES M., and ALISON T. TARLEAU: "Marching to a Different Drummer: Occupational and Political Correlates of Former Student Activists," *Social Forces,* 52:245–253, December 1973.

FENGLER, ALFRED P., and VIVIAN WOOD: "The Generation Gap: An Analysis of Attitudes," *Gerontologist,* 12:124–128, Summer 1972.

FERRELL, MARY ZEY, O. C. FERRELL, and QUENTIN JENKINS: "Social Power in a Rural Community," *Growth and Change,* 4:3–6, April 1973.

FESTINGER, L., A. PIPESTONE, and T. NEWCOMB: "Some Consequences of Deindividuation in a Group," *Journal of Abnormal and Social Psychology,* 47:382–389, 1952.

——, HENRY W. RIECKEN, and STANLEY SCHACHTER:

When Prophecy Fails, University of Minnesota Press, Minneapolis, 1956.

FETTERMAN, JOHN: *Stinking Creek: A Portrait of a Small Community in Appalachia,* E. P. Dutton & Company, Inc., New York, 1970.

FEUER, LEWIS S.: "The Risk is 'Juvenocracy,'" *New York Times Magazine,* Sept. 18, 1966, pp. 56ff.

———: *The Conflict of Generations,* Basic Books, Inc., New York, 1968.

FEY, HAROLD E.: "Let Us Possess the Land," *Christian Century,* 71:757–759, 1954.

FIERABEND, IVO, and ROSALIND L. FIERABEND: "Coerciveness and Change: Cross-national Trends," *American Behavioral Scientist,* 15:911–927, July 1927.

FINNIE, WILLIAM C., cited in research note: *Society,* January 1974, p. 11.

FIRESTONE, SHULAMITH: *The Dialectic of Sex: The Case for Feminist Revolution,* W. W. Morrow and Co., New York, 1970.

FIRST, ELSA: Review of Peter Tompkins and Christopher Bird, "The Secret Life of Plants," *New York Times Book Reviews,* Dec. 30, 1973, p. 15.

FISCHER, CLAUDE S.: "On Urban Alienations and Anomie: Powerlessness and Social Isolation," *American Sociological Review,* 38:311–326, June 1973a.

———: "Urban Malaise," *Social Forces,* 52:221–235, December 1973b.

FISH, JOHN HALL: *Black Power—White Control: The Struggle of the Woodlawn Organization in Chicago,* Princeton University Press, Princeton, N.J., 1973.

FLACKS, RICHARD: "Liberated Generation: An Explanation of the Roots of Student Protest," *Journal of Social Issues,* 23:52–75, July 1967.

FLIEGEL, FREDERICK C., and JOSEPH E. KIVLIN: "Attributes of Innovation as Factors in Diffusion," *American Journal of Sociology,* 72:235–248, November 1966.

FLINN, WILLIAM L.: "Influence of Community Values on Innovativeness," *American Journal of Sociology,* 75:983–991, May 1970.

FLUGEL, J. C.: *The Psychology of Clothes,* Hogarth Press, Ltd., London, 1930.

FOGELSON, ROBERT E.: "Violence as Protest," in ROBERT H. CONNERY (ed.), *Urban Riots: Violence and Social Change,* Random House, Inc., New York, 1969.

FONER, PHILIP S. (ed.): *The Black Panthers Speak,* J. B. Lippincott Company, Philadelphia, 1970.

FORD, ARTHUR M.: *Political Economics of Rural Poverty in the South,* Ballinger Publishing Co., Cambridge, Mass., 1973.

FOREMAN, GRANT: *Indian Removal,* University of Oklahoma Press, Norman, 1932.

FOREMAN, PAUL B.: "Panic Theory," *Sociology and Social Research,* 37:295–304, 1953.

FORM, WILLIAM H., and WARREN L. SAUER: *Community Influentials in a Middle-sized City,* Institute for Community Development, Michigan State University Press, East Lansing, 1960.

———: "Auto Workers and Their Machines: A Study of Work, Factory, and Job Satisfaction in Four Countries," *Social Forces,* 52:1–15, September 1973.

FORTUNE, R. F.: *The Sorcerers of Dobu,* E. P. Dutton & Co., Inc., New York, 1932.

FOSKETT, JOHN M.: "Social Structure and Community Participation," *American Sociological Review,* 20:431–438, 1955.

FOX, DOUGLAS M.: "The Identification of Community Leaders by the Reputational, and Decisional Methods: Three Case Studies and an Empirical Analysis of the Literature," *Sociology and Social Research,* 54:94–103, October 1969.

FOX, GREER LITTON: "Another Look at the Comparative Resources Model: Assessing the Balance of Power in Turkish Marriages," *Journal of Marriage & the Family,* 35:718–739, November 1973.

FOX, RUTH: "The Alcoholic Spouse," in VICTOR W. EISENSTEIN (ed.), *Neurotic Interaction in Marriage,* Basic Books, Inc., New York, 1956, pp. 148–167.

FRANCOIS, WILLIAM: "Where Poverty Is Permanent," *Reporter,* Apr. 17, 1961, pp. 38–39.

FRANK, RICHARD A.: "The Law at Sea," *New York Times Magazine,* May 18, 1975, pp. 14ff.

FRANKLIN, BRUCE (ed.): *From the Movement: Toward Revolution,* Van Nostrand Reinhold Company, New York, 1971.

FRAZIER, GRAHAM: *Fighting Back: Urban Renewal in Trefann Court,* A. M. Halpert, Ltd., Toronto, 1972.

FREDERICHS, ROBERT W.: *A Sociology of Sociology,* The Free Press, New York, 1970.

FREEDMAN, D. X.: "On the Use and Abuse of LSD," *Archives of General Psychiatry,* 18:330–347, 1968.

FREEDMAN, RONALD, PASCAL K. WHELPTON, and ARTHUR A. CAMPBELL: *Family Planning, Sterility, and Population Growth,* McGraw-Hill Book Company, New York, 1959.

——, ——, and JOHN W. SMIT: "Socio-Economic Factors in Religious Differentials in Fertility," *American Sociological Review,* 26:608–614, 1961.

FREEMAN, HARVEY R.: "The Generation Gap: Attitudes of Students and Their Parents," *Journal of Counseling Psychology,* 19:441–447, September 1972.

FREEMAN, HOWARD E.: "Attitudes Toward Mental Patients among Relatives of Former Patients," *American Sociological Review,* 26:59–66, 1961.

——, and CLARENCE C. SHERWOOD: *Social Research and Social Policy,* Prentice-Hall, Inc., Englewood Cliffs, N.J., 1970.

FREILICH, MORRIS: "The Natural Triad in Kinship and Complex Systems," *American Sociological Review,* 29:529–534, August 1964.

FREILICH, MORRIS, and LEWIS A. COSER: "Structured Inbalances of Gratification: The Case of the Caribbean Mating System," *British Journal of Sociology,* 23:1–19, March 1972.

FRIEDAN, BETTY: *The Feminine Mystique,* W. W. Norton & Company, Inc., New York, 1963.

FRIEDMAN, NORMAN L.: "Nativism," *Phylon,* 28:408–415, Winter 1967.

FRIEDMANN, JOHN: *Retracking America: A Theory of Transitional Planning,* Anchor Press, Doubleday & Company, Inc., Garden City, New York, 1973.

FROMM, ERICH: *Escape from Freedom,* Holt, Rinehart and Winston, Inc., New York, 1941.

——: "Individual and Social Origins of Neurosis," *American Sociological Review,* 9:380–384, 1944.

——: *The Art of Loving,* Harper & Row, Publishers, Inc., New York, 1956.

FUERST, J. S.: "Class, Family and Housing," *Society,* November 1974, pp. 48–53.

GALBRAITH, JOHN KENNETH: *American Capitalism: The Concept of Countervailing Power,* Houghton Mifflin Company, Boston, 1952.

GAMSON, WILLIAM A.: *The Strategy of Social Protest,* Dorsey Press, Homewood, Ill., 1975.

GANS, HERBERT J.: "We Won't End the Urban Crisis until We End 'Majority Rule,'" *New York Times Magazine,* Aug. 3, 1969, pp. 12ff.

GARDNER, MARTIN: *Fads and Fallacies in the Name of Science,* Dover Publications, Inc., New York, 1957.

GASSON, RUTH M., ARCHIBALD O. HALLER, and WILLIAM H. SEWELL: *Attitudes and Facilitation in the Attainment of Status,* American Sociological Association, Washington, D.C., 1972.

GEIS, GILBERT: "The Fable of a Fatty," *Issues in Criminology,* 3:211–214, Spring 1968.

——: "Rejoinder to Geis," *Issues in Criminology,* 3:215, Spring 1968.

GELLHORN, WALTER: *Ombudsmen and Others: Citizens' Protectors in Nine Countries,* Harvard University Press, Cambridge, Mass., 1967.

GERBERDING, WILLIAM P., and DUANE E. SMITH (eds.): *The Radical Left: The Abuse of Discontent,* Houghton Mifflin Company, Boston, 1970.

GERTH, HANS: "The Nazi Party: Its Leadership and Composition," *American Journal of Sociology,* 55:517–541, 1940.

GESCHWENDER, JAMES A.: "Explorations in the Theory of Social Movements," *Social Forces,* 47:127–135, December 1968.

——: "Internal Ideological Conflict and the Development of Splits within Social Movements: The Case of the League of Revolutionary Black Workers," paper presented at 36th annual meeting of the North Central Sociological Association, Windsor, Ontario, May 1974.

GIBBARD, GRAHAM S., JOHN J. HARTMAN, and RICHARD D. MANN (eds.): *Analysis of Groups,* Jossey-Bass, Inc., San Francisco, 1974.

GIBBARD, HAROLD: *Residential Succession: A Study in Human Ecology,* unpublished Ph.D. dissertation, University of Michigan, 1938.

GIDDINGS, F. H.: *The Principles of Sociology,* The Macmillan Company, New York, 1913.

GIL, DAVID G.: *Unraveling Social Policy: Analysis and Political Action towards Social Equality,* Schenkman Publishing Co., Cambridge, Mass., 1973.

GILES, ROBERT H.: "How to Become a Target City," *The Reporter,* June 15, 1967, pp. 38–41.

GILLIN, JOHN P.: *The Ways of Men,* Appleton-Century-Crofts, Inc., New York, 1948.

GILROY, HARRY: "Flight from East Germany: The People," *New York Times,* Aug. 13, 1961, sect. 4, p. 4.

GLAZER, NATHAN, and DANIEL P. MOYNIHAN: *Beyond the Melting Pot: The Negroes, Puerto Ricans, Jews, Italians and Irish of New York City,* M.I.T. Press, Cambridge, Mass., 1970.

—— and ——: "The Culture of Poverty: The View from New York City," in ALAN WINTER, *The*

Poor: A Culture of Poverty or a Poverty of Culture? William B. Eerdmans, Publishers, Grand Rapids, Mich., 1971, pp. 20–48.

———: "On 'Opening Up' the Suburbs," *The Public Interest*, 37:89–111, Fall 1974.

GLENN, NORVAL D., and RUTH HYLAND: "Religious Preference and Wordly Success: Some Evidence from a National Survey," *American Sociological Review*, 32:73–85, February 1967.

GLICK, CLARENCE: "Social Roles and Types in Race Relations," in ANDREW W. LIND, *Race Relations in World Perspective*, University of Hawaii Press, Honolulu, 1955.

GLOCK, CHARLES Y., and BENJAMIN B. RINGER: "Church Policy and the Attitudes of Ministers and Parishioners on Social Issues," *American Sociological Review*, 21:148–156, April 1956.

GLUECK, SHELDON, and ELEANOR GLUECK: *Predicting Juvenile Delinquency and Crime*, Harvard University Press, Cambridge, Mass., 1959.

GOFFMAN, ERVING: *Presentation of Self in Everyday Life*, Social Science Research Center, University of Edinburgh, 1956. Reprinted by Anchor Books, Doubleday & Company, Inc., Garden City, N.Y., 1959.

———: *Where the Action Is: Three Essays*, Doubleday & Company, Inc., Garden City, N.Y., 1967.

GOFFMAN, IRWIN W.: "Status Consistency and Preference for Change in Power Distribution," *American Sociological Review*, 22:275–281, April 1957.

GOLD, MARTIN: *Delinquent Behavior in an American City*, Brooks/Cole, Monterey, Calif., 1970.

GOLDBERG, EVELYN L.: "Crowd Hysteria in a Junior High School," *Journal of School Health*, 43:362–365, June 1973.

GOLDBERG, STEPHEN: *The Inevitability of Patriarchy*, William Morrow and Co., Inc., New York, 1973.

GOLDHAMER, HERBERT, and EDWARD A. SHILS: "Types of Power and Status," *American Journal of Sociology*, 45:171–182, September 1939.

——— and ANDREW MARSHALL: *Psychosis and Civilization: Two Studies in the Frequency of Mental Illness*, The Free Press, New York, 1953.

GOLDNER, FRED H.: Review of VANCE PACKARD: *The Pyramid Climbers, American Journal of Sociology*, 69:197, September 1963.

GOLDTHORPE, JOHN H., and DAVID LOCKWOOD: "Affluence and the British Class Structure," *Sociological Review* (New Series), 11:133–163, July 1963.

GOLEMBIEWSKI, ROBERT T., and ARTHUR BLUMBERG (eds.): *Sensitivity Training and the Laboratory Approach*, F. E. Peacock Publishers, Inc., Itaska, Ill., 1970.

GOOD, PAUL: "The Bricks and Mortar of Racism," *New York Times Magazine*, May 21, 1972, pp. 25ff.

GORDON, MILTON: *Social Class in American Society*, Duke University Press, Durham, N.C., 1958.

———: *Assimilation in American Life: The Role of Race, Religion and National Origins*, Oxford University Press, New York, 1964.

GORNICK, VIVIAN: "Consciousness," *New York Times Magazine*, Jan. 10, 1971, pp. 22ff.

GOTTLIEB, ANNIE: "Female Human Beings," *New York Times Book Review*, Feb. 21, 1971, sect. 2, pp. 1ff.

GOULD, HAROLD A.: "Modern Medicine and Folk Cognition in Rural India," *Human Organization*, 24:201–208, Fall 1965.

GOULDNER, ALVIN: "Cosmopolitans and Locals: Towards an Analysis of Latent Social Roles," *Administrative Science Quarterly*, 2:281–292, December 1957.

———: "Anti-Minotaur: The Myth of a Value-Free Sociology," *Social Problems*, 9:190–213, Winter 1962.

———: "Toward the Radical Reconstruction of Sociology," *Social Policy*, May–June 1970, pp. 18–25.

GREELEY, ANDREW M.: "The Protestant Ethic: Time for a Moratorium," *Sociological Analysis*, 25:20–33, Spring 1964.

———: *Why Can't They Be Like Us?*, Institute of Human Relations Press, New York, 1969.

———: "Intellectuals as an Ethnic Group," *New York Times Magazine*, July 12, 1970; reprinted in ROBERT K. YIN (ed.), *Race, Creed, Color, or National Origin*, F. E. Peacock Publishers, Inc., Itaska, Ill., 1973, pp. 113–123.

GREEN, ARNOLD: *Sociology*, McGraw-Hill Book Company, New York, 1972.

GREEN, GIL: *The New Radicalism: Anarchist or Marxist*, International Publishers, New York, 1971.

GREENE, SHELDON L.: "Somebody Is Always Offended," *The Nation*, 211:624–627, Dec. 14, 1970.

GREENE, WADE: "Triage," *New York Times Magazine*, Jan. 5, 1975, pp. 9ff.

GREENHOUSE, LINDA J.: "Constitutional Question: Is There a Right to Abortion?" *New York Times Magazine,* Jan. 25, 1970, pp. 30ff.

GREENWALD, HAROLD: *The Call Girl,* Ballantine Books, Inc., New York, 1959.

GREENWOOD, DAVYDD J.: "Tourism as an Agent of Change: A Spanish Basque Case," *Ethnology,* 11:81–91, January 1972.

GREER, COLIN: *The Great School Legend,* Basic Books, Inc., N.Y., 1972.

GREER, GERMAINE: *The Female Eunuch,* McGraw-Hill Book Company, N.Y., 1971.

GREER, SCOTT, and ELLA KUBE: "Urbanism and Social Structure: A Los Angeles Study," in MARVIN B. SUSSMAN (ed.), *Community Structure and Analysis,* Thomas Y. Crowell Company, New York, 1959.

GREGG, RICHARD B.: *The Power of Nonviolent Resistance,* Schocken Books, Inc., New York, 1966.

GRIER, EUNICE, and GEORGE GRIER: "Discrimination in Housing," *Anti-Defamation League,* New York, 1960.

GRIFFIN, C. W.: *Taming the Last Frontier: A Prescription for the Urban Crisis,* Pitman Publishing Co., New York, 1974.

GRIFFIN, JOHN H.: *Black Like Me,* Houghton Mifflin Company, Boston, 1961.

GROSS, BERTRAM M. (ed.): *Action under Planning: The Guidance of Economic Development,* McGraw-Hill Book Company, New York, 1967.

GROSS, EDWARD: "Some Functional Consequences of Primary Group Controls in Formal Work Organizations," *American Sociological Review,* 18:368–373, 1953.

GROVE, GENE: *Inside the John Birch Society,* Fawcett Publications, Inc., Greenwich, Conn., 1961.

GRUEN, VICTOR: *The Heart of Our Cities,* Simon & Schuster, Inc., New York, 1964.

GUMP, JANICE PORTER: "Sex-role Attitudes and Psychological Well-being," *Journal of Social Issues,* 28:2, 79–92, 1972.

GUSFIELD, JOSEPH R.: "Social Structure and Moral Reform: A Study of the Women's Christian Temperance Union," *American Journal of Sociology,* 56:221–232, 1955.

GUSTAFSSON, BERNDT: "The State of Sociology of Protestantism in Scandinavia," *Social Compass,* 12:359–365, 1965.

HACKER, ANDREW: "The Boy Who Doesn't Go to College," *New York Times Magazine,* June 24, 1962, pp. 11ff.

HACKETT, HERBERT: "The Flying Saucer," *Sociology and Social Research,* 32:869–873, 1948.

HADDEN, JEFFREY K.: *The Gathering Storm in the Churches,* Doubleday & Company, Inc., Garden City, N.Y., 1969.

HADDON, TOM: "Making People Good by Law," *New Society,* 13:79–81, January 1969.

HAGSTROM, WARREN O.: "Competition in Science," *Commentary,* February 1974, pp. 1–19.

HALBERSTAM, DAVID: *The Best and the Brightest,* Random House, Inc., New York, 1972.

HALL, EDWARD T.: *The Silent Language,* Doubleday & Company, Inc., Garden City, N.Y., 1959.

———: "Our Silent Language," *Americas,* 14:5–8, February 1962.

HALL, FLORENCE TURNBULL, and MARGUERITE PAULSEN SCHROEDER: "Effects of Family and Housing Characteristics on the Time Spent on Household Tasks," *Journal of Home Economics,* 62:23–29, January 1970.

HALLOWAY, MARK: *Heavens on Earth: Utopian Communities in America, 1680–1880,* Library Publishers, New York, 1951.

HALPERN, JOEL: *The Changing Village Community,* Prentice-Hall, Inc., Englewood Cliffs, N.J., 1967.

HAM, EVIYOUNG: "Urbanization and Asian Lifestyles," *The Annals of the American Academy of Political and Social Science,* 405:104–113, January 1973.

HAMBLIN, ROBERT L., R. BROOKE JACOBSEN, and JERRY L. MILLER: *A Mathematical Theory of Social Change,* John Wiley & Sons, Inc., New York, 1973.

HAMERSMA, RICHARD: Research note in *Behavior Today,* Nov. 23, 1970, p. 3.

HAMILTON, CHARLES V.: "The Nationalist vs. the Integrationist," *New York Times,* Oct. 1, 1972, pp. 37ff.

HAMILTON, RICHARD F.: "The Marginal Middle Class: A Reconsideration," *American Sociological Review,* 31:192–199, April 1966.

HANEY, C. ALLEN, ROBERT MICHIEULETTE, CLARK E. VINCENT, and CARL M. COCHRANE: "The Value

Stretch Hypotheses: Family Size in a Black Population," *Social Problems,* 21:206–219, Fall 1973.

HANSEN, MARCUS L.: "Third Generation in America: The Problem of the Third Generation Immigrant," *Commentary,* 14:492–500, November 1952.

HANSEN, W. LEE, et al.: "Schooling and Earnings of Low Achievers," *American Economic Review,* 60:409–418, June 1970.

HANSON, MARK: "The Improbable Change Agent and the Ph.B.," *Rural Sociology,* 38:237–242, Summer 1973.

HARDIN, GARRETT: "Lifeboat Ethics: The Case Against Helping the Poor," *Psychology Today,* September 1974, pp. 38–43.

HARE, A. PAUL, and HERBERT H. BLUMBERG (eds.): *Non-violent Direct Action; American Cases: Social-Psychological Analyses,* Corpus Books, Washington, D.C., 1968.

HARLOW, HARRY F., and MARGARET K. HARLOW: "A Study of Animal Affection," *Natural History,* 70:48–55, 1961.

HARRIS, C. D., AND E. L. ULLMAN: "The Nature of Cities," *Annals of the American Academy of Political and Social Science,* 242:7–17, 1945.

HARRIS, LOUIS: "Election Polling and Research," *Public Opinion Quarterly,* 11:111, 1957.

HARRIS, MARVIN: "What Goes Up May Stay Up," *Natural History,* 81:18–25, January 1973.

HARRIS, MICHAEL: interviewed by Carol Tavris in *Psychology Today,* January 1975, pp. 61–69.

HART, DONN V.: "The Philippine Cooperative Movement," *Far Eastern Survey,* 24:27–30, 1955.

HARTLEY, SHIRLEY FOSTER: "Our Growing Problem: Population," *Social Problems,* 21:190–205, Fall 1973.

HARTMAN, MOSHE: "On the Definition of Status Inconsistency," *American Journal of Sociology,* 80:706–721, November 1974.

HARTNAGEL, TIMOTHY F.: "Father Absence and Self-Conception Among Lower-class White and Negro Boys," *Social Problems,* 18:152–163, Fall 1970.

HARVEY, JESSE: Unpublished doctoral dissertation, reported in *Science News Letter,* Dec. 5, 1953, p. 360.

HAUG, MARIE: "Social Class Measurement: A Methodological Critique," in GERALD W. THIELBAR and SAUL D. FRIEDMAN, *Issues in Social Inequality,* Little Brown and Company, Boston, 1972, pp. 429–451.

HAUSER, PHILIP M.: *Population Perspectives,* Rutgers University Press, New Brunswick, N.J., 1960.

HAUSER, ROBERT M., and DAVID L. FEATHERMAN: "Trends in the Occupational Mobility of U.S. Men, 1962–1970," *American Sociological Review,* 38:310–320, June 1973.

HAVELOCK, RONALD G., and MARY C. HAVELOCK: *Training for Change Agents,* Center for Research on Utilization of Scientific Knowledge, University of Michigan, Ann Arbor, 1973.

HAYANAGI, TADASHI: "The Mother's Child-Rearing Attitudes and Her Child's Socialization—A Clinical Aspect in Child Socialization," *Journal of Educational Sociology,* 23:110–123, October 1968.

HAYS, WILLIAM C., and CHARLES H. MINDEL: "Extended Kinship Relations in Black and White Families," *Journal of Marriage and the Family,* 35:51–57, February 1973.

HEBERLE, RUDOLF: *Social Movements,* Appleton-Century-Crofts, New York, 1951.

———: Review of STANLEY HOFFMAN, "Le Mouvement Poujade," (Librairie Armand Colin, Paris), in *American Journal of Sociology,* 63:440–441, 1956.

HEDGEPETH, WILLIAM: *Communal Life in America,* The Macmillan Company, New York, 1970.

HEER, DAVID M.: "The Prevalence of Black-White Marriage in the United States 1960 and 1970," *Journal of Marriage and the Family,* 36:246–258, May 1974.

HEILBRONER, ROBERT L.: *An Inquiry into the Human Prospect,* W. W. Norton and Co., New York, 1974.

HEINO, JACK K.: "Finnish Influence on the Cooperative Movement in America," *Michigan Academician,* 3:55–60, Winter 1971.

HEISEL, DORELLE: *What Is Your Concept of Masculine and Feminine?* unpublished research study, University of Cincinnati, 1970.

HELFGOT, JOSEPH: "Professional Reform Organizations and the Symbolic Representation of the Poor," *American Sociological Review,* 39:475–491, August 1974.

HELFRICH, HAROLD W., JR.: *The Environmental Crisis: Man's Struggle to Live with Himself,* Yale University Press, New Haven, Conn., 1970.

HEMMER, CARL J.: "World Population Conference: Bucharest in Retrospect," *War on Hunger: A Report from the Agency for International Development,* 9:8–13, January 1975.

HENDIN, HERBERT: "A Psychoanalyst Looks at Student Revolutionaries," *New York Times Magazine,* Jan. 17, 1971, pp. 16ff.

HENNESSY, BERNARD C.: *Public Opinion,* Wadsworth Publishing Co., Belmont, Calif., 1970.

HERBERG, WILL: *Protestant, Catholic, Jew,* Doubleday & Company, Inc., Garden City, N.Y., 1960.

HERBERT, MURIEL: *The Snow People,* G. P. Putnam's Sons, New York, 1973.

"HERE'S WHERE CHURCH TRIED TO SWING AN ELECTION: WITH TEXT OF PASTORAL LETTER," *U.S. News and World Report,* Nov. 7, 1960, pp. 59–61.

HERMALIN, ALBERT L., and REYNOLDS FARLEY: "The Potential for Racial Integration in Cities and Suburbs: Implications for the Busing Controversy," *American Sociological Review,* 38:595–610, October 1973.

HERNANDEZ, JOSE: *People, Power, and Policy: A New View on Population,* National Press Books, Palo Alto, Calif., 1974.

HERRNSTEIN, RICHARD J.: *I.Q. in the Meritocracy,* Little, Brown and Company, Boston, 1973.

HERSKOVITZ, MELVILLE J.: *Man and His Works,* Alfred A. Knopf, Inc., New York, 1949.

HERTZLER, J. O.: *American Social Institutions,* Allyn and Bacon, Inc., Boston, 1961.

HERZOG, ELIZABETH: *Children of Working Mothers,* Children's Bureau Publication No. 382, U.S. Department of Health, Education, and Welfare, 1960.

HEUSSENSTAMM, F. K.: "Bumper Stickers and the Cops," *Trans-action,* February 1971, pp. 32–34.

HIGHAM, JOHN: *Strangers in the Land: Patterns of American Nativism, 1860–1925,* Rutgers University Press, New Brunswick, N.J., 1955.

HIGHTOWER, JIM: *Hard Tomatoes, Hard Times: The Failure of the Land Grant College Complex,* Schenkman Publishing Co., New York, 1973.

HILL, REUBEN, J. MAYONE STYCOS, and KURT W. BACK: *The Family and Population Control,* University of North Carolina Press, Chapel Hill, 1959.

HILL, ROBERT B.: "The Strengths of Black Families," in DAVID G. BROMLEY and CHARLES F. LONGINO, JR., *White Racism and Black Americans,* Schenkman Publishing Co., Cambridge, Mass., 1972, pp. 262–290.

HILL, W. W.: "The Status of the Hermaphrodite and Transvestite in Navaho Culture," *American Anthropologist* 37:273, 279, 1935.

HILLERY, GEORGE A.: "Definitions of Community: Areas of Agreement," *Rural Sociology,* 20:111–123, 1955.

HIMES, JOSEPH S.: *Social Planning in America: A Dynamic Interpretation,* Doubleday & Company, Inc., Garden City, N.Y., 1954.

HINDELAND, MICHAEL J.: "Equality Under the Law," *Journal of Criminal Law, Criminology, and Police Science,* 60:306–313, September 1969.

HINDUS, MAURICE: "Historical Trends in American Premarital Pregnancy," paper presented at the American Historical Association, New York, December 1971.

HIRSCH, N. D. M.: "An Experimental Study of the East Kentucky Mountaineers," *Genetics Psychology Monographs,* 3:239, 406, 1928.

HODGE, ROBERT W., and DONALD J. TREIMAN: "Class Identification in the United States," *American Journal of Sociology,* 73:535–547, March 1968.

HODGES, HAROLD M.: *Social Stratification: Class in America,* Schenkman Publishing Co., Cambridge, Mass., 1964.

HOEBEL, E. ADAMSON: *Man in the Primitive World,* McGraw-Hill Book Company, New York, 1949.

HOFFER, ERIC: *The True Believer,* Harper & Row, Publishers, Inc., New York, 1951.

———: *Working and Thinking on the Waterfront,* Harper & Row, Publishers, Inc., New York, 1969.

HOFFMAN, ABBIE: *Revolution for the Hell of It,* Dial Press, Inc., New York, 1968.

———: *Steal This Book,* Pirate Editions, New York, (distributed by Grove Press, Inc., New York), 1971.

HOFFMAN, GEORGE W.: "Migration and Social Change," *Problems of Communism,* 22:16–31, November 1973.

HOFFMAN, LOIS W.: "Research Findings on the Effects of Maternal Employment on the Child," in F. IVAN NYE AND LOIS W. HOFFMAN (eds.), *The Employed Mother in America,* Rand McNally & Company, Chicago, 1963, pp. 190–212.

HOFSTADTER, RICHARD: *Anti-Intellectualism in American Life,* Alfred A. Knopf, Inc., New York, 1963.

HOLDEN, DAVID: "A Bad Case of Troubles Called Londonderry," *New York Times Magazine,* Aug. 3, 1969, pp. 10ff.

HOLLINGSHEAD, AUGUST B.: *Elmtown's Youth,* John Wiley & Sons, Inc., New York, 1949.

—— and FREDERICK C. REDLICH: "Social Stratification and Psychiatric Disorders," *American Sociological Review,* 18:163–169, 1953.

—— and ——: *Social Class and Mental Illness: A Community Study,* John Wiley & Sons, Inc., New York, 1958.

HOLT, JOHN: *Escape from Childhood,* E. P. Dutton and Company, Inc., New York, 1974.

HOLZMAN MATHILDA, ZELLA LURIA, and HERBERT SHERMAN: "Adolescent Subculture: Endover, New England," *School Review,* 76:231–245, June 1968.

HOOK, SIDNEY: "War Against the Democratic Process," *Atlantic,* 223:45–49, April 1969.

——: "Real Crisis on the Campus," *Readers Digest,* 95:41–45, August 1969.

HOOTON, E. A.: *Crime and the Man,* Harvard University Press, Cambridge, Mass., 1939.

HOROWITZ, DAVID (ed): *Radical Sociology: An Introduction,* Canfield Press, San Francisco, 1971.

HOROWITZ, IRVING LOUIS (ed.): *The New Sociology: Essays in Social Science and Social Theory in Honor of C. Wright Mills,* Oxford University Press, Fair Lawn, N. J., 1964.

——: *Three Worlds of Development: The Theory and Practice of World Stratification,* Oxford University Press, New York, 1966.

HORTON, DONALD: "The Functions of Alcohol in Primitive Societies," *Quarterly Journal of Studies on Alcohol,* 4:293–303, 1943.

HORTON, PAUL B. and DONALD H. BOUMA: "The Sociological Reformation: Immolation or Rebirth," *Sociological Focus,* 4:25–41, Winter 1970–1971.

—— and GERALD R. LESLIE: *The Sociology of Social Problems,* Appleton-Century-Crofts, New York, 1974.

HOSTETTLER, JOHN A.: "Persistence and Change Patterns in Amish Society," *Ethnology,* 3:185–198, April, 1964.

HOULT, THOMAS FORD: *Dictionary of Modern Sociology,* Littlefield, Adams and Company, Totowa, N. J., 1969.

HOURIET, ROBERT: *Getting Back Together,* Coward-McCann & Geoghegan, New York, 1971.

HOWARD, JOHN R.: "Perspectives in Sociology," in STEVEN E. DEUTSCH and JOHN R. HOWARD, *Where It's At: Radical Perspectives in Sociology,* Harper & Row, Publishers, Inc., New York, 1970, pp. 1–9.

HOWARD, JOHN R. (ed.): *The Awakening Minorities: American Indians, Mexican Americans, Puerto Ricans,* Aldine Publishing House, Chicago, 1970a.

——: *The Cutting Edge: Social Movements and Social Change in America,* J. B. Lippincott Co., Philadelphia, 1974.

HOWELL, JOSEPH T.: *Hard Living on Clay Street,* Anchor Press, Doubleday and Company, Inc., Garden City, N.Y., 1973.

HOWTON, F. WILLIAM: "Cities, Slums, and Acculturative Process in Developing Countries," *Buffalo Studies,* 3:21–42, December 1967.

HOYT, HOMER: *One Hundred Years of Land Values in Chicago,* University of Chicago Press, Chicago, 1933.

HUANG, L. J.: "Some Changing Patterns in the Communist Chinese Family," *Marriage and Family Living,* 23:137–146, May 1961.

HUFF, DARRELL: *How to Lie with Statistics,* W. W. Norton & Company, Inc., New York, 1954.

HUIZINGA, J.: *The Waning of the Middle Ages,* Edward Arnold, Ltd., London, 1924.

HUMPHREYS, LAUD: *Out of the Closet: The Sociology of Sexual Liberation,* Prentice-Hall, Inc., Englewood Cliffs, N.J., 1972.

HUNT, CHESTER L.: "Catholicism and the Birth Rate," *Review of Religious Research,* 8:67–80, Winter 1967.

——: "The Treatment of 'Race' in Beginning Sociology Textbooks," *Sociology and Social Research,* 35:277–284, 1951.

——: "Japan's Answer to the Population Problem," *Antioch Review,* 32:461–474, Winter 1962–1963.

HUNT, MORTON: *Sexual Behavior in the Seventies,* Playboy Press, Chicago, 1974.

HUNTER, FLOYD: *Community Power Structure,* University of North Carolina Press, Chapel Hill, 1953.

HUNTINGTON, ELLSWORTH: *The Character of Races as Influenced by Physical Environment, Natural Selection and Historical Development,* Charles Scribner's Sons, New York, 1924.

HUREWITZ, J. C.: *The Struggle for Palestine,* Greenwood Press, Publishers, New York, 1968.

HURLEY, JOHN R., and DONNA P. PALONEN: "Marital Satisfaction and Child Density Among University Student Parents," *Journal of Marriage and the Family,* 29:483–484, August 1967.

HURLOCK, ELIZABETH B.: "The Use of Group Rivalry as an Incentive," *Journal of Abnormal and Social Psychology,* 22:278–290, 1927.

HUXLEY, ALDOUS: *Brave New World,* Doubleday & Company, Inc., Garden City, N.Y., 1932.

———: *Brave New World Revisited,* Harper & Row, Publishers, Inc., New York, 1958.

HYMAN, HERBERT H., and JOHN SHELTON REED: "'Black Matriarchy' Reconsidered: Evidence from Secondary Analysis of Sample Surveys," *Public Opinion Quarterly,* 33:346–354, Fall 1969.

——— and CHARLES R. WRIGHT: "Trends in Voluntary Associational Memberships of American Adults: Replication Based on Secondary Analysis of National Sample Surveys," *American Sociological Review,* 23:191–206, April 1971.

ILFELD, FRED, JR., and ROGER LAUER: *Social Nudism in America,* College and University Press Services Inc., New Haven, Conn., 1964.

INKLES, ALEX: "Social Stratification and Mobility in the Soviet Union: 1940–1950." *American Journal of Sociology,* 66:1–31, 1960.

INKLES, ALEX, and DAVID H. SMITH: *Becoming Modern: Individual Changes in Six Developing Countries,* Harvard University Press, Cambridge, 1974.

INNIS, ROY: "The Zero Population Game," *Ebony,* November 1974, p. 110.

INSTITUTE FOR CONTINUING EDUCATION SERVICE, MICHIGAN STATE UNIVERSITY: "Equal Protection Under the Law: It Means More in Ann Arbor," *Human Rights Information Service,* Vol.5, No. 10, Nov. 25, 1974.

ISAMBERT, FRANCOIS-ANDRE: "Is the Religious Abstention of the Working Classes a General Phenomenon?" in Louis Schneider, *Religion, Culture, and Society,* John Wiley & Sons, Inc., New York, 1964, pp. 400–402.

JACK, NANCY KOPLIN, and BETTY SCHIFFER: "The Limits of Fashion Control," *American Sociological Review,* 13:730–738, 1948.

JACKMAN, ROBERT W.: "Political Democracy and Social Equality: A Comparative Analysis," *American Sociological Review,* 39:29–45, February 1974.

JACKSON, ELTON F., and RICHARD F. CURTIS: "Effects of Vertical Mobility and Status Inconsistency: A Body of Negative Evidence," *American Sociological Review,* 37:701–713, December 1973.

JACOBS, JANE: *The Death and Life of Great American Cities,* Random House, Inc., New York, 1961.

JAFFE, FREDERICH S., and STEPHEN POLGAR: "Family Planning and Public Policy: Is the Culture of Poverty the New Cop-out?" *Journal of Marriage and the Family,* 30:228–235, May 1968.

JALNINE, V.: "Some Recent Developments in the Labor Field in the USSR," *International Labor Review,* 106:191–205, August/September 1972.

Japan Report: "Japanese Believe Further Population Expansion Undesirable, Says Health and Welfare Ministry Study," Vol. 20, No. 22, Nov. 16, 1972, p. 1.

JAY, KARLA, and ALLEN YOUNG (eds.): *Out of the Closets: Voices of Gay Liberation,* Pyramid Publications, New York, 1974.

JEFFREY, C. RAY: *Crime Prevention Through Environmental Design,* Sage Publishers, Inc., Beverly Hills, Calif., 1971.

JENCKS, CHRISTOPHER et al.: *Inequality,* Basic Books, Inc., New York, 1972.

JENSEN, ARTHUR R.: "Social Class, Race, and Genetics: Implications for Education," *American Education Research Journal,* 5:1–42, January 1968.

———: "How Much Can We Boost IQ and Scholastic Achievement?" *Harvard Educational Review,* 28:1–123, Winter 1969.

———: *Educability and Group Differences,* Harper & Row, Publishers, Inc., New York, 1973.

JENVEY, SUE: "Sons and Haters: Ulster Youth in Conflict," *New Society,* 21:125–127, July 20, 1972.

JOHNSON, BENTON: "Do Holiness Sects Socialize in Dominant Values?" *Social Forces,* 39:309–316, May 1961.

JOHNSON, DONALD M.: "The 'Phantom Anesthetist' of Mattoon: A Field Study of Mass Hysteria," *Journal of Abnormal and Social Psychology,* 40:175–186, 1945.

JOHNSON, NICHOLAS: "What You Can Do to Improve TV," *Harper's Magazine,* 238:14–20, February 1969.

———: *How to Talk Back to Your Television Set,* Little, Brown and Company, Boston, 1970.

JOHNSTON, DENIS F., and HARVEY R. HAMEL: "Educational Attainment of Workers," *Monthly Labor Review,* 89:250–257, March 1966.

JONASSEN, CHRISTEN T.: "Community Typology," in MARVIN B. SUSSMAN (ed.), *Community Struc-*

ture and Analysis, Thomas Y. Crowell Company, New York, 1959.

JUPPENLATZ, MORRIS: *Cities in Transformation: The Urban Squatter Problem of the Developing World,* University of Queensland Press, St. Lucia, Queensland, Australia, 1970.

KADUSHIN, CHARLES: "How and Where to Find the Intellectual Elite in the United States," *Public Opinion Quarterly,* 35:1–18, Spring 1971.

———: *The American Intellectual Elite,* Little, Brown and Company, Boston, 1974.

KAHN, ALFRED J.: *Theory and Practice of Social Planning,* Russell Sage Foundation, New York, 1969.

KAHN, H. A.: "The Dorn Study of Smoking and Mortality among U.S. Veterans: Report on 8½ Years of Observation," *National Cancer Institute Monographs,* No. 9, January 1966, pp. 1–125.

KAHN, ROBERT L.: "The Meaning of Work: Interpretation and Proposal for Measurement," in Angus Campbell and Philip E. Converse (eds.), *The Human Meaning of Social Change,* Russell Sage Foundation, New York, 1972.

KAMPF, LOUIS: "The Trouble with Literature," *Change Magazine,* May—June 1970, pp. 27–34.

KANDEL, DENISE B., and GERALD S. LESSER: *Youth in Two Worlds,* Jossey-Bass Inc., San Francisco, 1972.

KANE, JOHN J.: "The Irish Wake: A Sociological Appraisal," *Sociological Symposium,* 1:21–27, Fall 1968.

KANTER, ROSABETH M.: *Commitment and Community: Communes and Utopias in Sociological Perspective,* Harvard University Press, Cambridge, Mass., 1972.

KAPLAN, BERT: "A Study of Rorschach Responses in Four Cultures," *Papers of the Peabody Museum of American Archeology and Ethnology,* Vol. 42, No. 2, Harvard University Press, Cambridge, Mass., 1954.

KAPLAN, JOHN: *Marijuana—The New Prohibition,* Harcourt, Brace & World, Inc., New York, 1970.

KASARDA, JOHN D. and MORRIS JANOWITZ: "Community Attachment in Mass Society," *American Sociological Review,* 39:328–339, June 1974.

KATEB, GEORGE (ed.): *Utopia,* Aldine-Atherton Press, New York, 1971.

KATZ, ABRAHAM: *The Politics of Economic Reform in the Soviet Union,* Praeger Publishers, Inc., New York, 1972.

KATZ, DANIEL A., and ROBERT L. KAHN: "Open Systems Theory," *The Social Psychology of Organizations,* John Wiley & Sons, Inc., New York, 1966, pp. 14–29.

KATZ, JAY, et al.: *Experimentation with Human Beings,* Russell Sage Foundation, New York, 1972.

KAUFMAN, WALTER C.: "Status, Authoritarianism, and Anti-semitism," *American Journal of Sociology,* 52:379–382, 1957.

KEELY, CHARLES B.: "Immigration Composition and Population Policy," *Science,* 185:587–573, Aug. 16, 1974.

KEESING, ROGER M.: "Chiefs in a Chiefless Society: The Ideology of Modern Kwaio Politics," *Oceania,* 38:276–280, June 1968.

KELLER, SUZANNE: "Does the Family Have a Future?" *Journal of Comparative Family Studies,* 2:1–14, Spring 1971.

KELLEY, DENNIS K., and WILLIAM J. CHAMBLISS: "Status Consistency and Political Attitudes," *American Sociological Review,* 31:375–382, June 1966.

KELLOGG, W. N., and L. A. KELLOGG: *The Ape and the Child,* McGraw-Hill Book Company, New York, 1933.

KELMAN, HERBERT C.: "Deception in Social Research," *Trans-action,* 3:20–24, July—August 1966.

KELMAN, STEPHEN: *Push Comes to Shove: The Escalation of Student Protest,* Houghton Mifflin Company, Boston, 1970.

KENISTON, KENNETH: "The Sources of Discontent," in Walt Anderson (ed.), *The Age of Protest,* Goodyear Publishing Company, Pacific Palisades, Calif., 1969. Originally published in KENNETH KENISTON'S *Young Radicals: Notes on Committed Youth,* Harcourt, Brace & World, Inc., New York, 1968.

KEPHART, W. M.: *Family, Society, and the Individual,* Houghton Mifflin Company, Boston, 1966.

KERCHER, LEONARD, VANT W. KEBKER, and WILFRED C. LELAND, JR.: *Consumers' Cooperatives in the North Central States,* University of Minnesota Press, Minneapolis, 1941.

KERPELMAN, LARRY C.: "Student Political Activism and Ideology: Comparative Characteristics of Activists and Nonactivists," *Journal of Counseling Psychology,* 16:8–13, 1969.

KERR, CLARK: "Industrial Conflict and Its Mediation," *American Journal of Sociology,* 60:230–245, November 1954.

KESSIN, KENNETH: "Social and Psychological Consequences of Intergenerational Occupational Mobility," *American Journal of Sociology,* 77:1–18, July 1971.

KEY, WILLIAM H.: "Rural-Urban Differences and the Family," *Sociological Quarterly,* 2:49–56, 1961.

KHARCHEV, A. G.: "The Nature of the Russian Family," *Voporosy Filosofia,* no. 1, translated and abridged in *Soviet Review,* 2:3–19, 1961.

KIERNAN, BERNARD P.: *The United States, Communism, and the Emergent World,* Indiana University Press, Bloomington, 1972.

KIESTER, EDWIN, JR.: "Dr. Szasz: The Devil's Advocate," *Human Behavior,* July 1972, 16–23.

KIM, MO-IM: "Age at Marriage, Family Planning Practices, and Other Variables as Correlates of Fertility in Korea," *Demography,* 11:641–656, November 1974.

KINKADE, KATHLEEN: *A Walden Two Experiment: The First Five Years of Twin Oaks Community,* William E. Morrow and Co., New York, 1974.

KINSEY, ALFRED C., WARDELL B. POMEROY, and CLYDE E. MARTIN: *Sexual Behavior in the Human Male,* W. B. Saunders Company, Philadelphia, 1948.

———, et al.: *Sexual Behavior in the Human Female,* W. B. Saunders Company, Philadelphia, 1953.

KITAGAWA, EVELYN M., and PHILIP M. HAUSER: *Education and Income Differentials in Mortality, United States, 1960,* University of Chicago Population Center, Chicago, 1967.

KLAUSNER, SAMUEL Z.: *On Man in His Environment,* Jossey-Bass, Inc., San Francisco, 1971.

KLEMMACK, DAVID L., and JOHN N. EDWARDS: "Women's Acquisition of Stereotyped Occupational Aspirations," *Sociology and Social Research,* 57:510–525, July 1973.

KLINEBERG, OTTO: *Negro Intelligence and Selective Migration,* Columbia University Press, New York, 1935.

———: *Characteristics of the American Negro,* Harper & Row, Publishers, Inc., New York, 1944.

KLUCKHOHN, CLYDE: "Participation in Ceremonials in a Navaho Community," *American Anthropologist,* 40:359–369, 1938.

KNIBBS, GEORGE HANDLEY: *The Shadow of the World's Future: Or the Earth's Population Possibilities and Consequences of the Present Rate of Increase of the World's Inhabitants,* Ernest Benn, Ltd., London, 1928.

KNITTEL, ROBERT E.: "New Towns, Knowledge, Experience, and Theory: An Overview," *Human Organization,* 32:27–48, Spring 1973.

KNOTT, PAUL D. (ed.): *Student Activism,* William C. Brown Company, Publishers, Dubuque, Iowa, 1971.

KNUDSON, DEAN D.: "The Declining Status of Women: Popular Myths and the Failure of Functionalist Thought," *Social Forces,* 48:183–193, December 1969.

KOENIG, ROBERT P.: "An American Engineer Looks at British Coal," *Foreign Affairs,* 26:285–286, 1948.

KOHN, MELVIN, "Bureaucratic Man: A Portrait and an Interpretation," *American Sociological Review,* 36:461–474, June 1971.

———, and CARMI SCHOOLER: "Class, Occupation, and Orientation," *American Sociological Review,* 34:659–678, October 1969.

———, and ———: "Occupational Experience and Psychological Functioning: An Assessment of Reciprocal Effects," *American Sociological Review,* 38:97–118, February 1973.

KON, IGOR S.: "The Concept of Alienation in Modern Sociology," in PETER L. BERGER (ed.), *Marxism and Sociology,* Appleton-Century-Crofts, New York, 1969, pp. 146–167.

KORNHAUSER, WILLIAM: *The Politics of Mass Society,* The Free Press, New York, 1959.

KRAMER, RALPH M.: *Participation of the Poor: Comparative Community Case Studies in the War on Poverty,* Prentice-Hall, Inc., Englewood Cliffs, N.J., 1969.

———, and HARRY SPECHT (eds.): "Processes of Directed Change: Social Planning," in *Readings in Community Organization Practice,* Part II, Section D, Prentice-Hall, Inc., Englewood Cliffs, N.J., 1975.

KRETSCHMER, ERNEST: *Physique and Character,* Harcourt, Brace & World, Inc., New York, 1925.

KRIESBERG, LOUIS: *The Sociology of Social Conflict,* Prentice-Hall, Inc., Englewood Cliffs, N.J., 1973.

KRISTOL, IRVING: "About Equality," *Commentary,* November 1972, pp. 41–47.

KROPOTKIN, PETER: *Mutual Aid,* Alfred A. Knopf, Inc., New York, 1925.

KROUT, MAURICE A.: *Introduction to Social Psychology,* Harper & Row, Publishers, Inc., New York, 1942.

KUHN, MANFORD, H., and THOMAS S. MCPARTLAND: "An Empirical Investigation of Self-Attitudes," *American Sociological Review,* 19:68–75, February 1954.

KUO, ZING YANG: "Genesis of Cat's Responses to Rats," *Journal of Comparative Psychology,* 11:1–35, 1931.

LAM, BLAINE: "Black Officials Ask Total Effort to Fight Crime," *Kalamazoo Gazette,* Oct. 30, 1974.

LANDER, BERNARD: *Toward an Understanding of Juvenile Delinquency,* Columbia University Press, New York, 1954.

LANDIS, PAUL H.: *Social Control,* J. B. Lippincott Company, Philadelphia, 1956.

———: *Making the Most of Marriage,* New York: Appleton-Century-Crofts, New York, 1970.

LANE, ROBERT: *Political Ideology,* The Free Press, New York, 1962.

LANG, KURT, and GLADYS ENGEL LANG: *Collective Dynamics,* Thomas Y. Crowell Company, New York, 1961.

LAPIERE, RICHARD T.: *Collective Behavior,* McGraw-Hill Book Company, New York, 1938.

———: *A Theory of Social Control,* McGraw-Hill Book Company, New York, 1965.

———: *Social Change,* McGraw-Hill Book Company, New York, 1965.

LAQUEUR, WALTER: "The Gathering Storm," *Commentary,* August 1974, pp. 22–33.

LASSWELL, HAROLD D.: "The Strategy of Soviet Propaganda," *Proceedings of the Academy of Political Science,* 24:214–226, 1951.

———, and DOROTHY BLUMENSTOCK: *World Revolutionary Propaganda,* Alfred A. Knopf, Inc., New York, 1939.

LASSWELL, THOMAS E.: *Class and Stratum,* Houghton Mifflin Company, Boston, 1965.

LAUER, ROBERT H.: "Rate of Change and Stress: A Test of the 'Future Shock' Thesis," *Social Forces,* 52:510–516, June 1974.

LEAGINS, J. PAUL, and CHARLES P. LOOMIS (eds.): *Behavioral Change in Agriculture,* Cornell University Press, Ithaca, N.Y., 1971.

LEBON, GUSTAV: *The Crowd: A Study of the Popular Mind,* Ernest Benn, Ltd., London, 1896.

LEE, ALFRED M.: *Multivalent Man,* George Braziller, Inc., New York, 1966.

———, and ELIZABETH BRIANT LEE: *The Fine Art of Propaganda,* Harcourt, Brace & World, Inc., and the Institute for Propaganda Analysis, New York, 1939.

———, and NORMAN D. HUMPHREY: *Race Riot,* Holt, Rinehart and Winston, Inc., New York, 1943.

———, and ———: *Toward a Humanist Sociology,* Prentice-Hall, Inc., Englewood Cliffs, N.J., 1973.

LEE, DOROTHY: *Freedom and Culture,* Prentice-Hall, Inc., Englewood Cliffs, N.J., 1959.

LEE, MING T.: "The Founders of the Chinese Communist Party: A Study in Revolutionaries," *Civilizations,* 18:113–127, 1968.

LEEMAN, WAYNE A.: "Bonus Formulae and Social Managerial Performance," *Southern Economic Journal,* 36:431–439, April 1970.

LEHR, STAN, and LOUIS ROSSETTO, JR.: "The New Right Credo-Libertarianism," *New York Times Magazine,* Jan. 10, 1971, pp. 24ff.

LEJEUNE, ROBERT (ed.): *Class and Conflict in American Society,* Rand McNally Publishing Co., Chicago, 1973.

LELYFELD, JOSEPH: "Chinese Promote Job 'Enthusiasm,'" *New York Times,* Nov. 10, 1974, p. 13.

LEMERT, EDWIN M.: *Social Pathology,* McGraw-Hill Book Company, New York, 1951.

———: "The Concept of Secondary Deviation," in *Human Deviance, Social Problems, and Social Control,* Prentice-Hall, Inc., Englewood Cliffs, N.J., 1967, pp. 40–64.

LENSKI, GERHARD: "Status Crystallization: A Nonvertical Dimension of Social Status," *American Sociological Review,* 19:405–413, June 1954.

———: *The Religious Factor,* Doubleday & Company, Inc., Garden City, N.Y., 1961.

———: *Power and Privilege: A Theory of Social Stratification,* McGraw-Hill Book Company, 1966.

———: "Status Inconsistency and the Vote: A Four Nation Test," *American Sociological Review,* 32:298–301, April 1967.

———: *Human Societies,* McGraw-Hill Book Company, New York, 1970.

———: "The Religious Factor in Detroit: Revisited," *American Sociological Review,* 36:48–50, February 1971.

LEON, DAN: *The Kibbutz: A New Way of Life,* Pergamon Press, New York, 1970.

LERNER, MICHAEL: "Respectable Bigotry," *American Scholar,* 38:606–617, Autumn 1969.

LESLIE, GERALD R.: *The Family in Social Context,* Oxford University Press, New York, 1973.

LESSER, ALEXANDER: "Cultural Significance of the Ghost Dance," *American Anthropologist,* 35:108–115, January 1972.

LEVER, H.: "Changes in Ethnic Attitude in South Africa," *Sociology and Social Research,* 56:202–210, January 1972.

LEVINE, ROBERT A., and DONALD C. CAMPBELL: *Ethnocentrism: Theories of Conflict, Ethnic Attitudes, and Group Behavior,* John Wiley & Sons, Inc., New York, 1972.

LEVITT, THEODORE: *The Third Sector: New Tactics for a Responsive Society,* New York, 1973.

LEVY, MARION J.: *The Family Revolution in Modern China,* Harvard University Press, Cambridge, Mass., 1949.

———: "Social Patterns (Structures)," in WILBERT E. MOORE and ROBERT M. COOK (eds.), *Readings on Social Change,* Prentice-Hall, Inc., Englewood Cliffs, N.J., 1966.

LEWIS, JERRY M.: "A Study of the Kent State Incident Using Smelser's Theory of Collective Behavior," *Sociological Inquiry,* 42:87–96, Spring 1972.

LEWIS, OSCAR: *Five Families: Mexican Case Studies in the Culture of Poverty,* Basic Books, Inc., New York, 1959.

———: *The Children of Sanchez: Autobiography of a Mexican Family,* Vintage Books, Random House, Inc., New York, 1963 (a).

———: *Life in a Mexican Village: Tepoztlan Revisited,* with drawings by Alberto Beltram, University of Illinois Press, Urbana, 1963 (b).

———: *Village Life in Northern India: Studies in a Delhi Village,* with the assistance of VICTOR BARNOUW, Vintage Books, Random House, Inc., New York, 1965.

———: *La Vida: A Puerto Rican Family in the Culture of Poverty, San Juan and New York,* Random House, Inc., New York, 1966 (a).

———: "Culture of Poverty; with Biographical Sketch," *Scientific American,* 215:19–25, October 1966 (b).

LEWIS, SINCLAIR: *Babbitt,* Harcourt, Brace & World, Inc., New York, 1922.

LEYBURN, JAMES G.: *Frontier Folkways,* Yale University Press, New Haven, Conn., 1935.

LIEBERMAN, E. JAMES: "The Case for Small Families," *New York Times Magazine,* Mar. 8, 1970, pp. 86–89.

LIEBERMAN, MORTON A., IRWIN D. YOLOM, and MATTHEW B. MILES: *Encounter Groups: First Facts,* Basic Books, Inc., New York, 1973.

———: "The Leader Makes the Difference," *Psychology Today,* March 1973, pp. 70–76.

LIEBERSON, STANLEY, and ARNOLD R. SILVERMAN: "Precipitants and Conditions of Race Riots," *American Sociological Review,* 30:887–898, December 1965.

LIEBOW, ELLIOT: *Tally's Corner: A Study of Negro Streetcorner Men,* Little, Brown and Company, Inc., New York, 1967.

LILIENTHAL, ALFRED M.: *The Other Side of the Coin: An American Perspective of the Arab-Israeli Conflict,* Devin-Adair Company, Inc., New York, 1965.

LINCOLN, C. ERIC: *The Black Muslims in America,* Beacon Press, Boston, 1961.

———: "The Absent Father Haunts the Negro Family," *New York Times Magazine,* Nov. 28, 1965, p. 60ff.

LINDESMITH, ALFRED E.: "Social Problems and Sociological Theory," *Social Problems,* 8:98–102, 1960.

LINDZEY, GARDNER (ed.): *Handbook of Social Psychology,* Addison-Wesley Press, Inc., Cambridge, Mass., 1954.

LINTON, RALPH: *The Study of Man,* Appleton-Century-Crofts, Inc., New York, 1936.

LIPPMANN, WALTER: "On Freedom," *Newsweek,* Dec. 23, 1974, p. 45.

LIPSEDGE, M. S.: "The Poujade Movement," *Contemporary Review,* 189:83–88, 1956.

LIPSET, SEYMOUR M.: "Leadership and New Social Movements," in ALVIN W. GOULDNER (ed.), *Studies in Leadership,* Harper & Row, Publishers, Inc., New York, 1950, pp. 342–362.

———, A. THROW, and JAMES S. COLEMAN: *Union Democracy: The Internal Politics of the International Typographical Union,* The Free Press of Glencoe, Ill., Chicago, 1956.

———: "George Wallace and the U.S. New Right," *New Society,* 12:477–482, October 1968.

———: "Religion in America: What Religious Revival?" *Columbia University Forum,* Winter 1959, pp. 17–21.

———: "Social Mobility and Equal Opportunity," *The Public Interest,* 29:90–108, Fall 1972.

———, and EVERETT CARL LADD, JR.: "The Politics of

American Sociologists," *American Journal of Sociology,* 78:67–104, July 1972.

LITWAK, EUGENE: "Three Ways in which Law Acts as a Means of Social Control: Punishment, Therapy, and Education," *Social Forces,* 34:217–223, 1956.

LOHMAN, JOSEPH D.: *The Police and Minority Groups,* Chicago Park District, Chicago, 1947.

LOMBROSO, CESARE: *Crime, Its Causes and Remedies,* translated by H. P. Horton, Little, Brown and Company, Boston, 1912.

LONG, LARRY H.: "Women's Labor Force Participation and Residential Mobility of Families," *Social Forces,* 52:342–348, March 1974.

LOOMIS, CHARLES P., and J. ALLAN BEAGLE: "The Spread of German Nazism in Rural Areas," *American Sociological Review,* 11:724–734, 1946.

———, and ZONA KEMP LOOMIS: *Modern Social Theories,* D. Van Nostrand Company, Inc., Princeton, N.J., 1961.

———, and J. ALLAN BEAGLE: *A Strategy for Rural Change,* Halstead Publishers, New York, 1975.

LOPREATO, JOSEPH, and JANET E. SALZMAN: "Descriptive Models of Peasant Society: A Reconciliation from Southern Italy," *Human Organization,* 27:132–142, Summer 1968.

LORENZ, KONRAD: *On Aggression,* Harcourt, Brace & World, Inc., New York, 1966.

LOWE, SUSAN J.: "Abortion: The Facts," *Zero Population Growth National Reporter,* May 1975, p. 1.

LOWENTHAL, LEO, and NORBERT GUTERMAN: *Prophets of Deceit,* Harper & Row, Publishers, Inc., New York, 1949.

LOWIE, ROBERT H.: *Introduction to Cultural Anthropology,* Holt, Rinehart and Winston, Inc., New York, 1940.

LOWRY, RITCHIE P.: *Who's Running This Town? Community Leadership and Social Change,* Harper & Row, Publishers, Inc., New York, 1965.

LUBIN, JOANN S.: "Black Firm's Blues," *Wall Street Journal,* Apr. 1, 1975, pp. 1ff.

LUFT, JOSEPH: *Group Processes: An Introduction to Group Dynamics,* National Press, Palo Alto, Calif., 1970.

LUMLEY, FREDERICK E.: *Means of Social Control,* Century Company, New York, 1925.

LUNDBERG, FERDINAND: *America's Sixty Families,* Vanguard Press, Inc., New York, 1937.

———: *The Rich and the Super Rich: A Study in the Power of Money Today,* Lyle Stuart, Inc., New York, 1968.

LURIE, NANCY: "Winnebago Berdache," *American Anthropologist,* 55:708–712, 1953.

LYNCH, FRANK: *Social Class in a Bicol Town,* Philippines Studies Program, University of Chicago Press, Chicago, 1959.

LYND, ROBERT S., and HELEN M. LYND: *Middletown,* Harcourt, Brace & World, Inc., New York, 1929.

——— and ———: *Middletown in Transition,* Harcourt, Brace & World, Inc., New York, 1937.

LYND, STAUGHTON: "The New Left," *Annals of the American Academy of Political and Social Science,* 382:64–72, March 1969.

LYONS, RICHARD D.: "Psychiatrists in a Shift, Declare Homosexuality No Mental Illness," *New York Times,* Dec. 16, 1973, pp. 1ff.

MCBIRNIE, WILLIAM S.: *Who Really Rules America: A Study of the Power Elite,* Center for American Education and Research, Glendale, Calif., 1968.

MCCLELLAND, DAVID C.: "The Power of Positive Drinking," *Psychology Today,* January 1971, pp. 40ff.

MCCLOSKY, HERBERT, and JOHN H. SCHAAR: "Psychological Dimensions of Anomy," *American Sociological Review,* 30:14–40, February 1965.

MCCORMACK, ARTHUR: *The Population Problem,* Thomas Y. Crowell Company, New York, 1970.

MCELROY, ROGER: "Sex-role Orientations, Socioeconomic Status, and Intended Family Size," Paper presented at Annual Meeting of the Northcentral Sociological Association, Windsor, Ontario, May 1974.

MCFERRAN, DOUGLASS: "Christianity and the Religions of the Occult," *Christian Century,* 89:541–545, May 10, 1972.

MCGINNIS, ROBERT, and LOUISE SOLOMON: "Employment Prospects for Ph.D. Sociologists During the Seventies," *American Sociologist,* 8:57–63, May 1973.

MCGINTY, ALICE B.: "India: A House Divided," *Current History,* 13:288–289, 1947.

MCGOTHLIN, WILLIAM H., and DAVID O. ARNOLD: "LSD Revisited: A Ten-Year Follow-up of LSD Medical Use," *Archives of General Psychiatry,* 24:35–49, January 1971.

MCKEE, DAVID L., and GERALD H. SMITH: "Environmental Diseconomies in Suburban Expansion," *American Journal of Economics and Sociology,* 31:181–188, April 1972.

MCKEE, JAMES B.: "Status and Power in the Industrial Community: A Comment on Drucker's Thesis," *American Journal of Sociology,* 58:364–370, 1953.

MCKENZIE, R. D.: "The Ecological Approach to the Study of the Human Community," in ROBERT E. PARK, E. W. BURGESS, and R. D. MCKENZIE (eds.), *The City,* University of Chicago Press, Chicago, 1925, pp. 63–79.

MCKERN, SHARON S., and THOMAS W. MCKERN: "The Peace Messiah," in Raymond Friday Locke (ed.), *The American Indian,* Mankind Publishing Company, Los Angeles, 1970, pp. 147–176.

MCNALL, SCOTT G.: *The Sociological Experience,* Little, Brown and Company, Boston, 1974.

MCNAMARA, JOHN: *Bilingualism and Primary Education,* Edinburgh University Press, Edinburgh, 1966.

MCVAY, FRANK L.: "The Social Effects of the Eight Hour Day," *American Journal of Sociology,* 8:521–530, January 1903.

MACK, DOLORES E.: "Where the Black Matriarchy Theorists Went Wrong," *Psychology Today,* January 1971, pp. 24ff.

MACK, RAYMOND W.: "The Components of Social Conflict," *Social Problems,* 12:394–397, Spring 1965.

MACKAY, CHARLES: *Extraordinary Popular Delusions and the Madness of Crowds,* L. C. Page & Company, Boston, 1932.

MACKLIN, ELEANOR D.: "Cohabitation in College: Going Very Steady," *Psychology Today,* November 1974, pp. 53–59.

MAEROFF, GENE L.: "Students' Scores Again Show Drop," *New York Times,* Dec. 16, 1973, pp. 1ff.

MAHER, ROBERT F.: *The New Man of Papua: A Study in Cultural Change,* University of Wisconsin Press, Madison, 1961.

MAILER, NORMAN: "The Prisoner of Sex," *Harper's,* March 1971, pp. 41ff.

MALCOLM, ANDREW: *The Tyranny of the Group,* Clark, Irwin and Co., Ltd., Toronto, 1973.

MALEWSKI, ANDRZEJ: "The Degree of Status Incongruence and Its Effects," in REINHARD BENDIX and S. M. MILLER (eds.), *Class, Status, and Power,* The Free Press, New York, 1966, pp. 303–308.

MALINOWSKI, BRONISLAW: *Crime and Custom in Savage Society,* Routledge & Kegan Paul, Ltd., London, 1926.

MALIVER, BRUCE L.: "Encounter Groupers Up Against the Wall," *New York Times Magazine,* Jan. 3, 1971, pp. 4ff.

———: *The Encounter Game,* Stein and Day, New York, 1973.

MANGUS, A. R.: "Personality Adjustment of Rural and Urban Children," *American Sociological Review,* 13:566–575, 1948.

MANIS, JEROME, G., MILTON J. BRAWER, CHESTER L. HUNT, and LEONARD C. KERCHER: "Estimating the Prevalence of Mental Illness," *American Sociological Review,* 29:84–89, February 1964.

MANKOFF, MILTON: "Toward Socialism: Reassessing Inequality," *Social Policy,* March—April 1974, pp. 20–31.

MANN, RICHARD D., GRAHAM S. GIBBARD, and JOHN J. HARTMAN: *Interpersonal Styles and Group Development,* John Wiley & Sons, Inc., New York, 1967.

MANNHEIM, KARL: *Man and Society in an Age of Reconstruction,* Harcourt, Brace & World, Inc., New York, 1940.

———: *Man and Society in an Age of Reconstruction: Studies in Modern Social Structure,* Verry, Fischer, and Co., Inc., New York, 1949.

MANTELL, DAVID MARK: "Doves vs. Hawks: Guess Who Had the Authoritarian Parents," *Psychology Today,* September 1974, pp. 56–62.

———: *Three Americas: Green Berets and War Resistors, a Study of Commitment,* Teachers' College Press, New York, 1974.

MARCUSE, HERBERT: *An Essay on Liberation,* Beacon Press, Boston, 1969 (a).

———: "Student Protest Is Nonviolent Next to the Society Itself," *New York Times Magazine,* May 4, 1969, p. 137 (b).

MARRIOTT, MCKIM (ed.): *Village India,* University of Chicago Press, Chicago, 1955.

MARSHALL KAPLAN, GANS, and KAHN: *The Model Cities Program: The Planning Process in Atlanta, Seattle, and Dayton,* Frederick A. Praeger, Inc., New York, 1970.

MARSHALL, RAY: "Labor in the South," *Antioch Review,* 21:80–95, 1961.

MARSHALL, S. L. A.: *Men Under Fire,* William Morrow & Company, Inc., New York, 1947.

MARTIN, DEL, and PHYLLIS LYON: *Lesbian Woman,* Glide Publications, San Francisco, 1972.

MARTIN, GALEN: "New Civil Rights Act Coverages— Progress or Racism?" Mimeographed report presented to Conference of the National Association of Human Rights Workers, Oct. 8, 1974.

MARTINDALE, DON, and R. GALEN HANSON: *Small Town and the Nation: The Conflict of Local and Translocal Forces,* Greenwood Publishing Company, Westport, Conn., 1969.

MARTY, MARTIN: "The Occult Establishment," *Social Research,* 37:211–230, Summer 1970.

MARX, GARY T.: "Issueless Riots," *Annals of the American Academy of Political and Social Science,* 391:21–33, September 1970.

MARX, KARL, and FREDERIC ENGELS: *Basic Writings on Politics and Philosophy,* ed. by Lewis S. Feuer, Doubleday & Co., Inc., New York, 1959.

MASSIMO, TEODORI (ed.): *The New Left: A Documentary History,* Bobbs-Merrill Co., Indianapolis, 1969.

MASTERS, WILLIAM H., and VIRGINIA E. JOHNSON: *Human Sexual Response,* Little, Brown and Company, Boston, 1966.

——— and ———: *Human Sexual Inadequacy,* Little, Brown and Company, Boston, 1970.

MATZA, DAVID: *Becoming Deviant,* Prentice-Hall, Inc., Englewood Cliffs, N.J., 1969.

MAULDIN, W. PARKER, NAZLI CHOUCHI, FRANK NOTESTEIN, and MICHAEL TIETELBAUM: "A Report on Bucharest," *Studies in Family Planning,* 5:358–381, November 1974.

MAUSNER, BERNARD, and JUDITH MAUSNER: "A Study of the Anti-scientific Attitude," *Scientific American,* 192:35–39, 1955.

MAYBEE, C.: "Evolution of Non-Violence," *Nation,* 193:78–81, 1961.

MAYER, ALBERT J., et al.: *Pilot Project: India,* University of California Press, Berkeley, 1958.

MAYESKE, GEORGE W.: *On the Explanation of Racial-ethnic Group Differences in Achievement Test Scores,* Office of Education, Washington, D.C. (mimeo), 1973.

MEAD, GEORGE HERBERT: *Mind, Self and Society,* University of Chicago Press, Chicago, 1934.

MEAD, MARGARET: "The Implications of Culture Change for Personality Development," *American Journal of Orthopsychiatry,* 17:633–646, 1947.

———: *Cultural Patterns and Technical Change,* UNESCO, Mentor Books, New American Library, Inc., New York, 1955.

———: *New Lives for Old,* William Morrow & Company, Inc., New York, 1956.

———: *Culture and Commitment: A Study of the Generation Gap,* Natural History Press, New York, 1970.

MEADOWS, DONELLA H., et al.: *The Limits to Growth,* Universe Books, New York, 1972.

MECKLIN, JOHN H.: *The Ku Klux Klan,* Harcourt, Brace & World, Inc., New York, 1924.

MEEKER, MARCIA: "Status Aspirations and the Social Club," in W. Lloyd Warner (ed.), *Democracy in Jonesville,* Harper & Row, Publishers, Inc., New York, 1949, pp. 130–148.

MEISELS, MURRAY, and FRANCIS M. CANTER: "A Note on the Generation Gap," *Adolescence,* 6:523–530, Winter 1971.

MERCER, JANE R.: *Labeling the Mentally Retarded,* University of California Press, Berkeley, 1973.

MERRILL, FRANCIS E.: "The Self and the Other: An Emerging Field of Social Problems," *Social Problems,* 4:200–207, January 1957.

MERTON, ROBERT K.: "Social Structure and Anomie," *American Sociological Review,* 3:672–682, 1938.

———: "Bureaucratic Structure and Personality," in *Social Theory and Social Structure,* The Free Press, New York, 1949 (a), pp. 151–160.

———: "Spheres of Influence: Monomorphic and Polymorphic," in PAUL F. LAZARSFELD and FRANK R. STANTON (eds.), *Communications Research,* Harper & Row, Publishers, Inc., 1949 (b), pp. 148–149.

——— et al.: "Reader in Bureaucracy," The Free Press, New York, 1952.

———: "Social Theory and Social Structure," The Free Press, New York, 1957 (a).

———: "Manifest and Latent Functions: Toward a Codification of Functional Analysis in Sociology," in *Social Theory and Social Structure,* The Free Press, New York, 1957 (b), pp. 19–84.

———: "Priorities in Scientific Discovery: A Chapter in the Sociology of Science," *American Sociological Review,* 22:635–659, December 1957 (c).

MESSINGER, SHELDON L.: "Organizational Transformation: A Case Study of a Declining Social Movement," *American Sociological Review,* 20:3–10, February 1955.

METHVIN, EUGENE H.: *The Rise of Radicalism,* Arlington House, New Rochelle, N.Y., 1973.

MEYER, ROGER E.: "LSD: The Conditions and Consequences of Use and the Treatment of Users," in *Proceedings of the Rutgers Symposium on Drug Abuse,* compiled and edited by J. R. WITTENBORN et al., Charles C Thomas, Publisher, Springfield, Ill., 1969, pp. 199–208.

MICHEL, ANDREE, and FRANCOISE LAUTMAN FEYRABEND: "Real Number of Children and Conjugal

Interaction in French Urban Families: A Comparison with American Families," *Journal of Marriage and the Family,* 31:359–363, May 1969.

MICHELS, ROBERT: *Political Parties: A Sociological Study of the Oligarchial Tendencies in Modern Democracy,* translated by EDEN and CEDAR PAUL, The Free Press of Glencoe, Glencoe, Ill., 1949.

MICHENER, JAMES A.: *Centennial,* Random House, Inc., New York, 1974.

MICOSSI, ANITA LYNN: "Conversion to Women's Lib," *Trans-action,* November—December 1970, pp. 82–90.

MIKESELL, MARVIN W.: "The Deforestation of Mount Lebanon," *The Geographical Review,* 59:1–28, January 1969.

MILGRAM, STANLEY, and HANS TOCH: "Collective Behavior: Crowds and Social Movements," in GARDNER LINDZEY and ELLIOTT ARONSON (eds.), *Handbook in Social Psychology,* vol. IV, Addison-Wesley Publishing Company, Inc., Reading, Mass., 1969, pp. 507–610.

—— and ——: *Obedience to Authority: An Experimental View,* Harper & Row, Publishers, Inc., New York, 1974.

MILLER, ARTHUR S.: "Some Observations on the Political Economy of Population Growth," *Law and Contemporary Problems,* 25:614–632, 1960.

MILLER, DELBERT C.: *International Community Power Structures: Comparative Studies of Four World Cities,* Indiana University Press, Bloomington, 1970.

—— and WILLIAM H. FORM: *Industrial Sociology,* Harper & Row, Publishers, Inc., New York, 1964.

MILLER, MERLE: "What It Means to Be a Homosexual," *New York Times Magazine,* Jan. 17, 1971, pp. 9ff.

MILLER, S. M., and ELLIOT G. MISHLER: "Social Class, Mental Illness, and American Psychiatry," *Milbank Memorial Fund Quarterly,* 37:174–199, 1959.

—— and FRANK RIESSMAN: "The Working Class Subculture: A New View," *Social Problems,* 9:86–97, Summer 1961.

—— and PAMELA A. ROBY: *The Future of Inequality,* Basic Books, Inc., New York, 1970.

MILLER, WALTER B.: "Lower Class Culture as a Generating Milieu of Gang Delinquency," *Journal of Social Issues* (3), 14:5–19, 1958.

MILLET, KATE: *Sexual Politics,* Doubleday & Company, Inc., Garden City, N.Y., 1970.

MILLS, C. WRIGHT: *The Power Elite,* Oxford University Press, Fair Lawn, N.J., 1956.

MILLS, THEODORE M.: *The Sociology of Small Groups,* Prentice-Hall, Inc., Englewood Cliffs, N.J., 1967.

MILNER, MURRAY, JR.: *The Illusion of Equality,* Jossey-Bass, San Francisco, 1972.

MINER, HORACE (ed.): *The City in Modern Africa,* Frederick A. Praeger, Inc., New York, 1952, 1967.

MINTZ, ALEXANDER: "Non-adaptive Group Behavior," *Journal of Abnormal and Social Psychology,* 46:150–158, 1951.

MITCHELL, ROBERT EDWARD: "Methodological Notes on a Theory of Status Crystallization," *Public Opinion Quarterly,* 28:315–325, 1964.

MIYAMOTO, S. FRANK, and SANFORD M. DORNBUSCH: "A Test of Interactionist Hypothesis of Self-Conception," *American Journal of Sociology,* 61:399–403, 1956.

MOINET, SHERYL M, et al.: "Black Ghetto Residents and Rioters," *Journal of Social Issues,* 28:45–62, 1972.

MONROE, KEITH: "The New Gambling King and the Social Scientists," *Harper's Magazine,* January 1962, pp. 35–41.

MONTAGNA, PAUL D.: "Professionalization and Bureaucratization in Large Professional Organizations," *American Journal of Sociology,* 74:138–145, September 1968.

MONTAGU, ASHLEY: *Man: His First Million Years,* Mentor Books, New American Library, Inc., New York, 1958.

——: *Sex, Man and Society,* G. P. Putnam's Sons, New York, 1969.

MOORE, JOAN W., with ALFRED CUELLAR: *Mexican Americans,* Prentice-Hall, Inc., Englewood Cliffs, N.J., 1970.

MOORE, WILBERT E.: *Social Change,* Prentice-Hall, Inc., Englewood Cliffs, N.J., 1963.

MOREHOUSE, FRANCES: "The Irish Migration of the 'Forties,'" *American Historical Review,* 33:579–592, 1928.

MORENO, J. L.: "Psychodramatic Treatment of Marriage Problems," *Sociometry,* 3:2–23, 1940.

MORGAN, MIRIAM MARABEL: *The Total Woman,* Fleming H. Revell, Westwood, N.J., 1973.

MORGAN, THEODORE: "The Economic Development of

Ceylon," *Annals of the American Academy of Political and Social Science,* 305:92–100, 1956.

MORGAN, TED: "Cuba," *New York Times Magazine,* Dec. 1, 1974, pp. 27ff.

MORRIS, DESMOND: *The Naked Ape,* McGraw-Hill Book Company, New York, 1968.

MORRIS, PETER: *Loss and Change,* Pantheon Books, New York, 1974.

MORRIS, R. N., and JOHN MOGEY: *The Sociology of Housing,* Routledge and Kegan Paul, Ltd., London, 1965.

MORRISON, DELTON E., and ALLAN D. STEEVES: "Deprivation, Discontent, and Social Movement Participation," *Rural Sociology,* 32:414–434, December 1967.

—— and ——: "Some Notes Toward Theory on Relative Deprivation," *American Behavioral Scientist,* 24:675–690, November 1971.

MORRISON, RAYMOND L., JR., and JACK D. SALMON: "Population Control in China: A Reinterpretation," *Asian Survey,* 13:873–890, September 1973.

MOSK, STANLEY, and HOWARD H. JEWEL: "The Birch Phenomenon Analyzed," *New York Times Magazine,* Aug. 20, 1961, pp. 12ff.

MOTWANI, KEWAL: "The Impact of Modern Technology on the Social Structure of South Asia," *International Social Science Bulletin,* 3:783–793, Winter 1951.

MOYNIHAN DANIEL P.: "Behind Los Angeles: Jobless Negroes and the Boom," *The Reporter,* Sept. 9, 1965 (a), p. 31.

——: *The Negro Family: The Case for National Action,* U.S. Department of Labor, Washington, D.C., 1965 (b).

——: *Maximum Feasible Misunderstanding: Community Action in the War on Poverty,* The Free Press, New York, 1969.

——: "'Peace'—Some Thoughts on the 1960's and 1970's," *The Public Interest,* 32:3–12, Summer 1973.

MUNCH, PETER A.: "Culture and Super-Culture in a Displaced Community: Tristan deCunha," *Ethnology,* 3:369–376, October 1964.

——: *Crisis in Utopia,* Thomas Y. Crowell Company, New York, 1970.

MUNTS, RAYMOND, and IRWIN GARFINKEL: *The Work Disincentive Effects of Unemployment Insurance,* W. E. Upjohn Institute for Employment Research, Kalamazoo, Mich., 1974.

MURAMATSU, MINORU: "Effect of Induced Abortion on the Reduction of Births in Japan," *Milbank Memorial Fund Quarterly,* 38:153–166, 1960.

MURDOCK, GEORGE P.: *Our Primitive Contemporaries,* The Macmillan Company, New York, 1936.

——: *Social Structure,* The Macmillan Company, New York, 1949.

——: "Sexual Behavior: A Comparative Anthropological Approach," *Journal of Social Hygiene,* 36:133–138, 1950.

MURPHY, GARDNER, LOIS MURPHY, and THEODORE M. NEWCOMB: *Experimental Social Psychology,* Harper & Row, Publishers, Inc., New York, 1937.

MUSKRAT, JOSEPH: "Thoughts on the Indian Dilemma," *Civil Rights Digest,* 6:46–50, Fall 1973.

MUTH, RICHARD F.: *The Spatial Pattern of Urban Residential Land Use,* University of Chicago Press, Chicago, 1969.

MYERS, LENA WRIGHT: "Black Women: Selectivity Among Roles and Reference Groups in the Maintenance of Self-esteem," *Journal of Social & Behavioral Sciences,* Winter 1974–1975.

MYRDAL, GUNNAR: *An American Dilemma,* Harper & Row, Publishers, Inc., New York, 1944.

NADER, RALPH: *Unsafe at Any Speed: The Designed-in Dangers of the American Automobile,* Grossman Publishers, New York, 1965.

NAPPER, GEORGE: *Blacker Than Thou,* William B. Eerdmans Publishing Co., Grand Rapids, Mich., 1973.

NASH, DENNISON: "The Fate of Americans in a Spanish Setting: A Study of Adaptation," *Human Organization,* 26:157–163, Fall 1967.

NASH, JUNE: "The Logic of Behavior: Curing in a Maya Town," *Human Organization,* 26:132–140, Fall 1967.

NASH, PHILLEO: "The Place of Religious Revivalism. . . . ," in FRED EGGAN (ed.), *Social Anthropology of the North American Tribes,* University of Chicago Press, Chicago, 1937.

NATIONAL ADVISORY COMMISSION ON CIVIL DISORDERS: *Report,* Washington, D.C., 1968, Bantam Books, Inc., New York, 1968.

NATIONAL ADVISORY COMMISSION ON SELECTIVE SERVICE: *In Pursuit of Equity: Who Serves When Not All Serve?* Washington, D.C., 1967.

NATIONAL COMMISSION ON THE CAUSES AND PREVENTION OF VIOLENCE IN AMERICA: *Violence in America: Historical and Comparative Perspec-*

tives, Staff Report No. 1, Washington, D.C., 1969.

NATIONAL COUNCIL OF THE CHURCHES OF CHRIST: *Yearbook of American and Canadian Churches,* New York, 1964.

NATION'S BUSINESS: "Success with a Spanish Accent," March 1972, pp. 78–80.

NELSON, EDWARD W.: "The Eskimo about Bering Straits," *18th Annual Report, Bureau of American Ethnology,* part 1, Washington, D.C., 1899, pp. 268–270.

NETTLER, GWYNN: "A Measure of Alienation," *American Sociological Review,* 22:670–677, 1957.

NEWSWEEK: "The Philippines: The 51st State?" July 24, 1972, p. 50.

NIMKOFF, MEYER F., and RUSSELL MIDDLETON: "Types of Economy," *American Journal of Sociology,* 66:215–225, 1960.

NISBET, ROBERT A.: "The Decline and Fall of Social Class," *Pacific Sociological Review,* 2:11–17, Spring 1959.

———: "The University Had Better Mind Its Own Business," *Psychology Today,* 4:22–37, March 1971.

NORDHOFF, CHARLES: *The Communistic Societies of the United States, (1875),* Schocken Books, Inc., New York, 1965.

NORTMAN, DOROTHY: "Population and Program Planning: A Fact Book," *Reports on Population Planning,* September 1972, p. 2.

NUNN, W. C.: *Escape from Reconstruction,* Leo Potishman Foundation, Fort Worth, 1956.

NWOSU, S. N.: "Education and Economic Development," *African Studies,* 30:75–90, 1971.

NYE, F. IVAN: "Adolescent-Parent Adjustment: Age, Sex, Sibling Number, Broken Homes, and Employed Mothers as Variables," *Marriage and Family Living,* 14:327–332, November 1952.

———: *Family Relationships and Delinquent Behavior,* John Wiley & Sons, Inc., New York, 1958.

——— and LOIS W. HOFFMAN: *The Employed Mother in America,* Rand McNally & Company, Chicago, 1963.

———, JOHN CARLSON, and GERALD GARRETT: "Family Size, Interaction, Affect, and Stress," *Journal of Marriage & the Family,* 32:216–226, May 1970.

OAKLAND, LYNNE, and ROBERT L. KANE: "The Working Mother and Child Neglect on the Navajo Reservation," *Pediatrics,* 51:849–853, May 1973.

OBERSCHALL, ANTHONY: "The Los Angeles Riot of 1965," *Social Problems,* 15:322–341, Winter 1968.

———: *Conflict and Social Movements,* Prentice-Hall, Inc., Englewood Cliffs, N.J., 1973.

O'BRIEN, JAMES: "Beyond Reminiscences: The New Left in History," *Radical America,* 6:11–48, July 1972.

O'CONNELL, EDWARD J., JEROME B. DUSEK, and RICHARD J. WHEELER: "A Follow-up Study of Teacher Expectancy Effects," *Journal of Educational Psychology,* 66:325–328, 1974.

ODUM, HOWARD W.: *Understanding Society,* The Macmillan Company, New York, 1947.

OFFICE OF ECONOMIC OPPORTUNITY: *Further Preliminary Results: The New Jersey Graduated Work Incentive Experiment,* Institute for Research on Poverty, University of Wisconsin, Madison, May 1971.

OFFICIAL GAZETTE OF THE PEOPLE'S REPUBLIC OF SERBIA: Belgrad, No. 29, 1960.

OGBURN, WILLIAM F.: "The Influence of Invention and Discovery," in President's Research Committee on Social Trends, *Recent Social Trends,* McGraw-Hill Book Company, New York, 1933, pp. 122–166.

———: *Social Change,* Viking Press, Inc., New York, 1922, 1950.

———: "The Wolf Boy of Agra," *American Journal of Sociology,* 64:499–454, March 1959.

——— and MEYER F. NIMKOFF: *A Handbook of Sociology,* Routledge & Kegan Paul, Ltd., London, 1964.

OGLESBY, CARL (ed.): *The New Left Reader,* Grove Press, Inc., New York, 1969.

O'HANLON, THOMAS: "Anarchy Threatens the Kingdom of Coal," *Fortune,* January 1971, pp. 78–85.

OLSEN, MARVIN E.: *Power in Societies,* The Macmillan Company, New York, 1970.

OLSON, MANCUR: *The Logic of Collective Action,* Harvard University Press, Cambridge, Mass., 1965.

OLSON, PHILIP: "Rural American Community Studies: The Survival of Public Ideology," *Human Organization,* 23:342–350, Winter 1964–1965.

O'NEILL, WILLIAM L.: *Everyone Was Brave: The Rise and Fall of Feminism in America,* Quadrangle Books, Inc., Chicago, 1969.

ORDEN, SUSAN R., and NORMAN M. BRADBURN: "Working Wives and Marital Happiness," *American Journal of Sociology*, 74:392–407, January 1969.

ORUM, ANTHONY M.: *Black Students in Protest: A Study of the Origins of the Black Student Movement*, American Sociological Association, Washington, D.C., 1972.

OSSOWSKI, STANISLAW: "Old Notions and New Problems: Interpretations of Social Structure in Modern Society," in ANDRE BETEILLE (ed.), *Social Inequality: Selected Readings*, Penguin Books, Baltimore, 1969, pp. 79–89.

OTTEN, MICHAEL C.: *University Authority and the Student: The Berkeley Experiment*, University of California Press, Berkeley, 1970.

OTTENBERG, SIMON: "Ileo Receptivity to Change," in WILLIAM R. BASCOM and MELVILLE J. HERSKOVITZ (eds.), *Continuity and Change in African Cultures*, University of Chicago Press, Chicago, 1959, pp. 130–143.

PACKARD, VANCE: *The Hidden Persuaders*, David McKay Company, Inc., New York, 1957.

———: *The Status Seekers*, David McKay Company, Inc., New York, 1959.

———: *The Pyramid Climbers*, McGraw-Hill Book Company, New York, 1962.

———: *The Sexual Wilderness*, David McKay Company, Inc., New York, 1968.

———: *A Nation of Strangers*, David McKay Company, Inc., Chicago, 1972.

PADDOCK, WILLIAM, and PAUL PADDOCK: *Famine—1975!* Little, Brown and Company, Toronto, 1967.

PAGE, JOSEPH A.: "Law Professor Behind ASH, SOUP, PUMP and CRASH," *New York Times Magazine*, Aug. 23, 1970, pp. 32ff.

PARK, ROBERT E.: "Human Migration and the Marginal Man," *American Journal of Sociology*, 33:893, May 1928.

———: *Race and Culture*, The Free Press of Glencoe, Glencoe, Ill., 1949.

——— and ERNEST BURGESS: *Introduction to the Science of Sociology*, University of Chicago Press, Chicago, 1921.

———, ———, and R. D. MCKENZIE: *The City*, University of Chicago Press, Chicago, 1925.

PARSONS, TALCOTT: *Structure and Process in Modern Society*, The Free Press, New York, 1960.

———: "On the Concept of Political Power," *Proceedings of the American Philosophical Society*, 107:232–262, June 1963.

———: "Evolutionary Universals in Society," *American Sociological Review*, 29:339–357, June 1964.

———: *The System of Modern Societies*, Prentice-Hall, Inc., Englewood Cliffs, N.J., 1971.

PARTEN, MILDRED: *Surveys, Polls, and Samples: Practical Procedures*, Harper & Row, Publishers, Inc., New York, 1950.

PASLEY, VIRGINIA: *21 Stayed*, Farrar, Straus & Co., New York, 1955.

PATTERSON, BRADLEY H.: "The Federal Executive Branch and the First Americans," *Civil Rights Digest*, 6:51–54, Fall 1973.

PAVENSTEDT, ELEANOR (ed.): *The Drifters: Children of Disorganized Lower-Class Families*, Little, Brown and Company, Boston, 1967.

PEARSON, KARL: *The Grammar of Science*, A. & C. Black, Ltd., London, 1900.

PECK, JAMES: *Freedom Ride*, Simon & Schuster, Inc., New York, 1962.

PELLEGREN, ROLAND J., and CHARLES H. COATES: "Absentee-owned Corporations and Community Power Structure," *American Journal of Sociology*, 61:413–419, 1956.

PELLEGRINI, ROBERT J.: "Impressions of Male Personality as a Function of Beardedness," *Psychology*, 10:29–33, February 1973.

PERLMAN, DANIEL: "Self-esteem and Sexual Permissiveness," *Journal of Marriage & the Family*, 36:470–473, August 1974.

PERRUCCI, ROBERT, and MARC PILISUK: "Leaders and Ruling Elites: The Interorganizational Bases of Community Power," *American Sociological Review*, 35:1040–1057, December 1970.

PERRY, RALPH BARTON: *Puritanism and Democracy*, Vanguard Press, New York, 1944.

PESCATELLO, ANN (ed.): *Female and Male in Latin America: Essays*, University of Pittsburgh Press, Pittsburgh, 1973.

PESSEN, EDWARD: "The Equalitarian Myth and American Social Reality: Wealth, Mobility and Equality in the Era of the Common Man," *The American Historical Review*, 76:989–1034, October 1971.

PETERS, JOHN FRED: "Mate Selection Among the Shirishna," *Practical Anthropology*, 18:19–23, January—February 1971.

PETERSEN, WILLIAM: Review of Vance Packard: *The*

Status Seekers, American Sociological Review, 25:124–126, February 1960.

PETTIGREW, THOMAS R.: *Profile of the Negro American,* D. Van Nostrand Company, Inc., Princeton, N.J., 1964.

———: "Racially Separate or Together?" *Journal of Social Issues,* 25:43–69, January 1969.

———: *Racially Separate or Together,* McGraw-Hill Book Company, New York, 1971.

PHILBEAM, DAVID: "The Fashionable View of Man as a Naked Ape Is an Insult to Apes, Simplicistic Male-oriented Rubbish," *New York Times Magazine,* Sept. 3, 1972, pp. 10ff.

PHILLIPS, BERNARD S.: *Social Research,* The Macmillan Company, New York, 1966.

PHILLIPS, DEREK L., and KEVIN J. CLANCY: "Response Bias in Field Studies of Mental Illness," *American Sociological Review,* 35:503–505, June 1970.

PIERCY, MARGE: "The Grand Coolie Damn," in Robin Morgan, *Sisterhood Is Powerful,* Random House, Inc., New York, 1970, pp. 421–438.

PISKUNOV, V. P., and V. S. STESHENKO: "On the Demographic Policy of Socialist Society," *Soviet Sociology,* Spring 1975, pp. 42–59.

PIVEN, FRANCES SCOTT, and RICHARD A. CLOWARD: *Regulating the Poor: The Functions of Public Welfare,* Pantheon Books, New York, 1971.

PODALSKY, EDWARD: "The Sociopathic Alcoholic," *Quarterly Journal of Studies on Alcohol,* 21:292–297, June 1960.

PODHORETZ, NORMAN: "The New Inquisitors," *Commentary,* April 1973, pp. 7–8.

POMEROY, RICHARD, and LYNN C. LANDMAN: "American Public Opinion and Abortions in the Early Seventies," in HOWARD I. OSOFSKY, and JOY D. OSOFSKY, *The Abortion Experience,* Harper & Row, Publishers, Inc., New York, 1973, pp. 482–495.

PONTING, J. RICK: "Rumor Control Centers: Their Emergence and Operations," *American Behavioral Scientist,* 16:391–401, January 1973.

PORTERFIELD, AUSTIN L: *Youth in Trouble,* Leo Potishman Foundation, Fort Worth, Tex., 1946.

POWLEDGE, FRED: *Model City, A Test of American Liberalism: One Town's Efforts to Rebuild Itself,* Simon & Schuster, Inc., New York, 1970.

PRESSER, H. B.: "The Role of Sterilization in Controlling Puerto Rican Fertility," *Population Studies,* 23:343–361, March 1969.

PRESSMAN, JEFFREY L., and AARON B. WILDAUSKY: *Implementation: How Great Expectations in Washington Are Dashed in Oakland or Berkeley, or Why It Is Amazing That Federal Programs Work at All,* University of California Press, Berkeley, 1974.

PRESTON, JAMES D.: "The Search for Community Leaders: A Re-examination of the Reputational Technique," *Sociological Inquiry,* 39:39–47, Winter 1969.

PROPPER, ALICE MARCELLA: "The Relationship of Maternal Employment to Adolescent Roles, Activities, and Parental Relationships," *Journal of Marriage & the Family,* 34:417–442, August 1972.

PYLE, ERNIE: *Brave Men,* Holt, Rinehart and Winston, Inc., New York, 1943.

QUALTER, TERENCE H.: *Propaganda and Psychological Warfare,* Random House, Inc., New York, 1962.

QUEEN, STUART A., ROBERT W. HABENSTEIN, and JOHN B. ADAMS: *The Family in Various Cultures,* J. B. Lippincott Company, Philadelphia, 1961.

QUINN, ROBERT P., GRAHAM L. STAINES, and MARGARET R. MCCULLOUGH: "Job Satisfaction Has Been High over 15-year Period, Survey Findings Demonstrate," *ISR Newsletter,* Summer 1974, p. 5., University of Michigan, Institute for Social Research.

QUINNEY, RICHARD: *The Social Reality of Crime,* Little, Brown and Company, Boston, 1970.

RAKSTIS, TED J.: "Sensitivity Training: Fad, Fraud, or New Frontier?" *Today's Health,* January 1970, pp. 20ff.

RANSFORD, H. EDWARD: "Isolation, Powerlessness and Violence: A Study of Attitudes and Participation in the Watts Riot," *American Journal of Sociology,* 73:581–591, March 1968.

———: "Blue Collar Anger: Reactions to Student and Black Protest," *American Sociological Review,* 37:333–346, June 1972.

RAO, P. KODANDRA: *Bi-lingualism for India,* W. O. Judge, Bengal, India, 1956.

RAPER, ARTHUR F.: *The Tragedy of Lynching,* University of North Carolina Press, Chapel Hill, 1933.

"Red Torture Broke Few G.I.'s," *U.S. News and World Report,* Aug. 8, 1955, p. 8.

RATHJE WILLIAM L.: "The Garbage Project: The Archeology of Refuse and Relevance," paper presented at Annual Meeting of the Soc. for Amer. Archeol., Washington, D.C., May 1974.

RAWLS, JOHN: *A Theory of Justice,* Belknap Press of Harvard University, Cambridge, Mass., 1971.

RAY, J. J.: "Ethnocentrism: Attitudes and Behavior," *Australian Quarterly,* 43:89–97, June 1971.

REISS, ALBERT J., JR.: "Rural-Urban Status Differences in Interpersonal Contacts," *American Journal of Sociology,* 65:182–195, September 1959.

REISSMAN, LEONARD: Review of C. Wright Mills: *The Power Elite, American Sociological Review,* 21:513–514, August 1956.

———: "Readiness to Succeed: Mobility Aspirations and Modernism among the Poor," *Urban Affairs Quarterly,* 4:379–396, March 1969.

REUSCH, JURGEN: "Social Technique, Social Status, and Social Change in Illness," in CLYDE KLUCKHOHN and HENRY A. MURRAY, with D. M. SCHIENDER (eds.), *Personality in Nature, Society, and Culture,* 2d ed., Alfred A. Knopf, Inc., New York, 1953, pp. 123–136.

REYNOLDS, FRED D., and WILLIAM R. DARDEN: "Why the Midi Failed," *Journal of Advertising Research,* 12:39–44, August 1972.

RIBBLE, MARGARET A.: *The Rights of Infants,* Columbia University Press, New York, 1943.

RIEMER, SVEND: "Social Planning and Social Organization," *American Journal of Sociology,* 52:508–516, March 1947.

RIESMAN, DAVID, with NATHAN GLAZER and REUEL DENNEY: *The Lonely Crowd: A Study in the Changing American Character,* Yale University Press, New Haven, Conn., 1950.

RIGBY, ANDREW: *Alternative Realities: A Study of Communes and Their Members,* Routledge and Kegan Paul, Ltd., London, 1974.

RISNER, MASON: Quoted in "Life in a POW Camp," *Newsweek,* Feb. 26, 1973, p. 21.

RIST, RAY C.: "Social Class and Teacher Expectations: The Self-fulfilling Prophecy in Ghetto Education," *Harvard Educational Review,* 40:411–454, August 1970.

———: *The Urban School: A Factory for Failure,* MIT Press, Cambridge, Mass., 1973.

RIVERS, W. H. R.: "On the Disappearance of Useful Arts," in *Festkrift Tillägnad Edward Westermarck,* Helsingfors, 912, pp. 109–130, summarized in A. L. Kroeber, *Anthropology,* Harcourt, Brace & World, Inc., New York, 1949, p. 375.

——— (ed.): *Essays on the Depopulation of Melanesia,* Cambridge University Press, London, 1922.

ROACH, JACK L., and ORVILLE R. GURSSLIN: "An Evaluation of the Concept of the Culture of Poverty," *Social Forces,* 45:383–392, March 1967.

ROBBINS, JOHN: "Unmet Needs in Family Planning: A World Survey," *Perspectives,* 5:3–7, Fall 1973.

ROBERTS, RON: *The New Communes,* Prentice-Hall, Inc., Englewood Cliffs, N.J., 1971.

ROBINSON, IRA E., KARL KING, and JACK O. BALSWORTH: "The Premarital Sexual Revolution among College Females," *Family Coordinator,* 21:189–194, April 1972.

ROBY, THORNTON: *Small Group Performance,* Rand McNally & Company, Chicago, 1968.

ROCK, RONALD S., with MARCUS A. JACOBSON and RICHARD M. JANOPAUL: *Hospitalization and Discharge of the Mentally Ill,* University of Chicago Press, Chicago, 1968.

RODMAN, HYMAN: "The Value Stretch," *Social Forces,* 42:205–215, December 1963.

ROEBUCK, JULIAN, and S. LEE SPRAY: The Cocktail Lounge: A Study in Heterosexual Relations in a Public Organization," *American Journal of Sociology,* 72:388–395, January 1967.

ROETHLISBERGER, F. J.: *Management and Morale,* Harvard University Press, Cambridge, Mass., 1949.

——— and WILLIAM J. DICKSON: *Management and the Worker,* Harvard University Press, Cambridge, Mass., 1939.

ROGERS, CARL: *Carl Rogers on Encounter Groups,* Harper & Row, Publishers, Inc., New York, 1970.

ROGIN, RICHARD: "This Place Makes Bedford-Stuyvesant Look Beautiful," *New York Times Magazine,* Mar. 28, 1971, pp. 30ff.

"Rome and New Orleans," *America,* Aug. 24, 1957, p. 518.

ROMM, ETHEL GRODZINS: *The Open Conspiracy: What America's Angry Young Generation Is Saying,* Stackpole Books, Harrisburg, Pa., 1970.

ROSE, A. J.: *Patterns of Cities,* Thomas Nelson, Ltd., Melbourne, Australia, 1967.

ROSE, ARNOLD: *The Power Structure: Political Process in American Society,* Oxford University Press, New York, 1967.

ROSEN, BERNARD C.: "Conflicting Group Membership: A Study of Parent-Peer Group Cross-Pressure," *American Sociological Review,* 20:155–161, April 1955 (a).

———: "The Reference Group Approach to the Parental Factor in Attitude and Behavior Formation," *Social Forces,* 34:137–144, December 1955.

———: "Social Change, Migration, and Family Interaction in Brazil," *American Sociological Review,* 38:198–212, April 1973.

ROSENSTONE, ROBERT A.: "'The Times They Are A-Changing': The Music of Protest," *The Annals of the American Academy of Political and Social Science,* 382:131–144, March 1969.

ROSENTHAL, DONALD B., and ROBERT L. CRAIN: "Structure and Values in Local Political Systems: The Case of Fluoridation Decisions," *Journal of Politics,* 28:169–195, February 1966.

ROSENTHAL, ROBERT, and LENORE JACOBSON: "Teacher Expectations for the Disadvantaged," *Scientific American,* 218:16ff, April 1968.

ROSS, IRWIN: "Sweden: How Much Government Is Too Much?" *Readers Digest,* April 1974, pp. 18ff.

ROSS, MADELINE, AND FRED KERNER: "Stars and Bars Along the Amazon," *Reporter,* Sept. 18, 1958, pp. 34–36.

ROSSI, ALICE S. (ed.): *The Feminist Papers: From Adams to Beauvoir,* Columbia University Press, New York, 1973.

ROSSI, PETER H.: Review of C. Wright Mills, *The Power Elite, American Journal of Sociology,* 62:232–233, September 1956.

———: "Community Decision Making," *Administrative Science Quarterly,* 1:415–443, 1957.

ROSZAK, BETTY, and THEODORE ROSZAK: *Masculine-Feminine: Readings in Sexual Mythology and the Liberation of Women,* Harper & Row, Publishers, Inc., New York, 1970.

ROSZAK, THEODORE: *The Making of a Counter Culture: Reflections on the Technocratic Society and Its Youthful Opposition,* Doubleday & Company, Inc., Garden City, N.Y., 1969.

ROTHER, IRA S.: "The Righteous Rightists," *Transaction,* 4:27–35, May 1967.

ROUTH, FREDERICK B., and PAUL ANTHONY: "Southern Resistance Forces," *Phylon,* 18:50–58, 1957.

ROWE, WILLIAM L.: "The New Cauhāns: A Caste Mobility Movement in North India,' in JAMES SILVERBERG (ed.), *Social Mobility in the Caste System in India,* Mouton, The Hague, 1968, pp. 66–77.

ROY, DONALD: "Efficiency and 'The Fix': Informal Intergroup Relations in a Piecework Machine Shop," *American Journal of Sociology,* 60:255–266, November 1955.

RUBENSTEIN, RICHARD E.: *Rebels in Eden: Mass Political Violence in the U.S.,* Little, Brown and Company, Boston, 1970.

RUNCIMAN, STEPHEN: *Byzantine Civilization,* Meridian Books, Inc., New York, 1956.

RUSHING, WILLIAM A.: "Two Patterns in the Relationship between Social Class and Mental Hospitalization," *American Sociological Review,* 34:533–541, August 1969.

RUSTIN, BAYARD: "A Way Out of the Exploding Ghetto," *New York Times Magazine,* Aug. 13, 1967, pp. 16ff.

RYAN, BRUCE F.: *Social and Cultural Change,* Ronald Printing Co., New York, 1969.

RYDEN, HOPE: "On the Trail of the West's Wild Horses," *National Geographic,* January 1971, pp. 94–109.

SAGARIN, EDWARD: *Odd Man In: Societies of Deviants in America,* Quadrangle Books, Inc., Chicago, 1970.

SAHLINS, MARSHALL D.: "Land Use and the Extended Family in Moala, Fiji," *American Anthropologist,* 59:449–462, 1957.

SALOMONE, JEROME J.: "An Empirical Report on Some Aspects of American Funeral Practices," *Sociological Symposium,* 1:49–56, Fall 1968.

SAMUELSON, KURT: *Religion and Economic Action: A Critique of Max Weber,* Harper & Row, Publishers, Inc., New York, 1961.

SANDOZ, MARI: *The Buffalo Hunters,* Hastings House, Publishers, Inc., New York, 1954.

SANTROCK, JOHN W.: "Paternal Absence, Sex Typing and Identification," *Developmental Psychology,* 2:264–272, April 1970.

SCHACHTER, GUSTAV C., and EDWIN L. DALE, JR.: *The Economist Looks at Society,* Xerox, Lexington, Ky., 1973.

SCHACHTER, STANLEY: "Deviation, Rejection, and Communication," *Journal of Abnormal and Social Psychology,* 46:190–207, 1951.

SCHAFFER, FRANK: *The New Town Story,* MacGibbon and Kee, Ltd., London, 1970.

SCHAMP, GERALD: *Birchism Was My Business,* The Macmillan Company, New York, 1970.

SCHEFF, THOMAS J.: "The Role of the Mentally Ill and the Dynamics of Mental Disorder," *Sociometry,* 26:436–453, December 1963.

SCHEFLEN, ALBERT E.: *Body Language and the Social Order,* Prentice-Hall, Inc., Englewood Cliffs, N.J., 1973.

SCHEIN, EDGAR H.: "Interpersonal Communication,

Group Solidarity and Social Influence," *Sociometry,* 23:148–161, 1960.

SCHELLENBERG, JAMES A., and JOHN HALTEMAN: *Effects of Busing Upon Academic Achievement and Attitudes of Elementary School Children,* Center for Educational Studies, Western Michigan University, Kalamazoo, Mich., June 1974.

SCHINDLER, JOHN A.: *How to Live 365 Days a Year,* Prentice-Hall, Inc., Englewood Cliffs, N.J., 1954.

SCHLAFLY, PHYLLIS: *A Choice, Not an Echo,* Pere Marquette Press, Alton, Ill., 1964.

SCHLESINGER, ARTHUR M., JR.: *The Age of Roosevelt,* Vol. 3, *The Politics of Upheaval,* Houghton Mifflin Company, Boston, 1960.

SCHMIDT, GUNTER, and WOLKMUR SIGURSCH: "Changes in Sexual Behavior among Young Males and Females between 1960–1970," *Archives of Sexual Behavior,* 2:27–45, June 1972.

SCHNEIDER, HAROLD K.: "Pakot Resistance to Change," in WILLIAM R. BASCOM and MELVILLE J. HERSKOVITZ (eds.), *Continuity and Change in African Cultures,* University of Chicago Press, Chicago, 1959, pp. 144–167.

SCHNEIDER, LOUIS, and SVERRE LYSGAARD: "The Deferred Gratification Pattern: A Preliminary Study," *American Sociological Review,* 18:142–194, April 1953.

SCHOENHERR, RICHARD A., and ANDREW M. GREELEY: "Role Commitment Process and the American Catholic Priesthood," *American Sociological Review,* 39:407–426, June 1974.

SCHOOLER, CARMI: "Childhood Family Structure and Adult Characteristics," *Sociometry,* 35:255–269, June 1972.

SCHRAG, PETER: *The Decline of the WASP,* Simon and Schuster, Inc., New York, 1971.

SCHULER, EDGAR A., and V. J. PARENTON: "A Recent Epidemic of Hysteria in a Louisiana High School," *Journal of Social Psychology,* 17:221–235, 1943.

SCHUMAN, HOWARD: "The Religious Factor in Detroit: Review, Replication and Reanalysis," *American Sociological Review,* 36:30–48, February 1971.

SCHUR, EDWIN M.: "Crimes Without Victims: Deviant Behavior and Public Policy," Prentice-Hall, Inc., Englewood Cliffs, N.J., 1965.

SCHUR, EDWIN M. (ed.): *The Family and the Sexual Revolution,* Indiana University Press, Bloomington, 1964.

SCHUTZ, WILLIAM C.: *Joy-expanding Human Relationships,* Grove Press, Inc., New York, 1967.

SCHWARTZ, DAVID C.: "A Theory of Revolutionary Behavior," in JAMES C. DAVIES (ed.), *When Men Revolt and Why: A Reader in Political Violence and Revolution,* The Free Press, New York, 1971, pp. 109–132.

SCHWARTZ, MICHAEL, and SANDRA S. TANGRI: "A Note on Self-concept as an Insulator against Delinquency," *American Sociological Review,* 30:922–934, December 1965.

SCOTT, JAMES, and BEN KERKVLIET: "The Politics of Survival: Peasant Response to 'Progress' in Southeast Asia," *Journal of Southeast Asian Studies,* 4:241–267, September 1973.

SCOTT, JOHN FINLEY: *Internalization of Norms: A Sociological Theory of Moral Commitment,* Prentice-Hall, Inc., Englewood Cliffs, N.J., 1971.

SEABURY, PAUL: "HEW and the Universities," *Commentary,* February 1972, pp. 38–44.

SEARLE, JOHN R.: "A Foolproof Scenario for Campus Revolts," *New York Times Magazine,* Dec. 29, 1968, pp. 4ff.

SEGRE, V. D.: *Israel: A Society in Transition,* Oxford University Press, London, 1971.

SELIGMAN, DANIEL: "A Special Kind of Rebellion," *Fortune,* January 1969, pp. 67ff.; also, June 1959, p. 73.

SELIGMAN, RALPH: "How Equal Opportunity Turned into Employment Quotas," *Fortune,* 87:160–163, November 1973.

SELWYN, PERCY: "The Tyranny of the Technician," *International Development Review,* 15:17–20, 1973.

SELZNICK, PHILIP: "An Approach to the Theory of Bureaucracy," *American Sociological Review,* 8:47–54, February 1943.

SEWELL, WILLIAM H.: "Infant Training and the Personality of the Child," *American Journal of Sociology,* 58:150–159, September 1952.

———: "Inequality of Opportunity for Higher Education," *American Sociological Review,* 36:793–810, October 1971.

———, ARCHIBALD O. HALLER, and MURRAY A. STRAUSS: "Social Status and Educational and Occupational Aspirations," *American Sociological Review* 22:67–73, February 1957.

SHAFFER, HARRY G.: "New Winds in Soviet Planning," *Queen's Quarterly,* 75:402–409, August 1968.

SHANKER, ALBERT: "Must Federal Aid to Education

Mean Federal Control?" *New York Times,* Mar. 24, 1974, sect. 4, p. 9.

SHANNON, LYLE, and JUDITH L. MCKIM: "Mexican, American, Negro, and Anglo Improvement in Labor Force Status between 1960 and 1970 in a Midwestern Community," *Social Science Quarterly,* 15:91–111, June 1974.

SHARP, GENE: *The Politics of Nonviolent Action,* Porter Sargent, Boston, 1974.

SHARP, LAURISTON: "Steel Axes for Stone Age Australians," in Edward H. Spicer (ed.), *Human Problems in Technological Change,* Russell Sage Foundation, New York, 1952, pp. 69–90.

SHAW, CLIFFORD and M. E. MOORE: *The Natural History of a Delinquent Career,* The University of Chicago Press, Chicago, 1931.

———: *Varieties of Delinquent Youth,* Harper & Row, Publishers, Inc., New York, 1949.

SHELDON, WILLIAM H., and S. S. STEVENS: *The Varieties of Temperament,* Harper & Row, Publishers, Inc., New York, 1942.

SHELLOW, ROBERT, and DEREK V. ROEMER: "No Heaven for 'Hell's Angels,'" *Trans-action,* July-August 1966, pp. 12–19.

SHEPARD, MARTIN, and MARJORIE LEE: *Marathon 16,* G. P. Putnam's Sons, New York, 1970.

SHEPHER, JOSEPH: "Familism and Social Structure: The Case of the Kibbutz," *Journal of Marriage and the Family,* 31:567–573, August 1969.

SHERIF, MUZAFER A.: "A Study of Some Social Factors in Perception," *Archives of Psychology,* No. 187, 1935.

——— and CAROLYN SHERIF: *Groups in Harmony and Tension,* Harper & Row, Publishers, Inc., New York, 1953.

——— and ———: "Superordinate Goals in the Reduction of Intergroup Conflict," *American Journal of Sociology,* 63:349–356, 1958.

SHERMAN, MANDELL, and THOMAS R. HENRY: *Hollow Folk,* Thomas Y. Crowell Company, New York, 1933.

SHIBUTANI, TAMOTSU: *Society and Personality: An Interactionist Approach to Social Psychology,* Prentice-Hall, Inc., Englewood Cliffs, N.J., 1961.

———: *Improvised News: A Sociological Study of Rumor,* Bobbs-Merrill Co., Inc., Indianapolis, 1966.

SHILS, EDWARD A., and MORRIS JANOWITZ: "Cohesion and Disintegration in the Wehrmacht in World War II," *Public Opinion Quarterly,* 12:280–315, 1948.

———: "Primary Groups in the American Army," in ROBERT K. MERTON and PAUL LAZARSFELD (eds.), "Continuities in Social Research: Studies in the Scope and Method of the American Soldier," The Free Press of Glencoe, Glencoe, Ill., 1950.

SHORT, JAMES F., JR., and FRED L. STRODTBECK: *Group Process and Gang Delinquency,* University of Chicago Press, Chicago, 1965.

SHORTER, EDWARD: "Illegitimacy, Sexual Revolution, and Social Change in Modern Europe," *Journal of Interdisciplinary History,* 2:237–272, Autumn 1971.

SHOSTAK, ARTHUR B. (ed.): *Sociology in Action: Case Studies in Social Problems and Directed Social Change,* Dorsey Press, Homewood, Ill., 1966.

———: *Putting Sociology to Work: Case Studies in the Application of Sociology to Modern Social Problems,* David McKay Co., New York, 1974.

SHUVAL, JUDITH L.: "Class and Ethnic Correlates of Casual Neighboring," *American Sociological Review,* 21:453–458, August 1956.

SIEBER, SAM D.: "Toward a Theory of Role Accumulation," *American Sociological Review,* 39:567–578, August 1974.

SIEGLER, MIRIAM, and HUMPHREY OSMOND: *Models of Madness: Models of Medicine,* The Macmillan Company, New York, 1974.

SILBERMAN, CHARLES E.: *Crisis in Black and White,* Random House, Inc., New York, 1964.

———: "Negro Economic Gains, Impressive but Precarious," *Fortune,* 82:74–78, July 1970.

SIMMEL, GEORG: *Conflict,* translated by REINHARD BENDIX, The Free Press of Glencoe, Chicago, 1955.

———: *Georg Simmel,* translated and edited by KURT WOLFF, Ohio State University Press, Columbus, 1959.

SIMMONS, GEORGE B.: *The Indian Investment in Family Planning,* Population Council, New York, 1971.

SIMMONS, J. L.: *Deviants,* Glendessary Press, Berkeley, 1970.

SIMON, WILLIAM: Review of VANCE PACKARD, *The Sexual Wilderness,* American Sociological Review, 34:605–606, August 1969.

SIMPSON, GEORGE E.: "Darwinism and Social Darwinism," *Antioch Review,* 19:33–46, 1959.

SINGH, J. A. L., and ROBERT M. ZINGG: *Wolf Children*

and Feral Men, Harper & Row, Publishers, Inc., New York, 1942.

SIZEMORE, BARBARA A.: "Social Science and Education for a Black Identity," in JAMES A. BANKS and JEAN D. GRAMBS (eds.), *Black Self Concept,* McGraw-Hill Book Company, New York, 1972, pp. 141–170.

SJOBERG, GIDEON: *The Preindustrial City,* The Free Press, New York, 1960.

SKINNER, B. F.: *Walden Two,* The Macmillan Company, New York, 1948.

SKOLNIK, ARLENE: *The Intimate Environment: Exploring Marriage and the Family,* Little, Brown and Company, Boston, 1973.

—— and JEROME H. SKOLNIK (eds.): *Intimacy, Family, and Society,* Little, Brown and Company, Boston, 1974.

SKOLNIK, JEROME (ed.): *The Politics of Protest,* Ballantine Books, New York, 1969.

SLADEK, JOHN: *The New Apocrypha: A Guide to Strange Science and Occult Beliefs,* Hart-Davis, MacGibbon, London, 1973.

SMELSER, NEIL J.: *Theory of Collective Behavior,* The Free Press, New York, 1963.

SMIRENKO, ALEX: "From Vertical to Horizontal Inequality: The Case of the Soviet Union," *Social Problems,* 20:150–161. Fall 1972.

SMITH, CONSTANCE E., and ANNE FREEDMAN: *Voluntary Associations: Perspectives on the Literature.* Harvard University Press, Cambridge, Mass., 1972.

SMITH, DELBERT D.: "The Legitimacy of Civil Disobedience as a Legal Concept," *Fordham Law Review,* 336:707–730, May 1968.

SMITH, HELENA HUNTINGTON: *Cattle Barons and Range Wars: The War on Powder River,* University of Nebraska Press, Lincoln, 1967.

SMITH, RICHARD AUSTIN: "The Fifty-Million-Dollar Man," *Fortune,* November 1957, pp. 176ff.

SMITH, T. LYNN: "Some Major Current Rural Social Trends in the United States," *International Social Science Journal,* 21:272–285, 1969.

SMOLINSKI, LEON: "Planning Reforms in Poland," *Kyklos,* 21:498–513, 1968.

"Sociologists Invade the Plant," *Business Week,* Mar. 21, 1959, pp. 95ff.

SMOOT, DAN: *The Invisible Government,* The Dan Smoot Reports, Inc., Dallas, Tex., 1962.

SNOW, C. P.: *The Two Cultures: A Second Look,* Cambridge University Press, Cambridge, 1964.

SOROKIN, PITIRIM A., and CARLE C. ZIMMERMAN: *Principles of Rural-Urban Sociology,* Holt, Rinehart and Winston, Inc., New York, 1929.

——: *Contemporary Sociological Theories,* Harper & Row, Publishers, Inc., New York, 1928.

——: *Social and Cultural Dynamics,* American Book Company, New York, 1941.

——: *The Revolution of Humanity,* Beacon Press, Boston, 1948.

SPENGLER, OSWALD: *The Decline of the West,* translated by Charles Francis Atkinson, Alfred A. Knopf, Inc., New York, 1926–1928.

SPIRO, MELFORD E.: "Culture and Personality: The Natural History of a False Dichotomy," *Psychiatry,* 14:19–46, 1951.

——: *Children of the Kibbutz,* Harvard University Press, Cambridge, Mass., 1958.

SPITZ, RENE: "Hospitalism," in *The Psychoanalytic Study of the Child,* Vol. 1, International Universities Press, Inc., New York, 1945, pp. 53–74.

SPOCK, BENJAMIN: *The Pocket Book of Child Care,* Pocket Books, Inc., New York, 1945, 1957, 1974.

——: *Raising Children in a Difficult Time,* W. W. Norton and Co., New York, 1974.

SROLE, LEO: "Social Integration and Certain Corollaries: An Exploratory Study," *American Sociological Review,* 21:709–716, December 1956.

STAHL, SIDNEY M., and MORTY LEBEDUN: "Mystery Gas: An Analysis of Mass Hysteria," *Journal of Health and Social Behavior,* 14:44–50, March 1974.

STAINES, GRAHAM, CAROL TAVRIS, and TOBY E. JAYARANTE: "The Queen Bee Syndrome," *Psychology Today,* January 1974, pp. 55–60.

STANNARD, UNA: "Clothing and Sexuality," *Psychology Today,* May 1971, pp. 24ff.

STARKEY, MARION L.: *The Devil in Massachusetts,* Alfred A. Knopf, Inc., New York, 1949.

STEIN, DAVID LEWIS: *Toronto for Sale,* The New Press, Toronto, 1972.

STEIN, MAURICE, and ARTHUR VIDICH: *Sociology on Trial,* Prentice-Hall, Inc., Englewood Cliffs, N.J., 1964.

STEINBECK, JOHN: *The Moon Is Down,* The Viking Press, Inc., New York, 1942.

STEINER, STANLEY: *The New Indians,* Harper & Row, Publishers, Inc., New York, 1968.

STEPHENS, WILLIAM A.: "A Cross-cultural Study of Modesty and Obscenity," in *Technical Report of the Commission on Obscenity and Pornography,* Washington, D.C., Vol. IX, 1970.

STERLING, CLAIRE: "The Aswan Disaster," *National Parks and Conservation Magazine: The Environmental Journal,* August 1971, pp. 10–13.

STERN, BERNHARD J.: "Resistance to the Adoption of Technological Inventions," in U.S. National Resources Committee, *Technological Trends and National Policy,* 1937, pp. 39–66.

STERNLIEB, GEORGE: *The Tenement Landlord,* Rutgers University Press, New Brunswick, N.J., 1969.

—— and ROBERT W. BURCHELL: *Residential Abandonment: The Tenement Landlord Revisited,* Center for Urban Policy Research, Rutgers University, New Brunswick, N.J., 1973.

STEWART, CHARLES T., JR: "The Rural-Urban Dichotomy: Concepts and Uses," *American Journal of Sociology,* 64:152–158, September 1958.

STIEHM, JUDITH H.: "The Teacher's Millstone," *Progressive* 25:23–25, July 1961.

STOCKDALE, JERRY D.: "Structural Preconditions for Collective Action," paper presented at The Society for the Study of Social Problems, Washington, D.C., 1970.

STOLTZ, LOIS KEEK: "Effects of Maternal Employment upon Children: Evidence from Research," *Child Development,* 31:749–782, 1960.

STONE, CAROL: "Some Family Characteristics of Socially Active and Inactive Teenagers," *Family Life Coordinator,* 8:53–57, 1960.

STONE, DALE: "SDS and the Iron Law of Oligarchy," *Kansas Journal of Sociology,* 8:59–64, Spring 1972.

STONEQUIST, EVERETT H.: *The Marginal Man,* Charles Scribner's Sons, New York, 1937.

STOUFFER, SAMUEL A., et al.: *Studies in the Social Psychology of World War II,* Vol. 2, "The American Soldier: Combat and Aftermath," Princeton University Press, Princeton, N.J., 1949.

STRANGE, HEATHER, and JOSEPH MCCRORY: "Bulls and Bears in the Cell Block," *Society,* July 1974, pp. 51–59.

STRAUS, MURRAY A.: "Deferred Gratification, Social Class, and the Achievement Syndrome," *American Sociological Review,* 27:326–335, June 1962.

STRAUSS, ANSELM L.: "The Literature on Panic," *Journal of Abnormal and Social Psychology,* 39:317–328, 1944.

——, BARNEY G. GLASSER, and JEANNE C. QUINT: "Religion, American Values and Death Perspective," *Sociological Symposium,* 1:30–36, Fall 1968.

STREET, PEGGY, and PIERRE STREET: "In Iran, a New Group Challenges Us," *New York Times Magazine,* July 23, 1961, pp. 11ff.

STRICKLAND, STEPHEN P.: "Can Slum Children Learn?" in CARL SENNA (ed.), *The Fallacy of I.Q.,* The Third Press, New York, 1973.

STRODTBECK, FRED L.: "Husband-Wife Interaction over Revealed Differences," *American Sociological Review,* 16:468–473, August 1951.

—— and A. PAUL HARE: "Bibliography of Small Group Research," *Sociometry,* 17:107–178, May 1954.

STROTHER, GEORGE B.: "Creativity in the Organization," *Journal of Cooperative Extension,* 7:7–16, Spring 1969.

STUCKERT, ROBERT P.: "African Ancestry of the White American Population," *Ohio Journal of Science,* 58:155–160, 1958.

SUCZEK, BARBARA: "The Curious Case of the 'Death' of Paul McCartney," *Urban Life and Culture,* 1:61–76, April 1972.

Summary of the Report on Conditions of Women and Children Wage Earners in the United States, Bureau of Labor Statistics Bulletin No. 175, Washington, D.C.

SUMNER, WILLIAM GRAHAM: *Folkways,* (1906), Ginn & Co., Boston, 1940.

SURFACE, BILL: *The Hollow,* Coward-McCann, Inc., New York, 1970.

SUSSMAN, MARVIN (ed.): *Non-Traditional Family Forms in the 1970s,* National Council on Family Relations, Minneapolis, Minn., 1973; reprinting of series of articles from *Family Coordinator,* October 1972.

SUTTLES, GERALD D.: *The Social Order of the Slum,* University of Chicago Press, Chicago, 1968.

SYKES, GERALD (ed.): *Alienation: The Cultural Climate of Our Time,* George Braziller, New York, 1964.

SYZMANSKI, ALBERT: "The Inauthentic Sociology: A Critique of Etzioni's Activist Society," *Human Factor,* 9:53–63, Spring 1970.

SZASZ, THOMAS: *The Myth of Mental Illness: Foundations of a Theory of Personal Conduct,* Harper & Row, Publishers, Inc., 1961.

——: "The Psychiatrist as Double Agent," *Transaction,* 4:16–24, October 1967.

——: *The Manufacture of Madness,* Harper & Row, Publishers, Inc., New York, 1970.

TALMON, YONINA: "Pursuit of the Millennium: The Relation between Religious and Social Change," *European Journal of Sociology,* 3:125–148,

1962. Reprinted in JOSEPH R. GUSFIELD (ed.), *Protest, Reform, and Revolt,* John Wiley & Sons, Inc., New York, 1970, pp. 436–452, and in BARRY MCLAUGHLIN (ed.), *Studies in Social Movements,* The Free Press, New York, 1969, pp. 400–427.

——: *Family and Community in the Kibbutz,* Harvard University Press, Cambridge, Mass., 1972.

TAMBLYN, LEWIS R.: *Inequality: A Portrait of Rural America,* Rural Education Association, Washington, D.C., 1973.

TANNENBAUM, ARNOLD: *Hierarchy in Organizations: An International Comparison,* Jossey-Bass, Publishers, New York, 1974.

TAVRIS, CAROL: "Who Likes Women's Liberation: The Case of the Unliberated Liberals," *Journal of Social Issues,* 29:174–198, 1973.

TAYLOR, MILLER LEE, and A. R. JONES: *Rural Life in Urbanized Society,* Oxford University Press, Fair Lawn, N.J., 1964.

TAYLOR, TELFORD: *Nuremberg and Vietnam: An American Tragedy,* Quadrangle Books, Chicago, 1970.

THOMAS, RAY, and PETER CRESSWELL: *The New Town Idea,* The Open University Press, Milton Keynes, England, 1973.

THOMAS, W. I.: *The Unadjusted Girl,* Little, Brown and Company, Inc., Boston, 1923.

—— and FLORIAN ZNANIECKI: *The Polish Peasant in Europe and America,* Alfred A. Knopf, Inc., New York, 1918, 1927.

THOMPSON, VICTOR A.: *Modern Organizations,* Alfred A. Knopf, Inc., New York, 1961.

THOMPSON, WARREN S.: *Danger Spots in World Population,* Alfred A. Knopf, Inc., New York, 1929.

THOMPSON, WAYNE E., and JOHN E. HORTON: "Political Alienation as a Force in Political Action," *Social Forces,* 38:190–195, March 1960.

TIETZE, CHRISTOPHER, and DEBORAH A. DAWSON: "Induced Abortion: A Factbook," *Reports on Population Family Planning,* No. 14, December 1973, pp. 1–51.

TIGER, LIONEL: *Men in Groups,* Random House, Inc., New York, 1969.

—— and ROBIN FOX: *The Imperial Animal,* New York, Dell Publishers, 1972.

Time, "Puerto Rico Votes for Commonwealth," Nov. 27, 1972, p. 27.

TINBERGEN, NIKOLAAS: *Study of Instinct,* Oxford University Press, Fair Lawn, N.J., 1969.

TOFFLER, ALVIN: *Future Shock,* Random House, Inc., New York, 1970.

TOMASSON, RICHARD F.: "Religion is Irrelevant in Sweden," in JEFFERY K. HADDEN (ed.), *Religion in Radical Transition,* Aldine Press, Chicago, 1971, pp. 111–127.

TOMPKINS, PETER, and CHRISTOPHER BIRD, *The Secret Life of Plants,* Harper & Row, Publishers, Inc., New York, 1973.

TONNIES, FERDINAND: *Community and Society,* translated and edited by Charles A. Loomis, Michigan State University Press, East Lansing, 1957.

TOYNBEE, ARNOLD: *A Study of History,* Oxford University Press, London, 1935–1961.

TREIMAN, DONALD J.: "Status Discrepancy and Prejudice," *American Journal of Sociology,* 71:651–664, May 1966.

TRIMBLE, JOSEPH E.: "Say Good-bye to the Hollywood Indian," paper presented at Annual Meeting of American Psychological Association, New Orleans, August 1974.

TRIPP, MAGGIE (ed.): *Women in the Year 2000,* Arbor House, New York, 1974.

TROPMAN, JOHN E.: "Social Mobility and Marital Stability," Applied Social Studies, 3:165–173, 1971.

TROTTER, ROBERT J.: "Aggression: A Way of Life for the Quolla," *Science News,* 103:65–80, Feb. 3, 1973.

TUDDENHAM, READ D.: "The Influence of a Distorted Group Norm upon Judgments of Adults and Children," *Journal of Psychology,* 52:231–239, 1961.

TUMIN, MELVIN M.: "Some Unapplauded Consequences of Social Mobility," *Social Forces,* 36:21–37, September 1957.

TURNBULL, COLIN: *The Mountain People,* Simon & Schuster, Inc., New York, 1973.

TURNER, JAY R., and MORTON O. WAGENFELD: "Occupational Mobility and Schizophrenia: An Assessment of the Social Causation and Social Selection Hypothesis," *American Sociological Review,* 32:104–113, February 1967.

TURNER, RALPH H.: "Role-taking, Role Standpoint, and Reference Group Behavior," *American Journal of Sociology,* 61:316–338, 1956.

—— and LEWIS M. KILLIAN: *Collective Behavior,* Prentice-Hall, Inc., Englewood Cliffs, N.J., 1972.

——: "The Sense of Injustice in Social Movements," *Proceedings of the Southwestern Sociological Association,* 19:122–126, 1968.

TURNER, RALPH H., and SAMUEL J. SURACE: "Zoot-Suiters and Mexicans: Symbols in Crowd Behavior," *American Journal of Sociology,* 62:14–20, 1956.

TURNER, THOMAS B.: "The Liberal Arts in Medical Education," *Association of American Colleges Bulletin,* 44:71–77, 1958.

TWEETEN, LUTHER, and DEAN SCHREINER: "Economic Impact of Public Policy and Technology in Marginal Farms and on the Non-Farm Population," in Iowa State University Center for Agricultural and Economic Development, *Benefits and Burdens of Rural Development,* Iowa State University Press, Ames, 1970, pp. 41–76.

TYLER, EDWARD: *Primitive Culture: Researches into the Development of Mythology, Philosophy, Religion, Language, Art and Custom,* Vol. 1, John Murray (Publishers), Ltd., London, 1871.

U.S. COMMISSION ON CIVIL RIGHTS: *Stranger in One's Land,* Clearing House Publication No. 19, May 1970.

U.S. COMMISSION ON CIVIL RIGHTS: *Statement on Affirmative Action for Equal Employment Opportunities,* Clearing House Publications No. 41, February 1973.

U.S. News and World Report: "Here's Where Church Tried to Swing an Election; with Text of Pastor's Letter," Nov. 7, 1960, pp. 59–61.

U.S. PRESIDENT'S COMMISSION ON CAMPUS UNREST: *The Report of the U.S. President's Commission on Campus Unrest,* Arno Press, New York, 1970.

UNGER, IRWIN: *The Movement: A History of the American New Left, 1959–1972,* Dodd, Mead and Co., New York, 1974.

UNNI, K. P.: "Polyandry in Malabar," *Sociological Bulletin* (India), 7:62–79, 1958.

URBAN AMERICA, INC.: *One Year Later,* Frederick A. Praeger, Publishers, Inc., New York, 1969.

USEEM, JOHN: "South Sea Island Strike: Labor-Management Relations in the Carolina Islands, Micronesia," in EDWARD H. SPICER (ed.), *Human Problems in Technological Change,* Russell Sage Foundation, New York, 1952, pp. 149–164.

VANDERKOOI, RONALD: "The Main Stem: Skid Row Revisited," *Society,* September 1973, pp. 64–71.

VAN DER KROEF, JUSTUS M.: "Some Head-hunting Traditions of Southern New Guinea," *American Anthropologist,* 54: 221–235, April 1952.

VAN DER SCHALIE, HENRE: "Aswan Dam Revisited," *Environment,* November 1974, pp. 18–26.

VANDERZANDEN, JAMES W.: "Resistance and Social Movements," *Social Forces,* 37:312–315, May 1959.

———: "The Klan Revival," *American Journal of Sociology,* 65:456–462, March 1960.

———: *Sociology: A Systematic Approach,* The Ronald Press Company, New York, 1970.

VANE, JULIA R.: "Intelligence Test Results of Children in England, Ireland, and the United States," *Journal of Clinical Psychology,* 29:191–193, April 1973.

VAUGHN, JAMES: "An Experimental Study of Competition," *Journal of Applied Psychology,* 20:1–15, 1956.

VERMISHEV, K.: "The Stimulation of Population Growth," *Soviet Review,* Fall 1973, pp. 3–13.

VERNON, RAYMOND: *Metropolis 1985: An Interpretation of the Findings of the New York Metropolitan Study,* Harvard University Press, Cambridge, Mass., 1960.

VEYSEY, LAURENCE: *The Communal Experience,* Harper & Row, Publishers, Inc., New York, 1974.

VINCENT, CLARK E.: "An Open Letter to the 'Caught Generation,'" *Family Coordinator* 2:143–150, April 1972.

VON HENTIG, HANS: "Redhead and Outlaw," *Journal of Criminal Law and Criminology,* 38:1–6, May–June 1947.

VOORHIES, BARBARA: "Supernumerary Sexes," paper presented at 71st Annual Meeting of the American Anthropological Association, Toronto, Canada, November 1973.

WAGENFELD, MORTON O.: "The Primary Prevention of Mental Illness: A Sociological Perspective," *Journal of Health and Social Behavior,* 13:194–203, June 1972.

WAISANEN, F. B., and HIDEYA KUMATA: "Education, Functional Literacy, and Participation in Development," *International Journal of Comparative Sociology,* 13:21–35, March 1972.

WAKIL, S. PARVEZ: "Campus Mate Selection Preferences: A Cross-national Comparison," *Social Forces,* 51:471–476, June 1973.

WALLACE, A. F. C.: "The Modal Personality Structure of the Tuscarora Indians as Revealed by the Rorschach Test," *Bureau of American Ethnology,* Bulletin, No. 150, 1952 (a).

———: "Individual Differences and Cultural Uniformities," *American Sociological Review,* 17:747–750, December 1952 (b). WALLACE, SAM-

UEL E.: *Skid Row as a Way of Life*, Harper & Row, Publishers, Inc., New York, 1965.

WALLACE, SAMUEL E.: "The Road to Skid Row," *Social Problems,* 16:92–105, Summer, 1968.

WALLERSTEIN, JAMES S., and CLEMENT J. WYLE: "Our Law-abiding Law Breakers," *National Probation,* pp. 107–112, March–April 1947.

WALSH, BRENDAN M.: "Trends in Age at Marriage in Postwar Ireland," *Demography,* 9:187–202, May 1972.

WALSH, ROBERT H.: "Intergenerational Transmission of Sexual Standards," paper read at American Sociological Association, Washington, D.C., 1970.

WARD, HILEY, H.: *The Far-out Saints of the Jesus Communes,* Association Press, New York, 1972.

WARNER, LUCIEN: "A Survey of Psychological Opinion on E.S.P.," *Journal of Parapsychology,* 2:296–301, 1938.

WARNER, W. LLOYD: "Murngin Warfare," *Oceania,* 1:457–494, 1931.

—— and JAMES C. ABEGGLEN: *Big Business Leaders in America,* Harper & Row, Publishers, Inc., New York, 1955.

—— and PAUL S. LUNT: *The Social Life of a Modern Community,* Yale University Press, New Haven, Conn., 1941.

—— and ——: *The Status System of a Modern Community,* Yale University Press, New Haven, Conn., 1942.

WARREN, ROLAND, L.: "Comprehensive Planning and Coordination: Some Functional Aspects," *Social Problems,* 20:335–364, Winter 1973.

WARRINER, CHARLES K.: "The Nature and Functions of Official Morality," *American Journal of Sociology,* 64:165–168, September 1958.

WARWICK, DONALD P.: "Ethics and Population Control in Developing Countries," *The Hastings Center Report,* June 1964; reprinted in *Current,* November 1974, pp. 37–42.

WATSON, G. LLEWELLYN: "Social Structure and Social Movements: The Black Muslims in the United States and the Ras-Tafarians in Jamaica," *British Journal of Sociology,* 24:188–204, June 1973.

WATTENBERG, BEN J., and RICHARD M. SCAMMON: "Black Progress and Liberal Rhetoric," *Commentary,* April 1973, pp. 35–44.

WAX, MURRAY L.: *Indian Americans: Unity and Diversity,* Prentice-Hall, Inc., Englewood Cliffs, N.J., 1971.

WEBER, MAX: *From Max Weber: Essays in Sociology,* translated and edited by H. H. GERTH and C. WRIGHT MILLS, Oxford University Press, Fair Lawn, N.J., 1946.

WEIL, ANDREW: "Andrew Weil's Search for the True Andrew Geller," *Psychology Today,* June 1974, pp. 45–50; July 1974, pp. 74–82.

WEINER, BERNARD: "Getting Busted Abroad," *The Nation,* Feb. 14, 1972, pp. 198–199.

WEINTRAUB, LARRY: "Ministers Vow Fight on Inner-city Crime," *Chicago Sun-Times,* Apr. 7, 1974, p. 6.

WEINTRAUB, LEWIS: "Black Pastors to Fight Crime," *Chicago Sun-Times,* Aug. 5, 1974.

WELLER, LEONARD, and ELMER LUCHTERHAND: "Effects of Improved Housing on the Family Functioning of Large, Low-income Black Families," *Social Problems,* 20:382–389, Winter 1973.

WELLMAN, PAUL L.: *The Trampling Herd,* Carrick and Evans, New York, 1939.

WENGER, DENNIS: "The Reluctant Army: The Functioning of Police Departments During Civil Disturbances," *American Behavioral Scientist,* 16:326–342, January–February 1973.

WEST, JAMES: *Plainville, U.S.A.,* Columbia University Press, New York, 1945.

WESTIE, FRANK R.: "Social Distance Scales: A Tool for the Study of Stratification," *Sociology and Social Research,* 43:251–258, 1959.

WHELPTON, PASCAL K., ARTHUR A. CAMPBELL, and JOHN E. PATTERSON: *Fertility and Family Planning in the United States,* Princeton University Press, Princeton, N.J., 1966.

WHITTAKER, DAVID, and WILLIAM A. WATTS: "Personality Characteristics of a Nonconformist Youth Subculture: A Study of Berkeley Nonstudents," *Journal of Social Issues,* 25:65–88, Spring 1969.

WHITTAKER, JAMES O.: "Cognitive Dissonance and the Effectiveness of Persuasive Communication," *Public Opinion Quarterly,* 28:547–555, Winter 1964.

WHYTE, WILLIAM F.: *Street Corner Society,* University of Chicago Press, Chicago, 1955.

WHYTE, WILLIAM H., JR.: "Urban Sprawl," in EDITORS OF FORTUNE, *The Exploding Metropolis,* Doubleday & Company, Inc., Garden City, N.Y., 1958, pp. 115–139.

WILKES, PAUL: "Mother Superior to Women's Lib," *New York Times Mag.,* Nov. 29, 1970, pp. 27ff.

WILKINS, THURMAN: *Cherokee Tragedy: The Story of the Ridge Family and the Decimation of a People,* The Macmillan Company, New York, 1971.

WILKINSON, DORIS Y.: "Collective Behavior Theory and Research: A Critique of Smelser's Approach," Paper read at American Sociological Association, Washington, D.C., 1970.

WILLIAMS, ALLEN J., JR., NICHOLAS BABCHUCK, and DAVID R. JOHNSON: "Voluntary Associations and Minority Status: A Comparative Analysis of Anglo, Black, and Mexican Americans," *American Sociological Review,* 38:637–646, October 1973.

WILLIAMS, ROGER J.: *Biochemical Individuality,* John Wiley & Sons, Inc., New York, 1956.

WINFIELD, GERALD F.: "The Impact of Urbanization on Agricultural Process," *The Annals of the American Academy of Political and Social Science,* 405:65–74, January 1973.

WINICK, CHARLES: "Physician Narcotic Addicts," *Social Problems,* 9:174–186, Fall 1961.

———: "The Beige Epoch: Depolarization of Sex Roles in America," *Annals of the American Academy of Political and Social Science,* 376:18–24, March 1968.

———: *The New People: Desexualization in American Life,* Pegasus Press, Indianapolis, 1969.

WINSLOW, CHARLES N: "The Social Behavior of Cats," *Journal of Comparative Psychology,* 37:297–326, 1944.

WIRTH, LOUIS: *The Ghetto,* University of Chicago Press, Chicago, 1928.

———: "Urbanism as a Way of Life," *American Journal of Sociology,* 44:3–24, July 1938.

WISSLER, CLARK: "Depression and Revolt," *Natural History,* 41:108–112, 1938.

WITTFOGEL, KARL A.: *Oriental Despotism,* Yale University Press, New Haven, Conn., 1957.

WIXEN, BURTON N.: *Children of the Poor,* Crown Publishers, New York, 1973.

WOELFEL, JOSEPH, and ARCHIBALD O. HALLER: "Significant Others: The Self-reflective Act and the Attitude Formation Process," *American Sociological Review,* 36:74–87, February 1971.

WOLFF, MICHAEL: "Cheerleader for the Revolution," *New York Times Magazine,* July 21, 1974, pp. 11ff.

WOLFF, ROBERT J.: "Modern Medicine and Traditional Culture: Confrontation on the Malay Peninsu-la," *Human Organization,* 24:339–345, Winter 1965.

WOLFGANG, MARVIN E., and BERNARD COHEN: "The Convergence of Race and Crime," in *Crime and Race: Conceptions and Misconceptions,* Institute of Human Relations Press, New York, 1970.

WOMEN'S BUREAU: *Wives—Their Contribution to Family Income,* Document WB 67-271, U.S. Department of Labor, Washington, D.C., 1967.

———: *Background Facts on Women Workers in the U.S.,* U.S. Department of Labor, Washington, D.C., 1972.

WOODWARD, C. VANN: "What Became of the 1960s?" *New Republic,* 171:18–25, Nov. 9 1974.

WOODWARD, KENNETH L.: "Do Children Need Sex Roles?" *Newsweek,* June 10, 1974, pp. 79–80.

WORSLEY, PETER: *The Trumpet Shall Sound: A Study of "Cargo" Cults in Melanesia,* MacGibbon & Kee, London, 1957.

WRIGHT, GRACE S.: *Subject Offerings and Enrollments in Public Secondary Schools,* U.S. Government Printing Office, Washington, D.C., 1965.

WRIGHT, JAMES D.: "The Working Class, Authoritarianism, and the War in Vietnam," *Social Problems,* 133–149, Fall 1972.

WUTUNEE, W. I. C.: "The Long Trail to Integration," *Kalamazoo College Review,* 34:19, Spring 1974.

WYNDER, E. L., and A. GRAHAM EVARTS: "Tobacco as a Possible Etiological Factor in Bronchogenic Carcinoma: A Study of Six Hundred and Eighty-four Proved Cases," *Journal of the American Medical Association,* 143:329–336, May 27, 1950.

YABLONSKY, LEWIS: *The Hippie Trip,* Pegasus Press, New York, 1968.

YANG, C. K.: *The Chinese Family in the Communist Revolution,* M.I.T. Press, Cambridge, Mass., 1959.

YANKELOVICH, DANIEL: *The Changing Values on Campus: A Survey for the JDR Fund,* Pocket Books, New York, 1972.

YANOWITCH, MURRAY: "The Soviet Income Revolution," *Slavic Review,* 22:683–697, December 1963.

YINGER, J. MILTON: *Toward a Field Theory of Behavior,* McGraw-Hill Book Company, New York, 1965.

———: A Minority Group in American Society, McGraw-Hill Book Company, New York, 1965.

YOUNG, KIMBALL, and RAYMOND W. MACK: *Sociology and Social Life,* American Book Company, New York, 1959.

YOUNG, LEONTINE: *Out of Wedlock,* McGraw-Hill Book Company, New York, 1954.

YOUNG, MICHAEL D., and PETER WILLMOT: *The Symmetrical Family,* Pantheon Press, New York, 1973.

YOUNG, WHITNEY: *To Be Equal,* McGraw-Hill Book Company, New York, 1964.

ZABLOCKI, BENJAMIN: *The Joyful Community,* Penguin Books, Baltimore, 1971.

ZAHN, G. D.: *The Military Chaplaincy: A Study of Role Transition in the Royal Air Force,* University of Toronto Press, Toronto, 1969.

ZAJONC, ROBERT B.: "Dumber by the Dozen," *Psychology Today,* January 1975, pp. 37–43.

ZALD, MAYER N., and ROBERTA ASH: "Social Movement Organizations," in BARRY MCLAUGHLIN, *Studies in Social Movements,* The Free Press, New York, 1969, pp. 461–485.

ZANDER, ALVIN: "Productivity and Group Success: Team Spirit vs. the Individual Achiever," *Psychology Today,* November 1974, pp. 64–68.

ZARETSKY, IRVING I., and MARK P. LEONE (eds.): *Religious Movements in Contemporary America,* Princeton University Press, Princeton, N.J., 1974.

ZELNIK, MELVIN, and JOHN F. KANTNER: "The Probability of Premarital Intercourse," *Social Science Research,* 1:335–341, September 1972.

ZILBOORG, GREGORY: *Mind, Medicine, and Man,* Harcourt, Brace & World, Inc., New York, 1943.

ZIMMERMAN, CARLE C.: "The Future of the American Family, II, The Rise of Counterrevolution," *International Journal of the Sociology of the Family,* 2:1–9, March 1972.

ZOLLA, ELEMIRE: *The Eclipse of the Intellectual,* translated by RAYMOND ROSENTHAL, Funk and Wagnalls, a division of Reader's Digest Books, Inc., New York, 1968.

Glossary

Accommodation Peaceful adjustment between hostile or competing groups; "antagonistic cooperation."

Acculturation Acquisition by a group or individual of the traits of another culture.

Achieved role or **status** A role or status attained through individual choice, effort, action, or accomplishment.

Adjudication Resolution of role conflict by decision of a third party.

Affirmative action Programs legally requiring employers to follow specific procedures for reaching certain "goal" for the employment of minorities and women.

Aggregation A gathering of people without conscious interaction.

Alienation An emotional separation from a society or group, combining feelings of powerlessness, normlessness, and social isolation.

Amalgamation Biological interbreeding of two or more peoples of distinct physical appearance until they become one stock.

Anomie A situation in which a large number of persons lack integration with stable institutions, to the extent that they are left rootless and normless.

Anthropomorphism Process of attributing human feelings and motives to animals.

Applied science Scientific methodology applied to the search for knowledge which will be useful in solving practical problems.

Ascribed role or **status** A role or status assigned according to hereditary traits without regard to individual preference, ability, or performance.

Assimilation Mutual cultural diffusion through which persons or groups come to share a common culture.

Association A group with its own administrative structure, organized to pursue some common interest of its members.

Attitude A tendency to feel and act in a certain way.

Audience A crowd with interest centered on stimuli outside themselves.

Authority An established right to order the actions of other people.

Bias A tendency, usually unconscious, to see facts in a certain way because of one's wishes, interests, or values.

Bureaucracy A pyramid of officials who conduct rationally the work of a large organization.

Caste system A stratified social system in which social position is entirely determined by parentage, with no provision for change of position.

Category A number of people who share some common characteristics.

Charismatic leadership Type of leadership in which the personality and image of the leader give him great authority and influence.

Clique A small group of intimates with intense in-group feelings based on common sentiments and interests.

Cognitive dissonance The degree of difference one perceives between own beliefs or ideas and those of another person.

Collective behavior Behavior which originates spontaneously, is relatively unorganized, fairly unpredictable, and depends upon interstimulation among participants.

Collectivity A physical collection of people.

Commune A number of persons, usually not related, who live together collectively and cooperatively, as an alternative to the conventional family.

Community A local grouping within which people carry on a full round of life activities.

Compartmentalization Process of isolating parts of the personality from each other so that one is unaware of value conflicts; isolating roles from one another so that one is unaware of role conflicts.

Competition Process of seeking to obtain a reward by surpassing all rivals.

Compromise Form of accommodation in which each party accepts less than its full goal in order to avoid or end conflict.

Concept An idea or mental image that embodies generalized or common elements found in a number of specific cases.

Conflict The effort to obtain rewards by eliminating or weakening the competitors.

Conjugal family Family with the married couple and their children as its core, with a fringe of other relatives.

Consanguine family Family with a group of married sisters and their children, or a group of married brothers and their children, as its core, with a fringe of spouses and other relatives.

Cooperation Joint activity in pursuit of common goals or shared rewards.

Counterculture A subculture not merely different from, but in opposition to, the conventional and approved culture of the society; e.g., the hippie subculture.

Craze A temporary obsessive interest shared by a number of people.

Crescive change Gradual adaptation to changing conditions.

Cross-fertilization in social change Use in one field of discoveries and inventions from an entirely different field.

Crowd A temporary collection of people reacting together to stimuli.

Cult A religious group, usually of small membership, that stresses the ecstatic emotional experience of its members and ignores governmental, educational, or economic activities.

Cultural base for invention The accumulation of knowledge and techniques available to the inventor.

Cultural change Changes in the culture of a people; often used interchangeably with social change.

Cultural drift A broad, sweeping, gradual change in values or behavior in a society.

Cultural integration The degree to which the traits, complexes, and institutions of a culture are harmoniously adjusted to one another.

Cultural lag The time lag between a change or innovation and accomplishment of the social and cultural adjustments which the innovation makes necessary.

Cultural pluralism Toleration of cultural differences within a common society; allowing different groups to retain their distinctive cultures.

Cultural relativism Concept that the function, meaning, and "desirability" of a trait depend upon its cultural setting.

Cultural trait Smallest unit of culture as perceived by a given observer.

Culture Everything that is socially learned and shared by the members of a society; social heritage which the individual receives from the group; a system of behavior shared by members of a society.

Culture complex A cluster of related culture traits.

Deferred gratification pattern Postponement of present satisfactions for future rewards.

Demography Statistical study of population composition, distribution, and trends.

Denomination A fairly large religious group, usually supported by private gifts, and therefore not as pressured as the ecclesia to accept all majority social norms.

Deviation Failure to conform to the norms of a group or society.

Deviation, primary The deviant behavior of a person who is conformist in the rest of his or her life organization.

Deviation, secondary Deviant behavior which follows from one's public identification as a deviant.

Diffusion The spread of culture traits from group to group.

Discovery A shared human perception of an aspect of reality which already exists.

Discrimination A practice that treats equal people unequally; limiting opportunity or reward according to race, religion, or ethnic group.

Displacement Process of suspending one conflict by replacing it with another.

Ecclesia The most powerful form of religious organization, which accepts state aid and, in turn, sanctions the basic cultural practices of the society.

Ego According to Freud, the conscious and rational part of the self which oversees the restraint of the id by the superego.

Elite A small controlling clique within a group, association, or society.

Embourgeoisment Assumption of middle-class attitudes by people generally considered to be of working-class status.

Enacted change Rapid modification of social practices as a result of deliberate choice.

Encounter group Broadly defined to include all sensitivity groups whose purpose is meditative, therapeutic, body, or consciousness-expansion.

Endogamy Requirement that mates be chosen within some specified group.

Ethical neutrality in science Seeking knowledge but avoiding value judgments or recommendations.

Ethnic group A number of people with a common cultural heritage which sets them apart from others in a variety of social relationships.

Ethnocentrism Tendency of each group to take for granted the superiority of its own culture.

Ethology Science devoted to the comparative study of behavior, mainly animal behavior.

Ethos Unifying spirit running through various aspects of a culture.

Exogamy Requirement that mates be selected outside some specified group.

Extended family The nuclear family plus any other kin with whom important relationships are maintained.

Fact A descriptive statement of reality upon which all qualified observers are in agreement; a descriptive statement of reality which scientists, after careful examination and cross-checking, believe to be accurate.

Fad A trivial, short-lived, popular variation in speech, decoration, or behavior.

Family A kinship grouping which provides for the rearing of children and for certain other human needs.

Fashion A variation in speech, decoration, or behavior, of temporary duration but less trivial or brief than a fad.

Feral man Individual supposedly reared apart from human society and hence imperfectly socialized.

Folk society Small, isolated, often nonliterate, homogeneous society characterized by a high degree of group solidarity, traditionalism, and informal social control.

Folkways Customary, normal, habitual behavior characteristic of the members of the group.

Force Use or threat of physical coercion, or punishment.

Formal organization Associations of people with a definite structure, deliberately created to operate according to definite rules in order to pursue specific goals.

Gemeinschaft A society in which most relationships are either personal or traditional.

Generalized order The totality of values and standards of one's community or one's social group, whose judgments one applies to one's own behavior in forming the concept of self.

Geriatrics The study of the health problems of the aged.

Gerontology The study of the aged and their problems.

Gesellschaft A society based on contractual as contrasted with traditional relationships.

Ghetto Any part of a city in which the population is restricted to a particular ethnic group; historically applied to a Jewish district, but today often applied to Negro districts.

Group Any number of persons who share a consciousness of membership and of interaction; often used incorrectly to denote aggregation, collectivity, or category.

Group dynamics The scientific study of the interaction within small groups.

Human ecology The study of human beings in relation to their physical environment; a study of how people and institutions are located in space.

Hypothesis Tentative, unverified statement of the relationship of known facts; a reasonable proposition worthy of scientific testing.

Id According to Freud, the instinctive, anti-social, selfish desires and impulses of the individual.

Ideology A system of ideas which sanctions a set of norms.

In-group A group or category toward which one has a feeling of identity or belonging.

Influence The ability to affect the decision and actions of others without any formal authority to do so.

Innovation A new culture trait or complex, whether received through discovery, invention, or diffusion.

Instinct An inborn behavior pattern characteristic of all members of the species.

Institution An organized cluster of folkways and mores centered around a major human activity; organized system of social relationships which embodies certain common values and procedures and meets certain basic needs of society.

Intellectual One who is concerned primarily with ideas.

Invention A new combination or a new use of existing knowledge.

Labeling process The public identification of a person as a deviant (e.g., thief, rapist, homosexual).

Latent functions Unintended effects of a policy, program, or institution.

Law Regulations enforced by coercive power which is either organized or sanctioned by the society; sometimes referred to as "stateways."

Levirate Pattern in some societies whereby a widow

automatically becomes wife to her deceased husband's brother.

Longitudinal study A study that extends over time, describing a trend or making a series of before-and-after observations.

Looking-glass Perception of the self that one forms by interpreting the reactions of others to oneself.

Manifest functions Intended and realized effects of a program or institution.

Marginal man Individual torn between two or more cultures, partly assimilated into each and fully assimilated into neither; often an immigrant.

Marriage The approved social pattern whereby two or more persons establish a family.

Mass A relatively large number of people, spatially dispersed and anonymous, acting independently in response to the same stimuli.

Mass behavior The unorganized, unstructured, uncoordinated, individually selected behavior of masses in a mass society.

Mass hysteria An irrational, compulsive belief or behavior which spreads among a number of people.

Mass society A society in which primary-group, community-based, tradition-oriented relationships have been largely replaced by contractual, secondary-group, utilitarian relationships; characterized by anonymity, mobility, specialization, and individualism.

Mean Sum of all the items divided by the number of items; sometimes referred to as the "average."

Median The midpoint in a series of items arranged according to size.

Mob An emotionally aroused crowd taking violent action.

Modal personality A personality configuration which is typical of most members of a group or society.

Mode Value which appears most frequently in a series.

Monogamy Marriage form permitting only one mate (at a time).

Mores Strong ideas of right and wrong which require certain actions and forbid others.

Multivariate analysis Statistical procedures which allow a researcher to work with two or more variables at a time.

Nativism Rejection of contemporary culture, with a desire to return to traditional patterns; rejection of "foreign" groups and influences.

Norm A standard of behavior. Statistical norm is a measure of actual conduct; cultural norm states the expected behavior of the culture.

Normative To make something conform to or support some norm or pattern.

Norms of evasion Customary, recognized ways of violating certain of the norms of a society.

Nuclear family Also called the "conjugal family," consisting of a husband and wife, and their children.

Objectivity Observing and accepting facts as they are, not as one would wish them to be.

Oligarchy Rule of a group or organization by a small clique of self-perpetuating leaders.

Oppression psychosis Tendency for members of a group with a history of persecution to feel persecuted even in situations where they are not being mistreated.

Orgy Joyous revelry of a crowd which transgresses the normal mores.

Out-group A group or category toward which one has no feeling of identity or of belonging.

Panic A collective flight based on a hysterical belief.

Personality The totality of behavior of an individual with a given tendency system interacting with a sequence of situations.

Phenomenology and ethnomethodology Philosophical view that only those who personally experience a reality are equipped to study it—for example, that only a black scholar is equipped to study the black family.

Polyandry A form of polygamy in which two or more husbands share one wife.

Polygamy A plurality of mates.

Polygyny A form of polygamy in which one husband has two or more wives.

Position The rank one holds in an hierarchical series.

Power The ability to control the actions of others, regardless of their wishes.

Primary group Small group in which people come to know one another intimately as individual personalities; distinct from the impersonal, formal, utilitarian secondary group.

Primitive Descriptive term for societies which are (or were) culturally homogeneous and relatively isolated, with fairly simple technological and economic organization, and usually preliterate.

Progress Social or cultural change of a kind defined as desirable according to some set of values.

Proletariat A working class which is conscious of its underprivileged and propertyless status.

Propaganda All efforts to persuade others to an acceptance of a point of view.

Prospective study One that begins with the present and carries observations forward over a period of time.

Public A number of people who share an interest in a particular topic or activity, or are concerned about and divided upon an issue.

Public opinion An opinion held by a significant number of people; the dominant opinion among a population.

Pure science Search for knowledge for its own sake without primary regard to its practical usefulness or consequences.

Race A group of people somewhat different from other people in a combination of inherited physical characteristics, but the meaning of the term is also substantially determined by popular social definition.

Reference group Any group accepted as model or guide for our judgments and actions.

Relative deprivation Feelings of deprivation which tend to be proportionate to the gap between what one has and what one feels one should have, or between what one has and what others have.

Retrospective study One that works backward in time, using already recorded data.

Revolution A relatively sudden, usually violent, and relatively complete change in a social system.

Riot Action of a violently aggressive, destructive crowd. Motives may be race, religion, nationality, and the dramatization of grievances.

Rite of passage Any ritual which marks movement from one status to another, such as the ceremonies attending birth, death, puberty, or marriage.

Role Expected behavior of one who holds a certain status.

Role playing Acting out the behavior of a role which one actually holds, as when a couple marry and set up a household.

Role set A cluster of associated roles that together form a social status.

Role taking Assuming or acting out the behavior of a role which one does not actually hold, as when children "play house."

Rumor A rapidly spreading report unsubstantiated by authenticated fact.

Sacred society A society with a homogeneous set of folkways and unified moral values which are revered as sacred and eternal.

Science A body of organized, verified knowledge which has been secured through scientific investigation, a method of study whereby a body of verified knowledge is discovered.

Scientific methods Methods of study which produce organized, verified knowledge.

Secondary group Group in which contacts are impersonal, segmental, and utilitarian, as distinct from the small, intimate, highly personal primary group.

Sect A religious group, usually of small membership, that is concerned about all aspects of life and insists that its members follow its doctrines without deviation.

Secular society Society with a diversity of folkways and mores; society in which religious influence is minimized.

Secularization Movement from a sacred to a rationalistic, utilitarian, experimental viewpoint.

Segregation Separation of two or more groups based on a desire to avoid equal-status social contact.

Self An individual's awareness of, and attitudes toward, his or her own person.

Self-fulfilling prophesy A prediction which starts a chain of events which make the prediction come true.

Semite People of Middle-Eastern origin, perhaps represented in most nearly pure form by the Bedouins of Northern Arabia; often used as a synonym for Jewish, but equally applicable to most Arabs.

Significant others Those individuals whose approval one desires and whose judgments will affect one's attitudes and behavior.

Slum A deteriorated area of the city inhabited by poor people.

Social change Change in the social structure and relationships of a society; often used interchangeably with *cultural change.*

Social class A stratum of persons of similar position in the social-status continuum.

Social contagion Process whereby members of a crowd stimulate and respond to one another and thereby increase their emotional intensity and responsiveness.

Social control All the means and processes whereby a group or a society secures its members' conformity to its expectations.

Social disorganization Disruption of existing culture by social change, as evidenced by failure of traditional social controls, role confusions, and conflicting moral codes.

Social distance Degree of closeness to, or acceptance of, members of other groups.

Social mobility Movement from one class level to another.

Social order A system of people. relationships, and customs operating smoothly together to accomplish the work of a society.

Social planning Attempt at the intelligent direction of social change.

Social processes Repetitive interaction patterns which are commonly found in social life.

Socialization Process by which one internalizes the norms of his groups so that a distinct self emerges unique to this individual.

Society A relatively independent, self-perpetuating human group which occupies a particular territory, shares a culture, and has most activities within this group.

Sociocultural change Changes in either the social structure and relations or in the culture of a society.

Sociology The scientific study of human social life.

Sororate Pattern in some societies whereby a widowed husband automatically becomes husband to his deceased wife's sister.

Standardized birth- and death-rates Birth- and death-rates which are adjusted to what they would be if the population had the same age, sex, or other population characteristic as some "standard" population distribution which is used as a measure.

Status Position of an individual in a group, or of a group in relation to other groups.

Stereotype A group-shared image of another group or category of people.

Subculture A cluster of behavior patterns related to the general culture of a society and yet distinguishable from it; behavior patterns of a distinct group within the general society.

Superego According to Freud, the social ideals and values which one has internalized and which form the conscience.

Superordination Total, ruthless domination of one group by another.

Symbiosis (social) Mutual interdependence without conscious decision to cooperate.

Symbol That which stands for something beyond its own immediate meaning; especially a specific object representing a more diffused, generalized, or abstract concept. The flag, the cross, and Uncle Sam are examples.

Symbolic communication Exchanging meanings through words and other symbols which have no meaning in themselves, but to which agreed meanings have become attached; distinguished from exchange of meanings through instinctive barks and growls.

Toleration An agreement to disagree peaceably.

Utopia A perfect society.

Values Measures of goodness or desirability.

Variable Anything which differs from person to person, group to group, time to time, or place to place.

Voluntary association Formal organization directed toward some definite function which one supposedly enters voluntarily rather than by ascription.

Women's Liberation Movement A philosophical and legal movement for sex equality and the ending of role ascription by sex.

Name Index

Subject Index